JESUS IN JOHN'S GOSPEL

Jesus in John's Gospel

*Structure and Issues
in Johannine Christology*

William Loader

WILLIAM B. EERDMANS PUBLISHING COMPANY
GRAND RAPIDS, MICHIGAN

Wm. B. Eerdmans Publishing Co.
2140 Oak Industrial Drive N.E., Grand Rapids, Michigan 49505
www.eerdmans.com

© 2017 William Loader
All rights reserved
Published 2017

ISBN 978-0-8028-7511-2

Library of Congress Cataloging-in-Publication Data

A catalog record for this book is available from the Library of Congress

Contents

Foreword	vii
Acknowledgments	x
Introduction	1

PART ONE
The Structure of Johannine Christology — 39

1 **Identifying the Central Structure** — 41
   1. Issues of Method — 41
   2. Examining Select Passages — 46
   3. Common Elements of the Structure — 57
   4. Summary Statements Illustrating the Christological Structure — 63
   5. John 17 — 67

2 **A Survey of the Gospel** — 72
   1. John 1–5 in Review — 72
   2. John 6–12 in Review — 80
   3. John 13–14 in Review — 91
   4. John 15–16 in Review — 100
   5. John 17 in Review — 107
   6. John 18–21 in Review — 108

3 **The Structure: An Outline** — 121

CONTENTS

PART TWO
Issues of Johannine Christology — 145

4 **The Death of Jesus in John** — 147
   1. Jesus' Death—Vicarious, Sacrificial, Apotropaic? — 148
   2. Jesus' Death as Revelation and Judgment — 202
   3. Glorification, Exaltation, Ascension and the Son of Man — 213
   4. Conclusion — 280

5 **The Salvation Event in John** — 282
   1. The Salvation Event—Revelation? — 282
   2. The Salvation Event and Pre-existence — 303
   3. The Nature of the Son in Relation to the Father — 315
   4. The Nature of the Son as Jesus of Nazareth — 364

6 **The Fourth Gospel in the Light of its Christology** — 393
   1. The Gospel and the Jesus of History — 393
   2. The Gospel, its Christology and its Community — 421
   3. Johannine Christology and the Gospel Today — 460

Conclusion — 472

Bibliography — 485
Index of Modern Authors — 514
Index of Subjects — 522
Index of Ancient Sources — 526

Foreword

The scholarly work of Professor William R. G. Loader first came to my attention more than thirty years ago when I was working on a commentary on the Epistle to the Hebrews. One of the monographs that I found particularly helpful was a work in German, *Sohn und Hohepriester: Eine traditionsgeschichtliche Untersuchung zur Christologie des Hebräerbriefes*, based on a dissertation completed in Germany by an Australian scholar whom I had not previously encountered. That volume's treatment of the Christology of Hebrews was impressive in many ways. The author had mastered a vast array of literature from many different scholarly traditions, had assessed it judiciously, and, in critical dialogue with that literature, came to his own carefully considered judgment about what Hebrews was trying to say about the significance of Christ. His work helped me enormously in my own efforts to make sense of that intriguing piece of early Christian rhetoric.

Since his landmark study of the Christology of Hebrews, Prof. Loader has made other significant contributions to New Testament scholarship. Most notable perhaps is his multivolume analysis of the ways ancients thought about sexuality. Individual volumes in this series treated the Septuagint, Jewish pseudepigraphical literature, the Dead Sea Scrolls, Philo, Josephus, and the New Testament. Meticulous attention to detail and careful exegesis—with attention to the larger cultural context—characterized the scholarship in all these volumes. The results of this major effort are available in a one-volume synthesis published by Eerdmans, which offers a wonderful introduction for anyone interested in the treatment of sexuality that shaped the attitudes of early Christians (*Making Sense of Sex*).

While issues of sexuality engaged his interest, Prof. Loader also continued his interest in Christology. The precursor to the current monograph was a treatment of the *Christology of the Fourth Gospel* published in 1989.

FOREWORD

Since then he has also produced quite accessible studies of Jesus within his first-century Jewish context, *Jesus' Attitude toward the Law* and *Jesus and the Fundamentalism of His Day*. In this volume he returns to the Christology of John, building on his earlier work but engaged in critical dialogue with an abundance of more recent Johannine scholarship.

At the core of his treatment in this work is the argument that the Gospel exhibits a consistent and coherent vision of the character and significance of Jesus. He was the one sent by and authorized by the Father to offer to humankind a revelation of a relationship that brings light and life, a mission continued through the work of the Spirit in the life of the church. This summary of what John teaches about Jesus recalls the famous assessment of the Fourth Gospel by Rudolf Bultmann, but differs from it in significant ways. For Loader, Jesus is a revealer, but reveals more than the fact that he is such.

After laying out this Christological scheme and showing how it is articulated through the text of the Gospel, Loader analyzes a range of critical issues that have elicited widely divergent scholarly judgments. How, for instance, does the Gospel understand the claim that Jesus is the "lamb of God who takes away the sins of the world"? Does it presume a doctrine of atonement, of vicarious substitution, or does it offer a reinterpretation, a *"relecture,"* of early Christian formulations, to use a term coined by Jean Zumstein? Similarly, how does the Gospel understand the "glorification" of Christ? Is it, as Bultmann suggested, a paradoxical theology of the cross, finding the glorification of Christ precisely in his suffering, or is it an understanding of his exaltation to heaven and restoration to the presence of the Father which is somehow anticipated in the event of his death? The dichotomies in which these and many similar questions are framed do not define the limits of hermeneutical possibility, but merely point to the spectrum of opinion on issues with which Prof. Loader deals. He strongly resists reducing the interpretation of the Gospel to a simple set of binaries and remains open to the ways in which the evangelist subtly combines different perspectives.

After wrestling with these and other issues raised by the motifs of the text itself, Loader sets the Gospel and its creative synthesis of early Christian affirmations within the larger historical context of the development of the Johannine community and its relationships with the larger Christian world. This in turn leads to a profound theological reflection on the kinds of claims made in this Gospel, about the humanity and divinity of Jesus, the kind salvation that the evangelist believes he offers and the ways in which that message can be fruitful for the church today. This whole penetrating analysis is conducted in constant critical dialogue with a vast array of scholarly voices, all heard and acknowledged, even when their positions are rejected.

Foreword

Prof. Loader's extraordinarily learned and sensitive treatment of the Fourth Gospel models New Testament scholarship at its best, a trove of learning and insight. It will teach scholars things that they did not know and help any thoughtful reader of the Gospel to understand the power of its longstanding appeal to people of faith.

Harold W. Attridge
Sterling Professor,
Yale University Divinity School
June 29, 2016

Acknowledgments

The present study has a long history, reaching back over 40 years. Its predecessor, *The Christology of the Fourth Gospel: Structure and Issues* (Frankfurt: Peter Lang, 1989, 2nd ed., 1992), was already the fruit of 15 years of research. The latter has been incorporated—in part unchanged, in part extensively revised, rewritten, and expanded—in the present work on the basis of engagement with a further 25 years of international research on John and its Christology.

My initial concern had been to embark on a traditio-historical study of the Fourth Gospel's Christology, having completed such a study of the Christology of Hebrews in the monograph *Sohn und Hohepriester. Eine traditionsgeschichtliche Untersuchung zur Christologie des Hebräerbriefes*, WMANT 53 (Neukirchen: Neukirchener Verlag, 1981). My first endeavours in this regard appeared in: "The Central Structure of Johannine Christology," *NTS* 30 (1984): 188–216. The more I pursued this, the more I became aware of the need first to analyse the transmitted text as a whole. In my 1989 book I sought to offer an integrative study of Johannine Christology that identified an overall structure and examined the individual themes of ongoing research in its light. Positive responses to that work over the ensuing years then prompted this extensive reworking.

Research may have its primary focus on an ancient text and its world, but needs also to be a conversation with contemporary scholars in our own world. The conversation partners have become very numerous, but the engagement all the more enriching, so that there is a sense in which we work in communal indebtedness. I appreciate the generosity of Bill Eerdmans in welcoming the publication and editor-in-chief James Ernest's support in bringing it to completion. I also thank Mary J. Marshall for proofreading the penultimate draft, Trevor Thompson for giving it its final form, and, above all, my wife, Gisela, whose patience has supported me for over half a century.

Introduction

In his major review of Johannine research Robert Kysar describes Christology as "the heartbeat of the theology of the Fourth Gospel."[1] The investigation which follows seeks to listen for that "heartbeat," to detect its rhythm and feel its strength. In the introduction, I begin by examining one of the most sensitive and influential expositions of Johannine Christology, that of Rudolf Bultmann. I then explore the ways in which research has developed since Bultmann, partly in response to the issues which his synthesis raised.

In Part One, I turn directly to the transmitted text of the Gospel in order to listen for the patterns and themes. I hope to identify the underlying structure or structures of the author's Christology. On the basis of this reading of the text I return in Part Two to major issues of interpretation that have emerged in current Johannine christological research reviewed in the Introduction or that have arisen through the analysis in Part One.

Johannine Christology, one could say, is the Gospel. Its scope is very wide and the issues of Johannine Christology have been given attention in an increasing volume of literature. Many of its individual motifs and images have demanded monograph treatment. The present volume, which represents an extensive reworking of the 1989 edition, will, like it, not aim at comprehensive detailed treatment of every feature, but will seek an overview, a "map" of its contours, within which motifs and images are seen in perspective. This research has been undertaken in the confidence that a clarification of the overall structure of the Gospel's Christology will also facilitate a clearer understanding of its major themes and of the disputed issues which have arisen in its exposition.

---

1. Robert Kysar, "The Fourth Gospel: A Report on Recent Research," *ANRW* 25.3:2389–480 (2443).

INTRODUCTION

The investigation works with the present form of the Gospel as it has been passed down to us, but the issues of tradition and of the history of the Gospel's composition and its community are not ignored. I believe that a careful analysis of the Christology of the transmitted text necessarily raises such issues. I have adopted the method of first dealing primarily with the transmitted text as it stands. But in the final chapters I shall draw together questions and issues raised by the analysis concerning the history of Johannine Christology, of its community, and of the composition of the Gospel.

I have been mindful that the Fourth Gospel's Christology developed in the context of a community of faith and its preaching. A similar context remains the primary place of its use today. Accordingly I conclude with brief observations relating to this context. Sensitivity to the "heartbeat" of Johannine theology was surely a mark, above all, of Bultmann's work on John's Gospel. Accordingly I begin with a presentation of his exposition.

Bultmann on Johannine Christology

The importance of Bultmann's description of Johannine Christology is that he asked the question: what is at its centre?[2] His answer was seemingly simple: the sending of the Son. Expanded, the central story of Johannine Christology tells how the Father sent the Son into the world to tell what he had seen and heard, to be the revealer. The Son came in fulfilment of the Father's will, manifested the divine glory in human flesh and, having completed his

---

2. "Was ist seine zentrale Anschauung, seine Grundkonzeption?" in Rudolf Bultmann, "Die Bedeutung der neuerschlossenen mandäischen und manichäischen Quellen für das Verständnis des Johannesevangeliums," in *Johannes und sein Evangelium*, ed. K. H. Rengstorf, Wege der Forschung 82 (Darmstadt: WBG, 1973), 404. This article appeared first in 1925. It represents the foundational statement of Bultmann's interpretation of Johannine Christology developed later in his commentary, Rudolf Bultmann, *Das Evangelium des Johannes*, KEKNT (Göttingen: Vandenhoeck und Ruprecht, 1968; first published in 1941); ET: *The Gospel of John* (Oxford: Blackwell, 1971), and in his *Theologie des Neuen Testaments* (Tübingen: Mohr Siebeck, 1977; first published in 1953); ET: *Theology of the New Testament*, 2 vols. (London: SCM, 1952-1955). See also Rudolf Bultmann, "Der religionsgeschichtliche Hintergrund des Prologs zum Johannesevangelium," in *EUCHARISTERION. Festschrift für H. Gunkel*. 2. Teil (Göttingen: Vandenhoeck und Ruprecht, 1923), 3-26; Rudolf Bultmann, "Die Eschatologie des Johannes-Evangeliums," *Zwischen den Zeiten* 6 (1928): 4-22; Rudolf Bultmann, "Untersuchungen zum Johannesevangelium," *ZNW* 27 (1928): 113-63; Rudolf Bultmann, "Untersuchungen zum Johannesevangelium," *ZNW* 29 (1930): 169-92; Rudolf Bultmann, "Johannesevangelium," *RGG* 3:840-50, and the review article, Rudolf Bultmann, "Zur Interpretation des Johannesevangeliums," *TLZ* 87 (1962): 1-8.

task, returned in exaltation to the glory of the Father.[3] The basic pattern is that of the Redeemer-Revealer sent by God.

For Bultmann this pattern is drawn from the myth of the gnostic redeemer.[4] Bultmann believed that this myth was reflected in the various gnostic systems from the second century onwards, but existed already in the world of the Fourth Gospel. It told the following story. Human beings are captive in the material world. Their spirits were once part of the heavenly world and there they belong. The heavenly Redeemer-Revealer comes to make known to them their true nature and origin. As the heavenly man he calls his brothers and sisters out of this world to their true home. Those who accept this "gnosis" (knowledge), the "gnostics," rejoice in their identity and await their final departure from the shackles of the material at death, when they follow the path forged for them by the Redeemer-Revealer.

Bultmann could point not only to the similar pattern of the coming of a Redeemer-Revealer from heaven, but also to numerous motifs which occur both in the Fourth Gospel and in gnostic literature, particularly in the Mandean writings. In his view, this literature reflects gnostic traditions of the first century CE influential in the background of the Johannine church.[5]

But there are also differences. Bultmann points to the absence in John of the idea of souls once pre-existing in heaven, of the absolute dualism between spirit and material, and of the view that the Redeemer could not be a real human being as presupposed in the story of Jesus' incarnation and death.[6] Although following the same basic pattern, the christological story in the Fourth Gospel could not itself be gnostic but had developed under the influence of Gnosticism and in reaction against it.[7]

More significant still is Bultmann's view of how the author of the Fourth Gospel understood the christological story. He observes inconsistencies in the author's statements about the Redeemer-Revealer. One is that the Gospel repeatedly, and in numerous variations, speaks of the Son making known in the world what he had seen and heard in the heavenly world, but it never has the Son pass on such information.[8] The Son consistently and repeatedly presents himself as the Revealer, but, while using the formulations of revelation, never discloses revelation of heavenly words or events. Another is that

3. Bultmann, "Bedeutung," 407–55.
4. Bultmann, "Bedeutung," 406–7; Bultmann, *Theologie*, 365–66, 389.
5. Bultmann, "Bedeutung," 412–25, 459–65.
6. Bultmann, *Johannes*, 107; Bultmann, *Theologie*, 365, 369, 392–93.
7. Bultmann, *Johannes*, 41–42.
8. Bultmann, *Johannes*, 42, 103–4, 190.

sometimes John has Jesus speak in the present tense of telling what he sees and hears (as in 5:19–20), whereas usually Jesus refers to pre-existent seeing and hearing (as in 3:31–32).[9] Similarly, sometimes the Gospel portrays life as the gift of the incarnate one and of his earthly ministry (as in 6:35), while at other times it speaks of it as in some sense the fruit of his exaltation and return to the Father (as in 3:14–15; 6:27; 7:38–39).[10] These discrepancies lead Bultmann to conclude that the author does not mean us to take the pattern of the story literally. The prologue, and, indeed, the Gospel, remain an enigma until this is seen.[11]

Accordingly, unlike Gnosticism, Johannine religion is not primarily about a Revealer who gives information, brings words, coming down as an emissary of the heavenly world and then returning. It is rather about one who presents himself and in presenting himself presents the Father. He is the divine Word.[12] The story or myth serves the evangelist as a vehicle for expressing the significance of the breaking through of God's word in Jesus of Nazareth. Jesus was not a pre-existent heavenly being.[13] He was not sent from above in that sense. These elements give expression to the fact that in him it is God, the "other," who encounters us. That the Word, active at creation, became flesh is a way of saying that in Jesus we meet the possibility of finding our way to authentic existence, to becoming what we were created to be.[14]

The claim to present God, to offer the true bread, to be the giver of life, and to be life and light challenges human self-sufficiency, revealing human beings' inadequacy and confronting them with it. This "negative" revelation which takes place within the situation of being encountered with the word of Jesus is at the same time a call to authentic human existence in relationship with the Son and therefore with the Father. It restores us to our true humanity, to what we were meant to be. In the encounter the Son's claim to be one with the Father is a revelation of God, not in the sense of conveying information about him but in the sense of an epiphany. The self-presentation of the Son as Revealer effects thus a double-sided revelation, negative and positive. This absolute claim at the same time evokes crisis, for it divides the world of humanity into those who believe and those who do not believe. In this way, it constitutes darkness as what rejects the Son and light as what

---

9. Bultmann, *Johannes*, 190; Bultmann, *Theologie*, 191 n. 5.
10. Bultmann, *Theologie*, 387.
11. Bultmann, *Johannes*, 1, 103–4; Bultmann, *Theologie*, 364.
12. Bultmann, *Theologie*, 415–18.
13. Bultmann, *Johannes*, 191–92 n. 5; Bultmann, *Theologie*, 385–86, 414–15.
14. Bultmann, *Johannes*, 26–27, 39; Bultmann, *Theologie*, 420, cf. 379.

comes to him and so belongs to him. This is dualism based on decision ("Entscheidungsdualismus").[15]

Bultmann is not thereby denying incarnation in the author's scheme. But incarnation is not, for the author, the entry into human flesh, according to Bultmann's analysis. Rather it means that the event of the revelation of the Father by the Son takes place in the fully human person Jesus of Nazareth.[16] In John 1:14 the author sets himself clearly apart from the myths of the gnostic redeemer, just as he does not espouse a notion of revelation like theirs.[17] For Bultmann, the Johannine Christology holds fast to the paradox that the "glory" is manifest in the humanity. That is the meaning of incarnation. It does not refer to an event at the commencement of Jesus' earthly life; the incarnation is not the means of revelation, but is another way of talking of revelation itself. Accordingly, he argues that 1:51, which sees Jesus as the revelatory ladder, exegetes 1:14a. Incarnation refers to the human being of Jesus as the place where the divine-human encounter takes place.[18]

The centring of Johannine Christology on the event of Jesus of Nazareth leads Bultmann to the claim that elements of Jesus' earthly life receive a new evaluation in the Gospel. The author, he suggests, probably did not intend that the miracles, such as the turning water into wine, should be taken literally.[19] In his hands they are no longer miracles. They have been transformed into "signs" which proclaim that Jesus is the sent one. They are a "redender Hinweis" (verbal pointer), they are *verba visibilia*, and response to them is the first step of faith.[20] The historical details of Jesus' earthly life are not of importance to the author. They belong to the past and of themselves are of no salvific significance. Central is the fact that in Jesus revelation has taken place, in him God has spoken. The meeting with the Word in the event of proclamation, not knowledge of the details of Jesus' earthly life, is the central concern. The earthly Jesus, therefore, belongs to the past. The meeting with the Word is not with the historical Jesus or with his teaching; it is an encounter made possible through the Paraclete.[21]

The paradox of the "glory" made manifest in the flesh leads Bultmann to claim that in John it is the thoroughly human Jesus, about whom there was nothing extraordinary except his claim to be one with the Father, who is the

---

15. Bultmann, *Johannes*, 7–8; Bultmann, *Theologie*, 370, 373.
16. Bultmann, *Johannes*, 189.
17. Bultmann, *Johannes*, 41–42.
18. Bultmann, *Johannes*, 40–42, 75.
19. Bultmann, *Johannes*, 83.
20. Bultmann, *Johannes*, 79, 92; Bultmann, *Theologie*, 492.
21. Bultmann, *Johannes*, 232–33, 261, 377, 432.

place of the divine epiphany. This ordinariness reaches its climax in the passion and crucifixion. Jesus is presented as a pathetic figure ("Jämmergestalt") before Pilate.[22] Above all in the crucified one we meet the glory of the divine Word. In this way Bultmann attributes to the author a remarkable transformation of the conclusion to the story of the Redeemer-Revealer. Where the story told of exaltation and return to glory—glorification in the presence of the Father in heaven—the author has transposed the reference of exaltation so that now the crucifixion is paradoxically portrayed as the moment of exaltation and glorification.[23] Accordingly the allusion to ascension in 6:62 is taken by Bultmann to refer to a greater offence still to come: the crucifixion.[24] But even the glorification is no addition of glory; it is, rather, the completion and climax of the paradox of the divine glory in human flesh.[25] The glorification continues when the disciples believe and so are gathered into the community of faith.[26] Instead of following the pattern of the story as set out in the gnostic myth, the author achieves a challenging reinterpretation which redirects the focus to the encounter with the crucified, the incarnate one, as the place of revelation.

Similarly elements of the story which spoke of an actual return to the heavenly world and to the Father are reinterpreted as indicating the divine authority and source of Jesus' words. The fact that the Gospel sometimes relates the promise of the gift of life to Jesus' coming and sometimes to his going, indicates, according to Bultmann, that these elements are not to be understood literally. Both coming and going bear the same basic import for the Gospel: they serve to underline that in Jesus we meet God.[27]

Jesus' death is not only the climax of his earthly life as the event of revelation and therefore the climax of the crisis, the judgment which that revelation brings;[28] it is also the departure of Jesus which enables his true meaning to be comprehended.[29] Resurrection adds in itself nothing new to the revelation, at least, not as an inner-worldly event.[30] It is only the encounter with the Word that matters and this continues in the event of proclamation. Here Bultmann picks up the notion of the Paraclete, which makes

22. Bultmann, *Johannes*, 40; Bultmann, *Theologie*, 403.
23. Bultmann, *Johannes*, 325, 328, 330, 375–76, 379.
24. Bultmann, *Johannes*, 341.
25. Bultmann, *Johannes*, 328, 375–76; Bultmann, *Theologie*, 400.
26. Bultmann, *Johannes*, 25, 45.
27. Bultmann, *Johannes*, 189, 191 n. 5, 232.
28. Bultmann, *Theologie*, 387.
29. Bultmann, *Theologie*, 402; Bultmann, *Johannes*, 356.
30. Bultmann, *Theologie*, 408–9.

Introduction

the writing of the Gospel possible. The completion of Jesus' life opens the possibility of encountering the significance of that life, a significance obscured during the earthly ministry. By emphasising that distance from an event facilitates insight, Bultmann demythologises both Jesus' return and the coming of the Paraclete.[31] Here we must distinguish between Bultmann's own demythologising and that attributed by him to the evangelist. But Bultmann can appeal to the fact that already the author displays a similar radical hermeneutic in merging the parousia of Jesus with the coming of the Spirit.

In discussing the post-Easter perspective and the significance of the Paraclete for the Gospel, Bultmann also draws a parallel with the Markan "messianic secret."[32] Mark, or his tradition, had sought to bridge the gap between what faith affirmed of Jesus after Easter and what Jesus said during his ministry by attributing to the disciples a high degree of misunderstanding during Jesus' earthly ministry. This led to their not being able to affirm for themselves what Jesus claimed of himself, that is, what faith had come to affirm that Jesus affirmed of himself. In John, the Paraclete, the Spirit, while not guiding the pen of the evangelist in writing down exactly what the historical Jesus said, nevertheless brings into the present the word, the event, the encounter which then broke into the world in the person of Jesus. The Paraclete guarantees the continuity and its integrity. It is to this end that the Gospel is written. It so tells the story that the encounter may take place. That retelling involves the use of traditions, but they serve now neither to narrate what actually may have happened nor to reproduce what Jesus may have said, "das Was," the "what" of revelation. They are employed in the service of mediating that encounter with the Word which can take place because of the sheer fact ("das Dass") that in Christ God has broken into the world in a unique way.[33] In this manner, the incarnation, crucifixion, resurrection, ascension, Pentecost, and parousia become for the Gospel a single event with a single message. This is the "eschatological event," the moment of ultimate encounter.[34]

The centering upon the eschatological event is so consistently carried through by the evangelist that traditional Christian categories are thoroughly reinterpreted. Thus while Bultmann identifies the notion of vicarious suffering in 1:29, for instance, this idea can no longer be of great importance for the evangelist.[35] Forgiveness is the gift of the risen one through his word.[36]

---

31. Bultmann, *Johannes*, 430–31; Bultmann, *Theologie*, 437, 395.
32. Bultmann, *Theologie*, 400.
33. Bultmann, *Johannes*, 188; Bultmann, *Theologie*, 418.
34. Bultmann, *Johannes*, 410–11.
35. Bultmann, *Johannes*, 66; Bultmann, *Theologie*, 406 n. 1.
36. Bultmann, *Theologie*, 408.

For the whole life of Jesus is an offering, and then only in the sense that in love he has given himself in the service of making the Father known, even in the final hour when in love he lays down his life.[37]

Traditional notions of eschatology have been reinterpreted by the author, because eternal life and resurrection happen in the encounter with the word already in the person of Jesus.[38] Eschatology is subsumed under Christology. Because this is so, Bultmann sees no place within the author's thought for notions of future resurrection or judgment. What awaits the believer at death is the final fulfilment of the oneness already known on earth.[39] The few verses which, by contrast, speak in traditional eschatological terms, Bultmann attributes, on these and other grounds, to later redaction. He sees the author, indeed, deliberately countering traditional eschatology as he identifies the moment of the casting out of the prince of this world not with a future apocalyptic event but with the event of the cross,[40] just as he has similarly relocated the moment of the Son's glorification to the cross.[41] Bultmann also sees no place in this radical reinterpretation, with its emphasis on encounter with the word, for a sacramental understanding of salvation and accordingly attributes 6:51c–58 and "of water" in 3:5 to the hand of an ecclesiastical redactor.[42]

Bultmann's presentation of Johannine Christology is a consistent whole. His commentary has that quality, rare among exegetical works, of being able to bridge the gap between the reader and the Gospel. Bultmann achieves this, not primarily by reading into the Gospel his own theological concerns, but by reflecting upon the questions which the text of the Gospel raises, not least because of the discrepancies which arise from a literal reading. That Bultmann sees these questions leading in the same direction as his own existentialist theology is not to be denied, but he appears not to compromise the integrity of the text as he perceives it.

There are, indeed, discrepancies in the text. Why does the revealer reveal nothing but that he is sent as the revealer? How can the author narrate the raising of Lazarus, for instance, and present Jesus as speaking of a totally different kind of resurrection available in his person, so that the original story seems little other than a symbol?[43] How can Jesus claim at one time that he

---

37. Bultmann, *Johannes*, 293, 372; Bultmann, *Theologie*, 405–7.
38. Bultmann, *Theologie*, 391–92.
39. Bultmann, *Johannes*, 399; Bultmann, *Theologie*, 437.
40. Bultmann, *Johannes*, 330.
41. Bultmann, *Johannes*, 402.
42. Bultmann, *Johannes*, 412.
43. Bultmann, *Johannes*, 306–7.

proclaims what he has seen and heard and at another that he proclaims what he sees and hears in the present? Is not the idea of pre-existence thereby relativised? Is it merely symbolic? And when life is offered, on the one hand, as the gift of the one who goes and, on the other, as the gift of the one who has come, do not the sayings about coming and going appear to conflict if they are not understood as just two different ways of symbolising Jesus' absolute claims? How, further, is it possible to speak of Jesus' glorification at his return to the Father and at the same time to affirm that the glory was seen in the earthly Jesus?[44]

Bultmann's is a genuine attempt to face these issues. His synthesis is impressive. The *theologia crucis* is found in the fact of Jesus' earthly, ordinary existence as well as in the suffering on the cross.[45] This authentic human life is the place of divine revelation. The encounter which takes place in the preaching of the word demands not extensive cognitive reception of the historical details of the life of Jesus or of dogma, but faith in the fact that this word has broken through in history.[46] The anthropological correlate of the divine gift is human hunger and thirst, the basic existential, and in that sense, timeless needs of human beings.[47] Accordingly, the divine correlate—the gift in the person of Jesus—is bread, light, and life.[48] By seeking to show that the evangelist uses the elements of the story to this one end, to focus upon the encounter, Bultmann achieves a presentation of Johannine Christology which speaks with timeless relevance. For the evangelist, while using the revelation schema, has in fact abandoned the revelation model or transformed it into an encounter model.[49]

The synthesis, thus achieved, not only presents the Johannine Gospel as a contemporary challenge; it also meets many of the questions which the text raises for the modern reader. Miracles are seen by John as symbols, so too pre-existence, exaltation, glorification, and parousia. And the issue of the Jesus of history becomes irrelevant, for only the fact of his coming, the paradox of the divine glory in human flesh, as an act of divine love, is important for the Johannine Jesus. We need not therefore be concerned at the differences between the Johannine and the Synoptic portrait of Jesus' ministry or the anachronisms in the Johannine account; for it is a post-Easter presentation of the Jesus of faith's experience in the time of the church, not

44. Bultmann, *Johannes*, 376–77.
45. Bultmann, *Johannes*, 356 n. 24, 533; Bultmann, *Theologie*, 405.
46. Bultmann, *Johannes*, 298, 540.
47. Bultmann, *Theologie*, 418.
48. Bultmann, *Theologie*, 416–17.
49. Bultmann, *Theologie*, 419.

INTRODUCTION

a reconstruction of the past. It is a re-presentation of the glory which faith has seen and which abides.

With the exception of the few eschatological and sacramental passages which Bultmann attributes to a redactor, and despite his generally unconvincing theory of disorder in the Gospel as the result of displacement of original sheets, Bultmann's synthesis is achieved without sacrificing the integrity of the work as a whole. The key to the synthesis lies in Bultmann's answers to the questions outlined above, especially in his belief that the evangelist must have intended a transformation of the story or myth of the Redeemer-Revealer. To use Bultmann's own terms, the evangelist practised demythologising. Once this demythologising, for which Bultmann marshals strong arguments from within the Gospel, is called into question at any point, the synthesis weakens and the problems are exposed. Criticisms of Bultmann have frequently called into question various points of the synthesis, but have rarely faced the reexposed problems with the thoroughness of Bultmann. It is Bultmann's achievement to have faced these problems and sought for them a consistent explanation.

Since the publication of the first edition of this current study in 1989 there have been a number of discussions of Johannine Christology which have recognised Bultmann's achievement and so taken it as the inspiration or at least the starting point for their own contributions.[50]

Whenever any point in Bultmann's synthesis has been questioned, far-reaching problems have been thrown up which ultimately demand a totally new synthesis. This may be illustrated in the following overview of elements of the synthesis which have been called into question.

---

50. See, for instance, the discussion in John Ashton, *Understanding the Fourth Gospel*, 2nd ed. (Oxford: Oxford University Press, 2007 [1st ed. in 1991]), 2–11; Herbert Kohler, *Kreuz und Menschwerdung im Johannesevangelium. Ein exegetisch-hermeneutischer Versuch zur johanneischen Kreuzestheologie*, ATANT 72 (Zürich: TVZ, 1987), 21–45; Paul N. Anderson, *The Christology of the Fourth Gospel: Its Unity and Disunity in the Light of John 6*, 3rd ed. (Eugene: Wipf and Stock, 2010), 33–36; Stephen Voorwinde, *Jesus' Emotions in the Fourth Gospel: Human or Divine?* JSNTSup 284 (London: T&T Clark, 2005), 5–9; Johanna Rahner, *"Er aber sprach vom Tempel seines Leibes." Jesus von Nazaret als Ort der Offenbarung Gottes im vierten Evangelium*, BBB 117 (Bodenheim: Philo, 1998), 12–26; Margaret Davies, *Rhetoric and Reference in the Fourth Gospel*, JSNTSup 69 (Sheffield: Sheffield Academic Press, 1992), 116, who distances herself from what she seems mistakenly to depict as Bultmann's position, only to end up espousing a position close to Bultmann's. She writes: "In order to accept Bultmann's assertion that the Johannine story of Jesus is expressed in mythological language we are required to understand literally Jesus' statements about his descent, his mission from the Father, his coming into the world, his departure and ascension to the Father, and then de-mythologize them." But this mistakes what we must do, with what according to Bultmann (and herself) the author did.

Introduction

Miracles?

Did the fourth evangelist really not believe in miracles? Most likely he did.[51] This is not to deny that they were signs, that they were ultimately words about the Son; but, as Wilhelm Wilkens points out, the suffering which forms part of the paradox of the cross is in part the direct result of miracles according to the Johannine story; they demonstrate Jesus' glory and are as real as other signs which are not miracles, such as the cross itself.[52] They were not just symbols.[53] As well as symbolically pointing to the deeper reality, for instance, that Jesus is the bread of life, the feeding of the 5,000 also demonstrates Jesus' power which belongs to his being the Revealer. The miracles must accordingly be taken seriously in the presentation of Johannine Christology, and in their endeavour to do so scholars are divided over their significance.

---

51. Ernst Haenchen, "'Der Vater, der mich gesandt hat,'" in *Gott und Mensch* (Tübingen: Mohr Siebeck, 1965), 69; Ernst Haenchen, "Das Johannesevangelium und Sein Kommentar," in *Die Bibel und Wir* (Tübingen: Mohr Siebeck, 1968), 219; Ernst Haenchen, *Johannesevangelium. Ein Kommentar*, ed. U. Busse (Tübingen: Mohr Siebeck, 1980), 106; Ernst Käsemann, "The Structure and Purpose of the Prologue to John's Gospel," in *New Testament Questions of Today* (London: SCM, 1969), 161; Ernst Käsemann, *Jesu Letzter Wille nach Johannes 17*, 3rd ed. (Tübingen: Mohr Siebeck, 1971), 54; Günther Bornkamm, "Zur Interpretation des Johannesevangeliums," in *Geschichte und Glaube. Erster Teil. Gesammelte Aufsätze, Band III* (Munich: Kaiser, 1968), 116; Harald Hegermann, "'Er kam in sein Eigentum,'" in *Der Ruf Jesu und die Antwort der Gemeinde. Festschrift für J. Jeremias* (Göttingen: Vandenhoeck und Ruprecht, 1970), 113; Anderson, *Christology*, 3, who hypothesises that what he sees as the author's ambivalence reflects stages of the author's faith development (159); Ashton, *Fourth Gospel*, 182; James F. McGrath, *John's Apologetic Christology: Legitimation and Development in Johannine Christology*, SNTSMS 111 (Cambridge: Cambridge University Press, 2001), 188–89; Rainer Schwindt, *Gesichte der Herrlichkeit. Eine exegetisch-traditionsgeschichtliche Studie zur paulinischen und johanneischen Christologie*, HBS 50 (Freiburg: Herder, 2007), 294–301. On the use of miracles in John to promote recognition of Jesus as Messiah see Gilbert Van Belle, "The Signs of the Messiah in the Fourth Gospel: The Problem of a 'Wonder-Working Messiah,'" in *The Scriptures of Israel in Jewish and Christian Tradition: Essays in Honour of Maarten J. J. Menken*, ed. B. J. Koet, S. Moyise, and J. Verheyden, NovTSup 148 (Leiden: Brill, 2013), 168, who writes: "even though no miracles were expected in the Jewish tradition of the Messiah, it was a true 'dogma' for the Christians and certainly also for John that by his miracles Jesus would be recognised as Messiah."

52. Wilhelm Wilkens, *Zeichen und Werke*, ATANT 55 (Zürich: Zwingli, 1969), 27, 30, 32, 44, 49, 66.

53. So Haenchen, *Johannes*, 106; similarly Rudolf Schnackenburg, "Johannesevangelium als hermeneutische Frage," *NTS* 13 (1967): 205–6; Mark L. Appold, *The Oneness Motif in the Fourth Gospel*, WUNT 2.1 (Tübingen: Mohr Siebeck, 1976), 95, 100–101; Peter von den Osten-Sacken, "Leistung und Grenze der johanneischen Kreuzestheologie," *EvT* 36 (1976): 161; Willem Nicol, *The Semeia in the Fourth Gospel*, NovTSup 32 (Leiden: Brill, 1972), 106.

Many, like Rudolf Schnackenburg, argue that faith in miracles is a first step.[54] For Jürgen Becker it is not faith at all, but rather leads to a Christology the evangelist seeks to counter.[55] For Luise Schottroff miracle faith belongs to the irrelevant response to Jesus which sees him in this-worldly terms. True faith sees what the miracles symbolise and that alone.[56] For Ernst Käsemann the Gospel intends miracle faith and emphasises miracles as manifestations of Jesus' divine power and glory.[57]

The question about miracles opens a wider door. Was the evangelist at all concerned about the details of the earthly Jesus? Bultmann would answer: no. Schottroff also answers: no, but not in a way that denies the reality of the details.[58] On her analysis, the Christology of the Gospel of John considers the earthly Jesus irrelevant except insofar as one sees the heavenly Jesus as beyond the human. However, most other scholars seem to imply by their response to the miracle question at least some relevance of the picture of the earthly Jesus for the evangelist in composing the Gospel.

Ernst Käsemann and Naïve Docetism

It is not insignificant that Käsemann, who, one could say, reopened the issue of the historical Jesus, was the one who revived the nineteenth-century critical description of the Johannine Jesus as a god marching triumphantly across the world.[59] For not only the miracles, but also Jesus' sovereign knowledge

---

54. Rudolf Schnackenburg, *The Gospel according to John*, 3 vols. (London: Burns & Oates, 1968–1982), 1:517; similarly Nicol, *Semeia*, 99–103; J. Terence Forestell, *The Word of the Cross*, AnBib 57 (Rome: BibInst, 1974), 70; Appold, *Oneness*, 100.

55. Jürgen Becker, "Wunder und Christologie," NTS 16 (1969–1970): 144–48; Jürgen Becker, *Das Evangelium des Johannes*, OekTK 4.1, 2 (Gütersloh: Mohn, 1979–1981), 1:119–20; similarly Michael Lattke, *Einheit im Wort*, SANT 41 (Munich: Kösel, 1975), 143.

56. Luise Schottroff, *Der Glaubende und die feindliche Welt*, WMANT 37 (Neukirchen: Neukirchener Verlag, 1970), 258–59; similarly Wolfgang Langbrandtner, *Weltferner Gott oder Gott der Liebe*, BET 6 (Frankfurt: Lang, 1977), 93–96, for the Grundschrift see also 111.

57. Käsemann, *Letzter Wille*, 17, 53, 53 n. 59.

58. Schottroff, *Glaubende*, 252–59; similarly Lattke, *Einheit*, 143; Heinrich Schlier, "Zur Christologie des Johannesevangeliums," in *Das Ende der Zeit. Exegetische Aufsätze und Vorträge III* (Freiburg: Herder, 1971), 85–88.

59. Käsemann, *Letzter Wille*, 22, 53–54; cf. already Ferdinand Christian Baur, *Kritische Untersuchungen über die kanonischen Evangelien* (Tübingen: Fues, 1847), 87, 313; and Heinrich J. Holtzmann, *Lehrbuch der neutestamentlichen Theologie II*, 2nd ed. (Tübingen: Mohr Siebeck, 1911), 458; Wilhelm Bousset, *Kyrios Christos: A History of the Belief in Christ from the Beginnings of Christianity to Irenaeus*, trans. John E. Steely (Nashville: Abingdon, 1970), 217–18.

Introduction

in encounter with his opponents,[60] presents a Jesus who fails to meet Bultmann's ideal of an ordinary human being about whom there was nothing extraordinary except his claim to be the Revealer.[61] Käsemann's analysis was, in a very real sense, inevitable once he crossed the threshold—deemed by Bultmann as both irrelevant and inappropriate to the Johannine conception—and began to ask what kind of Jesus is portrayed here.[62]

In response to Käsemann, Günther Bornkamm pointed to and emphasized elements of the portrayal which present Jesus in the Gospel as a real man, especially those which centre the attention upon the death of Jesus, including, not least, the final discourses, to which Käsemann gives scant attention, and also the passion narrative.[63] An interpreter could, indeed, assert with Wilhelm Thüsing—as Martin Kähler had of Mark—that the Gospel of John is also a passion narrative with an extended introduction.[64] Above all, Bornkamm argued that the Johannine Jesus must be seen in the light of the work of the Paraclete as a post-Easter presentation of the Christ of faith.[65] But the issue raised by Käsemann is primarily whether the picture, so produced, has not overlaid the earthly Jesus with post-Easter perspectives of a certain developed Christology to an extent that beneath it all, the earthly Jesus ceases to be a real human being. This certainly was to happen in Gnosticism, which denied Christ a real humanity and a real death. For Käsemann the evangelist is not so blatant,[66] but nevertheless

---

60. Eduard Schweizer, "Jesus der Zeuge Gottes," in *Studies in John. Presented to J. N. Sevenster*, NovTSup 24 (Leiden: Brill, 1970), 162–63.

61. Bultmann, *Theologie*, 403.

62. On Käsemann's contribution see Kohler, *Kreuz*, 45–64; Anderson, *Christology*, 24.

63. Günther Bornkamm, "Zur Interpretation des Johannesevangeliums," in *Geschichte und Glaube. Erster Teil. Gesammelte Aufsätze, Band III* (Munich: Kaiser, 1968), 112, 114; similarly von den Osten-Sacken, "Leistung," 160; Wilkens, *Zeichen*, 51–52, 66; Appold, *Oneness*, 111; cf. also Schweizer, "Zeuge," 167.

64. Wilhelm Thüsing, *Die Erhöhung und Verherrlichung Jesu im Johannesevangelium*, 3rd ed., NTAbh 21 (Münster: Aschendorff, 1979), 335; similarly Klaus Haacker, *Die Stiftung des Heils. Untersuchungen zur Struktur der johanneischen Theologie*, AzTh 47 (Stuttgart: Calwer, 1972), 167–68. Cf. Martin Kähler, *The So-Called Historical Jesus and the Historic, Biblical Christ* (Philadelphia: Fortress, 1966), 80.

65. Bornkamm, "Interpretation," 114. On this see Jörg Frey, "Die 'theologia crucifixi' des Johannevangeliums," in *Die Herrlichkeit des Gekreuzigten. Studien zu den Johanneischen Schriften I*, ed. J. Schlegel, WUNT 307 (Tübingen: Mohr Siebeck, 2013), 506; Jörg Frey, "'dass sie meine Herrlichkeit schauen' (Joh 17,24). Zu Hintergrund, Sinn und Funktion der johanneischen Rede von der δόξα Jesu," in *Die Herrlichkeit des Gekreuzigten. Studien zu den Johanneischen Schriften I*, ed. J. Schlegel, WUNT 307 (Tübingen: Mohr Siebeck, 2013), 646.

66. As, for instance, Schottroff, *Glaubende*, suggests (279); similarly Ulrich B. Müller, "Die Bedeutung des Kreuzestodes im Johannesevangelium," *KD* 21 (1975): 52 n. 15.

does reflect a naive docetism,⁶⁷ a Johannine tendency also noted by Eduard Schweizer.⁶⁸

Accordingly Käsemann counters the central role given to 1:14a ("The Word became flesh") in Bultmann's Christology and much traditional Christology, arguing that it is of subordinate significance in the immediate context and means little more than that the Logos assumed fleshly attire as the vehicle for manifesting divine glory. The focus of the passage lies on 1:14c, "we beheld his glory."⁶⁹ Bornkamm countered with the Bultmannian thesis that the manifestation of glory is primarily in the cross as a paradox of real human suffering and divine glory and attacked Käsemann's exclusive dependence on 1:14c.⁷⁰ But for Käsemann the manifestation of glory in John is not confined to the cross. Jesus' life and ministry was one long manifestation of glory. The passion narrative, no longer relevant as passion, now portrays a triumphant exit.⁷¹ He also points out that Bultmann went primarily to the antidocetic statements of 1 and 2 John for support of his interpretation of 1:14, not to the Gospel itself.⁷²

Others have taken this further and suggested that 1:14a comes from the hand of a later redactor sharing the concerns of the Epistles.⁷³ On the

---

67. Käsemann, *Letzter Wille*, 61–62. See also Siegfried Schulz, *Das Evangelium nach Johannes*, NTD 4 (Göttingen: Vandenhoeck und Ruprecht, 1972), 211–12; von den Osten-Sacken, "Leistung," 157; Georg Richter, *Studien zum Johannesevangelium*, BU 13 (Regensburg: Pustet, 1977), 112, 114 (docetism in the Gospel; antidocetism in redaction); similarly Hartwig Thyen, "'. . . denn wir lieben die Brüder' (1 Joh 3,14)," in *Rechtfertigung. Festschrift für E. Käsemann*, ed. G. Friedrich et al. (Tübingen: Mohr Siebeck, 1976), 536; Langbrandtner, *Weltferner Gott*, 38, 95–96. Against docetism in John see Wilkens, *Zeichen*, 67; Günther Bornkamm, "Der Paraklet im Johannes-Evangelium," in *Geschichte und Glaube. Erster Teil. Gesammelte Aufsätze, Band III* (Munich: Kaiser, 1968), 68–89, 89; "Interpretation," 117–18.

68. Eduard Schweizer, "Der Kirchenbegriff im Evangelium und in den Briefen des Johannes," in *Studia Evangelica I*, TU 73 (Berlin: de Gruyter, 1959), 363–64.

69. Käsemann, *Letzter Wille*, 22–24.

70. Bornkamm, "Interpretation," 113, 117.

71. On this see Mavis M. Leung, *The Kingship-Cross Interplay in the Gospel of John: Jesus' Death as Corroboration of His Royal Messiahship* (Eugene: Wipf and Stock, 2011), 8–11; John Dennis, "Jesus' Death in John's Gospel: A Survey of Research from Bultmann to the Present with Special Reference to the Johannine Hyper-Texts," *CurBR* 4 (2006): 337–39; Rahner, *Tempel*, 26–39; Ashton, *Fourth Gospel*, 463–65. See also the critical discussion in Martinus C. de Boer, *Johannine Perspectives on the Death of Jesus*, CEBT 17 (Kampen: Pharos, 1996), 20–29.

72. Käsemann, *Letzter Wille*, 49 n. 53; Bultmann, *Theologie*, 392.

73. Richter, *Studien*, 152, 157–58, 170, 179–182; Hartwig Thyen, "Entwicklungen innerhalb der johanneischen Theologie und Kirche im Spiegel von Joh 21 und der Lieblingsjüngertexte des Evangeliums," in *L'Évangile de Jean. Sources, Rédaction, Théologie*, ed. M. de Jonge, BETL 44 (Leuven: Peeters, 1977), 259–99; "Brüder," 532.

Introduction

other hand, Schottroff argues for taking 1:14 to mean becoming real flesh but claims that the flesh is irrelevant for the author.[74] According to Ulrich B. Müller, John 1:14 belongs to the author's tradition and expresses a Christology centered in miracles, which he then sets in balance with the passion narrative.[75] Others, like Yu Ibuki—while acknowledging Käsemann's valid exegetical observations about the centrality of 1:14c—have explained the manifestation of glory in ways that seek to retain a strong emphasis on 1:14a as expressing a real humanity and have therefore interpreted the glory as the glory of the relationship of love between Father and Son.[76]

The issue of Jesus' humanity is also addressed by those who endeavour to remove pre-existence from the story of Johannine Christology altogether. Often noting, as Bultmann had, the discrepancy between statements of pre-existent seeing and hearing as the source of revelation and such passages as 5:19–20 which speak of the Son's seeing and hearing in the present, these scholars opt not for Bultmann's synthesis of demythologising but for a thoroughly humanised Christology. Thus John A. T. Robinson revives the suggestion that only an anhypostatic pre-existence of the Logos should be presupposed in John, so that Jesus is totally a human being like us and the model for all human relationships with God. Francis Watson has taken this further, arguing for an adoptionist Christology on the theory that the Logos joined Jesus at his baptism.[77] According to Margaret Davies, "The Gospel never states that the human being, Jesus, the 'I' of the request in 17:5, existed anywhere at any time before he was born and lived in Palestine,"[78] but "is portraying Jesus and his disciples as prophets like Moses."[79]

---

74. Schottroff, *Glaubende*, 272, 275; similarly Müller, "Bedeutung," 52 n. 15; Schulz, *Johannes*, 211–12.

75. Ulrich B. Müller, *Christologie in der Johanneischen Gemeinde*, SBS 77 (Stuttgart: KBW, 1975), 13–36; "Bedeutung," 66–67; similarly Becker, *Johannes*, 78.

76. Yu Ibuki, *Die Wahrheit im Johannesevangelium*, BBB 39 (Bonn: Hanstein, 1972), 193–98; similarly Heinrich Schlier, "In Anfang war das Wort: Zum Prolog des Johannesevangeliums," in *Die Zeit der Kirche: Exegetische Aufsätze und Vorträge* (Freiburg: Herder, 1968), 282.

77. John A. T. Robinson, *The Priority of John* (London: SCM, 1985), 368–89; Francis Watson, "Is John's Christology Adoptionist?" in *The Glory of Christ in the New Testament: Studies in Christology. In Honour of G. B. Caird*, ed. L. D. Hurst and N. T. Wright (Oxford: Clarendon, 1987), 113–24. See also Ludger Schenke, "Christologie als Theologie. Versuch über das Johannesevangelium," in *Von Jesus zum Christus. Christologische Studien. Festgabe für Paul Hoffmann zum 65. Geburtstag*, ed. R. Hoppe and U. Busse, BZNW 93 (Berlin: de Gruyter, 1998), 459–61.

78. Davies, *Rhetoric and Reference*, 133.

79. Davies, *Rhetoric and Reference*, 167.

INTRODUCTION

Faith and History

The question of Jesus' humanity is also closely bound to the issue of faith and history in John. The Johannine Jesus speaks Johannine language. Correspondingly there is a distinctive Johannine way of seeing, as Franz Mussner points out. The Paraclete not only brings to memory, but also inspires interpretation. This results in a portrayal of Jesus in which pre- and post-Easter perspectives are merged in the light of Jesus' glory. The Gospel is therefore speaking the language of epiphany and the evangelist becomes the mouthpiece for Christ, who speaks Johannine language in response to issues of the evangelist's day.[80] The work of Herbert Leroy and others on techniques of misunderstanding and double meaning shows that the Gospel depends on having an "in-group" for such techniques to be effective and speaks to and serves the interests of that group.[81] J. Louis Martyn has shown how at one level the miracle in the healing of the blind man in John 9 reflects the community's own conflicts with the synagogue.[82] He speaks of the author doubling Jesus with an early Christian preacher.[83] These and other studies raise all the more acutely the question: how did the evangelist intend that we should understand his Gospel?

Was it to be understood as a historical account with a few interpretative elements, inevitable in any historical work because of subjectivity and distance, and above all, because of the latter, of even greater value because of the perspective which elapse of time brings? Then we should expect to find evaluative interpretation beside, but separate from, faithfully reproduced words of Jesus. Were words of Jesus that are distinctive to the Fourth Gospel derived from a special memory tradition—as Harald Riesenfeld suggested[84]—preserving perhaps the private instruction of Jesus, the rabbi? An extreme form of this approach is found in Sydney Temple, who argues that

---

80. Franz Mussner, *Die johanneische Sehweise*, QD 28 (Freiburg: Herder, 1965), 42–43, 57, 81, 84.

81. Herbert Leroy, *Rätsel und Missverständnis*, BBB 32 (Bonn: Hanstein, 1968), 71; similarly Birger Olsson, *Structure and Meaning in the Fourth Gospel*, ConBNT 6 (Lund: Gleerup, 1974), 282–83.

82. J. Louis Martyn, *History and Theology in the Fourth Gospel*, 3rd ed. (Louisville: Westminster John Knox, 2003), 40, 124.

83. Martyn, *History and Theology*, 38; similarly Stephen S. Smalley, *John: Evangelist and Interpreter* (Exeter: Paternoster, 1978), 178, cf. also 194–95.

84. Harald Riesenfeld, "The Gospel Tradition and Its Beginnings," in *The Gospels Reconsidered: A Selection of Papers Read to the International Congress on the Four Gospels, 1957* (Oxford: Blackwell, 1969), 151–52; Leon Morris, *The Gospel according to John* (Grand Rapids: Eerdmans, 1971), 45–47.

a scribe wrote down the core of the Gospel shortly after the end of Jesus' ministry and that it came to light only some 50 years later.[85] Can, then, even the pre-existence sayings and those which are most commonly understood to reflect a post-Easter situation be explained as expressing Jesus' earthly experience of instruction from the Father and not pre-existence at all, in the one case, and as proleptic foreknowledge, in the other, as W. H. Cadman suggests?[86] This is most unlikely. It does not account for the fact that Jesus' language in John is so distinctly Johannine, his words, there, are mostly addressed to a public audience, and they include those which contain the developed Johannine Christology of which the Synoptics bear little trace.

The most thorough attempt in recent years to claim historical origins for the very different image of Jesus in John is that of Paul N. Anderson. He goes beyond the recognition that the Fourth Gospel in all probability preserves an underlay of early material. Anderson employs a psychological theory of the author's personal development through the stages of faith as outlined by James Fowler.[87] Anderson even speculates that we could be dealing with this one disciple's experience of Jesus as he passes through the processes of personal development and reflection which led to his very different portrait.[88] More credible than an individual's inner development is an interactive process of post-Easter reflection which took on distinctive traits in the creative hands of leadership within what in general terms we call the Johannine community. Even a trimmed version of a Jesus asserting openly his messiahship let alone his divine status is difficult to reconcile with what we find in the Jesus tradition of the first three Gospels. Were their disciples simply not listening?

Does the post-Easter perspective mean that the evangelist simply pro-

---

85. Sydney Temple, *The Core of the Fourth Gospel* (London: Oxford University Press, 1975), 286-87.

86. W. H. Cadman, *The Open Heaven* (Oxford: Blackwell, 1969), 203-4; similarly L. Brun, "Die Gottesschau des johanneischen Christus," *SO* 5 (1927): 1-22; cf. also Robinson, *Priority*, 368-89.

87. James Fowler, *Stages of Faith: The Psychology of Human Development and the Quest for Meaning* (San Francisco: HarperCollins, 1981); Anderson, *Christology*, 142-48.

88. Anderson, *Christology*, 255; see also Paul N. Anderson, "Interfluential, Formative, and Dialectical—A Theory of John's Relation to the Synoptics," in *Für und wider die Priorität des Johannesevangeliums*, ed. P. Hofrichter (Hildesheim: Olms, 2002), 19-58; Paul N. Anderson, "The Cognitive Origins of John's Unitive and Disunitive Christology," *HBT* 17 (1995): 1-24; Paul N. Anderson, "Aspects of Historicity in the Fourth Gospel: Consensus and Convergences," in *John, Jesus, and History, Volume 2: Aspects of Historicity in the Fourth Gospel*, ed. P. N. Anderson, F. Just, and T. Thatcher, ECL 2 (Atlanta: SBL, 2009), 379-86. See also his summary discussion in *Christology*, xxxv-lxxxiv.

jected back into the setting of the earthly ministry and onto earlier traditions an image of the post-Easter Jesus without regard for history, except the all-important single fact of the Word made flesh in history, as Bultmann suggests? Would the evangelist have known that he was projecting such a picture?[89] Or was it done unconsciously as the fruit of faith? Siegfried Schulz argued that the evangelist depends heavily on what had already been developed in apocalyptic Christian material.[90] Walter Grundmann spoke of visionary experiences of the Johannine church being reflected in the speeches of Jesus.[91] Klaus Haacker notes that many speeches of Jesus are not directed to the disciples.[92] Marinus de Jonge and others have pointed out that the author shows himself fully aware at points that certain insights about Jesus came to the disciples only after Easter (12:16; 13:7). Similarly the sayings about the Paraclete assume an awareness that true knowledge about Jesus came to the disciples only then.[93] John Ashton writes that "the difference between John's portrait of Christ and that of the Synoptics is best accounted for by the *experience* of the glorious Christ, constantly present to him and to his community."[94] Is it the case that the evangelist believed that he was recounting events as they happened with help of the divine "recall" of the Spirit? Or was it that he believed Jesus gave pointers during his earthly ministry and that post-Easter reflection simply elaborated these?[95]

Growing recognition of the author's skilful compositional techniques which touch every part of the Gospel, including especially the words of Jesus, suggests that the author must have been aware that his portrait was ahistorical. This is not to say that it was unhistorical, i.e., that it did not contain some reference to what the author believed had actually happened. It does, however, suggest that he was governed by another purpose. In that sense Bultmann is right that the details of history are not a priority, but Käsemann is also right to examine the resultant picture for its portrait of the earthly Jesus. The issues of the historicity of the picture of Jesus and of its humanity

89. Schnackenburg, *John*, 1:23.

90. Siegfried Schulz, *Untersuchungen zur Menschensohn-Christologie im Johannesevangelium* (Göttingen: Vandenhoeck und Ruprecht, 1957), 179.

91. Walter Grundmann, *Zeugnis und Gestalt des Johannes-Evangeliums* (Stuttgart: Calwer, 1960), 14.

92. Haacker, *Stiftung*, 59–60.

93. Marinus de Jonge, *Jesus: Stranger from Heaven and Son of God*, SBLMS 10 (Missoula: Scholars, 1977), 8, 11–12; Bornkamm, "Paraklet," 87–89; Onuki, *Gemeinde*, 194.

94. John Ashton, *The Gospel of John and Christian Origins* (Minneapolis: Fortress Press, 2014), 201–2; similarly in John Ashton, "The Johannine Son of Man: A New Proposal," *NTS* 57 (2011): 526.

95. So Haenchen, "Vater," 74.

Introduction

are not the same as the issue of how the author might have understood the historicity or humanity of his portrayal of Jesus. Both sets of questions must be seen in their distinctiveness and both deserve attention.

There are other important issues related to the question of faith and history. Bultmann bracketed out the historical questions about Jesus and also gave too little attention to the situation of the evangelist and its relationship to Christology. Bultmann's tendency to reduce elements of the story of the Gospel to symbol may be observed in his treatment of "the Jews" in John. They are allegedly mere symbols of the world of darkness, a world that rejects the light.[96] Investigation of the author's situation suggests strongly that the Jews are not just symbols of the world, but reflect in some way the conflicts of the Johannine community with contemporary Judaism.[97] Increased awareness of these issues lies behind the expansions in this new edition, not least in relation to the Gospel's depiction of the Law and its status, the relation of Law, Logos and Wisdom, the transfer of Torah images to Jesus acclaiming him as the true bearer of light, life and bread, and the significance of messianic claims.[98]

Gnostic Redeemer?

As Bultmann's reduction of the historical Jesus to a simple point in time has been largely given up in favour of a reexamination of the Johannine understanding of the earthly Jesus and his story, so Bultmann's reduction of

---

96. Bultmann, *Johannes*, 59.
97. See the discussion in Ashton, *Fourth Gospel*, 60–78.
98. On this see William Loader, "The Law and Ethics in John," in *Rethinking the Ethics of John: 'Implicit Ethics' in the Johannine Writings*, ed. J. G. van der Watt and R. Zimmermann, Contexts and Norms of New Testament Ethics, 3 vols. (Tübingen: Mohr Siebeck, 2012), 3:143–58; William Loader, "Jesus and the Law in John," in *Theology and Christology in the Fourth Gospel: Essays by Members of the Johannine Writings Seminar* ed. G. Van Belle, J. G. van der Watt, and P. Maritz, BETL 184 (Leuven: Leuven University Press; Leuven: Peeters, 2005), 135–54; William Loader, "'Your Law'—the Johannine Perspective," in *"was ihr auf dem Weg verhandelt habt": Beiträge zur Exegese und Theologie des Neuen Testaments. Festschrift für Ferdinand Hahn zum 75. Geburtstag*, ed. P. Müller, C. Gerber, and T. Knöppler (Neukirchen-Vluyn: Neukirchener Verlag, 2001), 63–74; William Loader, "The Significance of the Prologue for Understanding John's Soteriology," in *The Prologue of the Gospel of John: Its Literary and Philosophical Context*, ed. J. G. van der Watt and R. A. Culpepper, WUNT 359 (Tübingen: Mohr Siebeck, 2016), 46–54; William Loader, "The Significance of 1:14–18 for Understanding John's Approach to Law and Ethics," *Review of Rabbinic Judaism* 19 (2016): 194–201; and William Loader, "Wisdom and Logos Traditions in Judaism and John's Christology" (forthcoming).

the Johannine situation is increasingly being surrendered to a more differentiated analysis. This goes hand in hand with an increasing unwillingness to accept Bultmann's view that John's Gospel has demythologised the myth of the Redeemer-Revealer sent from heaven.

Schottroff remains close to Bultmann in denying that the evangelist places emphasis upon any temporal development in the story of the Revealer as presupposed in the myth.[99] For her, the evangelist, however, does not deny pre-existence. Nevertheless all the emphasis falls upon the call of the Redeemer. The Redeemer calls his own out of the hostile world.[100] Reality is polarised by the fact of the Redeemer. Like Bultmann's analysis, Schottroff's has a dualism of decision.[101] By decision the two spheres of light and darkness are established. Yet Schottroff also presupposes a modified cosmic dualism, for a real pre-existence implies it, as does the understanding of salvation as escape from this world, and it also lies behind her distinction between faith's vision of the truth about Jesus and the world's seeing him only as a miracle worker.[102] This dualism recalls Dodd's analysis where Platonic thought is employed to distinguish between two levels of reality in John.[103] Schottroff's conclusion is different from Bultmann's also in that it aligns John with Gnosticism. This is reflected not only in the role she presupposes for cosmic dualism, but also in the common dualism of decision, shared with Gnosticism.[104] As Ernst Haenchen had already pointed out, Bultmann's assumption that Gnosticism does not know the dualism of decision is questionable.[105]

Here it is interesting to observe that as soon as we give up demythologising as an explanation of the evangelist's method in interpreting the Redeemer's story, Bultmann's analysis drives us in the direction of gnosis, for he had maintained that the Johannine story pattern had been modelled on the gnostic. And once it is recognised that Gnosticism also used the dualism of decision, the differences between Johannine Christology and the

---

99. Schottroff, *Glaubende*, 230, 285–86. See also the discussion in Kohler, *Kreuz*, 64–84, 131–33; Rahner, *Tempel*, 39–52.

100. Schottroff, *Glaubende*, 228, cf. 232–33.

101. Schottroff, *Glaubende*, 228, 285.

102. Schottroff, *Glaubende*, 272–74, 279.

103. C. H. Dodd, *The Interpretation of the Fourth Gospel* (Cambridge: Cambridge University Press, 1953), 142–43, 445 n. 1. See the discussion in Jan G. van der Watt, "Symbolism in John's Gospel: An Evaluation of Dodd's Contribution," in *Engaging with C. H. Dodd on the Gospel of John: Sixty Years of Tradition and Interpretation*, ed. T. Thatcher and C. H. Williams (Cambridge: Cambridge University Press, 2014), 66–85.

104. Schottroff, *Glaubende*, 289, 295.

105. Haenchen, "Das Johannesvangelium," 223–34.

Introduction

gnostic myth are reduced considerably. Because he shares Bultmann's presuppositions about a gnostic background of the Gospel, Käsemann, too, finds himself acknowledging a more direct relationship with Gnosticism than Bultmann would allow.[106] Wolfgang Langbrandtner takes this development even further when he argues that notions such as the pre-existence of the soul are not of the *esse* of gnostic thought; they are myths spun out to underpin what is basically a theology of salvation, according to which faith means acceptance of the Redeemer who offers the way to the heavenly rest; the true gnostic is born only by faith, by decision.[107] Bultmann's position on the relationship of John and Gnosticism meets its antithesis in Roland Bergmeier who argues that in John's Gospel we have determinism, not the dualism of decision evident within Gnosticism.[108]

This is not the place to examine the case for the relationship between John and Gnosticism, but it is apparent that Bultmann's synthesis was so achieved that removal of the demythologising theory inevitably led to directly gnostic interpretations of the Gospel. The Nag Hammadi discoveries, which established the new understanding of gnostic dualism, have hastened the process.

Pre-existence and the Revealer

The assertion that the Johannine story or pattern is not to be demythologised gave to the ideas of pre-existence and sending a far greater importance than Bultmann had ever allowed. Scholars like Käsemann, Luise Schottroff, and Mark L. Appold have persisted in playing off the idea of Jesus' oneness with the Father against the idea of sending.[109] This is largely a legacy of Bultmann's synthesis. Haenchen and others are right when they recognise that the notions of pre-existence and sending are of central importance for the author of the Gospel of John. These dual notions raise crucial questions about how the relationship of Jesus to the Father is to be understood.[110] In contrast, Josef

---

106. Käsemann, *Letzter Wille*, 95–96 n. 36b. See also Kohler, *Kreuz*, 134–36.

107. Langbrandtner, *Weltferner Gott*, 91–93; but see the criticism of this assessment of Gnosticism by Onuki, *Gemeinde*, 53 and the review of Schottroff by Hans-Martin Schenke, "Review of L. Schottroff, *Der Glaubende und die feindliche Welt*," TLZ 97 (1972): 755.

108. Roland Bergmeier, *Glaube als Gabe nach Johannes*, BWANT 12 (Stuttgart: Kohlhammer, 1980), 213–36.

109. Käsemann, *Letzter Wille*, 30–31, 59; Appold, *Oneness*, 20, 272, 280–83; similarly Ibuki, *Wahrheit*, 149, 358.

110. Haenchen, *Johannes*, 107; similarly Bornkamm, "Paraklet," 69, 77–79; Juan P. Mi-

INTRODUCTION

Blank and Johannes Riedl, for instance, strongly emphasise the person of Jesus, his being and nature, as the clue to his revelation, so that to meet him is to meet the divine, and they consider Johannine Christology as thus treading a pre-trinitarian path. Riedl even speaks of a binitarian conception in John.[111] That seems a straightforward way of explaining such statements as: "he who has seen me has seen the Father" (14:9). But the Gospel does not argue in this way. Rather it relates revelation to what Jesus says and does. He says what he has heard from the Father in his pre-existence; he fulfils a commission given him; he does the Father's works not because of an innate deity, but because of obedience. And, above all, the notions of pre-existence and sending serve to portray Jesus' oneness as the oneness of the sent one who is subordinate to another. C. K. Barrett, in particular, argues this point strongly.[112] In that sense, Michael Theobald maintains that the author employs it to protect his christological claims against any accusation of ditheism or literal equality with God, while still asserting his substantial oneness.[113]

It is at this point that Bultmann's synthesis was at its strongest. For his observation is valid that Jesus does not in fact come with revelations from the Father. Haenchen, who stresses the importance of sending and its implied subordination, tries to counter this by arguing that Jesus in the Gospel of John reveals more than just the simple fact that he is the revealer. He also reveals the Father's love and offers both bread and life.[114] However, that was already implied in Bultmann's statements.[115] The problem of the Christology

---

randa, *Die Sendung Jesu im vierten Evangelium*, SBS 87 (Stuttgart: KBW, 1977), 37-38, 42; de Jonge, *Stranger*, 141-50. See also the discussion in William Loader, "John 5,19-47: A Deviation from Envoy Christology," in *Studies in the Gospel of John and Its Christology: Festschrift Gilbert Van Belle*, ed. J. Verheyden, G. van Oyen, M. Labahn, and R. Bieringer, BETL 265 (Leuven: Peeters, 2014), 149-64.

111. Johannes Riedl, *Das Heilswerk nach Johannes*, FTS 93 (Freiburg: Herder, 1973), 153, 201-5, 421-23; Josef Blank, *Krisis. Untersuchungen zur johanneischen Christologie und Eschatologie* (Freiburg: Lambertus, 1962), 36, 69, 72, 222-24. See also Udo Schnelle, "Trinitarisches Denken im Johannesevangelium," in *Israel und seine Heilstraditionen im Johannesevangelium. Festgabe für Johannes Beutler SJ zum 70. Geburtstag*, ed. M. Labahn, K. Scholtissek, and A. Strotmann (Paderborn: Ferdinand Schöningh, 2004), 376, 379-80.

112. C. K. Barrett, "'The Father Is Greater Than I': John 14.28: Subordinationist Christology in the New Testament," in *Essays on John* (Philadelphia: Westminster, 1982), 19-36; C. K. Barrett, "Christocentric or Theocentric? Observations on the Theological Method of the Fourth Gospel," in *Essays on John* (Philadelphia: Westminster, 1982), 1-18.

113. Michael Theobald, "Gott, Logos und Pneuma. 'Trinitarische' Rede von Gott im Johannesevangelium," in *Studien zum Corpus Iohanneum*, WUNT 267 (Tübingen: Mohr Siebeck, 2010), 366-68.

114. Haenchen, "Vater," 72; *Johannes*, 226.

115. See Bultmann, *Theologie*, 414, 418.

Introduction

of sending rests in its failure to do justice to the fact that Jesus is not the bearer of revelation. The model of information-revelation has been transformed into a model of revelation-encounter. The answer does not appear to lie in the direction of Riedl who would say that Jesus was the revelation himself because of his being and nature. That in turn fails to do justice to the sending and related motifs which are represented throughout the Gospel.

The Envoy Motif

A new and important way lies in a reexamination of the notion of sending in the light of judicial emissary patterns in Judaism and stereotypical protocols of emissaries and ambassadors in the ancient world, which were frequently applied to heavenly as well as earthly figures. The messengers present themselves in such a way that they may be much more than the bearers of a message. They are an extension of the sender, so that they mediate the presence of the sender. Earlier Karl H. Rengstorf and Josef Kühl—then Peder Borgen, Juan P. Miranda, and Jan Bühner—pointed to this circle of ideas.[116] These studies have explored the prophetic, rabbinic, and apocalyptic backgrounds of the sending idea and sought to relate the Fourth Gospel to them. Bühner even posits a Johannine Christology of a pre-existent ascension for authorisation and finds traces of this in 3:13.[117]

Further exploration and clarification is needed for statements which imply sending, subordination, and the reception of revelation and those which speak more directly of Jesus' relationship to God. Is Jesus analogous to Wisdom[118] or to apocalyptic eschatological figures,[119] a bearer of God's

---

116. Karl Heinrich Rengstorf, "ἀποστέλλω," *TDNT* 1:398–406; Josef Kühl, *Die Sendung Jesu und der Kirche nach dem Johannesevangelium* (St. Augustin: Steyler, 1967); Peder Borgen, *Bread from Heaven: An Exegetical Study of the Concept of Man in the Gospel of John and the Writings of Philo*, NovTSup 10 (Leiden: Brill, 1965), 158–62; also Peder Borgen, "God's Agent in the Fourth Gospel," in *Logos Was the True Light* (Trondheim: Tapir, 1983), 121–32; Juan P. Miranda, *"Der Vater, der mich gesandt hat,"* 2nd ed., EHS 23.7 (Frankfurt: Peter Lang, 1976); Jan Bühner, *Der Gesandte und sein Weg im 4. Evangelium*, WUNT 2.2 (Tübingen: Mohr Siebeck, 1977). See also Ferdinand Hahn, *Theologie des Neuen Testaments*, 2 Vols. (Tübingen: Mohr Siebeck, 2002), 1:606–7; Ashton, *Fourth Gospel*, 225–28, 297; Jan G. van der Watt, *Family of the King: Dynamics of Metaphor in the Gospel according to John*, BI 47 (Leiden: Brill, 2000), 296–302.

117. Bühner, *Gesandte*, 310, 373–78.

118. Haenchen, *Johannes*, 218.

119. Cf. Martin Hengel, *Der Sohn Gottes. Die Entstehung der Christologie und die jüdisch-hellenistische Religionsgeschichte* (Tübingen: Mohr Siebeck, 1977), 73–77.

INTRODUCTION

name and therefore "God" or a "second God"? Is he such only because of his representative function? But that would leave open the ontological question. Clearly the author presupposes an ontology which enables him to speak of Jesus' pre-existence and being with the Father in the beginning. How is this perceived in such a way that it is not made the basis of the scheme of revelation: "I am God: look at me"; but rather is integrated within a story of sending and revealing and representing another?

If the surrender of the Bultmannian reduction of the significance of the earthly Jesus leads in Käsemann to the issue of the reality of Jesus' humanity, the surrender of demythologising in relationship to pre-existence and sending leads to the issues of the relationship between the Father and the Son.

The solution of Bultmann that the revealer does not reveal, but is himself the gift in the fact of his being in the flesh, has been countered with alternative suggestions. For example, Haacker, acknowledging the legitimacy of Bultmann's observations about revelation, opts rather for the idea of Jesus as the founder.[120] However, this imports a foreign model into the discussion. In fact, Haacker reproduces the revealer model in much of his analysis.[121]

Revelation and Soteriology

Another alternative focusses upon the statements within the Gospel which use the language of vicarious suffering. Jesus is indeed the revealer, but what he reveals is what he does: his work; and his work and commission from the Father is to die on the cross offering his life as a vicarious sacrifice on the basis of which salvation and life are offered to all who believe. Theophil E. Müller has developed this thesis most fully, but many agree with him in giving the traditional notion of Jesus' atoning death a major role in the Gospel.[122]

---

120. Haacker, *Stiftung*, 34–60.

121. So, for instance, Haacker, *Stiftung*, 90–134.

122. Theophil E. Müller, *Das Heilsgeschehen im Johannesevangelium* (Zürich: Gotthelf, n.d.; Diss. Bern, 1961), 130–32; also Miranda, *Vater*, 125–26, 140; Miranda *Sendung*, 24–25; Thüsing, *Erhöhung*, 68 n. 1, 164; Haacker, *Stiftung*, 169–73; Riedl, *Heilswerk*, 313–14; Wilkens, *Zeichen*, 77; cf. also Richter, *Studien*, 305, 312 (for the Grundschrift); Langbrandtner, *Weltferner Gott*, 109 (for the redactor); similarly Becker, *Johannes*, 407. See the strong advocacy for this position in Roland Bergmeier, "ΤΕΤΕΛΕΣΤΑΙ Joh 19,30," *ZNW* 79 (1988): 281–90; Thomas Knöppler, *Die theologia crucis des Johannesevangeliums. Das Verständnis des Todes Jesu im Rahmen der johanneischen Inkarnations- und Erhöhungschristologie*, WMANT 69 (Neukirchen-Vluyn: Neukirchener Verlag, 1994); Rainer Metzner, *Das Verständnis der Sünde im Johannesevangelium*, WUNT 122 (Tübingen: Mohr Siebeck, 2000); Udo Schnelle, "Markinische und johanneische Kreuzestheologie" in *The Death of Jesus in the Fourth Gospel*, ed. G. Van Belle, BETL 200

Introduction

Bultmann did acknowledge the existence of such a tradition in the Gospel of John to a minimal extent. However, he denied it played a significant role.[123] There was a certain consistency which demanded this conclusion. If life is available in the encounter with the Redeemer, then what can the sacrifice on the cross add? The whole life of Jesus is an offering of love right to the end; and in that offering life is offered. This is a powerful argument, all the more so because of the paucity of references to Jesus' death as a sacrifice against the dominant emphasis throughout the Gospel of John on eternal life that is now available in the person of Jesus. The structure of Johannine Christology argued in the present work and which has been widely acknowledged in subsequent research also raises the issue.[124]

(Leuven: Peeters, 2007), 233-58; John A. Dennis, *Jesus' Death and the Gathering of True Israel: The Johannine Appropriation of Restoration Theology in the Light of John 11.47-52*, WUNT 2.217 (Tübingen: Mohr Siebeck, 2006), 351-53; Jörg Frey, "Edler Tod—wirksamer Tod—stellvertretender Tod—heilschaffender Tod. Zur narrativen und theologischen Deutung des Todes Jesu im Johannesevangelium," in *Die Herrlichkeit des Gekreuzigten. Studien zu den Johanneischen Schriften I*, ed. J. Schlegel, WUNT 307 (Tübingen: Mohr Siebeck, 2013), 555-84; and the same volume reflecting research to 2000: Frey, "Theologia crucifixi," 485-554.

123. Bultmann, *Johannes*, 188; *Theologie*, 418.

124. Rudolf Schnackenburg, *Die Person Jesu Christi im Spiegel der vier Evangelien*, HThKS 4 (Freiburg: Herder, 1993): "eine beachtliche einheitliche Gesamtschau" (274); Martinus J. J. Menken, "The Christology of the Fourth Gospel: A Survey of Recent Research," in *From Jesus to John: Essays on Jesus and New Testament Christology in Honour of Marinus de Jonge*, JSNTSup 84 (Sheffield: JSOT, 1993), 300: "To my mind, Loader's synthetic description of the Christology of the Gospel of John at the level of the redaction of the evangelist can broadly speaking be considered as successful"; Raymond E. Brown, *An Introduction to the Gospel of John: Edited, Updated, Introduced and Concluded by Francis J. Moloney, S.D.B.*, ABRL (New York: Doubleday, 2003), 252: "In a well-reasoned book, Loader describes a central structure of Johannine Christology that catches many of the motifs in a complementary manner"; Van Belle, "Signs of the Messiah," 174; George R. Beasley-Murray, *John*, 2nd ed., WBC 36 (Nashville: Thomas Nelson, 1999), cix: "Loader's book is a profound investigation into the Christology of John's Gospel"; Marinus de Jonge, "Christology and Theology in the Context of Early Christian Eschatology Particularly in the Fourth Gospel," in *The Four Gospels 1992: Festschrift Frans Neirynck: Volume III*, ed. F. van Segbroeck, C. M. Tuckett, G. Van Belle, and J. Verheyden, BETL 100 (Leuven: Peeters, 1992), 1845; see also Anderson, *Christology*, 331-33; McGrath, *Christology*, 60-64; Craig S. Keener, *The Gospel of John: A Commentary*, 2 vols. (Peabody: Hendrickson, 2003), 310-17; Andrew T. Lincoln, *The Gospel According to Saint John*, BNTC 4 (London: Continuum, 2005), 60-61; Otto Schwankl, "Aspekte der johanneischen Christologie," in *Theology and Christology in the Fourth Gospel: Essays by the Members of the SNTS Johannine Writings Seminar*, ed. G. Van Belle, J. G. van Der Watt, and P. Maritz, BETL 184 (Leuven: Peeters, 2005), 356.

INTRODUCTION

> The Father
> sends and authorises the Son,
> who knows the Father,
> comes from the Father, makes the Father known,
> brings light and life and truth,
> completes his Father's work,
> returns to the Father,
> exalted, glorified, ascended,
> sends the disciples
> and sends the Spirit
> to enable greater understanding,
> to equip for mission,
> and to build up the community of faith.

It is possible to argue that the gift of life was in fact available only after and because of the vicarious death, so that all statements about Jesus' offering life during his earthly ministry are proleptic of the post-Easter situation and were placed within the ministry by the evangelist in the light of this.[125] But this puts an enormous strain on the text. It might gain some support from 6:51-58 which interprets the bread of life as the eucharistic gift of the flesh and blood of Jesus, but this passage is not typical and its authenticity widely questioned. There are passages which speak of the promise of life in the future, especially those which allude to the future gift of the Spirit (7:37-39), but these are not usually related to the idea of sacrificial death.[126]

Nevertheless a text like John 1:29 cannot be ignored, especially because of its place in the Gospel. Even those like J. Terence Forestell—who rule out the notion of vicarious sacrifice elsewhere in the Gospel—recognise its presence here.[127] Though some—like Harald Hegermann and U. B. Müller—argue for a non-cultic interpretation, such as taking away of sin by exposing

---

125. So Thüsing, *Erhöhung*, 14, 164, 171; John Painter, "Eschatological Faith in the Gospel of John," in *Reconciliation and Hope: Festschrift for L. Morris*, ed. R. Banks (Exeter: Paternoster, 1974), 50-51; John Painter, "Christ and the Church in John 1,45-51," in *L'Évangile de Jean. Sources, Rédaction, Théologie*, ed. M. de Jonge, BETL 44 (Leuven: Gombleux, 1977), 361-62; Edward Schillebeeckx, *Christ: The Christian Experience in the Modern World* (London: SCM, 1980), 405-6, 410-11; Jörg Frey, *Die johanneische Eschatologie I-III*, WUNT 96, 110, 117 (Tübingen: Mohr Siebeck, 1997-2000), 3.241-46; Marianne Thompson, *The God of the Gospel of John* (Grand Rapids: Eerdmans, 2001), 178.

126. Contrast Alfons Dauer, *Die Passionsgeschichte im Johannesevangelium*, SANT 30 (Munich: Kösel, 1972), 39.

127. Forestell, *Word*, 191; similarly Käsemann, *Letzter Wille*, 23; John Painter, *John: Witness and Theologian*, 3rd ed. (Melbourne: Beacon Hill, 1986), 63; Smalley, *John*, 224-26.

Introduction

it or simply by being the saving one.[128] But, should the notion be present here, other more doubtful and ambiguous passages may well have to be seen in the light of it. There remains a tension, but hardly a convincing case that the central salvific act in John is vicarious death, as it is, for instance, for Paul.

Glorification and Exaltation

Bultmann had also seen demythologising in the way the author handled the elements of exaltation, glorification, and return in the story pattern of the Redeemer. For Bultmann the death of Jesus is the conclusion of the earthly paradox of divine glory and so the glorification of Jesus. Theo Preiss draws attention in particular to the forensic nature of much of the Fourth Gospel and since then much greater emphasis has been given to the death of Jesus as the climax of the world's judgment of Jesus and in reality Jesus' judgment of the world.[129] Forestell, too, emphasises the cross as the place of supreme revelation.[130] Similarly Bornkamm points to the repeated references to the death of Jesus from the beginning of the Gospel onwards in such a way that it becomes the climax of revelation.[131]

In Bornkamm, and in the work of many others, Bultmann's thesis persists, according to which the elements of glorification and exaltation to heaven are transferred by the author to the death of Jesus.[132] Wilhelm Thüsing retains this view to the extent that he spoke of Jesus' exaltation in

128. Hegermann, "Eigentum," 119–20, 126–27; Müller, "Bedeutung," 63.

129. Theo Preiss, *Life in Christ*, SBT 1.13 (London: SCM, 1954), 9–31; and more recently Andrew T. Lincoln, *Truth on Trial: The Lawsuit Motif in the Fourth Gospel* (Peabody: Hendrickson, 2000). See also Blank, *Krisis*, 92–93, 284–85; Dauer, *Passionsgeschichte*, 247–49, 261; Ferdinand Hahn, "Der Prozess Jesu im Johannesevangelium," in *EKK Vorarbeitsheft 2* (Neukirchen: Neukirchener; Zürich: Benziger Verlag, 1970), 23–96, 68–85; Nils A. Dahl, "The Johannine Church and History," in *The Interpretation of John*, ed. J. Ashton (Philadelphia: Fortress, 1986), 135; Wayne Meeks, "The Man from Heaven in Johannine Sectarianism," in *The Interpretation of John*, ed. John Ashton (Philadelphia: Fortress, 1986), 155.

130. Forestell, *Word*, 113; similarly Francis J. Moloney, *The Johannine Son of Man*, 2nd ed.; Bibl di Scienze Religiose 14 (Rome: Las, 1978), 38, 41.

131. Bornkamm, "Interpretation," 114; "Paraklet," 60.

132. Bornkamm, "Interpretation," 113; Moloney, *Son of Man*, 176–78; Barnabas Lindars, *Jesus Son of Man* (London: SPCK, 1983), 147; similarly Ibuki, *Wahrheit*, 140–41, 196, 230; Forestell, *Word*, 15, 36–37; Dauer, *Passionsgeschichte*, 40, 238–40; Dwight M. Smith, *The Theology of the Gospel of John* (Cambridge: Cambridge University Press, 1997), 121; Thomas Söding, "Kreuzerhöhung. Zur Deutung des Todes Jesu nach Johannes," *ZTK* 103 (2006): 13–15; Udo Schnelle, *Das Evangelium nach Johannes*, THNT 4 (Berlin: Evangelische Verlagsanstalt, 1998), 74; Christian Dietzfelbinger, *Das Evangelium nach Johannes*, 2nd ed. (Zurich: TVZ, 2004), 1.86.

the event of the cross; but he saw it as something separate within the total event of his return to the Father, for which he saw the word glorification being used. In that sense he made a distinction between the foci of exaltation and glorification and so broke the connection affirmed by Bultmann's line of interpretation.[133] For Thüsing, glorification, applied in its specific sense to the climax of Jesus' earthly ministry, meant glorification in the presence of the Father. He identified two stages: the work of glorification in the broader sense, by the Son of the Father and by the Father of the Son, in his earthly ministry up to and including death and exaltation on the cross; and secondly, the ministry of Jesus through the Spirit after Easter, glorifying the Father and being glorified by him and in the disciples, in the community of faith.

Blank challenged Thüsing's separation of exaltation and glorification, arguing, as did Godfrey C. Nicholson subsequently, that exaltation must also include its traditional meaning of exaltation on high to the Father,[134] and Thüsing's response acknowledged the validity of challenge. Yet he has done so in a manner which leaves a certain ambiguity. He retains statements about the distinction, but also speaks of Jesus' exaltation as his elevation to the throne of glory[135] and draws attention to the cross as a symbol of the crowning, the crowning taking place subsequently in heaven.[136] It seems to me that in effect the distinction has almost disappeared. It is true, and frequently ignored, that the passion narrative is just as symbolically suggestive as the rest of the Gospel. But the crown of thorns, for instance, and the regal imagery are manifestly symbolic of Jesus' messiahship, not of a post-mortal crowning. The author does not use royal messianic imagery in association with Jesus' exaltation, glorification and return to the Father, but uses it in association with Jesus' claim during his earthly ministry to be God's sent one. The themes of exaltation and glorification have continued to receive attention in recent scholarship with no clear consensus emerging between those who equate both as referring simultaneously to cross and resurrection, those who see exaltation as referring only to the cross and glorification to both, and those who see both referring only to the cross.[137]

The surrender of Bultmann's thesis of demythologising also means, therefore, the surrender of one of the most challenging features of his anal-

---

133. Thüsing, *Erhöhung*, 15, 21, 24-28, 33, 233, 240-41.

134. Blank, *Krisis*, 139, 268-69; Godfrey C. Nicholson, *Death as Departure: The Johannine Descent-Ascent Schema*, SBLDS 63 (Chico: Scholars, 1982), 99-101, 132-36, 141-51; similarly Riedl, *Heilswerk*, 160-62; Rudolf Schnackenburg, *Das Johannesevangelium*, 4 vols, HThKNT 4.1-4 (Freiburg: Herder, 1977-84), 2.499-502; Schnackenburg, *John*, 1.394-97.

135. Thüsing, *Erhöhung*, 300, cf. 302-7.

136. Thüsing, *Erhöhung*, 302, 308.

137. See the detailed discussion below.

ysis: the idea of the death of Jesus as the paradox of glory and humanity in suffering. This Pauline insight remains, of course, theologically valid, even though we have to admit it is not intended in John.[138]

Taking the glorification seriously as the return to be glorified with the glory which Jesus had with the Father before the world began raises important issues about the nature of Jesus' revelatory glory on earth as expressed in 1:14 and elsewhere. Here Bultmann had harmonised, arguing that it would be inconsistent to suggest that Jesus received glory when he already had it from the beginning. Hence a demythologised solution: the cross is glorification, in end effect in exactly the same way as the whole life bears glory.[139] Without Bultmann's solution a tension remains. Are we to speak of degrees of glory, the one hidden or more obscured and the other open?[140] But that is not the author's formulation. It is those who have truly seen who testify to the glory of 1:14; and 2:11 scarcely means anything different. Further, Jesus' glorification at the climax of his ministry is not an unveiling, but a receiving.[141] These appear to be different uses and need further exploration.

The death and departure of Jesus have also been an important special instance of the problem of the nature of Jesus' humanity, which I mentioned in general terms earlier. Here, having given up Bultmann's premise, Käsemann saw the triumphant exit of the divine being, the transformation of a passion narrative of real suffering, for which the author's scheme, according to Käsemann, could have no place, into a virtual parody of suffering.[142] He is followed by Schulz[143] and U. B. Müller.[144] Jesus comes and goes, having power and authority to lay down his life and take it up again. What they explicate is what Bultmann affirmed as myth, but then demythologised. Here, too, the danger of oversystematisation lies close at hand. Do the texts support this view—even though it may be logically demanded by the myth? For instance, Hebrews assumes Jesus has the power of an indestructible life and makes his return to the Father upon accomplishment of his work (7:16), but it recounts side by side with this the story of one who sheds real tears and knows real suffering (5:7). Is it similar with John's Jesus? Only a careful analysis of the texts will prove to what degree he holds to a human or real view of the passion, perhaps even holds it in tension.

---

138. So correctly Becker, *Johannes*, 144.

139. Bultmann, "Interpretation," 3–4; *Johannes*, 398.

140. So Felix Porsch, *Pneuma und Wort*, FraTS 16 (Frankfurt: Knecht, 1974), 75, 77–78; Schnackenburg, *Johannesevangelium*, 2.503; Riedl, *Heilswerk*, 155, 169.

141. So Thüsing, *Erhöhung*, 206–8.

142. Käsemann, *Letzter Wille*, 22.

143. Schulz, *Johannes*, 209, 238.

144. Müller, "Bedeutung," 54, 58.

INTRODUCTION

Life Only Post-Easter?

In the story the Son's return is linked with the giving of the Spirit which makes the continuing work of Jesus possible, not by adding to, but by bringing clear understanding of who Jesus was and is. As Thüsing has clearly shown, this means that the work of glorification which marked the earthly ministry continues after Easter.[145] This makes mission possible, the fruit-bearing which is achieved through the witness of the disciples who love one another. All this means that the death of Jesus is not seen as simply the "end," but rather as the "turning point," as Blank puts it, using the German "Ende" and "Wende."[146] Haenchen, too, emphasises the important hermeneutical function of the coming of the Spirit in the thought of the author.[147] He rejects Bultmann's grouping of parousia, Pentecost, ascension, resurrection, death, and incarnation as one single event. Rather the event of Jesus' death belongs with the complex of exaltation, glorification, and return. It is evident in the coming of the Spirit. This is a new stage in the story, the real story of God's action in Christ.[148]

Because this "turning point" makes greater understanding possible of who Jesus is, it makes possible true sight and salvation. It is, in that sense, what makes the gift of life accessible. The logic of the story suggests that this is because of the work of the Spirit enabling true sight because of the completed work of revelation.[149] Others presuppose that this life is available post-Easter because it is the result of Jesus' vicarious death, as I have already noted. But that does not seem to be the main line of the story and Bultmann's objection remains that it was in the person of the revealer that this life was available, and therefore already before Easter.[150]

In a sense the problem is not peculiarly Johannine. We might also ask: was the word of life present in its fullness in the person of the earthly Jesus? Was justification—or whatever other term we use to describe salvation—already possible then? The Jesus tradition points strongly in the affirmative direction. If it was all there before Easter in the person of Jesus, then Bultmann's comments concerning the Fourth Gospel—that in fact the resurrection adds nothing to the content of revelation[151]—touch on a problem

---

145. Thüsing, *Erhöhung*, 141–42, 191–92.
146. Blank, *Krisis*, 282.
147. Haenchen, *Johannes*, 109.
148. Haenchen, "Johannesevangelium," 226–27.
149. So Forestell, *Word*, 19.
150. Cf. Müller, *Heilsgeschehen*, 25, 33.
151. Haenchen, *Johannes*, 356; similarly Dodd, *Interpretation*, 442.

Introduction

that was already implicit in the Jesus tradition. Yet, just as the resurrection of Jesus before the eschaton was celebrated as God's vindication of what he claimed to be in his earthly ministry and so performed for the disciples the all-important hermeneutical function that finally made their faith possible, so in John the event—death, resurrection, exaltation, glorification, and giving of the Spirit—has primarily a hermeneutical role. To that role belongs not only the coming of the Spirit who leads the disciples to the truth, but also the Johannine portrait of Jesus' death as the place of judgment by the world of Jesus and judgment by Jesus of the world. In this sense the death of Jesus cannot simply be the end or even just the climax of Jesus' ministry. It is the point at which the conflict and controversy with the world reaches its climax and its verdict. It is therefore the final exposure of the world for what it is and thus the victory over the devil. The ascent of Jesus to the Father is at the same time his vindication and the confirmation that the world has been judged and Jesus has been justified. Yet precisely because this is so for the evangelist, he can point to the gift of life as already being present during Jesus' earthly ministry and highlight the climax of the story as the means by which this became truly known and, in that sense, available.

Salvation History?

The Spirit also brings to light the relationship between Jesus and the OT. Bultmann refers to the OT fulfilment within the Gospel,[152] but rejects a salvation-historical perspective. This is consistent with his demythologising theory which treats the story or myth symbolically as a statement about a single event in history and not as a narrative of events.[153] The prologue does not, according to Bultmann, tell of the Logos's encounter with Israel. Its activity in creation is symbolic of the inner unity of redemption and creation.[154]

This is not the place to discuss the Gospel's understanding of the OT—which is primarily based upon tradition—or to examine the role of the history of the people of God in John. But a number of scholars see in the prologue some reference to the Logos "asarkos" in pre-Christian history. The abandonment of the demythologising principle for interpreting John inevitably raises the issue afresh. Nevertheless it remains a matter of dispute whether the Gospel intends such a continuity with Israel. John 4:22 was for

---

152. Bultmann, *Theologie*, 389.
153. Bultmann, *Theologie*, 360.
154. Bultmann, *Johannes*, 26–28.

Bultmann an oddity with its claim that salvation came from the Jews, who are otherwise so frequently symbols of the hostile world; it was a later gloss.[155] But there has been increasing dissatisfaction with his solution of attributing it to a later hand. Ferdinand Hahn shows convincingly that the verse belongs well within its context and within the theology of the author.[156]

John and Judaism

The opening up of the question of salvation-historical perspectives in John, which Bultmann's theory virtually forbad, has also led to a new evaluation of the role both of the OT and of the Jewish traditions in the Fourth Gospel. We have already noted the works of Borgen, Miranda and Bühner on the background of the sending idea. Borgen especially has drawn our attention anew to rabbinic and Philonic use of early Jewish traditions which appear also to lie behind Johannine material.[157] Wayne Meeks argued for a strong Moses typology behind the Gospel and sought to trace behind the Gospel a prophetic-messianic hope which has left traces both in the Samaritan episode and in 6:14–15.[158] Bultmann had already noted similarities between the christological story's words of Jesus telling what he had seen and heard and the picture of the Mosaic prophet of Deut 18:15–18.[159] But, he countered, the Johannine model does not ground Jesus' authority in inspiration and call but in oneness with the Father and the fact of his person.[160] The alternatives are no longer so simple, as the monograph studies of Bühner and Miranda, for instance, on the sending motif have shown.

With the increasing awareness of the Jewishness in much of the Johannine material has come an awareness that there is a twofold orientation in the Gospel in relation to Israel. There is the strong negative reaction against contemporary Judaism represented in the Jews of John's Gospel. This shows all the marks of a reaction of a group which has been forcibly separated from a wider community. Probably the dualistic determinism which comes

---

155. Bultmann, *Johannes*, 139.
156. Ferdinand Hahn, "'Das Heil kommt von den Juden'. Erwägungen zu Joh 4,22b," in *Wort und Wirklichkeit. Festschrift für E. L. Rapp*, Vol. 1 (Weisenheim: Anton Hain, 1976), 67–84; Ferdinand Hahn, "Die Juden im Johannesevangelium," in *Kontinuität und Einheit. Für Franz Mussner* (Freiburg: Herder, 1981), 430–38.
157. Borgen, *Bread from Heaven*; *Logos Was the True Light*.
158. Wayne Meeks, *The Prophet-King*, NovTSup 14 (Leiden: Brill, 1967).
159. See also Anderson, *Christology*, 185–92.
160. Bultmann, *Johannes*, 187–88; *Theologie*, 415.

to expression in parts of the Gospel is a fruit of the Johannine community's coming to terms with the break. The same phenomenon repeats itself in the inner divisions of the Christian community evident behind 1 John and recalls the response of the Qumran community to the Jerusalem hierarchy.

On the other hand, there is a strong positive concern to maintain the validity of the Christian cause as fulfilment of Scripture and its intention. Scripture witnesses on Jesus' behalf in the great trial carried through in Jesus' ministry. Moses takes the stand against the Jews. Isaiah and Abraham know Jesus in his pre-existence. But the concern seems less with establishing historical continuity as God's people and more with establishing scriptural warrant. Thus the manna story is but a springboard for the claim that Jesus is the bread of life and the temple is left in irrelevance as Jesus goes on to speak of his body as the temple; for he is now the true bread and the true temple has arrived. Cornelis Bennema has pointed to the model of saving wisdom as informing the author's Christology and soteriology.[161]

Sources and Traditions

The question of the author's perception of how Jesus is to be understood in history is different from the question of what historical factors played a role in the development of the author's Christology. Bultmann made important suggestions about the background of the Christology, but his synthesis of Johannine Christology is primarily won from the text itself. This is the great value of his work. Yet he did posit written sources: a gnostic discourse collection, a source of miracles, and a passion narrative. Of greatest influence has been the signs source which has been taken up by a number of scholars and variously defined, the most thoroughgoing attempt being Fortna's.[162] It is not my concern to evaluate these constructions.[163] My question is rather their importance for establishing the Christology of the author.

In the works of M.-E. Boismard, Jürgen Becker, U. B. Müller, Georg Richter, Martyn, Raymond E. Brown, Haenchen, Langbrandtner and others, attempts are made to lay bare a history of Christology within the Johannine

---

161. Cornelis Bennema, *The Power of Saving Wisdom: An Investigation of Spirit and Wisdom in relation to the Soteriology of the Fourth Gospel*, WUNT 2.148 (Tübingen: Mohr Siebeck, 2002).

162. Robert T. Fortna, *The Gospel of Signs: A Reconstruction of the Narrative Underlying the Fourth Gospel*, SNTSMS 11 (Cambridge: Cambridge University Press, 1970).

163. See the thoroughgoing critique of attempts to reconstruct a "signs source" in Gilbert Van Belle, *The Signs Source in the Fourth Gospel*, BETL 116 (Leuven: Peeters, 1994), 370-77.

community.¹⁶⁴ That endeavour has continued since the publication of the first edition of the current work.¹⁶⁵ A development is usually traced from a model of a miracle-oriented messianic, prophetic, "theios aner" Christology to a revelational Christology (analogous or related to gnostic patterns), mostly also seen in the context of conflict with Judaism, finally to a Christology which more carefully avoids docetic characteristics or suggestions. The latter is linked with the stance of the author of the first epistle against opponents who have followed an alternative development from the second stage.

It seems to me very likely that some such development took place with the Johannine community, but questions arise for me in the way each stage is related to the other and, significantly, it is here that these scholars are least united. The relevance of these hypotheses for understanding the Christology of the author lies in their ability to open a new way of solving the problems and discrepancies within the Gospel. But this is a procedure fraught with difficulty. How can we know that what does not fit our system of Johannine Christology must either be from a later hand or represent the residue of older tradition? And in the latter case what is gained by establishing that this or that saying is traditional when the question to be faced is: how does the author integrate it? In addition, what assumptions are being made about the level of consistency and coherence to be expected of the author? The procedure is even more complicated by the distinctive Johannine style which according to Ruckstuhl permeates the whole Gospel.¹⁶⁶ And more recently Georg Strecker and Udo Schnelle have proposed what amounts to a reversal of traditional understanding of the order in which the Gospel and Epistles were written. Schnelle has sought to support this hypothesis in his recent analysis of the Gospel on the assumption that it is dealing with the problems

---

164. M.-E. Boismard and A. Lamouille, *L'Évangile de Jean. Synopse des Quatres Évangiles en Français*, Vol. 3 (Paris: Cerf, 1977); Becker, "Wunder"; *Johannes*; Müller, *Christologie*; Richter, *Studien*; J. Louis Martyn, "Source Criticism and Religionsgeschichte in the Fourth Gospel," in *The Interpretation of John*, ed. J. Ashton (Philadelphia: Fortress, 1986), 99–121; Langbrandtner, *Weltferner Gott*; Raymond E. Brown, *The Community of the Beloved Disciple* (New York: Paulist, 1979); Haenchen, *Johannes*; cf. also Judith M. Lieu, *The Second and Third Epistles of John* (Edinburgh: Clark, 1986), 171–216.

165. So, for instance, de Boer, *Johannine Perspectives*, who adapts Martyn's theory of four stages and seeks to identify the distinctive Christology of each; Ashton, *John*, who sees development from a missionary signs source to the Gospel and then to corrections (11, 126–35); see also Ashton, *Fourth Gospel*, 35–53; Jerome H. Neyrey, *An Ideology of Revolt: John's Christology in Social-Science Perspective* (Philadelphia: Fortress, 1988), 117–47; Urban C. von Wahlde, *The Gospel and Letters of John*, 3 vols. (Grand Rapids: Eerdmans, 2010).

166. Eugen Ruckstuhl, *Die literarische Einheit des Johannesevangeliums*, Studia fribourgensia, NF 3 (Freiburg, Switzerland: Paulus, 1951).

Introduction

of docetism already addressed in the first epistle.¹⁶⁷ To my mind he fails to demonstrate his case. As often happens in Johannine research hypotheses, the thesis is weak where one would want it to be strongest: in the discourse material.

The diversity of reconstructions is evidence of a high degree of subjectivity in such research, but the obverse of this is also true: the persistence of such a range of proposals indicates that the material must be recognised as demanding such a treatment. This is so, even when with Anderson, one assumes a single author undergoing stages of spiritual growth reflected in different levels posited within the next, as a way of explaining "the tensions associated with the uniting and disunitive aspects of John's Christology."¹⁶⁸ The strength of the proposals of Martyn and Brown is that they seek to relate source theories, history of the community and development and diversity of Christology. Inevitably such reconstructions entail speculation and are vulnerable to criticism on these grounds. Klaus Wengst's impressive reconstruction is too harshly put aside as akin to "science fiction."¹⁶⁹ There is no question of the importance of seeking the sociological context of Johannine Christology. In this regard Meeks's essay on the social function of the myth of the descending and ascending redeemer¹⁷⁰ has contributed importantly to the discussion of the nature of the community, raising the question of its sectarian character. Takashi Onuki's study takes this further detecting a twofold movement of mission and withdrawal reflected in the pattern of coming and returning of the Son.¹⁷¹ Becker's insistence on the basically dualistic world view of the Gospel also has important implications for understanding the community and not least its Christology.¹⁷² Martinus C. de

---

167. Georg Strecker, "Die Anfänge der johanneischen Schule," *NTS* 32 (1986): 31-47; Udo Schnelle, *Antidoketische Christologie im Johannesevangelium. Eine Untersuchung zur Stellung des vierten Evangeliums in der johanneischen Schule* (Göttingen: Vandenhoeck und Ruprecht, 1987).

168. Anderson, *Christology*, 252.

169. Klaus Wengst, *Bedrängte Gemeinde und verherrlichter Christus* (Neukirchen: Neukirchener, 1981); cf. Joachim Kügler, "Das Johannesevangelium und seine Gemeinde. Kein Thema für Science Fiction," *BN* 23 (1984): 48-62. See the critical evaluation in Jürgen Becker, "Das Johannesevangelium im Streit der Methoden (1980-1984)," *ThR* 51 (1986): 53-54; and the more positive responses of Schnackenburg, *Johannesevangelium*, 4.229; Günter Reim, "Zur Lokalisierung der johanneischen Gemeinde," *BZ* 32 (1988): 73-74; cf. also Hans-Josef Klauck, "Gemeinde ohne Amt? Erfahrungen mit der Kirche in den johanneischen Schriften," *BZ* 29 (1985): 193-220.

170. Meeks, "Man from Heaven."

171. Onuki, *Gemeinde*, 110-14; cf. also de Jonge, *Stranger*, 99-100.

172. Jürgen Becker, "Beobachtungen zum Dualismus im Johannesevangelium," *ZNW* 65 (1974): 71-87; Becker, "Streit der Methoden," 46-47; Becker, *Johannes*, 147-51.

INTRODUCTION

Boer's observations on the possible connection between seeing the cross as glorification and disciples' facing the prospect of needing to follow the same path are instructive.[173]

Literary Perspectives

Studies of the transmitted text from a literary perspective, such as those of R. Alan Culpepper, Paul D. Duke, and Gail R. O'Day,[174] have not only expanded our awareness of the literary forms and devices of the work. They have also raised important questions about the nature of the document itself and its relationship to the community in which it was produced.[175] This is particularly so, when they highlight the importance of irony, double meaning, misunderstanding, and symbolism, all of which function most naturally within a community which "knows" and so enhance the fellowship of knowing and belonging. These raise, in turn, significant questions about the nature of the Gospel itself, its portrait of Jesus, and its use, even in our own day.

---

173. De Boer, *Johannine Perspectives*, 172, 185.

174. R. Alan Culpepper, *The Anatomy of the Fourth Gospel* (Philadelphia: Fortress, 1983); R. Alan Culpepper, "Reading Johannine Irony," in *Exploring the Gospel of John: In Honor of D. Moody Smith*, ed. R. A. Culpepper and C. C. Black (Louisville: Westminster John Knox, 1996), 193-207; Paul D. Duke, *Irony in the Fourth Gospel* (Atlanta: Knox, 1985); Gail R. O'Day, *Revelation in the Fourth Gospel* (Philadelphia: Fortress, 1986); Craig Koester, *Symbolism in the Fourth Gospel: Meaning, Mystery, Community* (Minneapolis: Fortress, 1995). See also Dorothy Lee, *The Symbolic Narratives of the Fourth Gospel*, JSNTSup 95 (Sheffield: JSOT Press, 1994); Derek Tovey, *Narrative Art and Act in the Fourth Gospel*, JSNTSup 151 (Sheffield: Sheffield Academic Press, 1997); Ruben Zimmermann, *Christologie der Bilder im Johannesevangelium. Die Christopoetik des vierten Evangeliums unter besonderer Berücksichtigung von Joh 10*, WUNT 171 (Tübingen: Mohr Siebeck, 2004); Jörg Frey, Jan G. van der Watt, and Ruben Zimmermann, eds., *Imagery in the Gospel of John: Terms, Forms, Themes, and Theology of Johannine Figurative Language*, WUNT 200 (Tübingen: Mohr Siebeck, 2006); Cornelis Bennema, *Encountering Jesus: Character Studies in the Gospel of John* (Milton Keynes: Paternoster, 2009); Christopher W. Skinner, ed., *Characters and Characterization in the Gospel of John*, LNTS (London: T&T Clark, 2013). See also Bennema's revised edition (Philadelphia: Fortress, 2014) and Jason S. Sturdevant, *The Adaptable Jesus of the Fourth Gospel: The Pedagogy of the Logos* (Leiden: Brill, 2015), both of which became available to me only after completion of this manuscript.

175. Cf. Richard Bauckham, "For Whom Were the Gospels Written?" in *The Gospels for All Christians* (Grand Rapids: Eerdmans, 1998), 9-48, who goes beyond caution in playing down the relevance of contextuality against speculative reconstructions.

Conclusions

These reflections underline the importance of Bultmann's starting point. He sought the central structure of the author's thought. I hope to show that he was fundamentally right in his outline of the Johannine story. But I cannot agree that the author demythologised the story to the extent that Bultmann presumes. It seems to me that Bultmann's insight that the model of revelation and information has been transformed into a model of revelation and encounter is correct and of abiding worth for interpreting the Gospel today. By allowing the story to stand un-demythologised and so by facing anew the author's understanding of pre-existence, sending, oneness with the Father, humanness, death, exaltation, glorification, and return to the Father, both new problems and discrepancies come into focus and also new possibilities are opened for understanding the Christology of the author within the Gospel and within the context of early Christianity.

The problems include the significance of Jesus' death. Has vicarious sacrifice a place in Johannine Christology? In what way does his death relate to his work? Was it real suffering or merely triumphant exit? What is the relationship between Jesus' death, his exaltation, and his glorification? They include also the question of the significance of his earthly life as a whole. What constitutes the saving event in John? In what sense does the revealer reveal? What is the nature of his divinity? What role has pre-existence? How human is the Johannine Jesus? How real his passion? What role do miracles play in John's Christology? They also include consideration of the nature of the Gospel in the light of its Christology. Do the Jesus of history and the details of his life matter any longer to the author? What is the life setting of Johannine Christology? Is it still possible to do as Bultmann did and relate it the modern world? I shall return to many of these issues in Part Two. The way to these issues must lie first of all in a reexamination of Bultmann's fundamental question: what is the central structure of the author's Christology? To this we now turn.

PART ONE

The Structure of Johannine Christology

1 Identifying the Central Structure

1.1 Issues of Method

In reviewing research into Johannine Christology since Bultmann I have shown that the major issues of dispute which have arisen, often against Bultmann, have concentrated on elements within the story which Bultmann saw as forming the centre of Johannine Christology. Bultmann's interpretation of each element of the story sought to retain a consistency and coherence with the story as a whole. In discussing the major areas of dispute in Johannine Christology I want similarly to take into account the Johannine story as a whole, in particular, what I describe as the central structure of Johannine Christology. For it is only when we have been able to see the overall structure that we are able to gain a perspective for evaluating the role of individual elements.

The Fourth Gospel contains a wide variety of christological sayings, motifs and narratives. Most have been subjected to minute analysis, both for their role within the Gospel and for their background in Christian tradition and in the religio-historical traditions of the day. On the surface of the text of the Gospel we see rich and varied expressions of christological thought. The search for the central structure of the author's Christology is the search for what holds these various motifs and images together. What structure or structures lie beneath the surface manifestations in the text?

In looking for the basic story of Johannine Christology I am not wanting to find a central structure which we can then use to rule out the significance of other motifs or into which we might force other motifs and patterns of thought on the assumption that the author's Christology must be consistent and unified. It is rather that we seek an overall perspective, a christological map that will enable us to see the way particular motifs function within the whole. This is particularly important in a writing which contains a wide variety of christological themes and in which it is very easy to isolate a particular motif—like, for instance, Jesus' death as an act of vicarious atonement—and elevate it to the major theme of the Gospel. Tracing the christological map that emerges from the text must not be undertaken on the presupposition that there is a single unified structure. That can only emerge from the text itself. We may assume consistency, but with caution.

Our concern at this stage is therefore not with individual motifs but with what integrates them or with the way they are related to one another. Similarly I am not interested at this stage in classifying the Johannine christological material into a systematic arrangement of, for instance, titles or themes. As far as possible I want to listen for structures and patterns that emerge from the text itself.

Some have presented Johannine Christology by identifying a key text or texts. The prologue with the Logos motif might, by its very position, be seen as an appropriate key or starting point for understanding the author's christological thought. We may assume its meaning would have been clear to its first readers for whom it functioned as the overture or key to the Gospel,[1] unlocking its messianic secret, the directive for how the Gospel should be understood, the window through which it should be viewed, the script for its main character. But for us, as Bultmann points out, it is an "enigma" which only makes sense after we have read the Gospel as a whole.[2] Furthermore, many of its major motifs, including its chief motif, Logos, the theme of Christ and creation, the incarnation of the Word, to name only a few, do not occur elsewhere in the Gospel and it contains no direct reference to Jesus' death and ascension. Nor can "the Word became flesh" (1:14a) on its own function as a summary of the author's Christology, as it had for Bultmann, especially since Käsemann challenged its traditional interpretation and suggested that it intended little more than to describe how the glory appeared (1:14b).[3] Similarly Haacker's attempt to make 1:17, with its contrast between Moses and Jesus Christ, "law" and "grace and truth," the centre of the author's Christology[4] proves an inadequate starting point, because it puts the focus

---

1. Holtzmann, *Lehrbuch*, 446; Haacker, *Stiftung*, 17-18; Bultmann, *Johannes*, 1; T. E. Pollard, *Johannine Christology and the Early Church*, SNTSMS 13 (Cambridge: Cambridge University Press, 1970), 13-14; Wengst, *Gemeinde*, 101-3; Schnelle, *Christologie*, 246; and see the discussion in 5.3.2 below.

2. Bultmann, *Johannes*, 1; also Pollard, *Christology*, 6-7.

3. Käsemann, *Letzter Wille*, 23-25. See also Jürgen Becker, "Ich bin die Auferstehung und das Leben. Eine Skizze der johanneischen Christologie," *TZ* 39 (83): 138-40. Contrast Hans Weder, "Die Menschwerdung Gottes," *ZThK* 82 (1985): 352.

4. Haacker, *Stiftung*, 21, 25-36.

too much on the salvation-historical perspective which is not dominant in John. Accordingly Haacker emphasises Jesus as "founder," though his own expositions make the motif of revealer much more central.

Richter makes the christological formulation in 20:31, "Jesus is the Christ, the Son of God," into a criterion of the evangelist's concerns and uses it, for instance, in arguing that 1:14a is a redactional addition,[5] but this confession is also too narrow a base for such assertions. Numerous other passages have been described from time to time as embodying the essence of the author's Christology. Stephen S. Smalley sees the Gospel as a kind of midrash based on the Son of Man saying of 1:51.[6] Similarly the wedding at Cana (2:1-11), as the first sign and as one standing without interpretation, is seen by some as a programmatic statement of the evangelist's theology.[7] Ruckstuhl, arguing for the integrity of 6:51c-58, maintains that it contains within a confined space a summary of the whole Gospel in form and content,[8] Hans Weder argues that John 6 as a whole should be seen as representative of Johannine Christology,[9] and Anderson makes it the basis for his exploration of the genesis and development of Johannine Christology.[10] Appold focusses on the brief statements in 10:30 ("I and the Father are one") and 17:11-12 as abbreviations of Johannine Christology.[11] Some choose the briefer formulation, "It is finished" (19:30), as their centre.[12]

It is not our intention to dispute that these passages or formulations may reflect the centre of Johannine Christology. Many are, however, too succinct.

---

5. Richter, *Studien*, 152, 173, 196; cf. also 66, 101–103, 141. McGrath, *Christology*, points to it at least as the author's aim (145); similarly Silke Petersen, "'. . . wieso sagt ihr: "Du lästerst", weil ich gesagt habe: "Sohn des Gottes bin ich"?' (Joh 10,36)—oder: Wie 'göttlich' ist der johanneische Jesus?" in *Fragen wider die Antworten*, ed. K. Schiffner, S. Leibold, M. L. Frettlöh, J.-D. Döhling, and U. Bail (Gütersloh: Gütersloher Verlagshaus, 2010), 476.

6. Stephen S. Smalley, "Johannes 1,51 und die Einleitung zum vierten Evangelium," in *Jesus und der Menschensohn. Für Anton Vögtle*, ed. R. Pesch and R. Schnackenburg (Freiburg: Herder, 1975), 313; similarly Francis J. Moloney, "The Johannine Son of God," *BTB* 6 (1976): 180.

7. Josef Breuss, *Das Kana-Wunder. Hermeneutische und pastorale Überlegungen aufgrund einer phänomenologischen Analyse von Johannes 2,1-12*, BibB 12 (Fribourg, Switzerland, 1976), 26; Wilhelm Lütgert, *Die Johanneische Christologie*, 2nd ed. (Gütersloh: Bertelsmann, 1916), 18; Sebald Hofbeck, *Semeion. Der Begriff des "Zeichens" im Johannesevangelium unter Berücksichtigung seiner Vorgeschichte*, 2nd ed. (Münsterschwarzach: Turme, 1970), 105. Cf. also Olsson, *Structure*, 101.

8. Ruckstuhl, *Einheit*, 249.

9. Weder, "Menschwerdung," 325.

10. Anderson, *Christology*.

11. Appold, *Oneness*, 11–12, 272, 280.

12. Paolo Ricca, *Die Eschatologie des Vierten Evangeliums* (Zürich: Gotthelf, 1966), 106; Alf Corell, *Consummatum Est: Eschatology and Church in the Gospel of John* (London: SPCK, 1970).

They need expanding and this expanded outline or structure needs to be identified. In many ways scholars who have analysed the Christology of the Fourth Gospel, presenting systematic outlines, have also noted patterns and structures in the text.

Wetter, for instance, created a list of Johannine christological statements, above all, of the enormous variety of statements which I have classed under the heading: "The Son makes the Father known." He speaks of an almost tiresome monotony in such Johannine material.[13] Wilhelm Lütgert made similar lists, but tried to force them all into a theory according to which Jesus' claims amounted primarily to a claim to be a man inspired by the Spirit.[14] Bultmann also listed the variations before arguing that the author had a demythologising interpretation of the pattern of coming and sending.[15] Forestell surveys the Gospel for statements illustrating the centrality of revelation,[16] and lists motifs which follow the verbs to believe and to know: Jesus is sent by God, the Father; he comes from God; he is in the Father and the Father in him; and the enigmatic statement, "I am."[17] The sending sayings have been listed by many.[18] Ibuki places 8:28; 12:49-50; and 14:10bc in parallel columns,[19] texts which, as we shall see, reflect the central structure. He does the same for 3:32; 8:26; 8:40; 1:18; 6:66; and 15:15b.[20] Schnackenburg lists motifs associated with "Father" and "Son";[21] de Jonge and Moloney do similarly, the latter contrasting these with motifs associated with the Son of Man title.[22] Bühner lists the elements which belong to the traditional motif of the envoy and finds the pattern expressed in 13:3 and 3:35.[23] Becker draws on Bühner in applying the pattern to the christological statements in the Gospel as a whole.[24] Bornkamm uses 3:31-36 and also 8:21-29 to trace a pattern of christological thought.[25]

---

13. Gillis P. Wetter, *Der Sohn Gottes*, FRLANT 26 (Göttingen: Vandenhoeck und Ruprecht, 1916), 49-52, 155.

14. Lütgert, *Christologie*, 23-30, 36-40.

15. Bultmann, *Johannes*, 103-4, 188-90; Bultmann, *Theologie*, 386-87, 403-4, 414.

16. Forestell, *Word*, 19-57.

17. Forestell, *Word*, 45-46.

18. E.g., Kühl, *Sendung*, 77-78, 82-88; Miranda, *Vater*, 18-52; Miranda, *Sendung*, 29-35; Riedl, *Heilswerk*, 51 n. 41; Haacker, *Stiftung*, 92-97.

19. Ibuki, *Wahrheit*, 43.

20. Ibuki, *Wahrheit*, 146-149.

21. Schnackenburg, *Johannesevangelium*, 2.153-57; cf. also Nicholson, *Death*, 52-60.

22. de Jonge, *Stranger*, 41, 132-35, 142-48; Moloney, *Son of Man*, 208.

23. Bühner, *Gesandte*, 198-99, 212-13; cf. also 202, 233, 261; similarly Robinson, *Priority*, 368-69.

24. Becker, *Johannes*, 403-6.

25. Bornkamm, "Paraklet," 77-79.

Identifying the Central Structure

Much of the work done thus far has rarely gone beyond listing the elements or focussing upon particular elements (especially the sayings about sending). The work of identifying similar material and listing it is essential for any careful analysis of Johannine Christology, as is individual investigation of particular elements. But beyond that it is important to identify patterns or structures of thought which show the ways the various elements interrelate. It is particularly valuable if these structures can be shown to exist already within the text itself and not simply be a structure systematised out of the gathered material. This is the strength of the approaches like Bornkamm's. Both the systematic review and the tracing of patterns in particular passages of the text itself are important for identifying the central structure of the author's Christology.

In the investigation which follows I have sought to establish the basic structure of the author's Christology by noting:

1. Motifs and images that occur frequently within the Gospel
2. Combinations or patterns of motifs and images that occur frequently
3. Summary statements, especially those within which the common motifs and groups of motifs occur
4. Motifs or groups of motifs made the subject of attention and development, especially in discourses of Jesus about himself

Any such posited underlying structure should be shown to integrate, or, at least, to relate coherently to the variety of motifs within the Gospel. As well as these general criteria there may also be indications of the author's special christological interests in the way the author structures the Gospel, inasmuch as such structures are visible and generally agreed. It is also important to take into account not only the thematic statements in the sayings material, but also the way the narrative material functions.

I have spoken of the author's Christology. Strictly speaking it is only the Christology of the text before us to which we have access and we assume it reflects that of the author. But a greater problem arises in the light of the question whether the text which we have should be treated as a whole or be seen as a multi-layered document in which we can detect a pre-Gospel or miracle source, the Gospel itself, and redactional expansions and additions. I want to treat the text as it stands as a unity and to take our readings of its Christology from the whole text. But we also want to be aware of the (to my mind convincing) view that the present Gospel text has behind it a history of development. Rather than frustrate the reader with a maze of "ifs" and "buts" in the light of the various source and redaction theories proposed,

THE STRUCTURE OF JOHANNINE CHRISTOLOGY

I shall press ahead with the text as we have it, and return to consider the author's Christology in the light of source theories in 6.2 below. The viewing of the text for traces of the central christological structure will, in turn, raise questions of tradition and redaction, but they are not the primary subject of this study.

Frequency of motifs alone could be established on the basis of statistics; but then we should be in danger of losing the individual contours of the text which give each motif its setting and specific meaning. The ideal would be a careful sifting verse by verse and passage by passage of the whole Gospel from beginning to end, but this—which I have indeed done—will have to be assumed as background to what follows. Instead I propose to begin by looking at some sample passages and to examine what emerges as a common christological structure. The elements of this structure will be examined in the light of the criteria of frequency and combination outlined above, including occurrence in summary statements. In a further step, I shall review the Gospel as a whole for indications of particular attention and development of the structure and finally consider the way in which the structure integrates, or relates to, the various christological motifs of the Gospel. On this basis, I return in Part Two to the wider issues of Johannine Christology.

1.2 Examining Select Passages

1.2.1 John 3:31–36

I choose to begin with John 3:31–36. It comes at the conclusion of the first major dialogue and functions as a summary.[26]

Schnackenburg considers the passage a piece of Johannine writing, probably by the author of the Gospel, which, together with 3:13–21, has been secondarily added to chapter 3; but at the same time sees in this material a condensation of the principal assertions of Johannine theology.[27] He frequently uses it as such a reference point.[28] Olsson includes this passage and 12:44–50, which I shall consider below, in his list of Johannine "footnotes"

---

26. So Dodd, *Interpretation*, 309, 386; Johannes Beutler, *Martyria. Traditionsgeschichtliche Untersuchungen zum Zeugnisthema bei Johannes*, FraTS 10 (Frankfurt: Knecht, 1972), 313–15; Richter, *Studien*, 314, 337; Bornkamm, "Paraklet," 77–78; Meeks, "Man from Heaven," 150.

27. Schnackenburg, *John*, 1.380; also Blank, *Krisis*, 53–56; Moloney, *Son of Man*, 42.

28. Schnackenburg, *John*, 1.4, 278, 280.

which reflect the author's theology.[29] For Schulz it is the author's composition and reflects his characteristic Christology.[30] J. N. Sanders and B. A. Mastin see in it the author's own meditation.[31] Significantly it was 3:31–36 which Bornkamm used when highlighting the parallel thought structure between the author's Christology and his pneumatology.[32] Becker challenges its use as a starting point for investigating Johannine Christology, rightly drawing attention to its loose connection within the Gospel.[33] Some scholars in more recent times have read 3:31–36 as continuing the witness of John the Baptist.[34] For our purposes, whether these are seen as John's words, Jesus' words,[35] or, as more likely, those of the evangelist,[36] does not finally alter the fact that they can be seen as a significant summary. According to John Painter, John 3:13–21, 31–36 "are to be understood as the word of the narrator where an ascension perspective is not surprising."[37]

Its usefulness as a starting point is its compactness and summary character. Comparison with the rest of the Gospel will indicate how well its Christology fits within the Gospel. It serves as a starting point, not a concluding summary of our investigation. The following are its major christological statements:

29. Olsson, *Structure*, 262.

30. Schulz, *Johannes*, 66.

31. J. N. Sanders and B. A. Mastin, *A Commentary on the Gospel according to St. John*, BNTC (London: Black, 1968), 135; similarly Beasley-Murray, *John*, 53.

32. Bornkamm, "Paraklet," 77–78.

33. Becker, "Streit der Methoden," 11.

34. Elizabeth Harris, *Prologue and Gospel: The Theology of the Fourth Evangelist*; JSNTSup 107 (Sheffield: Sheffield Academic Press, 1994), 49; Hartwig Thyen, *Das Johannesevangelium*, HNT 6 (Tübingen: Mohr Siebeck, 2005), 233; Michael Theobald, *Das Evangelium nach Johannes. Kapitel 1–12* (Regensburg: Pustet, 2009), 289–91; J. Ramsey Michaels, *The Gospel of John*, NICNT (Grand Rapids: Eerdmans, 2010), 221–22; Martin Rese, "Johannes 3,22–36: Der taufende Jesus und das letzte Zeugnis Johannes des Taufers," *Studies in the Gospel of John and Its Christology: Festschrift Gilbert Van Belle*, ed. J. Verheyden, G. van Oyen, M. Labahn, and R. Bieringer, BETL 265 (Leuven: Peeters, 2014), 94–97.

35. Ulrich Wilckens, *Das Evangelium nach Johannes*, NTD 4 (Göttingen: Vandenhoeck und Ruprecht, 1998), 76–77.

36. So Ben Witherington III, *John's Wisdom: A Commentary on the Fourth Gospel* (Louisville: Westminster John Knox, 1995), 110; Francis J. Moloney, *The Gospel of John*, SP 4 (Collegeville: Liturgical, 1998), 106–7; Schnelle, *Johannes*, 81; Martin Schmidl, *Jesus und Nikodemus. Gespräch zur johanneischen Christologie. Joh 3 in schichtenspezifischer Sicht*, BU 28 (Regensburg: Pustet, 1998), 387; Lincoln, *John*, 161; Keener, *John*, 581; Ashton, *John*, 117; Johannes Beutler, *Das Johannesevangelium* (Freiburg: Herder, 2013), 147, 150; Frey, *Eschatologie*, who writes of chapter 3 as "*mehrschichtige Kommunikation*" written from a post-Easter perspective (3.247, 300).

37. Painter, *Quest*, 330.

> Ὁ ἄνωθεν ἐρχόμενος ἐπάνω πάντων ἐστίν·
> He who comes from above is above all. (3:31a)[38]

This statement is expanded in two ways. Negatively:

> ὁ ὢν ἐκ τῆς γῆς ἐκ τῆς γῆς ἐστιν καὶ ἐκ τῆς γῆς λαλεῖ.
> He who is of the earth is of the earth and speaks of the earth. (3:31b)

The contrast is not with John the Baptist.[39] That would devalue his informed witness to Jesus in the preceding verses (3:27–30!), not to speak of 1:15 and what he is about to say, were he to be understood as speaking. Rather the contrast is with Nicodemus, the teacher of Israel who cannot see because he is not born from above (3:3), and with those like him who involve themselves in disputes about purification (3:25).[40] The first statement is then reformulated: ὁ ἐκ τοῦ οὐρανοῦ ἐρχόμενος ("he who comes from heaven"). At this point the textual witness is divided between continuing directly into 32 (P^{75} ℵ*) or repeating the formulation from 31a ἐπάνω πάντων ἐστίν ("is above all"; P$^{36.66.75}$ A B). Whichever text we follow, we can see that 31 contains two major statements about Jesus: he comes from above, from heaven; and he is above all (either people or both people and things). The verse also associates his origin with his superiority ("from above" and "above all") and relates this to his speaking, which follows directly in 32, but is indirectly implied in 31 where the one who is "of the earth speaks of the earth."

> ὃ ἑώρακεν καὶ ἤκουσεν τοῦτο μαρτυρεῖ
> What he has seen and heard, to this he bears witness. (3:32a)

With this we may associate:

> ὃν γὰρ ἀπέστειλεν ὁ θεὸς τὰ ῥήματα τοῦ θεοῦ λαλεῖ

---

38. Unless otherwise indicated, translations are the author's.

39. Cf. Raymond E. Brown, *The Gospel according to John*, 2 vols., AB 29/29A (New York: Doubleday, 1966–1970), 161; Barnabas Lindars, *The Gospel of John* (London: Oliphants, 1972), 169; Boismard and Lamouille, *Jean*, 125 (for the redactor, not the "IIA" Gospel: so 119); Haenchen, *Johannes*, 232; Rodney A. Whitacre, *Johannine Polemic*, SBLDS 67 (Chico: Scholars, 1982), 97; Gary M. Burge, *The Anointed Community: The Holy Spirit in the Johannine Tradition* (Grand Rapids: Eerdmans, 1987), 83; Donald A. Carson, *The Gospel according to John* (Grand Rapids: Eerdmans:, 1991), 212; Michaels, *John*, 222.

40. So Schnackenburg, *John*, 1.382; Blank, *Krisis*, 66; Beutler, *Martyria*, 316; Beasley-Murray, *John*, 53; Keener, *John*, 581; Theobald, *Johannes*, 1.291–92; Beutler, *Johannes-evangelium*, 148.

Identifying the Central Structure

He whom God sent speaks the words of God. (3:34a)

The first of these statements casts Jesus in the role of someone reporting what he has experienced. It uses the specifically forensic motif of witness, and forensic imagery also lies behind 3:33 ("seal"; "true"). The second also alludes to Jesus' speaking, but uses the envoy imagery. Both confirm the focus on speaking, already present in 3:31. Both are to be seen as relating the validity of Jesus' speaking to his origin in heaven. He has come from there as witness and envoy.

καὶ τὴν μαρτυρίαν αὐτοῦ οὐδεὶς λαμβάνει.
and no one accepts his witness. (3:32b)
ὁ λαβὼν αὐτοῦ τὴν μαρτυρίαν ἐσφράγισεν ὅτι ὁ θεὸς ἀληθής ἐστιν.
He who has accepted his witness has set his seal to the fact that God is true. (3:33)

The first is a statement about response to Jesus and his communication (see above), now expressed in forensic terms as "witness." As such, it is also a statement about Jesus and his rejection. The "no one" cannot be inclusive because 3:33 tells of those who do accept him (like 1:11-12). The seal image is also forensic language.

ὃν γὰρ ἀπέστειλεν ὁ θεὸς τὰ ῥήματα τοῦ θεοῦ λαλεῖ,
οὐ γὰρ ἐκ μέτρου δίδωσιν τὸ πνεῦμα.
ὁ πατὴρ ἀγαπᾷ τὸν υἱὸν
καὶ πάντα δέδωκεν ἐν τῇ χειρὶ αὐτοῦ.
For he whom God sent speaks the words of God (3:34a)
for he does not give the Spirit by measure. (3:34b)
The Father loves the Son (3:35a)
and has given all things into his hand. (3:35b)

Jesus receives his authorisation as envoy from God (3:34a). The three statements which follow expand the meaning of the Son's authority. It is best to take God as the subject of all three.[41] Jesus' authority rests on God's equipping

---

41. So Bultmann, *Johannes*, 119; C. K. Barrett, *The Gospel according to St. John*, 2nd ed. (London: SPCK, 1978), 226; Schnackenburg, *John*, 1.386-87; Lindars, *Gospel of John*, 170-71; F. F. Bruce, *The Gospel of John* (Grand Rapids: Eerdmans, 1983), 97; George Johnston, *The Spirit Paraclete in the Gospel of John*, SNTSMS 12 (Cambridge: Cambridge University Press, 1970), 14; Ibuki, *Wahrheit*, 149-50, 153; Beasley-Murray, *John*, 53-54; Burge, *Anointed Community*, 83-84; Moloney, *John*, 107; Schnelle, *Johannes*, 82; Lincoln, *John*, 162; Thyen, *Johannesevangelium*, 237; Michaels, *John*, 225.

him with the Spirit, loving him, and giving all things into his hands. Three further motifs are thus employed to express Jesus' authority: pneumatic or charismatic authority, familial or filial authority, and delegated authority. "All things" echoes "above all" in 3:31. There, too, authority is the focus.

In itself the text, οὐ γὰρ ἐκ μέτρου δίδωσιν τὸ πνεῦμα ("for he does not give the Spirit by measure" in 3:34b) is ambiguous. The following grounds have been offered for taking Jesus as the subject: (i) the present tense, δίδωσιν ("give"); compare the aorist and perfect in 3:34a and 35b; (ii) elsewhere πνεῦμα and ῥήματα are associated as gifts of Jesus (6:63), so that 3:34b could be treated as a parallel to 34a; (iii) 3:35b can be read as explaining why the Son can give the Spirit: he has been given all things; (iv) one might expect a γάρ ("for") in 3:35 if the Father were the giver of the Spirit; (v) the coming of the Spirit upon Jesus in 1:32-33, while reflecting earlier christological tradition, now serves merely as a sign for John the Baptist to help him recognise the one who was authorised and empowered already in his pre-existence; (vi) the promise that Jesus would baptise with the Spirit (1:33b) is being reflected here; (vii) the chapter had begun with reflection on the receiving of the Spirit by those who are born again (3:5-8). The case is argued strongly by Thüsing and Felix Porsch.[42]

None of these arguments is finally convincing. John 3:35 uses the present tense ἀγαπᾷ immediately after 3:34b and the use of the perfect δέδωκεν also puts the focus on the present relationship. It may be that 1:32 is in mind, but hardly as the event when Jesus first received the Spirit; rather, it is a sign that Jesus has the Spirit. The words ῥήματα and πνεῦμα are associated, but this is so because Jesus has received the Spirit—the word—which he can then give. The conjunction of the two words in 3:34 is best explained as a statement, first of all, of Jesus' sending to speak the words and then of his complete equipping to do so, hence the γάρ of 34b. This best explains οὐ ... ἐκ μέτρου ("without measure"); for, like 3:34a (ὃν γὰρ ἀπέστειλεν ὁ θεός ("whom God sent") and especially 3:35 (πάντα "all things"), it emphasises Jesus' complete authorisation. The focus of the context is not the giving of the Spirit and the equipping of the disciples, but the authorisation and equipping of Jesus, though earlier in the chapter the Spirit is related both to Jesus and to the disciples (3:3-8). Further, the passage clearly refers to Jesus' earthly work of revelation, not his work as the exalted one who gives the Spirit or has the Spirit sent. Strictly speaking, the Son is described as sending the Paraclete (15:26), but only the Father "gives" it (14:16).

---

42. Thüsing, *Erhöhung*, 153-56, 321; Porsch, *Pneuma*, 104-105. See also Brown, *John*, 158, 161-62.

Identifying the Central Structure

However the issue is settled, the question of the basic structure of thought in 3:31–36 is largely unaffected. A third hypothetical alternative might take πνεῦμα as subject, but this is less convincing and would be without parallel in John. The variant reading in a few manuscripts (apparently including B) which omits πνεῦμα would most naturally require God as subject and this is probably why other manuscripts include the word θεός ("God") in the text (this reading is supported by an impressive number of witnesses but is probably outweighed by those that omit it, including such as P⁶⁶, P⁷⁵ and ℵ).

Within these verses we also note for the first time the terms "Father" and "Son" for Jesus and God in the words, "The Father loves the Son" (3:35a), and the way the relationship is described as one of love. "The Son" also appears twice in 3:36.

The expression "giving all things into his hands (τῇ χειρί literally: 'hand')" (3:35b) reflects the OT idiomatic expression, "to fill the hands," meaning to ordain (e.g., a priest; Exod 29:9, 29, 35; Lev 8:33). It is used here by extension in the sense of authorisation.[43] A variant occurs in 13:3 "knowing that the Father had given all things into his hands" (compare also Matt 11:27a par. Luke 10:22a). The same idea is reflected in 17:2, "you have given him authority over all flesh." πάντα ("all things") is neuter, though John seems primarily concerned with people, as also the parallel in 17:2 indicates. πάντων in 3:31 may also be neuter, especially if the two references form an *inclusio*, and not masculine as Schnackenburg and Brown suggest.[44]

> ὁ πιστεύων εἰς τὸν υἱὸν ἔχει ζωὴν αἰώνιον·
> ὁ δὲ ἀπειθῶν τῷ υἱῷ οὐκ ὄψεται ζωήν,
> ἀλλ' ἡ ὀργὴ τοῦ θεοῦ μένει ἐπ' αὐτόν.
> He who believes in the Son has eternal life;
> he who does not obey the Son shall not see life,
> but the wrath of God abides upon him. (3:36)

While our concern is Christology not soteriology, we note that this is a statement of judgment and so recalls the forensic motifs of 3:32–33. The sentence of judgment falls according to people's response to the Son and his words. The Son's coming and speaking is decisive for the future of people.

Within 3:31–36 we may trace the following christological statements:

1. Jesus comes from above, from heaven.

---

43. Schnackenburg, *John*, 1.388.
44. Schnackenburg, *John*, 1.381; Brown, *John*, 157.

2. Jesus is above all.
3. Jesus has been sent by God.
4. Jesus tells/bears witness to what he has seen/heard, the words of God.
5. Jesus faces rejection, disobedience or belief.
6. Jesus is equipped fully with the Spirit.
7. Jesus is loved as Son by the Father.
8. Jesus has been given all things.
9. Response to Jesus brings judgment to life or death.
10. Jesus is the Son, God is the Father.

When we set these main christological points alongside the findings from other passages, a common pattern emerges. I shall illustrate this first by looking at another passage of summary character, 12:44-50.

1.2.2   John 12:44-50

In its present position within the Gospel it carries considerable weight. Olsson lists it as one of the evangelist's "footnotes,"[45] while Brown considers it a variant of 3:31–36.[46] Edward Schillebeeckx considers it a resumé of Johannine Christology.[47] There are grounds for seeing it as at one time an independent piece of Johannine writing written by the author,[48] perhaps on the basis of earlier Jesus tradition,[49] or by an earlier author of the Johannine school,[50] or by a redactor using motifs and ideas who added it to the Gospel as a summary of the message of the earthly ministry.[51] But without doubt its place within the transmitted text makes it Jesus' final public statement of any length, a summary statement of the purport of chapters 1–12.[52] In taking it as another starting point beside 3:31–36 I am not making a particular claim in relationship to its authorship, but using it to trace patterns within the existing text.

---

45. Olsson, *Structure*, 262.
46. Brown, *John*, 160.
47. Schillebeeckx, *Christ*, 399–400.
48. Schnackenburg, *Johannesevangelium*, 2.523–24.
49. Peder Borgen, "The Use of Tradition in John 12.44-50," in *Logos Was the True Light* (Trondheim: Tapir, 1983), 54–66.
50. So M.-E. Boismard, "Le caractère adventice de Jo., XII, 45-50," in *Sacra Pagina II* (Paris: Gemloux, 1959), 189–92; see also Schnackenburg, *Johannesevangelium*, 2.523–25.
51. So Becker, *Johannes*, 413–15.
52. So Dodd, *Interpretation*, 381–83; Barrett, *John*, 433.

Identifying the Central Structure

The following points emerge:

> ὁ πιστεύων εἰς ἐμὲ οὐ πιστεύει εἰς ἐμὲ ἀλλ᾽ εἰς τὸν πέμψαντά με,
> καὶ ὁ θεωρῶν ἐμὲ θεωρεῖ τὸν πέμψαντά με.
> He who believes in me believes not in me but in him who sent me
> and he who sees me sees him who sent me. (12:44–45)

Already these opening statements contain much that is repeated or developed in the rest of the passage:

> τὸν πέμψαντά με
> him who sent me (12:44, 45, 49; ὁ πέμψας με)
> ὁ πιστεύων εἰς ἐμέ
> He who believes in me (cf. 3:36; 12:44, 46–47)
> ὁ θεωρῶν ἐμέ
> he who sees me (12:45)

and its opposite:

> καὶ ἐάν τίς μου ἀκούσῃ τῶν ῥημάτων καὶ μὴ φυλάξῃ
> If anyone hears my words and does not keep them. (12:47)
> ὁ ἀθετῶν ἐμὲ καὶ μὴ λαμβάνων τὰ ῥήματά μου
> He who rejects me and does not receive my words. (12:48)

Of more directly christological interest is the coupling of response to Jesus with response to God: "The one who believes in me believes not in me but in him who sent me" (12:44) and "he who sees me sees him who sent me" (12:45). This coupling receives an explanation in 12:49–50.

> ὅτι ἐγὼ ἐξ ἐμαυτοῦ οὐκ ἐλάλησα,
> ἀλλ᾽ ὁ πέμψας με πατὴρ αὐτός μοι ἐντολὴν δέδωκεν
> τί εἴπω καὶ τί λαλήσω. . . . ἃ οὖν ἐγὼ λαλῶ,
> καθὼς εἴρηκέν μοι ὁ πατήρ, οὕτως λαλῶ.
> I do not speak on my own authority,
> but the Father who sent me has given me commandment
> what I am to say and what I am to speak. . . .In regard to what I speak,
> as the Father has spoken to me, so I speak. (12:49–50)

This recalls the statements in 3:31–36 about Jesus bearing witness to what he had seen and heard (32) and speaking the words of God as the one sent and authorised by the Father (34). Seeing Jesus as seeing the Father may be another way of saying this; it may go beyond it.

> ἐγὼ φῶς εἰς τὸν κόσμον ἐλήλυθα,
> ἵνα πᾶς ὁ πιστεύων εἰς ἐμὲ ἐν τῇ σκοτίᾳ μὴ μείνῃ. . . .
> οὐ γὰρ ἦλθον ἵνα κρίνω τὸν κόσμον,
> ἀλλ᾽ ἵνα σώσω τὸν κόσμον.
> I have come as light into the world,
> that all who believe in me may not walk in darkness. . . .
> I did not come that I might judge the world,
> but that I might save the world. (12:46–47)

We note the statement, repeated in abbreviated form in 12:47, that Jesus came into the world. 12:46 also contains the contrasting imagery of light/darkness and identifies Jesus himself with light. 12:47 speaks of Jesus' saving and contrasts this with the role of judging, i.e., condemning. When 12:50 speaks of the Father's commandment being "eternal life," it probably means that, as the Son carries out the Father's commission, he brings to the world the opportunity for people to believe and so have life (like 3:36). The Son brings not condemnation, but light, life, salvation.

> ὁ ἀθετῶν ἐμὲ καὶ μὴ λαμβάνων τὰ ῥήματά μου ἔχει τὸν κρίνοντα αὐτόν·
> ὁ λόγος ὃν ἐλάλησα ἐκεῖνος κρινεῖ αὐτὸν ἐν τῇ ἐσχάτῃ ἡμέρᾳ.
> Anyone who rejects me and does not accept my words has one who judges him.
> The word which I have spoken, it shall judge him on the last day. (12:48)

The verse speaks of a future judgment day and "the one judging" is not God but Jesus' own word. John 12:49–50 explains (ὅτι, "because") this along the lines that rejection of Jesus' word is nothing other than rejection of God's word. Response to Jesus is response to God.

Within 12:44–50 we may trace the following christological statements:

1. Jesus has come into the world.
2. Jesus has been sent by the Father.
3. Jesus says what he has been commanded to say by God.
4. To see Jesus is to see the one who sent him.
5. Jesus is rejected or accepted.
6. Jesus brings light, life, salvation and indirectly also judgment.
7. God is the Father.

Identifying the Central Structure

The third passage to be considered, 8:12–19, is typical of much of the material portraying Jesus' dialogue with the Jews. Here their concern is the validity of his self-testimony, and within Jesus' response a number of christological statements are made.

1.2.3   John 8:12–19

> ἐγώ εἰμι τὸ φῶς τοῦ κόσμου·
> ὁ ἀκολουθῶν ἐμοὶ οὐ μὴ περιπατήσῃ ἐν τῇ σκοτίᾳ, ἀλλ' ἕξει τὸ φῶς τῆς ζωῆς.
> I am the light of the world;
> he who follows me shall not walk in darkness but shall have the light of life. (8:12)

This recalls 12:46 where Jesus will speak of his coming as light into the world. Instead of "I have come" here we have one of the "I am" sayings of Jesus' self-presentation. As in the passage just considered, response to Jesus determines whether one abides or walks in darkness or has the light of life.

The Pharisees challenge Jesus' claim about himself. Forensic language dominates the discussion that follows: "witness," "judging," "truth" (all three also in 3:31–36). Jesus' witness is true (8:14; cf. 17) and should he judge, his judgment is true (8:16). By contrast, the Pharisees make their assessment according to the flesh. Unlike 3:31–36 the "witness" here refers not to what Jesus has seen and heard (3:32) but to his self-claim to be light coming into the world. Beyond the evidential dispute is the claim itself, expressed not only in terms of light but also in the following ways:

> κἂν ἐγὼ μαρτυρῶ περὶ ἐμαυτοῦ, ἀληθής ἐστιν ἡ μαρτυρία μου,
> ὅτι οἶδα πόθεν ἦλθον καὶ ποῦ ὑπάγω·
> ὑμεῖς δὲ οὐκ οἴδατε πόθεν ἔρχομαι ἢ ποῦ ὑπάγω.
> If I witness concerning myself, my witness is true
> because I know where I come from and where I am going;
> you do not know where I come from and where I am going. (8:14)

> καὶ ἐὰν κρίνω δὲ ἐγώ, ἡ κρίσις ἡ ἐμὴ ἀληθινή ἐστιν,
> ὅτι μόνος οὐκ εἰμί, ἀλλ' ἐγὼ καὶ ὁ πέμψας με πατήρ.
> And if I judge, my judgment is true,
> because I am not alone, but there is me and the Father who sent me. (8:16)

> ἐγώ εἰμι ὁ μαρτυρῶν περὶ ἐμαυτοῦ
> καὶ μαρτυρεῖ περὶ ἐμοῦ ὁ πέμψας με πατήρ.
> I am witnessing concerning myself
> and my Father who sent me witnesses concerning me. (8:18)

> οὔτε ἐμὲ οἴδατε οὔτε τὸν πατέρα μου·
> εἰ ἐμὲ ᾔδειτε, καὶ τὸν πατέρα μου ἂν ᾔδειτε.
> You neither know me nor my Father.
> If you had known me, you would have known my Father. (8:19)

Jesus has come from the Father and returns to the Father. The Father sent him and witnesses concerning him. In this sense Jesus is his own authority, but is also ultimately authorised by the Father. Knowing Jesus is knowing God. This is a variant of what appears in 12:45, seeing the Son is seeing the Father.

Within 8:12–19 we may trace therefore the following christological statements:

1. The Son comes from the Father.
2. The Son returns to the Father.
3. The Son knows where he comes from and where he is going.
4. The Father has sent the Son.
5. The Son witnesses concerning himself.
6. The Father witnesses concerning the Son.
7. The Son presents himself: "I am the. . ."
8. The Son offers the light of life or darkness.
9. To know Jesus is to know the Father.
10. Jesus as Son speaks of God as the Father.

The most consistent elements to emerge from all three passages taken together are: the use of "Father" for God and, by implication, "Son" for Jesus; the sending of the Son by the Father; the coming of the Son into the world from the Father (from above, from heaven) and, by implication, his return; his authorisation by the Father (variously expressed: given the Spirit, "all things," being commanded, borne witness to, as well as sent); his self-claim expressed variously to be the one who represents the Father, speaks his words, bears his message and therefore brings life, light and salvation to those who believe in him. The pattern which emerges may be set out schematically as follows:

1. The Son comes from the Father.

2. The Father has sent the Son.
3. The Father has authorised the Son.
4. The Son makes the Father known.
5. Jesus is the Son and God is the Father.
6. The Son returns to the Father.

I shall use this as a framework for the next section in which I shall explore each of these and, in doing so, take into account other motifs and elements, including those noted in the three passages above. In proceeding in this way, having sampled three brief passages, I am not making the claim that they, alone, are sufficient evidence on which to assert that the outline does in fact represent the central structure of Johannine Christology. Only the following steps can establish the extent to which this may be so. In these I will show how extensive this pattern is within the Gospel and how the indicators outlined above support the claim. The one element which will be shown to require a more expansive treatment is the sixth element, "The Son returns to the Father," for it entails a discussion of the very complex variety of images used in the Gospel to express the significance of Jesus' death and the events associated with it. This emerges especially when I run through the Gospel as a whole in the light of the findings concerning the patterns.

1.3 Common Elements of the Structure

This section considers the elements of the above structure in turn, examining the ways they are expressed and their frequency within the Gospel.

1.3.1 The Son Comes from the Father

This takes many forms, but the most common are:

> He comes (ἔρχομαι):
> from above (3:31; 8:23)
> from heaven (3:31; with καταβαίνω: 3:13)
> and as the bread also (6:33, 41, 42, 50, 51, 58)
> from God (3:2; 8:42–43; 13:3; 16:30)
> from the Father (16:27–28; cf. 1:14; 17:8)
> Similarly, he is not from this world. (8:23; 15:19; 17:14, 16)

The coming stands on its own:
without a statement of origin (10:10; 12:27; cf. 10:18)
with a denial that he comes of his own accord (7:27-29; 8:42-43; cf. 5:43)
or with the addition that he comes
into the world (1:9; 3:19; 9:39; 12:46-47; 18:37; 16:28)
or to his own (1:11)

Sometimes the coming is expressed in association with motifs:
light (1:9; 3:20; 12:46-47; cf. 8:12, 14)
or judgment (9:39; 12:46-47)
The coming is associated with hopes for
a prophet (6:14)
or a Messiah who is coming (1:15, 27, 30; 4:23; 7:27, 31, 42; 11:27; 12:13, 15)

Often the Son's coming is alluded to in the form of a question about Jesus' origin, usually introduced by πόθεν ("whence?"). Both in relationship to Jesus' messianic claims (7:27-28, 42) and more generally (8:14; 9:29-30) the Jews are shown to be perplexed about where Jesus has come from. Pilate, too, asks the question (19:9). The issue of Jesus' origin is crucial for the author's Christology. This is evident also in the way he introduces it into other narratives: "Whence do you know me?" (1:48); whence does Jesus get the wine? (2:9), the water? (4:11), and the bread? (6:5; cf. 4:33). Often the author associates the "whence" question with the "whither" question (3:8; 8:14) or associates a statement about origin with one about his return (8:42-43; 13:3; 16:27-28; cf. 3:13).[53]

1.3.2 The Father Has Sent the Son

The words, ὁ πέμψας με ("the one who sent me"), are almost a standard formula for God on the lips of the Johannine Jesus (4:34; 5:30; 6:38, 39; 7:18, 28, 33; 8:26; 9:4; 12:44, 45; 13:16, 20; 16:5), sometimes directly linked with the designation of God as "Father" (5:37; 6:44; 8:16, 18, 29; 12:49; 14:24), and usually presuming a reference to Jesus and God as "Son" and "Father" (5:23-24; cf. 5:30, 37 and most of the above references).

Apart from the aorist active participle no other form of πέμπω is used of the sending of the Son by the Father (cf. 13:20; 15:21, 26; 16:7; 20:21). Instead

---

53. On "whence" and "whither" sayings see further: Nicholson, *Death*, 53-55; de Jonge, *Stranger*, 142; R. Kieffer, "L'Espace et le Temps dans l'Évangile de Jean," *NTS* 31 (1985): 400-404; Culpepper, *Anatomy*, 170-71; L. M. Dewailly, "'D'où est tu?' (Jean 19,9)," *RB* 92 (1985): 489-92.

the verb ἀποστέλλω is used, either on its own in the indicative with implicit reference to "Father" and "Son" (5:38; 7:29; 8:42; 11:42; 17:8, 18, 21, 23, 25) or with explicit reference to "God" (3:34; 6:29; 17:3), to "Father" (6:57; 10:36; 20:21), to "God" and "Son" (3:17), or to "Father" and "Son" (5:36; cf. 3:34–35). But it is never used in the active aorist participial form, the form preserved exclusively for πέμπω.

This makes it likely that the use of one or the other verb is for the author a matter of stylistic preference and that both mean the same thing.[54] I find no evidence in John for Rengstorf's claim that ἀποστέλλω stresses authority and πέμπω indicates God's involvement.[55] Nor do I accept Jean Radermakers's or Jean Seynaeve's respective claims that the former or the latter focusses more on the purpose of the sending.[56] The same two verbs are used in the same way in relation to the sending of the disciples (πέμπω: 13:16, 20; 20:21; ἀποστέλλω: 4:38; 17:18; cf. 1:6 and 3:28 of John the Baptist). The words of Jesus' commission to the disciples in 20:21 bring both verbs together: "As my Father has sent me (ἀπέσταλκέν), even so I send (πέμπω) you."

Closely associated with the motif of sending is that of the giving of the Son (3:16; cf. 3:17). Both terms are also associated in the promise of the coming of the Spirit, the Paraclete (giving: 7:39; 14:16; cf. 3:34; sending: 14:26; 15:26; 16:7).

1.3.3 The Father Has Authorised the Son

The notion of authorisation belongs closely with that of sending, especially with the envoy motif. Most statements that speak of the Son coming from the Father also assume authorisation. It is also related to statements about the Son receiving something which he can pass on or seeing something to which he can bear witness. I shall turn to these in the next section below.

Both 3:35 and 13:3 speak of the Father's giving all things into the hand(s) of the Son in association with the task to be fulfilled by the Son. This is best understood as authorisation in much the same way as 17:2 ("you have given

---

54. So Kühl, *Sendung*, 54; Haenchen, *Johannes*, 107; Miranda, *Sendung*, 29; de Jonge, *Stranger*, 165.

55. Rengstorf, "ἀποστέλλω"; similarly Blank, *Krisis*, 70 n. 61; Bühner, *Gesandte*, 412–13; Frank J. Matera, "Christ in the Theologies of Paul and John: A Study in the Diverse Unity of New Testament Theology," *TS* 67 (2006): 250.

56. Jean Radermakers, "Mission et Apostolat en Jean," in *Studia Evangelica II* (Berlin: de Gruyter, 1964), 100–21; similarly Riedl, *Heilswerk*, 55–57; Jean Seynaeve, "Les verbes ἀποστέλλω et πέμπω dans le vocabulaire théologique de Saint Jean," in *L'Évangile de Jean. Sources, Rédaction, Théologie*, ed. M. de Jonge, BETL 44 (Leuven: Peeters, 1977), 389.

him authority over all flesh"). Thüsing and Schnackenburg relate 17:2 only to Jesus' exaltation and its fruit, the giving of eternal life (17:3);[57] but while the giving does indeed relate to the Easter event, this need not mean that 17:2a refers to anything other than the authorisation which sent Jesus on his course in the beginning.[58] A distinction must be drawn, as we shall see, between Jesus' authorisation "authority," and his exaltation and glorification. This is already clear from 17:1, which portrays Jesus as praying for glorification in the immediate future (its hour has come). Similarly 3:31 ("above all") is associated with Jesus as the one who has come from above, from heaven.

The author often uses the word "given" to express authorisation. Jesus says to Pilate: "You would have no authority over me except it was given to you from above" in 19:11, and of disciples: "no one can come to me unless it is given to him by the Father" in 6:65. John the Baptist uses a similar formulation in discussing Jesus' authority: "No one can do anything except it is given him from heaven" (3:27). The phrase "from heaven" recurs shortly afterwards in the designation of Jesus as the one who is "from heaven" (3:31). The verb δίδωμι occurs a number of times in ch. 17 in relation to authorisation. We have already noted 17:2a. Jesus speaks of "having completed the work you gave me to do" (17:4). Authorisation is also present where Jesus speaks of being given the Father's name (17:11–12) and is also associated with Jesus' being given God's word (17:8, 14) and glory (17:22, 24). The same chapter also speaks of believers as given to the Son in a way that recalls 6:65, already noted, which speaks of authorisation of disciples to come to Jesus (17:6, 9; cf. also 6:37, 39; 18:9). Disciples may also be meant in the enigmatic phrases, "all that you have given him" in 17:2, "all that you have given me" in 17:7 and "what my Father has given me" in 10:29. Jesus also refers to his commissioning in these words in 18:11: "The cup which my Father has given me, am I not to drink it?"

In 5:26–27 being authorised and being equipped are linked: the Son is given life in himself and the authority to judge. 5:20–21 express this authorisation in close association with the Father's love for his Son, as in 3:35 ("the Father loves the Son and has given all things into his hands"; cf. 3:34 which speaks of the giving of the Spirit). Love and authorisation are also linked in 10:17–18, where the Son speaks of his authority to lay down and take up his life again in accordance with his Father's will. In 15:10 the Son's remaining in the Father's love is linked with his keeping the Father's commandments. Authorisation and receiving commandments are also closely linked and will

---

57. Thüsing, *Erhöhung*, 231–32; Schnackenburg, *Johannesevangelium*, 3.193–94.
58. So Becker, *Johannes*, 518; Barrett, *John*, 502; Brown, *John*, 740.

be dealt with in the following section. Authorisation is also expressed where Jesus emphasises that he has not come of his own accord (7:27-29; 8:42-43) nor does he do anything of his own accord (7:17; 8:28; 5:30; 14:10).

1.3.4 The Son Makes the Father Known

This idea is fundamental and widespread, but expressed in a variety of ways. There are two aspects: receiving and giving. Under receiving we may list statements which speak of the Son knowing, having seen, having been told, taught, given, and commanded. Under giving we might list: making known, giving, witnessing, teaching, and doing works which function in these revelatory ways. The following illustrate the bringing together of both aspects:

> The Son witnesses to what he has seen and heard (3:32),
> tells of what he has seen (8:38; cf. 1:18; 5:37; 6:46; 3:11),
> of what he has heard (8:26, 40; cf. 5:37; 3:8)
> or makes it known (15:15).

> He speaks as he has been taught (8:28: cf. 7:16, 35; 3:2),
> been told (12:50)
> or commanded (12:49).

> As he has been given, so he gives the Father's words (17:8),
> the Father's name (17:6, 11-12, 26),
> the Father's glory (17:22, 26).

> He also does on earth what he has been commanded to do by the Father. (15:10; cf. 17:4; 5:36)
> This includes laying down his life and taking it up again. (10:18; cf. 14:31; 18:37)
> The Son does the works of the Father. (6:38-40; cf. 10:32, 37; 5:17, 20)
> The Son's concern is to complete the work given him to do. (4:34)
> This he does. (17:4; 19:30, "it is finished")
> Thus the Son does not act of his own accord. (7:17; 8:28; 5:30; 14:10)

Because it is in the authority and the power of the Father that the Son does the works he has been commanded to do, it can equally be said that the Father is doing the works (14:10). Accordingly to have seen and known the Son is to have seen and known the Father (14:7-11; cf. also 1:18).

The unity of the Father and the Son is expounded in association with this Christology of revelation, both in 10:32–38 and in 14:7–11. Jesus' being one with the Father (10:30) and his being in the Father and the Father in him (10:38; 14:10–11; cf. 14:20) is argued on the basis that he does the works of the Father, which he had been given to do (similarly 5:17–18, 20). Other factors play a role in the author's understanding of Jesus' relation to God and these will be examined below, but it is noteworthy that the author consistently returns to the model of the Son making the Father known.

This is also both the central thrust and the climactic claim of the prologue. Jesus is the Word. He has seen God and makes him known (1:18). He was with God, was θεός (1:1), θεός, the only Son, in the bosom of the Father (1:18), and, as only Son from (παρά) the Father (1:14), he became flesh, manifested his glory (1:14) and made the Father known (1:18).

Correspondingly the Gospel frequently records that a response to the Son is a response to the Father. To believe in (12:44), see (12:45), honour (5:23), receive (13:20), know (14:7) or hate (15:23) the Son is to believe in, see, honour, receive, know or hate the Father who sent him. For the Son knows the Father and has made him known (14:7; 15:24; cf. 16:3; 17:3; 8:19; 15:21). In this sense the Son has made known the truth (8:32, 40; 17:17; cf. 5:33). For this purpose he came (18:37–38). Grace and truth came through him (1:14, 16). Therefore he can be identified as "the truth" (14:6). Here, too, belong the enigmatic "I am" sayings in which Jesus presents himself as the revealer.

Within the variety of motifs listed there is a consistent pattern. It is that the Son makes the Father known. The Son has come as revealer, sent by the Father and authorised by him to speak and act in accordance with what he has been shown and been commanded. He does this in the power and authority given him by the Father and in unity with him. The effect of his making the Father known is to provoke crisis, to bring a turning point, for some to life, for others to death. Because the Son comes from the Father—as the one sent and authorised to make the Father known, he can claim: I am the source of water, the bread, the light, the shepherd, the door, the bread, the resurrection and the life, the way, the truth, and the life for those who believe. For those who do not believe he is the bearer of judgment.

1.3.5 Jesus as "Son" and God as "Father"

It is beyond dispute that these terms occur with great frequency throughout the Gospel, so that I see no need other than to state this fact and point to the evidence of a concordance.

1.3.6 Review

The elements of the structure identified in the three passages considered occur extensively within the Gospel and often take a variety of forms. They also occur frequently in association with one another in much the same way as in the three passages considered earlier. This can be shown by first considering the summary statements within the Gospel.

1.4 Summary Statements illustrating the Christological Structure

We have already considered the summary passages, 3:31–36 and 12:44–50. Apart from these the following shorter summary statements illustrate the conjunction of the elements of the christological structure noted above.

At the beginning of the second major section of the Gospel after the conclusion of the public ministry, Jesus is introduced as:

> εἰδὼς ὅτι πάντα ἔδωκεν αὐτῷ ὁ πατὴρ εἰς τὰς χεῖρας
> καὶ ὅτι ἀπὸ θεοῦ ἐξῆλθεν καὶ πρὸς τὸν θεὸν ὑπάγει.
> Knowing that the Father had given all things into his hands
> and that he had come from God and was going to God. (13:3)

In his dialogue with the Jews, Jesus says that after they have lifted up the Son of Man they would come to understand who Jesus is:

> ὅταν ὑψώσητε τὸν υἱὸν τοῦ ἀνθρώπου, τότε γνώσεσθε ὅτι ἐγώ εἰμι,
> καὶ ἀπ' ἐμαυτοῦ ποιῶ οὐδέν, ἀλλὰ καθὼς ἐδίδαξέν με ὁ πατὴρ ταῦτα λαλῶ.
> καὶ ὁ πέμψας με μετ' ἐμοῦ ἐστιν· οὐκ ἀφῆκέν με μόνον,
> ὅτι ἐγὼ τὰ ἀρεστὰ αὐτῷ ποιῶ πάντοτε.
> When you have lifted up the Son of Man, then you shall know that I am the one
> and that I do nothing of myself, but as the Father taught me, these things I speak.
> And he who sent me is with me. He has not left me alone,
> because I always do what is pleasing to him. (8:28–29)

A little earlier Jesus had stated in similar terms:

> κἀμὲ οἴδατε καὶ οἴδατε πόθεν εἰμί·

> καὶ ἀπ' ἐμαυτοῦ οὐκ ἐλήλυθα, ἀλλ' ἔστιν ἀληθινὸς ὁ πέμψας με,
> ὃν ὑμεῖς οὐκ οἴδατε·
> ἐγὼ οἶδα αὐτόν, ὅτι παρ' αὐτοῦ εἰμι κἀκεῖνός με ἀπέστειλεν.
> And you know me and you know where I come from.
> I have not come of my own accord, but he who sent me is reliable,
> whom you do not know. I know him, because I came from him and he
> sent me. (7:28–29)

At the conclusion of his first farewell discourse Jesus says:

> ἀλλ' ἵνα γνῷ ὁ κόσμος ὅτι ἀγαπῶ τὸν πατέρα,
> καὶ καθὼς ἐνετείλατό μοι ὁ πατήρ, οὕτως ποιῶ. ἐγείρεσθε, ἄγωμεν
> ἐντεῦθεν.
> But, that the world may know that I love the Father
> and as he has commanded me so I act, arise, let us go hence. (14:31)

At the climax of the second farewell discourse he says:

> αὐτὸς γὰρ ὁ πατὴρ φιλεῖ ὑμᾶς, ὅτι ὑμεῖς ἐμὲ πεφιλήκατε
> καὶ πεπιστεύκατε ὅτι ἐγὼ παρὰ [τοῦ] θεοῦ ἐξῆλθον.
> ἐξῆλθον παρὰ τοῦ πατρὸς καὶ ἐλήλυθα εἰς τὸν κόσμον·
> πάλιν ἀφίημι τὸν κόσμον καὶ πορεύομαι πρὸς τὸν πατέρα.
> The Father loves you, because you have loved me
> and believed that I came from God.
> I came from the Father and have come into the world.
> Again I am leaving the world and I am going to the Father. (16:27–28)

These are significant not just for what they say but where they say it, at strategic points of the narrative. The disciples find in this previous statement a clarity no longer masked in parable. Accordingly, they declare that Jesus knows all things and has unquestionable credentials. They add: ἐν τούτῳ πιστεύομεν ὅτι ἀπὸ θεοῦ ἐξῆλθες ("In this we believe that you are from God" in 16:30).

Within the passion narrative there are few utterances of Jesus, so that it is all the more significant that before Pilate Jesus declares:

> ἐγὼ εἰς τοῦτο γεγέννημαι καὶ εἰς τοῦτο ἐλήλυθα εἰς τὸν κόσμον,
> ἵνα μαρτυρήσω τῇ ἀληθείᾳ·
> I was born for this and for this I came into the world
> to bear witness to the truth. (18:37)

Identifying the Central Structure

Jesus' final word on the cross is: τετέλεσται ("It is finished" [19:30]). Near the beginning of his ministry Jesus had declared to his disciples:

ἐμὸν βρῶμά ἐστιν ἵνα ποιήσω τὸ θέλημα τοῦ πέμψαντός με
καὶ τελειώσω αὐτοῦ τὸ ἔργον.
My food is to do the will of him who sent me
and to finish his work. (4:34; cf. also 9:3–4)

Jesus' prayers sometimes summarise the aims of his ministry such as the one before Lazarus' grave. He prays, ἵνα πιστεύσωσιν ὅτι σύ με ἀπέστειλας ("that they may believe that you sent me" in 11:42). Jesus' prayer for his own, also of strategic importance in the narrative, contains similar summaries:

νῦν ἔγνωκαν ὅτι πάντα ὅσα δέδωκάς μοι παρὰ σοῦ εἰσιν·
ὅτι τὰ ῥήματα ἃ ἔδωκάς μοι δέδωκα αὐτοῖς,
καὶ αὐτοὶ ἔλαβον καὶ ἔγνωσαν ἀληθῶς ὅτι παρὰ σοῦ ἐξῆλθον,
καὶ ἐπίστευσαν ὅτι σύ με ἀπέστειλας.
Now they know that all that you have given me is from you,
because the words which you gave me I have given to them,
and they have received and know truly that I came from you
and they have believed that you sent me. (17:7–8; cf. also 21, 23, 25)

Nicodemus is also unwittingly the bearer of the christological statement if his words are understood at the Johannine level of faith:

ῥαββί, οἴδαμεν ὅτι ἀπὸ θεοῦ ἐλήλυθας διδάσκαλος·
οὐδεὶς γὰρ δύναται ταῦτα τὰ σημεῖα ποιεῖν ἃ σὺ ποιεῖς,
ἐὰν μὴ ᾖ ὁ θεὸς μετ' αὐτοῦ.
Rabbi, we know that you have come as a teacher from God.
For no one can do these signs which you do
unless God is with him. (3:2)

These are by no means all the summary statements of the Gospel, but they represent a significant portion[59] and the extent to which they are expressed in terms of the central structure and located at strategic points is striking, confirming this as the author's framework of thought. Of those which remain perhaps the most distinctive are:

---

59. Compare also the list of summary statements in Culpepper, *Anatomy*, 87–88.

ταῦτα δὲ γέγραπται ἵνα πιστεύ[σ]ητε
ὅτι Ἰησοῦς ἐστιν ὁ χριστὸς ὁ υἱὸς τοῦ θεοῦ,
καὶ ἵνα πιστεύοντες ζωὴν ἔχητε ἐν τῷ ὀνόματι αὐτοῦ.
These things are written that you may believe
that Jesus is the Christ, the Son of God,
and that believing you may have life in his name. (20:31)

ἐγὼ πεπίστευκα ὅτι σὺ εἶ ὁ χριστὸς ὁ υἱὸς τοῦ θεοῦ
ὁ εἰς τὸν κόσμον ἐρχόμενος.
I have believed that you are the Christ, the Son of God,
coming into the world. (11:27)

Later I shall show that such messianic confessions are consistently interpreted by the author within the framework of his basic christological structure. This is also the case with Thomas's acclamation ὁ κύριός μου καὶ ὁ θεός μου ("My Lord and my God" in 20:28) and the Johannine confession of Peter, where already the focus falls upon the words of eternal life which Jesus brings (6:68–69).

κύριε, πρὸς τίνα ἀπελευσόμεθα; ῥήματα ζωῆς αἰωνίου ἔχεις,
καὶ ἡμεῖς πεπιστεύκαμεν καὶ ἐγνώκαμεν ὅτι σὺ εἶ ὁ ἅγιος τοῦ θεοῦ.
Lord, to whom shall we go? You have the words of eternal life,
And we have believed and know that you are the holy one of God.
(6:68–69)

Statements within the prologue, as well as the prologue as a whole, and indeed the motif, Logos, reflect the same basic structure:

Ἦν τὸ φῶς τὸ ἀληθινόν, ὃ φωτίζει πάντα ἄνθρωπον,
ἐρχόμενον εἰς τὸν κόσμον.
He was the true light, which enlightens every man, coming into the world. (1:9)
εἰς τὰ ἴδια ἦλθεν, καὶ οἱ ἴδιοι αὐτὸν οὐ παρέλαβον.
He came to his own, and his own people did not accept him. (1:11)
Καὶ ὁ λόγος σὰρξ ἐγένετο καὶ ἐσκήνωσεν ἐν ἡμῖν,
καὶ ἐθεασάμεθα τὴν δόξαν αὐτοῦ, δόξαν ὡς μονογενοῦς παρὰ πατρός,
πλήρης χάριτος καὶ ἀληθείας.
And the Word became flesh and tented among us,
and we saw his glory, glory as of the only Son from the Father,
full of grace and truth. (1:14)

Θεὸν οὐδεὶς ἑώρακεν πώποτε·
μονογενὴς θεὸς ὁ ὢν εἰς τὸν κόλπον τοῦ πατρὸς ἐκεῖνος ἐξηγήσατο.
No one has ever seen God;
God, the only Son, who is in the bosom of the Father has made him known. (1:18)

Within the summary statements considered we have clear evidence that the elements of the christological structure identified above frequently occur in combination. In no one brief summary do they all occur. What we do find is that the basic thought structure is presupposed in clear summary statements at strategic points within the Gospel. This indicates that we are dealing with an important outline of the Christology underlying the Gospel.

1.5 John 17

In examining selected passages, finding a common underlying structure of christological thought, and testing its frequency within the Gospel as a whole, we have been able to support the claim that this structure underlies the Gospel's Christology. This does not exclude the possibility that there are other such structures nor does it mean that the structure itself does not need expanding with further elements. Before turning now to a review of the Gospel as a whole I want first to test our findings in relationship to John 17, the passage Käsemann took as his starting point for discussing Johannine Christology. Hubert Ritt describes this text as a compendium and *summa* of Johannine theology.[60] By its position as the climax of Jesus' words before his disciples, it carries significant weight. In it we find not only strong confirmation of what I have defined so far as the central structure but also a focus on the significance of Jesus' death and return to the Father.

The prayer begins with the address to God as "Father" and immediately focusses upon the "hour" of Jesus' death and glorification:

πάτερ, ἐλήλυθεν ἡ ὥρα· δόξασόν σου τὸν υἱόν, ἵνα ὁ υἱὸς δοξάσῃ σέ
Father the hour has come, glorify your Son, that your Son may glorify you. (17:1)

---

60. Hubert Ritt, *Das Gebet zum Vater,* FB 36 (Würzburg: Echter, 1979), 5, 13; similarly Cadman, *Open Heaven,* 203. See also its central role in the depiction of Jesus' mission of love in Francis J. Moloney, *Love in the Gospel of John: An Exegetical, Theological, and Literary Study* (Grand Rapids: Baker, 2013).

The request is repeated in 17:5:

καὶ νῦν δόξασόν με σύ, πάτερ, παρὰ σεαυτῷ τῇ δόξῃ
ᾗ εἶχον πρὸ τοῦ τὸν κόσμον εἶναι παρὰ σοί.
And now, Father, glorify me with yourself with the glory
which I had with you before the world began. (17:5)

In the christological structure we have traced thus far the focus has not been upon Jesus' death and departure, but on his coming and earthly work. But we have already noted that statements about "whence" are often linked with statements about "whither" he goes, and ones about his coming with ones about his going. Here Jesus looks forward to his death and return to the Father, using the motif of glorification. The motif of pre-existent glory also appears in 17:24.

Πάτερ, ὃ δέδωκάς μοι, θέλω ἵνα ὅπου εἰμὶ ἐγὼ κἀκεῖνοι ὦσιν μετ' ἐμοῦ,
ἵνα θεωρῶσιν τὴν δόξαν τὴν ἐμήν, ἣν δέδωκάς μοι
ὅτι ἠγάπησάς με πρὸ καταβολῆς κόσμου.
Father, with regard to what you have given me, I wish that where I am they also might be with me,
so that they may see my glory, which you gave me
because you loved me before the foundation of the world. (17:24)

In 17:2 the pattern of the revealer-envoy appears in the words: καθὼς ἔδωκας αὐτῷ ἐξουσίαν πάσης σαρκός ("as you have given him authority over all flesh"). This refers not to an authorisation yet to come as a result of Jesus' death and return, as Thüsing and Schnackenburg suggest, much along the lines of Matt 28:18,[61] but rather, with Barrett and Becker,[62] to the fact that as the sent one Jesus was authorised ἵνα πᾶν ὃ δέδωκας αὐτῷ δώσῃ αὐτοῖς ζωὴν αἰώνιον ("that he might give eternal life to what was given to him" in 17:2b), his disciples. It carries much the same meaning as the giving of all things into the Son's hands in 3:34–35 and 13:3. We have noted the two uses of "give," one more directly christological and referring to authorisation of the Son, the other related to the granting of disciples to Jesus.

The "eternal life" (17:2) is then explained:

αὕτη δέ ἐστιν ἡ αἰώνιος ζωὴ ἵνα γινώσκωσιν σὲ τὸν μόνον ἀληθινὸν θεὸν

---

61. Thüsing, *Erhöhung*, 231–32; Schnackenburg, *Johannesevangelium*, 3.193–94.
62. Becker, *Johannes*, 518; Barrett, *John*, 502; Brown, *John*, 740.

καὶ ὃν ἀπέστειλας Ἰησοῦν Χριστόν.
This is eternal life that they may know you are the only true God
and Jesus Christ whom you have sent. (17:3)

Knowing the Father and knowing the Son are not two separate acts, but to be understood in the light of the basic christological structure. The Son is the Father's envoy. Similarly 17:4 reflects that structure when it speaks of Jesus finishing the work he had been given to do and having so glorified the Father.

17:6 continues to draw upon the revealer-envoy structure:

Ἐφανέρωσά σου τὸ ὄνομα τοῖς ἀνθρώποις οὓς ἔδωκάς μοι ἐκ τοῦ κόσμου.
I have manifested your name to the people whom you have given me from the world. (17:6a)

"Name," like "glory," entails something of the power and the person of the Father. This is how the disciples know the Father. This is the "word" of revelation to which they hold (17:6b). The extrapolation of the central structure is also evident in 17:7–8.

νῦν ἔγνωκαν ὅτι πάντα ὅσα δέδωκάς μοι παρὰ σοῦ εἰσιν·
ὅτι τὰ ῥήματα ἃ ἔδωκάς μοι δέδωκα αὐτοῖς,
καὶ αὐτοὶ ἔλαβον καὶ ἔγνωσαν ἀληθῶς ὅτι παρὰ σοῦ ἐξῆλθον,
καὶ ἐπίστευσαν ὅτι σύ με ἀπέστειλας.
Now they know that all that you have given me is from you,
because the words which you gave me I have given to them,
and they received and know truly that I came from you
and they believed that you sent me. (17:7-8)

The following verses contain Jesus' prayer for his disciples and their future protection and unity. But here, too, the structure surfaces. When 17:10 begins by affirming that all that belongs to the Father belongs to the Son, it does so with a view to the disciples' belonging both to the Son and to the Father; but the broader statement with which the verse begins (using neuter forms: καὶ τὰ ἐμὰ πάντα σά ἐστιν καὶ τὰ σὰ ἐμά, "all that is mine is yours and yours is mine") may well reflect the motif of the structure according to which the Father has given all things into the Son's hands. This element is certainly present in 17:11–12 when Jesus speaks of having been given the Father's name.

In 17:11 Jesus refers again to his return to the Father, κἀγὼ πρὸς σὲ ἔρχομαι ("I am coming to you") and repeats this in 17:13. The revealer-envoy structure is also apparent where the Son and disciples are compared. As the Son, who gave them the Father's word, is hated, so the disciples will be hated; as the Son is not of this world, so the disciples do not belong to this world (17:14, 16). The Son came from the Father and is therefore not of the world. But because the disciples received his word, they, though coming from the world, now no longer belong to it. The analogy is not exact, but sufficient for the structure to be used also of the sending of the disciples into the world:

καθὼς ἐμὲ ἀπέστειλας εἰς τὸν κόσμον,
κἀγὼ ἀπέστειλα αὐτοὺς εἰς τὸν κόσμον·
As you sent me into the world,
so I sent them into the world. (17:18)

The motif of sanctification, also applied both to Jesus and to his disciples (17:17–18), should be taken in close association with the sending and thus echo the notion of equipping (cf. 10:36). What equips the disciples is the word the Son has given, the truth to which he came to bear witness (17:17, 19; cf. 18:37). In the case of the disciples there is no indication that what they will achieve should be interpreted cultically, nor need this be the case when Jesus sanctifies himself (17:19), though some see here an allusion to his death as a sacrifice (see 4.2 below).

In 17:20–23 the parallel is continued in the prayer that the unity which exists between Father and Son may exist between Son and disciples and among the disciples together, all with the common goal expressed in terms of the structure:

ἵνα γινώσκῃ ὁ κόσμος ὅτι σύ με ἀπέστειλας
καὶ ἠγάπησας αὐτοὺς καθὼς ἐμὲ ἠγάπησας.
That the world may know that you sent me
and that you have loved them as you have loved me. (17:23)

The climax of the prayer expresses the desire that the disciples might join the Son in the glory and love given him before the world began. This reflects the equipping and authorising of the Son, but in a manner consistent with the basic christological structure which sees the Son not as an impersonal emissary, but as the one who has been loved, authorised and commissioned (cf. 3:34–35). The structure surfaces also in the concluding two verses which speak of the Son's knowing the Father, and, as the one whom the Father sent, making his name known. Jesus twice referred to his coming to the Father (17:11, 13). In this final segment Jesus' desire that his disciples might be where he is and see his heavenly glory to which he returns, forms an *inclusio* with his prayer for glorification in 17:1 and 5.

The review of John 17 confirms that the christological structure I have outlined functions as the basic structure beneath the text. At the same time we have noted that the events forming the climax of Jesus' ministry are described in two ways: one speaking simply of his return to the Father and the other of his glorification. None of the passages considered thus far had thematised this element in relation to the central structure beyond speaking simply of the Son's return to the Father. Associated with Jesus' death and return are his commissioning of the disciples and his concern for their unity in the future. In the context of speaking of their sanctification and sending, Jesus speaks of sanctifying himself. A cultic interpretation of Jesus' death (e.g., vicarious sacrifice) may, but need not, be implied by this. In the review of the Gospel which follows we shall find further expansion or different ways of speaking of Jesus' death and return.

2 A Survey of the Gospel

The purpose of this survey is to examine the extent to which the structure of Johannine Christology outlined above is reflected in the rest of the Gospel and to note where it needs expansion or elaboration. Detailed discussion of particular passages where there is a divergence of views will follow in the thematic discussion of issues in Part Two of this book.

2.1 John 1–5 in Review

The prologue, the Gospel's "overture," reflects the underlying structure of the author's Christology. The Logos/Son—with the Father, in the bosom of the Father, and even bearing the name "God"—comes into the world, becomes flesh, tents among us, manifests glory, and makes the Father known. Many of the surface manifestations here are unique and may add nuances of meaning not found elsewhere in John. These include: the Logos motif itself, his being "in the beginning with God," that he "was God" (cf. 20:28), his role as mediator of creation, his possible other activity "asarkos" in salvation history (if this is present, though I shall argue below that it is not), his becoming flesh, his tenting among us, his being "full of grace and truth," his fullness, and his being in the bosom of the Father, and his status as μονογενὴς θεός ("God, the only Son"). To many of these we shall return in 5.3, but the structure beneath the unusual text as it stands in the Gospel is clearly and predominantly that of the revealer pattern but with a strong emphasis also on the being of the Son which becomes fundamental for what follows in the Gospel. The focus on the Son's making the Father known is so much the centre of attention that the prologue does not even mention Jesus' death, return to the Father and events associated with it. The references to John the Baptist will be taken up in what follows.

A Survey of the Gospel

In 1:19–34 John the Baptist witnesses that he, himself, is neither the Christ, nor Elijah, nor the Prophet. Instead he points to Jesus, the one who comes after him. Jesus is "the lamb of God who takes away the sin of the world" (1:29). He comes after John, but is before him in rank and time (1:30; cf. 1:15), as the hearer well knows on the basis of what the prologue has said about him. Through John he becomes manifest to Israel (1:31). John knows who he is only after he sees the Spirit descend and abide upon him: he is the one who will baptise with the Spirit; he is the Son of God or the elect one (1:33–34). The Son's pre-existence, coming and being manifest to Israel, reflects generally the central structure. The messiahship of Jesus will be shown below to be fully integrated within it.

Two features of the text do not relate to the central structure as I have delineated it: the lamb of God taking away sin and the giving of the Spirit. The former may function as an *inclusio* with 19:26 if it contains Passover allusions in relation to Jesus' death. We shall see that both potentially relate to the significance of Jesus' death and will be treated in detail in that context.

In 1:35–51 Jesus' first disciples come to him. John repeats, "Behold the lamb of God!" (1:36). The two disciples ask where Jesus stays and are invited to come and see (1:38–39). Probably more than the literal sense is intended by the narrative. Where he stays, where he is from, and where he is going to become regular features of the Johannine narrative pointing beyond the literal to the symbolic, understood within the framework of the central structure. Messianic affirmation is the focus of the encounters which follow, depicting Jesus as fulfilment of promises in Scripture (1:45). The narrative of Jesus' meeting with Nathanael employs irony. Both Nathanael's words about Jesus' town of origin and his question about where Jesus obtains the ability to know about him suggest to the reader the truth of the central structure: Jesus is the Son who has come from the Father. Jesus accepts Nathanael's messianic affirmation: "You are the Son of God; you are the king of Israel" (1:49). It will find its echo in the passion narrative with the superscription of the cross, but also in 20:31, the statement of the Gospel's aim.

John 1:50–51 suggests there is more to be seen: "'You shall see greater things than these.' And he said, 'Truly truly I say to you, you shall see the heaven opened and the angels of God ascending and descending upon the Son of Man.'" We return to this passage in detail in 4.3.3, but for the present we may note two main interpretations. The one sees Jesus promising Nathanael that he will see Jesus as the medium of revelation between heaven and earth in the ministry that is to follow. The other, which makes better sense of the imagery, sees here a reference to the outcome of Jesus' death and exaltation. The former interpretation would interpret this saying as giving expression to the central thrust of the christological structure we have identified. The latter would need to include this saying as another example of the variety of motifs, yet to be examined, which speak of Jesus as Son of Man and expand upon the meaning of Jesus' death and return to the Father, to which we return in ch. 3 below.

The narrative of the wedding feast at Cana and the account of the temple expulsion both appear to interpret Jesus' death and resurrection.[1] The clues in the former are probably the dating "on the third day,"[2] the reference to Jesus' hour as having not yet come,[3] and perhaps also a eucharistic allusion in the wine imagery. In the latter it is explicit in the reference to Jesus' being consumed because of his zealous act in regard to the temple (2:17) and in the author's interpretation of Jesus' saying about the destroying and raising of the temple (2:21–22; cf. 2:19). The symbolism of the wedding feast also suggests that eschatological hope, often expressed as a feast, sometimes a wedding feast, is fulfilled. The mention of jars for purification may indicate that both passages have to do with the replacement of the Jewish cult through Jesus (discussed in ch. 6).

While both passages serve to expand symbolically the meaning of Jesus' death and resurrection, there may be traces of the structure in the irony concerning the origin of the wine, unknown to the chief steward, but known to the servants (2:9).[4] This is more likely to be so if a eucharistic allusion is not present and what is being celebrated under the symbol is the nourishment that Jesus brings as the revealer. An allusion to both is possible, as both are present in the use of the bread imagery in ch. 6. The structure is, however, reflected in 2:11, where the author remarks that in this first sign of Cana Jesus

---

1. So Olsson, *Structure* 72; Nicol, *Semeia*, 129; Wilkens, *Entstehung*, 39–40; Porsch, *Pneuma*, 35; Dodd, *Interpretation*, 297; Smalley, *John*, 178; Martin Hengel, "The Interpretation of the Wine Miracle at Cana: John 2:1–11," in *The Glory of Christ in the New Testament: Studies in Christology. In Memory of G. B. Caird*, ed. L. D. Hurst and N.T. Wright (Oxford: Clarendon, 1987), 95–99.

2. So Breuss, *Kana-Wunder*, 30; Dodd, *Interpretation*, 299–300; Boismard and Lamouille, *Jean*, 105–106; Nicholson, *Death*, 46; Schnelle, *Christologie*, 88, 190; as the work of the redactor: Hans-Peter Heekerens, *Die Zeichen-Quelle der johanneischen Redaktion. Ein Beitrag zur Entstehungsgeschichte des vierten Evangeliums*, SBS 113 (Stuttgart: KBW, 1984), 72.

3. Barrett, *John*, 191; Oscar Cullmann, *Early Christian Worship*, SBT 1.10 (London: SCM, 1953), 66; Brown, *John*, 99–100; Olsson, *Structure*, 101, 259; de Jonge, *Stranger*, 124; Heekerens, *Zeichen-Quelle*, 69; Schnelle, *Christologie*, 89. Cf. Hofbeck, *Semeion*, 95–97; Becker, *Johannes*, 111; Beasley-Murray, *John*, 35, for a contrary view.

4. So Schnackenburg, *John*, 1.333; Nicholson, *Death*, 53; Kieffer, "L'Espace," 401; Peter F. Ellis, *The Genius of John: A Compositional Critical Commentary on the Fourth Gospel* (Collegeville: Liturgical, 1984) 43–44; Schnelle, *Christologie*, 90, 95; cf. Barrett, *John*, 193.

manifested his glory. This is doubtless the same as the "glory of the only Son of the Father" of 1:14 and thus interprets the miracle at one level as part of the Son's revelation. We shall consider in ch. 3 below the way the author integrates signs within the structure of his Christology. Perhaps Jesus' behaviour in the temple should also be seen as an expression of judgment in fulfilment of Malachi's warning that the Lord would suddenly appear in his temple in judgment (Mal 3:1), and so we should interpret his coming as confrontation.[5]

The concluding verses of ch. 2 show Jesus refusing to acknowledge as having true faith those who respond to him merely at the level of the miraculous. Chapter 3 begins with the Pharisee, Nicodemus, making an equivalent response: "You are a teacher come from God, because no one can do these miracles which you do unless God is with him" (3:2). This is another example of Johannine irony. For, understood at the right level, they do indeed express the truth about Jesus and echo the basic structure. He is indeed a teacher come from God and does indeed do the signs because God is with him (3:2). But this statement must be understood in the light of 3:11–21, 31–36.[6]

The teacher motif remains important in what follows, where attention is being drawn both to Jesus and his disciples at the same time. Thus, the true teacher is the one who can see the kingdom of God because he is (born) from above (3:2–3). Nicodemus is not a true teacher (3:10); a person born of the Spirit is (3:8). The contrast from 3:3 onwards is between Nicodemus and anyone who is born of the Spirit. But implicitly there is also a link between those born of the Spirit and Jesus of whom this is uniquely so.[7] This association with Jesus explains the use in the wind/spirit image of the "Whence-Whither" motif, employed ironically elsewhere to express the Christology of the central structure. People like Nicodemus hear the sound of Jesus' words but do not know where he comes from or where he goes (he is "from above"! 3:31); nor do they comprehend the witness of people of the Spirit. They bear witness to what they have known and have seen (3:11). In 3:32 a similar formulation is used directly of Jesus. The central structure is of major importance in 3:1–11, as it is also in 3:31–36 in which a number of its themes are echoed.

John 3:12 introduces a contrast between what Jesus has been saying thus far, about his coming to earth, and what he might say about "heavenly things" (3:12). This recalls the promise to Nathanael of "greater than these" (1:50). The heavenly things are the events associated with his death (3:13–15).

---

5. So Bultmann, *Johannes*, 91; Brown, *John*, 121.
6. So de Jonge, *Stranger*, 40–41; Nicholson, *Death*, 65.
7. So Meeks, "Man from Heaven," 147; Nicholson, *Death*, 81–82.

We explore these, including the post-Easter perspective represented already in 3:11 and 3:13 and their relationship to the argument of the context, in 4.3.3 below, but for the present we note: ascent and descent of the Son of Man; the lifting up of the Son of Man. Descent refers to Jesus' coming to earth; the rest add to a range of motifs associated with Jesus' death and return.

In 3:16–21 the motifs of the coming and the sending of the Son into the world reappear in passages highlighting the crisis of life and condemnation which the Son brings. In 4.1.2 we shall explore the extent to which 3:16 is primarily a reference to Jesus' coming to earth as revealer, as in the central structure and the previous reference to him as the only Son (1:14, 18), or whether it does not (perhaps, also) make reference to Jesus' death and its significance, possibly with allusion to the sacrifice of Isaac. John 3:17 refers directly to God's sending his Son into the world; John 3:18 refers to faith in him as the only Son; and John 3:19–21 repeat the reference to his coming into the world, using the imagery of light, a further echo of the prologue and of a common motif in passages in which the underlying christological structure of the Gospel comes to expression.

John 4 continues the contrast between the old and the new, above all in the assurance that now old centres of worship are superfluous and true worship is in spirit and is now possible. The Samaritan makes her faltering journey of faith from acknowledgment of Jesus as a prophet (4:19) to tentative proclamation of his messiahship (4:29), which leads to the acclamation by her kinsfolk that he is "the saviour of the world" (4:42). Apart from these messianic affirmations, the narrative subtly portrays Jesus as the giver of the water of life and its brilliant irony has been well set out in Duke's study.[8] This is the life he brings as the one sent from the Father. In the dialogue with the disciples the structure is also apparent when Jesus refers to his food as doing the will of him who sent him and completing his work (4:34). The context relates this work to mission and speaks in turn of Jesus' sending the disciples (4:31–38).

The episode of the healing of the official's son (4:46–54) illustrates the life Jesus brings as well as appropriate and inappropriate faith. The miracle story which follows in ch. 5 illustrates the same healing life, but also leads to major controversy with the Jews. In reply to the accusation that he had caused someone to break the Sabbath, Jesus says: "My Father is working up till now and I am working" (5:17). The Jews accuse him further of calling God his own Father and making himself equal with God (5:18). Jesus' reply speaks of himself in family apprenticeship terms: "The Son cannot do anything of

---

8. Duke, *Irony*, 101–3.

himself but only what he sees his Father doing. For what he does, this the Son likewise does. The Father loves the Son and shows him all which he himself is doing, and greater works than these will he show him, that you may marvel" (5:19-20). Thus the central structure is visible where the Son argues his "equality" with the Father on the grounds of his obedient subordination. The motif of family apprenticeship, which is developed christologically in 5:19-20, probably explains the change to the present tense, where the usual model of Jesus doing or telling what he has seen and heard is replaced by one that speaks of continuing observation and instruction during Jesus' earthly ministry. In addition, the focus here is not on the giving of revelation once received but on the unity of will and action in the present. This change has occasioned considerable discussion in treatments of Johannine Christology which we shall address in Part Two below.

The structure is also apparent when the Son speaks of his being authorised to judge and to give life (5:22, 26-27), and of his doing the will of him who sent him (5:23-24, 30). The activity of the Son in giving life encompasses his present ministry. In that sense raising the lame man has become the springboard for a discourse about Jesus' raising the dead and giving life. But 5:28-29 extend the focus to the eschaton, one of the few such references to Jesus' activity in the future resurrection. The central structure of the author's Christology does not extend to include references to future parousia, resurrection and judgment, though these need not be seen as incompatible with it. We shall return to this below (6.2.4).

Finally two further elements are to be noted. The words "Son of Man" appear in 5:27 in reference to Jesus as judge. We shall note elsewhere the association of the title "the Son of Man" and judgment motifs in John (9:35-39; 12:31). The other feature is the promise to which the Son alludes when he says that the Father "will show him greater things than these that you may marvel" (5:20). Could the contrast here be similar to the one in 3:13 and possibly behind 1:50-51 so that present ministry and the events associating with the Son's death and return to the Father are being alluded to here as well?[9] What is promised is future—something to be shown to Jesus—and precedes the statements about judgment (5:21-28). This suggests that what is to be shown is Jesus' role as judge, which he was already exercising in the present but will also exercise in the future.[10] So we have another instance of something greater to come linked with the designation of Jesus as the Son of Man (5:27). This makes better sense than seeing the contrast here as

---

9. So Thüsing, *Erhöhung*, 59-61, 115; Brown, *John*, 88; Lindars, *Gospel of John*, 220, 222.
10. See Loader, "John 5,19-47," 158; Keener, *John*, 648.

between the miracle as a literal act of healing and the resurrection life the revealer offers, an interpretation which would cohere with seeing in 1:50–51 a contrast between seeing Jesus as Messiah because of miracles and seeing him as the ladder between heaven and earth.

In the discourse about Jesus' self-testimony and the testimony borne to him by others (5:31–47), the content of each testimony is expressed using the language of the central structure. "The works which the Father has given that I should complete, the works themselves that I do, bear witness that the Father sent me" (5:36). Unlike the Son, the Jews have never "heard his voice or seen his form" (5:37). They have not believed in "him whom he sent" (5:38). Jesus has come in the name of his Father (5:43). But they do not accept him nor do they accept the glory which comes from God alone (5:44). The Son will not be their accuser before God. Moses will be their accuser as he bears witness to the Son (5:45). This recalls 12:47–48 according to which Jesus will not judge, but his word will. The passage as a whole also recalls 8:12–19 considered above and similarly reflects the basic christological pattern.

John 1–5 Conclusions

Within these chapters the revealer-envoy pattern clearly underlies much of both the discourse and the narrative material. From the prologue we learn that the Son may be described as the Logos, with God in the beginning, in the bosom of the Father, "God," mediator of creation, the only Son, and possibly active in salvation history. The pre-existence is reiterated by John the Baptist (1:15, 30) and presupposed by the many statements which reflect the revealer-envoy pattern of Christology. The Son comes as the one sent by the Father to make him known (1:18; 3:2, 16–19, 31–35; 4:34; 5:17–20, 22–24, 26–27, 30, 36–38, 43–44). In John 4:34—and especially in 5:17–30—Jesus' mission is described as doing the works of the Father (cf. also 5:36; 3:2). The uniqueness of the Son is also expressed in 3:16, 18. John 5:17–20 reflects in particular on the relationship of the Son and Father, explaining it in terms of an equality in which Jesus shares the Father's tasks in obedient submission to him, and speaks also of a present relationship on earth, rather than the usual pattern of the revelation model where the Son reports what he has seen and heard. This reflects the focus in the context upon the exercise of judgment rather than revelation. Sometimes the author playfully alludes to Jesus' origin: in Nathanael's comment about Jesus' town of origin and the source of his knowledge about him (1:46, 48); in the origin of the wine (2:9); in Nicodemus's "from God" (3:2); in the mysterious whither and whence of the wind/Spirit, and in the question of the Samaritan woman about where Jesus draws his water (4:11).

What Jesus brings is represented in the prologue as word, light (also 3:19–21), life, authority to become God's children (also 3:3, 5), glory (also 2:11), grace and truth, and, supremely, knowledge of God. It is also symbolically represented in the wine of a wedding feast replacing the jars of purification water (2:1–10), the living water (4:10), the raising of the near dead (4:46–54), and the healing of the lame (5:1–9). The miracles display the glory of the Son of the Father (1:14; 2:11) and this is understood within the framework of the revealer-envoy pattern, so that true faith goes beyond hailing the miraculous quality of deeds and sees in them a sign that he is the Son come from the Father (cf. 2:23–25; 3:1–3; 4:48). By contrast even with simple faith in miracles which may move on, unbelief means refusal of light and condemnation to judgment (3:18–21, 36).

At a number of points the motif of messiahship appears (1:20, 25, 41, 45–49; 4:29; cf. the Son of God, 1:34, 49; a prophet, 4:19; the prophet or Elijah, 1:21, 25; saviour of the world, 4:42). The episode with the Samaritan shows clearly that ultimately all such expressions mean Jesus is the bearer of life in terms of the pattern of the revealer-envoy.

At some points the material goes beyond the pattern of the revealer-envoy and focusses on the significance of Jesus' death, his return to the Father, and events associated with it. In particular we noted three places where a contrast is made between what is now available or to be seen during Jesus' ministry and something greater which lies ahead. The first is 1:51 which I take to refer not to Jesus' earthly ministry of revelation, as some do, but to his heavenly glorified status as Son of Man. The second is 3:12 which introduces a contrast between earthly things and heavenly things in Jesus' words and in the latter includes: the ascension of the Son of Man, who descended, and the exaltation of the Son of Man, so that all who believe may have life. The third is 5:22, a text that associates Jesus' role as judge with the title Son of Man and sees him exercising it in the future both during his ministry and at the final judgment (also reflected indirectly in 5:45).

The event of Jesus' death and return to the Father is heralded in the words about the hour yet to come in 2:4 and Jesus prophesies his death in the words of Ps 69:9 in 2:17. The resurrection of Jesus, probably hinted at in 1:51, is also prophesied in the temple saying (2:19).

The author notes also that after this event the disciples would remember both Jesus' words and the applicability to him of the Scripture in which he prophesied his death because of his zeal for God's house (2:17). Other benefits associated with this coming event include the sending of the disciples, alluded to in 3:11; 4:35–38, and, perhaps, given a model in mission by the Samaritan woman (4:29); possibly the Eucharist (if the wine also refers to it in 2:1–11) and the gift of the Spirit (1:33), which in ch. 3 is spoken of in association with new birth imagery in such a way that the conversation moves from Jesus the true teacher—in contrast to Nicodemus the teacher of Israel—to the disciples as true teachers born from above, an anachronistic allusion to the witness they would fulfil after Easter.

In addition there is a saying which is widely understood as highlighting the significance of Jesus' death in itself (1:29). Speaking of Jesus as the lamb of God taking away the sin of the world may imply a sacrificial interpretation of Jesus' death, but this is debated. Passover imagery may be implied. The full significance of the verse must be considered in the light of the Gospel as a whole because nothing in the context develops the theme further. Some also see a sacrificial reference in 3:14 ("lifting up of the Son of Man") and 3:16 (given up to death, perhaps like Abraham giving up Isaac). So much depends, here, too, on use of terms elsewhere in the Gospel ("lifting up" and "Son of Man"), so that we will consider all three passages within the systematic survey of alleged references to vicarious atonement and its role in the Gospel in 4.2 below.

2.2 John 6–12 in Review

The feeding of the 5,000 in John 6 forms the basis for a presentation of Jesus as the bread of life in the discourse which follows. The messianic response of those who were fed in the miracle (6:14–15) fails to grasp Jesus' true significance. It remains at the level that Nicodemus reached, the level of the material. There is a faint echo of the deeper reality when Jesus is hailed as the prophet "coming into the world" and faith would have its deeper understanding of messiahship, as the passion narrative shows. The feeding miracle is primarily a sign of the true nourishment which comes from God.

The narrative of Jesus walking on the water confirms to the eyes of faith that Jesus acts with divine power. As in Mark Jesus presents himself to his anxious disciples with the declaration, "It is I (ἐγώ εἰμι). Do not be afraid" (6:20; cf. Mark 6:50). He is not a ghost or the like. Nothing in the immediate passage (nor its parallel in Mark) suggests ἐγώ εἰμι specifically alludes to the divine name, even though a divine claim is implied by Jesus' miracle, expressed in the Matthean parallel by acclamation of Jesus as Son of God (Matt 14:33). Whether, however, such a meaning would be given to the text

A Survey of the Gospel

by the author or the first readers depends upon wider consideration of its use throughout the Gospel, to which we return in 5.3.11 below.

In the present state of the text the discourse presents two foci when expounding nourishment symbolised in the feeding miracle. In 6:27 Jesus speaks of "the food which endures to eternal life, which the Son of Man will give you; for on him the Father has set his seal." This corresponds to 6:51–58. Here Jesus speaks of the bread which he will give (6:51). It is the flesh and blood of the Son of Man (6:53), the true food and drink (6:55). The eucharistic allusions here and probably elsewhere in the chapter (6:11, 23) confirm that the use of the future "he will give" (6:27, 51) is intentional. Probably the occurrence of the title "Son of Man" suggests the same, namely, that these passages refer to Jesus' post-Easter activity. The words, "and the bread which I give is my flesh for the life of the world" (6:51), may refer primarily to Jesus' eucharistic gifts of his flesh (and blood); they may also, or perhaps also refer to his death as a vicarious act. We return to this question in 4.1.2 below. In terms of our analysis, the sayings which represent this first focus belong among the motifs associated with Jesus' death and return to the Father and not with what I have delineated so far as the central structure.

There is another focus of the text, found in particular in the contrast made between the manna which came down from heaven and Jesus as the bread come down from heaven (6:31–51b).[11] Jesus offers this bread now in his person, much as he had offered living water to the woman of Samaria. Within the discussion elements of the structure appear frequently. The Son has come, has descended, as bread from heaven (6:33, 38, 41, 42, 50, 51). Irony underlines Jesus' heavenly origin, when the Jews claim to know his parentage (6:42). Jesus declares: "I have not come from heaven to do my own will, but the will of him who sent me" (6:38). The sending motif occurs frequently (6:38, 39, 44). The structure also surfaces in the words: "Not that anyone has seen the Father except the one who is from God, he has seen the Father" (6:46). Jesus, the Son, sent by the Father, has come into the world with the offer of life, presenting himself as God's representative, and using the "I am" presentation formula.

The sequel to the discourse (6:59–71) presents a reaction of certain disciples to Jesus' "hard saying" (6:60). This may refer to Jesus' requirement that people eat his flesh and drink his blood (6:53–57);[12] or it may refer to

---

11. On the two foci of John 6 see Brown, *John*, 272–75; Wilckens, "Lebensbrot," 226–27. Weder, "Menschwerdung," 329, identifies three levels: messianic, Christ the true bread and the Eucharist.

12. Dodd, *Interpretation*, 341–42; Ellis, *Genius*, 128.

Jesus' claim to have come down from heaven (6:31–51, 58).[13] In 6:62–63 Jesus contrasts what offends them with something greater: "What if you were to see the Son of Man ascending where he was before? The spirit is what makes alive, the flesh is not at all profitable. The words which I have spoken to you are spirit and life."

These words recall the dialogue with Nicodemus and represent a challenge to a way of perceiving Jesus which sees him only at the level of the flesh, as Nicodemus had done. In this sense they pick up the response of the Jews who failed to see the meaning of the sign, earlier in the chapter (6:14–15, 26). Jesus' words are spirit and life because Jesus has come down from heaven. This, then, is another way of saying his words are bread from heaven. This recalls the contrast in 3:31 between the one from heaven and the one from the earth. It would seem that the second focus forms the immediate background for the saying. They refer primarily to the words of the Son come from the Father and not directly to the promised offer of life in Jesus' flesh and blood.[14] A reference to the latter would have been awkward because of the two different uses of the word "flesh."

This means that probably what offended some disciples is the notion of Jesus' descent from heaven. This receives confirmation in the fact that Jesus sets in contrast to it a reference to his ascent as Son of Man to where he was before. If they cannot "stomach" his claim of descent, what will they do when he ascends? The presumed reader knows well that this ascent will be by way of the cross: the offence will then be even greater;[15] the reader also knows that the ascent will bring greater benefit,[16] including an understanding through the Spirit of Jesus' words. Both levels operate here: greater offence

---

13. Lindars, *Gospel of John*, 272; *Son of Man*, 219–20; Schnackenburg, *Johannesevangelium*, 3.104; Bruce, *John*, 163; Beasley-Murray, *John*, 96; Weder, "Menschwerdung," 344.

14. Brown, *John*, 300; Günther Bornkamm, "Vorjohanneische Tradition oder nachjohanneische Bearbeitung in der eucharistischen Rede Johannes 6," in *Geschichte und Glaube. Zweiter Teil. Gesammelte Aufsätze, Band IV* (Munich: Kaiser, 1971), 51–64, 58 n. 16; Wilckens, "Lebensbrot," 244; Weder, "Menschwerdung," 345; Becker, *Johannes*, 216; Schnelle, *Christologie*, 214. Against Schnackenburg, *Johannesevangelium*, 2.105–106; Barrett, *John*, 304–5; Burge, *Anointed Community*, 105, 187.

15. So Bultmann, *Johannes*, 341; Günther Bornkamm, "Die eucharistische Rede im Johannes-Evangelium," in *Geschichte und Glaube. Erster Teil. Gesammelte Aufsätze, Band III* (Munich: Kaiser, 1968), 64; Schulz, *Johannes*, 110–11; Meeks, "Man from Heaven," 153; Nicholson, *Death*, 58; Weder, "Menschwerdung," 344.

16. So Thüsing, *Erhöhung*, 261–62; Hofbeck, *Semeion*, 121 n. 144; Lindars, *Gospel of John*, 273; Bruce, *John*, 163. Affirming both: Barrett, *John*, 303; Heinz Schürmann, "Joh 6,51c— ein Schlüssel zur grossen johanneischen Brotrede," *BZ* 2 (1959): 258–59; Schnackenburg, *Johannesevangelium*, 2.105; Porsch, *Pneuma*, 206–7; Beasley-Murray, *John*, 96.

at the level of the flesh, greater benefit at the level of the spirit. Accordingly we find here a further example of the other, more positive, contrast in ch. 3 between Jesus' earthly revelation and the heavenly things related to his ascent and exaltation as Son of Man (3:12–13; cf. also 1:50–51; 5:21).

What I have described as the central structure describes primarily the coming and revealing. Consistently, however, we also find another field of concepts describing what comes next—the events surrounding Jesus' death and return—as something greater.

Peter voices the faith of those who perceive Jesus in his true role as the revealer-envoy: "To whom shall we go? You have the words of eternal life, and we have believed and know that you are the holy one of God" (6:68–69). Probably related to the tradition of Peter's confession in the Synoptic Gospels, the confession is understood fully within the frame of reference of the revealer-envoy pattern.

Jesus' brothers operate at the level of the flesh in suggesting Jesus go to Judea to display his wonder-working powers. Jesus responds with reference to his "time" not yet having come (7:6, 8). While the immediate reference is to when Jesus will go to Jerusalem, readers would doubtless recall the use of "hour" in Jesus' response to his mother at Cana: "My hour has not yet come" (2:4) and connect this, in turn, with the hour of Jesus' death, exaltation, and glorification referred to explicitly later (12:23, 27, 31–32; 17:1). Perhaps even the use of the word "to go up, to ascend" contains hints of Jesus' ascension (7:8).[17] The narrative contributes thus to the material concerned with Jesus' death and return to the Father.

In the Jerusalem scenes which follow, the Jews voice their questions and their objections to Jesus and in both the questions and the answers the central structure has been determinative. "My teaching is not mine but his who sent me" (7:16). Jesus "seeks the glory of him who sent him" (7:18). The author's use of irony is present, when he pictures some Jews wondering if Jesus is the Christ, but being disturbed that he did not fit the expectation that the origin of the Christ was to be unknown (7:27). Jesus responds: "You know me and you know where I come from; I have not come of my own accord, but he who sent me is true, whom you do not know. I know him, because I am from him and he sent me" (7:28–29).

Noting Jesus' escape from the Jews' hostile response, the author refers again to Jesus' death: "His hour had not yet come" (7:30). And in response to a delegation sent to arrest him Jesus continues: "A little while I am with

---

17. So Thüsing, *Erhöhung*, 90–91; Porsch, *Pneuma*, 75; cf. Haenchen, "Vater," 75; Lindars, *Gospel of John*, 284–85.

you and I am going to him who sent me. You will seek me and not find me, and where I am you cannot come" (7:33-34). The perplexed Jews speculate whether Jesus is going into the diaspora to teach the Greeks (7:35-36). The irony of this is that the Christian mission will indeed reach the Gentile world, but the reader knows that this will happen as a result of Jesus' death and return to the Father. The promise of the Spirit which follows in 7:37-39 also belongs to this complex of events to come, as the author indicates by the explanation in 7:39 that the promised Spirit was not yet available to the disciples at the time of speaking, except in the person of Jesus himself (cf. 14:17), because Jesus was not yet glorified. Yet the saying of Jesus also offers something to the listeners of the time: "If anyone thirsts, let him come to me and drink." As in ch. 6 we find here a double focus, one which views the gifts brought by the revealer (37); the other (38) takes this further and overlays it with reference to the post-Easter gift of the Spirit. The former belongs within the revealer pattern traced out in the central structure; the second belongs to the material associated with Jesus' death and return to the Father.

Irony features again in the discussions among the Jews of Jesus' origin in 7:40-52. We have already considered 8:12-19 and traced in it the emergence of the central structure. John 8:20 again refers to Jesus' hour not yet having come. The following verses show Jesus returning to the theme of his going away and using again the language of the central structure: "You are from below, but I am from above; you are from this world, I am not from this world" (8:23); "He who sent me is true and what I heard from him, this I speak to the world" (8:26). In the same context Jesus warns: "If you do not believe that I am, you will die in your sins" (8:24). The Jews ask, "Who are you?" They understand Jesus to have meant something like: "I am who I claim to be." This may be an ironical allusion to Jesus as "I am," i.e., bearing the name of Yahweh, but Jesus responds by saying he is what he has been saying to them all along from the beginning (8:25) and obviously alludes to the repeated variant explanations that derive from the central structure and must mean something like: "I am the sent one," as in 8:28.

John 8:28-29 gives an answer to the question who Jesus is by using the central structure: "Then you shall know that I am (who I claim to be), and I do nothing of myself, but as the Father taught me, so I speak and he who sent me is with me; he has not left me alone, because I always do what is pleasing to him." The introduction to this formulation is equally interesting. It should not be read with Bultmann to indicate that Jesus' response implies that they will see him as Son of Man and judge.[18] The rest of the verse shows that the

---

18. Bultmann, *Johannes*, 265-66; Riedl, *Heilswerk*, 365; Josef Coppens, "Le Fils de

focus is on coming to know he is the sent revealer. It speaks rather of the lifting up of the Son of Man as the event which will make such knowledge available. Again two levels operate. At one level the verse refers to the Jews' crucifixion of Jesus. At another, it refers to Jesus' exaltation. Again, as in 3:14 and 6:62, where this greater event is looked forward to, we have the Son of Man title. Again the affirmation of the central structure is set beside a further complex of ideas which concentrate on Jesus' death and return to the Father.

The dispute with the Jews heightens in the rest of ch. 8. Again Jesus defends himself, using terms familiar to us from the central structure: "What I have seen with the Father, I speak and what you have heard from the Father you do not do" (8:38); "now you seek to kill me, a human being, who has spoken the truth to you which I heard from God" (8:40); "If God were your Father, you would love me, because I came out from the Father and have arrived here; I have not come of my own accord, but he sent me" (8:42). Jesus does not seek his own glory, but God's (8:50, 54). "The Father is the one who glorifies me, of whom you say, 'he is our God,' and you have not known him, but I know him. If I were to say I do not know him, I should be a liar like you. But I do know him and I keep his word" (8:54–55). The conflict reaches its climax when Jesus asserts his pre-existence: "Before Abraham came into being, I am" (8:58). Again the precise meaning of "I am" will depend on factors outside the immediate passage. The attempted stoning (8:59) might suggest blasphemous utterance of the divine name, but need not either here or elsewhere. Need it mean more than the stupendous claim: I am in existence since before Abraham? We explore this further in Part Two below.

John 9 is primarily narrative material, though within it the central structure appears explicitly in Jesus' affirmation that he must work the works of him who sent him while it is day (9:3–4) and is implicit in the ironical treatment of the Jews' discussion of Jesus' origins: "this man is not from God" (9:16); "we know that God has spoken to Moses, but this man, we do not know where he comes from" (9:29) and the blind man's response: "If he were not from God, he could not do anything" (9:33). It should also be seen in the etymology of Siloam: "the sent one," as a symbolic reference to Jesus as the fount of healing. The symbolism of light and darkness, blindness and sight, lifts the story into being a proclamation of Jesus, the light come into the world (so explicitly, 9:5) and by implication also the bearer of judgment when people refuse the light: "For judgment I have come into this world, that those who do not see may see and that those who see may become blind"

---

l'Homme dans l'Évangile johannique," *ETL* 52 (1976): 54; E. D. Freed, "The Son of Man in the Fourth Gospel," *JBL* 86 (1967): 405; cf. Schnackenburg, *Johannesevangelium*, 2.256.

(9:39). The chapter also contains an affirmation of Jesus as "a prophet" (9:17) and mention of confessing Jesus as the Christ (9:22); only here in John the faith called for ultimately by Jesus is faith in "the Son of Man" (9:35). The presence of the judgment theme probably explains this somewhat sudden appearance of "Son of Man" (9:35), linked already with judgment in 5:27 and in tradition.[19]

John 10 is marked by its use of shepherd imagery. Beneath it we detect the basic christological pattern when Jesus speaks of his coming (10:10), of his being recognised for who he is (10:2, 4, 5, 14, 27), of his knowing the Father and being known by him (10:15) and of his receiving authority to lay down his life and take it up again (10:11, 17–18). Jesus, the shepherd, lays down his life for the sheep (10:11, 15) and promises a future gathering of sheep not of this fold into a single flock (10:16). Both of these statements belong to the complex of events concerned with Jesus' death and return to the Father. Their possible relation to Jesus' death understood as vicarious atonement will be discussed below in 4.1.2.

John 10:19–39 contains many christological statements and again they reflect the central structure. Jesus responds to the question about his messiahship (10:24) by appealing to the works he does in his Father's name (10:25). The Jews do not believe and are not Jesus' sheep. Those who are Jesus' sheep will be kept by the Father (10:29). Immediately there follow Jesus' famous words: "I and the Father are one" (10:30). The preceding context relates these words to at least a common interest between the Father and the Son as the basis for the Son's claim that the Father will look after his sheep. The Jews sense blasphemy and gather stones. Jesus responds by appealing again to the many works which he has shown them from the Father (10:32). The Jews specify the grounds of their charge: "You, being a human, make yourself God" (10:33).

We shall be exploring more fully the possible meanings of both the accusation and Jesus' reply, which equates it to the claim to be the Son of God, in 5.3.7. At this stage we note however that Jesus uses the language of the central structure in making his reply, as he had done earlier in drawing attention to the work he had done in the Father's commission (10:25, 32). Jesus appeals to the use of "gods" in Ps 82:6 to address those to whom the word of God came (10:35), then continues in typically Johannine christological terms: "Of the one whom the Father sanctified and sent into the world you say, 'You

---

19. So Brown, *John*, 375; Robert L. Maddox, "The Function of the Son of Man in the Gospel of John," in *Reconciliation and Hope. Festschrift for L. Morris*, ed. R. Banks (Exeter: Paternoster, 1974), 199; Duke, *Irony*, 124; Schnelle, *Christologie*, 138–40.

blaspheme,' because I said I am Son of God. If I do not do the works of my Father, do not believe in me. If I do, and you do not believe in me, believe in the works, so that you may come to know and realise that the Father is in me and I in the Father" (10:36–38). For the first time we have the language of mutual indwelling as a way of expressing the relationship between Father and Son. The same language is used in the first farewell discourse (14:10–11, 20) and the final prayer (17:21, 23), both of the Father-Son relationship and of the relationship between disciples and the Son and the Father. We discuss the implications of such unity statements for the author's Christology in 5.3.7.

John 11, like John 9, is primarily discourse, but again we can understand it within the framework of the central structure. Martha's messianic affirmation, "I have believed that you are the Christ, the Son of God coming into the world" (11:27), follows Jesus' summation of his mission as an offer of resurrection and life. Like earlier miracle stories, the raising of Lazarus is made to symbolise the gift that Jesus brings. Jesus' prayer functions as a demonstration of his relationship with the Father: "Father, I thank you that you have heard me. I knew that you always hear me, but I am speaking because of the crowd standing around, that they may believe that you sent me" (11:41–42). In the miracle, the crowds can see the glory of God that Jesus had predicted would be seen (11:4; cf. 11:40 for Jesus' reminder to Martha). To see the glory of God in the miracle and to read it as a manifestation of the Son sent from the Father to bring life is to read the story in the light of the central structure.

The references to glory almost certainly function at two levels. One relates to the revelation of glory in the miracle just mentioned. The other relates to something yet to come, namely Jesus' death and return to the Father. For in John's account it is this miracle which leads ultimately to Jesus' arrest and thus to his crucifixion, and, through his death, to his return to the glory of the Father. In other words we meet here the same twofold structure, presenting Jesus as the revealer and Jesus as the one who will die and return to the Father. The latter focus of the Lazarus episode finds confirmation in the account of the Sanhedrin meeting in 11:47–54 where with splendid irony the author portrays the high priest Caiaphas unwittingly prophesying that Jesus' death would be for the nation and for the gathering into unity of all God's children (11:51–53). Does "dying for" imply vicarious atonement or indicate representative action in some other way? The immediate context offers no answer. We return to this in 4.1.2 below.

John 12 continues the focus on Jesus' death and resurrection as the reader is reminded in the first verse of Lazarus' resurrection and again in 12:9. The anointing at Bethany is symbolic preparation for Jesus' burial (12:7).

Jesus enters Jerusalem as Zion's king upon a foal. The royal messianic overtones are also present in the crowd's acclamation, "Hosanna. Blessed is he who comes in the name of the Lord, the king of Israel" (12:13). This imagery runs strongly through the Johannine passion narrative and, as we shall see, the author interprets it within the framework of the central structure (see 6.2.5 below).

The author makes the important footnote: the disciples did not understand the messianic significance of what the crowds did nor the fulfilment of messianic prophecy in this event until after Jesus was glorified (12:16). This is similar to 2:22 where the author notes that understanding of Scripture and of Jesus' words in relation to the expulsion from the temple did not come to the disciples until after Jesus was raised from the dead. The same idea was present in the claim that the Jews would be able to know who Jesus was after his exaltation (8:28).

The significance of events associated with Jesus' death and return to the Father form the central focus of 12:20–33. The Pharisees' fear that the world was going after him (12:19) and the request by Greeks to see Jesus, relayed through two disciples, Philip and Andrew (12:20–22), point, through the author's irony and symbolism, to the Gentile mission which would come as a fruit of Jesus' death and return to the Father and be carried out through such disciples.[20] That hour has come. It is the hour of Jesus' glorification (12:23). Continuing the metaphor of bearing fruit, Jesus interprets his death as the falling of a seed into the ground, which should bear fruit (12:24). Appropriately the disciples are also encouraged to follow their master on this path and promised the same shared honour with the Father (12:25–26).

In 12:27 the author returns to Jesus' facing his "hour": "Now is my soul troubled, and what shall I say? Father, save me from this hour? But for this I came to this hour. Father, glorify your name." The Son came to this hour to face death and does not ask to be saved from it, but that what he will do will bring glory to God. In what way Jesus' facing death fulfils the task (e.g., as an act of revelation or of atonement) is not stated and will engage us in 4.1 and 2 below. God's reassurance follows: "I have glorified it and will glorify it again" (12:28). This reflects the same twofold character of Johannine Christology: the earthly ministry up to the passion and the passion and return to the Father. The author has these words function as christological commentary when he has Jesus declare that they were spoken not for his sake but for the crowd's (12:30).

The focus returns to the event itself, the "hour." It is the hour of the

---

20. Nicholson, *Death*, 152–53.

A Survey of the Gospel

judgment of this world when the ruler of this world will be cast out (12:31), a motif associated here with Jesus as Son of Man (12:34), as already in 5:27; 9:35–39. It is also the hour for Jesus to be lifted up, resulting in the drawing to himself of all people (12:32). This picks up again the motif of mission already expressed through the metaphor of bearing fruit and the symbolic use of the coming of the Greeks. Finally the literal truth of the saying about Jesus' being lifted up is underlined: it indicates crucifixion. 18:32 will make reference back to this as a prophetic prediction. The following verses in ch. 12 show the crowd understanding "lifting up" to mean death. It does not fit with their ideas of messiahship. Interestingly they report Jesus as saying, "The Son of Man must be lifted up" (12:34), and then ask who this Son of Man is. The title does indeed occur in association with "lifting up" in 3:14 and 8:28 and the narrative presupposes it also behind 12:32.

There emerges from this passage in ch. 12 a range of images associated with Jesus' death and return to the Father, which we have met already. They will be drawn together and explored in detail in chs. 3 and 4.

The elements of the central structure reappear in the remaining verses of ch. 12 where response to Jesus' ministry is in view. Jesus has come into the world as the light (12:35–36). The invitation to believe in him has been refused, despite the signs (12:37). The author uses Isa 53:1 to bemoan this lack of response: "Lord, who has believed our report (what we have heard) and to whom has the arm of the Lord been revealed?" We should probably interpret this within the framework of the central structure as the words of Jesus so that it means: Who has believed the report the Son has brought of what he heard from the Father and who has accepted the revelation he offered? This is in contrast to the prevailing interpretation which treats the words as those of Christian preachers bemoaning response to what they have heard from Jesus.

Using Isa 6:10, the author explains the inability to believe and alludes to the wider context of this passage, identifying Isaiah's temple vision as a vision of the pre-existent glory of the Son (12:41–42). John 12:43 berates those who through fear fail to confess Christ, as preferring the glory (praise) from people (i.e., that people give) to the glory of God. It is possible that "the glory of God" may not mean any more here than praise from God, though the immediate parallel suggests this. In the light of the reference to Isaiah's seeing Christ's glory in the temple it is tempting to see here another reference to the glory of God seen in Jesus' earthly ministry by the eyes of faith: "we beheld his glory, glory as of the only Son of the Father" (1:14).[21]

The concluding passage, 12:44–50, functions as a summary of the mean-

---

21. Cf. Barrett, *John*, 443.

John 6–12 Conclusions

Two things have emerged clearly from the review of John 6–12. Firstly, the pattern of the revealer-envoy has been confirmed as underlying the statements about Jesus' coming and his earthly ministry. The pre-existent Son (with the Father before his descent, 6:62; before Abraham, 8:58; seen by Isaiah, 12:41), was authorised and sent by the Father into the world. The Son who knows the Father comes from the Father and makes him known (7:16, 18; 8:28); and returns to the Father. These motifs occur frequently throughout, fuelling irony concerning Jesus' origin (e.g., 6:41–42; 7:27, 40–52; 9:16, 29, 33) and destination (7:33–34; 8:21–22). It is Jesus' prayer that people will know he is sent by the Father (11:41–42; cf. 12:30).

The oneness of the Father and Son is asserted and argued along the lines we found in John 5, namely, that the oneness finds expression in the Son doing the works of the Father and so remains within the framework of the christological pattern of the revealer-envoy (10:29–39). The same is true of the concepts of mutual knowledge (10:15) and indwelling (10:36–39).

Jesus' messiahship (7:27: 9:22; 10:24; 11:27; 12:13–15) and occasional references to him as prophet (9:17; 6:14–15) are understood within the framework of the central structure, when they are correctly interpreted (cf. 6:14–15; 12:34). The reworking of Peter's traditional confession illustrates this also (6:68–69).

In John 6:20; 8:25, 28 and 58 Jesus uses the absolute, ἐγώ εἰμι (lit. "I am"). In 8:25, 28 the context favours the meaning, "I am what I claim to be," understood in terms of the revealer pattern (so: esp 8:28). In 6:20 Jesus is identifying himself: "It is I (not a ghost or the like)" and in 8:58 the text need mean no more than "I am and was in existence before Abraham," still a majestic unique claim but not an allusion to the divine name. Wider meanings may be present, but this will be determined by other uses in the Gospel and be discussed in 5.3.11 below.

In particular the coming of the Son brings nourishment (6:31–51b, 58), light (8:12; 9:5; 12:35–36, 46), and life (7:38; 11:25). The sent one "Siloam" (9:7) is the source of healing. Of these gifts the miracles are signs. In them God's glory is seen (11:4, 40), but ultimately they are not believed (12:37) or they are responded to inappropriately (6:14–15). Isaiah 53:1 expresses what could be the words of the revealer-envoy himself: "Who has believed what we have heard?" (12:38). Isaiah 6:10 explains it. Faith is to recognise Jesus as the true shepherd and this too means seeing him as the revealer sent by the Father (10:2, 4, 5, 14, 27).

Secondly, the death of the Son and his return to the Father is an event looked forward to during the Son's earthly ministry and his revelatory activity expressed through the central structure. As a total event it is portrayed as something greater and more significant yet to come (6:62). The total event, signalled by "the hour" (12:23, 27; cf. 7:6, 8; 12:31), encompasses Jesus' death (12:24, 27, 33–34), resurrection (12:24; cf. 2:22), exaltation (8:28; 12:32–34), glorification (7:39; 12:16, 23; cf. 11:4, 40; 12:28), ascent (6:62), and the judgment of the world (12:31; cf. 9:39). The event is also associated with the sending of the Spirit (7:39; cf. 6:63), with mission (7:35–36; 10:16; 11:51–53; 12:19–24, 32), eucharistic nourishment (6:51–58; cf. 6:27), and a new understanding of Scripture and the events of Jesus' life (12:16; cf. 6:62; 8:28–29). The title "Son of Man" occurs often in these contexts (6:27, 53, 62; 8:28; 9:35; 12:23, 34).

Some passages speak of Jesus' dying as an event in itself "for" (ὑπέρ) the sheep (10:11, 15), "for" the nation (11:51), or "for" the world (6:51c). In John 12:27 Jesus states that for "this" (suffering death) he came to this hour. These formulations raise the question of the extent to which the author thinks of these texts as expressing a notion of vicarious atonement or whether they should be seen as expressing a representative action of some kind on behalf of others (e.g., act of revelation?). To this we return when we consider all such passages (4.1).

2.3 John 13–14 in Review

John 13 begins with two statements about what Jesus "knew" as he faced his disciples for the last time: "Jesus, knowing that the hour had come for him to depart from this world to the Father" (13:1) and "knowing that the Father had given all things into his hands and that he had come from God and was going to God" (13:3). Both reflect the central structure, yet both focus on the implications of Jesus' impending death, as the context demands. Schnackenburg takes the reference to the Father giving all things into the Son's hands as more directly a statement about power and control in the light of the assault of the devil through Judas, just mentioned in 13:2, and, like Becker, sees 13:3 as a redactional addition.[22] Brown refers it to Jesus' salvific mission.[23]

---

22. Schnackenburg, *Johannesevangelium*, 3.18; similarly Becker, *Johannes*, 420–21.
23. Brown, *John*, 564; similarly Barrett, *John*, 439; Beasley-Murray, *John*, 233.

The fact that the phrase occurs in 3:35—also in association with elements of the pattern of the revealer-envoy—suggests that this context should also be borne in mind here. Authorisation for mission and being given authority over all for that purpose need not exclude here some reference to the devil's threat. But the verse is primarily saying that nothing will prevent the obedient fulfilment of the commission given in pre-existence.

Jesus washes his disciples' feet. Peter questions Jesus, who replies: "What I am doing you do not understand now, but afterwards you will understand" (13:7). The "afterwards" indicates that what we have here follows the pattern we have already observed: only after the event of Jesus' death and return to the Father is the meaning of some words and events in Jesus' ministry able to be understood. Will he understand then because of a better knowledge of who Jesus was? Will it be because of Jesus' atoning death as the basis for the granting of forgiveness? The answer cannot be considered in isolation from other passages in the Gospel and we shall return to it in 4.1 below.

The second interpretation (13:12–17), which sees in the act an example to be followed, uses the familiar language of the central structure in saying that "the apostle is not greater than the one who sent him" (13:16). In 13:19 Jesus comments on his prediction of Judas's betrayal: "From now on I am telling you before it happens, so that you may believe, when it happens, that I am (who I claim to be?)." This is another example of the enigmatic "I am" use which we shall consider below in 5.3.11. It need mean no more than "I am who I claim to be." It could be a deliberate self-identification using the divine name. In 13:20 the envoy language is used in making a parallel between the response to Jesus and the response to his disciples: "He who accepts anyone I send accepts me and he who accepts me accepts him who sent me."

On the exit of Judas, the event which sets the events of the passion night in motion, Jesus declares: "Now is the Son of Man glorified and God is glorified in him. If God is glorified in him, God will also glorify him in himself, and will glorify him immediately" (13:31–32). These words echo 12:23: "The hour has come for the Son of Man to be glorified." The simplest explanation of the use of the word "glorify" in the aorist in 13:31 and the first clause of 13:32 and in the future in the remaining two clauses of 13:32 is that they relate to the one single event. John 13:31 views it as having happened, now that Judas has departed, even though Judas's activities are but its beginning; for Jesus now sees his death as inevitable. Both John 13:31 and 32a use the punctiliar aorist. John 13:32a repeats 31b and reflects back on both how and when 31a will take place. This is preferable to delineating two events in 13:31–32a and 32b. Some interpreters understand glorification through the cross and glorification through future mission or glorification through Jesus' ministry up to this point, including the foot washing and glorification through the event of the cross.

"Now is the Son of Man glorified" (13:31a). The author places the words: "and God is glorified in him" (13:31b). John 13:32a reflects on 13:31b, repeating its substance, "if God is glorified in him," to suggest that God's glorification of Jesus is a response to his glorification of God: "(then) God will glorify him in himself," that is, God will reward Jesus by taking him into his own intimate glory. God has been glorified in and through Jesus' obedience and will in turn glorify him in the glory of his own being.[24] John 13:32c adds: this will happen immediately. The way this text relates to others which use the glorification motif is the subject of a separate discussion in 4.3. Coming at the beginning of the last discourses these statements about glorification form an *inclusio* with the prayer with which they conclude. We hear of Jesus' prayer that God might be glorified (17:1), that he might be glorified with the glory that he had with the Father before the world began (17:1, 5), and that his disciples might see and share with him in that glory (17:24).

The following verse speaks of Jesus' departure: "Little children, yet a little while I am with you; you shall seek me, and as I said to the Jews: where I am going you cannot come, so I am telling you now" (13:33). The Jews had heard (7:33–34) and misunderstood the saying (7:35–36; 8:14, 21–22). It belongs with the sayings of "whence-whither," for to know where Jesus is going is to know where he came from (8:14). It reflects the pattern of the revealer-envoy.

The differences between 7:33–34 and 13:33 are noteworthy:

> I will be with you a little while longer, and then I am going to him who sent me.
> You will search for me, but you will not find me; and where I am, you cannot come. (7:33–34)
> Little children, I am with you only a little longer. You will look for me; and as I said to the Jews so now I say to you, "Where I am going, you cannot come." (13:33)

The author adds "little children" because these are Jesus' disciples. He omits the reference to where Jesus is going because this becomes a major question which will dominate the discourse to follow (13:36a; 14:5). He also omits "you will not find me," because this will not be true of the disciples. The Jews will die in their sins; the disciples will indeed find Jesus. The final part of the saying is modified in Jesus' answer to Peter's question two verses later,

---

24. Schnackenburg, *Johannesevangelium*, 3.57.

"Lord, where are you going?" Jesus replies: "Where I am going you cannot follow now, but you will follow later" (13:36). At the level of literal meaning this connects with the description of Peter's death in 21:18–19: "'When you become old, you will stretch out your hands and another will gird you and carry you where you do not want to go.' He said this indicating by what death he would glorify God. And having said this he says to him, 'Follow me!'" But at a deeper level it is true for all disciples, for Jesus goes to prepare a place for them (14:2) and prays that they may be where he is (17:24). Already in 12:25 Jesus had identified his path with the path to be taken by the disciples who would then share his destiny to be with him forever.

The announcement in 13:33 has therefore important sequels. The first is an instruction about loving one another (13:34–35), a typical instruction by a parting one to those who are left. There follow Peter's question, Jesus' answer, and his prediction of Peter's denial. With typical Johannine irony the narrative tells how Peter wants to go so far as to lay down his life. The irony works because of what we know from 21:18–19, but the readers may well have known this independently. The denial warns of the difficulty in following Jesus.

John 14 begins with Jesus addressing the disciples' grief, which is assumed to have arisen because of his words in 13:33. The basis of their comfort is to be their belief in the Father and the Son: "Believe in God and believe in me" or possibly: "You believe in God, believe also in me" (14:1). The "and" which joins these two statements (or alternatively the "also") is more than a simple juxtaposition. The central structure makes it clear that we can know the Father only by knowing the Son. It speaks not only of the Son's coming, but also of his return to the Father and it is the latter which is immediately expounded here. The Son goes to the Father to prepare a dwelling place for his own. He will then come again and take them so that, as he was with them on earth ("a little while I am with you" 13:33), so he will be with them in the presence of the Father (14:3). We are not told in these verses when or how the Son will come again, but just that he will do so and that the ultimate goal of that coming will be to take the disciples to himself, to where he has gone, to his Father's house.

The comfort is twofold: the hope of a place with the Son where he goes and the coming again of the Son; not only the place, also the coming. In fact, because he goes to prepare a place, he comes again. This emphasis returns in 14:18–23. But first, in a way characteristic of the dialogue in ch. 14, Jesus concludes response to one issue by opening another: "And where I am going you know the way" (14:4; further issues are introduced similarly in 14:7b, 11b, 21b). John 14:5–11 expounds the issue, using the pattern of the revealer-envoy: Jesus the revealer is the way, the truth and the life (14:6), because to know him is to know the Father (14:6–7). Philip's request to be shown the Father (14:8) is used to underline the central theme of the revealer-envoy pattern: to have seen the Son is to have seen the Father (14:9). "Do you not believe that I am in the Father and the Father in me; otherwise believe me because of the works themselves" (14:10). This is the same mutual indwelling formula and appeal to the works which we found already in 10:38. To believe in the Son is the way to the Father, so that he is the way, the life, the truth. In these verses we have an expansion therefore of what is meant in the opening exhortation: "believe in God and believe in me" (14:1). It also goes beyond the envoy pattern by focussing on mutual indwelling.

Comfort consists in the promise of a place with the Son in the Father's presence. That is future. It also consists in Jesus' coming and in comfort for the disciples as they face life on earth. It is this need which the author addresses from 14:12 onwards. Because Jesus goes to the Father, the disciples will do the works of Jesus and will do even greater works (14:12). This is another of the occasions where Jesus contrasts his earthly ministry with something greater that will come as a result of his death and return to the Father (cf. 1:50–51; 3:12; 5:21; 6:62). The works of Jesus were to make the Father known. The works of the disciples will do that to an even greater extent. The primary focus is not greater miracles, but mission, not in the sense of winning larger numbers or of achieving greater geographical spread, but in the sense that the Spirit will cause new fruit. The fruit of a community of faith bears witness in accordance with its commission.[25]

Immediately associated with this promise is a saying which features also in the later discourses: "Whatever you ask in my name I will do it, that the Father may be glorified in the Son. Whatever you ask of me in my name I will do" (14:13–14; cf. in variant forms: 15:7; 16:23–24, 26). This is not a blank cheque to fulfil all manner of whims and wishes, but a promise related to the "works." As Untergassmair points out, "in my name" means more than motivation; it refers also to the commission undertaken by the community in love and obedience.[26] The Father is glorified by the Son's fulfilment of his Father's commission and also by the disciples' fulfilment of theirs. The

---

25. So Bultmann, *Johannes*, 471–72; Hofbeck, *Semeion*, 154–55; Thüsing, *Erhöhung*, 114f; Schnackenburg, *Johannesevangelium*, 3.81; Brown, *John*, 633; Riedl, *Heilswerk*, 288; Ibuki, *Wahrheit*, 279–80; Johannes Beutler, *Habt keine Angst. Die erste johanneische Abschiedsrede (Joh 14)*, SBS 116 (Stuttgart: KBW, 1984), 49; Christian Dietzfelbinger, "Paraklet und theologischer Anspruch im Johannesevangelium," *ZTK* 82 (1985): 397.

26. Franz Untergassmair, *Im Namen Jesu*, FB 13 (Stuttgart: KBW, 1973), 86–87, 123–24; similarly Thüsing, *Erhöhung*, 115.

commission is understood according to the central structure and this also influences the way he perceives the disciples' role.

The introduction of the love theme in 14:15 continues the focus on commission: "If you love me, keep my commandments." The same complex of thought, linking mission, prayer, glorification of the Father, and love, is present in 15:7-10: "If you remain in me and my words remain in you, ask what you want and it shall happen for you. In this is my Father glorified that you bear much fruit and become my disciples." To be a disciple means following Jesus in fulfilling the commission he had and passed on. A similar connection to the one found in 15:9-10—between the love commandment and the result that people recognise the disciples for who they are—occurred already in 13:34-35. In 14:15 the commandment is more directly related to keeping the commission. The commission is to make the revelation known and so to bear fruit. This the disciples are to do in Jesus' name, that is, with the authorisation that belongs to the commission.

The promise and the commission to do the same and greater things than the Son relate closely to the promise of the Paraclete which will give the disciples the sure knowledge they will need for mission. "I will ask the Father and he will give you another Paraclete to remain with you forever, the Spirit of Truth whom the world cannot receive because it neither sees nor knows it. You know it, because it remains with you and shall be in you" (14:16-17). Jesus, who was with the disciples a little while (as 13:33), is contrasted with another Paraclete who will be with them forever. The disciples are being comforted for the Son's absence by the promise of the Spirit's presence. They are not abandoned as orphans (14:18a). Yet at the point where we might want to see the Paraclete as a replacement for Jesus, the author has Jesus assert: "I will come to you" (14:18b) and returns to the saying which introduced the discourse in 13:33, "Yet a little while and the world will see me no more, but you will see me; because I live, you will live also. In that day you will know that I am in my Father and you in me and I in you" (14:19-20).

The statements concerning the Paraclete and those concerning the Son can be paralleled:

> And I will ask the Father, and he will give you another Advocate, to be with you for ever. This is the Spirit of truth, whom the world cannot receive, because it neither sees him nor knows him. You know him, because he abides with you (παρ' ὑμῖν), and he will be in you. (14:16-17)
>
> I am coming to you. In a little while the world will no longer see me, but you will see me; because I live, you also will live. On that day you

will know that I am in my Father, and you in me, and I in you. (ἐν ὑμῖν in 14:18–20)

Both the Spirit and the Son come. Neither will be able to be seen by the world, but each will be seen or known by the disciples. Both are currently with the disciples: the Paraclete "remains with you" (παρ᾽ ὑμῖν) and Jesus is with the disciples for "a little while" (14:19; alluding to "a little while I am with you," 13:33; see also 14:25, "while I remain with παρ᾽ ὑμῖν"). Both will be in them.[27] Johannes Beutler relates the promise of the indwelling of the Spirit to the covenant hope of Jeremiah.[28] There is no indication here that the promise should refer to the Spirit's presence only among certain believers, such as Christian prophets, as M. Eugene Boring suggests.[29] John 14:3 had promised the Son's coming. In 14:18–24 this coming coincides with the coming of the Spirit. "Because I live" (14:19) probably includes an allusion to the resurrection, but, as Porsch rightly points out,[30] the promised presence of the Son is not limited to the time of resurrection appearances. Primarily it refers to the life he has in himself which enables him both to lay down his life and take it up again. Because he lives, the disciples will live. Nor does this refer primarily to life with the Son in the heavenly mansions promised in association with the Son's coming in 14:3, but to life through the gift of the Spirit and the risen Christ.[31] The extent to which Johannine eschatology still had a place for parousia eschatology will be discussed in 6.2 below. This passage implies that it is the Spirit who mediates this presence of the Son and the Father to the believer.[32]

These promises are all seen within the context of the Son's commission so that 14:21 returns us to the theme of loving the Son by keeping his commandments: "He who has my commandments and keeps them, he it is who loves me; and he who loves me will be loved by my Father and I will love him and manifest myself to him" (14:21). The words, "manifest myself to him," are the cue for Judas's question and for wider exploration of the theme of the Son's manifestation. John 14:23 rephrases 14:21, "If anyone loves me, he will keep my word and my Father will love him and we shall come to him

27. So Porsch, *Pneuma*, 247.
28. Beutler, *Angst*, 64–65.
29. M. Eugene Boring, "The Influence of Christian Prophecy in the Johannine Portrayal of the Paraclete and Jesus," *NTS* 25 (1978): 114 n. 1.
30. So Porsch, *Pneuma*, 249–50, 384.
31. Lodewijk van Hartingsveld, *Die Eschatologie des Johannesevangeliums* (Assen: Van Gorcum, 1962), 117.
32. So Porsch, *Pneuma*, 389; Onuki, *Gemeinde*, 73; Burge, *Anointed Community*, 138–39.

and make our dwelling with him." The author then expounds the meaning of keeping the word of the Son by using the familiar pattern of the central structure: "He who does not love me does not keep my words; and the word which you hear is not mine but the Father's who sent me" (14:24).

In 14:25 Jesus returns to the thought of 13:33 in saying: "These things I have spoken to you while remaining with you." The "these things" could refer to "the word" received from the Father, following the pattern of the central structure. More likely they refer to the content of the discourse as a whole. In the light of 14:18–23 we might expect the author to have Jesus continue: "but when I come to you and dwell in you." Instead the author has Jesus return to speak of the Spirit: "The Paraclete, the Holy Spirit, whom the Father will send in my name, he shall teach you all things and remind you of all I have said to you" (14:26). The elements of the central structure are present: "the Father," sending, the teaching role; but the Spirit is not a second revealer. He acts on Jesus' authority ("in his name") and reminds of his words. Only the statement "he will teach you all things" could suggest something more.

With 14:27 we come full circle. Jesus gives his disciples peace. The words, "Let not your heart be troubled, neither let it be afraid" (14:27c), echo 14:1. John 14:28 is a summary: "You heard that I said, I am going away and I am coming to you. If you love me, you would rejoice that I go to the Father, because the Father is greater than I." In it, as in the discourse as a whole, the departure motif of the central structure, which had been introduced through the saying in 13:33, is expanded in two ways: by the promise of Jesus' coming (as 14:3, 17b–23) and by the fact that Jesus is going to the greater one. In the summary, this reference to the Father as the greater one picks up the promise of 14:12. On the Son's return the Father will enable the disciples to do greater things and will send the Paraclete which will enable true knowledge of who Jesus is and of his abiding presence with the disciples. Jesus will refer back to this promise when he tells Mary Magdalene of the good news for the disciples that he is going to his Father (20:17). The perspective of something more, which will come through the death and the return of the Son, is also expressed in the words that follow: "I have spoken these things to you now before they happen, so that when they happen you may believe" (14:29). They are almost an exact echo of 13:19, though there they refer to the prediction of Judas's betrayal, and here to the promise of greater things to come.

The closing verses allude to the coming confrontation with the ruler of this world (14:30), already mentioned in 12:31 (cf. also 16:8–33), and have Jesus summarise his purpose, using the pattern of the revealer-envoy: "that the world may know that I love the Father, and as the Father commanded me, so I act" (14:31).

John 13–14 Conclusions

In these chapters the pattern of the central structure continues to determine the way the author expounds the coming of the Son into the world. This is so in the opening verses (13:1, 3) and in the final words of the discourse (14:31). It is particularly present in 14:5–11 and is doubtless in mind in the command to the disciples: "Believe in God and believe in me" (14:1). Elements of the pattern are also applied to the sending of the Spirit (14:26) and the disciples (13:16, 20). Behind much of ch. 14 is the assumption that the disciples are entrusted with a commission to do the works Jesus did and to spread them more widely (14:12, 15, 21, 23).

Much of these two chapters concentrates on the event of Jesus' death and return to the Father. The return belongs within the central structure as 13:1, 3 indicate, but it comes to particular expression in 13:33, a saying already used in conflict with the Jews. This is almost like the preaching text for the discourse and its elements keep recurring throughout. It is used by the author as a starting point for interpreting this event. Jesus' return is to prepare a place with the Father in heavenly dwellings for the disciples who will follow the path of his return if they believe in him (14:3; 13:36b; 14:6). This might be little more than an exposition of the central structure. It recalls sayings such as Jesus is the door. But the author expands the meaning of Jesus' return in two ways.

First, he shows that the Son's return will enable the disciples to do greater things than Jesus, as they fulfil their mission at his command (14:12) and rely on his help in answer to their prayers in this regard (14:13-14). Then the return also brings the Paraclete, the Spirit, already present among the disciples during Jesus' ministry, but in future to be in them (14:15–17) and to inform them of all things, especially the words Jesus had spoken to them (14:26). The Father to whom Jesus goes is "greater" according to the summary in 14:28 and this doubtless connects back to the promise of the Spirit which will make the achievement of greater works possible (cf. also the promise of greater things in 1:50–51; 3:12; 5:21; 6:62).

The second and surprise development is that the Son's return to the Father will be followed by the Son's return with the Father to dwell in those who love him and carry out his commission (14:18–24). The context suggests strongly that the presence of the Son is made possible by the presence of the Spirit. The disciples' life will derive from Jesus' life (14:19) and the day of Jesus' coming will be the day of greater understanding both about the relationship of indwelling of the Father in the Son and mutually of the Son and the disciples.

Other elements related to Jesus' death and return to the Father which feature briefly are the motif of mutual glorification between God and the Son of Man (13:31–32) and the two occasions when Jesus makes predictions so that their fulfilment may confirm the disciples' knowledge. In the case of the prediction about Judas (13:19) it is that they may know "that I am." This could mean "I am who I claim to be" or it could be a revelatory claim in itself through use of the divine name. The second (14:29) expresses no object of what the disciples will come to believe, though the context suggests something along the lines of what is expressed in the pattern of the revealer-envoy (so 14:31).

As in previous sections we have noted that the central structure as initially outlined needs to be supplemented by a cluster of notions associated with Jesus' death and its significance as something greater. This includes reference to it as the hour or "now" and to Jesus as Son of Man. In addition, the author depicts the event as glorification, ascent, and return, the turning point where the Spirit is given, and the moment the disciples are sent in the inauguration of mission.

2.4 John 15–16 in Review

John 15:1–8 is dominated by the motif of the vine and emphasises the need for the disciples to abide in the Son. John 14:20 had spoken of a future perception made possible for the disciples through the Son's return: "On that day you will know that I am in the Father and you in me and I in you." The "I in you and you in me" is now subject of further reflection and exhortation. It is assumed that the disciples are not diseased unfruitful branches (15:2–3), because they have received Jesus' word: "you are clean through the word which I have spoken to you" (15:3). The pattern of the revealer-envoy also informs the use of this imagery. Being clean means receiving the Son's revelation. This is evident also in 15:7, "If you abide in me and my words abide in you, you shall ask what you want and it shall happen for you." The goal of such abiding is the glorification of the Father through the bearing of much fruit: "By this is my Father glorified that you bear much fruit" (15:8).

In ch. 14 the author links glorification of the Father, the promise of answered prayer, and the disciples' future greater works, a reference to their mission (14:12–14). Here the same motifs are present, only mission is expressed through the image of bearing fruit (as already in 12:24; 4:35–38). Thus Rainer Borig's dichotomy here between fruit as deeds of love and fruit as mission, with the suggestion that primarily the former are intended in this

A Survey of the Gospel

passage,[33] must be rejected. Thüsing shows how the notion of fruit-bearing and mission are interrelated. Fruit-bearing is not primarily about numbers but about manifesting the life that by its quality continues the mission of Jesus the vine.[34] The vine image is being used not primarily with a focus on Jesus as the source of life, though without this the image scarcely works. Nor is its focus on the office of ordained ministry alone, as Mussner suggests,[35] nor on a select group of charismatic leaders, as Paul S. Minear suggests,[36] to whom he sees the last discourses primarily addressed. Its focus is that, for all, abiding in the vine and its life makes fruit-bearing possible.[37]

The connections with the passage in ch. 14 continue with the reference to the love theme and the commands in 15:9 (cf. 14:15). In 15:10 abiding in the Son's love is defined as keeping his commands and grounded by using the language of the pattern of the revealer-envoy: "as I have kept the commands of my Father and remain in his love." John 15:11-17 recalls 13:34-35 when it calls for the disciples to love one another, as the Son has loved them. The Son's love is illustrated: "No one has greater love than this, that someone lays down his life for his friends" (15:13). We note a possible reference to Jesus' atoning death here, but it is not the subject of further reflection. The statement could simply mean that in carrying out the task of revelation on their behalf Jesus went even so far as to die. As a generalisation it means little more than the extent to which people go to benefit others. It is therefore hard to be sure from the context to what extent expiatory ideas may be present. We shall return to this in the context of discussion of similar statements in 4.1.2. In what follows the author stays close to the revealer-envoy pattern: "I have called you friends, because all that I heard from the Father I made known to you" (15:15). The imagery of "master-servant," chosenness, and the example of Jesus' love, recall 13:12-20, where similar focus is given to the way the commissioned ones relate to one another. John 15:16-17 return directly to the commission to bear fruit and the promise of answered prayer associated with it (as already 15:7-8).

The parallels between the Son's commission and that of the disciples

---

33. Rainer Borig, *Der wahre Weinstock*, SANT 16 (Munich: Kösel, 1967), 65-66.

34. Thüsing, *Erhöhung*, 106-12, 119-21; similarly Bultmann, *Johannes*, 391; Onuki, *Gemeinde*, 126-30.

35. Franz Mussner, "Die johanneischen Parakletsspruche und die apostolische Tradition," in *Praesentia Salutis* (Düsseldorf: Patmos, 1967), 154-55; cf. Thüsing, *Erhöhung*, 329.

36. Paul S. Minear, *John: The Martyr's Gospel* (New York: Pilgrim, 1985), 84-85, 92-93. Similarly by implication also Boring, "Christian Prophecy," 113-14.

37. So Schnackenburg, *Johannesevangelium*, 3.113; Porsch, *Pneuma*, 194; Thüsing, *Erhöhung*, 119.

continues through 15:18–25 and the elements of the central structure feature throughout. The world hated the Son and hates them (15:18). Like the Son, they are not of the world, for he has chosen them (15:19). The issue is whether people respond to and keep the word, whether the Son's or theirs, for it is the word of revelation (15:20). The disciples will operate with Jesus' authority, so that their rejection will be on account of that authority, that name: "They will do these things to you because of my name, because they do not know him who sent me" (15:21). Jesus has come and has spoken the word and done the deeds of revelation (15:22, 24); negative response to this revelation constitutes sin: "If I had not come and spoken to them, they would have no sin" (15:22). Such rejection is rejection of the Father (15:23–24).

John 15:26–27 shifts the attention from rejection to the coming of the Paraclete: "When the Paraclete comes, whom I shall send from the Father, the Spirit of Truth which proceeds from the Father, he will bear witness concerning me; and you will bear witness, because you have been with me from the beginning." As in 14:26, the sending of the Spirit reflects the central structure. Here the forensic language of evidence, "witness," and the fulfilment of the formal legal requirement of two witnesses for valid testimony may reflect forensic concerns in the rejection of the disciples, just mentioned. This also may reflect the original setting of the motif of the Paraclete in relation to the Spirit (Mark 13:11).[38] It may however simply reflect John's wider use of the term, such as in 3:32–33. Bearing witness is another way of speaking about bearing the word of revelation. Both the witness of the Paraclete and that of the disciples are firmly tied to Jesus. Both are sent by Jesus, the former directly from the Father and bearing the designation "Spirit of Truth," the latter through historical association with the earthly Jesus.

The persecution theme continues into John 16. Persecution occurs "because they have come to know neither my Father nor me" (16:3). Jesus makes these predictions "so that when their hour comes, you may remember that I told you of them" (16:4a). This is not unlike the statements about prediction in 13:19 and 14:29, except that the purpose remains simply remembering that Jesus had said so. Presumably this is to function as comfort.

The following statement is enigmatic, almost as if the exalted Jesus speaks: "These things I did not tell you from the beginning because I was with you." Read in the present context, it must mean that Jesus had not spoken of such things earlier in the ministry when the prospect of his departure was still some time away. Now departure is imminent and Jesus continues:

---

38. So Porsch, *Pneuma*, 269–70; Ibuki, *Wahrheit*, 291; Robin Scroggs, *Christology in Paul and John* (Philadelphia: Fortress, 1988), 88.

A Survey of the Gospel

"But now I am going to the one who sent me" (16:5a). This is a return to the statement of 13:33. It is as though the former conversation begins all over again. "No one asks me, 'Where are you going?'" (16:5b). It is as though Thomas's question, using exactly these words (14:5), had not occurred. In 16:6 there is a similar assumption that Jesus' departure would distress the disciples as we find behind 14:1. Similar comfort is offered: the coming of the Paraclete (16:7; cf. 14:16-17). Within the present text of the Gospel John the evangelist (or a later hand) is repeating themes of ch. 14 with variation.

John 16:8-11 offers a succinct summary of the Paraclete's work. The language is forensic (as already in 15:26) and this is consistent with the forensic use of the word Paraclete, meaning advocate. Here the world is on trial and the Paraclete presents convincing evidence so as to lead to a conviction of the world in relation to three themes.[39] It will establish the world's guilt on the basis that it has not believed in Jesus. This is similar to 15:22 which defines guilt as negative response to the revelation Jesus brings. Second, it will provide convincing evidence of Jesus' righteousness. This evidence lies in the fact of Jesus' return to the Father, the people (including the disciples) no longer seeing Jesus as he was on earth. Why this counts as evidence of righteousness is that Jesus' return to the Father shows the Father has vindicated him.[40] Third, evidence will be laid on the table proving that the world's judgment has taken place. The cross on which the world condemned the Son is the place where the world is condemned. The hour of Jesus' judgment is the hour of the judgment of the world, when the ruler of this world would be cast out, as already 12:31 suggests (cf. also 16:33).

The author has constructed a neat summary of the Gospel,[41] using the pattern of the central structure and the theme of the cross as the hour of judgment. In effect the Paraclete will hold before the world the implications of its response to Jesus' coming, understood in accordance with the central structure. The primary focus of the Paraclete's work here is, as the text

---

39. So Schnackenburg, *Johannesevangelium*, 3.147; John Painter, "The Farewell Discourses and the History of Johannine Christianity," *NTS* 27 (1981): 538-39; A. A. Trites, *The New Testament Concept of Witness*, SNTSMS 31 (Cambridge: Cambridge University Press, 1977), 49-50; Beasley-Murray, *John*, 280-81; cf. the review of alternatives in Donald A. Carson, "The Function of the Paraclete in John 16:7-11," *JBL* 98 (1979): 547-66, who agrees that "convict of" or "convince of" gives the best sense, but, as Burge, *Anointed Community*, 209, notes, presses too hard for a conformity of meaning among the genitives in having "righteousness" refer ironically to the world's righteousness (558).

40. So Bultmann, *Johannes*, 434-35; Blank, *Krisis*, 337; Schnackenburg, *Johannesevangelium*, 3.149; Dietzfelbinger, "Paraklet," 391-92; Onuki, *Gemeinde*, 145; Beasley-Murray, *John*, 282.

41. So Preiss, *Life in Christ*, 21-22.

explicitly states, the confrontation of the world,[42] not a court action in the consciences of the disciples for their comfort and reassurance.[43] The disciples will indeed share the verdict, but the focus is the address to the world, the work of the Paraclete, doubtless through their preaching.

In the verses which follow, the author has Jesus use the language of the central structure also to describe the role of the Spirit of Truth: "He shall not speak on his own authority, but what he shall hear he shall speak. . . . He shall glorify me, because he shall take from me and announce it to you. All that the Father has is mine; therefore I said, he shall take what is mine and announce it to you." The Spirit's revelation is derivative and the author emphasises its secondary role in subordination to the Son. At two points this dependence may seem to falter: "When he, the Spirit of Truth, comes he will lead you into all truth"; and "he will announce to you what is to come" (literally: "the coming things" in 16:13). They echo 14:26 which spoke of the Paraclete teaching the disciples all things. But the context in which these are set demands that such truth and prediction will not come without being authorised by the Son. In 6.1.3 below we discuss the implications for our understanding of the Gospel writing itself.

Taken as a whole, 16:7–15 shows the Paraclete fulfilling a crucial role in relationship to both the world and the disciples. He expounds the meaning of Jesus' coming. Both in the exposition of Jesus' coming and in the manner in which the Paraclete exercises his ministry, the author employs the pattern of the central structure. The open-endedness of the Paraclete's ministry to the disciples leaves room for creative developments and growth in understanding and exposition of "the things" of Jesus—past, present and future.

John 16:16 returns us again to 13:33 except that the "little while" is now related to the interim between Jesus' departure and the disciples' seeing him again. The transition from the coming of the Paraclete (16:7-15) to the coming of the Son recalls the abrupt transition in 14:18. The manner in which the author has the disciples puzzle over the departure saying recalls the Jews' puzzlement after its first use in 7:33 (cf. 7:35; 8:21–22). Jesus addresses the grief of the interim by using the motif of birthpangs which are fulfilled in the joy of the birth of a child. He promises his disciples similar joy (16:22).

---

42. So Bultmann, *Johannes*, 433; *Theologie*, 442; Blank, *Krisis*, 335; Barrett, *John*, 488–89; Müller, *Heilsgeschehen*, 84; Thüsing, *Erhöhung*, 143; Painter, "Farewell Discourses," 539–40; Onuki, *Gemeinde*, 146; Carson, "Paraclete," 553; Dietzfelbinger, "Paraklet," 391–92.

43. Against Porsch, *Pneuma*, 222-24, 274–75, 280–86; I. de la Potterie, *La Vérité dans Saint Jean*, 2 vols., AnBib 73/74 (Rome: BibInst, 1977), 410; M. F. Berrouard, "Le Paraclete, Défenseur du Christ devant la conscience du croyant (Jo. XVI.8–11)," *RSPT* 33 (1949): 301-49, 361–89; Brown, *John*, 712; Ulrich B. Müller, "Die Parakletenvorstellung im Johannesevangelium," *ZTK* 71 (1974): 76; Becker, *Johannes*, 495.

As it stands, 16:16–22 is unusual in that it purports to address the problem of the days between Jesus' departure from the disciples and his resurrection appearance to them, a problem of only very indirect relevance to the readers. It is probably dealt with here with such emphasis (the repetition of the question!) because other disciples may feel themselves in a similar situation later.

In 16:23–27 the author returns to the other logion which occurs frequently in the last discourses, the promise of answered prayer. Like the variant of 13:33 in 16:16–22, this saying is repeated a number of times. In 14:13–14 Jesus had said that he himself would answer prayer requests. In 15:16 it is the Father who does so. Here the emphasis falls upon the fact of the disciples' having direct access to the Father independent of Jesus (16:26–27). This is not in any way meant to denigrate Jesus. Rather it demonstrates to the disciples the Father's love. This love is then explained as the Father's response to the way the disciples have responded to Jesus. Predictably, at this strategic point, we meet the pattern of the central structure again: "The Father himself loves you, because you have loved me and believed that I came from God. I came from the Father and have come into the world. Again I am leaving the world and am going to the Father" (16:27–28).

Jesus had introduced this promise of a direct relationship with the Father by announcing that he was now going to speak plainly and not in a veiled way as before (16:25). The disciples respond to Jesus' clear word of promise with a somewhat baffling affirmation: "Now we know that you know all things and have no need for anyone to ask you. In this we believe that you have come from God" (16:30). In 16:29 the disciples indicate that this awareness has come to them since Jesus announced he was speaking plainly to them, namely, from 16:25 onwards. Having no need to be asked sounds similar to the language of the prayer requests, but there is no apparent connection between Jesus not being prayed to directly, the theme of 16:26–27, and his knowing all things. Jesus has already affirmed their adequate faith in 16:27–28. It is hard to interpret 16:30 as an improvement beyond that.

In all likelihood, the author is deliberately presenting the disciples as expressing their faith inadequately at this point in order to explain Jesus' prediction of their imminent failure. Their affirmation that Jesus has come from God on the basis of knowing all things could be seen as the kind of inferior faith exhibited by Nicodemus and by Peter in 21:15–17, a miracle-based faith responding here to Jesus' supernatural knowledge.[44] Such faith will not stand. They will be scattered to their homes and will abandon Jesus.

---

44. So Barrett, *John*, 497; Schnackenburg, *Johannesevangelium*, 3.185; Becker, *Johannes*, 505.

The Father will not abandon him. Alternatively their faith had grasped Jesus' descent (16:30b), but not the meaning of his ascent.[45] Within the transmitted text of the Gospel the disciples have advanced beyond a faith based in miracle, so that this second alternative is to be preferred.

The discourse concludes abruptly after this warning. Jesus explains that their peace is the intention of his words and encourages them to face persecution in the world confident that ultimately it has been overcome. This functions as a rudimentary summary, recalling the persecution theme and the interpretation of the cross as the world's judgment (16:11).

John 15–16 Conclusions

The pattern of the central structure of the author's Christology features often within these two chapters (directly 15:10, 15, 22, 24; 16:27–28) and it lies behind the image of clean and healthy branches (15:3, 7)—the way the Paraclete presents evidential content in 16:7–11—and the paralleling of the response to Jesus and the response to disciples in 15:18–25. Its structure also determines the way the commission of the Paraclete is described, especially in 16:12–15 (see also 15:26). Twice the pattern of the revealer-envoy is used in defining sin as rejection of Jesus as the sent one (15:22, 24; 16:7–8).

As in chs. 13–14, however, much of the material focusses on the events surrounding Jesus' death and return to the Father. We find again an extensive use of the saying found in 13:33, especially from 16:5 onwards where a lot of the substance of the discussion in 13:33–14:31 is repeated in variant form (16:16–19; cf. 16:7, 28). John 16:19–22 primarily address the distress of the disciples between the passion and Easter. Mostly however the departure is shown to be the basis for new promising events, like the coming of the Paraclete (16:6–11, 12–15).

This is the fullest exposition of the Paraclete's role. The Paraclete presents convincing evidence about Jesus' coming as having exposed what sin is and about the significance of his death and departure as vindication and judgment. The Paraclete will also be the source of knowledge both about and from the Son (16:12–15). This is a key passage for understanding how the author would understand the source of the material presented in the Gospel.

Already 15:26 connects the witness of the Spirit and the witness of the disciples, the latter's witness tied to their having been with the earthly Jesus. The discourse also assumes that the disciples receive the Paraclete's wisdom.

---

45. So Lindars, *Gospel of John*, 573; Nicholson, *Death*, 68–69; Brown, *John*, 736.

This enables them in mission. John 16:7–11 assumes missionary confrontation with the world and 15:18–25 assumes rejection and persecution (very specifically: 16:1–3). Missionary fruit-bearing also underlies the vine image (15:2, 4, 5, 7–8, 16) and the exhortation to mutual love in the community (15:12–17; cf. 13:34–35).

John 15:1–17 reads as a direct address to the post-Easter community. The vine image assumes the mutual indwelling promised by 14:20 for the future, speaks of the fruit-bearing as a present reality, and looks back on Jesus' self-sacrifice (15:13). It lacks any reflection on the difference in time perspective. As it stands in the text it is timeless advice to the disciples applicable already pre-Easter. Time-specific references are otherwise common from 15:18 onwards and quite extraordinarily so in 16:16–22 and possibly in 16:29–32 where the disciples seem to be shown as having an incomplete faith which will lead to their downfall in the face of the immediate crisis of the passion.

The promise of answered prayer appears a number of times in these chapters. In 15:1–18 it relates directly to the tasks of mission in much the same way as it did in 14:13–14 (15:7–9, 16). In ch. 16 it is used quite differently as a way of describing the new relationship that disciples may now have with the Father (16:23–26).

We note a further use of the judgment motif to describe the death of Jesus, first encountered in 12:31 (16:11 and probably 16:33). Apart from that there also occurs the brief generalised reference to Jesus' death in the word "someone lays down his life for his friends" (15:13). How it should be weighted (vicarious atonement? total commitment to benefit others?) cannot be decided from the context. It is not the subject of further reflection in the context.

2.5 John 17 in Review

John 17 was considered in the initial discussion of the central structure above. There it was shown that the pattern of the central structure is present throughout. Accordingly Jesus announces that he has completed his task of making the Father known and so bringing eternal life (17:2–3). The author varies the core theme, having Jesus describe that task as giving eternal life (17:2–3), making known God's name (17:6, 11–12, 26), giving God's words (17:8), God's word (17:6, 14), and God's glory (17:22) and as a mission for which he was authorised (17:2, 7), loved by God (17:23, 26), sent (extensively: 17:3, 8, 18, 21, 23, 25) and came from God (17:8). He has Jesus also refer to the greater event to come: his return to the Father (17:11, 13), his glorification by the Father with the glory he shared with God before the world began (17:5, 24), his sanctifying himself as the disciples are similarly to be sanctified and sent (17:17–19), which some take as a reference to his death as a cultic sacrifice, and their mutual indwelling with him (17:23), living in unity (17:11, 21–22), and joining him ultimately where he is (17:24).

2.6 John 18–21 in Review

In the account of Jesus' arrest in the garden (18:1–11) the outstanding feature is the way those who had come with Judas to arrest Jesus backed away and fell to the ground when he identified himself. Twice Jesus asked them whom they sought (18:4, 7); twice they answered, "Jesus of Nazareth" (18:5, 7); and twice Jesus replied: "I am (he)" (18:5, 8). After the first exchange the author mentions the falling to the ground in response to Jesus' words, "I am" (18:6). On the second occasion Jesus continues after the words "I am" to say, "If you are looking for me, let these go!" (18:8).

Is this the effect of the overwhelming numinous power of the presence of him, whom the reader knows to be the revealer, so that "I am" was the point of the identification and therefore the point when its impact struck the bystanders? In that case "I am" means: "I am Jesus of Nazareth whom you seek." The reaction of the bystanders was occasioned, therefore, not merely by surprise, but by a holy presence outside their control, the holy presence of the revealer. Or, is it that the expression, "I am," represents a statement of divine revelation or a statement of the divine name, the revealer presenting himself as the presence of Yahweh?

It is in this event that Judas betrays Jesus and it may be of significance that Jesus appended to the prediction the words, "From now on I tell you before it happens, so that you may believe, when it happens, that I am (he)" (13:19). Is the "I am" here meant to connect with the "I am" in the arrest scene? It could however be nothing more than the claim that when my prediction comes true, "then you will know that I am who I claim to be." Nothing in the text forces one to conclude one way or the other, including the repetition of the event twice and of the words "I am" three times in the text. Only if the second use is evident elsewhere in the Gospel, and particularly if it is already established by this point in the Gospel, is the case for the second interpretation strong and this has not proved so. For the present we can note that, one way or another, the dignity of the revealer is presupposed here. We return to the issue of "I am" in both passages below in 5.3.11.

In 18:11 Jesus employs a metaphor of commissioning: "The cup which the Father has given me, am I not to drink it?" This reflects (and corrects) the tradition of his Gethsemane prayer as in 12:27 (cf. Mark 14:36). Jesus sees therefore not only the passing on of the words of the Father, following the pattern of the central structure, as his commission. He must also face suffering and death. Only then is the task complete (cf. "It is finished," 19:30). In 18:14 the author recalls the prophecy of Caiaphas, "It is fitting that one man die for the people" (cf. 11:50). The reader is receiving an interpretation of the task which lies ahead. As with 15:13, the precise interpretation depends upon factors which lie outside the immediate context of the passage. We shall therefore return to the question of whether this belongs to notions of vicarious atonement and of its role in the Gospel's Christology in 4.2 below.

In the interview with Annas (18:19-24) the focus is entirely upon Jesus as teacher. Jesus refuses to refer to the content of his teaching and remains with the affirmation that he has spoken openly for all to hear. This is consonant with the strong emphasis, following the revealer model, on the centrality of Jesus' words. Meanwhile Peter has been denying Jesus three times, as predicted (13:38b). Neither here, nor in Judas's fulfilment of Jesus' prediction concerning him (cf. 13:18-19), is direct reference made back to the fulfilled prediction. But both confirm for the reader Jesus' supernatural knowledge (also 18:4).

The trial before Pilate (18:28-19:16) is a carefully structured narrative highlighting the theme of Jesus the royal messiah, the king of the Jews. The author notes in the introduction that the Jews remain outside the praetorium, so that they would not defile themselves before eating the Passover (18:28). Already 13:1 made reference to the Passover and further references will follow. They may carry more weight than simple indicators of time, but an evaluation can be made only in the light of all such references and allusions.

The first scene (18:29-32) has Pilate ask the Jews the grounds of their accusation. They give a very shifty, indirect answer, part of the extremely negative characterisation of the Jews during the trial. Their assertion that Jesus has committed a capital crime for which only the Romans could carry out the sentence allows the author to note Jesus' prediction about the manner of his death, deduced in 12:33 from the words "lifted up." The particular phrase is not repeated in the passion narrative, neither in its literal nor in its metaphoric sense, nor are the other terms associated with it (Son of Man, glorification). This may well indicate that it is not seeking to portray the passion events as an act of exaltation, or as the prefiguration of a heavenly exaltation or enthronement, or as the simultaneous earthly representation of a heavenly event, as some have suggested. The Son of Man, and the motifs of exaltation and glorification should then not be synthesised with the messianic kingship motifs in this way and, in any case, the kingship motifs of the trial function as they do elsewhere in the Gospel: they focus on Jesus as the revealer, who, as such, is already the messiah, the king. The king motif in the trial would belong, therefore, within the language of royal messianic expectation, as the sequence of images to follow amply testifies.

Pilate asks Jesus if he is "the king of the Jews" (18:33), a phrase recalling Nathanael's messianic affirmation: "You are the Son of God. You are the king of Israel!" (1:49). Jesus effectively affirms the question with reservations and safeguards it against misinterpretation: "My kingdom is not of this world; if my kingdom were of this world, my servants would fight so that I might not be handed over to the Jews. But now my kingdom is not from here" (18:36). This is not a reference to impending enthronement of Jesus in heaven, but to Jesus' present messianic status. It does refer to the heavenly world, the world above, in the sense that Jesus has come from above, but the reference is not primarily topographical, but qualitative. The kingdom, to be seen and entered by those born from above (3:3, 5), is the realm of the Spirit present in the exercise of Jesus' ministry, but invisible to those like Nicodemus who see only at the earthly level.

In response to Pilate's reply, "Then you are a king," the author has Jesus underscore the nature of his kingship by using words which reflect the central structure of John's Christology: "You say I am a king. I was born for this and came into the world for this, to witness to the truth. All who are of the truth hear my voice" (18:37). Beutler and Ibuki draw attention to the similarity between 18:37 and 3:31.[46] When Pilate asks, "What is truth?," the reader knows it is the revelation brought by the Son from the Father. This confirms what we have already found elsewhere: the author interprets the royal messianic confession within the framework of the central structure of his Christology. Similarly Hahn and Alfons Dauer, who both emphasise the importance of royal messianic motifs in the passion narrative, stress that the focus of the messianic claim in the passion narrative is not rule but revelation.[47]

In 18:38b-40 Pilate offers the brigand Barabbas in exchange for Jesus. The motif of the royal messianic pretender thus continues to dominate. Jesus' claim to kingship is also the focus of the mockery and presentation which follow (19:1-5). Pilate repeats the affirmation of Jesus' innocence (19:4; cf. 18:38b) and presents the mock king with the words: "Behold the man!"

46. Beutler, *Martyria*, 324; Ibuki, *Wahrheit*, 144-45.
47. Dauer, *Passionsgeschichte*, 259-60; Hahn, "Prozess," 40-41.

A Survey of the Gospel

(19:5). At the level of Pilate within the narrative the statement must mean something like: "Look at the man. Here he is, your king!" The force of this comment is that it is spoken of Jesus in a state of humiliation and ridicule. He is just a pathetic human being. The Jews are also being ridiculed in the act. The power of this scene for the reader is twofold. Precisely this mocked king is the only true king and messiah and precisely this human person is the Son come from the Father.

The passage raises a number of questions to which we return in the thematic discussion in Part Two below. These include whether in playing on enthronement the author means us to understand the mockery or the crucifixion itself as paradoxically the actual enthronement of Jesus as Messiah or as foreshadowing it as happening at his return to the Father. Or does the royal imagery now serve, as it does earlier in the Gospel, to underline the claims made in the central structure of the author's Christology into which it is integrated? Similarly, the words, "Behold the man!" have elicited a range of responses. Is there an allusion here to Jesus as Son of Man, a new Adam, the Man-Messiah, the gnostic Anthropos, or primarily to his state of humiliation?

Pilate repeats his statement of Jesus' innocence a third time (19:6) and the Jews for the first time name their accusation: "He made himself Son of God" (19:7). The numinosity of this claim frightens Pilate; the numinosity had already thrown his captors back at the arrest. Introduction of the sonship theme brings us more directly within the framework of the central structure of the author's Christology. Accordingly we note the irony in Pilate's next question: "Where do you come from?" (19:9), which as elsewhere plays on deeper meaning. Similarly Jesus asserts his awareness of Pilate's relative authority: "You would have no authority over me, unless it had been granted you from above" (19:11; cf. 3:35). The royal messianic theme returns when Pilate seeks to release Jesus and the Jews respond: "Anyone who makes himself a king speaks against Caesar" (19:12).

Pilate succumbs. He takes his seat (ἐκάθισεν) to declare the verdict (19:13). It has long been noted that the Greek could be read to mean either that Pilate himself sat down or that he made Jesus sit down on the seat. The latter could mean that Jesus himself is being portrayed as the judge (cf. similarly, Gos. Pet. 3:7; Justin *1 Apol.* 35:6).[48] This would cohere with the tenor of the narrative which in effect has Pilate and the Jews on trial before Jesus,

---

48. Beutler, *Martyria*, 319; Boismard and Lamouille, *Jean*, 430-31; Haenchen, *Johannes*, 541; Meeks, *Prophet-King*, 74-75; and as one side of an instance of double meaning: Barrett, *John*, 544.

an orientation of the narrative brought out strongly by Dauer and Hahn.[49] Alternatively, or perhaps in addition, it influences the powerful irony of Pilate enthroning Jesus, with the seat understood not as the tribunal seat itself but as a mock throne.[50] Perhaps the author intends us to see in Pilate's act a further act of mockery of Jesus' kingship, following it, as had the first, by a statement of presentation: "Behold your king!" (cf. "Behold the man!" 19:5). Both acts of mockery are also a mockery of the Jews, and their response is the same: "Away with him, away with him! Crucify him!" (cf. 19:6, "crucify him! crucify him!").

While the motif of setting Jesus up as judge coheres broadly with the tenor of the narrative, it is not supported specifically, apart from the suggested action itself, by any further gesture of Pilate, Jesus, or the Jews. There is more to be said for the second interpretation which sees the seating as a further act of mockery, particularly because the events which follow reflect the same structure as the earlier mockery. On this interpretation the seat is not a judgment seat and the judgment motif is not in focus. Had Pilate taken this seat to declare a verdict, why does he not do so immediately? On the other hand, the preceding exchange had reached a point where Pilate was forced to declare judgment so that, at least from what precedes, we should take βῆμα (seat) to be a seat of judgment. In support of this is the formal characterisation of its setting in the Gabbatha. No such concern about location is evident in the first mockery (19:1–5). Similarly the dating given in 19:14 suggests a formally significant event has taken place. On balance, therefore, it is best to read the text as describing how Pilate took his seat for judgment.[51]

We note the further reference to the Passover, which together with 18:28 may form an *inclusio* and we will return to it below. Pilate mockingly presents Jesus a second time to the Jews as king, this time using the word "king" explicitly (cf. 19:5): "Behold your king." We have already noted the similarity in structure between the two scenes. The Jews reject their king, their Messiah, and Pilate hands him over to crucifixion.

---

49. Dauer, *Passionsgeschichte*, 247, 249, 261; Hahn, "Prozess," 68–85; similarly Porsch, *Pneuma*, 223–27; Beutler, *Martyria*, 365–66; Appold, *Oneness*, 108–9.

50. I. de la Potterie, "Jésus roi et juge d'après Jn 19,13," *Bibl* 41 (1960): 217–47; C. H. Giblin, "John's Narration of the Hearing Before Pilate," *Bib* 67 (1986): 234–35; Nicholson, *Death*, 164.

51. Blank, "Verhandlung," 64–65; *Krisis*, 269–74; Josef Blinzler, *Der Prozess Jesu*, 4th ed. (Stuttgart: KBW, 1969), 346–56; Brown, *John*, 880–81; Forestell, *Word*, 86 n. 115; Appold, *Oneness*, 134; Dauer, *Passionsgeschichte*, 155, 269–74; Hahn, "Prozess," 48–50; Schnackenburg, *Johannesevangelium*, 3.304–5; Rosel Baum-Bodenbender, *Hoheit in Niedrigkeit. Johanneische Christologie im Prozess Jesu vor Pilatus (Joh 18,28–19,16a)*, FB 49 (Würzburg: Echter, 1984), 78–79; Beasley-Murray, *John*, 341–42; Keener, *John*, 1129; Beutler, *Johannesevangelium*, 493–94.

A Survey of the Gospel

The royal messianic imagery continues in the account of the crucifixion, especially in the insistence by Pilate that the superscription, "Jesus of Nazareth, the king of the Jews," should stand (19:19–22). Pilate's "What I have written I have written" has a finality about it which speaks to the reader at a level Pilate himself would not have realised.

The author emphasises that Jesus' robe was seamless (19:23), perhaps only to explain why lots were cast, perhaps to emphasise his perfection. Some suggest it is, like the unbroken net in 21:11, an allusion to the unity of the Church,[52] or that it alludes to the seamless robes of high priests (cf. Josephus, *A.J.* 3.161) and so to Jesus as high priest,[53] but there is no convincing evidence of this motif in the Gospel and certainly none that it played a central role in the author's Christology.[54] Jesus commends his mother to the care of the beloved disciple, an enormous credit to and benefit for the disciple's community (19:25–27) and thus also for the reader indirectly, who will benefit from this Gospel's community. Having not only the Paraclete but also this disciple—with his special connection to Mary—assures the reader that the portrait of Jesus in the Gospel is true. A similar reassurance comes a few verses later in the author's noting of a report from an eyewitness (19:35).

In 19:28–30 the author describes how Jesus, knowing he had completed all, fulfilled Scripture by declaring his thirst, announced the mission complete: "It is finished," bowed his head and gave up his spirit (19:30). The "It is finished" (τετέλεσται) might mean little more than "I am dying" (colloquially: "I am finished!"), but the repetition in the narrative and the underlying revealer pattern of the author's Christology determine that we should see in these words Jesus' declaration that he had completed his commission (cf.

---

52. Boismard and Lamouille, *Jean*, 442.

53. So Franz Mussner, "'Kultische' Aspekte im Johanneischen Christusbild," in *Praesentia Salutis* (Düsseldorf: Patmos, 1967), 143–44; Brown, *John*, 921; J. T. Williams, "Cultic Elements in the Fourth Gospel," in *Studia Biblica 1978. II. Papers on the Gospels. Sixth International Congress on Biblical Studies*, ed. E. A. Livingstone (Sheffield: JSOT, 1980), 342–43; Helen Bond, "Discarding the Seamless Robe: The High Priesthood of Jesus in John's Gospel," in *Israel's God and Rebecca's Children: Christology and Community in Early Judaism and Christianity: Essays in Honor of Larry W. Hurtado and Alan F. Segal*, ed. D. B. Capes, A. D. DeConick, H. K. Bond, and T. A. Miller (Waco: Baylor University Press, 2007), 183–94, who argues that its removal symbolises that "the entire system of traditional Jewish worship, with its feasts and cultic activities centred in the Jerusalen temple, has been fulfilled (and, therefore, superseded) by Christ" (190–91) and reflects the Johannine community's response to the destruction of the temple (193).

54. Critical appraisal of both in Schnackenburg, *Johannesevangelium*, 3.317–18. See also John W. Pryor, *John: Evangelist of the Covenant Community: The Narrative and Themes of the Fourth Gospel* (Downers Grove: IVP, 1992), 80.

17:4: "I have glorified you on earth, having completed the work you gave me to do"; also 4:34). This passage forms an *inclusio* with 13:1, where the author notes that Jesus loved his own to the end. There is no indication that his death is being singled out as an accomplishment on its own, for example, as an act of sacrifice or atonement. Rather it is best to see these words in relation to the total commission, which, of course, also included his suffering and death (so, specifically, 18:11). We return in 4.1 and 2 to the question of how elements of that commission were understood.

Some read the words παρέδωκεν τὸ πνεῦμα in 19:30 not as "he gave up the (his) spirit," a reference to death, but as "he handed over the Spirit." Should this be so, it is extraordinary that nothing further in the context, before or after, reflects such a meaning. It is best to read the promise of the Spirit being fulfilled in 20:22, not here. We return to this in 4.1.2.11 below.

In 19:31–37 two further motifs appear and the meaning of both is disputed. The first is that Jesus' bones are left unbroken, fulfilling the Scripture quoted in John 19:36. The Scripture is either Ps 34:21: which refers to the righteous sufferer or Exod 12:10, 46 referring to the Passover lamb. It is unlikely to be both, much as both might be applicable christological interpretations. Some suggest a former reference to the psalm has now been overlaid by the author's concern to emphasise Jesus as the Passover lamb. In favour of reference to Ps 34:20 is the frequency of allusions to the suffering righteous of the psalms in the passion narratives of the Gospels generally and the marked omission of any reference to the Passover imagery in the immediate context here. Should a Passover reference have been intended, it is hard to see why the author missed the opportunity in 19:31 to mention that the great Sabbath was the day of the Passover, and this immediately before Pilate's command to break the legs! The case for a reference to the Passover lies wider afield, including a possible inclusion with John the Baptist's hailing Jesus as Son of God in 1:29. We shall return to the broader discussion in the context of discussing the theme of Jesus' death in John in 4.1 below.

The second disputed image is the spear thrust and in particular the words of 19:34, "there immediately flowed out blood and water." The matching text is in 19:37: "They will look on him whom they have pierced." The weight lies on the details of what was seen, blood and water, as the elaborate guarantee of the eyewitness report in 19:35 confirms. Is the focus on Jesus' real humanity and his death as therefore normal, on his superhumanity and his death as exceptional, or on the symbolic significance of blood and water, for which a range of possibilities have been proposed? We shall return to the discussion in 5.4.3 below.

Jesus is placed in the tomb (19:38–42). Two days later, Mary Magdalene finds the stone removed and the body gone. She tells Peter and the beloved disciple. Both run to the tomb, the latter arriving first, peering in and seeing the lying graveclothes. Peter goes right in and observes enough detail to suggest Jesus himself might have arranged them. The beloved disciple enters, sees the same and the headband in a place on its own, and believes. The author hastens to add: "For they did not yet know the Scripture that he must rise from the dead" (20:9). This reflects the notion expressed earlier in the Gospel that the applicability of Scripture to Jesus comes to the disciples only after Easter (2:22; 12:16), doubtless in particular: after the Spirit was given.

The narrative leaves us up in the air about the extent of the disciples' understanding. At this point Peter does not seem to have read what he saw in such a way as to believe Jesus had risen, whereas the beloved disciple—seeing the same evidence (or did Peter not see the headband?)—does believe. The interposition of 20:9 makes good sense after Peter's response, but is difficult after the response of the beloved disciple. Either we must reduce the meaning of "believed" in 20:8[55] or 20:9 means only the disciples' understanding of Scripture.[56] The beloved disciple already fully believes without it; Peter does not.[57] Brendan Byrne links the disciple's faith with 20:29 and sees in the beloved disciple a model for the later church which will have to believe without encountering appearances of the risen Lord.[58] Perhaps we should be pressing the narrator too far if we ask why the beloved disciple did not tell Peter what he was thinking or what he saw if it was that which made the difference!

Mary Magdalene's dramatic encounter with Jesus concludes with Jesus' enigmatic words: "Do not hold on to me (or "touch me"; μή μου ἅπτου), for I have not yet ascended to my Father; but go to my brothers and say to them, 'I am ascending to my Father and to your Father, to my God and to your God'" (20:17). Jesus had already spoken of his ascent to the Father in the Gospel (3:13; 6:62) and of his going to the Father many times. This must

---

55. So I. de la Potterie, "Genèse de la Foi Pascal d'après Jn 20," *NTS* 30 (1984): 26-49, 30-31; Paul S. Minear, "'We Don't Know Where. . .' John 20:2," *Int* 30 (1976): 125-29; Nicholson, *Death*, 70-71.

56. So Boismard and Lamouille, *Jean*, 459; Dieter Zeller, "Der Ostermorgen im vierten Evangelium," in *Auferstehung Jesu und Auferstehung der Christen*, ed. H. Oberlinner, QD 105 (Freiburg: Herder, 1986), 158-59.

57. So Brown, *John*, 987; Lindars, *Gospel of John*, 602; Schnackenburg, *Johannesevangelium*, 3.368; Jacob Kremer, *Die Osterevangelien: Geschichten um Geschichte* (Stuttgart: KBW, 1981), 168.

58. Brendan Byrne, "The Faith of the Beloved Disciple and the Community in John 20," *JSNT* 23 (1985): 87-89, 92.

be our guide, and not Luke's story of Jesus' visible assumption into heaven on the fortieth day (Acts 1:11), for the Fourth Gospel nowhere indicates that Jesus' ascent or return to the Father is an observable event.

Within the Johannine context, therefore, the most natural reading is that Jesus is in the process of completing his return to the Father and has not done so yet. The person he is—able to be touched at this moment—has yet to complete the journey. The emphasis on God being God and Father of both Jesus and the disciples must allude to the benefit which will come to the disciples because of Jesus' return. In the light of the last discourses this benefit would include at least the gift of the Paraclete. Accordingly the message to the disciples is the promise of greater things to come, once Jesus has returned. Jesus must therefore be referring here to an event soon to be fulfilled, after which and as a result of which blessing will come to the disciples. In the context of the Gospel this most naturally refers to an event which will take place before Jesus appears to his disciples in the following episode (20:19-23). We return to a fuller discussion in 4.3.3.7 below.

The fact that Jesus was willing to be touched in 20:24-29 might be confirmation that this has by that time happened, since it contrasts with Jesus' command to Mary not to touch him.[59] It is more likely that Mary is being told not to hold on and therefore the possible touching in 20:24-29 is less relevant to the interpretation of 20:17.[60] There may also be the message here that true Easter faith does not try to hold onto the form of the earthly visible Jesus,[61] so that there emerges a certain similarity between the behaviour of Mary and that of Thomas.[62]

The miraculous appearance of Jesus (despite closed doors) to his disciples (20:19-23) establishes once and for all his resurrection. Seeing the Lord

---

59. So Sanders and Mastin, *John*, 428.

60. So also Thüsing, *Erhöhung*, 265; Brown, *John*, 992-94, 1011; Schnackenburg, *Johannesevangelium*, 3.376; Onuki, *Gemeinde*, 86; but see also the suggestion of Mary Rose D'Angelo, "A Critical Note: John 20.17 and Apocalypse of Moses 31," *JTS* 41 (1990): 529-36, that it reflects the kind of belief found in Apoc. Mos. 31:3-4 where Adam asks that he not be touched till he had ascended.

61. So de Jonge, *Stranger*, 4; Schnackenburg, *Johannesevangelium*, 3.377; Kremer, *Osterevangelien*, 172; Pheme Perkins, *Resurrection: New Testament Witness and Contemporary Reflection* (New York: Doubleday, 1984), 176; de la Potterie, "Genèse," 34-35; Byrne, "Beloved Disciple," 84; cf. also Sandra Schneiders, *The Johannine Resurrection Narrative: An Exegetical and Theological Study of John 20 as a Synthesis of Johannine Spirituality* (Rome: GregUniv, 1975), who sees in Mary's quest for the body an echo of the bride's quest in the Song of Solomon 3:1-4 (47-56).

62. So de la Potterie, "Genèse," 34-35; Byrne, "Beloved Disciple," 84; Dauer, *Johannes und Lukas*, 257, 259.

alive with the marks of his ordeal in hands and side ensures secure identification; they rejoice. The double greeting of peace recalls the peace given in 14:27. The author then has Jesus use the sending language of the central structure to apply it, in turn, to them: "As my Father has sent me, so I send you" (20:21). This recalls 17:18 and the consistent way in which the author applies the pattern of the Son's commission to the disciples.

Jesus then gives the Spirit, thus fulfilling the promise made in the last discourses where the Spirit is described as the Paraclete and Spirit of Truth, and echoing the breathing of the Spirit at creation (Gen 2:7). It also fulfils the reader's expectation from texts like 7:39 which indicated the gift of the Spirit would come after Jesus was glorified. It connects, too, with 3:34 where Jesus' own authorisation is associated with his full endowment with the Spirit (symbolised already in the descent of the dove at his baptism, 1:32–33). Here Jesus also fulfils the divine message to the Baptist that the one on whom the Spirit descends and remains would baptise with the Spirit (1:33), so that the two references function as an *inclusio*. The authorisation relates to the sending. It relates also to the releasing and withholding of sins (20:23), a link which echoes 1:29–34.

The episode with Thomas focusses primarily on the nature of faith and reaches its climax as a statement about faith in the conclusion: true faith is not dependent primarily upon literally having seen, even though that was Thomas's experience and the experience of those who first passed on the witness of the Gospel. The theme of faith and its basis continues in the two verses that follow. They should be taken therefore closely with what precedes. The readers do not have Thomas's advantage and there are many signs which Jesus did, which are not recorded in this Gospel, but what is written here is with the intention that "you may believe that Jesus is the Christ the Son of God and that believing you may have life in his name" (20:30–31).

We have passed over Thomas's acclamation, "My Lord and my God" (ὁ κύριός μου καὶ ὁ θεός μου in 20:28), because it, too, should be seen within the connection between the Thomas episode and what follows. Sometimes such heights are supposed to have been reached in Thomas's words that the confession sought in 20:31 would represent a sudden anticlimax. This is surely not the case. "My Lord and my God" will not have been sensed as being any more or less adequate than "Jesus is the Christ, the Son of God." Both belong within the framework of the central structure and in various ways give expression to its key affirmation that Jesus is the Son who has come from the Father to make him known. In this sense he bears the designation θεός already in the prologue, within which it forms an *inclusio* and from which it forms one here with 20:28. "Christ, the Son of God" (20:31), the language of royal messianism which so dominates the passion narrative, means also nothing other than that Jesus is the one who has come into the world to bear witness to the truth.

The final chapter points in particular to the nature of the Christian community after Easter. There are symbolic references to universal mission in the fish catch (21:11), to the unity of believers in the untorn net (21:11), and to the Eucharist in the meal shared on the lakeside (21:13). They occur within a narrative which is also emphasising Jesus' resurrection (21:14) and his appearing (21:1; "the third time," 21:14). The second half of the chapter regulates the community's leadership and relates it to the leadership of the wider church. Jesus commissions Peter with pastoral leadership and foretells his death. He also indicates to Peter the longevity of the beloved disciple, doubtless indicative also of his enduring influence. The author notes that this had led some to think the beloved disciple would not die before the parousia, but had obviously been proved wrong by events. He then claims the enduring influence of the disciple as witness, "the one having written these things," and does so in much the same way as he appeals to the eyewitness in 19:35. The Gospel ends with a note indicating the necessarily selective nature of what is presented because of the abundance of what is available. Of course the very selection and its ordering are in themselves important statements about the author's Christology, and this review has sought to bring them out.

John 18–21 Conclusions

Reviewing the passion narratives we note first the extensive use of royal messianic imagery in the trial and crucifixion scenes and the way it is thoroughly integrated within the central structure of the author's Christology. This is the point of the irony throughout, in Pilate's questioning, the mockery, the two presentations of Jesus as king, the offer of Barabbas, the contrast with Caesar, and especially the supreme irony of the superscription. The royal messianic imagery of the passion narrative is not presented as depicting an enthronement of Jesus at his trial or in his crucifixion nor as foreshadowing a heavenly enthronement of Jesus as king on his return to the Father. That he is already. The language usually associated with Jesus' return to the Father—exaltation, glorification, ascent, and Son of Man—is absent, and conversely, the royal messianic language is nowhere used to describe Jesus' return to the Father. The only use of exaltation language is in the literal sense of lifting up as a reference back to the prediction of the manner of Jesus' death (18:32; cf. 12:33).

Messianic language also appears in the confession, "the Christ, the Son of God," in 20:31. Both this confession and that of Thomas, "my Lord and my God," are to be understood as different ways of giving expression to the same underlying faith, namely that expressed in the central structure of the author's Christology.

Sometimes that central structure surfaces directly in the passion narrative, especially where Jesus speaks of who he is. Thus he translates kingship into a statement about coming into this world to bear witness to the truth (18:36–37). Similarly at the end he views his task as "finished" (19:30). John 18:11 had already expressly included his suffering as part of that commission. The central structure lies also behind Pilate's question: "Where are you from?" (19:9) and the Jews' accusation that he made himself Son of God (19:7), recalling the discussion in 5:17–23; 10:31–39.

At a number of points exegesis is divided or uncertain. "Behold the man" in 19:5 we saw primarily as mockery of both Jesus and the Jews that their king looked such a pathetic figure and not as symbolic of Jesus as Son of Man or representative man. We understood "Pilate sat" intransitively and not as reference to Jesus' being made to sit down. If at all, the case for seeing the action as expressing mock enthronement is stronger than suggestions that Jesus is being made judge. "Giving up the spirit" (19:30) we saw as referring to Jesus' death not the gift of the Spirit. Jesus' interpretation of Passover in 19:37 we held to be inconclusive and, on balance, unlikely. We were similarly uncertain about the reference of "blood and water" in 19:34, though these probably serve to emphasise either Jesus' real death or his real humanity. The arrest of Jesus raised again the question of what meaning "I am" conveys in the author's Christology. The numinosity seems best understood as relating to the person of Jesus as revealer rather than to an alleged pronouncement of the divine name. A similar fear overcomes Pilate when he hears the title "Son of God" in relation to Jesus (19:7).

A number of passages related to the benefits of Jesus' death and return to the Father. These included Jesus' words to Mary in which the familiar ascension language reappears (20:17). These are most naturally understood to refer to an event about to occur as a result of which God would bring blessing to the disciples. The sending of the disciples for mission (following the model of the central structure) and the gift of the Spirit (20:21–22) reflect promises made in the last discourses. Mission is also symbolically represented in the fish catch in ch. 21. The benefit of the Son's return is also implied in the note that the disciples would come to understand how Scripture foretold the resurrection (20:9).

It is not surprising that the concluding chapters, especially those depicting the appearances, should contain much that pertains to the life of the post-Easter community and the Johannine community in particular. These include the benefits mentioned in the previous paragraph. We also note the symbolism of unity, the untorn net (21:11), the Eucharist (21:13), and Peter's pastoral leadership (21:15–17). The author also includes more particular references relevant to the Gospel and the first readers. They assure the reader of the authority and integrity of the material in the Gospel and include the beloved disciple's commission to care for Jesus' mother (19:25–28), his longevity, and his function as guarantor and witness, having been the beloved disciple and the one who leant on Jesus' breast (21:20–24). The reader is assured of the full adequacy of faith on the basis of the reporting of the Gospel alone (20:29–31). This represents the author's selection from a vast quantity of available material (21:25).

3   The Structure: An Outline

What has emerged from the review and the earlier investigations of the "central structure" may be set out as follows:

> The Father
> sends and authorises the Son,
> who knows the Father,
> comes from the Father,
> makes the Father known,
> brings light and life and truth,
> completes his Father's work,
> returns to the Father,
> exalted, glorified, ascended,
> sends the disciples
> and sends the Spirit
> to enable greater understanding,
> to equip for mission,
> and to build up the community of faith.

We shall use this structure to integrate the findings of chs. 1 and 2. In doing so, we are concerned to list the salient features and, where interpretation of particular motifs has demanded consideration of their use in a number of passages, to give an overall assessment of their likely meaning. These findings will then form the basis for the systematic consideration of issues of Johannine Christology in Part Two. The earlier clauses of the statement have to a large degree already been the subject of attention in ch. 1 above. Their treatment below will be brief. Later clauses will demand fuller consideration.

THE STRUCTURE OF JOHANNINE CHRISTOLOGY

"The Father..."

The Son was in the beginning with God (1:1–2; 17:5), in the bosom of the Father (1:18), θεός (1:18), only Son of the Father (1:14; 3:16, 18), sharing the Father's glory and his love before the foundation of the world (17:5, 24), mediator of creation (1:3, 10), before John the Baptist (1:15, 30), before Abraham (8:58), and seen in his pre-existent glory by Isaiah (12:41).

The terms "Father" for God and "Son" for Jesus are most common throughout the Gospel, particularly in describing the relationship of the two and the Son's revelatory task. While pre-existence is presupposed throughout when the author speaks of the Son's coming and being sent, the direct references are the few noted above and are found especially in the prologue in association with motifs not recurring later in the Gospel.

"...sends and authorises the Son..."

The references to the Father sending the Son are extensive and have been listed above. John 3:16 also speaks of the Father giving the Son. Because sending entails authorisation we include here other authorisation motifs. The Father has given all into the Son's hands (3:35; 13:3), given him authority over all flesh (17:2), given him authority to judge and to give life (5:22), given him his name (17:11–12), given him command (10:18; 12:49–50; 15:10), given him instruction (8:28), and given him a task to complete (4:34; 5:36; 17:4; 18:11; 19:30). Accordingly the Son does not act of his own accord (5:30; 7:17; 8:28; 14:10).

"...who knows the Father..."

This is primarily related to the Son's having been with the Father. Jesus refers to what he has seen and heard (3:32; 6:46; 8:26, 38, 40; 15:15). No one has seen God, but the Son has (1:18; 5:37; 6:46). This relates also to his having been given instruction in the context of authorisation and to his receiving the Father's name and words (see above).

This follows the model of the revealer-envoy, where the sent one comes from, reports, and acts for the sender. This is also the framework within which the unique relationship of Father and Son is usually expounded (so mostly in 10:32–38 and 14:7–11). Jesus is one with the Father and to have seen him is to have seen the Father because he does the works the Father has given him to do. John 5:17–20 is similar in emphasising unity expressed through the Son's obedience to the Father, but it departs from the revelation envoy model

The Structure: An Outline

by speaking of the Father showing the Son in the present what he is doing and thereby giving him a pattern to follow (an apprentice model). The Son's knowing the Father is also implied in the concept of mutual indwelling (10:38; 14:10, 20) and is stated explicitly as mutual knowledge in 10:15 (cf. also 17:25).

". . .comes from the Father. . ."

The references are extensive and have been gathered above. The Son comes from the Father, from God, from above, and from heaven into the world. Coming thence is more than explanation of change of place; it implies authority and superiority in contrast to those who are of the earth. It relates closely to the elements of the statement we have already dealt with to this point. The coming is often linked with the going, as we shall see below. Failure to perceive the one is the same as failure to perceive the other. In association with the manna imagery the author also speaks of the descending of Jesus from heaven as bread, a motif used of Jesus elsewhere only in 3:13, which speaks of descent and ascent of Jesus as Son of Man. The other distinctive formulation for the Son's coming as revealer is in the prologue: "The word became flesh and tented among us and we beheld his glory" (1:14). The author is particularly fond of irony in relation to Jesus' origin and frequently portrays unknowing questioners discussing Jesus' origin, while the reader knows all along the true answer (1:46, 48; 2:9; 3:2, 8; 4:11; 6:5, 41–42; 7:27, 40–52; 9:16, 29, 33; 19:9). Sometimes both the whence and the whither questions occur together in this way (8:14; cf. 3:8).

". . .makes the Father known. . ."

The extensive and varied formulations by which this is expressed and the references are listed in ch. 1 above. This is the climactic statement of the prologue (1:18) and appears throughout the Gospel as Jesus is portrayed as speaking, telling, witnessing to, or making known what he has seen and heard, been commanded, told, and instructed. Accordingly, to have seen the Son is to have seen the Father, for he has made him known (1:18; 14:7–11). Response to Jesus is thus response to the Father. This is the revelation model and is primarily expounded within the framework of the pattern of the revealer-envoy. Closely associated with it are the two elements which follow.

". . .brings light and life and truth. . ."

This is a selection of the most important images and within the statement they also represent many others which occur within the Gospel. Jesus has come as light into the world (1:4–5, 7–9; 3:19–21; 8:12; 9:5; 11:9–10; 12:35–36, 46). Light and life are sometimes linked (1:4; 8:12). Jesus comes as life into the world. References to people receiving "eternal life" through faith in the Son are common throughout the Gospel and this corresponds to the Gospel's aim (20:31). Eternal life or life (they mean the same as 5:39–40 show) is a gift given by the Son during his ministry. Sometimes it is spoken of as a future gift available after Jesus' death and return (3:15; cf. 6:27, 51c–58). But mostly it represents what Jesus brings in his person. He offers living water (4:10) and he is also the bread of life, the light of life, the resurrection and the life, the way, the truth, and the life. These are, above all, images traditionally associated with Torah. They are now transferred to Jesus. 17:3 explains that this life is to know God and Jesus Christ whom he sent. 6:63 identifies Jesus' words as spirit and life, and Peter's confession is introduced with the affirmation that Jesus has the words of eternal life (6:68). The link between the gift of life and the giver as life is evident in 5:26–27 where the Father has granted the Son to have life in himself, as he has life in himself, and given him authority to bring judgment (to death or life). Life is a gift brought by and also inherent in the Son and derived from the Father, and to offer this life is the purpose of the Son's coming (10:10).

The offer of life, when refused, brings judgment. The Son did not come to judge the world (3:17–21; 5:45; 8:15; 12:47), yet his very coming brought judgment, so that sometimes in apparent contradiction Jesus can affirm that it is for judgment that he has come (9:39). The word he has spoken (12:47), and even the word bearing witness to him (5:46), effectively condemns those who refuse its truth (3:18–21, 36). Accordingly the final rejection of Jesus on the cross becomes the final act of judgment for the world. It thinks it judges Jesus; but in the cross God judges it and its ruler (16:11; 12:31; cf. 16:33), manifests its sin as rejection of the Son (16:9) and demonstrates Jesus' righteousness, because his return to the Father through death has vindicated him (16:10). The Son's offer brings therefore the judgment of life or death now to people (5:21–27), as well as judgment in the future (5:28–29).

Truth (and grace) also came through the Son (1:14, 17). Jesus has come to bear witness to the truth (18:37) and is the truth (14:6). This is closer to the revelation imagery, but has the same basic structure as the statements about light and life. These are all ways of expressing what the Son brings by his very presence. They present his salvific significance and do so within the framework of the revealer-envoy pattern.

The "I am" statements with a simple predicate (without a qualifier such as "true" or "good") belong here. In each case they are to be understood

The Structure: An Outline

within the framework of the revealer-envoy Christology and frequently this is quite explicit (e.g., 6:35; cf. 6:36–51b; 8:12; cf. 8:13–19; and 14:6; cf. 14:7–11). There are also parallels for the use of "I am" in this way by envoy and emissary figures outside the Gospel which strengthen the possibility that this is its context here. Statements with qualifiers are in part polemical, in contrast to claims made of Torah, but also represent Jesus as the source of life, almost in a popularly Platonic sense,[1] even though more, it seems, from the perspective of the time after Jesus' death and return to the Father. The simple "I am" of 8:24, 28 and 13:19 seems also best understood as a statement that Jesus is the one he claims to be: the one sent from God. Of the other absolute uses, John 6:20—like its Markan parallel—has Jesus simply identify that it is he not a ghost. In the account of the arrest, Jesus uses the words "I am (he)" (18:5, 6, 8) to identify himself as the one for whom they are looking in much the same way as the former blind man also owns up to his identity in 9:9 by saying, "I am (he)." This is in no way to diminish the impact on the bystanders; but it explains "I am" as the self-identification which triggered it. In 4:26 Jesus identifies himself with the Messiah, just as, by contrast, John the Baptist had rejected such an identity for himself with the words "I am not" in 1:21. Finally, John 8:58 means the equivalent of "I was and have been in existence since before Abraham."

None of the "I am" sayings demands the explanation that Jesus is pronouncing the divine name, and such an interpretation reads most unnaturally in contexts where it is supposed to occur. On the other hand, some influence from Isa 43:10 must not be ruled out in the sense that Jesus speaks in the same manner as Yahweh does when identifying himself as the one who will save Israel.[2] This manner of self-claim is being used by analogy. It was also used by analogy negatively of demiurges in gnostic literature, but not as a statement of the divine name itself; it also occurs there frequently in a positive sense with predicates.[3] This usage is consistent with the revealer-envoy background noted above.

Here, too, belong the messianic statements of the Gospel, to which we return in 6.2.5 below. Jesus is presented as the Messiah (1:41, 45–49; 4:29; 7:27; 9:22; 11:27; 12:13–15; 20:31) and this theme is developed with powerful irony in the passion narrative. When we look for clues about how this messiahship is understood, we find that Jesus' messiahship is consistently expounded

---

1. So David W. Wead, *The Literary Devices in John's Gospel* (Basel: Reinhardt, 1970), 76–77.
2. So Barrett, "Theocentric," 13; Barrett, "Symbolism," 69–70; Barrett, *John*, 342; Lindars, *Gospel of John*, 320–21.
3. So George W. MacRae, "The Ego Proclamations in Gnostic Sources," in *The Trial of Jesus. In Honour of C. F. D. Moule*, ed. E. Bammel, SBT 2.13 (London: SCM, 1970), 129, 132–34.

in terms of his being the Son sent from the Father and come to make him known. Sometimes there is a movement from messianic titles to Son of Man (e.g., 1:49–51; 12:34), as Martyn has shown especially in relation to ch. 9,[4] but this is not corrective supplementation. Rather it reflects the way the author uses Son of Man tradition in relation to Jesus' death and return to the Father. Thus the author employs confessional messianic statements that Jesus is the Christ and the Son of God, but integrates them primarily within his overall Christology of Jesus as the Son of the Father whose coming was the event of revelation.

"…completes his Father's work…"

The words "It is finished" (19:30) issue from Jesus on the cross. He had expressed himself similarly in 17:4; and in 4:34 Jesus describes his task as completing the work he had been given to do. I have listed references above which describe how the Son does on earth what he has been commanded to do by the Father, doing the works of the Father, and so not acting on his own authority. Accordingly it may also be said that the Father, himself, is doing the works in the Son (14:10).

What is the work and what are the works? The work refers to the commission to be the revealer-envoy and to return to the Father. The work of the revealer-envoy is to make the Father known, and the goal of his ministry is that people may come to believe that this is God's envoy, at least on the basis of his deeds, his works, even if not on the basis of his direct claims (5:36; 10:37; 14:11).

The works refer to Jesus' deeds. They include in particular Jesus' miracles. The miracle at the wedding feast and the miracle of the raising of Lazarus are both said to manifest Jesus' glory and, while this word does not appear in other miracle stories in John, the same basic idea is present. The miracles manifest, for eyes that can see, who Jesus is, namely the one sent from the Father (so explicitly as Jesus' purpose for the miracle, 11:42; cf. also 5:36). Therefore, the author describes them as signs. Failure to read them as signs reflects an inadequate faith which sees, like Nicodemus, only at the earthly level.

At this point I want also to mention those texts scattered throughout the Gospel which, with varying degree of probability or uncertainty, may refer to Jesus' death as vicarious or cultic sacrifice. They are 1:29; 6:51c; 10:11, 15; 11:51–53 (cf. 18:14); and 15:13. Others sometimes linked with such an interpre-

---

4. So Martyn, *History and Theology*, 126–28.

tation are 3:14, 16; 12:27; 17:19; 18:11. Accordingly some would include this act of atonement as a major part of Jesus' work which he had to complete, and so find it also alluded to in 19:30 ("it is finished") and in 17:4 ("I have finished the work you have given me to do"). The context of 17:4 suggests that the work of revelation is primarily in view, not the work of atonement, and the association of the two texts makes it therefore likely for 19:30. Similarly in 10:17 Jesus says that his Father loves him because he lays down his life that he might take it up again. This suggests the task lies in passing through death and returning to the Father rather than in an act of atonement. Nevertheless the presence of the texts which appear to attribute soteriological significance to Jesus' death would necessarily mean that this was an element in the task to be completed. We discuss the extent to which this is so in 5.2 below. The primary focus of the Son's work is as the previous two sections have indicated: to make the Father known and so to bring life to the world (17:3).

"...returns to the Father..."

Often Jesus' going is mentioned in the context of coming, as in the summary statement of 13:3 ("knowing that the Father had given all things into his hands and that he had come from God and was going to God"; cf. also 13:1). The Son knows whence he came and where he is going (8:14). Jesus tells his disciples: "I have come from the Father and have come into the world; again I am leaving the world and going to the Father" (16:28). In the last discourses in particular and in the final prayer Jesus speaks of his going to the Father (14:12, 28; 16:7; 17:11, 13).

As with the theme of Jesus' origin, so also with that of his destination, the author makes full use of irony. In particular the saying 7:34 ("where I am going you cannot come; you shall seek me and not find me") is used in this way with the Jews (7:34, 36; 8:21–22). We saw that in the last discourses a variant of the same saying becomes the subject of reflection at a number of points from 13:33 onwards, and in particular in chs. 14 and 16. By contrast with the use of the saying in relation to the Jews, Jesus promises Peter and the disciples that where he goes they will come later. 14:2–3 uses the image of heavenly dwellings. In 17:24 Jesus prays that his disciples may come to be where he is and see the heavenly glory he shares with the Father. The same thought also lies behind 12:26, "If anyone serves me, let him follow me, and where I am, there also will my servant be." This is true, notwithstanding the promise that the Son and Father will also take up their abode in the disciples after Easter (14:20–23). They refer to two different modes of being.

The author associates other benefits with the return of the Son to the

Father, benefits which result from it, and we shall consider these below. The return completes the Son's movement undertaken in fulfilling the task of revelation on which he was sent. But our survey of the Gospel also demonstrated that this is of much greater significance than the completion of a cycle. Throughout the Gospel some significant patterns and motifs occurred which interpreted the significance of this event and to these we turn in the remaining elements of our summary.

"...exalted, glorified, ascended..."

Under this heading I want also to gather associated motifs.

The first is "the hour," sometimes "the time" or referred to simply as "now." These terms refer throughout the Gospel to the moment of Jesus' death and return to the Father, and to events associated with it. The salient texts are:

οὔπω ἥκει ἡ ὥρα μου.
My hour has not yet come. (2:4)
   (Jesus, speaking to his mother at the wedding feast)

ὁ καιρὸς ὁ ἐμὸς οὔπω πάρεστιν.
My time is not yet here. (7:6)
ὁ ἐμὸς καιρὸς οὔπω πεπλήρωται.
My time is not yet fulfilled. (7:8)
   (Jesus, speaking to his brothers, referring to his going up to
   Jerusalem and possibly indirectly to his ascent to the Father)

οὔπω ἐληλύθει ἡ ὥρα αὐτοῦ.
His hour had not yet come. (7:30 and 8:20)
   (The author, telling us why the Jews were unable to arrest Jesus)

ἐλήλυθεν ἡ ὥρα ἵνα δοξασθῇ ὁ υἱὸς τοῦ ἀνθρώπου.
The hour has come for the Son of Man to be glorified. (12:23)
   (Jesus in Jerusalem and in response to the approach of the Greeks)

Νῦν ἡ ψυχή μου τετάρακται, καὶ τί εἴπω;
πάτερ, σῶσόν με ἐκ τῆς ὥρας ταύτης;
ἀλλὰ διὰ τοῦτο ἦλθον εἰς τὴν ὥραν ταύτην.
πάτερ, δόξασόν σου τὸ ὄνομα.
Now is my soul troubled. And what shall I say?
Father, save me from this hour?

The Structure: An Outline

But for this I came to this hour.
Father, glorify your name! (12:27–28)
    (Jesus in the same setting, facing the prospect of death)

νῦν κρίσις ἐστὶν τοῦ κόσμου τούτου,
νῦν ὁ ἄρχων τοῦ κόσμου τούτου ἐκβληθήσεται ἔξω·
κἀγὼ ἐὰν ὑψωθῶ ἐκ τῆς γῆς, πάντας ἑλκύσω πρὸς ἐμαυτόν.
Now is the judgment of this world,
now shall the ruler of this world be cast out;
and I, if I am lifted up from the earth, will draw all people to myself. (12:31–32)
    (Jesus in the same setting. The author adds: "he said this to indicate by what kind of death he would die," 12:33).

εἰδὼς ὁ Ἰησοῦς ὅτι ἦλθεν αὐτοῦ ἡ ὥρα
ἵνα μεταβῇ ἐκ τοῦ κόσμου τούτου πρὸς τὸν πατέρα.
Jesus, knowing that the hour had come
for him to pass out of this world to the Father. (13:1)
    (The author, introducing the scene of the foot washing and the farewell discourses)

νῦν ἐδοξάσθη ὁ υἱὸς τοῦ ἀνθρώπου καὶ ὁ θεὸς ἐδοξάσθη ἐν αὐτῷ·
[εἰ ὁ θεὸς ἐδοξάσθη ἐν αὐτῷ], καὶ ὁ θεὸς δοξάσει αὐτὸν ἐν αὐτῷ,
καὶ εὐθὺς δοξάσει αὐτόν.
Now is the Son of Man glorified and God is glorified in him.
[If God is glorified in him,] God will glorify him in himself
and will glorify him immediately. (13:31–32)
    (Jesus at the beginning of the farewell discourses)

νῦν δὲ ὑπάγω πρὸς τὸν πέμψαντά με.
Now I am going to him who sent me. (16:5)
    (within the second discourse; this sense of time is present throughout especially ch. 14 and ch. 16)

πάτερ, ἐλήλυθεν ἡ ὥρα· δόξασόν σου τὸν υἱόν, ἵνα ὁ υἱὸς δοξάσῃ σέ.
Father, the hour has come; glorify your Son, that your Son may glorify you. (17:1)
καὶ νῦν δόξασόν με σύ, πάτερ, παρὰ σεαυτῷ τῇ δόξῃ
ᾗ εἶχον πρὸ τοῦ τὸν κόσμον εἶναι παρὰ σοί.
And now glorify me, Father, in yourself with the glory

which I had when I was with you before the foundation of the world. (17:5)

νῦν δὲ πρὸς σὲ ἔρχομαι.
But now I am coming to you. (17:13)
   (Jesus, in his final prayer)

There is a remarkable consistency in usage here of the "hour," "time" concept. I note in particular the presence of the following motifs in association with it:

Son of Man
glorification
lifting up/exalted
ascension
judgment
going to the Father

The second motif, "something greater," consists more of a structure of thought, whereby the present of the speaker is compared with something greater to come, and this something greater is associated with Jesus' death and return to the Father.

ὅτι εἶπόν σοι ὅτι εἶδόν σε ὑποκάτω τῆς συκῆς, πιστεύεις;
μείζω τούτων ὄψῃ.
καὶ λέγει αὐτῷ· ἀμὴν ἀμὴν λέγω ὑμῖν, ὄψεσθε τὸν οὐρανὸν ἀνεῳγότα
καὶ τοὺς ἀγγέλους τοῦ θεοῦ ἀναβαίνοντας
καὶ καταβαίνοντας ἐπὶ τὸν υἱὸν τοῦ ἀνθρώπου.
Because I said to you (sg), "I saw you under the fig tree," do you believe? You shall see greater things than these.
And he said to him,
"Truly, truly, I tell you (pl), you shall see the heaven opened
and the angels of God ascending
and descending upon the Son of Man. (1:50–51)
   (Jesus, responding to Nathanael's confession of Jesus as Son of God
   and king of Israel)

εἰ τὰ ἐπίγεια εἶπον ὑμῖν καὶ οὐ πιστεύετε,
πῶς ἐὰν εἴπω ὑμῖν τὰ ἐπουράνια πιστεύσετε;
καὶ οὐδεὶς ἀναβέβηκεν εἰς τὸν οὐρανὸν
εἰ μὴ ὁ ἐκ τοῦ οὐρανοῦ καταβάς, ὁ υἱὸς τοῦ ἀνθρώπου.

The Structure: An Outline

Καὶ καθὼς Μωϋσῆς ὕψωσεν τὸν ὄφιν ἐν τῇ ἐρήμῳ,
οὕτως ὑψωθῆναι δεῖ τὸν υἱὸν τοῦ ἀνθρώπου,
ἵνα πᾶς ὁ πιστεύων ἐν αὐτῷ ἔχῃ ζωὴν αἰώνιον.
If I told you earthly things and you do not believe,
how will you believe if I tell you heavenly things?
And no one has ascended into heaven
except he who descended from heaven, the Son of Man.
And as Moses lifted up the serpent in the wilderness,
even so the Son of Man must be lifted up,
so that all who believe might have eternal life in him. (3:12–15)
    (Jesus, having faced Nicodemus with his word of revelation on earth)

τοῦτο ὑμᾶς σκανδαλίζει; ἐὰν οὖν θεωρῆτε τὸν υἱὸν τοῦ ἀνθρώπου
ἀναβαίνοντα ὅπου ἦν τὸ πρότερον;
Does this offend you? What if you were to see the Son of Man
ascending where he was before? (6:61b–62)
    (Jesus, responding to the disciples' difficulty with his claim to have
    descended and become a human being)

Ἀμὴν ἀμὴν λέγω ὑμῖν, ὁ πιστεύων εἰς ἐμὲ τὰ ἔργα ἃ ἐγὼ ποιῶ κἀκεῖνος
ποιήσει καὶ μείζονα τούτων ποιήσει, ὅτι ἐγὼ πρὸς τὸν πατέρα
πορεύομαι·
καὶ ὅ τι ἂν αἰτήσητε ἐν τῷ ὀνόματί μου τοῦτο ποιήσω, ἵνα δοξασθῇ ὁ
πατὴρ ἐν τῷ υἱῷ.
Truly, truly, I say to you, he who believes in me, the works which I do he
also shall do
and greater works than these shall he do because I go to the Father.
And whatever you ask in my name I shall do it, that the Father may be
glorified in the Son. (14:12–13)
    (Jesus, speaking during the last discourse about the disciples' future
    work and about the promise of the Paraclete)

ἠκούσατε ὅτι ἐγὼ εἶπον ὑμῖν· ὑπάγω καὶ ἔρχομαι πρὸς ὑμᾶς.
εἰ ἠγαπᾶτέ με ἐχάρητε ἂν ὅτι πορεύομαι πρὸς τὸν πατέρα,
ὅτι ὁ πατὴρ μείζων μού ἐστιν.
You have heard that I said to you, "I go away and I am coming to you."
If you loved me you would rejoice that I go to the Father,
because the Father is greater than me. (14:28)
    (Jesus, at the conclusion of the discourse in ch. 14, having assured the
    disciples of the gift of the Spirit)

καὶ μείζονα τούτων δείξει αὐτῷ ἔργα, ἵνα ὑμεῖς θαυμάζητε.
Greater works than these he will show him, so that you may marvel. (5:20b)
>(possibly alluding to Jesus' exercise of judgment as Son of Man [5:27!] in the future)

These passages bear similarity with those concerning the "hour." Both refer to the event associated with Jesus' death and return to the Father. These promise in different ways that this event will bring something greater for the disciples. There is also a striking similarity in many of the motifs associated with both sets of passages. In particular the following should be noted:

Son of Man
ascent (and descent; language present also in 1:51 but about angels)
lifting up/exalted
going to the Father

In turning to the motifs "exalted, glorified, and ascended," I note that these have already appeared in the texts considered and within them form a cluster of motifs together with the title Son of Man. The following are passages not cited thus far (see already 3:12–15, above; cf. also 1:50–51; 6:62) in which these motifs appear.

ὅταν ὑψώσητε τὸν υἱὸν τοῦ ἀνθρώπου, τότε γνώσεσθε ὅτι ἐγώ εἰμι, καὶ ἀπ' ἐμαυτοῦ ποιῶ οὐδέν, ἀλλὰ καθὼς ἐδίδαξέν με ὁ πατὴρ ταῦτα λαλῶ.
When you have lifted up the Son of Man, then you shall know that I am the one and I do nothing of myself, but as the Father taught me, so I speak. (8:28)
>(Jesus, addressing the Jews)

πῶς λέγεις σὺ ὅτι δεῖ ὑψωθῆναι τὸν υἱὸν τοῦ ἀνθρώπου;
How can you say that the Son of Man must be lifted up? (12:34)
>(The Jews, perturbed by Jesus' prediction of being lifted up because it does not fit their messianic expectation)

οὔπω γὰρ ἦν πνεῦμα, ὅτι Ἰησοῦς οὐδέπω ἐδοξάσθη.
For the Spirit was not yet (present), because Jesus was not yet glorified. (7:39)
>(The author, noting that Jesus' promise in 7:38 of rivers of water from within could apply only after Easter)

The Structure: An Outline

αὕτη ἡ ἀσθένεια οὐκ ἔστιν πρὸς θάνατον ἀλλ' ὑπὲρ τῆς δόξης τοῦ θεοῦ,
ἵνα δοξασθῇ ὁ υἱὸς τοῦ θεοῦ δι' αὐτῆς.
This sickness is not to death but for the glory of God,
so that the Son of God might be glorified through it. (11:4)
> (This refers initially to the glory manifest in the raising of Lazarus but also to the ultimate glorification through Jesus' death and return to the Father, the event to which the Lazarus miracle leads in John's account. John 11:40 refers to "seeing the glory of God" in the same way.)

ταῦτα οὐκ ἔγνωσαν αὐτοῦ οἱ μαθηταὶ τὸ πρῶτον,
ἀλλ' ὅτε ἐδοξάσθη Ἰησοῦς τότε ἐμνήσθησαν ὅτι ταῦτα ἦν ἐπ' αὐτῷ γεγραμμένα
καὶ ταῦτα ἐποίησαν αὐτῷ.
His disciples did not understand these things at first,
but when Jesus was glorified, then they remembered that these things were written concerning him
and that they did these things to him. (12:16)
> (The author's comment about messianic fulfilment of Scripture and messianic implications of the behaviour of the crowd at Jesus' entry into Jerusalem)

πάτερ, δόξασόν σου τὸ ὄνομα. ἦλθεν οὖν φωνὴ ἐκ τοῦ οὐρανοῦ·
καὶ ἐδόξασα καὶ πάλιν δοξάσω.
"Father, glorify your name." A voice came from heaven:
"I have glorified it and will glorify it again." (12:28)
> (Jesus' prayer concerning his hour and God's response)

The motif "glorify" also occurs in 8:54 (Jesus does not glorify, seek honour for, himself, the Father does that; similarly using the word "glory": 5:41, 44; 7:18; 8:50; 12:43; 15:8 (the Father is glorified through the disciples' bearing fruit); 16:14 (the Paraclete will glorify Jesus); 17:4 (Jesus has glorified God on earth); and 17:10 (Jesus has been glorified among his disciples). "Glory" is also used to describe the revelation Jesus brought (1:14; 2:11; 11:4, 40; cf. 12:43). John 12:41 refers to Jesus' pre-existent glory (cf. 17:5, 24).

The only other reference to ascent outside the passages already quoted (see 3:13; 6:62 above; and cf. 7:9) is:

μή μου ἅπτου, οὔπω γὰρ ἀναβέβηκα πρὸς τὸν πατέρα·

THE STRUCTURE OF JOHANNINE CHRISTOLOGY

> πορεύου δὲ πρὸς τοὺς ἀδελφούς μου καὶ εἰπὲ αὐτοῖς·
> ἀναβαίνω πρὸς τὸν πατέρα μου καὶ πατέρα ὑμῶν
> καὶ θεόν μου καὶ θεὸν ὑμῶν.
> Do not hold onto me, for I have not yet ascended to the Father;
> but go to my brothers and tell them,
> "I am ascending to my Father and your Father,
> to my God and your God." (20:17)
> (The risen Jesus, addressing Mary Magdalene)

The passages, taken all together, show how "hour," the promise of greater things, exaltation, glorification, ascent (descent), and the title "Son of Man" form a distinctive semantic cluster in the author's language and he uses them to describe Jesus' death and return to the Father. Some of the texts are the author's footnotes, so that we may be confident in speaking of the author's particular interest in using this language in this way. The only motif in this cluster not yet considered is the title Son of Man. Outside the texts cited above it occurs in 5:27 (where the author speaks of Jesus' role in judgment), in 9:35 (also linked with Jesus in a judging role, cf. 9:39), and in ch. 6. Here we saw it is used of future nourishment (6:27), in particular of the Eucharist (6:53). The motif of judgment, already appearing in 12:31, may also belong to the semantic cluster. The ch. 6 sayings are consistent with the use of Son of Man in most of the texts cited above to refer not primarily to Jesus' ministry, but to the greater event and what flows from it.

In 4.3 below we shall examine a number of these motifs in greater detail. In what follows we shall examine the result of Jesus' death and return. Already a number of elements in this have appeared in the texts cited, illustrating that the motif of Jesus' return, the Son of Man cluster, and the fruits of the event should be considered together.

"...sends the disciples..."

The commissioning of the disciples occurs when the risen Jesus appears to them on the evening of the resurrection day and declares: "As my Father has sent me, so I send you" (20:21). A similar analogy between the Son's own sending and that of the disciples is expressed in 17:18. The same parallel structure lies behind 3:3–11, where there is a shift from Jesus the teacher come from God to a generalised discussion of all who are born of the Spirit and so qualified to be teachers and to bear witness. The wind metaphor in 3:8 uses language elsewhere associated with the Son: people hear his voice, but no one knows where he comes from or where he is going; "so is everyone who is born of the Spirit." The distinction lies

The Structure: An Outline

within the use of the birth metaphor in 3:3, 5. Whereas Jesus is the only Son who has come from above (3:31; cf. 3:16, 18), the disciples are born (3:3, 5), given the authority to become children of God (1:12–13). They are from above, but not in the same sense. Nevertheless ch. 3 shows how the author interprets the sending of the disciples within the framework provided by the central structure.[5]

Accordingly they are not of this world and will face the same hatred and rejection the Son has faced (15:19; 17:14, 16). They, too, have been authorised (20:21, 23). Their authorisation is associated with the giving of the Spirit (20:22; 3:5) and it is with the Spirit's authority they will bring to the world the evidence concerning Jesus (esp. 16:8–11). They, too, have been loved by the Father (17:23, 26), been given the Father's glory (17:22), his name (17:6, 26; cf. 17:11–12), his words (17:8, 14), and his command (15:10). In their own way, they know the Son as the Son knows the Father and therefore also know the Father (14:7–11; 17:3, 25). They, too, bear witness (15:27). They, too, manifest oneness to the world that the world may know the Son by knowing them (17:20–23; cf. 13:34–35). They, too, must be willing to follow their master to death (12:25; cf. 13:36; 21:18–19) and know the reward that their path will finally lead to his heavenly presence (12:26; 17:24). We explore further the purpose of their sending under "mission" below.

". . .and sends the Spirit. . ."

Jesus gives the Spirit directly after commissioning of the disciples: "Saying this, he breathed on them and said to them: 'Receive the Holy Spirit; whosoever sins you release they are released, and whoever you retain they are retained'" (20:22–23). The authority to release or retain sins is referred to here only; the giving of the Spirit, on the other hand, has been prepared for at a number of points in the Gospel. Already 1:33 designates Jesus the one who will baptise in the Spirit and 3:3–8 assumes the situation when it will be fulfilled. John 7:39 identifies the rivers of water (7:38) as a reference to the Spirit, noting that it will be given after Jesus' glorification. This promise is to all who believe and this counts against those who suggest that the promise of the Paraclete is for an apostolic[6] or prophetic[7] office or only for the disciples as distinct from the wider circle of believers.[8]

---

5. See also Schnackenburg, *Johannesevangelium*, 4.62–64; de Jonge, *Stranger*, 152–59; Bühner, *Gesandte*, 251–56, 317; Marie E. Isaacs, "The Prophetic Spirit in the Fourth Gospel," *HeyJ* 24 (1983): 404.

6. Against Mussner, "Parakletssprüche," 154–55.

7. Boring, "Christian Prophecy," 120, 122.

8. Minear, *John*, 8–23.

It is above all in the last discourses that the promise is expounded in detail. In 14:16–17 (as in 20:21–22), it is associated with the mission of the disciples and doubtless explains how their greater works will be possible. In particular the Spirit is designated as the Paraclete (14:16, 26; 15:26; 16:7) and the Spirit of Truth (14:17; 15:26; 16:13) and in 14:16 as "another Paraclete."

This signals an analogy between the Son and the Spirit similar to the one which exists between the Son and the disciples and a similar use of the pattern of the revealer-envoy. The analogy has been emphasised by Bornkamm,[9] who also suggests that behind it lies an adaptation of the forerunner successor model.[10] Gary M. Burge puts it well when he writes that Johannine Christology is the "template" for the Spirit in the Gospel.[11] The pattern of the revealer-envoy is evident in the following statements. The Spirit also comes from the Father (15:26), is sent (14:26) or given (14:16) by the Father, but also by the Son (15:26; 16:7). When the Spirit comes (16:7), he will expound to the world the significance of the Son: the world's rejection of him as sin, his vindication before God, and the meaning of the climax of Jesus' life as judgment of the world (16:8–11). Thus, as the Son makes the Father known, so the Spirit makes the Son known.

The coming of the Son (and the Father) to dwell in the disciples after Easter is almost certainly to be seen as something the Spirit makes possible (14:16–23). Similarly the Spirit will represent the Son according to 16:12–15. "When he comes, the Spirit of Truth, he will lead you into all truth; for he will not speak his own authority, but what he hears he will speak" (16:13). Similarly the Son did not speak his own authority, but only what he had heard from the Father (8:26, 28). The similarity continues: "He will glorify me, because he will take what is mine and declare it to you" (16:14). The pattern of coming, being sent, receiving and giving knowledge, is clearly discernible. The witnessing (14:26) and teaching (14:26) functions are as central as they are for the Son. The Spirit is the second Paraclete; the Son was the first.

The Spirit is, however, not another revealer-envoy independent of Jesus, but as 16:13–15 carefully points out, the truth into which he leads, including his words about things that are to come, is not original. They all derive from Jesus. This means in turn, however, that the Spirit both calls Jesus' words and deeds into remembrance, and tells more truth about (and from) Jesus. The witness of both the Spirit and the disciples (15:26–27) is the explanation for

---

9. Bornkamm, "Paraklet," 77–79; Porsch, *Pneuma*, 237–39; Eskil Franck, *Revelation Taught: The Paraclete in the Gospel of John*, CCBTNT 14 (Lund: Gleerup, 1985), 80, 83–84; Burge, *Anointed Community*, 140–42; Isaacs, "Prophetic Spirit," 393–401.

10. So also Bornkamm, "Paraklet," 87.

11. Burge, *Anointed Community*, 41.

The Structure: An Outline

what lies before us in the Gospel. The Spirit enables us to know the heart of the Gospel: the message of the Son come from the Father, sent to make him known. Because Jesus goes away and the Spirit is sent, the full import of who he was may be known (16:7–11).

"...to enable greater understanding..."

In the previous section we noted how it is above all through the Spirit Paraclete that greater understanding comes of who the Son was and is, what he said and is saying. This belongs together with other statements which indicate a change of understanding which will follow the event of Jesus' death and return.

In 2:22 the author notes that Jesus' temple word was remembered and understood only after Easter: "When Jesus therefore was raised from the dead, his disciples remembered that he said this and believed the Scripture and the word which Jesus said." "The Scripture," Ps 69:9, reformulated into the future tense, was read as a prediction of Jesus' death. This, too, was remembered by the disciples (2:17), and again it is likely this refers to remembering after Easter, as the link with 2:22 suggests. John 12:16 is similar. Referring to the messianic application of Zech 9:9 to Jesus' entry into Jerusalem and to the crowd's welcoming him as Messiah, the author notes: "His disciples did not understand these things at first, but when Jesus was glorified, then they remembered that these things were written concerning him and that they had done these things to him." Both verses refer to knowledge of two kinds gained after Easter: greater understanding about Jesus and about Scripture in relation to Jesus.

A similar prediction of greater understanding comes in the words of Jesus to the Jews in 8:28–29, "When you have lifted up the Son of Man, then you shall know that I am the one and that I do nothing on my own authority, but as the Father taught me, so I speak these things. And the one who sent me is with me. He has not left me alone, because I always do what is pleasing to him." What the Jews will (may) come to know is spelled out in the language of the revealer-envoy Christology. In 14:19–20 Jesus promises the disciples special knowledge: "A little while and the world will see me no more, but you will see me; because I live you will live also. And in that day you will know that I am in my Father and you in me and I in you." A similar idea seems present in the prediction of Judas's betrayal which is given: Jesus says, "So that when it has happened, you may believe that I am the one" (13:19). Jesus speaks similarly in 14:29, "And now I have told you before it happens, so that when it happens you may believe." What they should believe is doubtless not just that Jesus was right in his predictions, but that he is the one he claims to be (so 14:31). The prediction that the disciples will come to understand the application of Scripture to Jesus, noted already in discussing 2:17, 22 and 12:16, occurs also in 20:9 in a note of the author about the disciples' not yet achieving resurrection faith, "For they did not yet know the Scripture that he must rise from the dead."

Taken together with the Paraclete sayings, these passages indicate that the event of Jesus' death and return, taken as a whole, will bring about greater understanding of who Jesus was and of the way Scripture is fulfilled in him and that this knowledge comes in particular through the gift of the Spirit. Perhaps this is already hinted at in 6:62–63, where—after challenging the disciples with the words, "What if you see the Son of Man ascending where he was before?"—Jesus says, "The Spirit is the life giver, the flesh is of no profit; the words which I have spoken to you are spirit and life." While the primary reference is to Jesus' words during his earthly ministry (he is bearer of the Spirit!), there may also be the suggestion that after his ascension the Spirit would help them remember his words. When 3:3 speaks of "seeing the kingdom of God" and relates it to those born from above, born of the Spirit (3:5, 8), we also have reference to this special post-Easter knowledge.

So far, we have related the greater understanding primarily to the sending of the Spirit. Indirectly the sending of the disciples also increases knowledge. Both are witnesses according to 15:26 and the author takes particular care to emphasise the importance and reliability of the disciples' knowledge of the earthly Jesus. Faith can trust fully in their witness and thus the witness of the Gospel and need not be preoccupied, as Thomas was, with material evidence. The author emphasises that his Gospel is only a selection of much more material that is available (20:30; 21:25).

He stresses especially the role of the beloved disciple who "wrote" the Gospel with the claim that he was the source of special tradition from an eyewitness. In this role he foreshadows the roles claimed in later Gospels for Thomas, Mary, and Judas. Thus he is portrayed as the one who leant on Jesus' chest at the Last Supper (13:25), so that he is almost pictured as relating to Jesus the way Jesus related to God ("in the bosom of the Father," 1:18) and certainly as being privy to special knowledge on that occasion. A similar special claim to knowledge lies behind his receiving the commissioning to care for Jesus' mother, his inside knowledge of the high priestly courts, his racing first to the tomb and first looking in, and his position of special honour independent of Peter. He is also probably understood as the source of the report from an eyewitness of the piercing of Jesus' side.

The claim on knowledge in the Gospel combines recall and understanding given by the Spirit, on the one hand, and the connection of tradition through the disciples, the beloved disciple in particular, on the other. It is not the case that the disciples had no knowledge of Jesus during his earthly ministry, any more than it is the case that the gifts of light and life were not to be had then. What comes through the event of Jesus' death and return is greater understanding of what was already there. In particular Jesus' death focusses the issue of who he was and so becomes an act of judgment and an occasion for discernment (so 16:7–11). The Son carries his claim to the end and in the passion narrative this claim is driven to its climax particularly through ironic use of messianic motifs. Jesus' vindication (return to the Father) is a revelation of the rightness of his claim. The Spirit, therefore, not only aids recall and works beside the disciples in this; it also presses home the implications of the death and return of Jesus for understanding who he is. The ultimate focus is therefore who he is: the Son, sent from the Father, who came as the revealer-envoy offering the gift of life, and then returned.

". . .to equip for mission. . ."

Both the sending of the disciples and the sending of the Spirit are closely related to mission. The theme of the disciples' mission appears at a number of points through the Gospel. It is present in ch. 4, both in the Samaritan woman's "mission" to her townspeople (4:29) and in Jesus' words to his disciples about sowing and harvesting (4:35–38). It is present in the irony of the Jews' response to Jesus' saying he would go and they would not find him, where they speculate whether he would go to the Greeks (7:33–36). This clearly foreshadows the Gentile mission, which in John as in Matthew and Luke-Acts is a post-Easter phenomenon. The same is true in 10:16 when Jesus speaks of other sheep not of this fold and in 11:50–52 when Caiaphas predicts that Jesus' death will benefit not only the Jewish people but all God's scattered children.

The Gentile mission theme also lies behind the approach of the Greeks to Jesus in 12:20. The verse before has the Pharisees bemoaning that "the world has gone after him." The irony is obvious when immediately the author tells of the Greeks requesting to see Jesus. Between them and Jesus are Philip and Andrew, perhaps symbolic of the role the disciples will have in carrying the Gospel to the Gentiles. Jesus' acclamation that the hour of glorification had come refers primarily to his death and return, but also to what would flow from it, namely the mission of the disciples to the world. 12:24 makes the link specific: "Truly, truly I tell you, unless a grain of wheat falls into the ground and dies, it remains alone; if it dies, it bears much fruit." The same theme appears a few verses later where Jesus exclaims: "And I, if I be lifted up, will draw all people to me" (12:32).

Jesus' going away (7:33-34), his death (10:15-16; 11:51-52; 12:24, 32-33), his exaltation (12:32) and glorification (12:23), will result in the sending of the disciples, equipped by the Spirit, for mission to the world. This is doubtless the background for the promise of Jesus that the disciples will do the works he does and "greater works than these" (14:12). In such work Jesus promises them answered prayer (14:13-14), adding that this is so in order that the Father may be glorified in the Son. Mission brings glory to the Father and the Son. The same thought reappears in 15:7-8: "If you remain in me and my words remain in you, ask what you will and it shall be done for you. In this is my Father glorified that you bear much fruit and become my disciples." Similarly fruit bearing and prayer are linked in 15:16. In 15:1-17 fruit bearing is related to the vine image. In both contexts Jesus speaks of the commandments he gives the disciples (14:15, 21, 24; 15:10, 12, 14, 16, 17). These include the commandment to mission, as 15:16 illustrates: "I have appointed you that you go and bear fruit and that your fruit remain." "To build up the community in faith" links the love commandment closely with the command to mission (15:12; cf. 13:34-35).

John 14:16 directly relates this commission (14:15) to the promise of the Paraclete. The promise of the Paraclete is here the promise of indwelling presence (14:16-17). Beside it (and mediated through it) is the promise of the indwelling presence of Jesus and the knowledge which that brings (14:18-20). Then the author returns to the commission theme (14:21). The structure confirms the importance of the promises of presence for the mission theme. The promise is repeated in 14:23-24 in the same connection, this time speaking of both Father and Son indwelling. The words promising the teaching ministry of the Paraclete (14:26) should also be seen as connected to the mission theme.

The Paraclete is promised in 15:26-27 amid ominous predictions of violent opposition to the disciples' mission (reflected also in 17:14). In 16:5-15 the Paraclete's work is also to be seen in relation to the mission. In particular the Paraclete's case about sin, righteousness and judgment in expounding Jesus' death represents central preaching themes of the mission.

Mission is probably reflected symbolically in the miracle of the fish catch in ch. 21, perhaps its universality in the number 153. It is also likely that the accounts of healed people telling others of their healings have situations of missionary witness and opposition in mind (e.g., the lame man in ch. 5 and the blind in ch. 9). Mission is above all the fruit of Jesus' death and return, because through this event the Spirit is given and the disciples are commissioned.

The Structure: An Outline

"...and to build up the community of faith."

A particularly strong feature of the last discourses is the exhortation to unity and, as we have seen, it is frequently related to the impact this has on the world. The most celebrated examples are: "A new commandment I give to you that you love one another as I have loved you, that you love one another. By this shall all people know that you are my disciples, if you have love one for another" (13:34–35) and the prayer of Jesus for his disciples and those to follow them:

> that they may all be one, as you Father are in me and I in you, that they also may be in us, that the world may believe that you sent me. The glory you have given me I have given to them, that they may be one as we are one, I in them and you in me, that they may be completely one, so that the world may know that you sent me and that you loved them as you loved me. (17:21–23)

Recognition that they are Jesus' disciples and recognition that the Father sent the Son are connected, the one being a witness of the other. The connection between mission and community is also present in 15:1–18. Here, too, we find through the image of the vine the theme of indwelling. The unity derives from the unity which already exists between Father and Son and from the life that flows from the Son. We saw that 15:1–18 stands as a timeless statement of the continuing basis of unity with the Son and of disciples with one another for mission. The commandments Jesus gives include the fruit bearing of mission and loving one another. Both are possible because of the life in the vine, the love shown in Jesus' giving himself for them. This love-unity-mission theme is most strongly represented in 13:34–35; 15:1–18; and ch. 17.

A similar concern for unity in relation to mission is found in 10:16–17 and 11:51–52, though here the gathering of the one flock and the benefit for all the scattered children of God seem rather to come at the other end of the perspective, i.e., unity is the goal of the mission as well as its means.

In John 14 the focus of community is that between Father and Son and, through the Paraclete, that between the disciples and the Son. After Easter the Spirit—once present to the disciples through the person of Jesus in his earthly ministry—will come to dwell in the disciples (14:17). They will also see the Son, know that he is in the Father (as already affirmed as mutual indwelling between the two in 14:11), and know that he dwells in them and they in him (14:19–20). Similarly the Father and Son will dwell in the disciples, according to 14:23. The focus here is communion with Father and Son.

The narrative of foot washing emphasises community as serving, especially through the second interpretation. As it stands, the juxtaposition of this interpretation with that of the washing as Jesus' cleansing his disciples connects the community of disciples with Jesus and the community of disciples with one another. The second flows from the love shown in the first. The emphasis on community of disciples, not articulated in ch. 14, becomes a major focus in John 15 and in Jesus' final prayer in John 17, perhaps reflecting changing situations in the Johannine community, but it is always connected to the theme of communion first with the Son and the Father. This community or communion with the Son and the Father through the Son is important in the light of Jesus' going away. Apart from 14:16–17, the promise of the Paraclete relates to knowledge rather than presence, but presence—particularly empowering presence—is also presupposed in the account of the giving of the Spirit in 20:22.

Communion with the Father and the Son is already possible through the ministry of the earthly Jesus. He is light and life and bread. To follow him and to believe in him is to receive the gift. The issue, therefore, of mediating his presence after Easter is of great importance. We have seen that the Spirit does this both by presence and also by mediating his word. In ch. 6 we find reference to the future gift of life through the Son of Man, a term used of Jesus predominantly in association with his death and return: "Do not labour for the food which perishes but for the food which endures to eternal life, which the Son of Man will give you" (6:27). The future tense is to be taken seriously and refers to the nourishment as it will be given in the post-Easter period by the ascended Son of Man (cf. 6:62). In 6:53 this is identified more closely as eating the flesh and drinking the blood of the Son of Man in what is doubtless a reference to the Eucharist. The Eucharist is then a way in which the communion is established and maintained. A similar reference to the future mediation of life through Jesus as Son of Man is found in 3:14–15: "As Moses lifted up the serpent in the wilderness, so it is necessary that the Son of Man be lifted up, so that all who believe might have life in him."

It may be that the wine imagery in the wedding feast at Cana contains a eucharistic allusion as well as reflecting on the wine which has come with the Son's coming. We have also noted the promise of a new temple in Jesus' resurrection (2:21), probably carrying with it an allusion to the new communion in him. The irrelevance of Jerusalem and Samaritan temples according to 4:19–26 similarly points to the new worshipping community of the Spirit. The narratives of the wedding feast, the temple expulsion, the exchange with Nicodemus, and the meeting with the Samaritan woman seem to have been written with a constant dual reference to the situation before and after Easter.

The result is a higher degree of anachronism than elsewhere in the Gospel (see especially 3:3-13 and 4:35-38).

We have also noted the possibility that the issuing of water and blood from Jesus' side may allude to the Eucharist and baptism (also in 3:5). The Eucharist may also be suggested in the meal in 21:9-13, as it seems to be already in the narrative of the feeding of the 5,000. Possibly the mention of Jesus' seamless robe is meant as a symbol of unity, but this is uncertain.

I began by noting how in many passages unity is related to mission. We saw how community is frequently portrayed as derived from the communion with the Son (and the Father) through the Spirit, through Jesus' word and through Eucharist. The final chapter, in specifying Peter's pastoral role and the distinctive position of the beloved disciple (and by implication his community), represents a concrete working out of the community issue in history. The author is concerned for the unity of the Church.

The ultimate community to which all this leads is, for the author, the fulfilment of Jesus' prayer that his disciples follow him right through to the goal of the Father's presence: "I wish that where I am they may also be, so that they may see the glory which you have given me because you loved me before the foundation of the world" (17:24). This is the place Jesus goes to prepare for them (14:2) and to which he shall come to take them (14:3). The same promise expressed in other words appears in 12:26: "If anyone serves me, let him follow me, and where I am there will my servant also be. If anyone serves me, him will my Father honour." Thus the story ends where it began: the Son with the Father, but now the disciples will share this glory. This is the implicit focus of the author's eschatology. Explicit references to a future parousia of the Son are few (14:3; 21:22-23). References to a future judgment day (5:28-30; 12:48; cf. 5:45) and to a future resurrection of the dead (5:28-29; 6:39-40, 44, 54) also appear. However, they are incidental to the primary concern: the relationship with Father and Son now and ultimately being with them in glory in heaven.

Conclusion

We have reached the conclusion of the outline of the structure of the author's Christology. The central event is the Son's making the Father known, bringing light and life and truth, and completing the Father's work. All else focusses on this. His having been with the Father, being sent and coming from the Father, is what makes this possible. His return to the Father—exalted, glorified, and ascended—and his sending the disciples and the Spirit is what makes it possible for this to be understood, announced to the world in mission and lived out in the community of faith. The sending of the disciples and the Spirit is parallel to the sending of the Son, but not independent of it. There are not two revelatory events, the revelation of the Son and the revelation of the disciples and the Spirit. There is one single revelatory event; the work of the disciples and the Spirit is revelatory only in the sense that it reveals the revelation of the Son. The Father sends and authorises the Son, who knows the Father, comes from the Father, makes the Father known, brings light and life and truth, completes his Father's work, returns to the Father—exalted, glorified, and ascended—sends the disciples, and sends the Spirit to enable greater understanding, to equip for mission, and to build up the community of faith.

PART TWO

Issues of Johannine Christology

In the Introduction we examined Bultmann's Christology of John and briefly reviewed research since Bultmann, which—partly in response to Bultmann and partly independent from him—has raised and revived major issues for any new attempt to understand Johannine Christology. Renewed attention has been given to questions concerning the meaning of Jesus' death. Was it a real death, preceded by real suffering? Was it a work of salvific significance, the achievement of atonement, a moment of change in world power, or primarily a portal for a triumphant Son of God? What is the meaning of exaltation and glorification in relation to Jesus' death and return to the Father? How significant is the notion of his return to the Father and the giving of the Paraclete? What is the saving event in John? His death, his incarnation, his returning? Some of the major issues concern the nature of Jesus himself. What role does pre-existence play? What is the character of his oneness with the Father? Is it subordination? Is it such that the glory submerges Jesus' humanity? Is he a god striding the earth? Do miracles play a central role in Johannine thought? Has the earthly historical Jesus still a place? These raise, in turn, questions about the nature of the portrait in the Gospel itself, its setting, and its use in our own world.

In Part One we examined the text of the Gospel, following Bultmann's agenda of first seeking to identify the central structure of the christological story. The outline—published in 1989 in the first edition of this book—has been widely acclaimed as providing a framework within which to consider the author's Christology. While it employs the model of the revealer-envoy, the outline makes it clear that the primary focus of the author's Christology is not the giving of revelation as information. Rather, it is the offer of life in the person of Jesus, an initiative of divine love. Within this structure the author integrates images of Jesus as prophet, and especially as the Messiah.

On its basis the author differentiates this unique offer of life from God's gift of the Law through Moses, so that he alone, portrayed as embodying the qualities of Wisdom once attributed to Torah, is the true bread, light and life. Within this framework belong also the reflections on the meaning of Jesus' death and the greater event to which it belongs, including traditions of vicarious suffering.

While the central structure of the author's Christology gives a strong measure of coherence to the whole, this should not lead us to assume that we have before us a thoroughly systematised work or one in which no tensions or issues for clarification remain. The thematic section of this work will seek to examine key elements of the author's christological statements in greater detail to uncover the extent of such coherence and the way in which the author has incorporated key ideas and images within the whole. We begin with the major focus given to the death of Jesus and associated motifs. We then turn to how the author depicts the salvation event in the person of Jesus, looking at divine and human aspects of his portrayal, and finally turning to historical issues that relate both to Jesus and to the author and his first readers.

4 The Death of Jesus in John

The pattern of the author's Christology puts as the central act the Son's making the Father known, bringing light and life and truth, and completing the works of the Father. For this the Son came from the Father. After this the Son returns to the Father. The cycle is complete. The Son returns where he was with the Father before the world began. Therefore at its simplest, Jesus' death is the mode of his return to the Father.

To know the Son comes from and returns to the Father, his whence and his whither, is to know who he is, for it is to know him as the sent one. His return to the Father, like his coming from the Father, authenticates his claim. The Paraclete declares his righteousness on the grounds that he returned to the Father (16:10).

Seen in this perspective, Jesus' death is his exit. This is primarily how Käsemann and Schulz see the meaning of Jesus' death in John. They are followed by many others. It is the triumphant exit of the revealer.[1] The following sections will show that this too quickly ignores other aspects.[2] As Max Turner notes,

> If Forestell had not (correctly) argued that John has focused the cross as the supreme revelation of God's saving love, it may have been possible to agree with Bultmann that the death of Jesus is itself of little soteriological import in John. But having made this point, Forestell's own account successfully focuses the importance of the cross without

---

1. Käsemann, *Letzter Wille*, 124, 135; Schulz, *Johannes*, 209, 238; Lattke, *Einheit*, 142; Müller, "Bedeutung," 54, 68; Appold, *Oneness*, 135; Becker, *Johannes*, 406–7; Langbrandtner, *Weltferner Gott*, 97; cf. already Bultmann, *Theologie*, 406.

2. So rightly Frey, "Edler Tod," 556.

explaining why *this death* of Jesus is necessary at all, or *how* it can reveal God's love.³

4.1 Jesus' Death–Vicarious, Sacrificial, Apotropaic?

Jesus' death is more than simply the exit route of the revealer. The suffering and death is itself part of the Father's commission. It is the cup the Father has given for him to drink (18:11) and the hour before which he was distressed, but to which he had come to face suffering and death (12:27). The Father commanded the Son to lay down his life (10:18) and Jesus concludes the first discourse with the words: "That the world may know that I love the Father and that as the Father has commanded, so I act, arise let us go hence!" (14:31). The Son has come to do the Father's will and complete fully the task set before him (4:34; 5:36). In 17:4 he declares he has done so; his last words, "It is finished" (19:30), set the seal on his ministry.⁴

Facing suffering and death belongs to the commission of the Son. But why?⁵ A number of scholars see the final task of this commission as an act of vicarious atonement.⁶ Accordingly, Jesus singles out vicarious atonement as a second task by adding the words "and to complete his work" after "to do the will of him who sent me" in 4:34.⁷ The grounds for seeing atonement as the completion of the task are basically threefold: the alleged presence of allusions to Jesus' death as vicarious sacrifice in the Gospel, the presence of other texts which suggest that the gift of life becomes available only after Easter and so imply that it is available only as a result of the work of Jesus' death, and the singling out of the passion as a distinctive task in the passages mentioned above. We shall consider these three arguments in turn.

In Part One we noted a number of passages that—with varying degrees of certainty and uncertainty—might refer to Jesus' death as an act of vicar-

---

3. Max Turner, "Atonement and the Death of Jesus in John—Some Questions to Bultmann and Forestell," *EvQ* 62 (1990): 118.

4. Frey, "Edler Tod," 556, points to the threefold reference to completion in the immediate context, of the Son's task in accordance with Scripture and the will of the Father for which he was sent, picking up the earlier references in 4:34 and 17:4.

5. Frey, "Edler Tod," 555–84, discusses the various ways in which the author depicts the significance of Jesus' death as seen from a post-Easter perspective not as failure but triumph. He cautions against making any single motif the key to unlock all the others (561).

6. Thüsing, *Erhöhung*, 68–69, 100; Wilkens, *Zeichen*, 73, 77; Müller, *Heilsgeschehen*, 34, 50, 74, 130–31; Richter, *Studien*, 60, 291; Riedl, *Heilswerk*, 15; Miranda, *Vater*, 139–41; Miranda, *Sendung*, 20, 28; Dauer, *Passionsgeschichte*, 282–92; Schnelle, "Kreuzestheologie," 242–55.

7. So Thüsing, *Erhöhung*, 58; Riedl, *Heilswerk*, 62–63; Miranda, *Vater*, 126.

ious atonement. We postponed assessing that degree of probability in each case because the extent to which one reference might carry that meaning depends on the extent to which it is present elsewhere. In other words, they need to be considered as a whole. It is also easier, having considered them as a whole, to examine their overall role and function, their weight and valency, within the Gospel's Christology.

4.1.1 John 1:29 (36): Its Role and Status in the Gospel

The first potential reference is 1:29, ἴδε ὁ ἀμνὸς τοῦ θεοῦ ὁ αἴρων τὴν ἁμαρτίαν τοῦ κόσμου ("Behold the lamb of God who takes away the sin of the world"). It stands without further interpretation in the immediate context. On the other hand, at least its opening statement, ἴδε ὁ ἀμνὸς τοῦ θεοῦ ("Behold, the lamb of God"), is repeated in 1:36. It represents the first words of the first witness, John the Baptist, on seeing Jesus, and on the second occasion in 1:36 it is his first word to the first potential disciples of Jesus. In that sense it holds a position of significant prominence in the Gospel,[8] yet its imagery is completely absent in the rest of the Gospel.

Some have therefore suggested that the author makes use of a traditional statement whose meaning would be known to his readers.[9] Becker accounts for it as tradition added by the Johannine redactor.[10] Ashton sees it having been part of a signs Gospel where it had no relation to Jesus' death. He suggests that the words about taking away sin are "a later addition" on the basis of 1 John 3:5.[11] Lindars suggests that in it "John also carries forward the traditional interpretation of Jesus' death as an atonement sacrifice which belongs to earliest Christianity (cf. 1 Cor 15.3), and which is accepted in the Johannine church (1 John 2.2)."[12] At whatever stage such tradition entered the Gospel, the case for it as tradition is strong.

It is another question to ask what role it now plays in the Gospel. The

---

8. Frey, "Theologia Crucifixi," 517, points out that John the Baptist's witness is reinforced in 10:41–42 where many are reported as affirming that it was true.

9. Käsemann, *Letzter Wille*, 23 n. 7; Appold, *Oneness*, 79; Haenchen, "Johannesevangelium," 230; Haenchen, *Johannes*, 166–67; Müller, "Bedeutung," 63; Forestell, *Word*, 15–16; cf. also Bultmann, *Theologie*, 406.

10. Becker, *Johannes*, 91–92.

11. Ashton, *Fourth Gospel*, 162; similarly 466.

12. Barnabas Lindars, *John*, NTG (Sheffield: JSOT Press, 1990), 82. See also Ulrich B. Müller, *Die Menschwerdung des Gottessohnes. Frühchristliche Inkarnationsvorstellungen und die Anfänge des Doketismus*, SBS 140 (Stuttgart: KBW, 1990), 73.

possibility that it reflects tradition does not justify relegating its significance.[13] Nor is to be treated atomistically, as though it stands apart from its context, as too often happens. The major contribution of Reimund Bieringer's study of 1:29 is that he insists that it be read in its literary and traditio-historical context.[14] Already in the prologue we have reference to John's witness to Jesus as the light (1:6-8) and as the one who will follow after him but was before him (1:15).[15] While not yet citing the content of John's witness, the prologue makes it clear that Jesus as the Logos came as light into the world (1:9), enabling those who received him to be born as God's children (1:10-13), became flesh to enable people to see his glory (1:14) and so to offer them the gift of making God known to them (1:16-18).

All this lies in the background as John the Baptist denies that he is the Christ or Elijah or the prophet and points to the one coming after him (1:19-27). It also therefore lies in the background when John the Baptist finally declares: "Behold the lamb of God who takes away the sin of the world" (1:29). The author makes this clear by pointing to that fact directly when he has John declare: "This is the one of whom I said that the one coming after me was before me" (1:30). He then has John twice declare that he did not know the identity of the coming one until given instruction about how to recognise him: the Spirit would descend and abide on him. This is then more than a mechanism for informing John. It clearly identifies what the coming one would do and on what basis. His having the Spirit is what enables him to baptise with the Spirit. The Baptist concludes his witness by affirming that Jesus truly is the Son of God.

When he simply repeats "Behold the lamb of God" (1:36), those hearing the Gospel know how to fill out its meaning—namely with what had just been said. In the call episodes which follow, the author has those who heeded John's declaration that Jesus is the lamb of God declare to others not that he is "the lamb of God," but what is assumed to be at least in a broad sense the equivalent: he is "the Messiah, which is translated, 'the Christ'" (1:41, 45) and "the Son of God, the king of Israel" (1:49). The latter acclamation is greeted with the promise that there is more to know: he is the Son of Man (1:51).

---

13. So rightly Frey, "Theologia crucifixi," 499-500, who prefers to speak of "relecture," a category developed by Jean Zumstein.

14. Reimund Bieringer, "Das Lamm Gottes, das die Sünde der Welt hinwegnimmt (Joh 1,29): Eine kontextorientierte und redaktionsgeschichtliche Untersuchung auf dem Hintergrund der Passatradition als Deutung des Todes Jesu im Johannesevangelium," in *The Death of Jesus in the Fourth Gospel*, ed. G. Van Belle, BETL 200 (Leuven: Peeters, 2007), 199-232.

15. Dietrich Rusam, "Das 'Lamm Gottes' (Joh 1,29.36) und die Deutung des Todes Jesu im Johannesevangelium," *BZ* 49 (2005): 72.

Thus the acclamation "lamb of God" and the role, taking away the sin of the world, must be understood in association with the context in which the author uses it. "Lamb of God" not only occurs alongside "Christ," "Messiah," "Son of God," and "King of Israel," but appears within the narrative to be used as an equivalent of these both by John the Baptist—who denies that he is the Christ and instead identifies Jesus as the Christ, using "lamb of God"—and by the disciples—who equate Jesus' being lamb of God with his being the Christ.[16] Whatever else the designation "lamb of God" might have conveyed, a designation not previously attested,[17] we are on secure ground in beginning with its equivalence in broad terms to what John understands by messiahship.[18] The image of a ram (ἀρνίον) is used for the Messiah, indeed as slain (Rev 7:17; 17:14; similarly 1 En. 90:38), but, while close, is not the same. As Leung notes, "It is sufficient to note that despite the limited pre-Christian evidence of the use of 'lamb' as a messianic title, the strong messianic tenor surrounding the Baptist's testimonies in John 1:29 and 1:36 suggests that these testimonies most likely pertain to Jewish messianic hopes."[19]

Reading "who takes away the sin of the world" in the light of the context is less clear except that in the immediate context it stands in parallel to baptising with the Spirit.[20] In the Markan form of the baptism tradition this is fulfilled in Jesus' ministry not least through exorcism, to deny which is thus to blaspheme the Spirit (3:23–30). In John the gift of the Spirit to the disciples on the day of resurrection is associated with the authority to forgive sins (20:22–23).[21] But clearly, as in Mark, Jesus' having the Spirit is referring to the basis for his actions which he will do through the Spirit during his ministry. Indeed the author (or perhaps, again, the Baptist) points to Jesus, the Son, being given the Spirit without measure in order to fulfil the task for which he was sent, namely to speak the words of God (3:34), and 14:17 has Jesus explain that the Spirit that was with the disciples in his person will, after his return, be in them.[22]

---

16. On the concentric structure which gives prominence to 1:29 see Bieringer, "Lamm Gottes," 215–17, 220–21.

17. The use in T. Jos. 19:8–9 is likely to be a secondary Christian addition.

18. John Painter, "Sacrifice and Atonement in the Gospel of John," in *Israel und seine Heilstraditionen im Johannesevangelium. Festgabe für Johannes Beutler SJ zum 70. Geburtstag*, ed. M. Labahn, K. Scholtissek, and A. Strotmann (Paderborn: Ferdinand Schöningh, 2004), 293–94. Larry W. Hurtado, *Lord Jesus Christ: Devotion to Jesus in Earliest Christianity* (Grand Rapids: Eerdmans, 2003), 359, writes of "lamb of God" and "Son of God" that they are "complementary ways of referring to Jesus as Messiah."

19. Leung, *Kingship-Cross*, 53.

20. So rightly Bieringer, "Lamm Gottes," 218; Rusam, "Lamm Gottes," 75.

21. Rusam, "Lamm Gottes," 75; Theobald, *Johannes*, 1.169–70.

22. On this see Rusam, "Lamm Gottes," 75–80.

The verb αἴρω in "taking away" (αἴρων)—not a word commonly used in cultic contexts[23]—can have various meanings: destroying sin, removing sin from the land, tasks traditionally assigned to the Messiah in Jewish hope,[24] or possibly carrying away its burden.[25] Forestell shows that it can mean simply "forgive," like ἀφίημι.[26] This would accord with the usual Johannine way of dealing with sin, either by the word of the Son (cf. 15:3) or by overpowering the prince of the world (12:31; 16:11).[27] Hegermann suggests that it means to take away sin by exposing it for what it is.[28] For Boismard taking away sin means enabling people to stop sinning through giving them the revelation of God.[29] J. Ramsey Michaels notes that 1:29 depicts the lamb not as a victim but as active, bringing purification. Michaels notes how this parallels the prediction in the tradition by John the Baptist about the coming one cleansing the threshing floor (Matt 3:12; Luke 3:17).[30]

The singular "sin" could simply be generic to cover all sins or, more likely, refers to the sin of rejecting God and rejecting the light, to which the prologue already alludes.[31] There is a universal dimension in the fact that it is "the world" whose sin is to be removed (cf. "he shall save his people from their sins" [Matt 1:21]). The universal dimension is already present in the prologue.

Thus, read within the context of the author's reworking of the baptismal tradition, being "the lamb of God" and "taking away the sin of the world" appear most naturally to refer to Jesus as the Christ, but understood in the light of the prologue, and to the task which he was sent to fulfil during his ministry, namely, to baptise with the Spirit, understood as making the Father known and so offering light and life and truth.[32] It is surely not insignificant

---

23. Painter, "Sacrifice and Atonement," 292.

24. Already Dodd, *Interpretation*, 237.

25. So Frey, "Theologia crucifixi," 518–19, who sees this symbolised in Jesus' carrying his own cross in John.

26. Forestell, *Word*, 160–61.

27. Forestell, *Word*, 148–49, 154; cf. similarly Porsch, *Pneuma*, 40–41; Barnabas Lindars, "The Passion in the Fourth Gospel," in *God's Christ and His People: Studies in Honor of N. A. Dahl*, ed. J. Jervell and W. Meeks (Oslo: Universitetsforlaget, 1977), 72.

28. Hegermann, "Eigentum," 119–20, 126–27.

29. Boismard and Lamouille, *Jean*, 47–60, 91–92.

30. Michaels, *John*, 109–11.

31. Harris, *Prologue and Gospel*, 56; Rusam, "Lamm Gottes," 68–69, emphasising the concern is therefore not moral sin. Cf. Zimmermann, *Christologie*, 117, who sees it as referring above all to the power of sin and this as the author's distinctive contribution.

32. Brown, *John*, 61–63, holds open the possibility that John the Baptist may have intended

that what in tradition is attributed to John the Baptist—namely offering baptism with repentance for the forgiveness of sins—is here transferred to Jesus and broadened to embrace both sin as a whole and the world, not just Israel.[33] He is bringing light into the darkness of sin. Sin is an issue in John from which Jesus brings liberation through his ministry (8:21-24, 32-36).[34] This coheres with the author's concern, evident also elsewhere, to give John the Baptist his proper place and to correct understandings which give him higher status, a corrective tendency already exercised in the prologue and in John the Baptist's denials in 1:19-28.[35]

The image of the lamb is, however, striking. We can understand the royal messianic imagery and its integration within the author's Christology of divine sonship,[36] but "lamb of God" is, as noted above, thus far unattested as a title or designation.[37] The literary context suggests that it was a term which could be used of the Messiah and the tradition-historical context suggests that it also belonged to discourse about Jesus' baptism, whether in traditional material which the author then highlights or as the author's innovation. Baptismal tradition imagined the heavenly attestation as an adaptation of Isa 42:1 ("You are my servant, in whom I am well pleased"), Ps 2:7 ("You are my son; today I have begotten you") and possibly the image of Isaac as Abraham's beloved son: "You are my beloved Son in whom I am well pleased" (Mark 1:11; cf. Matt 3:17; Luke 3:22).[38]

---

a messianic sense, but argues that this is no longer determinative in the context; similarly Riedl, *Heilswerk*, 174-75, 199; Beasley-Murray, *John*, 24-25; Carson, *John*, 150.

33. Bieringer, "Lamm Gottes," 224; Theobald, *Johannes*, 1.170.

34. Cf. Frey, "Edler Tod," 582, who uses these texts to argue for a narrower understanding, namely that only Jesus' death achieves such forgiveness.

35. The dismissal of this contextual reading by Frey, "Edler Tod," 577, on the basis that it is "gezwungen" (forced) is not cogent. He argues that even though there is no specific reference to Jesus' death in the context, it must be assumed as the only point of reference that makes sense.

36. Painter, "Sacrifice and Atonement," 293, writes: "The best we can do with this text is to suggest that it refers to Jesus as the messianic deliverer of his people, indeed, of the world. Nevertheless, the text raises a question that it does not answer. *How* does the Lamb of God take away the sin of the world?"

37. Painter, "Sacrifice and Atonement," 292.

38. Charles F. Burney, *The Aramaic Origin of the Fourth Gospel* (Oxford: Clarendon, 1922), 107-8, followed by Joachim Jeremias, "παῖς θεοῦ," *TDNT* 5.702, and Cullmann, *Worship*, 63-65, who proposed that the same Aramaic word טליא, which could mean lamb or servant, lies behind the "Son" of the Synoptics and the ἀμνός "lamb" of John. Dodd, *Interpretation*, has shown, however, that the theory lacks adequate evidence. Similarly Barrett, *John*, 176; Bruce, *John*, 52-53; Lindars, *John*, 109; Forestell, *Word*, 162-63; Painter, "Sacrifice and Atonement," 294.

The allusion to Isa 42:1 would be all the stronger if we were to read with Sinaiticus ἐκλεκτός ("chosen one") instead of υἱός ("Son") in 1:34. "Lamb" and "chosen one" would then form an *inclusio* in John 1:29-34.[39] The Akedah motif—the binding of Isaac—could lie behind the formulation here. Other evidence for it could be found, perhaps, in the references to the designation "the only Son" (1:14; 3:16, 18) and some would see it also behind the action implied in 3:16 ("God . . . gave his only Son"; cf. Rom 8:32) and in the fact that Jesus carries his own cross in John. The word ἐκλεκτός ("chosen one") in 1:34 is closely related to "beloved" (ἀγαπητός) and "only/unique" (μονογενής) as epithets of the Son, and is perhaps to be preferred over the reading υἱός ("Son").[40]

Or one might see the reworking as preserving the traditional reference to sonship now in 1:34, where John the Baptist attests to Jesus as "Son of God," and the notion of intimacy and vulnerability in 1:29, where he is described as "the lamb of God."[41] Read in the light of the baptismal tradition which the author is adapting, the motif "lamb of God" is most naturally read as expressing both vulnerability[42] and a sense of being beloved by God as God's son. Bieringer draws attention to the use of ἀμνός in 2 Sam 12:3 to give expression to intimate relationship.[43] Given the use of μονογενής, ἀγαπητός, and possibly ἐκλεκτός, this would be a reworking of the baptismal tradition to express σὺ εἶ ὁ υἱός μου ὁ ἀγαπητός ("You are my beloved son") in an image. Given the allusion to Isa 42:1 in the tradition, the use of the "lamb" image to convey vulnerability may well have evoked the allusion to the vulnerability of God's servant as a "lamb" (ἀμνός) in Isa 53:7. We shall

---

39. So Forestell, *Word*, 162-63; Porsch, *Pneuma*, 40; Catrin H. Williams, "'He Saw His Glory and Spoke about Him': The Testimony of Isaiah and Johannine Christology," in *Honouring the Past and Shaping the Future: Religious and Biblical Studies in Wales. Essays in Honour of Gareth Lloyd Jones* (Leominster: Gracewing, 2003), 61-62; see also the discussion in Ashton, *Fourth Gospel*, 157-58.

40. See the assessment in Tze-Ming Quek, "A Text-Critical Study of John 1.34," *NTS* 55 (2009): 22-34, who argues that on the basis of transcriptional probability Son of God is secondary, but not for dogmatic reasons, since it is present in Q tradition and that the reading ἐκλεκτός preserved in P^{106} and probably in p^5 is original, also given John's emphasis on the servant image of Isaiah 42 and 53.

41. Painter, "Sacrifice and Atonement," 294.

42. Christine Schlund, *"Kein Knochen soll gebrochen werden": Studien zu Bedeutung und Funktion des Pesachfests in Texten des frühen Judentums und im Johannesevangelium*, WMANT 107 (Neukirchen-Vluyn: Neukirchener Verlag, 2005), 175; Painter, "Sacrifice and Atonement," 294.

43. Bieringer, "Lamm Gottes," 222, 230-31. He also draws attention to the presence of sheep and shepherd motifs in 1:35-51 echoed in ch. 10 of hearing and following (225-30).

return below to the suggestion that the image invokes not only this but also vicarious suffering. It may, but the use of Isa 53:7 to convey suffering without any explicit reference to vicariousness is present elsewhere (Acts 8:32), so that it should not be automatically assumed here. The author will then have interpreted messiahship in association with the image of Jesus as the Son of God who is beloved of the Father and who has made himself vulnerable, much as already in the Synoptic tradition, but understood now in the broader sense given through the prologue. In this sense the lamb motif associated with messiahship suggests not the victorious ram,[44] but rather the paradox of vulnerability in a manner which may recall other traditions present in Rev 5:6, 12; 14:1.

While the most natural reading of 1:29 in its context has it refer to Jesus as the Messiah and the role he will fulfil in his ministry,[45] especially for a first time hearer, it is important not to succumb to the first reader fallacy, as though all or most hearers would approach 1:29 having only the resources given in the chapter thus far. For we have to assume that most hearers of the Gospel and intended hearers would not be coming to this Gospel without prior knowledge and with no familiarity with the Christian tradition. We may and probably should assume that they would hear John the Baptist's declaration as referring to Jesus' status as the Christ, the Logos, Son of God, of the prologue and his taking away the world's sin, as referring to what he was about to do in his ministry through the power of the Spirit. There is, however, no reason why they might not have heard more than that in the imagery or why the author might not have intended more.

Here a note of caution is necessary because we must distinguish between what interpreters of modern times have brought to the text and what first-century hearers might have done. Over centuries, especially where soteriology has been framed primarily in relation to the cross, usually as a sacrificial or vicarious transaction, to the point where for some it becomes a shibboleth of orthodoxy,[46] Christians have interpreted these words in 1:29

---

44. Dodd, *Interpretation*, 233, 236-38. Cf. also the discussion in E. W. Burrows, "Did John the Baptist call Jesus 'Lamb of God'?" *ExpT* 85 (1974): 245-49; Painter, "Sacrifice and Atonement," 294.

45. Jens Schröter, "Sterben für die Freunde: Überlegungen zur Deutung des Todes Jesu im Johannesvangelium," in *Religionsgeschichte des Neuen Testaments. Festschrift für Klaus Berger zum 60. Geburtstag*, ed. A. von Bobbeler et al. (Tübingen: Francke, 2000), 286, speaks of only an indirect reference in 1:29 to Jesus' death.

46. On this see Frey, "Edler Tod," 581-82, who argues that dogmatic concerns have led others to deny such motifs play a role in John. See also Frey, "Theologia crucifixi," 492-96.

almost automatically as a reference to the death of Jesus as a sacrificial lamb. Against this, circumspection is called for in assessing what first-century hearers for their part might have brought to the text, so that we do not read our own dogmas into the text. The following discussion explores some of the additional associations which John the Baptist's declaration might have evoked (or been intended to evoke) for first-century hearers, while acknowledging the primary focus which its literary and traditio-historical context gives it, namely as referring to Jesus' vulnerable servanthood as Son and the role which he as bearer of the Spirit was about to exercise. There is no *prima facie* reason why one should limit this role to Jesus' ministry and exclude reference to Jesus' death or vice versa. The task he was to finish ended in death. It is therefore appropriate to consider what 1:29 might evoke in relation to Jesus' death, as long as one does not exclude its relevance for Jesus' ministry.

Many see a sacrificial motif in the use of ἀμνός "lamb" and therefore interpret αἴρων ("taking away") accordingly. Even Forestell, who vigorously denies a cultic interpretation of Jesus' death elsewhere in the Gospel, assumes its presence here.[47] Some, therefore, see in 1:29 the author's announcement of the major focus of his soteriology, namely the death of Jesus for his own, which accordingly informs all subsequent references to the death of Jesus.[48]

There have been various suggestions about the background of the motif of the sacrificial lamb, many seeing allusion to more than one text or idea.

---

47. Forestell, *Word*, 158.
48. So, for instance, Müller, *Heilsgeschehen*, 112-13, 130-31, 134-35; Schnackenburg, *John*, 1.29; *Johannesevangelium*, 4.223; Thüsing, *Erhöhung*, 19-21, 51, 164; Blank, *Krisis*, 133-34; Porsch, *Pneuma*, 42; Dauer, *Passionsgeschichte*, 292-94; Riedl, *Heilswerk*, 112-13, 313-14; F.-M. Braun, *Jean Le Théologien. Tome III* (Paris: Gabalda, 1966), 137-38, 216-18; Stephen Pancaro, *The Law in the Fourth Gospel: The Torah and the Gospel, Moses and Jesus, Judaism and Christianity according to John*, NovTSup 42 (Leiden, Brill, 1975), 441-42; Haacker, *Stiftung*, 169-73; Richter, *Studien*, 42-45, 53, 58-59, 291, 305, 312; Kühl, *Sendung*, 109-10; Günter Reim, *Studien zum alttestamentlichen Hintergrund des Johannesevangeliums*, SNTSMS 22 (Cambridge: Cambridge University Press, 1974), 179; Miranda, *Vater*, 125-26, 130, 132-41; Miranda, *Sendung*, 20, 24-25, 28; Franz Schnider and Werner Stenger, *Johannes und die Synoptiker* (Munich: Kösel, 1971), 169; Williams, "Cultic Elements," 340-41; Wilkens, *Zeichen*, 72-74, 77, especially for the "signs Gospel," but not for the "Reden,"; Turner, "Atonement," 121-22; Schnelle, "Kreuzestheologie," 244; Metzner, *Sünde*, 131; Klaus Scholtissek, "'Eine grössere Liebe als diese hat niemand, als wenn einer sein Leben hingibt für seine Freunde' (Joh 15,13): Die hellenistische Freundschaftsethik und das Johannesevangelium," in *Kontexte des Johannesevangeliums: Das vierte Evangelium in religions- und traditionsgeschichtlicher Perspektive*, ed. J. Frey and U. Schnelle, WUNT 175 (Tübingen: Mohr Siebeck, 2004), 434; Dennis, *Death and Gathering*, 352-53; Frey, "Theologia crucifixi," 517, 519; Frey, "Edler Tod," 578, 582.

They include: Jesus as the Passover lamb,[49] the lamb in terms of Isa 53,[50] or of Isa 53:7 (the silent vulnerable lamb),[51] the lamb as servant of Yahweh (usually combining Isaiah 53 and 42),[52] the lamb of the story of Abraham's willingness to sacrifice Isaac,[53] the tradition of Moses as a lamb,[54] the lamb of the daily sacrifice,[55] and the goat sent away into the wilderness to Azazel (Lev 16:10).[56]

49. So Bultmann, *Johannes*, 66-67; *Theologie*, 406; Barrett, *John*, 176; Schnackenburg, *John*, 1.299; Brown, *John*, 61-63; Lindars, *Gospel of John*, 109; Becker, *Johannes*, 97; Joachim Gnilka, "Zur Christologie des Johannesevangeliums," in *Christologische Schwerpunkte*, ed. W. Kasper (Düsseldorf: Patmos, 1980), 106; Ellis, *Genius*, 33-34; Bruce H. Grigsby, "The Cross as an Expiatory Sacrifice in the Fourth Gospel," *JSNT* 15 (1982): 54; Beutler, "Heilsbedeutung," 192; Beasley-Murray, *John*, 24-25; Wilkens, *Zeichen*, 73-77; Forestell, *Word*, 165; also earlier: Lütgert, *Christologie*, 108-12. Against this: Ferdinand Hahn, "Das Verständnis des Opfers im Neuen Testament," in *Das Opfer Jesu Christi und seine Gegenwart in der Kirche*, ed. K. Lehmann and E. Schlink (Freiburg: Herder; Göttingen: Vandenhoeck und Ruprecht, 1983), 75; Hahn, *Theologie*, 1.633; Appold, *Oneness*, 79 n. 1; Ashton, *John*, 143; *Fourth Gospel*, 80, 163; Schnackenburg, *Person Jesu Christi*, 312; Frey, "Theologia crucifixi," 519, 527; Frey, "Edler Tod," 582; Knöppler, *Theologia crucis*, 86-89; Davies, *Rhetoric and Reference*, 234; Schnelle, *Johannes*, 49-50; Lincoln, *John*, 113; Hans-Ulrich Weidemann, *Der Tod Jesu im Johannesevangelium. Die erste Abschiedsrede als Schlüsseltext für den Passions- und Osterbericht*, BZNW 122 (Berlin: de Gruyter, 2004), 423; Metzner, *Sünde*, 22-23, 132-37.

50. So Barrett, *John*, 176; Schnackenburg, *John*, 1.300; Brown, *John*, 61-63; Lindars, *Gospel of John*, 109; Beasley-Murray, *John*, 24-25; Riedl, *Heilswerk*, 179-80; Haacker, *Stiftung*, 170-71; Hahn, "Verständnis des Opfers," 75; Hahn, *Theologie*, 1.633; Joachim Jeremias, "ἀμνός," *TDNT* 1.338-41; Dietzfelbinger, *Johannes*, 1.53; Schnelle, *Johannes*, 49-50; Lincoln, *John*, 113.

51. Brown, *John*, 61; Lindars, *Gospel of John*, 109; Jeremias, "ἀμνός." Against this: Schnackenburg, *John*, 1.298-99; Haenchen, *Johannes*, 166.

52. Porsch, *Pneuma*, 40-42; Jeremias, "ἀμνός"; Jeremias, "παῖς θεοῦ," 5.702; Boismard and Lamouille, *Jean*, 92; Burge, *Anointed Community*, 61.

53. Geza Vermes, *Scripture and Tradition in Judaism* (Leiden: Brill, 1961), 223-24; Roger Le Déaut, *La nuit pascale*, AnBib 22 (Rome: BibInst, 1963), 158; Martin J. McNamara, *The New Testament and the Palestinian Targum to the Pentateuch*, AnBib 27 (Rome: BibInst, 1966), 164-68; Braun, *Jean*, 137-38, 162-65, 216-18; Th. C. de Kruijf, "'The Glory of the Only Son' (John I 14)," in *Studies in John. Presented to J. N. Sevenster*, NovTSup 21 (Leiden: Brill, 1970), 118, 122-23; Lindars, *Apologetic*, 139, 146; Grigsby, "Cross," 60; Schnackenburg, *Johannesevangelium*, 4.192; Thyen, *Johannesevangelium*, 119-23; Mary L. Coloe, *God Dwells with Us: Temple Symbolism in the Fourth Gospel* (Collegeville: Liturgical, 2001), 191-92; Steven A. Hunt, "And the Word Became Flesh—Again? Jesus and Abraham in John 8:31-59," in *Perspectives on Our Father Abraham: Essays in Honor of Marvin R. Wilson*, ed. S. A. Hunt (Grand Rapids: Eerdmans, 2010), 100.

54. Boismard and Lamouille, *Jean*, 92.

55. Beutler, "Heilsbedeutung," 192; Ulrich Wilckens, *Das Evangelium nach Johannes*, NTD 4 (Göttingen: Vandenhoeck und Ruprecht, 1998), 40-41; see also Peter Stuhlmacher. *Biblische Theologie des Neuen Testaments*, 2 vols. (Göttingen: Vandenhoeck und Ruprecht, 1992-1999), 2.222-25, in relation to the imagery of lamb in Revelation.

56. Ulrich Busse, "Theologie oder Christologie im Johannesprolog?" in *Studies in the*

While the motif of carrying sin to Azazel might fit 1:29b, the animal there is a goat not a lamb. Similarly unconvincing is an allusion to the daily offering of a lamb since it was not a sin offering.[57] Nothing in the context suggests an allusion to Moses. As noted above, the reference to Jesus as God's only son in 1:14; 3:16, 18 and the voice from heaven in the Synoptic baptismal tradition addressing him as God's beloved Son may allude to the special relationship between Abraham and Isaac. This might then have evoked and have been meant to evoke for hearers the Jewish tradition which saw the binding of Isaac as having vicarious effect, thus as an allusion to Jesus' death. One might then see corroboration in the detail that Jesus carried his own cross, unlike in the Synoptic passion narratives. The evidence is not substantial and remains speculative. The other proposals are more substantial.[58] We turn first to the motif of the Passover lamb.

4.1.1.1 John 1:29 and Passover

In the instructions concerning the celebration of the Passover, Exod 12 (LXX) requires that the lamb be slain, which is then consumed in the Passover meal.[59]

> πρόβατον τέλειον ἄρσεν ἐνιαύσιον ἔσται ὑμῖν· ἀπὸ τῶν ἀρνῶν καὶ τῶν ἐρίφων λήμψεσθε.
> Your lamb shall be without blemish, a year-old male; you may take it from the sheep or from the goats. (Exod 12:5 LXX)

Strictly speaking, the animal can be a sheep or goat, hence the use of πρόβατον and not the word used in John 1:29 for "lamb," ἀμνός, which does not appear in these instructions.[60] By contrast it appears regularly in the

---

Gospel of John and Its Christology: Festschrift Gilbert Van Belle, ed. J. Verheyden, G. van Oyen, M. Labahn, and R. Bieringer, BETL 265 (Leuven: Peeters, 2014), 30–31; Wilckens, *Johannes*, 40–41. See also Dorothy A. Lee, "Paschal Imagery in the Gospel of John: A Narrative and Symbolic Reading," *Pacifica* 24 (2011): 16–17; Keener, *John*, 456.

57. So Painter, "Sacrifice and Atonement," 292; Frey, "Theologia crucifixi," 527.

58. Frey, "Theologia crucifixi," 525, 527, nevertheless acknowledges that it is not possible to reach a definite conclusion concerning its background.

59. See discussion of Exod 12 LXX in Schlund, "*Kein Knochen soll gebrochen werden*," 28. She concludes that the LXX translation is careful not to import cultic imagery. It understands the Hebrew root פסח as meaning to cover and protect (σκεπάζω) and so presents Passover as a festival remembering Israel's protection from the destroyer (ὀλεθρεύων) and so its successful escape out of Egypt.

60. Painter, "Sacrifice and Atonement," 293.

instructions concerning the daily offering in Exod 29:38–41 and frequently in other instructions about sacrifice (e.g., Lev 9:3; 12:6; 14:10–13, 21–24; 23:18–20) and means a young sheep, usually up to a year old.[61]

In itself and within its narrative context John 1:29 appears best taken as a reference to what Jesus was about to do in his ministry up to and including his death,[62] and not as a reference exclusively or even primarily to his death, nor to his death as a Passover lamb. Neither in its appellation of Jesus as "lamb of God," nor in its depiction of his role as "taking away the sin of the world" does it reflect the language of Exod 12. It remains a fact that the killing of the lamb for Passover, which could be described as a sacrifice (e.g., Josephus, *A.J.* 2.312; 1 Cor 5:7), though different in kind from other sacrifices, was not a sacrifice for sins.[63] Much later Jewish tradition attributed atoning qualities to it, but the evidence that this was so at the time of the Fourth Gospel is slender. The language used in 1:29b does not cohere well with such an understanding.[64]

While this is all true, the possibility should not be ruled out that the author and hearers of the Gospel could have brought Passover imagery to their understanding of the text.[65] There are two main lines of argument, one related to intratextual links and one related to wider early Christian discourse reflected in Johannine writings. The first is to note the author's apparent interest in relating Jesus to the Jewish festivals in a way that employed, for instance, the imagery of the Hanukkah, in portraying Jesus as the light of the world and the bringer of the water of life. Passover receives mention at a number of points in the Gospel (2:13, 23; 6:4; 11:55; 12:1; 13:1) and plays a particular role in the passion narrative tradition and its distinctive presentation in the Gospel.

---

61. Frederick W. Danker, Walter Bauer, and William F. Arndt, *A Greek-English Lexicon of the New Testament and Other Early Christian Literature*, 3rd ed. (Chicago: University of Chicago Press, 2000), 54.

62. According to Rusam, "Lamm Gottes," 78, what makes Jesus' death special is that it brings to a climax what he was doing during his earthly ministry.

63. Painter, "Sacrifice and Atonement," 292–93; Coloe, *God Dwells with Us*, 194–95. Similarly on the basis of detailed investigation of Jewish sources Schlund, "*Kein Knochen soll gebrochen werden*," shows that the focus there was on Israel's being confronted with a destroying power, depicted at various levels of connection with God (156). She argues that fixation with relating 1:29 to Jesus' death led to attempts on the basis of very late rabbinic texts to argue that an understanding of the Passover lamb as bringing atonement must have already been present in the first century, which the extant evidence simply does not support (174). See also Weidemann, *Tod Jesu*, 426–40. Cf. Notker Füglister, *Die Heilsbedeutung des Pascha*, SANT 8 (Munich: Kösel, 1963).

64. On this see Weidemann, *Tod Jesu*, 432.

65. Rusam, "Lamm Gottes," 78.

The distinctive emphasis meets us already in 11:55–57 where John makes reference to people coming to Jerusalem before the feast to purify themselves and their wondering whether Jesus would come to the feast, and to the authorities' seeking information which might lead to his arrest. The dramatic irony plays with what the author and hearers know. The reference to the Passover in 12:1 before the account of Jesus' anointing matches the account in Mark 14:1, as does 13:1 where John again mentions the Passover and Jesus' impending death. Thus, the dating of Jesus' last days to the time of the Passover was already well rooted in the passion narrative tradition. By comparison with the Synoptic Gospels, John's account has at one level fewer references. We find nothing about preparation for Jesus and his disciples to celebrate the Passover, nor anything about the last meal as a Passover meal (cf. Mark 14:12–25; Luke 22:15). In John it was apparently not. We do, however, find literary exploitation of the motif. This is particularly striking in the way the author has composed the trial before Pilate where on the basis that the Jewish authorities would not want to contaminate themselves before the feast by entering a Gentile building (18:28) the author has Pilate move to and fro between Jesus inside and them outside over 7 scenes (18:28–19:16).

This sevenfold literary construct at no point suggests that Jesus is being portrayed as a Passover lamb, but it does conclude by noting that it was the Day of Preparation for the Passover at around the sixth hour when Pilate passed judgment on Jesus (19:14). References to timing were probably already a feature of John's passion narrative tradition, such as we find in Mark, whose sets of threes in relation to crucifixion at the third hour (15:25) and the death at the sixth and darkness till the ninth (15:33) reflect the storyteller's art. John's different timing—day in relation to the Passover and time of day— may well reflect early tradition, indeed greater historical accuracy. The next Johannine reference is incidental, explaining why the Jews took down the bodies from the cross: "Since it was the day of Preparation, the Jews did not want the bodies left on the cross during the Sabbath, especially because that sabbath was a day of great solemnity" (19:31). It was a special Sabbath because on John's chronology the Passover fell on that day (not the day before as in the Synoptic Gospels).

What remains unstated, but may be deduced is that Jesus, according to John's timing, would have been executed at the time when the Passover lambs were slain.[66] The author might have drawn attention to it with a more

---

66. Schlund, *"Kein Knochen soll gebrochen werden,"* 130, notes the importance of the issue of timing in relation to the Passover, pointing to Num 9:2–3; Jub. 49:1, 12, 14–15; John 11:55; 18:28; 19:14.

specific reference to the Passover and not just the great Sabbath. On the other hand, two signals in the context of Jesus' death may well indicate intent on the part of the author to draw his hearers' attention to the Passover and to Jesus being killed like the Passover lambs. In that sense, Jesus would be the new Passover lamb. The first is the reference to hyssop (19:29)—a plant in the mint family used for medicinal purposes but also, because of its sturdiness, for sprinkling or brushing, often for ritual purification (Lev 14:4–6, 49–52; Num 19:18).⁶⁷ Hyssop was to be used to sprinkle blood on the lintel and the doorposts of the house of the Israelites in the first Passover (Exod 12:22) in order to protect them from the killing of their firstborn. Was it common enough to be on hand and sufficiently sturdy to be used to bring sour wine to the lips of Jesus or is the image so unrealistic that we must conclude that the author intended symbolism, at least to evoke association with the Passover?⁶⁸

The second possible allusion is in the details that the soldiers found that Jesus was already dead so did not break his legs in relation to which the author declares: "These things happened so that the Scripture might be fulfilled, 'None of his bones shall be broken'" (19:36). This might well allude to the instruction concerning the Passover lamb: καὶ ὀστοῦν οὐ συντρίψετε ἀπ' αὐτοῦ ("You shall not break any of its bones" in Exod 12:46 LXX).⁶⁹ It might equally allude to Ps 34:19–20 (33:20–21 LXX).⁷⁰

> πολλαὶ αἱ θλίψεις τῶν δικαίων, καὶ ἐκ πασῶν αὐτῶν ῥύσεται αὐτούς.
> κύριος φυλάσσει πάντα τὰ ὀστᾶ αὐτῶν, ἓν ἐξ αὐτῶν οὐ συντριβήσεται.
> Many are the afflictions of the righteous, but he rescues them from them all.
> The Lord keeps all their bones; not one of them will be broken.
> (Ps 33:20–21 LXX)

---

67. The plant referred to here as hyssop is probably Syrian hyssop, *Origanum syriacum*, a small shrub not sufficiently substantial to function as a means of conveying a sponge, but possibly used in association with a sponge.

68. Lee, "Paschal Imagery," 25; Weidemann, *Tod Jesu*, 424, 447; Schlund, "*Kein Knochen soll gebrochen werden*," 123–24, who sees the use of the mention of hyssop in 19:29 to prove a Passover typology as overly subtle.

69. Thüsing, *Erhöhung*, 171; Mussner, "Kultische Aspekte," 142–43; Herbert Klos, *Die Sakramente im Johannesevangelium*, SBS 46 (Stuttgart: KBW, 1970), 75; Grigsby, "Cross," 57–59; Baum-Bodenbender, *Hoheit*, 54, 171; Bruce, *John*, 377; Ellis, *Genius*, 277–78; Weidemann, *Tod Jesu*, 424; Schlund, "*Kein Knochen soll gebrochen werden*," 128–29. She also notes that the context of Zech 12:10 cited in this passage is about the protection of Jerusalem.

70. Dodd, *Interpretation*, 230–38; Forestell, *Word*, 90; Dauer, *Passionsgeschichte*, 139–42; Alfons Dauer, *Johannes und Lukas*, FB 50 (Würzburg: Echter, 1984), 230; Robinson, *Priority*, 152–53.

Although one cannot rule out multivalent allusions, it is unlikely to be both,[71] much as both might be applicable christological interpretations. Some suggest a former reference to Ps 34:19-20 has now been overlaid by the author's concern to emphasise Jesus as the Passover lamb.[72] One might also see in the flow of blood from Jesus' side an allusion to the blood of the paschal lamb.[73]

Again the evidence is inconclusive and accounts for the very differing interpretations. One interpretation is to dismiss altogether the presence of a Passover typology and take the references to Passover as simply part of the temporal description.[74] Against that, the fact that the author elsewhere sets Jesus in typological relation to the feasts would lead one to suspect that he would do so also in relation to the Passover, depicting Jesus as the true paschal lamb.[75] One might argue that his dating of the events, far from reflecting early historical memory, is a deliberate attempt to develop a Passover typology. Aside from the question whether John invented the chronology or not, many do read the Johannine narrative as subtly depicting Jesus as a Passover sacrifice. It is then natural to assume that John 1:29 would be understood by the author and hearers as including not just a reference to Jesus' ministry up to and including his death, but also to his death, in particular, as a Passover lamb.

If one does, there still remains the issue of how the author might have understood such a typology. The blood of the Passover lamb sprinkled on the lintel and doorposts was to ward off danger, in tradition interpreted as warding off the destroying angel, thus apotropaic.[76] Purification is associated

---

71. Against Boismard and Lamouille, *Jean*, 452; Brown, *John*, 953; Whitacre, *Polemic*, 62-63.

72. So Bultmann, *Johannes*, 677; Barnabas Lindars, *New Testament Apologetic* (London: SCM, 1961), 96; Lindars, *Gospel of John*, 590; Barrett, *John*, 558; Schnackenburg, *Johannesevangelium*, 3.342.

73. Weidemann, *Tod Jesu*, 447; Lee, "Paschal Imagery," 26; but see Schlund, "*Kein Knochen soll gebrochen werden*," 113.

74. Rusam, "Lamm Gottes," 66.

75. Ashton, *John*, 143; Michel Gourgues, "'Mort pour nos péchés selon les écritures': Que reste-t-il chez Jean du credo des origines? Jn 1,29, Chaînon unique de continuité," in *The Death of Jesus in the Fourth Gospel*, ed. G. Van Belle, BETL 200 (Leuven: Peeters, 2007), 181-97, 190; Brian D. Johnson, "'Salvation is from the Jews': Judaism in the Gospel of John," in *New Currents through John. A Global Perspective*, ed. F. Lozada and T. Thatcher, SBLRBS 54 (Atlanta: SBL, 2006), 95-96; Coloe, *God Dwells with Us*, 192, 196; Bond, "Seamless Robe," 191; Lee, "Paschal Imagery," 26, who writes: "Passover—the greatest of all the feasts in its iteration throughout the narrative—is essential for understanding the Johannine Jesus."

76. Weidemann, *Tod Jesu*, 426-29, 433-40, 448; Schlund, "*Kein Knochen soll gebrochen werden*," 113-14, 156, who notes the broad potential which contemporary understandings of Passover presented, as a symbol of apotropaic protection and of belonging.

with Passover but primarily in preparation for it (as in 11:55; 18:28; cf. also 13:10), not as something which Passover achieved.[77] Safety and protection of the believing community and belonging are major themes in John.[78] As Mary L. Coloe notes, "In the hour the fullness of this gift of love is revealed as Jesus gives himself over to death as a new Passover lamb, whose death creates a new household/Temple of God, and whose blood is the sign of those belonging to this household."[79]

Within the narrative of the last days of Jesus in John we have no direct references which tell us how the author might have understood what the death of Jesus as the Passover lamb achieved.[80] The closest probably relates to the casting out of the ruler of this world, to which we return below, and which is alluded to in 12:31, 14:30 and 16:11.[81] Read in the light of such an understanding of the typology, John 1:29 would refer to removing sin from the world by removing its ruler,[82] and so not as a sacrifice for sin.[83]

Those who believe that the author and his hearers would have already assumed that the killing of the Passover lamb achieved atonement in the sense of a sacrifice for sins, or at least had made this association in relation to Jesus, see the typology as pointing by implication to Jesus as the sacrificial lamb. They argue that the author and his hearers would already have understood John 1:29, 36 in that light, despite the singular of "sin," and the use of the non-cultic word, "taking away,"[84] so that in fact an *inclusio* is present linking 1:29 and the passion narrative.[85] John A. Dennis, who

---

77. So Schlund, "*Kein Knochen soll gebrochen werden*," 139–40, who points also to 2 Chr 35:3 and 1 Esd 1:3 (30–50). She adds that there is no clear focus on the aspect of the sprinkling of blood in contemporary tradition (113). See also Weidemann, *Tod Jesu*, 431.

78. So Schlund, "*Kein Knochen soll gebrochen werden*," who emphasises the importance of protection of believers from evil (130–33), noting how in 17:11 Jesus prays for the safety of his own (138). Security and belonging are key elements of Passover and concerns of the Fourth Gospel, for which the disempowering of the ruler of this world is a significant aspect of what Jesus' death achieved (170–71).

79. Coloe, *God Dwells with Us*, 196.

80. So Painter, "Sacrifice and Atonement," 293.

81. Painter, "Sacrifice and Atonement," 311; Weidemann, *Tod Jesu*, 26; Coloe, *God Dwells with Us*, 191–92.

82. Coloe, *God Dwells with Us*, 199.

83. So also Ashton, *Fourth Gospel*, 466.

84. Cf. Schnelle, "Kreuzestheologie," 245, who relates "takes away" to Jesus' carrying his cross in 19:17; and Keener, *John*, 456, who connects it to lifting sin up onto the cross.

85. Jean Zumstein, "L'interpretation johannique de la mort du Christ," in *The Four Gospels 1992. Festschrift for Frans Neirynck*, ed. F. Van Segbroeck, C. M. Tuckett, G. Van Belle, and J. Verheyden (Leuven: Peeters, 1992), 2120; Frey, "Theologia crucifixi," 519, 527; Beutler, *Johannesevangelium*, 494; Lee, "Paschal Imagery," 19, who writes: "There are literary reasons

understands 1:29 as also lying behind 11:51-52, argues that the author sees Christ's death as a Passover sacrifice in the light of restoration eschatology. Because Israel's sins resulted in the dispersion,[86] "as Israel's Passover Lamb, Jesus' death 'takes away sin' (1.29) and brings about a second exodus deliverance."[87] While Dennis uses this observation to make a claim for the importance of vicarious atonement in John,[88] his argument in fact makes a stronger case for understanding 1:29 not as dealing with the sins of individuals but corporately as dealing with Israel's sin. This, however, does not sit well with the formulation of 1:29 which focuses not on Israel but the world. Yet it does raise the possibility that taking away sin may have different aspects: dealing with the sins of individuals and dealing with the sin of the nation, the one available already during Jesus' ministry, the other achieved only through his death.

The case for arguing that 1:29 might have been intended or heard as also including an allusion to Passover typology and then understanding it as a sacrifice for sins may find some support in the observation that it is highly unlikely that the author and his hearers would have been unfamiliar with the notion of Jesus' death as like a sacrifice for sins. This notion is present in other literature considered to be the product of the Johannine community and its distinctive discourse, not least 1 John.[89] This argument carries weight even when one recognises different authorship of the writings and differences in theology and soteriology though expressed in the community's distinctive language. In addition, the presence of cultic or vicarious interpretations of Jesus' death elsewhere in the Gospel itself would strengthen the case.

In some sense the weight of the argument cannot be assessed until we have considered all such references. In the broader sense one needs also

---

for arguing that, within the shape of the Johannine narrative, it is temple, as well as Passover, imagery that carries the iconography of the lamb." She points to the temple expulsion, Johannine irony in having a lamb expel other animals, and argues that John is portraying the message that because of Jesus' sacrifice no further sacrifices are necessary (19-20). She also sees a parallel between "Behold the lamb" (1:29) and "Behold the man" (19:5) and irony in the leaders' concern with purification when now before them "the prolepsis of the Baptist's initial christological declaration is here fulfilled, since what we see on the cross is none other than the Lamb of God" (25).

86. Dennis, *Death and Gathering*, 351.
87. Dennis, *Death and Gathering*, 357.
88. Dennis, *Death and Gathering*, 353.
89. Frey, "Theologia crucifixi," 522, 530; Frey, "Edler Tod," 574, 581; Keener, *John*, 454. Weidemann, *Tod Jesu*, 442-44, notes that the focus in Rev 12 on blood relates to the notion of victory over the devil.

to take into account use of paschal imagery elsewhere in relation to Jesus' death. Many point to 1 Cor 5:7, ἐκκαθάρατε τὴν παλαιὰν ζύμην, ἵνα ἦτε νέον φύραμα, καθώς ἐστε ἄζυμοι· καὶ γὰρ τὸ πάσχα ἡμῶν ἐτύθη Χριστός ("Clean out the old yeast so that you may be a new batch, as you really are unleavened. For our paschal lamb, Christ, has been sacrificed"). The focus there is cleansing the congregation from contamination. It does not explicate Christ's role as paschal sacrifice.[90] Paschal imagery is applied to the blood of Christ as an unblemished lamb in 1 Pet 1:19.[91] The tradition of Jesus' last meal, at least in the Synoptic Gospels, associates Jesus' death with the Passover.[92] The specific reference to Passover in the context of the feeding of the 5,000 (6:4) may symbolically allude to a Passover significance of Jesus' death and the eucharistic meal it provided (6:51–58).

In the interim we may draw some tentative conclusions. A contextual reading of 1:29, 36 suggests that the primary focus is Jesus' status as Messiah, but understood in the light of the prologue as the Word made flesh, the only Son of the Father, and his mission, alternatively expressed in the context as bringing light and life and making the Father known. The image of lamb gives expression both to the special relationship of sonship and to the element of vulnerability. There is no reason to limit the role of "taking away the sin of the world" to Jesus' death, nor to exclude from it any reference to his death. If the balance of probability suggests the intention of a Passover typology in the passion narrative, then an allusion to that typology should not be excluded in 1:29, 36, though the case remains tentative.[93] That includes

90. Painter, "Sacrifice and Atonement," 292; Weidemann, *Tod Jesu*, 441–42.
91. Keener, *John*, 454.
92. Barrett, *John*, 176; Hans Hübner, *Biblische Theologie des Neuen Testaments*, 3 vols. (Göttingen: Vandenhoeck und Ruprecht, 1990–1995), 3.160; David D. C. Braine, "The Inner Jewishness of St. John's Gospel as the Clue to the Inner Jewishness of Jesus," *StNTU* 13 (1988): 124. Both Painter, "Sacrifice and Atonement," 293, and Schlund, *"Kein Knochen soll gebrochen werden,"* 174, challenge this conclusion on the basis that any Greek-speaking Jew of the time would have seen Passover imagery in this way. It becomes, however, credible if we see the context as Jewish Christian, where originally separate motifs have been drawn into service to depict the event of Christ's death and remember it in the Eucharist.
93. So Dodd, *Interpretation*, 230–38, 424; Bultmann, *Johannes*, 524; Forestell, *Word*, who interprets the Passover typology only to mean *Jesus* passes to the Father (90–92); similarly Boismard and Lamouille, *Jean*, 337–38 for 13:1, but not for 19:34; Dauer, *Passionsgeschichte*, 137–43, who identifies Passover typology as belonging only in the author's tradition; *Johannes und Lukas*, 230; Robinson, *Priority*, 152–53. Wilkens, *Zeichen*, sees "the signs Gospel" constructed around the Passover motif, with the signs corresponding to the plagues on Egypt and the cross as the Passover lamb sacrifice (73–74, 77). Others who support a Passover interpretation include: Thüsing, *Erhöhung*, 19–21; Pancaro, *Law*, 350; Reim, *Studien*, 52, 179; Schnackenburg, *Johannesevangelium*, 3.16; Robert Fortna, "Christology in the Fourth Gospel:

both the possibility that it alludes to Jesus' death as a sacrifice to deal with sin and the possibility that it alludes to protecting people from the destroyer, as light "breaking the power of darkness."⁹⁴ The broader question is then what the presence of such motifs implies about the author's soteriology, but this can be considered only after we have investigated further relevant data. First we return to other possible motifs which may have played a role in the author's and hearers' understanding of 1:29, 36.

4.1.1.2 John 1:29 and Isaiah 53 and 42

The case for seeing in 1:29 the announcement of a Passover theme of importance for the Gospel as a whole is not strong. This does not rule out the possibility that it is still the background for the formulations we have before us in 1:29. This may also be the case in relation to Isa 53, where the image of the lamb occurs:

> ὡς πρόβατον ἐπὶ σφαγὴν ἤχθη
> καὶ ὡς ἀμνὸς ἐναντίον τοῦ κείροντος αὐτὸν ἄφωνος
> οὕτως οὐκ ἀνοίγει τὸ στόμα αὐτοῦ.
> As a sheep is brought to slaughter
> and as a lamb is silent before its shearer,
> so he did not open his mouth. (Isa 53:7)

The following arguments support a possible allusion to this text. As noted above, the motif lamb, used in the reworking of the baptismal tradition, may well be expressing both intimate affection and vulnerability, perhaps implied in the allusion to Isa 42:1 in the Markan tradition where the voice from heaven declares: σὺ εἶ ὁ υἱός μου ὁ ἀγαπητός, ἐν σοὶ εὐδόκησα ("You are my Son, in whom I am well pleased" in Mark 1:11):

> Ιακωβ ὁ παῖς μου, ἀντιλήμψομαι αὐτοῦ·
> Ισραηλ ὁ ἐκλεκτός μου, προσεδέξατο αὐτὸν ἡ ψυχή μου·
> ἔδωκα τὸ πνεῦμά μου ἐπ' αὐτόν, κρίσιν τοῖς ἔθνεσιν ἐξοίσει.
> Jacob is my child/servant; I will help him,
> Israel my chosen one, my soul has accepted him;

Redaction-Critical Perspectives," *NTS* 21 (1975): 502; Wengst, *Gemeinde*, 109; Williams, "Cultic Elements," 340–41; Duke, *Irony*, 128; Beasley-Murray, *John*, 674.

94. Painter, "Sacrifice and Atonement," 311.

I have put my spirit upon him, and he will bring judgment to the
nations. (Isa 42:1)

If one sees the reworking as preserving the reference to sonship, now in 1:34, and the notion of intimacy and vulnerability in 1:29, where he is described as "the lamb of God," then such vulnerability would apply not only to Jesus' ministry but also and especially to his death. In his use of the motifs of exaltation and glorification, the author appears elsewhere to stand directly or indirectly under the influence of Isa 52:13, as we shall see in 4.1.2 and 4.3.2 below.

Ἰδοὺ συνήσει ὁ παῖς μου καὶ ὑψωθήσεται καὶ δοξασθήσεται σφόδρα.
Behold my servant shall understand and shall be exalted and glorified
exceedingly. (Isa 52:13)

The author also cites Isa 53:1 "Lord, who has believed our report and to whom has the arm of the Lord been revealed?" (κύριε, τίς ἐπίστευσεν τῇ ἀκοῇ ἡμῶν; καὶ ὁ βραχίων κυρίου τίνι ἀπεκαλύφθη;) in 12:38, though there the focus is not on Jesus' death but on his ministry.

In relation to John 1:29 the question is whether an allusion to Isa 53:7 would be limited to its depiction of vulnerability, as apparently the use of Isa 53:7–8 in Acts 8:32–33, or include also the content of the context, especially Isa 53:4–6,

οὗτος τὰς ἁμαρτίας ἡμῶν φέρει καὶ περὶ ἡμῶν ὀδυνᾶται, ...
αὐτὸς δὲ ἐτραυματίσθη διὰ τὰς ἀνομίας ἡμῶν
καὶ μεμαλάκισται διὰ τὰς ἁμαρτίας ἡμῶν·
παιδεία εἰρήνης ἡμῶν ἐπ᾽ αὐτόν, τῷ μώλωπι αὐτοῦ ἡμεῖς ἰάθημεν.
πάντες ὡς πρόβατα ἐπλανήθημεν, ἄνθρωπος τῇ ὁδῷ αὐτοῦ ἐπλανήθη·
καὶ κύριος παρέδωκεν αὐτὸν ταῖς ἁμαρτίαις ἡμῶν.
He bears our sins and suffers pain for us ...
He was wounded because of our acts of lawlessness,
and has been weakened because of our sins.
The punishment for our peace was on him and by his bruising we were
healed.
All of us like sheep went astray, each person strayed his own way;
and the Lord gave him up for our sins. (Isa 53:4–6)

Given that it makes best sense in the context to interpret 1:29b as referring to Jesus' ministry, the allusion to Jesus as lamb of God who takes away the sin of the world could also have been intended and heard as evoking traditions which spoke of Jesus' death as for sins. The language and concept of 1:29b ὁ αἴρων τὴν ἁμαρτίαν τοῦ κόσμου ("who takes away the sin of the world") do not appear to stand under the influence of Isa 53:4-6, but speak of taking away (αἴρων) and of sin (τὴν ἁμαρτίαν) in the singular and of "the world" (τοῦ κόσμου), not of someone suffering on our behalf.[95] It may seem closer to Isa 53:12,[96] but even then the same differences are evident.

καὶ αὐτὸς ἁμαρτίας πολλῶν ἀνήνεγκεν καὶ διὰ τὰς ἁμαρτίας αὐτῶν παρεδόθη.
And he bore the sins of many and was given up for their sins. (Isa 53:12)

Scholars are divided over whether to see here an allusion to Isa 53:4-6 and its concept of one suffering for the sins of others, which one might see as one allusion beside other allusions, such as to the Passover lamb,[97] or to deny such an allusion and understand it as referring only to vulnerability.[98] The evidence thus far is tenuous. Thus de Boer concludes: "The idea that Jesus' death is being regarded as a blood sacrifice expiating sins is not clearly discernible in 1:29 and has very little support (in the remainder of the Gospel, including in ch. 19)."[99] On the other hand, should discussion of the rest of the Gospel lead to the conclusion of Christ suffering for sins, whether understood as in cultic sacrificial terms or as vicarious suffering in others' stead, this would need to be weighed in assessing how John 1:29 might have been intended or heard.

---

95. Cf. Frey, "Edler Tod," 577.
96. Frey, "Edler Tod," 577.
97. Lee, "Paschal Imagery," 18; Williams, "He Saw His Glory," 61; Schnackenburg, *Person Jesu Christi*, 312; Schnelle, *Johannes*, 49-50; Wilckens, *Johannes*, 40-41; Thyen, *Johannesevangelium*, 119-23; Frey, "Theologia crucifixi," 527-28; Frey, "Edler Tod," 576-77; John F. McHugh, *John 1-4*, ICC (London: T&T Clark, 2009), 132, who speaks of multivalence. Zimmermann, *Christologie*, 107-17, similarly speaks of multiple semantic allusions at play including notions of expiation (117).
98. So Rusam, "Lamm Gottes," 65, 77-78, who argues that taking away sin refers not to carrying away the burden of sin but to how through the gift of the Spirit, the church can remove the world's sin (79); similarly Ashton, *Fourth Gospel*, 163.
99. De Boer, *Johannine Perspectives*, 280.

4.1.2 Other Alleged Allusions to Vicarious or Sacrificial Atonement

4.1.2.1 John 6:51c

In its present form[100] John 6 appears to allude to the Eucharist in 6:51c–58.[101] This allusion is also likely present earlier in 6:35[102] and in the account of the feeding of the 5,000. The words καὶ ὁ ἄρτος δὲ ὃν ἐγὼ δώσω ἡ σάρξ μού ἐστιν ὑπὲρ τῆς τοῦ κόσμου ζωῆς ("the bread which I give is my flesh for the life of the world" at 6:51c) are best understood as referring directly to the nourishment the Son will give in the flesh (and blood) of the Eucharist in the verses that follow.[103] Thus the response of the Jews in 6:52 focusses upon the giving of flesh to eat, not upon vicarious dying. This may reflect Johannine irony, though it would be more usual to see the irony work in the way that the focus is the same action, giving to eat, with the Jews then failing to comprehend the spiritual nourishment. This is confirmed by what follows, so that the primary reference of 6:51c is most likely not to Jesus' vicarious death, but the gift of his flesh (and blood) in the Eucharist. In the light of this connection it is also improbable that it refers simply to Jesus' giving himself (non-vicariously) for the benefit of others, as Forest-

---

100. On developments behind the present form of the text and issues of redaction see Anderson, *Christology*, who argues that there is "insufficient stylistic and contextual evidence for identifying John 6:51c–58 as a redactor's interpolation, neither are there sufficient *ideological* (sic) grounds" (135), but see also Ashton, *Fourth Gospel*, 466.

101. De Boer, *Johannine Perspectives*, 234.

102. Painter, "Sacrifice and Atonement," writes: "The extension of the metaphor to include drinking suggests that the eucharistic life of the believing community has impacted on the development of the discourse (6:35). This is very clear in the language of 6:53-55" (298). Cf. Martinus J. J. Menken, "John 6.51c–58. Eucharist or Christology?" in *Critical Readings of John 6*, ed. R. A. Culpepper (Leiden: Brill, 1997), 185, who uses the allusion to 6:35 to argue the opposite, that it cannot be eucharistic because eating and drinking at this point relate to responding in faith to the person of Jesus.

103. So Ulrich Wilckens, "Der eucharistische Abschnitt der johanneischen Rede vom Lebensbrot (Joh 6,51c–58)," in *Neues Testament und Kirche. Festschrift für R. Schnackenburg*, ed. J. Gnilka (Freiburg: Herder, 1974), 224, 227, 232; Brown, *John*, 285, 291; Boismard and Lamouille, *Jean*, 204-5; Haenchen, *Johannes*, 326; Beutler, "Heilsbedeutung," 191–92; Beutler, *Johannesevangelium*, 225–26; Theobald, *Johannes*, 1.477–78; Peder Borgen, *The Gospel of John: More Light from Philo, Paul and Archaeology: The Scriptures, Tradition, Exposition, Meaning*, NovTSup 154 (Leiden: Brill, 2014), 164. On the eucharistic allusion see also Jörg Frey, "Das Bild als Wirkungspotential. Ein rezeptionsgeschichtlicher Versuch zur Funktion der Brot-Metapher in Johannes 6," in *Die Herrlichkeit des Gekreuzigten. Studien zu den Johanneischen Schriften I*, ed. J. Schlegel, WUNT 307 (Tübingen: Mohr Siebeck, 2013), 406; Frey, "Edler Tod," 576.

ell suggests.¹⁰⁴ We have seen that 6:51c–58 belongs closely with 6:27. The latter speaks of a future gift of food given by the "Son of Man"(!), who, as the ascended "Son of Man"! (6:62), will give his flesh and blood (as "Son of Man"! 6:53) to his own, reflecting the focus in the cluster about the Son of Man cluster. John 6:27, too, therefore, best fits the post-Easter gift of life through the Eucharist.¹⁰⁵ On the other hand, this should not exclude indirect allusion in 6:51c to Jesus' offering himself vicariously, sacrificially, or otherwise, by his death on the cross,¹⁰⁶ especially since an understanding of Jesus' death as in some sense vicarious or for others underlies the eucharistic tradition, even though it is not the major focus of the context nor of 6:51c. This leaves open in what sense the author would have understood Jesus' death as for others. De Boer writes: "The substitutionary (or vicarious) meaning ('instead of') certainly does not seem applicable to John 6:51c; the meaning seems to be 'for the sake of the life (salvation) of the world.'"¹⁰⁷ By contrast Knöppler sees in 6:51c, in contrast to all other ὑπέρ sayings, an unambiguous reference to Jesus' death as an atoning sacrifice which is also vicarious.¹⁰⁸

The alternative view sees no allusion to the Eucharist, but rather a variation on the metaphor already employed variously in the preceding discourse according to which Jesus both gives the bread of life and is the bread of life.¹⁰⁹ Then John 6:51c might simply be expanding on this and what follows offering

---

104. Forestell, *Word*, 76; similarly in a non-sacrificial sense: Schürmann, "Schlüssel," 249–51, 255.

105. Schnackenburg, *Person Jesu Christi*, 299. Cf. Benjamin E. Reynolds, *The Apocalyptic Son of Man in the Gospel of John*, WUNT 2.249 (Tübingen: Mohr Siebeck, 2008), who sees a eucharistic allusion as at most secondary compared with the response of faith (156–57); similarly Dorothy Lee, *Flesh and Glory: Symbolism, Gender and Theology in the Gospel of John* (New York: Crossroad, 2002), 40.

106. So Müller, *Heilsgeschehen*, 106; Hofbeck, *Semeion*, 120; Barrett, *John*, 298; Schnider and Stenger, *Johannes*, 163; Riedl, *Heilswerk*, 314; Ruckstuhl, *Einheit*, 357; Haacker, *Stiftung*, 173; Lindars, "Passion," 73; Lindars, *Gospel of John*, 267; Lindars, *Son of Man*, 152; Williams, "Cultic Elements," 341; Bruce, *John*, 158; Weder, "Menschwerdung," 348; Rudolf Schnackenburg, "Ist der Gedanke des Sühnetodes Jesu der einzige Zugang zum Verständnis unserer Erlösung durch Jesus Christus?" in *Der Tod Jesu. Deutungen im Neuen Testament*, ed. K. Kertlege, QD 74 (Freiburg: Herder, 1978), 222; Schnackenburg, *Johannesevangelium*, 2.61–62; Schnackenburg, *Person Jesu Christi*, 313; Beasley-Murray, *John*, 94; Schnelle, *Christologie*, 223; Frey, "Theologia crucifixi," 531.

107. De Boer, *Johannine Perspectives*, 233; similarly Painter, "Sacrifice and Atonement," 300.

108. Knöppler, *Theologia crucis*, 94–95, 202.

109. So Menken, "John 6.51c–58," 187–88, though he acknowledges that the author "used a version of the words spoken by Jesus at the Last Supper," but does not believe that we can therefore conclude that 6:51–58 is about the Eucharist (189). He sees the reference to the bread in 6:51c–58 as differing from its use in the eucharistic tradition to refer to a piece of bread (191).

another variation on the metaphor about receiving this life, here under the image of eating and drinking. One could on that basis argue that there is no reference to Jesus' death at all or that, if there is, it should be understood as what he had been doing all along and now, as in 13:1, intimating that he would love them even to the point of death,[110] but it would still be open to see the death as an additional act, namely as vicarious or as a cultic sacrifice on their behalf. On balance, I consider an allusion to eucharistic tradition more likely and find it already alluded to in the account of the wedding at Cana. It is likely, however, that the Johannine community knew a form of the eucharistic tradition which contained elements interpreting Jesus' death as vicarious. This means we must leave open the possibility that 6:51c might include an allusion to Jesus' death as in some sense vicarious, even though that is not its primary reference.

4.1.2.2 John 10:11, 15, 17 (18)

The author has Jesus employ the metaphor of the shepherd to speak of his impending death.

> ὁ ποιμὴν ὁ καλὸς τὴν ψυχὴν αὐτοῦ τίθησιν ὑπὲρ τῶν προβάτων·
> The good shepherd lays down his life for the sheep. (10:11)
> τὴν ψυχήν μου τίθημι ὑπὲρ τῶν προβάτων.
> I lay down my life for the sheep. (10:15)
> Διὰ τοῦτό με ὁ πατὴρ ἀγαπᾷ ὅτι ἐγὼ τίθημι τὴν ψυχήν μου,
> ἵνα πάλιν λάβω αὐτήν. οὐδεὶς αἴρει αὐτὴν ἀπ' ἐμοῦ,
> ἀλλ' ἐγὼ τίθημι αὐτὴν ἀπ' ἐμαυτοῦ. ἐξουσίαν ἔχω θεῖναι αὐτήν,
> καὶ ἐξουσίαν ἔχω πάλιν λαβεῖν αὐτήν·
> ταύτην τὴν ἐντολὴν ἔλαβον παρὰ τοῦ πατρός μου.
> For this the Father loves me, because I lay down my life
> in order that I might take it up again. No one takes it from me,
> but I lay it down of myself. I have authority to lay it down
> and I have authority to take it up again.
> This command I received from my Father. (10:17–18)

In John 10:11–13 the focus is on real caring for the sheep as opposed to those

---

110. Painter, "Sacrifice and Atonement," 300–302, relates Jesus' death on behalf of the disciples, particularly in relation to 10:11, 17–18, to Jesus' action at his arrest in surrendering himself to enable the disciples to go free (18:8).

who do not care and abandon the sheep. In 10:14-18 the attention moves to the Son fulfilling the Father's mission and the special relationship between the two. In this context we find the only specific reference to the purpose of his laying down his life. He does so in order to take it up again, clearly with a focus on the benefits which will flow from his return to the Father. This reflects the basic structure of the author's Christology, according to which his return will mean that he will empower the disciples with the Spirit for mission, a perspective highlighted in 10:16.[111]

Nothing is said of his death as being an act of cultic atonement or being vicarious on their behalf. Nonetheless these possibilities should not be too summarily dismissed. Within the metaphor a good shepherd may well risk mortal danger to protect the sheep from danger, though his death would be a disaster leaving the sheep without protection.[112] Clearly, as is often the case, the metaphor is fractured by factors which transcend it. Jesus as shepherd laid down his life for his sheep, but, again, it is not immediately clear what the author understood or intended that hearers might understand about how his death benefitted them.[113] The options include, that his death served as an atoning sacrifice,[114] that it was on their behalf, vicariously, in their stead,[115] that it was the part of his commitment to them to make the Father known even when to do so finally meant facing rejection and execution, that it refers to Jesus' surrendering himself to death at the arrest at the hands of the authorities understood as wolves (cf. 10:12) to enable his disciples to go free (18:8),[116] or that it was, as explained in 10:17-18, a means of returning to the Father by which he could then benefit them with the blessings of the Spirit.

---

111. Dennis, *Death and Gathering*, 302, writes that the author "highlights Jesus as Israel's ideal Shepherd, the one who fulfils Ezekiel's vision of bringing back dispersed Israel and unifying all Israel under the Davidic King (Ezek 37.19-22, 24-28)."

112. Zimmermann, *Christologie*, 391.

113. So also Zimmermann, *Christologie*, 394-95, though he argues that the imagery and rest of the Gospel imply that the shepherd's giving his life is vicarious.

114. So Wilkens, *Zeichen*, 98-99; Müller, *Heilsgeschehen*, 56; Thüsing, *Erhöhung*, 279; Schnider and Stenger, *Johannes*, 164; Miranda, *Sendung*, 20; Haacker, *Stiftung*, 169; Barrett, *John*, 376; Schulz, *Johannes*, 151; Schnackenburg, "Gedanke des Sühnetodes," 223; Lindars, *John*, 82; Beutler, "Heilsbedeutung," 190-91; Williams, "Cultic Elements," 341; Lincoln, *John*, 297.

115. So Bultmann, *Johannes*, 293; Schnackenburg, *Johannesevangeliums*, 2.372; 4.110; Boismard and Lamouille, *Jean*, 271; Forestell, *Word*, 74-75; Lattke, *Einheit*, 119-21; Müller, "Bedeutung," 63-64; Riedl, *Heilswerk*, 110; Becker, *Johannes*, 332; Ulrich Busse, "Offene Fragen zu Johannes 10," *NTS* 33 (1987): 522-23; Theobald, *Johannes*, 1.676-77; Beutler, *Johannesevangelium*, 342; Smith, *Theology*, 119; Thomas Söding, "Einsatz des Lebens: Ein Motiv johanneischen Soteriologie," in *The Death of Jesus in the Fourth Gospel*, ed. G. Van Belle, BETL 200 (Leuven: Peeters, 2007), 380.

116. Painter, "Sacrifice and Atonement," 300-302; Knöppler, *Theologia Crucis*, 95.

While this last option certainly fits 10:17–18, it is unlikely to be all that was meant in 10:11, 15. Similarly the reference to 18:8, itself probably symbolic of more, is unlikely to exhaust the meaning.[117] While 13:1 would support an interpretation of seeing the death as showing the full extent of the love, in that sense its revelation—a noble death to benefit others[118]—is unlikely to explain the singling out of the death, so that the first two options remain possibilities. Even so, the primary focus in the context is not what the death achieved, but that it demonstrated the goodness of the shepherd and his care for his own, including his protection of them.[119] This might sit well with Jesus' death understood apotropaically as the Passover lamb, but neither this notion nor that of Jesus' death as a sacrifice for sins or as vicarious in a non-cultic sense is the primary focus of 10:11, 15[120] and clearly not the focus of the sayings in 10:17–18.[121]

4.1.2.3 John 11:50–52; 18:14

The unwitting prophecy of Caiaphas both provides a rationale for having Jesus executed and, under alleged inspiration, indicates the purpose of his death.

> οὐδὲ λογίζεσθε ὅτι συμφέρει ὑμῖν ἵνα εἷς ἄνθρωπος ἀποθάνῃ ὑπὲρ τοῦ λαοῦ καὶ μὴ ὅλον τὸ ἔθνος ἀπόληται.
> τοῦτο δὲ ἀφ' ἑαυτοῦ οὐκ εἶπεν,
> ἀλλ' ἀρχιερεὺς ὢν τοῦ ἐνιαυτοῦ ἐκείνου ἐπροφήτευσεν
> ὅτι ἔμελλεν Ἰησοῦς ἀποθνῄσκειν ὑπὲρ τοῦ ἔθνους,
> καὶ οὐχ ὑπὲρ τοῦ ἔθνους μόνον
> ἀλλ' ἵνα καὶ τὰ τέκνα τοῦ θεοῦ τὰ διεσκορπισμένα συναγάγῃ εἰς ἕν.
> You do not realise that it is better for you that one should die for the people and the whole nation not perish.
> He did not say this of his own accord,

---

117. Painter, "Sacrifice and Atonement," 303–4, 308.
118. For the categories, noble death, which is widely reflected in John, and beyond that the noble death to benefit others, see Frey, "Edler Tod," 561–72, who gives the term "wirksamer Tod"/"effective death" to the latter (see 564–66 on the extent of the noble death motif in John).
119. Christine Schlund, "Schutz und Bewahrung als ein soteriologisches Motiv des Johannesevangeliums," in *The Death of Jesus in the Fourth Gospel*, ed. G. Van Belle, BETL 200 (Leuven: Peeters, 2007), 533–34.
120. Cf. Frey, "Edler Tod," 575.
121. So also Appold, *Oneness*, 194, 271; Dauer, *Passionsgeschichte*, 39; Lindars, "Passion," 73.

but the high priest that year prophesied
that Jesus was going to die for the nation,
and not for the nation only,
but that he might gather all the dispersed children of God into one.
(11:50-52)

As in 10:16-18, Jesus' death is depicted as achieving the unity of the people of God, there, the creation of one flock, here, the restoration of the dispersed children of God.[122] There, it is explicitly stated that he laid down his life in order to take it up again—which within the structure of the author's Christology refers to what his return to the Father would make possible through the gift of the Spirit, namely the sending of the disciples in mission. But, again, this is not to be taken as exhausting what the author might have meant.[123] The author is concerned with the corporate dimension, now fulfilled in the community of faith and expressed in imagery belonging to Israel's identity.[124] At a literal level there is clearly the notion that having the Romans execute Jesus would remove the danger that they would react violently toward the nation in response to seeing Jesus as a disturbance, probably an accurate assessment of the situation. Killing one man instead of having others killed makes his death vicarious in that sense. Johannine subtlety makes it likely that there is more, not least because mission clearly also includes mission to Gentiles.[125] It may also allude here to Jesus' death as a sacrifice for sin[126] or as a vicarious act in more than a literal sense[127] or as something which would ward off danger also in more than a literal sense, namely in an apotropaic

---

122. Dennis, *Death and Gathering*, 260-62; similarly Leung, *Kingship-Cross*, 149-50. Dennis sees the gathering also symbolically foreshadowed in the gathering of the loaves after the feeding of the 5,000 (201); also Leung, *Kingship-Cross*, 148-49.

123. So rightly Dennis, *Death and Gathering*, 258.

124. Pryor, *John*, 127-28, argues on the basis of an allusion to Ps 80:14-17 that the association of the Son of Man and the image of the vine points to concern with Israel as an entity. He also points to the role of the servant in Isa 49:5 of gathering Israel and the imagery of light in Isa 49:6, 9-10.

125. Dennis, *Death and Gathering*, argues that neither 10:15-16 nor 11:52 is referring to Gentiles (258, 296, 300), but then acknowledges that the Greeks in 12:20 and 7:35 most likely refer to godfearers (307) and that "the Johannine designation 'children of God' allows for an extension beyond its primary referent to 'Israel'" (309-10). On the likely Gentile inclusion see also Painter, "Sacrifice and Atonement," 305.

126. So Müller, *Heilsgeschehen*, 59-60; Miranda, *Sendung*, 20, 25; Schnackenburg, "Gedanke des Sühnetodes," 223; Lindars, "Passion," 73; Beutler, "Heilsbedeutung," 190; Bruce, *John*, 251; Williams, "Cultic Elements," 341; Ellis, *Genius*, 188; Lincoln, *John*, 297.

127. De Boer, *Johannine Perspectives*, 233; Söding, "Einsatz des Lebens," 365-66.

sense.¹²⁸ Dennis suggests that Jesus' death could be understood as atoning for the sins of Israel's past which had brought about the dispersion, giving it more of the character of a national act of atonement than one concerned with individuals' sins.¹²⁹ Although possible, such a limitation is not evident elsewhere. The literal level requires the notion of the death of one to avert the death of many and this is probably also the metaphorical sense, rather than the notion of a cultic sacrifice,¹³⁰ but the issue is not clear and may well include the non-cultic vicarious notion of Jesus' death as on behalf of Israel and ultimately also the Gentiles.¹³¹ In John 18:14 the author has a cross-reference to Caiaphas' prophecy, just a few verses after Jesus makes mention of the cup of suffering which he is to take, but this provides no further clarity on the issue.¹³²

4.1.2.4 John 12:24, 32; Isa 52:13

The same notion of Jesus' death bearing the fruit of mission is evident in 12:24, the saying about the dying seed, and in 12:32 about the lifting up of the Son of Man from the earth who will draw all people to him.¹³³ Within the frame of reference of the central structure of the author's Christology this is made possible through the Son's death and return in exaltation to the Father and what this makes possible: revelation, the sending of the Spirit and of the disciples, and, above all, mission.¹³⁴ It is nevertheless possible that the author would also have in mind that part of this process, namely Jesus'

---

128. Schlund, "Schutz und Bewahrung," 533-34. Knöppler, *Theologia crucis*, 95; Painter, "Sacrifice and Atonement," 309.

129. Dennis, *Death and Gathering*, 72, 116. "Therefore, it would seem that Jesus' death in John 11.51-52, a death that effects the restoration of the true Israel, would have to deal with sin in some way.... As Israel's Passover Lamb, Jesus' death 'takes away' sin (1.29) and brings about a second exodus deliverance" (357).

130. So with hesitation, Dodd, *Interpretation*, 233, 246; Schnackenburg, *Johannesevangelium*, 2.451; and confidently, Appold, *Oneness*, 121-22, 194, 240, 272-73; Forestell, *Word*, 82.

131. So Frey, "Edler Tod," 571-72.

132. Lindars, "Passion," 73.

133. Hurtado, *Lord Jesus Christ*, 378, notes that "throughout Isaiah 40–66 in particular, 'glory' is frequently used in statements about a future manifestation of God that will involve redemption for Israel and eventually the illumination of Gentile nations."

134. Dennis, *Death and Gathering*, 204, writes: "It is crucial to emphasize here that these eschatological and soteriological effects of Jesus' death in 12.24 (cf. 4.36; fruit), 12.32 (drawing), and 11.52 (gathering) are at the same time restorational effects."

death on the cross, also had a salvific effect which informed the mission and was part of the substance which it proclaimed. Again it is not possible to go beyond this to identify a particular model for understanding death as lying behind these statements, whether as an expiatory sacrifice for sins,[135] as vicarious in others' stead, or as apotropaic, the last the only option to receive some support from the context, namely the reference to the death as an act of judgment which casts out the ruler of this world in 12:31. We discuss in 4.2 below the possible background in Isa 52:13 LXX to the author's use of exaltation and glorification motifs, present here in the contexts of both 12:24 and 13:32. In itself this need not imply that the author therefore uses them here and elsewhere with the references to vicarious suffering in Isa 53.[136] There is a citation of Isa 53:1 in John 12:38, but it refers to Jesus' ministry not his death.

4.1.2.5 John 15:13

The saying in 15:13, "Greater love has no one more than this that someone lays down his life for his friends," reflects the common motif of dying in the interests of others as evidence of friendship.[137] Again this raises the question: in what way might the author have understood Jesus' death as benefitting his disciples as friends? Was it in expiating their sins, dying vicariously in their stead, facing suffering and death while acting in their interests, engaging the battle for them with the ruler of this world, or some or all of the above? It does not require an expiatory understanding,[138] but nor does it exclude it.[139] The language of laying down one's life (τὴν ψυχὴν αὐτοῦ θῇ ὑπέρ, "that he lay down his life for" in 15:13) occurs similarly in the shepherd discourse (10:11, 15) where the same issues of interpretation arise. It occurs also in 1 John 3:16 as part of a letter emanating from broadly the same Johannine context,

---

135. On 12:24: Lütgert, *Christologie*, 65, 169; Müller, *Heilsgeschehen*, 60-62; Haacker, *Stiftung*, 65, 169; Miranda, *Sendung*, 20; Beutler, "Heilsbedeutung," who sees in 12:23 a reference to vicarious atonement (193). Cf. also Becker, *Johannes*, 400, who sees this as the work of the redactor. On 12:32: Thüsing, *Erhöhung*, 24-28; Braun, *Jean*, 175.

136. Rightly Maddox, "Function," 188.

137. So Söding, "Einsatz des Lebens," 363-66. Frey, "Edler Tod," 569.

138. So Schnackenburg, *Johannesevangelium*, 3.124-35; Hartwig Thyen. "'Niemand hat grössere Liebe als die, dass er sein Leben für seine Freunde hingibt' (Joh 15,13)," in *Theologia Crucis—Signum Crucis. Festschrift für E. Dinkler*, ed. C. Andresen and G. Klein (Tübingen: Mohr Siebeck, 1979), 467-68, 481; Forestell, *Word*, 75.

139. Appold, *Oneness*, 194, recognises it as tradition but carrying no weight in the context; similarly Lindars, *John*, 82. Forestell, *Word*, 75, rejects the atonement motif here altogether.

though of different authorship and in some respects a different theology. It reads:

> ἐν τούτῳ ἐγνώκαμεν τὴν ἀγάπην, ὅτι ἐκεῖνος ὑπὲρ ἡμῶν τὴν ψυχὴν αὐτοῦ ἔθηκεν·
> καὶ ἡμεῖς ὀφείλομεν ὑπὲρ τῶν ἀδελφῶν τὰς ψυχὰς θεῖναι.
> In this we know love because he laid down his life for us.
> And we ought to lay down our lives for our brothers. (1 John 3:16)

There it is being used in an appeal to the recipients to engage in support for the needy in their midst, implying not literal death on their part, but sacrificial generosity. We find the same language used by Peter of his willingness to be faithful even to death in his loyalty to Christ.

> λέγει αὐτῷ ὁ Πέτρος· κύριε, διὰ τί οὐ δύναμαί σοι ἀκολουθῆσαι ἄρτι;
> τὴν ψυχήν μου ὑπὲρ σοῦ θήσω.
> ἀποκρίνεται Ἰησοῦς· τὴν ψυχήν σου ὑπὲρ ἐμοῦ θήσεις;
> ἀμὴν ἀμὴν λέγω σοι, οὐ μὴ ἀλέκτωρ φωνήσῃ ἕως οὗ ἀρνήσῃ με τρίς.
> Peter said to him, "Lord, why am I not able to follow you now?
> I will lay down my life for you."
> Jesus replied. "Will you lay down your life for me?
> Truly, truly, I tell you, the cock will not crow before you deny me three times." (John 13:37–38)

The notion of following Jesus—including into death—appeared already in 12:26 in association with the reference to the dying of the seed, just discussed. De Boer has made a strong case that this juxtaposition of Jesus' death and that of disciples may well be addressing a context where dying for one's faith has become a real possibility.[140]

The focus of these statements about dying for another appears to relate strongly to remaining faithful and acting in the interests—for the benefit—of others. This need not exclude the possibility that the disciples' potential deaths and that of Christ were understood differently, or at least that this might be so with elements related to Christ's death which would not apply in the case of the disciples. These include a potential reference to Jesus' death as expiatory—a motif more clearly present in the wider context of 1 John—or as vicarious on their behalf (symbolised by his surrendering himself at the

---

140. De Boer, *Johannine Perspectives*, 172, 185, 189–97; similar Frey, "Theologia crucifixi," 509.

arrest and letting them go free),[141] or as averting danger on their behalf by disempowering the ruler of this world.

In none of the instances where the motif of laying down one's life for others occurs are these potential functions of Jesus' death the primary focus. Frey rightly observes that these sayings need to be considered for what each contributes to the understanding of laying down one's life,[142] including in relation to Peter.[143] Each, in various ways, contains the notion of vicarious death for others by undergoing death on their behalf. However, this is to be distinguished from the motif of an expiatory sacrificial death,[144] even though the two are occasionally linked in tradition and are probably assumed in 1 John 3:16. He also notes that laying down one's life—Jesus' vicarious death—in John is not as clearly linked to dealing with forgiveness of sin as in Pauline tradition, but, he argues, largely on the basis of its presence in 1 John, must have been known to the author.[145] Accordingly, he argues that anyone having heard 1:29 and 6:51, which he understands as expiatory, would have to bring this meaning into all other statements about Jesus' dying for others.[146]

4.1.2.6 John 3:14–16

Other alleged references to Jesus' death as expiatory or as vicarious are even less certain. John 3:16 speaks of God so loving the world "that he gave his only Son" (ὥστε τὸν υἱὸν τὸν μονογενῆ ἔδωκεν). The author probably draws here upon a traditional formulation found elsewhere in the NT: "God sent his Son" (ἐξαπέστειλεν ὁ θεὸς τὸν υἱὸν αὐτοῦ in Gal 4:4); "God, sending his own Son" (ὁ θεὸς τὸν ἑαυτοῦ υἱὸν πέμψας in Rom 8:3); "as Christ loved us and gave himself up for her" (καθὼς καὶ ὁ Χριστὸς ἠγάπησεν ἡμᾶς καὶ παρέδωκεν ἑαυτὸν ὑπὲρ ἡμῶν in Eph 5:2). These are all in one way or another associated with Christ's salvific death, clearly so in 1 John 3:16:

---

141. Frey, "Edler Tod," 569, cautions against reading these statements as necessarily alluding to Christ's death as expiatory.

142. Frey, "Theologia crucifixi," 529–30.

143. Frey, "Edler Tod," 570, 575.

144. Frey, "Edler Tod," 570, 573.

145. Frey, "Theologia crucifixi," 530; "Edler Tod," 574, 576, 581, but he also notes the absence of the terminology of cultic atonement, including in what he sees as the Passover typology (582). Frey then seeks to strengthen the case for assuming an expiatory understanding of Jesus' death in John by pointing to cultic imagery in 17:19 and 13:10–11, though acknowledging that there the Word is what purifies, and in references to Jesus' body as a temple (583).

146. Frey, "Theologia crucifixi," 531.

ἐν τούτῳ ἐγνώκαμεν τὴν ἀγάπην,
ὅτι ἐκεῖνος ὑπὲρ ἡμῶν τὴν ψυχὴν αὐτοῦ ἔθηκεν.
In this we know love,
that he laid down his life for us. (1 John 3:16)

It could therefore be so in John 3:16.[147] Some also see Isaac typology here.[148] John 3:16, usually cited atomistically, needs to be interpreted in its context. When we do so, the meaning is not as unambiguous as may first seem. On the one hand, John 3:14-15 clearly refer to the lifting up of the Son of Man, which must include a reference to his death. As we shall consider below, it may well function at two levels, referring both to the literal lifting up in crucifixion (as also in 8:28 and 12:32) and to the exaltation of Jesus through that event to the Father's glory. Some see the lifting up of the serpent as an allusion to Jesus' death as expiatory or vicarious[149] and some do not.[150] In any event its primary focus is the greater event associated with Jesus' death, which constitutes the "heavenly things" that Nicodemus will surely not grasp if he cannot understand what is said during Jesus' ministry, as outlined in what precedes (3:12). The purpose of that lifting up according to 3:15, namely ἵνα πᾶς ὁ πιστεύων ἐν αὐτῷ ἔχῃ ζωὴν αἰώνιον ("that all who believe may have eternal life in him"), matches 3:16b ἵνα πᾶς ὁ πιστεύων εἰς αὐτὸν μὴ ἀπόληται ἀλλ' ἔχῃ ζωὴν αἰώνιον ("that all who believe in him may not perish but have eternal life"). The verses which follow 3:16, however, repeat its formulation negatively and expound it in terms of the coming of light into the world and not in relation to Jesus' death as vicarious at all (3:17-21). This strongly suggests that we should read 3:16 in this way, too, as another way of saying that the Father sent the Son to save the world by bringing the gift of light and life.[151] This coheres with the previous reference to Jesus as God's only

---

147. Müller, *Heilsgeschehen*, 51-52; Thüsing, *Erhöhung*, 9, 14-15; Riedl, *Heilswerk*, 145-46; Miranda, *Vater*, 125-26, 135-39; *Sendung*, 19; Lindars, *Gospel of John*, 159; Haenchen, *Johannes*, 225; Schulz, *Johannes*, 60; Beasley-Murray, *John*, 51.

148. So Braun, *Jean*, 157; Lindars, *Gospel of John*, 159; Meeks, "Man from Heaven," 156; Grigsby, "Cross," 60; Ellis, *Genius*, 55-56; Margaret Pamment, "The Meaning of Doxa in the Fourth Gospel," *ZNW* 74 (1983): 15; Schillebeeckx, *Christ*, 307.

149. So Müller, *Heilsgeschehen*, 50; Schnider and Stenger, *Johannes*, 163; Frey, "Theologia crucifixi," 546; Kohler, *Kreuz und Menschwerdung*, 258; Bergmeier, "ΤΕΤΕΛΕΣΤΑΙ," 288; indirectly, Dauer, *Passionsgeschichte*, 39.

150. Maddox, "Function," 192; Wilckens, "Lebensbrot," 224; Schnackenburg, *John*, 1.395-97; Nicholson, *Death*, 99-101; Beutler, *Johannesevangelium*, 140.

151. So Lütgert, *Christologie*, 24; Bultmann, *Theologie*, 365; Müller, "Bedeutung," 58-59; Lattke, *Einheit*, 77, 84-85, while acknowledging an originally vicarious tradition (70, 75); Fernando F. Segovia, *Love Relationships in the Johannine Tradition*, SBLDS 58 (Chico: Scholars,

Son in 1:14, where again the focus is on his salvific presence and his making the Father known (1:18).

The resolution of what appear to be two different foci may not be to choose one or the other, but, as is often the case in John, to see both as present.[152] He does indeed come as light into the world and is rejected by the darkness, giving himself and being given up to death. The question is then again the familiar one from texts considered thus far. Does being given up to death mean more than loving his own to the end (13:1)? Does it imply an understanding of Jesus' death as expiatory or vicarious?[153] Does it also include the notion that this death effected significant change? The answer is surely that it does, and how it does will depend to some extent upon what we believe hearers would bring to the text — not just in the light of what precedes but in the light of being in a community where the themes of the Gospel and its attitudes towards Jesus' death were known and could be assumed. Even so, a certain ambiguity remains in the fact that in 3:14-15 eternal life is promised in the one lifted up to those believing, whereas in 3:17-21 and elsewhere it is promised to those who believe in Jesus because of who he is, though in both the focus is his person. As we shall see, resolving this ambiguity by denying that the author would have believed Jesus could offer eternal life before his death does injustice to the text, so that, again, we are required to hold both notions together. Indeed as a result of the cross and the event it inaugurates — including the return of the Son to the Father and the sending of the Spirit and the disciples in mission — eternal life will be offered far and wide. However, it will be the same eternal life which is available wherever one encounters the light come into the world, God's Son, and was available in his person during his earthly ministry.

1982), 167-69; Klaus Wengst, *Christologische Formeln und Lieder des Urchristentums* (Gütersloh: Mohn, 1972), 76; Nicholson, *Death*, 77; Scroggs, *Christology*, 75-76; Painter, "Sacrifice and Atonement," 295, 305; cf. also Schnackenburg, *John*, 1.399.

152. Hahn, *Theologie*, 1.613; Müller, *Menschwerdung des Gottessohnes*, 70-71; George R. Beasley-Murray, "The Mission of the Logos-Son," in *The Four Gospels 1992: Festschrift for Frans Neirynck*, ed. F. Van Segbroeck, C. M. Tuckett, G. Van Belle, and J. Verheyden (Leuven: Peeters, 1992), 1858; Carson, *John*, 206; Cf. Frey, *Johanneische Eschatologie*, 3.286-88, who argues that the tradition of the sending of the Son (3:17) has been modified in 3:16a to refer now directly to Jesus' death.

153. Bergmeier, "ΤΕΤΕΛΕΣΤΑΙ," 290, argues that the tradition taken up in 3:16-17 had already been focused on Jesus' death and led to the integration of this perspective in the author's envoy Christology; see also Frey, "Edler Tod," 582; Smith, *Theology*, 115; Keener, *John*, 566; Thyen, *Johannesevangelium*, 213; Michaels, *John*, 202-3.

4.1.2.7 John 17

Jesus' final prayer contains cultic imagery relating to the completion of his task through death. He prays:

> καὶ ὑπὲρ αὐτῶν ἐγὼ ἁγιάζω ἐμαυτόν,
> ἵνα ὦσιν καὶ αὐτοὶ ἡγιασμένοι ἐν ἀληθείᾳ.
> For their sake I sanctify myself,
> so that they also may be sanctified in truth. (17:19)

Many read this text to mean that Jesus is envisaging his death as an expiatory sacrifice.[154] Traditionally it helped give the prayer its designation as Jesus' high priestly prayer and led to reading it in the light of Hebrews, where Christ is both high priest and once-for-all sacrifice.[155] While the traditional view reflects canonical harmonisation, seeing a reference to expiatory sacrifice in the text also goes beyond the evidence. Jesus has just prayed for the disciples in similar terms:

> ἁγίασον αὐτοὺς ἐν τῇ ἀληθείᾳ· ὁ λόγος ὁ σὸς ἀλήθειά ἐστιν.
> καθὼς ἐμὲ ἀπέστειλας εἰς τὸν κόσμον, κἀγὼ ἀπέστειλα αὐτοὺς εἰς τὸν κόσμον·
> Sanctify them in the truth. Your word is truth.
> As you sent me into the world, I, too, have sent them into the world. (17:17–18)

Their sanctification remains in focus in 17:19b: "that they may be sanctified in truth" (ἵνα ὦσιν καὶ αὐτοὶ ἡγιασμένοι ἐν ἀληθείᾳ). His sanctification and theirs are clearly connected. Similarly, he spoke of his own sending in these terms:

> ὃν ὁ πατὴρ ἡγίασεν καὶ ἀπέστειλεν εἰς τὸν κόσμον.
> The one whom the Father sanctified and sent into the world. (John 10:36)

---

154. Müller, *Heilsgeschehen*, 61–65; Lindars, *Gospel of John*, 528–29; Miranda, *Vater*, 125–26; Miranda, *Sendung*, 25; Thüsing, *Erhöhung*, 187; Ibuki, *Wahrheit*, 137; Ritt, *Gebet*, 337; Porsch, *Pneuma*, 368; Riedl, *Heilswerk*, 109–10; Ellis, *Genius*, 243; Beasley-Murray, *John*, 301; Coloe, *God Dwells with Us*, 202; Frey, "Edler Tod," 575. Arguing against this: Forestell, *Word*, 81; de la Potterie, *Vérité*, 767–71; Appold, *Oneness*, 195.

155. See William Loader, *Sohn und Hohepriester. Eine traditionsgeschichtliche Untersuchung zur Christologie des Hebräerbriefes*, WMANT 53 (Neukirchen: Neukirchener Verlag, 1981), 142–250.

There is no need to read this in terms of Hebrews as depicting Jesus as high priest as some have, nor to see this in the confession, ὁ ἅγιος τοῦ θεοῦ ("holy one of God" in 6:69), the reference to Jesus' seamless garment (19:23),[156] or his being placed between two thieves (19:18b) as between the two cherubim. This is all little more than speculation.[157]

Sanctification in relation to Jesus in 10:36 and 17:19 and to the disciples in 17:17-18 is about setting people apart in a state of holiness for some special task or action. The special task or action need not be cultic or have to do with sacrifice,[158] and in the case of the disciples in 17:17-18 and Jesus in 10:36 clearly does not. The question remains: for what task was Jesus at this point setting himself apart? With the merged temporal horizon which characterises John 17,[159] it might allude to his finishing the task for which he was sent (17:4), to glorify God on earth. It must allude to the "hour" which in some sense has already begun and towards which Jesus is giving his attention in the prayer. That would seem particularly apt in view of Jesus returning to the ultimate of holiness, the glory of the Father's presence, a key focus of Jesus' prayer (17:1, 24). It would be similarly fitting in 17:19b in relation to the disciples, since the oneness for which Jesus prays for his disciples will also

---

156. See the discussion in Bond, "Seamless Robe," 187, who speculates that "John's Jewish readers might well interpret the χιτών as a priestly garment." She writes: "In 17:19 Jesus behaves as the high priest, as he both consecrates the sacrifice (himself) and intercedes with the Father" (192). "I would not wish to claim that John has a strongly developed, high priestly Christology, rather that his treatment of the high priesthood links with his treatment of other Jewish feasts and institutions" (189); Coloe, *God Dwells with Us*, 204; Jacob Chanikuzhy, *Jesus, the Eschatological Temple. An Exegetical Study of Jn 2,13-22 in the Light of the Pre-70 C.E. Eschatological Temple Hopes and the Synoptic Temple Action*, CBET 58 (Leuven: Peeters, 2012), 395, who writes: "Jesus' claim to be the consecrated one could be understood as his claim to be the temple. Jesus' consecration as the temple is far more superior to the other events of the consecration of the previous temples since Jesus is consecrated by God himself," but this depends heavily on indirect evidence. Cf. Pryor, *John*, 80.

157. Cf. Ellis, *Genius*, 131, 175, 268, 270; Thüsing, *Erhöhung*, 187; Brown, *John*, 767; Coloe, *God Dwells with Us*, 201-6, who also sees the author intimating Jesus' high priesthood in the Jewish "trial" (203), as temple builder and as interceding high priest.

158. So de la Potterie, *Vérité*, who shows that this is not its usage in the LXX (761-62); Chanikuzhy, *Jesus, the Eschatological Temple*, 382; cf. Bultmann, *Johannes*, 391; Bultmann, *Theologie*, 407, who sees in ἁγιάζω the language of sacrifice. Similarly Barnabas Lindars, "Word and Sacrament in the Fourth Gospel" *SJT* 29 (1976): 62; Lindars, *Gospel of John*, 375, 528-29; Ellis, *Genius*, 243; Beasley-Murray, *John*, 301.

159. Gail R. O'Day, "'I Have Overcome the World' (John 16:33): Narrative Time in John 13-17," *Semeia* 53 (1991): 159, argues that 16:33 is not proleptic, but is part of "the fourth evangelist's attempt to freeze the time of the hour in order to explain what the hour will mean before the events of the hour play themselves out in full." I find the proleptic reading which understands the final act as already underway more convincing.

find its fulfilment in that presence, a key theme in what follows (17:20–26). In itself this gives a coherent explanation of the use of sanctification imagery in 17:19. It need have no relation to seeing Jesus' death as a cultic act, an expiatory sacrifice. It is however wise in this Gospel never to rule out the possibility that allusions may be multivalent. This means here that we also need to bear in mind that "hour" also includes the death. It is then possible that there could be secondary allusions to one or more interpretations of the death itself, discussed in the passages above,[160] whether as expiatory sacrifice, or vicarious on behalf of others, or apotropaic, or as love revealed even in the face of death. There is insufficient evidence to claim any one of these to be the definitive explanation and any of these needs to be placed beside the better secured allusion to the holiness of God's glory for which the Son prepares himself and which he prays his own may share.

4.1.2.8 Other Cultic Imagery

Cultic imagery also appears in the motif of cleansing, which is probably implied in the reference to jars of purification in 2:6 and in the baptismal imagery of ch. 3, and is certainly present in the narrative of the foot washing in ch. 13. Lindars links 1:29 with the promise that Jesus would baptise with the Spirit (1:33), suggesting this entails the element of cleansing. He thus finds cleansing linked with vicarious sacrificial atonement in the reference to the jars and to Jesus' hour in 2:4–6, and especially also in the episode about the foot washing in addition to the ὑπέρ sayings, even though he sees it not as central to the author's concerns.[161] The link however is tenuous and cleansing need not imply expiatory sacrifice. Purification rites were often quite independent of sacrifice. Here there is possibly a play on purification before partaking in Passover (cf. also 18:28)[162] but also on purification before entering the temple[163]

---

160. Frey, "Edler Tod," 576, argues that statements about Jesus' death "for" others need to be read in relation to each other.
161. Lindars, "Passion," 72–73.
162. Schlund, *"Kein Knochen soll gebrochen werden,"* 159–66.
163. Schlund, *"Kein Knochen soll gebrochen werden,"* 164–65; Birger Olsson, "The Meanings of John 13,10: A Question of Genre?" in *Studies in the Gospel of John and Its Christology: Festschrift Gilbert Van Belle*, ed. J. Verheyden, G. van Oyen, M. Labahn, and R. Bieringer, BETL 265 (Leuven: Peeters, 2014), 322. While a literal sense of the longer text of 13:10 could relate to requirements in relation to approaching the temple, immersion and then only the need to wash one's feet, its symbolic sense has been open to debate. See the discussion in Otfried Hofius, "Die Erzählung von der Fusswaschung Jesu: Joh 13,1–11 als narratives Christuszeugnis," *ZTK* 106 (2009): 167–70, who affirms the better attested long text and suggests that the focus is not

(cf. *P.Oxy.* 840).¹⁶⁴ Many have taken the episode about the foot washing as foreshadowing Jesus' death as a sacrifice.¹⁶⁵ The context is certainly looking towards his death, loving his own to the end, and returning to the Father (13:1-3) reflecting the central structure of the author's Christology, but these introductory verses do not necessarily suggest sacrifice. Jesus' laying aside his garments could symbolise his death. But this is far from certain.¹⁶⁶ Dunn sees an allusion to washing by the Spirit which as water will flow from the side of Jesus.¹⁶⁷ Fernando F. Segovia sees the washing as rather an indication of the fruit which flows from Jesus' glorification¹⁶⁸ and Schnackenburg understands the act as life and love given the disciples.¹⁶⁹ Bultmann rightly connects the foot washing with 15:3, cleansing through Jesus' word,¹⁷⁰ acknowledged also by Frey.¹⁷¹

---

on two purifications, but only one so that the sense is: if I washed your feet that's all you need, nothing more except that (171-72). This is to be preferred to seeing a purification at conversion followed by the need to confess sins (as 1 John 1:9) and receive forgiveness in addition to this later. Cf. Olsson, 324; Ruth Edwards, "The Christological Basis of the Johannine Footwashing," in *Jesus of Nazareth: Lord and Christ. Essays on the Historical Jesus and New Testament Christology*, ed. J. B. Green and M. Turner (Grand Rapids: Eerdmans, 1994), 376.

164. On this see William Loader, *Jesus' Attitude towards the Law: A Study of the Gospels*, WUNT 2.97 (Tübingen: Mohr Siebeck, 1997), 503-4.

165. R. Alan Culpepper, "The Johannine *Hypodeigma*: A Reading of John 13," *Sem* 53 (1991): 147, who writes: "The footwashing is a proleptic and metaphorical interpretation of Jesus' death"; Carson, *John*, 463; de Boer, *Johannine Perspectives*, 314; Edwards, "Johannine Footwashing," 374; Smith, *Theology*, 118; Schnelle, "Kreuzestheologie," 246; Francis J. Moloney, "The Johannine Son of Man Revisited," in *Theology and Christology in the Fourth Gospel: Essays by the Members of the SNTS Johannine Writings Seminar*, ed. G. Van Belle, J. G. van der Watt, and P. Maritz, BETL 184 (Leuven: Peeters, 2005), 177-202, 199; Keener, *John*, 909; Hofius, "Fusswaschung," 156-57, 161-62, 172-74; Lee, "Paschal Imagery," 24; *Flesh and Glory*, 208; Jörg Frey, "'Ethical' Traditions, Family Ethos, and Love in the Johannine Literature," in *Die Herrlichkeit des Gekreuzigten. Studien zu den Johanneischen Schriften I*, ed. J. Schlegel, WUNT 307 (Tübingen: Mohr Siebeck, 2013), 796.

166. Against Brown, *John*, 551; Georg Richter, *Die Fusswaschung im Johannesevangelium*, BU 1 (Regensburg: Pustet, 1967), 289; Culpepper, *Anatomy*, 118; Bruce, *John*, 283; Beutler, "Heisbedeutung," 198; Edwards, "Johannine Footwashing," 372, noting the similar language to 10:17-18 of Jesus' laying down and taking up his life.

167. James D. G. Dunn, "The Washing of the Disciples' Feet," *ZNW* 61 (1970): 249-50, 252; similarly de Boer, *Johannine Perspectives*, 289.

168. Fernando F. Segovia, "John 13:1-30. The Footwashing in the Johannine Tradition," *ZNW* 73 (1982): 43-45.

169. Schnackenburg, *Johannesevangelium*, 3.19, 21; Schnackenburg, "Gedanke des Sühetodes," 223.

170. Bultmann, *Johannes*, 358.

171. Frey, "Edler Tod," 583.

4.1.2.9 John 19:34-35

Some see a symbolic allusion in the reference to the flow of water and blood from Jesus' side in 19:34-35. Some see it as alluding to Jesus' death as an expiation.[172] De Boer sees it as belonging to the latest stage of the Gospel and reflecting the concern he sees in 1 John that dissenters had been downplaying the significance of Jesus' death.[173] Gilbert Van Belle sees it fulfilling the promise of forgiveness of sins foreshadowed in the announcement of Jesus as the lamb of God (1:29).[174] Others see it as apotropaic.[175] The blood and water may symbolise Eucharist and baptism, which in a sense come to the church as a result of Jesus' death,[176] or may symbolise the blood of redemption and the gift of the Spirit, often repre-

---

172. Coloe, *God Dwells with Us*, 207, writes: "A writer familiar with the Jerusalem Temple and its altar, who had already brought together architecture and anatomy, in speaking of Jesus' body as the Temple (2:21), may here be further exploiting the rich symbolism of Jewish sacrifice"; see also Chanikuzhy, *Eschatological Temple*, 354, who sees Jesus not as sacrifice but as the new temple from which the streams of water flow; similarly Stephen T. Um, *The Theme of Temple Christology in John's Gospel*, LNTS 312 (London: T&T Clark, 2006), 166.

173. De Boer, *Johannine Perspectives*, 314, similarly 77, 281; earlier: Brown, *John*, 774. See also Tom Thatcher, "Remembering Jesus: John's Negative Christology," in *The Messiah in the Old and New Testaments*, ed. S. E. Porter (Grand Rapids: Eerdmans, 2007), 184-85; Jörg Frey, "'Die Juden' im Johannesevangelium und die Frage nach der 'Trennung der Wege' zwischen der johanneischen Gemeinde und der Synagoge," in *Die Herrlichkeit des Gekreuzigten. Studien zu den Johanneischen Schriften I*, ed. J. Schlegel, WUNT 307 (Tübingen: Mohr Siebeck, 2013), 361. On de Boer see the critique in John Painter, "The Death of Jesus in John: A Discussion of the Tradition, History, and Theology of John," in *The Death of Jesus in the Fourth Gospel*, ed. G. Van Belle, BETL 200 (Leuven: Peeters, 2007), 341, who argues persuasively that 1 John should not be taken as informing the tensions in the Gospel, which have a different background.

174. Gilbert Van Belle, "Christology and Soteriology in the Fourth Gospel: The Conclusion to the Gospel of John Revisited," in *Theology and Christology in the Fourth Gospel: Essays by the Members of the SNTS Johannine Writings Seminar*, ed. G. Van Belle, J. G. van der Watt, and P. Maritz, BETL 184 (Leuven: Peeters, 2005), 448-49; similarly Beutler, *Johannesevangelium*, 508.

175. Weidemann, *Tod Jesu*, 421-22, 448; cf. also Lee, "Paschal Imagery," 26.

176. Bultmann, *Johannes*, 525; Jacob Kremer, *Die Osterevangelien: Geschichten um Geschichte* (Stuttgart: KBW, 1981), 162-63; Francis J. Moloney, "When Is John Talking about the Sacraments?" in Francis J. Moloney, *"A Hard Saying": The Gospel and Culture* (Collegeville: Liturgical, 2001), 117; Moloney, *Love*, 156; Moloney, *John*, 505; Ellis, *Genius*, 275-76; Schnelle, *Christologie*, 229; *Johannes*, 292-93; Dietzfelbinger, *Johannes*, 2.312; cf. also Brown, *John*, 951-52.

sented by water (cf. 7:37–39),[177] or the gift of life and of the Spirit,[178] or the Eucharist and the Spirit.[179]

These symbolic interpretations seem not to give sufficient weight, however, to the importance of the eyewitness claim in 19:35. The claim appears to be concerned with what literally happened, as if to disclaim something else that might have happened or some other view of Jesus as a human being. Probably, therefore, the author is emphasising that Jesus really did die and therefore really did rise again from the dead[180] or, more likely, really was a human being[181] and did not in any docetic sense escape real human death.[182] This is similar to, though also different from, 1 John 5:6: "This is he who came by water and blood, Jesus Christ, not by water only but by water and blood." With the Spirit these are then the three witnesses, testifying that Jesus is the Son of God and the source of eternal life (1 John 5:7–12). Behind both texts may lie a concern to say that Jesus was no bloodless non-human person, against those who deny his full humanity, and by association a concern to argue that Jesus really did die, the flow of blood and water being what one would expect. 1 John would be saying he was not only baptised, but also died.[183] Some such direct concern with the human reality of Jesus, including a real death, seems a more convincing background to both texts, especially given the huge emphasis on the reliability of the eyewitness, than symbolism of the sacraments or Jesus' spiritual gifts, especially in the light of 19:34, although further allusions should not be excluded.[184]

The interpretation of sacramental or spiritual gifts would connect to other passages in the Gospel which promise life to come and food (especially

---

177. Wilkens, *Zeichen*, 74; Thüsing, *Erhöhung*, 167–68; Klos, *Sakramente*, 78–79; Minear, *John*, 75–78; Schnackenburg, *Johannesevangelium*, 3.345; Burge, *Anointed Community*, 94; de Boer, *Johannine Perspectives*, 302; Weidemann, *Tod Jesu*, 421; Koester, *Symbolism*, 181; Keener, *John*, 1153–54; Beutler, *Johannesevangelium*, 508.

178. Brown, *John*, 948–50; *Beloved Disciple*, 118–19; Forestell, *Word*, 89–90; Porsch, *Pneuma*, 338–39; Busse, "Theologie oder Christologie," 10; Chanikuzhy, *Eschatological Temple*, 354.

179. Lincoln, *John*, 479.

180. So Brown, *John*, 948–49; Boismard and Lamouille, *Jean*, 451.

181. So Richter, *Studien*, 134; Carson, *John*, 624.

182. So Barrett, "Theocentric," 13–14; de Jonge, *Stranger*, 210–11; Klos, *Sakramente*, 80; Eduard Schweizer, "Das johanneische Zeugnis vom Herrenmahl," *EvT* 12 (1952–1953): 350–51; Bruce, *John*, 376; Beasley-Murray, *John*, 356–57; Gnilka, "Christologie," 105; Schnelle, *Christologie*, 229.

183. For a full discussion of alternative interpretations of 1 John 5:6, see Raymond E. Brown, *The Epistles of John*, AB 30 (New York/London: Doubleday/Chapman, 1983), 575–78; William Loader, *The Johannine Epistles* (London: Epworth, 1992), 62–68.

184. Cf. Thyen, *Johannesevangelium*, 750, appealing to Origen and understanding the flow of water beside blood as pointing to a miraculous symbolic event.

6:51–58). The concern with Jesus' humanity or real death would represent a concern which may have left traces elsewhere, and we shall pursue this possibility in the discussion of the nature of Jesus' humanity below which will also investigate further alternatives for understanding the literal meaning.

4.1.2.10   John 18:28; 19:29, 31, 33, 36; 20:20, 23

We have noted above the possible presence of Passover typology in the allusions to timing in 18:28, 19:31, to hyssop in 19:29, and to unbroken bones in 19:33, 36, which may imply a particular soteriological interpretation of Jesus' death. De la Potterie suggests that authority to forgive sins (20:23) and Jesus' showing the disciples his hands and side (20:20) are linked through the notion of Jesus' death as vicarious sacrifice, but this is far from certain.[185]

4.1.2.11   "It is finished" (19:30)[186]

The last utterance of Jesus before his death, "It is finished" (τετέλεσται in 19:30) is open to a variety of interpretations.[187] The immediate context prepares the hearer for what is to follows:

> Μετὰ τοῦτο εἰδὼς ὁ Ἰησοῦς ὅτι ἤδη πάντα τετέλεσται,
> ἵνα τελειωθῇ ἡ γραφή, λέγει· διψῶ.
> After this, Jesus knowing that already everything was finished,
> in order to fulfil Scripture, said, "I thirst." (19:28)

"Finished" (τετέλεσται), the same word as in 19:30, is qualified by the adverb

---

185. De la Potterie, "Genèse," 38-39. Cf. Theobald, *Johannes*, 1.169-70, who argues that it is not through the cross as a sacrifice for sins but as the disempowering of the world's ruler and through the promised Spirit (1:33; 20:22) that forgiveness of sins is made possible in 20:23 and so sin taken away (1:29); similarly Weidemann, *Tod Jesu*, 423-50. Kohler, *Kreuz und Menschwerdung*, 171, who emphasises that the author's understanding of sin is totally defined by his understanding of the Son's coming. Sin is to reject him.

186. For what follows see also the discussion in William Loader, "What Is 'Finished'? Revisiting Tensions in the Structure of Johannine Christology," in *The Death of Jesus in the Fourth Gospel*, ed. G. Van Belle, BETL 200 (Leuven: Peeters, 2007) 457-68.

187. Frey, "Edler Tod," 583, follows Hengel's suggestion that it may allude to Gen 2:1; cf. Martin Hengel, "The Old Testament in the Fourth Gospel," in *The Gospels and the Scriptures of Israel*, ed. C. A. Evans and R. W. Stegner, JSNTSup 104 (Sheffield: Sheffield Academic Press, 1994), 394.

"already/now" (ἤδη) and given a subject: "all/everything" (πάντα). Nothing was left undone. In addition, not only the commission, but also through it, scriptural prediction had been fulfilled, underlined by this last request, "I thirst" (διψῶ).[188] The allusion is to a text in the Psalms that had informed the passion narrative tradition, Ps 69:22, a psalm already cited in relation to Jesus' death in the expulsion from the temple (2:17; Ps 69:9). As noted in the discussion above, the reference to hyssop—an unlikely instrument for extending a sponge to Jesus' lips, though not impossible—may evoke associations with the Passover and Jesus' death as a Passover lamb, but this cannot be known for sure.

The detail which immediately follows Jesus' utterance is also subject to diverse interpretation: "and bowing his head he gave up his spirit" or "gave the Spirit" (καὶ κλίνας τὴν κεφαλὴν παρέδωκεν τὸ πνεῦμα). It could be simply another way of saying: he died, and as such is paralleled in Mark, where similarly after the offer of sour wine "he expired" (ἐξέπνευσεν in Mark 15:37; also Luke 23:46); similarly Matt 27:50 (ἀφῆκεν τὸ πνεῦμα). Some read it as saying much more, namely that at this point Jesus bestows the Spirit.[189] The bestowal of the Spirit might then be seen as the final act in which Jesus finishes his commission. If there is an allusion to the bestowal of the Spirit here it is more likely to be symbolising what was to come and would occur in 20:22. This would remove the tensions which would otherwise rise with the claim that Jesus had already done so at 19:30 and with the promise of 7:39, according to which Jesus would give the Spirit only after he as Son of Man had been glorified.[190] It is impossible to rule out a reference to Jesus' giving the Spirit here, but also to prove it, since nothing in the context which follows indicates that anything more than expiry in death is intended. On balance, the reading which sees a reference to the promised Spirit here seems less likely.[191]

The question remains what Jesus' finishing his commission actually en-

188. Bergmeier, "ΤΕΤΕΛΕΣΤΑΙ," 286.

189. Porsch, *Pneuma*, 327–30, 370; Braun, *Jean*, 151–52; Breuss, *Kana-Wunder*, 24; Brown, *John*, 931; Brown, *Beloved Disciple*, 118; Dunn, "Washing," 250; Moloney, *Son of Man*, 176–78; Moloney, *Love*, 156; Culpepper, *Anatomy*, 134, 195; Schnackenburg, *Person Jesu Christi*, 315; Van Belle, "Christology and Soteriology," 448–49; Coloe, *God Dwells with Us*, 189; Schnelle, *Johannes*, 290–91; Beutler, *Johannesevangelium*, 506.

190. Moloney, *Love*, 168–69, does not resolve the issue when he writes that "recognising that both 19:30 and 20:22 form part of Jesus' 'hour' makes the question of 'two gifts of the Spirit' irrelevant" and argues that the latter is about the specific gift of forgiveness of sins.

191. Forestell, *Word*, 135; Riedl, *Heilswerk*, 112; Johnson, *Paraclete*, 11–12; Schnackenburg, *Johannesevangelium*, 3.332–33; Beasley-Murray, *John*, 353; Burge, *Anointed Community*, 134; Weidemann, *Tod Jesu*, 388; Carson, *John*, 621.

tailed. Might the author have wanted us to hear these words as referring to his death as an expiatory sacrifice, a vicarious death on behalf of others—an act which would bring victory over the ruler of this world, or an act which revealed the extent of his revelation of the Father's love? How one answers this question will depend on how one assesses the presence and strength of these motifs in the author's work, in particular in the passages discussed above. There are, however, some intratextual indicators which take us some way towards a better understanding. The language of commissioning belongs to the central structure of the author's Christology and the specific reference to finishing occurs on two separate occasions. Of particular relevance is the reference in 17:4 where Jesus declares:

ἐγώ σε ἐδόξασα ἐπὶ τῆς γῆς τὸ ἔργον τελειώσας ὃ δέδωκάς μοι ἵνα ποιήσω.
I have glorified you on earth having finished the work you gave me to do. (17:4)

This is not a fictional statement by the post-Easter Jesus as though it looks back on his death, resurrection, glorification, and bestowal of the Spirit, let alone his death as an expiatory or vicarious sacrifice.[192] The temporal integrity remains intact. The final event has begun. The hour has come and what happens is now part of it. Thus, as in 13:31–32 with which 17:1–5 forms an *inclusio*, the author can have Jesus speak of the event as already happening but, without surrendering the notion that there are still aspects of the immediate future which the hour holds, have Jesus claim that he has completed his work. The context spells that out in many variations, as we have seen, and in essence has referred to Jesus having done what he was authorised and sent to do (17:2), to offer the eternal life that comes through knowing God (17:3).[193] Similarly in 4:34 Jesus declares:

ἐμὸν βρῶμά ἐστιν ἵνα ποιήσω τὸ θέλημα τοῦ πέμψαντός με
καὶ τελειώσω αὐτοῦ τὸ ἔργον.
My food is to do the will of him who sent me
and to finish his work. (4:34)

Both the overall structure of the author's Christology, which repeats itself so regularly throughout the Gospel, as we have seen, and the specific reference

---

192. So Thüsing, *Erhöhung*, 231–32; contrast Schnackenburg, "Frage," 208.
193. Brown, *John*, 740; Becker, *Johannes*, 518; Moloney, *Love*, 136.

to completing his work suggest that the commission to be fulfilled was indeed to make the Father known as the prologue states in 1:14 and expresses in its image of Jesus as the Word. This will almost certainly be its primary reference also in 19:30.[194] Nothing in these contexts suggests a focus on expiatory or vicarious sacrifice. Accordingly, the author introduces the chapters leading to Jesus' death with the words:

ἀγαπήσας τοὺς ἰδίους τοὺς ἐν τῷ κόσμῳ εἰς τέλος ἠγάπησεν αὐτούς.
Having loved his own in the world he loved them to the end. (13:1)

Whatever else it was, this was an act and revelation of love. However, we should not rule out secondary allusions. The death is a climax towards which the narrative points forward, so that it seems hardly adequate simply to depict it as a finishing, even a very painful, love-revealing final act of vulnerability as part of offering eternal life.[195] His dying is for his own in that sense, but the cumulative evidence suggests that it is more than that and that this event is itself salvific.[196] In the chapters related to Jesus' final days the most specific reference to what the death achieves speaks of it as victory over the ruler of this world (12:31; 14:30; 16:11). This might have been in the author's mind, especially if linked to imagery of the Passover and dealing with the angel of death. We cannot know for sure. Assessment of this and other options must be undertaken in the light of all other statements about Jesus' death.

4.1.2.12 Life Available Only after the Cross? John 3:14–15; 6:27, 53; 7:38–39

Before drawing this to a conclusion I want to note a few other texts which, together, form the second argument for the role of Christ's death as an expiatory or vicarious sacrifice in the Gospel, namely those which speak of eternal life as a gift available to all who believe after the event of his death. We have already considered one of these, 3:14–15, where the author clearly has Jesus state that, when people look at the Son of Man lifted up like the snake and believe, they will receive eternal life. As we saw, many would also see this

---

194. Moloney, *Love*, 30, 136; Yung Suk Kim, *Truth, Testimony, and Transformation: A New Reading of the I Am Sayings of Jesus in the Fourth Gospel* (Eugene: Cascade, 2014), 6.

195. De Boer, *Johannine Perspectives*, 27–29, recognises this as an important difference between my approach and that of Käsemann and Bultmann.

196. Bergmeier, "ΤΕΤΕΛΕΣΤΑΙ," 287; Schnelle, *Johannes*, 290–91; cf. Schnackenburg, *Person Jesu Christi*, 315; Dietzfelbinger, *Johannes*, 2.304.

The Death of Jesus in John

sequence informing 3:16 so that there, too, it is Jesus' death which is the basis for people believing and so receiving eternal life, notwithstanding the fact that the verses which follow also speak of the light as already bringing life during Jesus' ministry. While lacking the reference to faith and eternal life, 12:32 may reflect the same perspective when the author has Jesus declare: "And I, if I am lifted up from the earth, will draw all people to me" (κἀγὼ ἐὰν ὑψωθῶ ἐκ τῆς γῆς, πάντας ἑλκύσω πρὸς ἐμαυτόν).

A second instance is to be found in the discourse about the bread of life:

ἐργάζεσθε μὴ τὴν βρῶσιν τὴν ἀπολλυμένην ἀλλὰ τὴν βρῶσιν τὴν
μένουσαν εἰς ζωὴν αἰώνιον,
ἣν ὁ υἱὸς τοῦ ἀνθρώπου ὑμῖν δώσει·
τοῦτον γὰρ ὁ πατὴρ ἐσφράγισεν ὁ θεός.
Work not for the food which perishes but the food that lasts for eternal life
which the Son of Man will give you.
For God, the Father, has set his seal on him. (6:27)

It is possible to read this as a logical future and so as referring to what Jesus would offer any who responded to him in his earthly ministry. That would cohere well with what follows where Jesus is presented as the bread of life already during his ministry and as offering life to his hearers. Perhaps that is the author's understanding. At least its formulation suggests, however, that it refers to the future after Christ's death. Possibly it reflects a tradition which did this but which the author now treats as referring already to Jesus' ministry.[197] The case for taking it as referring to the post-Easter period is its relationship with 6:51–58 where the author has Jesus speak of the future gifts of his flesh and blood, best taken as an allusion to the Eucharist. In the discourse about bread, the title Son of Man occurs only in 6:53 and in 6:27, making an intended link likely and thus supporting the reading of 6:27 as referring to the post-Easter period.[198]

It is noticeable that both here in 6:27, 53 and in 3:14–15 we are in the realm of discourse which I have identified as a cluster of ideas about the

---

197. De Boer, *Johannine Perspectives*, observes that both 3:14–15 and 6:27, 53, 62 "stand awkwardly in their immediate literary context" (103), and writes that "6:51c–56, along with 6:27 and 6:62, may with some confidence be assessed as secondary elaboration (Jn III) of the Bread of Life discourse" (226).

198. Barrett, *John*, 286–87; Schnackenburg, *Johannesevangelium*, 2.49; Ludger Schenke, "Die literarische Vorgeschichte von Joh 6,26–58," *BZ* 29 (1985): 74, 86–87; Wilckens, "Lebensbrot," 226.

Son of Man. They focus in particular on the hour to come, Jesus' exaltation, glorification, and ascent to the Father as something greater in the future and in which judgment will take place. We are therefore probably dealing with tradition where the gift of eternal life is expressed as its fruit, but that does not mean it carries no weight in the author's composition. That event would surely open the opportunity of faith to all in a way not previously possible, including through missional expansion but also in reflection on Jesus' life and death (as in 14:12). What one should not do is use these isolated instances to explain away the much more extensive evidence that Jesus was already light and life and bread during his ministry, as equally that one should not use that fact to ignore them.

There are further instances where the author draws attention to what was not present in Jesus' ministry and would come only after the event of his death, many of them also expressed in the language characteristic of the cluster of ideas about the Son of Man. These include the reference to the gift of the Spirit in 7:39, where the author notes:

> τοῦτο δὲ εἶπεν περὶ τοῦ πνεύματος ὃ ἔμελλον λαμβάνειν οἱ πιστεύσαντες εἰς αὐτόν·
> οὔπω γὰρ ἦν πνεῦμα, ὅτι Ἰησοῦς οὐδέπω ἐδοξάσθη.
> He said this about the Spirit which those who had believed in him were going to receive.
> For the Spirit was not yet (available to them) because Jesus had not yet been glorified. (7:39)

In 7:37–39 Jesus offers water, much as he had to the woman of Samaria and much as he had offered bread (7:37). But then he adds a promise relating to the future about flowing rivers (7:38). The author identifies these abundant rivers as the Spirit to be given after Jesus was glorified (7:39). As Jesus in ch. 6 offers bread in his person and also promises food to come, so here there is a twofold focus; but, unlike in ch. 6, here it is not related directly to the Eucharist and Jesus' death, but to the coming of the Spirit. The future gift of the Spirit becomes a theme in the last discourses. It is not claiming that the Spirit did not exist before then nor that eternal life was not available in Jesus' ministry, a claim to which we return below (4.3.3.6 and 6.2.2). It clearly was and the Spirit did exist and rested on Jesus (1:32–33) without measure (3:34) and so was with the disciples in his person enabling him to offer life. As 14:17 put it:

> ὑμεῖς γινώσκετε αὐτό, ὅτι παρ' ὑμῖν μένει καὶ ἐν ὑμῖν ἔσται.

You know it because it remains with you and will be in you. (14:17)

It was *with* them in the person of Jesus. It will be *in* them.

Associated with the future gift of the Spirit to the disciples is also the promise that they will have greater understanding, both of Scripture's application to Jesus and of the import of events in his ministry, also sometimes expressed in cluster language:

ὅτε οὖν ἠγέρθη ἐκ νεκρῶν, ἐμνήσθησαν οἱ μαθηταὶ αὐτοῦ ὅτι τοῦτο ἔλεγεν, καὶ ἐπίστευσαν τῇ γραφῇ καὶ τῷ λόγῳ ὃν εἶπεν ὁ Ἰησοῦς.
When he had been raised from the dead his disciples remembered that he was saying this and came to believe the Scripture and the word which Jesus said. (2:22)

ταῦτα οὐκ ἔγνωσαν αὐτοῦ οἱ μαθηταὶ τὸ πρῶτον, ἀλλ' ὅτε ἐδοξάσθη Ἰησοῦς τότε ἐμνήσθησαν ὅτι ταῦτα ἦν ἐπ' αὐτῷ γεγραμμένα καὶ ταῦτα ἐποίησαν αὐτῷ.
His disciples did not recognise this at first, but when Jesus was glorified then they remembered that these things were written in relation to him and that they had done these things to him. (12:16)

None of these implies that eternal life was not available in the person of Jesus before his death.

We can observe a similar phenomenon in those sayings which use the expression, "The hour is coming and now is." In John 4:23 it refers to true worship in spirit and in truth. This would surely be heard in the context of the destruction of the Jerusalem temple in 70 CE, but it is about something much more, namely the person of Jesus.[199] In 2:19 Jesus confounds his hearers by claiming already to be the temple which they would destroy and God would raise up, not, it should be noted, that he would be the new temple only after his resurrection. In 5:25 Jesus uses the introduction "The hour is coming and now is" to claim that already resurrection can happen as people hear and receive the life the Father has authorised him to offer, a claim echoed in his assertion: "I am the resurrection and the life" in 11:25, which is not to be read as "I will be so" after my death, but I am so—because of who I am.

---

199. Frey, *Eschatologie*, 2.282, observes that for the author Christ's presence alone makes true worship possible, explaining the proleptic "and now is" used of the earthly Jesus.

4.1.3 Concluding Assessment

This section has been dealing with what for many has been a vexed question: what role does Jesus' death play in Johannine soteriology? The debate has often been framed in alternatives.[200] If Jesus' death, as an expiatory sacrifice or a vicarious death or an apotropaic act, made salvation and eternal life possible, then it must follow, it would seem, that all statements portraying Jesus as offering eternal life during his ministry, as most do, as we have seen in tracing the central structure of the author's Christology, are consciously proleptic on the part of the author, who knows and intends the hearer to understand that this is the case. It would also follow that all statements referring to Jesus' death—of which there are many in the Gospel—must ultimately be pointing to his death as the moment when salvation was made possible.[201]

The problem with this assessment is not so much that statistically statements showing Jesus offering eternal life during his ministry are much more numerous, but that the author grounds them in a way that points not to a future event but both to the nature of the Son and to the commission given him. The logic of the central structure of the author's Christology is not to be denied or explained away as proleptic. For he is the Word and was the Word made flesh in his ministry, offering life and light and truth. The Christology in the strictest sense is the basis for the soteriology.[202]

This, however, has led others to argue an alternative exclusive position, along the lines that since Jesus offered life in his person, one cannot treat Jesus' death as achieving something already achieved by who Jesus was. Therefore references to his death must be explained as simply bringing to a climax what he had always been doing, exposing how darkness did not receive the light and showing that his giving of life extended also to his willingness to carry through his love for his friends to the limit, dying for them. On this basis, allusions to expiatory or vicarious death are either to be explained in a way that gives them no weight by denying them altogether,[203] relegating them to the status of relics of tradition,[204] or seeing them as redactional ad-

---

200. See the discussion in Frey, "Theologia crucifixi," 485-92.
201. So Frey, *Eschatologie*, 2.241-46.
202. Frey, *Eschatologie*, observes that merged horizons result from the unity which the person of Jesus constitutes (2.297) and historical encounter with him is decisive (3.487).
203. Against George B. Stevens, *The Theology of the New Testament* (Edinburgh: Clark, 1889), 224-33; E. F. Scott, *The Fourth Gospel. Its Purpose and Theology* (Edinburgh: Clark, 1908), 207-12; Forestell, *Word*.
204. Cf. Lindars, *John*, 82.

ditions,²⁰⁵ thus giving them an interpretation which in effect discounts their playing any role in the author's soteriology. Is this really credible?

This is an impasse,²⁰⁶ made all the more difficult by the fact that wider theological concerns sometimes appear to motivate conclusions, whether of those for whom the only valid understanding of the Christian Gospel is one based on making the cross the transaction that changes everything, or those whose theology finds the notion of a soteriological transaction best avoided in favour of speaking of the nature of God's generosity.²⁰⁷ Whatever conclusions one may decide to reach in relation to our contemporary appropriation of the biblical texts, the exegete serves those engaged in such processes best by seeking as clearly as possible to describe what the text actually says, whether it is favourable to one's theology or not, and to do so in dialogue with others to help subvert the distortions of the subjectivity we cannot ever fully avoid.

In that spirit this conclusion seeks to draw together the findings from what we have considered. First, there are some basic assumptions which must be borne in mind. We are dealing with a situation where in all probability the author could assume that few among his hearers would be hearing the story and its significance for the first time and so we should avoid the "first hearer" fallacy which might otherwise lead us to assume that when hearers listen, for instance to 1:29, they have no idea of potentially related ideas in the rest of the Gospel. It is also reasonable to assume that hearers would have some familiarity with Christian tradition which in various ways saw soteriological significance in Jesus' death,²⁰⁸ including sometimes merging expiatory and vicarious perspectives.²⁰⁹

It is not inappropriate in this regard to point to 1 John,²¹⁰ but one should not assume necessarily a common mind or emphasis between the two different authors. There are significant differences. A number of scholars note the comparative change in emphasis on sacrificial atonement in the Johannine

---

205. As Theobald, *Johannes*, 1.65; cf. Frey, "Theologia crucifixi," 521–22.

206. On this see Dennis, "Jesus' Death." Frey, "Theologia crucifixi," 492, poses the dilemma as whether one sees salvation achieved by his death or his incarnation, but this is too focused on events and not sufficiently on the person who in himself brings salvation because of who he is.

207. On this see, for instance, Frey, "Theologia crucifixi," 492–96; Frey, "Edler Tod," 581.

208. Lindars, *John*, 82; Jörg Frey, "Das vierte Evangelium auf dem Hintergrund der älteren Evangelientradition. Zum Problem Johannes und die Synoptiker," in *Die Herrlichkeit des Gekreuzigten. Studien zu den Johanneischen Schriften I*, ed. J. Schlegel, WUNT 307 (Tübingen: Mohr Siebeck, 2013), 286.

209. Frey, "Theologia crucifixi," 530.

210. So Frey, "Theologia crucifixi," 522, 530; Frey, "Edler Tod," 581.

Epistles[211] and suggest this is either a counterbalance to the Gospel's lack of emphasis on this aspect[212] or the cause of redactional additions of the motif within the Gospel itself.[213] Schnelle's suggestion that the statements about vicarious atonement carry significant weight for the author in countering the docetism already evident behind the Epistles is unconvincing.[214]

The extent to which the author and his hearers would have been familiar with wider early Christian tradition[215] is difficult to determine. Some assume knowledge of, if not direct access to, Mark.[216] Some would also add Luke[217] and Matthew.[218] We should take into account that the author and many of his hearers had a Jewish religious background. Thus for understanding both individual motifs but also how various expressions about receiving eternal life could be appropriated, this background should be borne in mind, a factor, which, as we shall see can play a key role in dealing with what is deemed an impasse.

It is appropriate to begin with what emerged from our analysis of the central structure of Johannine Christology. Statements pertaining to eternal life—whether on the lips of Jesus or about Jesus—relate to his identity, including, of course, who he was during his ministry. While the author often employs the envoy model, his Christology is much more than that. He is the Son of the Father, the Word, who became flesh to make the Father known, to offer light and life and truth. This is so well documented, recurring time and time again through the account of Jesus' earthly ministry, that it is implausible to deny it or relegate it to the category of prolepsis.

The author's Christology is certainly something which was developed in the post-Easter period.[219] It is in that sense read back into the ministry of Jesus. To some degree this is true of all the Gospels, but markedly so in John. These are insights of historical analysis which have helped us understand what they were doing. This should not, however, be confused with what the author himself might have thought. We can be very sure that he did not

---

211. E.g., Whitacre, *Polemic*, 157.
212. So Brown, *Beloved Disciple*, 119; Brown, *Epistles*, 79.
213. Segovia, *Love Relationships*, 196; Becker, *Johannes*, 407.
214. Schnelle, *Christologie*, 256.
215. So, for instance, Metzner, *Sünde*, 131.
216. Frey, "Johannes und die Synoptiker," 289–90; Frey, "Theologia crucifixi," 508.
217. On this see Frey, "Johannes und die Synoptiker," 289.
218. See Van Belle, "Death of Jesus," 3, on the Leuven hypothesis, which assumes knowledge of all three.
219. Bornkamm, "Interpretation," 114. On this see Frey, "Theologia crucifixi;" 506, Frey, "Herrlichkeit," 646.

The Death of Jesus in John

see his claims about the nature of the Son and his offer of life as proleptic. While exercising considerable freedom in composing his account and so to that degree being aware that he had constructed and shaped it to suit his emphases,[220] the author presents Jesus as speaking on one or two occasions with the voice of the post-Easter church (e.g., 3:11; 9:4a).[221] The author would almost certainly have believed that the Word really did offer life in his encounter with contemporaries. In fact, as we shall see in greater detail below and have noted above, the author does intimate stages in understanding that some things were not understood and some echoes of Scripture and its relevance not heard until after the disciples received the Spirit (2:22; 12:16). What, however, he portrays as their recollection would have been for him true. Faith in the Son enabled one to receive and have eternal life already in the period before Easter. It did not simply mean a promise that they would receive it later.

How then does this relate to the passages we have considered? It has long been observed that statements about Jesus' death as having saving significance do not appear to be central, at least on the surface. While identifying the presence of vicarious atonement in the Gospel, William Wrede, for instance, observed that, in contrast to the idea of life through the revelation of the word, it was a concept which had sprouted on a different field.[222] Holtzmann argued that the concern of the evangelist was with healing and forgiveness through revelation, a revelation so complete that it already offered what is traditionally attributed to vicarious atonement.[223] On the other hand, Bultmann's suggestion that the whole life of Jesus is a sacrifice from beginning to end is an interpretation he brings to the text, not that of the evangelist.[224]

In more recent times de Boer observes that "the idea that Jesus' death is being regarded as a blood sacrifice expiating sins is not clearly discernible in 1:29 and has very little support (in the remainder of the Gospel, including in ch. 19)."[225] Van der Watt concludes "that although John does not emphasize

---

220. Frey, "Johannes und die Synoptiker," 283–84, 286.

221. Frey, *Eschatologie*, notes the merging of horizons in the last discourses and also in John 3:11 and 9:4a (3.254–56, 266, 268, 281), but wrongly denies the application of "now is" to the pre-Easter earthly Jesus except proleptically (3.281).

222. William Wrede, *Charakter und Tendenz des Johannesevangeliums*, 2nd ed., Sammlung gemeinverständlicher Vorträge und Schriften aus dem Gebiet der Theologie und Religionsgeschichte 37 (Tübingen: Mohr Siebeck, 1933), 29.

223. Similarly Holtzmann, *Lehrbuch*, 523–26.

224. Bultmann, *Theologie*, 407.

225. De Boer, *Johannine Perspectives*, 280, similarly 234; Moloney, *John*, 59.

or focus on substitution or sacrifice, there are some insinuations in that direction. However, these references do not come into focus at all. They are secondary to the revelatory function of the cross events."[226] Dwight M. Smith notes that it is "surprising that such an understanding and interpretation of Jesus' death does not find a larger place in the Gospel of John. Yet several passages in the Gospel clearly allude to the primitive Christian interpretation of Jesus' death as a vicarious sacrifice."[227] Even Frey, who strongly argues for the centrality of Christ's death in John's soteriology, acknowledges that expiatory imagery in John, as such we find in 1 John 2:1, is not present in John.[228]

On the other hand, the Johannine narrative unmistakably points towards Jesus' death as the climax of his ministry[229] so that it must carry significance over and above being the consequence of love and faithfulness to his task. For some this must indicate that it is central to the author's soteriology.[230] Once one finds a single indication that the author viewed it as expiatory or vicarious, then, it is argued, this understanding must for the hearer fill out the substance of all allusions to Jesus' death.[231] As an argument this does not hold, if it is used to claim that expiatory or vicarious death is the centre of the author's soteriology, and certainly not if it is used to dismiss the offer of life which the Son brings in his ministry. It is, nevertheless, a valid observation, to the extent that once we can establish it as one way that the author (and potentially his hearers) saw Jesus' death, then it should at least be taken into account in considering other texts.[232]

---

226. Jan G. van der Watt, "Salvation in the Gospel According to John," in *Salvation in the New Testament. Perspectives on Soteriology*, ed. J. G. van der Watt, NovTSup 121 (Leiden: Brill, 2005), 116. Similarly David Rensberger, "The Messiah Who Has Come into the World: The Message of the Gospel of John," in *Jesus in Johannine Tradition*, ed. R. Fortna and T. Thatcher (Louisville: Westminster John Knox, 2001), 19; Lindars, *John*, 82, "Atonement is not stressed in the Fourth Gospel, however, because the essential point for the argument is the concept of Jesus' union with the Father"; Schnackenburg, *Person Jesu Christi*, 314-15.

227. Smith, *Theology*, 116.

228. On this see Frey, "Theologia crucifixi," 522; Frey, "Edler Tod," 582; similarly Painter, "Sacrifice and Atonement," 287, 289.

229. So, for instance, Schnelle, "Kreuzestheologie," 244-49.

230. Frey, "Theologia crucifixi," 515; Michael Labahn, "Bedeutung und Frucht des Todes Jesu im Spiegel des johanneischen Erzählaufbaus," in *The Death of Jesus in the Fourth Gospel*, ed. G. Van Belle, BETL 200 (Leuven: Peeters, 2007), 434.

231. So Frey, "Edler Tod," 576.

232. Frey, "Theologia crucifixi," 499-501, who sees 1:29 as atoning as fundamental for all sayings which follow (533); similarly Scholtissek, "Liebe," 434. See also Schnackenburg, *Person Jesu Christi*, 313; Dennis, *Death and Gathering*, 353, writes: "the burden of proof, I believe, remains squarely on those who argue that Jesus' death in John's Gospel has nothing to do with *Jewish* atonement theology or the elimination of sin."

Our analysis of 1:29 concluded that its primary focus was Jesus' taking away sin and doing so as part of his identity as Israel's Messiah, the image of Lamb evoking both vulnerability and intimacy with the Father, and that he was to do so by the Spirit. We noted however that it was certainly possible the author's aim and the hearers' listening might have associated that vulnerability at a secondary level with his death. Further reflection may have created a connection with the vicarious suffering of the servant depicted as a lamb in Isa 53 or with the motif of the Passover lamb whose blood warded off danger.

In the case of 6:51c the matter was to some extent equally unsure. One could see the reference to Jesus' flesh given for the life of the world as referring to what he had been doing all along and would do even unto death or, as we think more likely, having reference to eucharistic tradition. Hearers sensing this would surely have had some awareness of eucharistic traditions and possibly those which reflected an understanding of Jesus' death as a sacrifice or as for sins, again in probable allusion to Isa 53. Should this be present, it is appropriate to bear it in mind when considering the other main passages which speak of Jesus' death as "for" others,[233] but not necessarily as the author's primary reference. When Jesus declares in 10:17 that he lays down his life in order to take it up again, this is clearly not the case. It may however be in the background when earlier he simply speaks of laying down his life. A notion of vicarious death is certainly present in the words of advice of the high priest in 11:50, but is likely also to be present in the symbolic sense which the author sees as the inspired meaning. The matter is further complicated by the fact that this could be seen as dealing not with the sins of the world, but specifically with Israel's past sin. The reference to Jesus' dying for his friends in 15:13 is illustrative or exemplary of how the disciples should love one another, similar to the way it is used in 1 John 3:16, and in that sense incidental, but assumes that the death was not just an exit or an example of vulnerability, but something which was for the benefit of the disciples. That could have meant that it was the climax of the loving which had brought benefit to them, but, more likely, that it also singles out the death as an achievement benefiting them.[234]

It is a mark of the extent to which expiatory and vicarious death and its effects are not central that nowhere in the accounts of the passion, indeed from ch. 12 onwards, do we find any reference to what Jesus' death achieved expressed in those terms. The only explanation, significantly, relates to the judgment of the ruler of this world (12:31; 14:30; 16:11), a moment of realised

---

233. Frey, "Theologia crucifixi," 531.
234. Scholtissek, "Liebe," 432–33.

eschatology typical of the author, so that what was expected at the end of time has now happened in Jesus' death.[235] There may be links with Passover typology, but these are not explicit. As Dennis notes, John 8—a text that speaks of liberation from Satan's slavery—would also feed into the hearers' understanding of these texts.[236] The closest we come to an explanation of how this was achieved comes in 16:9-11 where on the basis of Jesus' death the Spirit will show up the world's sin, Christ's vindication as righteous, and the judgment of the ruler of this world. In other words judgment of the ruler of this world takes place in the cross because sin and righteousness, hate and love, are exposed. Such exposure is deemed not to annihilate but to disempower this world's ruler. This is clearly a component in what that death achieved.

If then it is likely that the author and his hearers were aware of traditions about Jesus' death as vicarious[237] and perhaps as expiatory and also as a triumph over the world's ruler, how does this relate to what is also clearly present and indeed central, namely that eternal life was the gift which the Word brought into the world and offered in his person already during his ministry?[238] Rather than seek to deny any of these perspectives, it is better to ask how the author and his hearers could have held this range of beliefs together. It is easier to hold together the affirmation that the Son brought life and that his death was an act of judgment, because the two would not be in conflict.[239] Those who received the gift of eternal life would also look forward to the gift of the Spirit, according to John, so that the judgment on the world's ruler, like the gift of the Spirit and ultimately their joining Jesus in glory, is not something which need imply that they could not have received the gift of life through faith in the Son.

The issue is more problematic with the notion of Jesus' death as atoning

---

235. So Müller, *Menschwerdung*, 76; Rusam, "Lamm Gottes, 80; John A. Dennis, "The 'Lifting Up of the Son of Man' and the Dethroning of the 'Ruler of This World': Jesus' Death as the Defeat of the Devil in John 12,31-32," in *The Death of Jesus in the Fourth Gospel*, ed. G. Van Belle, BETL 200 (Leuven: Peeters, 2007), 677-92; *Death and Gathering*, 208; see also Judith Kovacs, "'Now Shall the Ruler of This World Be Driven Out': Jesus' Death as Cosmic Battle in John 12:20-26," *JBL* 114 (1995): 227-47; Ashton, "Intimations of Apocalyptic," 13.

236. Dennis, *Death and Gathering*, 135.

237. Beutler, "Heilsbedeutung," 203-4; *Johannesevangelium*, 342; Culpepper, *Anatomy*, 87-88; Schnackenburg, *John*, 1.157; *Johannesevangelium*, 2.451; 4.110, 114; "Frage," 208; "Gedanke des Sühnetodes," 219-20, 224; Walter Klaiber, "Die Aufgabe einer theologischen Interpretation des vierten Evangeliums," *ZTK* 82 (1985): 312.

238. Hahn, *Theologie*, 1.612-13, asserts that both belong together.

239. Theobald, *Johannes*, 1.812-13, notes that 12:31 is not about individual judgment but is about the myth of exorcism of the world's ruler.

which could be seen to imply that people could not have been brought into a life-giving relationship of oneness with God before then.²⁴⁰ To some degree, scholarship on Matthew faces a similar impasse. Matthew 1:21 suggests that Jesus would save his people from their sins, which many see him achieving in his death, where his blood is poured, as his addition to eucharistic tradition states, "for the forgiveness of sins" (26:28). Yet at the same time Matthew has Jesus offer such forgiveness already during his ministry (9:2, 5–6), and indeed assumes that John the Baptist would have also done so (3:2, 6), since otherwise people's repentance would have made no sense.

Here an understanding of the Jewish background of both communities can help. Jewish traditions support the idea that the death of a suffering servant (Isa 53) or a martyr (2 Macc 7:14) might have vicarious effect, whether or not described in cultic terms.²⁴¹ This idea could be combined with the affirmation that God was a forgiving God and the practices of the temple in which forgiveness was offered. Indeed, the issue with John the Baptist was not that he offered a different means of forgiveness as though he thereby contravened the Law, but one of demarcation and suspicion. In other words it was possible to hold diverse traditions together.

One of the reasons why it was possible to hold diverse traditions together in relation to dealing with sins, was that sins were not such a central issue as they later became in historical Christianity.²⁴² When so much emphasis is given to forgiveness of sins as though that is the heart of what a relationship with God entails, this distorts one's understanding of Jewish spirituality and that of early, largely Jewish, Christian communities. In Matthew the primary focus is on relating to Jesus as the one authorised to interpret Torah. In John it is on relating to Jesus, who in himself now carries the roles attributed to Torah. Jesus offers himself as light, life, and truth. The author has transferred the images associated with Torah/Wisdom to Jesus, so he is the Word, the bread of life, the one who offers water for the thirsty. That is the primary focus, not sins. This then means that the author can happily embrace diverse traditions relating to sin without apparently sensing the contradiction Christians of the latter half of church history see and which their scholars consider as so incompatible that they have sought to resolve the impasse by dismissing what is reasonably clear in the text, adopting exclusive alternative positions.

---

240. So, for instance, Reynolds, *Apocalyptic Son of Man*, 158; Thompson, *God*, 178.

241. Scholtissek, "Liebe," 429.

242. Cf. Metzner, *Sünde*, 23, 30–113, 129, who argues that sin is a central concern for the evangelist, who includes reference to it at either end of the Gospel (1:29; 20:23), but then on his understanding the concern is not sins but the *totality of sin* whose power is once and for all broken at the cross.

On balance, two alternatives must be avoided. The references to Jesus the Son offering eternal life during his ministry because of who he was—such texts are numerous and extensive—must not be explained away as proleptic in favour of the scattered references which suggest that the author also embraced traditions that spoke of his death as a vicarious or expiatory sacrifice or as judgment on the world's ruler. It is simply not credible that the author would have so emphasised the person of the Son as embodying what Torah had offered as the source of life only to envisage that in reality he had nothing but promises of life to offer before his death. This view frequently arises from a confusion between what were doubtless the historical processes of reading post-Easter values into the pre-Easter earthly Jesus and his ministry and what the author, who was very aware of that time difference, would have believed—and could and did for instance in relation to the Spirit.

At the same time we must avoid the reverse, namely explaining away all likely or even indirect allusions to Jesus' death as carrying soteriological significance in the interests of claiming that only a Christology of Jesus as the sent one counted for the author. While it should be acknowledged that these allusions are in many cases ambiguous and certainly few in comparison with statements about the Son as the Sent One, there is sufficient evidence to indicate that the author was aware of them, used them, and could embrace them. In some instances that may have posed little difficulty if they were seen as dealing with corporate sin or with disempowerment of the devil, but there remains the likelihood that they included at least allusion to vicarious sacrifice. Even then it is unlikely that the author would have sensed the tension of many scholars of later times who could understand salvation almost exclusively as dealing with sin and sins. An author schooled in the Judaism of his time could well have embraced both belief in Jesus as doing already in his ministry what Torah was claimed to do and as having endured death to benefit his own and deal with sin. Such an author would have had no more difficulty doing so than his fellow Jews had in embracing Torah, sacrifice, and vicarious suffering as all playing a role in one's relation to God.

4.2 Jesus' Death as Revelation and Judgment

If the task to be completed through Jesus' suffering and death is not seen *primarily* as an expiatory or vicarious sacrifice, how is it to be understood? The answer must at first be related to the Son's commission overall. The Son came to make the Father known (1:18). This task, repeated so often throughout the

Gospel in so many variants as we have seen in Part One, did not cease before the passion, but remained the Son's task until the end. This is precisely the kind of understanding we find in ch. 17 where completion of the task stands within a context which speaks of Jesus' having given the disciples his Father's words, name, and glory in obedience to the Father's command. Its opening words in 17:1–5 form an *inclusio* with 13:1, which speaks of the Son's love:[243]

> Πρὸ δὲ τῆς ἑορτῆς τοῦ πάσχα εἰδὼς ὁ Ἰησοῦς ὅτι ἦλθεν αὐτοῦ ἡ ὥρα
> ἵνα μεταβῇ ἐκ τοῦ κόσμου τούτου πρὸς τὸν πατέρα,
> ἀγαπήσας τοὺς ἰδίους τοὺς ἐν τῷ κόσμῳ εἰς τέλος ἠγάπησεν αὐτούς.
> Before the feast of the Passover, Jesus, knowing that his hour had come to depart from this world to the Father,
> having loved his own in the world he loved them to the end. (13:1)

Accordingly, Moloney writes that "what is said and what happens in the narrative suggest that the Johannine cross should be understood as the consummate (εἰς τέλος: 13:1; 17:1; 19:28–30) revelation of God's love (ἀγάπη: 13:1, 34–35; 15:12, 13, 27; 19:28–30)."[244] Had expiatory or vicarious sacrifice been the author's primary focus, we should have read something like "Jesus, knowing the hour of his sacrifice had come," but this is not where the emphasis lies. As Nicole Chibici-Revneanu notes, it also makes no sense to see the hour reaching completion in Jesus' death, given that 20:17 makes it clear that he had at that point not yet returned to the Father.[245] Nor is this the case in John 17. As Jesus' final words before his disciples and his final prayer, John 17 carries significant weight within the author's composition so that it is here above all that we should expect a clear emphasis on what the task was, of which Jesus reports that it is complete. In turn it must inform 19:30 τετέλεσται ("It is finished").[246] As noted above (4.1.2.11), the key intratextual links to the notion of finishing his task are the following:

> ἐγώ σε ἐδόξασα ἐπὶ τῆς γῆς τὸ ἔργον τελειώσας ὃ δέδωκάς μοι ἵνα ποιήσω·
> I have glorified you on earth having finished the work which you gave me to do. (17:4)

---

243. Boismard and Lamouille, *Jean*, 338, 443; Painter, "Death of Jesus," 328; Michaels, *John*, 757.

244. Moloney, *Love*, 11.

245. See also Nicole Chibici-Revneanu, *Die Herrlichkeit des Verherrlichten. Das Verständnis der δόξα im Johannesevangelium*, WUNT 2.231 (Tübingen: Mohr Siebeck, 2007), 327.

246. Moloney, *Love*, 30.

and

ἐμὸν βρῶμά ἐστιν ἵνα ποιήσω τὸ θέλημα τοῦ πέμψαντός με
καὶ τελειώσω αὐτοῦ τὸ ἔργον.
My food is to do the will of him who sent me
and to finish his work. (4:34)

In the latter verse there is no suggestion of difference between the will to be done and the work to be completed.

4.2.1   The Cross the Climax of the Revelatory Task

To the end of his life the Son continued to make the Father known. As he says to Pilate: for this he came into the world, to bear witness to the truth (18:37). The passion is therefore part of the revelatory life on earth of the Son. As Bornkamm has emphasised, it looms on the horizon throughout the Gospel.[247] It is the ultimate end of the Son's faithful obedience to this task, the ultimate expression of love for his own and the love he has for the Father.[248] In this sense it reveals the character of the relationship between Father and Son which has been there throughout the ministry. The passion and death belong to the total life and ministry of revelation and therefore, of necessity, to the completion of the commission.

Forestell goes beyond this in claiming that the cross completes the revelation of love and the destruction of sin, so that it is not until this event that the benefits of divine salvation are available to believers.[249] But this runs in the face of the evidence of the Gospel according to which the life is available already in the presence of the revealer.[250] The climax of revelation comes to expression particularly in the drama of the passion narrative, where Jesus is mockingly set forth as royal messiah and crucified under the accusation, "King of the Jews" (19:19). This is a powerfully ironic presentation of Jesus as, in truth to the eyes

---

247. Bornkamm, "Interpretation," 114; similarly von den Osten-Sacken, "Leistung," 160; Haacker, *Stiftung*, 167; and Thüsing, *Erhöhung*, 222, uses Kähler's phrase concerning Mark to describe *John*, too, as a "passion narrative with an extended introduction." Kähler, *Historical Jesus*, 80.

248. So Schnackenburg, "Gedanke des Sühnetodes," 224; Lindars, *Gospel of John*, 322; "Passion," 81–82; Klaiber, "Interpretation," 312.

249. Forestell, *Word*, 19–20, 113, 191–92; similarly Onuki, *Gemeinde*, 169–70.

250. So Nicholson, *Death*, 4–5; J. E. Morgan-Wynn, "The Cross and the Revelation of Jesus as ἐγώ εἰμι in the Fourth Gospel," in *Studia Biblica 1978. II, Papers on the Gospels. Sixth International Congress on Biblical Studies*, ed. E. A. Livingstone, JSNTS 2 (Sheffield: JSOT, 1978), 221–23.

of faith, the one who has been the Christ, the Son of God, the King throughout his ministry.[251] It is not that Jesus becomes these by enthronement or exaltation on the cross,[252] nor that the events foreshadow or represent a heavenly enthronement,[253] as our treatment of exaltation and glorification below in 4.3 will demonstrate, nor is a simultaneous earthly and heavenly enthronement envisaged.[254] As we shall see below (4.3.1.3), the language of royal messianism is not used of Jesus' heavenly exaltation and glorification. Rather, while the mockery plays on enthronement ritual, the passion narrative presents him as what he was and had been throughout his ministry, the Son of God and King of Israel, understood within the framework of the author's Christology: the Son who makes the Father known, and in this way the author appropriates the irony which was already well rooted in the tradition of the passion narrative.

4.2.2 Paradox of Revelation in Wretchedness?

Bultmann emphasises that the cross is the necessary completion of what had begun in 1:14, the truth and paradox of the incarnation.[255] This belongs to his strong emphasis on the divine glory of the ordinariness of Jesus. "Behold the man" (19:5) is a call to see this revelation in wretchedness. Without question Jesus is presented as facing suffering and humiliation in the passion narrative. This belongs to his obedience. It is the suffering whose prospect disturbed him (12:27), the cup he had to drink (18:11). It is another

---

251. So de Jonge, *Stranger*, 66-69; Schnackenburg, *Johannesevangelium*, 3.287, 296; Baum-Bodenbender, *Hoheit*, 66-67; Beasley-Murray, *John*, 361.

252. So Schnackenburg, *Johannesevangelium*, 3.569-70; also Baum-Bodenbender, *Hoheit*, 66-67; against Thüsing, *Erhöhung*, 33, 260, 290-91; Blank, "Verhandlung," 62-63; Dauer, *Passionsgeschichte*, 249-50, 259-60, 274-75; Hahn, "Prozess," 40-41; Wilkens, *Zeichen*, 72, 112; Schillebeeckx, *Christ*, 413; Robert Kysar, *John's Story of Jesus* (Philadelphia: Fortress, 1984), 60; Duke, *Irony*, 106, 114, 132; van Hartingsveld, *Eschatologie*, 64-65; Kühl, *Sendung*, 118-19; Eugen Ruckstuhl, "Abstieg und Erhöhung des johanneischen Menschensohnes," in *Jesus und der Menschensohn. Für Anton Vögtle*, ed. R. Pesch and R. Schnackenburg (Freiburg: Herder, 1975), 333-34; Ruckstuhl, *Einheit*, 257; Braun, *Jean*, 137-38, 216-18; Porsch, *Pneuma*, 76-77, 206; Lindars, "Passion," 77-78; Meeks, "Man from Heaven," 159; Frey, *Eschatologie*, 3.278; Frey, "Edler Tod," 559; McGrath, *Christology*, 214-15; Udo Schnelle, "Cross and Resurrection in the Gospel of John," in *The Resurrection of Jesus in the Gospel of John*, ed. C. Koester and R. Bieringer (Tübingen: Mohr Siebeck, 2008), 147; Dennis, *Death and Gathering*, 207; Schwindt, *Herrlichkeit*, 316; Reynolds, *Apocalyptic Son of Man*, 195; Lee, *Flesh and Glory*, 207.

253. Against Forestell, *Word*, 36, 61, 71, 73; Moloney, *Son of Man*, 62-63; cf. also Bühner, *Gesandte*, 397.

254. Against Bühner, *Gesandte*, 397; similarly Dodd, *Interpretation*, 442.

255. Bultmann, *Johannes*, 293, 356; Bultmann, *Theologie*, 405, 408.

thing to suggest that it is precisely the paradox of suffering and divinity which constitutes the revelation, his wretchedness and ordinariness as human being, or even as servant of God. Real wretchedness is portrayed and motifs of servanthood are present, but they serve to reveal not Jesus as the "real" man or the predicted "suffering servant" of Isa 53.[256] Rather they portray the obedient Son, Israel's Messiah, sent from the Father to make him known and the lengths to which people went to reject him. And even the abuse and rejection serve ironically to expound who he truly is, to the eyes of faith. Rosel Baum-Bodenbender argues for an emphasis on humiliation on the part of the author in the passion narrative and we shall argue in 5.4 below that this motif is present. But it must not be stressed at the expense of elements emphasising Jesus as king, which, despite Baum-Bodenbender's claims, continue to play a dominant role in the narrative.[257]

There is also nothing here to suggest that "man" should be read as an alternative way of saying "Son of Man" and so to see here a Johannine instance of the suffering, humiliated Son of Man,[258] nor that this scene fulfils Jesus' prediction of 1:51, as Moloney suggests,[259] or deliberately echoes the statement about incarnation in 1:14.[260] The author uses "Son of Man" frequently and in association with concepts quite absent from the passion narrative and no indication exists within the Gospel of an alternative use of "man" for "Son of Man." Nor does the Gospel elsewhere indicate that "the man" here presents Jesus as the human being *par excellence* (not even because "the man" occurs six times),[261] or as the new Adam,[262] or the Man-Messiah,[263] or the counter to the Gnostic Anthropos.[264]

---

256. So Schnackenburg, *Johannesevangelium*, 3.85.

257. Baum-Bodenbender, *Hoheit*, 79, 81, 83, 85.

258. So rightly Rudolf Schnackenburg, "Die ecce-homo-Szene und der Menschensohn," in *Jesus und der Menschensohn. Für Anton Vögtle*, ed. R. Pesch and R. Schnackenburg (Freiburg: Herder, 1975), 377–80; Schnackenburg, *Johannesevangelium*, 3.295–96; against B. F. Westcott, *The Gospel according to John* (London: Clarke, 1958), 269; Dodd, *Interpretation*, 437; Meeks, *Prophet-King*, 70–71; Blank, "Verhandlung," 75–77; Dauer, *Passionsgeschichte*, 264–65; C. F. Evans, "The Passion of John," in *Explorations in Theology* 2 (London: SCM 1977), 60; Giblin, "Hearing," 230; John Suggit, "John 19:5. 'Behold the Man,'" *ExpT* 94 (1983): 333.

259. Moloney, *Son of Man*, 188; Love, 143–44.

260. So rightly Müller, *Menschwerdung*, 76.

261. Against Boismard and Lamouille, *Jean*, 434.

262. Against Suggit, "Behold the Man," 334; and more recently M. David Litwa, "Behold Adam: A Reading of John 19:5," *HBT* 32 (2010): 138–43, who argues for an echo of Gen 3:22 LXX (135–37) and possibly Life of Adam and Eve 13:3 and reverse irony in which to the eyes of unbelief there is humiliation but to the eyes of faith, glory.

263. Against Brown, *John*, 876; Meeks, *Prophet-King*, 69–72.

264. Against Gnilka, "Christologie," 106–7. See also the discussion of alternatives in Schnackenburg, "Ecce Homo."

4.2.3 Completion of the Commission

Jesus' death is therefore not only his return as Son to the Father. It also brings to a climax the Son's claim and brings his commission and work to its completion. Because this work is seen as a whole—the earthly ministry up to and including death, the evangelist can speak of God's sending the Son with all this in mind. This is the sense in which 3:16 is to be understood. The following verses continue with the obverse side of the sending: judgment in response to the light come into the world (3:17–21). The author does not isolate the death of Jesus as a work of revelation, though it brings that work to its climax and in it we see manifested the Son's complete obedience and love (13:1; 14:31). It manifests the extent of the Son's love also for his friends (15:13). It brings the Son's work of glorification of God to a climax, but in these contexts it is not considered a separate work, either as a work of atonement or as a work of revelation or as a work of glorification of the Father. It is completion of the ministry in which both the latter are already present. In that sense Bultmann is right in saying that it does not add to what has already been there.[265] But this is far from saying that the passion is lost sight of in the Gospel and tags along somewhat irrelevantly at the end as Käsemann's analysis suggests.[266] Martyn characterises rather the "Grundschrift" of the Gospel in this way.[267] Nor does this dominant perspective of how the author portrays Jesus' death in relation to his commission within the framework of the central structure of his Christology exclude the presence of other perspectives which are not explicitly expressed in the narrative of his last days in Jerusalem, such as the tradition that his death was an atoning sacrifice. As we have seen, however, there is one perspective concerning the death itself which does find expression: that it was an act of judgment.

4.2.4 The Moment of Truth: the Judgment of Jesus and of the World

There is a sense in which the passion is different in revelatory character from the rest of Jesus' earthly ministry. For by its very nature as a climax of the conflict which Jesus' coming brought, the death of Jesus has a special quality and brings an intensity to the encounter. It is the moment of truth. Jesus' claim to be the Son sent from the Father has been meeting rejection. The trial begins long before Jesus' appearance before Pilate. This is the

---

265. Bultmann, *Johannes*, 356; Bultmann, *Theologie*, 400.
266. Against Käsemann, *Letzter Wille*, 19–20.
267. Martyn, "Source Criticism," 110.

strength of A. E. Harvey's portrayal of the Gospel as the trial of Jesus from beginning to end.[268] Appold notes that the cross brings to a climax the note of rejection already announced in the prologue: "He came to his own and his own did not receive him" (1:11).[269] Andrew T. Lincoln observes that in John the passion "unlike that of the Synoptics, has no account of a Jewish trial before the Sanhedrin. Instead, throughout his public ministry, Jesus can be viewed as on trial before Israel and its leaders."[270] He also observes that it is "highly likely ... that the experience of expulsion from the synagogue, with its interrogations and trials, was a major factor in the choice of the trial motif, with its distinctive perspectives, to shape the Fourth Gospel's narrative."[271] At the conclusion of his ministry Jesus faces the final hour. It will be an hour of suffering and pain, because the threats of rejection will now fulfil themselves in crucifixion. For here the world finally passes its verdict of rejection on Jesus; and Jesus, facing suffering and death, maintains his obedience to the end and is vindicated. But the verdict passed against him is also a verdict passed against the world and its ruler (12:31). The world is revealed in all its lostness and sin.[272]

As noted above, this is the only way from ch. 12 onwards that the author goes beyond the cross as the climax to Jesus' ministry of offering life, to give the death itself a specific interpretation, judgment on the ruler of this world (12:31; 14:30; 16:11; cf. also 16:33).

νῦν κρίσις ἐστὶν τοῦ κόσμου τούτου,
νῦν ὁ ἄρχων τοῦ κόσμου τούτου ἐκβληθήσεται ἔξω·
Now is the judgment of this world;
now is the ruler of this world cast out. (12:31)

---

268. A. E. Harvey, *Jesus on Trial: A Study in the Fourth Gospel* (Atlanta: Knox, 1976), 53, 55, 57; see also Preiss, *Life in Christ*, 8–31; Dahl, "Church," 135; Meeks, "Man from Heaven," 155; Trites, *Witness*, 79–124; Dauer, *Passionsgeschichte*, 247, 249, 261; Hahn, "Prozess," 68–85; Dorothy A. Lee, "Witness in the Fourth Gospel: John the Baptist and the Beloved Disciple as Counterparts," *ABR* 61 (2013): 2–7.

269. So Appold, *Oneness*, 110, 119; similarly Hegermann, "Eigentum," 127; Nicholson, *Death*, 49.

270. Lincoln, *Truth on Trial*, 23.

271. Lincoln, *Truth on Trial*, 302; similarly de Boer, *Johannine Perspectives*, 172; Thomas Söding, "'Ich und der Vater sind eins' (Joh 10,30). Die johanneische Christologie vor dem Anspruch des Hauptgebotes (Dtn 6,4f)," *ZNW* 93 (2002): 181; Thomas Söding, "Die Macht der Wahrheit und das Reich der Freiheit: Zur johanneischen Deutung des Pilatus-Prozess (Joh 18,28–19,16)," *ZTK* 93 (1996): 37.

272. So Appold, *Oneness*, 108, 111; Hegermann, "Eigentum," 126; Dauer, *Passionsgeschichte*, 264, 267, 269; Dennis, *Death and Gathering*, 208.

ὅτι ὁ ἄρχων τοῦ κόσμου τούτου κέκριται.
The ruler of this world has been judged. (16:11)

In 12:31 the author uses the traditionally apocalyptic motif of casting out Satan and applies it to the event of Jesus' death and return to the Father. In 16:11 he depicts this as judgment. It cannot mean that all evil has been banished from the world, since the disciples are to face rejection as had their master. But Jesus promises,

ἐν τῷ κόσμῳ θλῖψιν ἔχετε· ἀλλὰ θαρσεῖτε, ἐγὼ νενίκηκα τὸν κόσμον.
In this world you have trouble; but be of good cheer; I have overcome the world. (16:33)

This is best understood as stating what the event which has begun would achieve.[273] Elsewhere he guarantees that no one will pluck his own from his hand (10:29). In this light the power of the ruler of this world—the devil—is limited but still active. It reflects, indeed, the author's priorities that when he depicts the message of the Paraclete, he focuses not on Jesus' death as expiatory or vicarious, but as an act of judgment.

ἀλλ᾽ ἐγὼ τὴν ἀλήθειαν λέγω ὑμῖν, συμφέρει ὑμῖν ἵνα ἐγὼ ἀπέλθω.
ἐὰν γὰρ μὴ ἀπέλθω, ὁ παράκλητος οὐκ ἐλεύσεται πρὸς ὑμᾶς·
ἐὰν δὲ πορευθῶ, πέμψω αὐτὸν πρὸς ὑμᾶς.
Καὶ ἐλθὼν ἐκεῖνος ἐλέγξει τὸν κόσμον περὶ ἁμαρτίας καὶ περὶ δικαιοσύνης καὶ περὶ κρίσεως·
περὶ ἁμαρτίας μέν, ὅτι οὐ πιστεύουσιν εἰς ἐμέ· περὶ δικαιοσύνης δέ, ὅτι πρὸς τὸν πατέρα ὑπάγω καὶ οὐκέτι θεωρεῖτέ με·
περὶ δὲ κρίσεως, ὅτι ὁ ἄρχων τοῦ κόσμου τούτου κέκριται.
But I tell you the truth. It is fitting for you that I go away.
For if I were not to go away, the Paraclete would not come to you.
If I depart, I will send it to you.
And coming it will convince the world about sin, about vindication, and about judgment:
about sin, because they did not believe in me; about vindication, because I go to the Father and you no longer see me;
and about judgment, because the prince of this world stands judged.
(16:7–11)

---

273. Cf. O'Day, "I Have Overcome the World," 162.

The climax of the conflict with its sequel reveals what is at a stake. It unmasks sin as rejection of the revealer. It reveals righteousness as belonging to the Son, because it is he who comes out of the conflict vindicated, shown by his return to the Father.[274] And the event is also revealed as judgment, because through its revelation the ruler of the world is disempowered. This passage is crucial for revealing how the Gospel understands Jesus' death. The conflict of light and darkness had been introduced already in the prologue. It continues as a theme linked with judgment throughout the Gospel. Judgment to life or death is determined by one's response to Jesus. Jesus does not come to judge, yet by implication his coming brings judgment and his death drives it into the open. The judgment (12:31; 16:11) seems then to be understood as exposure.[275] The devil is exposed for who he is and therefore, for believers, disempowered to the extent that they can recognise his works and not serve him.[276]

As noted above, the motif should not be thrust into the centre of Johannine soteriology as though only here in this act salvation is achieved and eternal life possible and not before, any more than should notions of expiatory or vicarious sacrifice. This would be to deny the perspective which governs the central structure of the author's Christology, namely that the Son came offering life because of who he was. I think it most unlikely that the author meant by casting out the ruler of the world a change in the power structure of the universe as a prerequisite before salvation could be offered,[277] or a disempowerment of the devil and thus achievement of access to transmortal salvation only thereafter,[278] or a casting out of Satan from heaven replaced now by the Son of Man.[279] Nor is it likely that the author means the casting out to be understood proleptically of the climax of history, as van Hartingsveld proposes.[280] John 16:11 links it too closely with the event of Jesus' death and return to the Father. Nor is it clear that we have here, as Hermann Strathmann suggests,[281] the idea of overcoming the devil who had

---

274. Dennis, *Death and Gathering*, 208-9, notes that the perfect tense indicates a post-Easter perspective.

275. Painter, "Sacrifice and Atonement," 292; Dietzfelbinger, *Johannes*, 2.308.

276. So Becker, *Johannes*, 392, 406; Blank, *Krisis*, 282; Schnackenburg, *Johannesevangelium*, 2.491; Dauer, *Passionsgeschichte*, 241.

277. So Forestell, *Word*, 165; cf. also Nicholson, *Death*, 131.

278. So Becker, "Auferstehung," 144, 149-50.

279. So Lütgert, *Christologie*, 140; Preiss, *Life in Christ*, 19; Beasley-Murray, *John*, 214; cf. also the discussion in Blank, *Krisis*, 282-84.

280. van Hartingsveld, *Eschatologie*, 44.

281. Hermann Strathmann, *Das Evangelium nach Johannes*, 10th ed., NTD 4 (Göttingen: Vandenhoeck und Ruprecht, 1963), 183.

prevented people being drawn to Christ, or the notion that like a gnostic redeemer Jesus pioneers the way to the Father by overcoming the barrier through death, as Bultmann suggests.[282] The motif of the way is used in John, but relates to Jesus himself as the way, inasmuch as he is also the truth and the life who by the gift of his person opens the way to the Father (14:1–11).

As noted above (4.1.1), some see the author as having employed Passover typology to reflect on this theme—already in John 1:29, 36—to depict Jesus' death as apotropaic by warding off the destroyer by his blood. As we have seen, this is not impossible. The author does not, however, provide us with evidence that he connected his notion of Jesus' death as judgment with that typology, but, as 16:7–11 suggests, appears rather to have linked it with his understanding of Jesus' role as the bearer of life, so that its rejection amounts to a revelation and exposure of sin and a disempowering of the world's ruler.

The Turning Point in Revelation

Yet the death is more than a negative revelation, i.e., a revelation of the world's sin in rejecting Jesus and so an exposure of its ruler. The death also belongs to the total event which includes Jesus' death, return to the Father, exaltation, glorification, ascension, and sending of the Spirit.[283] The result of this total event is greater understanding both of who the Son is and of Scripture. The death is therefore not only the "Ende," but also the "Wende" (turning point).[284] This "greater thing" resulting in greater understanding began with the passion and death of Jesus. The structure of the Gospel's Christology is such that the greater knowledge and revelation comes as a result of the work of the Paraclete, which comes, in turn, as a result of the total event, Jesus' death and return to the Father's glory. We see this connection in 7:39 ("The Spirit was not yet, because Jesus was not yet glorified") and 12:16

---

282. Bultmann, *Theologie*, 366; similarly Theobald, *Johannes*, 1.814 (similarly 1.64), who sees in 12:31–32 a soteriology according to which through the Son's exaltation the Father pioneers a way of escape from this earth of death. Cf. also Schnackenburg, *John*, 1.157–58; Schnackenburg, *Johannesevangelium*, 2.493–94; Becker, "Auferstehung," 149–50.

283. Frey, *Eschatologie*, 2.218–19, comments that while glorification is strictly referring to Jesus' death and not something separate from that event, yet it also implies more, namely Jesus' resurrection and living presence. Thus the "hour" takes in everything from the last meal with the foot washing, trial, crucifixion, burial, through to the Easter appearances, including the giving of the Spirit and the commissioning of the disciples; similarly Frey, "Theologia crucifixi," 511; Ashton, *Fourth Gospel*, 470; Reynolds, *Apocalyptic Son of Man*, 192; Carson, *John*, 484; Theobald, *Johannes*, 1.64–65.

284. Blank, *Krisis*, 282; cf. also Bultmann, *Johannes*, 330.

("When Jesus was glorified, then they remembered that these things were written about him and that they had done these things to him"). The death of Jesus must not be isolated from the total event in which there is also the positive revelation through the return of the Son to the Father in vindication, and the dynamic activity of revealing and bringing greater understanding about Jesus made possible by the gift of the Paraclete, the Holy Spirit.

John 14:30–31 illustrates this emphasis: Jesus says,

> Οὐκέτι πολλὰ λαλήσω μεθ᾽ ὑμῶν, ἔρχεται γὰρ ὁ τοῦ κόσμου ἄρχων·
> καὶ ἐν ἐμοὶ οὐκ ἔχει οὐδέν, ἀλλ᾽ ἵνα γνῷ ὁ κόσμος ὅτι ἀγαπῶ τὸν πατέρα,
> καὶ καθὼς ἐνετείλατό μοι ὁ πατήρ, οὕτως ποιῶ. ἐγείρεσθε, ἄγωμεν ἐντεῦθεν.
> No longer shall I speak much with you, for the ruler of the world comes; and he has no part in me, but that the world may know that I love the Father,
> and as the Father commanded me, so I act; arise, let us go hence. (14:30–31)

The relationship between the Son and the Father, the Son's having been sent to do the Father's will, remains the central revelatory concern. The cross is the climax of the encounter which the Son's revelation has brought. But the climax makes possible a deeper understanding of what that revelation is about, for it exposes for the eyes of faith who the players are. John 14:30–31 belongs with 16:7–11 and 8:28, where we have the same promise in other words,

> ὅταν ὑψώσητε τὸν υἱὸν τοῦ ἀνθρώπου, τότε γνώσεσθε ὅτι ἐγώ εἰμι,
> καὶ ἀπ᾽ ἐμαυτοῦ ποιῶ οὐδέν, ἀλλὰ καθὼς ἐδίδαξέν με ὁ πατὴρ ταῦτα λαλῶ.
> When you have lifted up the Son of Man, then you shall know that I am the one and that I do nothing on my own accord but speak these things just as my Father taught me. (8:28)

Jesus' death, exaltation, and return to the Father are a revelation about revelation. They unfold to the eyes of faith that Jesus truly is the revealer and that those who have rejected him have committed sin and are condemned. To reveal this will be the work of the Spirit. When 10:17 says that the Son lays down his life that he may take it up again, it throws the emphasis forward from the death to what will come as a result of his return to the Father. While the previous verse sets this in the context of mission, the wider context also relates it to Jesus' return to the Father and the giving of the Spirit, which enables knowledge and therefore mission.

4.2.5 Conclusion

Jesus' death and return represents both a positive and a negative revelation, a judgment of vindication and of condemnation. It brings to sharp focus what is already at stake in each encounter with Jesus in his ministry. The one who believes has eternal life; the one who does not stands condemned (3:16–18, 36). Aside from the revelatory nature of the encounter, the "Entscheidungsdualismus," and the promise of life now as the gift to those who believe, the author shows little interest in either future aspects of judgment or present aspects of condemnation. There will be future resurrection and judgment (5:28–29; 6:39–40, 44). The criterion is response to the Son's revelation. But whereas believers presently enjoy life, unbelievers receive no sentence beyond being condemned not to have life and light. They remain in darkness and death. It is not that the positive rewards of traditional eschatology are available to believers whereas the negative rewards or punishments are not available until later for unbelievers. For the focus of John is not rewards and punishments, but life in relationship. The author may well have had something to say about future rewards or punishments, but these are peripheral to the concerns of the Gospel.

4.3 Glorification, Exaltation, Ascension, and the Son of Man

In the Fourth Gospel Jesus' death is both the climax of his work on earth and the event of his return to the Father. Two of the motifs used by the author to describe this are glorification and exaltation. In this section we shall consider these and related motifs, their precise reference, and their significance for understanding the event of Jesus' death.

4.3.1 Glorification

4.3.1.1 Bringing Glory to God by Obedience to His Will

The Gospel sometimes uses the word δοξάζω ("glorify") to describe what happens when the Son fulfils the Father's commission. Thus in the Johannine version of the Gethsemane prayer (12:28), Jesus, facing the challenge of the hour which awaits him, prays, πάτερ, δόξασόν σου τὸ ὄνομα ("Father, glorify your name"). The Father promises in response that he will make this possible, having done so already in Jesus' earthly ministry: καὶ ἐδόξασα καὶ πάλιν δοξάσω ("I have both glorified and will glorify again"). There is no need, with Thüsing, to read ἐδόξασα ("have glorified") against its natural sense as an allusion to Jesus' death as well as his ministry and to read δοξάσω ("will glorify") as a reference only to the future mission of the disciples.[285] The latter may include the work of the disciples indirectly, but primarily it refers to the immediate events by which Jesus will glorify God by his obedience, just as he has done in his ministry to this point.[286] In the hour of his passion and death Jesus, the Son of Man, will glorify God by his faithful obedience:

νῦν ἐδοξάσθη ὁ υἱὸς τοῦ ἀνθρώπου καὶ ὁ θεὸς ἐδοξάσθη ἐν αὐτῷ·
Now is the Son of Man glorified and God is glorified in him. (13:31)

Peter, too, will glorify God by his death:

Ἀμὴν ἀμὴν λέγω σοι, ὅτε ἦς νεώτερος, ἐζώννυες σεαυτὸν
καὶ περιεπάτεις ὅπου ἤθελες· ὅταν δὲ γηράσῃς, ἐκτενεῖς τὰς χεῖράς σου,
καὶ ἄλλος σε ζώσει καὶ οἴσει ὅπου οὐ θέλεις.
τοῦτο δὲ εἶπεν σημαίνων ποίῳ θανάτῳ δοξάσει τὸν θεόν.
Truly I tell you, when you were younger, you girded yourself
and walked where you chose; but when you become old, you will stretch out your hands
and another will gird you and carry you where you do not want.
This he said indicating by what kind of death he would glorify God.
(21:18–19)

To glorify God is also the task of the disciples as they fulfil the commission given them.

ἐν τούτῳ ἐδοξάσθη ὁ πατήρ μου, ἵνα καρπὸν πολὺν φέρητε
καὶ γένησθε ἐμοὶ μαθηταί.
In this is my Father glorified that you bear much fruit

285. Thüsing, *Erhöhung*, 194–95; similarly Brown, *John*, 476–77; Nicholson, *Death*, 129; Pamment, "Doxa," 13.
286. So Bultmann, *Johannes*, 328; Schnackenburg, *Johannesevangelium*, 2.486; Blank, *Krisis*, 278–79; Riedl, *Heilswerk*, 173; Wilkens, *Zeichen*, 103; Untergassmair, *Im Namen Jesu*, 98–99; Schillebeeckx, *Christ*, 412; Bruce, *John*, 266; Beasley-Murray, *John*, 212.

and become my disciples. (15:8)

Their witness and work is made possible by the Paraclete and by answer to prayer:

καὶ ὅ τι ἂν αἰτήσητε ἐν τῷ ὀνόματί μου τοῦτο ποιήσω,
ἵνα δοξασθῇ ὁ πατὴρ ἐν τῷ υἱῷ.
Whatever you ask in my name I will do it,
that the Father may be glorified in the Son. (14:13)

Similarly Jesus prays that he may continue to glorify God in the future beyond his death and return:

πάτερ, ἐλήλυθεν ἡ ὥρα· δόξασόν σου τὸν υἱόν, ἵνα ὁ υἱὸς δοξάσῃ σέ.
Father, the hour has come; glorify your Son, that your Son may glorify you. (17:1)

This future work of glorification is doubtless perceived as the same work of the Son's, but now carried out through the Paraclete in the disciples as they fulfil their commission. At the same time, therefore, Jesus can say of the Paraclete:

ἐκεῖνος ἐμὲ δοξάσει, ὅτι ἐκ τοῦ ἐμοῦ λήμψεται καὶ ἀναγγελεῖ ὑμῖν.
He shall glorify me, because he shall take what is mine and declare it to you. (16:14)

And already during his earthly ministry Jesus was glorified by the disciples' response: "I have been glorified in them" (δεδόξασμαι ἐν αὐτοῖς in 17:10).

In all the passages considered thus far, "glorify" means "to bring honour or praise to someone." On occasion the noun δόξα ("glory") is used similarly in the expressions, "give glory to" or "receive glory from." Jesus is "one who seeks the glory of him who sent him" (ὁ δὲ ζητῶν τὴν δόξαν τοῦ πέμψαντος αὐτόν in 7:18), not his own. The focus here is on Jesus' glorifying God. In 8:49b–50 the movement is reciprocal:

ἀλλὰ τιμῶ τὸν πατέρα μου, καὶ ὑμεῖς ἀτιμάζετέ με.
ἐγὼ δὲ οὐ ζητῶ τὴν δόξαν μου· ἔστιν ὁ ζητῶν καὶ κρίνων.
I honour my Father and you do not honour me.
I do not seek my own glory. There is one who seeks it and judges.
(8:49b–50; cf. also 8:54)

> ἐὰν ἐγὼ δοξάσω ἐμαυτόν, ἡ δόξα μου οὐδέν ἐστιν·
> ἔστιν ὁ πατήρ μου ὁ δοξάζων με,
> If I glorify myself, my glory is nothing;
> my Father is the one who glorifies me. (8:54)

In 5:44 Jesus confronts the Jews,

> πῶς δύνασθε ὑμεῖς πιστεῦσαι δόξαν παρὰ ἀλλήλων λαμβάνοντες,
> καὶ τὴν δόξαν τὴν παρὰ τοῦ μόνου θεοῦ οὐ ζητεῖτε;
> How is it you cannot believe, you who receive glory from one another,
> and you do not seek the glory which comes from God alone? (5:44; cf. also 5:41)

This may refer simply to praise from God; it may possibly refer directly to Jesus as the embodiment of glory (cf. 1:14); and we shall return to this possibility below. Finally the meaning "honour, praise" is represented also in the comment about secret believers who "loved the glory of people more than the glory of God" (ἠγάπησαν γὰρ τὴν δόξαν τῶν ἀνθρώπων μᾶλλον ἤπερ τὴν δόξαν τοῦ θεοῦ at 12:43) and in the Jews' exhortation to the blind man, "Give glory to God" (δὸς δόξαν τῷ θεῷ in 9:24).

4.3.1.2 God Glorifies the Son of Man with His Heavenly Glory

To glorify God means to honour him, not to add anything to him, such as light or power. But when God glorifies a person there is often some way in which he does give something which that person did not previously have. This may not be the case where the meaning is simply "praise," as in many of the texts above; but there are other texts where this fuller meaning is present. They usually relate in some way to God's glory as belonging to his divine presence and more closely reflect the meaning of כבוד ("glory") in the OT and Jewish literature. This is particularly so in texts relating to Jesus' death and return to the Father in heaven.

Jesus' Glorification with Pre-existent Glory: 17:1, 5; 12:41

This is most evident in 17:5 where Jesus prays:

> καὶ νῦν δόξασόν με σύ, πάτερ, παρὰ σεαυτῷ τῇ δόξῃ

ἣ εἶχον πρὸ τοῦ τὸν κόσμον εἶναι παρὰ σοί.
And now, Father, glorify me with yourself with the glory
which I had with you before the world existed. (17:5)

and similarly in the opening words of the prayer:

πάτερ, ἐλήλυθεν ἡ ὥρα· δόξασόν σου τὸν υἱόν, ἵνα ὁ υἱὸς δοξάσῃ σέ.
Father, the hour has come; glorify your Son, that your son may glorify you. (17:1)

It is also Jesus' prayer that the disciples may share this:

Πάτερ, ὃ δέδωκάς μοι, θέλω ἵνα ὅπου εἰμὶ ἐγὼ κἀκεῖνοι ὦσιν μετ᾽ ἐμοῦ,
ἵνα θεωρῶσιν τὴν δόξαν τὴν ἐμήν,
ἣν δέδωκάς μοι ὅτι ἠγάπησάς με πρὸ καταβολῆς κόσμου.
Father, I wish that where I am they may be with me,
that they may see my glory,
which you have given me, because you loved me before the foundation
of the world. (17:24)

The closest parallel to these texts lies in the prologue which speaks of the Word being with God in the beginning (1:1–2) and of the Son being in the bosom of the Father (1:18). On earth, facing his death, the Son looks forward to returning to this glory he once shared and will share again as the gift of the Father.[287] He also looks forward to those who will believe in him, to their being with him and seeing this glory.[288] It is probably also this pre-existent glory to which the author refers in 12:41:[289]

---

287. Beutler, *Johannesevangelium*, 452; Schwindt, *Herrlichkeit*, 282; Lincoln, *John*, 435.

288. Frey, "Herrlichkeit," argues that 17:24 differs from 17:5 in putting the focus not only on Jesus' pre-existent glory, but on the whole story of Jesus including his death (654 n. 68 and 659–60). Accordingly he writes that the goal indeed of the Gospel as a whole is that future believers thus see Jesus' glory (662). This runs contrary to the natural sense of the text whose focus is clearly on being with Jesus in the future as the goal of the journey, as in 12:26, and seeing the glory from which he came and to which he returned.

289. Thüsing, *Erhöhung*, 218–19; de Jonge, *Stranger*, 137; Schnackenburg, *Johannesevangelium*, 2.175–76; 4.451; Boismard and Lamouille, *Jean*, 329; Jacques Dupont, *Essais sur la Christologie de Saint Jean* (Bruges: Saint-Andre, 1951), 269–73; Moloney, *Son of Man*, 278; Günter Reim, "Targum und Johannesevangelium," *BZ* 27 (1983): 8; Wolfgang J. Bittner, *Jesu Zeichen im Johannesevangelium*, WUNT 2.26 (Tübingen: Mohr Siebeck, 1987), 96; Hahn, *Theologie*, 1.621; Delbert Burkett, *The Son of Man in the Gospel of John*, JSNTSup 56 (Sheffield: Sheffield Academic Press, 1991), 127.

ταῦτα εἶπεν Ἡσαΐας ὅτι εἶδεν τὴν δόξαν αὐτοῦ.
Isaiah said these things, because he saw his glory. (12:41)

Some take Isaiah's vision as one also of the future glory of the incarnation[290] or of its reward.[291]

God Glorifies the Son of Man in Himself (God): 13:31-32

13:31-32 must also be understood in this context.

νῦν ἐδοξάσθη ὁ υἱὸς τοῦ ἀνθρώπου καὶ ὁ θεὸς ἐδοξάσθη ἐν αὐτῷ·
[εἰ ὁ θεὸς ἐδοξάσθη ἐν αὐτῷ], καὶ ὁ θεὸς δοξάσει αὐτὸν ἐν αὐτῷ,
καὶ εὐθὺς δοξάσει αὐτόν.
Now is the Son of Man glorified and God is glorified in him.
[If God is glorified in him,] God will also glorify him in himself
and will glorify him immediately. (13:31-32)

Our discussion above showed that these verses are best understood as referring to one single event, seen under two aspects.[292] As Benjamin E. Reynolds puts it,

> Since Jesus' hour has now come and that hour includes the Son of Man's glorification (12.23; 13.1, 31), it would seem that the past glorification can denote the realized aspect of Jesus' hour. In the 'now' of his hour, Jesus can say that this glorification is completed because the hour has begun and the events are in motion.[293]

---

290. Dahl, "Church," 129; Edwyn C. Hoskyns and Francis N. Davey, eds., *The Fourth Gospel* (London: Faber and Faber, 1967), 501; Lindars, *Gospel of John*, 439; Whitacre, *Polemic*, 47; Ellis, *Genius*, 206; Williams, "He Saw His Glory," 66-67, 142.

291. Bultmann, *Johannes*, 346 n. 2; Pamment, "Doxa," 13; Carl J. Bjerkelund, *TAUTA EGENETO. Die Präzisierungssätze im Johannesevangelium*, WUNT 2.40 (Tübingen: Mohr Siebeck, 1987), 142.

292. So also Lindars, *Gospel of John*, 462; R. G. Hamerton-Kelly, *Pre-Existence, Wisdom and the Son of Man*, SNTSMS 21 (Cambridge: Cambridge University Press, 1973), 235; Schnackenburg, *Johannesevangelium*, 3.54-57; Schulz, *Johannes*, 178-79; Bruce, *John*, 292-93; Nicholson, *Death*, 149-50; Beasley-Murray, *John*, 246; Frey, "Herrlichkeit," 653; Painter, *Quest*, 341; Fernando F. Segovia, *The Farewell of the Word: The Johannine Call to Abide* (Minneapolis: Fortress, 1991), 71-72.

293. Reynolds, *Apocalyptic Son of Man*, 209.

It does not refer to two events, such as the hour and the mission to follow,[294] or the ministry to this point and beyond it,[295] or earthly and heavenly glorification,[296] or to the foot washing and then to what is to follow.[297] Nor is it a statement about the revelation of glory, as George B. Caird suggests in reading the passives of δοξάζω in a reflexive or causative sense when referring to God, so that God causes himself to be revealed in the Son of Man.[298] It is one event, which has virtually happened, now that Judas has set it in motion (13:30)[299] and could be spoken of as having happened (13:31, 32a); yet Jesus still faced its reality ahead of him with its consequences as a future event (13:32bc).[300] In this sense one need not see it as a merging of pre- and post-Easter horizons within the author's narrative world.[301]

There is an *inclusio* between 13:32a and 17:5.[302]

ὁ θεὸς δοξάσει αὐτὸν ἐν αὐτῷ.
God will glorify him in himself. (13:32a)

καὶ νῦν δόξασόν με σύ, πάτερ, παρὰ σεαυτῷ.
And now, Father, glorify me with yourself. (17:5)

To deny this connection, as does Moloney, on the grounds that here "Son of Man" appears and there, "Father," and by implication, "Son," is to drive an artificial distinction into the text.[303] In 13:31–32 there is a mutuality: the Son of Man will glorify God through his obedience in fulfilling his commission by facing suffering and death. This is the meaning "honour" noted above. In response, the Father will "glorify the Son of Man." God's act of glorifying adds weight as it were to the honouring, for it is restoration to the gift of glory in the divine heavenly presence. There is a similar mutuality evident in 17:4–5, where Jesus' prayer for glorification follows his affirmation that he had glorified God:

---

294. Against Thüsing, *Erhöhung*, 236; Brown, *John*, 610.
295. Against Kysar, *Jesus*, 67.
296. Against Moloney, *Son of Man*, 195–97, 277.
297. Sanders and Mastin, *John*, 315; cf. also Barrett, *John*, 450.
298. George B. Caird, "The Glory of God in the Fourth Gospel," *NTS* 15 (1968/1969): 270–71; against this: Schnackenburg, *Johannesevangelium*, 3.57.
299. Weidemann, *Tod Jesu*, 101–2.
300. Painter, *Quest*, 340–41; Lincoln, *John*, 387; Carson, *John*, 484.
301. Cf. Frey, "Theologia crucifixi," 510.
302. Schwindt, *Herrlichkeit*, 379; similarly 282; Beutler, *Johannesevangelium*, 389; Ashton, *Fourth Gospel*, 472; Michaels, *John*, 757.
303. Moloney, *Son of Man*, 199–201, 277; Moloney, "Son of Man Revisited," 296; Moloney, *Love*, 87.

ἐγώ σε ἐδόξασα ἐπὶ τῆς γῆς τὸ ἔργον τελειώσας ὃ δέδωκάς μοι ἵνα ποιήσω·
καὶ νῦν δόξασόν με σύ, πάτερ, παρὰ σεαυτῷ τῇ δόξῃ
ᾗ εἶχον πρὸ τοῦ τὸν κόσμον εἶναι παρὰ σοί.
I have glorified you on earth, having completed the work you have given me to do.
And now, Father, glorify me with yourself with the glory which I had with you before the world existed. (17:4–5)

The Hour of Glorification of the Son of Man: 12:23

John 12:23 is similar:

ἐλήλυθεν ἡ ὥρα ἵνα δοξασθῇ ὁ υἱὸς τοῦ ἀνθρώπου.
The hour has come for the Son of Man to be glorified.

Here Jesus' glorification is associated in the context with the mission theme, the coming of "the world," specifically, the Greeks (12:19–22), the dying seed bearing fruit (12:24), and the Son of Man drawing all to himself through his exaltation (12:32). The glorification in 12:23 does not mean primarily the glory which will come to the Son through mission, as Thüsing suggests.[304] Rather the Son of Man's glorification by the Father which begins with his death will ultimately lead to mission, through the gift of the Spirit, the sending of the disciples and their bearing fruit. 17:1 preserves this connection when Jesus prays:

πάτερ, ἐλήλυθεν ἡ ὥρα· δόξασόν σου τὸν υἱόν, ἵνα ὁ υἱὸς δοξάσῃ σέ.
Father, the hour has come; glorify your Son that the Son may glorify you.

We saw above how mission is associated with glorifying God.[305] So also here in 12:23 the primary reference of glorification is to returning to the glory of

---

304. Thüsing, *Erhöhung*, 106; similarly Bultmann, *Johannes*, 325. H. B. Kossen, "Who Were the Greeks of John 12,20?" in *Studies in John. Presented to J. N. Sevenster*, NovTSup 21 (Leiden: Brill, 1970), 97–110, sees an allusion to the servant imagery of Isa 49:3, 5 here, so that *Jesus* represents Israel as a light to the Gentiles (103–9).

305. Reynolds, *Apocalyptic Son of Man*, 209, fails to hold the hour and the total act of glorification together when he writes: "The future glorification of the Johannine Son of Man looks beyond Jesus' hour to the time after Jesus' return to the Father, to the heavenly splendour of his place in the bosom of the Father (17,5b)."

the Father,[306] not the mission itself. Nor is it primarily a reference to the cross on the grounds that 12:16 and 7:39 promise the Spirit after Jesus' glorification and that 19:30 be read as fulfilment of this promise, as Moloney suggests.[307] Apart from the doubtful exegesis of 19:30, this interpretation also flounders on the understanding of the giving of the Spirit in the last discourses and in ch. 20 and on its assumption that the glorification of the Son of Man must mean something entirely different from 17:5.

"Jesus had not yet been glorified" (7:39; 12:16)

The connection between the glorification of the Son and the sending of the Spirit is made explicit in 7:39.

> οὔπω γὰρ ἦν πνεῦμα, ὅτι Ἰησοῦς οὐδέπω ἐδοξάσθη.
> The Spirit was not yet, for Jesus was not yet glorified. (7:39)

It was when he returned to the glory he shared with the Father that Jesus would send the promised Spirit, the Paraclete. This is a common theme in the last discourses. Jesus will return to the Father and send the Paraclete to enable them to do greater works (14:12–17, 26–28; 15:26; 16:7–11). Those who see 19:30 as a reference to his giving of the promised Spirit and not to Jesus' expiry must in turn limit the understanding of Jesus' glorification strictly to his dying at which the giving occurs.[308] Should 19:30 allude to the Spirit, it makes more sense to see it as some also see the flow of water in 19:34,[309] as proleptic, referring to the giving of the Spirit in 20:22, not least because the last discourses (14:12–17), Jesus' prayer (17:1, 5), and the narrative sequence (cf. 20:17) clearly show that the gift of the Spirit comes only after Jesus has returned to the glory of the Father. Similarly 12:16 notes Jesus' glorification as the turning point in the disciples' perception of Jesus' ministry and of the Scripture:

> ταῦτα οὐκ ἔγνωσαν αὐτοῦ οἱ μαθηταὶ τὸ πρῶτον,
> ἀλλ' ὅτε ἐδοξάσθη Ἰησοῦς τότε ἐμνήσθησαν

---

306. Lindars, *Gospel of John*, 427; Schnackenburg, *Johannesevangelium*, 2.479–80; Nicholson, *Death*, 151; Beasley-Murray, *John*, 211.

307. So Scroggs, *Christology*, 73; Reynolds, *Apocalyptic Son of Man*, 193; cf. Moloney, *Son of Man*, 176–78; Moloney, "Son of Man Revisited," 197; Moloney, *Love*, 53, 87, 95–96, 152, 156.

308. Moloney, "Son of Man Revisited," 197; Van Belle, "Christology and Soteriology," 446–48.

309. Weidemann, *Tod Jesu*, 114; Thatcher, "Remembering Jesus," 184.

> ὅτι ταῦτα ἦν ἐπ' αὐτῷ γεγραμμένα καὶ ταῦτα ἐποίησαν αὐτῷ.
> The disciples did not understand these things at first,
> but when Jesus was glorified, then they remembered that these things were written concerning him and that they had done these things to him. (12:16)

John 2:22 stands as a parallel:

> ὅτε οὖν ἠγέρθη ἐκ νεκρῶν, ἐμνήσθησαν οἱ μαθηταὶ αὐτοῦ ὅτι τοῦτο ἔλεγεν,
> καὶ ἐπίστευσαν τῇ γραφῇ καὶ τῷ λόγῳ ὃν εἶπεν ὁ Ἰησοῦς.
> When therefore he was raised from the dead, his disciples remembered that he said this and believed the Scripture and the word which Jesus spoke. (2:22)

This confirms that glorification has not just Jesus' death, but the total event of resurrection and return to the glory of the Father in mind.

"...that the Son may be glorified through it" (11:4, 40)

This glorification of Jesus as he returns through his death to the Father is also alluded to in the Lazarus story, where Jesus declares:

> αὕτη ἡ ἀσθένεια οὐκ ἔστιν πρὸς θάνατον ἀλλ' ὑπὲρ τῆς δόξης τοῦ θεοῦ,
> ἵνα δοξασθῇ ὁ υἱὸς τοῦ θεοῦ δι' αὐτῆς.
> This sickness is not to death but for the glory of God,
> that the Son of God may be glorified through it. (11:4)

The author has Jesus recall this saying in 11:40:[310]

> οὐκ εἶπόν σοι ὅτι ἐὰν πιστεύσῃς ὄψῃ τὴν δόξαν τοῦ θεοῦ;
> Did I not tell you that if you believed you would see the glory of God? (11:40)

---

310. So Nicol, *Semeia*, 129; Brown, *John*, 431; Schnackenburg, *Johannesevangelium*, 2.404-5; Moloney, *Son of Man*, 210; Jacob Kremer, *Lazarus. Die Geschichte einer Auferstehung* (Stuttgart: KBW, 1985), 30, 35-36, 56-57; Ellis, *Genius*, 184; cf. Lindars, *Gospel of John*, 400, who takes 11:4 to refer to the cross (387) and 11:40 to the glory of resurrection.

The Death of Jesus in John

Beyond its immediate reference to the glory in the miracle, this is doubtless a prediction of what the miracle would ultimately lead to according to John's account: Jesus' death and so his departure to the Father.³¹¹

Other Possible Glorification Texts: 5:44; 8:50, 54

Earlier we noted some passages where already during his ministry Jesus speaks of glorifying God and receiving glory from him. Most likely these refer primarily to praise and honour to God and from God, as the contexts suggest. In some texts, however, it is possible that the hour of glorification may also be in view. This might be the case in the following, though this is far from certain:

τὴν δόξαν τὴν παρὰ τοῦ μόνου θεοῦ οὐ ζητεῖτε.
You do not seek the glory which comes from God alone. (5:44)

ἐγὼ δὲ οὐ ζητῶ τὴν δόξαν μου· ἔστιν ὁ ζητῶν καὶ κρίνων.
I do not seek my own glory. There is one who seeks it and judges. (8:50)

ἐὰν ἐγὼ δοξάσω ἐμαυτόν, ἡ δόξα μου οὐδέν ἐστιν·
ἔστιν ὁ πατήρ μου ὁ δοξάζων με.
If I glorify myself my glory is nothing;
my Father is the one who glorifies me. (8:54)

Conclusion

The major passages considered represent a consistent pattern, even to some degree a consistent terminology (as well as "glorify," note the title, "Son of Man" in 13:31–32; 12:23). Glorification means primarily God's restoration of Jesus to glory in heaven, the glory which belongs to God himself and which he shared with the Father before the world began,³¹² an event which para-

---

311. Labahn, "Bedeutung und Frucht des Todes Jesu," 440; Dennis, *Death and Gathering*, 244, who notes that "Lazarus' resurrection therefore is an anticipation of the restoration of the children of God, of the creation of a new people, in 11.52, thus, the vision of Ezekiel will be fulfilled in Jesus, although in John's own unique vision of things."

312. So also Brown, *John*, 610; Schnackenburg, *Johannesevangelium*, 2.480; 3.54–57; Schnackenburg, *Person Jesu Christi*, 295; Hamerton-Kelly, *Pre-Existence*, 23–24; Schulz, *Johannes*, 178–79; Bruce, *John*, 292–93; Nicholson, *Death*, 149–51; Beasley-Murray, *John*, 211, 246.

doxically begins with his death. Jesus' glorification, including his death like a seed, and his return to the Father, is also associated with the fruits which flow from his presence in heaven: the giving of the Spirit, greater knowledge, and mission. The Father's glorification of the Son is also a response to the Son's glorification of the Father by carrying out his commission even to death.

4.3.1.3 Glorification and the Cross

The consistent pattern of passages referring to Jesus' return to the Father as glorification counts, in turn, against a number of common interpretations of glorification for which there is inadequate foundation in the text. These include seeing glorification in the sense of Jesus' passion being "his finest hour," the moment of heroic suffering,[313] and Bultmann's interpretation, followed by many, which reads John in the Pauline sense of the cross as the paradox of glory in suffering.[314] This depends both on Bultmann's understanding of the revelatory paradox of glory in human flesh as he sees it already in 1:14 and on his demythologising of Jesus' return to the Father. We shall see below that the relationship between the glory of the only Son on earth and the glorification by the Father with pre-existent glory is to be perceived differently. There is glory in the ministry of revelation and this continues to the end, to the cross, but the glorification texts are not referring primarily to glorification with this glory on the cross. They speak of glorification with heavenly glory awaiting the Son who completes his commission by revealing the glory of revelation up to and through his passion and death. As Ashton puts it, "It is not, as Bultmann affirms, that the glory is to be found in humiliation, but rather that what the world sees as a defeat is really a triumph, and what the world sees as the end of Jesus' hopes and aspirations is really the beginning of his ascent into glory."[315]

At the same time, there is an element of irony and paradox that this humiliating shameful event of crucifixion is seen by the eyes of faith as anything but shameful. For believers know that it is the beginning of a total event

---

313. Hamerton-Kelly, *Pre-Existence*, 199, "whose finest hour was the hour of his death," and Dodd, *Interpretation*, 373-74, who speaks of a progressive self-renunciation reaching its climax at the cross.

314. Bultmann, *Johannes*, 330; Bultmann, *Theologie*, 408. Similarly Bornkamm, "Interpretation," 113; von den Osten-Sacken, "Leistung," 162; Lindars, *Gospel of John*, 122, 157; Lindars, *Son of Man*, 146-47, 156; Moloney, *Son of Man*, 63-64; Wendy E. Sproston, "'Is Not This Jesus, the Son of Joseph?' (John 6:42): Johannine Christology as a Challenge to Faith," *JSNT* 24 (1985): 79.

315. Ashton, *Fourth Gospel*, 471.

which will see Jesus restored to his former glory.³¹⁶ In addition, there is also an element of truth in the observation that already the death itself is seen defiantly as a moment of glory, the glory of Jesus' total obedience glorifying God and the glory God affirms in this event as the completion of his will.³¹⁷ De Boer points to the probability that as such it would also have served to help Johannine believers come to terms with what might lie in prospect for them, so that Jesus becomes a model. Their potential martyrdom could also be seen as a moment of glory.³¹⁸ In both cases, this should not be seen as exhausting the meaning of glorification, but it is to be seen as typical of the author's creativity to have extended the application of glorification to include also the death. For both, this moment of glory in suffering and death only makes sense because it belongs to a sequence in which they are confident of reaching the presence of God's glory. This is clearly the focus in 17:5, where in praying to be glorified Jesus is praying that he may be glorified with the glory which he had with the Father before all time, not that he would have a glorious martyrdom. The irony of the cross or martyrdom as a moment of glory is not to be seen as something independent of this hope, but forming part of it.³¹⁹

The author writes among believers who face persecution and have faced it in the past. The last discourses promise that, as the Son faced hatred, so the disciples would face rejection in the world. This theme is particularly strong in 15:18–16:4. John 16:19–22, which addresses primarily the gap between Jesus' death and his resurrection appearance, is probably intended to bring comfort for disciples facing situations of suffering. Similarly the comfort to

---

316. Keener, *John*, 1052, 55; Peter Ensor, "The Glorification of the Son of Man: An Analysis of John 13:31–32," *TynBul* 58 (2007): 234, 245. Cf. Reynolds, *Apocalyptic Son of Man*, 210, who writes of "two moments" of glorification: "For John there is a realized glorification of the Son of Man (in his hour) but there remains an expectation of his future glorification." It makes better sense to me to see it as a single complex event.

317. De Boer, *Johannine Perspectives*, writes: "In 12:23 and 13:31, however, this language of glorification has manifestly been applied to Jesus' death on the cross" (182). "The language of glorification, proper to Jesus' resurrection-ascension, has been extended, as had the language of exaltation (ὑψωθῆναι), to Jesus' death-crucifixion" (188). Similarly in M. de Boer, "Johannine History and Johannine Theology: The Death of Jesus as the Exaltation and the Glorification of the Son of Man," in *The Death of Jesus in the Fourth Gospel*, ed. G. Van Belle, BETL 200 (Leuven: Peeters, 2007), 313; similarly Weidemann, *Tod Jesu*, 120; Michaels, *John*, 688.

318. De Boer, *Johannine Perspectives*, 185; similarly 172, 188–89; Ashton, "Johannine Son of Man," 525–26.

319. Hurtado, *Lord Jesus Christ*, 376 n. 56, affirms: "Loader has the better of it contending that in GJohn the glorification of Jesus is not simply his suffering, but *through* his suffering to a heavenly status with God." See also Frey, "Edler Tod," 559, who writes of exaltation as having double reference, to the cross and the return to the Father, depicted as glorification (cf. 655–56); Frey, *Eschatologie*, 2.218–19.

the troubled disciples who face the Son's departure in John 14 also brings comfort to the troubled lives of disciples in later generations. To them the second Paraclete will come (14:16). In the same way Jesus prays for the care of future disciples in John 17.

The parallel pattern between Jesus and the disciples is already apparent in 12:25-26. Jesus had just spoken of the necessity of his own death as a seed falling into the ground (12:24). He continues:

> ὁ φιλῶν τὴν ψυχὴν αὐτοῦ ἀπολλύει αὐτήν,
> καὶ ὁ μισῶν τὴν ψυχὴν αὐτοῦ ἐν τῷ κόσμῳ τούτῳ
> εἰς ζωὴν αἰώνιον φυλάξει αὐτήν.
> ἐὰν ἐμοί τις διακονῇ, ἐμοὶ ἀκολουθείτω,
> καὶ ὅπου εἰμὶ ἐγὼ ἐκεῖ καὶ ὁ διάκονος ὁ ἐμὸς ἔσται·
> ἐάν τις ἐμοὶ διακονῇ τιμήσει αὐτὸν ὁ πατήρ.
> He who loves his life loses it
> and he who hates his life in this world
> will keep it to eternal life.
> If anyone serves me, let him follow me,
> and where I am, there will my servant be also;
> if anyone serves me, him will my Father honour. (12:25-26)

The exchange with the disciples and Peter in 13:33, 36 also intimates that following will lead through suffering and then ultimately to the presence of Jesus with the Father in heaven: the disciples cannot at that time go where Jesus goes, but, unlike the Jews (cf. 7:34), they will follow him later (as in 17:24).

> τεκνία, ἔτι μικρὸν μεθ' ὑμῶν εἰμι·
> ζητήσετέ με, καὶ καθὼς εἶπον τοῖς Ἰουδαίοις
> ὅτι ὅπου ἐγὼ ὑπάγω ὑμεῖς οὐ δύνασθε ἐλθεῖν, καὶ ὑμῖν λέγω ἄρτι.
> Little children, I am with you for a little while.
> You will look for me, but as I said to the Jews,
> "Where I am going you cannot come," I am saying this also to you.
> (13:33)

> Λέγει αὐτῷ Σίμων Πέτρος· κύριε, ποῦ ὑπάγεις;
> ἀπεκρίθη [αὐτῷ] Ἰησοῦς· ὅπου ὑπάγω οὐ δύνασαί μοι νῦν ἀκολουθῆσαι,
> ἀκολουθήσεις δὲ ὕστερον.
> Simon Peter said to him, "Lord, where are you going?"
> Jesus responded: "Where I am going you cannot follow me now,
> But you will follow later." (13:36)

The Death of Jesus in John

Coming before the passion narrative, these promises and warnings suggest that the passion narrative must also be seen as, in some sense, a pattern for the disciples. They do not have the same power and knowledge, but they have the same confidence that their end is with God. Wengst suggests that the author develops as a major theme the presence of God in the suffering of Jesus in order to offer comfort and strength to his church facing the prospect of suffering.[320] U. B. Müller also sees an aim of the passion narrative as comfort for believers, but takes the author to task for its illusory nature.[321] Hegermann stresses the importance of such suffering in the light of the missionary situation where the disciples can look to the passion and be reassured that fruit comes through suffering.[322] Martyn notes that by transferring the temple expulsion to the beginning of the Gospel the author effectively has Jesus face the same issues as those confronting the Johannine church: the charge of ditheism and the prospect of martyrdom.[323]

There is no indication within the narrative itself that it should function in this way, though texts like 12:25–26 make it probable. This at least implies that the author would understand Jesus' suffering as real suffering and not illusory, as U. B. Müller suggests, and the following verse, 12:27, which speaks of Jesus being deeply troubled, would confirm this. We shall return to the theme of the reality of Jesus' suffering in discussing the reality of his humanity in 5.4 below. The understanding of Jesus' death as a pattern for the disciples may also be present in the narrative of the foot washing. The disciples are to serve one another as Jesus serves them (13:12–17). A more explicit link is made in 15:13 where Jesus uses his death as an illustration of love to be shown among disciples. There is also evidence that the author expands the use of OT passages in order to show God's hand through Scripture fulfilment and thus deal with the offensiveness of a suffering, crucified Messiah.[324]

Paradox

The Son is therefore the pattern in his suffering, just as he is in his sending (20:21). Jesus' suffering also represents a paradox, at least, to the world. For here is the unique Son of the Father, he who was in the beginning with God, facing suffering and death. For all the statements about return, ex-

---

320. Wengst, *Gemeinde*, 114–15, 120.
321. Müller, "Bedeutung," 68–69.
322. Hegermann, "Eigentum," 130–31.
323. Martyn, "Source Criticism," 111–13; see also Minear, *John*, passim.
324. See Craig A. Evans, "On the Quotations Formula in the Fourth Gospel," *BZ* 26 (1982): 82.

altation, glorification, ascension, to which his death leads, and for all the supremely confident self-awareness of the Son before his accusers and Pilate, the narrative still reads as an account of genuine suffering. Nowhere does the evangelist hint that the scourging had no impact, the thorns, no sting, his appearance, when Pilate presents him with the words, "Behold the man" (19:5), a mere disguise; nor should his cry of thirst be read simply as an attempt to fulfil Scripture. There was a cup of suffering to be drunk (18:11), an hour of pain to be faced (12:27), however triumphantly. From this dead body issued the same water and blood one would expect from any other, for he was human flesh (19:34). The author especially emphasises this (19:35).

This emphasis on real suffering and death is there. It is there beside a much more dominant one, which overlays the narrative with constant allusion to Jesus as the one sent from the Father. Yet this has not been done to the degree that the passion narrative ceases to be a passion narrative, his suffering, real suffering, and his death, a real death. It is, on the one hand, by no means the central theme that Bultmann makes it, where he sees in it the paradox of the glory in the flesh present throughout the whole ministry and in particular in the pathetic figure presented by Pilate with the words, "Behold the man!" Yet, on the other, it remains part of the story and for the disciples qualifies the nature of the pattern. For they, too, who have found in him the way to the Father, the light and the life, must face darkness and death in this world if they are to follow him. The Johannine paradox lies less in the juxtaposition of glory and suffering which confronts human confidence and challenges human self-sufficiency and more in the notion that the pathway to glory for the Son as for the believers is the pathway of obedience that leads through suffering.

The Cross: Glorification, Exaltation, Enthronement?

Many interpret the cross as both glorification and exaltation, usually in association with the royal motifs of the passion either as enthronement,[325] or symbolising Jesus' continuing kingship.[326] The resultant picture which emerges from both alternatives is one of Jesus the enthroned glorified one who rules from the cross of shame. There is no denying the theological

---

325. Dauer, *Passionsgeschichte*, 249–50; Porsch, *Pneuma*, 79; Moloney, *Son of Man*, 63–64, 206–7; Lindars, "Passion," 77–78; Lindars, *Son of Man*, 147; Lincoln, *John*, 478; Frey, "Edler Tod," 559; Schnelle, "Cross and Resurrection," 147, who writes that "sitting at God's right hand is sitting on the cross."

326. Bittner, *Zeichen*, 248; Petr Pokorny, "Der irdische Jesus im Johannesevangelium," *NTS* 30 (1984): 218, 222; Schnelle, *Christologie*, 208, 256.

and devotional power of such an image, but it is not the Gospel's. Nor is it supported by the conjunction of δοξάζω and ὑψόω in Isa 52:13, which in all probability lies in part behind the author's use of these terms,[327] since there it refers to the response to the servant's suffering, not to the suffering of death itself. The interpretation of the cross alone as exaltation and glorification misreads the clear meaning of the glorification passages; and in the case of one alternative it reads in the enthronement idea. As noted above the royal messianic motifs of the passion probably do not indicate enthronement and should not be merged with exaltation and glorification concepts. The latter concepts are in any case strikingly absent from the passion narrative.[328] Messianic motifs are consistently related in John to the status of the Son as the revealer, not to any notion of his death or his return to the Father as enthronement. Return to the Father and what it entails is never interpreted using messianic or royal enthronement motifs.

Glorious Triumphant Exit?

By contrast Käsemann emphasises Jesus' supreme confidence and might in his triumphant exit from the world and sees this as his glory and glorification.[329] But this fails to take into account the passive voice in so many of the glorification sayings and the fact that they speak of something not available for the Son on earth. It is the Father who glorifies the Son and he does so with the glory once shared with himself before the world was made, to which the Son returns and which the disciples will see only when they join him in the heavenly presence of the Father.

---

327. So Dodd, *Interpretation*, 247; Schnackenburg, "Son of Man," 130; Schnackenburg, *John*, 1.397, 536; Schnackenburg, *Johannesevangelium*, 2.505; Schnackenburg, *Person Jesu Christi*, 294; Thüsing, *Erhöhung*, 36; Brown, *John*, 146; Smalley, "Son of Man," 291; Reim, *Studien*, 174-76; Forestell, *Word*, 64-65; Johannes Beutler, "Psalm 42/43 im Johannesevangelium," *NTS* 25 (1979): 57; E. Richard, "Expressions of Double Meaning and Their Function in the Gospel of John," *NTS* 31 (1985): 105; Beasley-Murray, *John*, lxxxiv; Burkett, *Son of Man*, 120, 127; Robert Rhea, *The Johannine Son of Man*, ATANT 76 (Zürich: Theologischer Verlag, 1990), 70; Frey, "Theologia crucifixi," 540-41; Frey, "Edler Tod," 566; Williams, "He Saw His Glory," 68; Keener, *John*, 873; Thyen, *Johannesevangelium*, 210.

328. So Meeks, "Man from Heaven," 159; Paul S. Minear, "Diversity and Unity: A Johannine Case Study," in *Die Mitte des Neuen Testaments. Festschrift für E. Schweizer*, ed. U. Luz and H. Weder (Göttingen: Vandenhoeck und Ruprecht, 1983), 162.

329. Käsemann, *Letzter Wille*, 23, 49 n. 3, 124, 135; Müller, "Bedeutung," 48, 54, 65, 67-68; Schulz, *Johannes*, 209, 237-38; Appold, *Oneness*, 29, 54, 103, 123, 135; Becker, *Johannes*, 406; cf. already Bultmann, *Theologie*, 406.

ISSUES OF JOHANNINE CHRISTOLOGY

Glorious Love Revealed? Glory Reflected?

Others speak of the glory manifest on the cross as the glory of the oneness shared by Father and Son.[330] This is doubtless consistent with Johannine Christology elsewhere, for the Son continues as the revealer to the end and as the revealer he manifests God's glory to the world. But it is a misinterpretation of the glorification passages to read them as speaking of God's glorification of Jesus by revealing the glory of the divine relationship they share. This harmonises and distorts the text and seems influenced by the concern to avoid saying that the Son on earth lacked glory in any way.[331] In 17:1, 5 Jesus clearly looks forward to and asks for glorification as something to come not as a timeless state of being in relationship. This view depends in turn on a mistaken view of the relationship between 1:14 and the glorification sayings, as we shall presently see. It is better to speak with Blank and others of Jesus' subsequent glorification casting its light upon the Jesus of the cross.[332] This may be allowed in the sense that Jesus faced death confidently, assured of the glorification to follow (cf. 12:28). The Gospel portrays his bearing as a reflection of such confidence, much as it is also true of believers facing martyrdom.[333] For the evangelist, this perspective is by no means limited to the passion, but belongs rather to the Son's confidence in the Father throughout his ministry.

4.3.1.4 Glorification in Heaven and Glory Manifest on Earth

Having noted the consistent pattern of meaning in the glorification texts and the many interpretations which have led scholars to deny it, we turn to another group of sayings which have lain in part behind these attempts at harmonisation. By allowing the glorification texts to say what they say, these other passages may also be seen to have a consistent meaning and not to conflict with the former.

---

330. So Ricca, *Eschatologie*, 131; Forestell, *Word*, 15; de la Potterie, *Vérité*, 198–99, 771; Appold, *Oneness*, 32; Lindars, "Passion," 79–81; Ibuki, *Wahrheit*, 141, 158; Moloney, *Son of Man*, 227–28; Moloney, "Son of Man Revisited," 186; Schillebeeckx, *Christ*, 419; Harald Hegermann, "δόξα, δοξάζω," *EWNT* 1.840–43; Dietzfelbinger, *Johannes*, 2.203–4; Smith, *Theology*, 121.

331. Marianus Pale Hera, *Christology and Discipleship in John 17*, WUNT 2.342 (Tübingen: Mohr Siebeck, 2013), 131, writes: "Jesus possesses a pre-existent glory which he now asks the Father to grant him," but then argues that the former was not lost. This is so because of the nature of the Son's being and unity with the Father, but there is an obvious "plus" implied in the prayer for glorification. He asks for what he did not then have.

332. Blank, *Krisis*, 269; Dauer, *Passionsgeschichte*, 237; Dupont, *Christologie*, 263–37.

333. So Riedl, *Heilswerk*, 155.

The Glory of the Sent One: 11:4, 40–42

We have already noted that at one level Jesus' words in 11:4 refer to the glory to be manifest through his raising Lazarus from the dead:

> αὕτη ἡ ἀσθένεια οὐκ ἔστιν πρὸς θάνατον ἀλλ᾽ ὑπὲρ τῆς δόξης τοῦ θεοῦ,
> ἵνα δοξασθῇ ὁ υἱὸς τοῦ θεοῦ δι᾽ αὐτῆς.
> This sickness is not to death but for the glory of God,
> that the Son of God may be glorified through it. (11:4)

a saying which Jesus recalls again in 11:40,

> οὐκ εἶπόν σοι ὅτι ἐὰν πιστεύσῃς ὄψῃ τὴν δόξαν τοῦ θεοῦ;
> Did I not say to you that if you believe you will see the glory of God? (11:40)

What is this glory? At the level of the event, an important clue is to be found in Jesus' prayer which follows:

> πάτερ, εὐχαριστῶ σοι ὅτι ἤκουσάς μου. ἐγὼ δὲ ᾔδειν ὅτι πάντοτέ μου ἀκούεις,
> ἀλλὰ διὰ τὸν ὄχλον τὸν περιεστῶτα εἶπον,
> ἵνα πιστεύσωσιν ὅτι σύ με ἀπέστειλας.
> Father, I thank you that you have heard me. I know that you always hear me,
> but I spoke for the sake of the crowd standing around,
> so that they may come to believe that you sent me. (11:41–42)

Beyond the fact that Jesus has the power to perform the miracle is its central significance as a sign that he is the sent one, or, as he puts it in response to Martha, "I am the resurrection and the life" (ἐγώ εἰμι ἡ ἀνάστασις καὶ ἡ ζωή in 11:25). The glory is the glory of the sent one, the revealer, who brings life, and, through the manifestation of the glory of God, the Son also is glorified.

Manifesting the Glory: 2:11

A similar idea lies in 2:11, where the author writes:

Ταύτην ἐποίησεν ἀρχὴν τῶν σημείων ὁ Ἰησοῦς ἐν Κανὰ τῆς Γαλιλαίας καὶ ἐφανέρωσεν τὴν δόξαν αὐτοῦ, καὶ ἐπίστευσαν εἰς αὐτὸν οἱ μαθηταὶ αὐτοῦ.
This was the first of the signs which Jesus did in Cana of Galilee and manifested his glory, and his disciples believed in him. (2:11)

We have noted in 2.1 above that this miracle conveys much more than Jesus' power to change water to wine. A level of symbolism is present at least to the extent that Jesus is portrayed as the giver of new wine.

"We beheld his glory, glory as of the only Son of the Father" (1:14)

The clearest statement about the Son's glory, and the one which forms the background for both passages we have considered, is found in the prologue.

Καὶ ὁ λόγος σὰρξ ἐγένετο καὶ ἐσκήνωσεν ἐν ἡμῖν, καὶ ἐθεασάμεθα τὴν δόξαν αὐτοῦ, δόξαν ὡς μονογενοῦς παρὰ πατρός, πλήρης χάριτος καὶ ἀληθείας.
The Word became flesh and tented among us and we beheld his glory, glory as of the only Son of the Father, full of grace and truth. (1:14)

This is revelatory glory as the context confirms. It is explicated as grace and truth, set in contrast with the Sinai revelation, and expanded in 1:18:

Θεὸν οὐδεὶς ἑώρακεν πώποτε·
μονογενὴς θεὸς ὁ ὢν εἰς τὸν κόλπον τοῦ πατρὸς ἐκεῖνος ἐξηγήσατο.
No one has ever seen God;
God the only Son, who is in the bosom of the Father, he has made him known. (1:18)

The revelatory glory derives from the being of the Son in relationship to the Father: he is the unique Son, bears the "θεός" designation, and was in the bosom of the Father. It was in the flesh, as he tented among us, that the glory became visible.[334] In the exposition which follows of the days of Jesus' flesh,

---

334. Müller, *Menschwerdung*, observes that the depiction of the incarnation as enabling glory to be seen contrasts with the image of humiliation in Philippians 2 (50), but also with myths of temporary epiphany (62). He notes that there is no explanation of 1:14 in the rest of the Gospel, but instead a focus on the motif of authorised sending and return (63-65, 71).

the author shows how the Son's glory was there to see in word and deed, right up to and including suffering on the cross.[335] Finally, mention should be made of the judgment passed on the secret believers:

ἠγάπησαν γὰρ τὴν δόξαν τῶν ἀνθρώπων μᾶλλον ἤπερ τὴν δόξαν τοῦ θεοῦ.
They loved the glory of people more than the glory of God. (12:43)

It is possible that here, too, there is a hint of Jesus as the bearer of divine glory.[336]

4.3.1.5 Relating the Two Uses of Glory

How then does this glory relate to the glory which Jesus enjoyed in his pre-existence and to which he returned? Both are related. Both derive from God. Both are different.[337] The heavenly glory is not on earth, but belongs to the being of the Father in his heavenly state and to the relationship of Father and Son in that state. It is a glory not seen on this earth. Seeing it is Jesus' prayer for believers when they follow the path Jesus trod at his death and join him with the Father (17:24; 12:26; 14:3).

It is not inconsistent that the author also uses "glory" of the Son on earth.

κἀγὼ τὴν δόξαν ἣν δέδωκάς μοι δέδωκα αὐτοῖς.
The glory which you have given me I have given them. (17:22)

Here "glory" stands parallel to "word" (17:6, 14), "words" (17:8), "name" (17:6, 26), and, like 1:14, is the glory of revelation.[338] The revelatory glory derives from the Father and belongs to Jesus' being as Son. To see this glory is to know that he is the Son of the Father, the sent one, the life and the light (17:8, 21, 23, 25). In his coming he does not cease to be that Son and, therefore, does not

---

335. There is no need to exclude Jesus' death from how his glory was seen. So rightly Thomas Söding, "Kreuzerhöhung. Zur Deutung des Todes Jesu nach Johannes," *ZTK* 103 (2006): 15.

336. So Moloney, *Son of Man*, 228.

337. See also in agreement Chibici-Revneanu, *Herrlichkeit*, 34–36, who distinguishes between glory with the Father in pre- and post-existence and glory from the Father, always the same glory but related to differently (325). Beutler, *Johannesevangelium*, 452, suggests that behind the text lies a "relecture" of tradition originally referring only to earthly glory.

338. Schwindt, *Herrlichkeit*, 301; Hurtado, *Lord Jesus Christ*, 388, writes: "GJohn expresses the direct claim that God *has* given glory to Jesus, *because* he is the 'light' promised in Isaiah 42:6 (John 1:4–9; 12:35–36) and the 'name' pointed to in Isaiah 42:8."

cease to have that glory. It adheres to the status and being which is his. And to see him is to see the Father (14:8-11) and to see in him the glory of God.

Yet the author has not collapsed eschatology into a timeless Christology or abandoned spatial dimensions.[339] There remain a not yet and a not here in the author's theology and this applies equally to his portrait of the earthly Jesus during his ministry. It relates to much more than the motif "glory." The author consistently maintains a distinction between the event of Jesus' ministry and the greater event of his return to the Father. The difference between the revelatory glory and the glory with which he will be glorified corresponds to the difference between his being on earth and his return to the Father.[340] It is not that the Son manifests only a certain proportion of the divine glory. He manifests divine glory. But the author reserves a spatial and temporal distinction between the fullness of divine glory possible on earth and the fullness of divine glory possible in heaven, just as he retains and does not demythologise the notion of the Son's coming and going. This constitutes the difference between the two uses of glory.

The Two Uses of Glory: Interpretations in Research

The two uses have long been recognised. Holtzmann spoke of two uses.[341] Schnackenburg acknowledges the tension which exists,[342] and similarly, Käsemann.[343] Schnelle speaks of the paradox of the one unchanged glory manifest in different ways to which the Son also returns.[344] But this does

---

339. So rightly Frey, *Eschatologie*, 2.203, 207; Jan G. van der Watt, *An Introduction to the Johannine Gospel and Letters* (London: T&T Clark, 2007), 34, who sets out the spatial and temporal frame of reference diagrammatically (43); cf. Schillebeeckx, *Christ*, 368-69.

340. John Painter, "The Prologue as an Hermeneutical Key to Reading the Fourth Gospel," in *Studies in the Gospel of John and Its Christology: Festschrift Gilbert Van Belle*, ed. J. Verheyden, G. van Oyen, M. Labahn, and R. Bieringer, BETL 265 (Leuven: Peeters, 2014), 57-58; Carson, *John*, 484.

341. Holtzmann, *Lehrbuch*, 503-5; similarly Westcott, *John*, 240-41; J. H. Bernhard, *A Critical and Exegetical Commentary on the Gospel of St. John*, 2 vols., ICC (Edinburgh: T & T Clark, 1929), 563; Hoskyns, *John*, 506.

342. Schnackenburg, *Johannesevangelium*, 2.505.

343. Käsemann, *Letzter Wille*, 22.

344. Schnelle, *Christologie*, 93, 182, 254. On the one hand, he can insist that the incarnation does not mean a surrender of glory, and on the other, can speak of a return to glory (Schnelle, "Trinitarisches Denken," 377); similarly in Schnelle, "Tempelreinigung," 372, he writes of cross, exaltation and glorification not as distinct acts, but then explains that exaltation, which he confines to the cross, makes possible his return to the glory of the Father.

little more than restate the problem. Appold comes closer to defining the Johannine use when he explains the two uses along the lines that only the place changes, not the glory itself.[345] But this fails to take into account the return of the Son to a glory awaiting him. Better is Bühner's use of the envoy model to relate the two uses. The envoy bears the glory that belongs to his commission and to his being the sent one; but he returns to the source of this glory.[346] Weiss spoke of the earthly as a Platonic reflection of the heavenly glory.[347] Chibici-Revneanu's distinction between glory with the Father and glory from the Father is useful in preserving the sense of a glory from which the Son comes and to which he returns, and the glory he manifests on earth as glory given from the Father. The latter is also a glory inherent in his oneness with the Father in being, as set out in the prologue.[348]

Proleptic Glory?

Thüsing speaks of the manifestation on earth of the love which belongs to this glory, but not the full power of its light. From this the Son departs and to it he returns.[349] He distinguishes the two as the glory of the relationship of oneness and love[350] and the pre-existent and post-existent glory,[351] but also speaks of the former as a proleptic use of glory of the earthly Jesus in the light of the post-Easter glory.[352] Bultmann and Willem Nicol consider texts like 2:11 to relate both to Jesus' earthly ministry and, proleptically, to Jesus' post-Easter glory.[353] This may be so, given the levels of meaning in the Cana wedding narrative and the continuity of glory in the person of Jesus, pre- and post-Easter. But it will not do to interpret 1:14 and 2:11 proleptically as referring not to earthly, but only to post-Easter heavenly glory as a way of relaxing the tension, as does George Johnston.[354] This is to confuse what we

345. Appold, *Oneness*, 30–31; similarly Eric Osborn, "Negative and Positive Theology in John," *ABR* 31 (1983): 76.
346. Bühner, *Gesandte*, 294.
347. Bernhard Weiss, *Lehrbuch der Biblischen Theologie des Neuen Testaments*, 5th ed. (Berlin: Wilhelm Kerk, 1888), 609; similarly Dodd, *Interpretation*, 141.
348. Chibici-Revneanu, *Herrlichkeit*, 326–27, 572.
349. Thüsing, *Erhöhung*, 214–15, 222.
350. Thüsing, *Erhöhung*, 185, 227–28, 242–43.
351. Thüsing, *Erhöhung*, 233, 240–41.
352. Thüsing, *Erhöhung*, 181–86.
353. Bultmann, *Johannes*, 376–77, and Nicol, *Semeia*, 128.
354. George Johnston, "Ecce Homo. Irony in the Christology of the Fourth Evangelist,"

see as the historical processes of retrojection with what the author believes of his narrative world. It is misleading to relate 1:14 primarily to the events from John 13 onwards, on the basis of a division of the prologue into two parts matching two halves of the Gospel, as does Theobald.[355]

One Unchanging Glory?

It is also harmonising when F. F. Bruce and Onuki assert that Jesus' glorification means no addition of glory after Easter, but only greater ability on the part of the disciples to behold it,[356] or when Schillebeeckx—not unlike Käsemann and Appold who stress the constant glory of divine oneness—argues that the whole life of Jesus from 1:14 onwards is glory so that no glorification is needed,[357] or when Hegermann claims that the glory remains constant because it represents the presence of God who is always with the Son.[358] Nor is it likely that the glory for which the Son of Man prays is corporate glory for his own, as Caird suggests.[359] Any discussion must take into account that the incarnation implies both manifestation of glory and departure from glory to which the Son will return.[360]

Those who dispute that Jesus could have received more glory than he already had must deny the clear statements such as 17:5. They speak of the crucifixion as an unveiling of the glory that had always been there. This is true of Bultmann, who demythologises the concept of glorification, so that it means, in effect, that Jesus remains the revealer.[361] At most, like Cadman, he uses glorification in a future sense in relationship to fruit being born in mission and the gathering of Jesus' own, one of the uses evident in the Gospel (16:14), but not the major one.[362]

---

in *The Glory of Christ in the New Testament: Studies in Christology. In Memory of G. B. Caird*, ed. L. D. Hurst and N. T. Wright (Oxford: Clarendon, 1987), 131-32, 135.

355. Theobald, *Anfang*, 37-38; cf. also Becker, *Johannes*, 29-30; Bornkamm, "Paraklet," 117.
356. Bruce, *John*, 36; Onuki, *Gemeinde*, 106, 197-99, 210.
357. Schillebeeckx, *Christ*, 419; Käsemann, *Letzter Wille*, 48-54, 59; Appold, *Oneness*, 27-28; see also Dietzfelbinger, *Johannes*, 2.203-204, who sees glorification as a process which embraces all the elements from pre-existence, earthly ministry and death, to glorification in post-existence.
358. Hegermann, "δόξα," 839-40.
359. Caird, "Glory," 269-70, 272.
360. So Schnackenburg, *John*, 1.267; Schnackenburg, *Johannesevangelium*, 2.505.
361. Bultmann, *Johannes*, 376, 398; similarly Appold, *Oneness*, 27-28; Cadman, *Open Heaven*, 206; Bornkamm, "Interpretation," 113; Smalley, *John*, 221; de la Potterie, *Vérité*, 459; and earlier: Baur, *Kritische Untersuchungen*, 203; Lütgert, *Christologie*, 21.
362. Bultmann, *Johannes*, 325; Cadman, *Open Heaven*, 38, 40.

The Death of Jesus in John

Glory, Veiled and Unveiled?

The idea of the cross as revelation or as unveiling has often been used to suggest that during Jesus' ministry his glory was veiled, either in humility or in ambiguity.[363] Those who posit a Semeia source usually see it treating Jesus' miracles as an unveiling of his glory.[364] For the Gospel, both Thüsing and Nicol argue that this glory is seen only after the gift of the Spirit.[365] Sebald Hofbeck counters that this is not so, for the life promised in the signs is more than proleptic. It is a present reality in the person of Jesus. The glory of the signs is veiled to unbelievers, but not to the eyes of faith.[366] Schottroff argues that the manifestation takes place through the flesh and the signs in a way that leaves them untouched and in themselves irrelevant.[367] By contrast, Käsemann sees the humanity of Jesus seriously called into question by the manifestation of glory. The miracles are not irrelevant; they are demonstrations of the divine glory. Thus he denies a future glorification adds anything to what is already there.[368] Ibuki also points to the glory as manifest not only in the signs, but reinterprets glory to mean the glory of the relationship of love between Father and Son.[369] Forestell emphasises that the glory is manifest throughout the earthly life up to and including the cross and Easter event.[370]

The latter are surely correct in seeing 1:14 and 17:22 referring to a glory present in the ministry and veiled only to the eyes that will not see. There is, therefore, no need to harmonise the two uses of glory along the lines that the one glory is veiled, then unveiled. Jesus' glorification is not an unveiling, but a return to the glory he had with the Father in the beginning. The same must be said of those attempts which define glory as the oneness and love shared by Father and Son, always present but fully visible at Easter.[371] Without question the cross as the climax of the obedient life reveals in a unique way

---

363. Thüsing, *Erhöhung*, 246–47; Lütgert, *Christologie*, 31; Nicol, *Semeia*, 122; de la Potterie, *Vérité*, 193; Blank, *Krisis*, 272; Ruckstuhl, "Abstieg," 335.

364. So Müller, "Bedeutung," 67–68.

365. Thüsing, *Erhöhung*, 324; Nicol, *Semeia*, 122, 128.

366. So Hofbeck, *Semeion*, 104–5, 143, 173–78; Wilkens, *Zeichen*, 110; Braun, *Jean*, 206–7; Schnackenburg, *Johannesevangelium*, 2.503; similarly Käsemann, *Letzter Wille*, 22 and earlier Lütgert, *Christologie*, 21.

367. Schottroff, *Glaubende*, 272–77.

368. Käsemann, *Letzter Wille*, 19–20.

369. Ibuki, *Wahrheit*, 191.

370. Forestell, *Word*, 70–71.

371. Ibuki, *Wahrheit*, 192–96; Schlier, "Prolog," 282; Riedl, *Heilswerk*, 138–39. cf. also Thüsing, *Erhöhung*, 182, 242–43, 246; de la Potterie, *Vérité*, 198–99.

the relation of Father and Son, the love which constitutes it and the glory, the grace and truth, manifest through it.³⁷² But this should not be confused with the glorification of Jesus which his death inaugurates as the first step in his return to the glory he had with the Father before the world was and for which he prays.³⁷³

Glory: Tradition and Redaction

Some have explained the two uses as coming from different sources or levels of composition. Wilkens attributes the earthly use to the narrative source and the heavenly use to the sayings source.³⁷⁴ For Richter 2:11 and 11:40 come from the Semeia source, pre- and post-existent glory sayings from the evangelist, and 1:14 from the redactor.³⁷⁵ Becker sees glory linked with sending as the view of the evangelist, the idea of post-existent glory, as in ch. 17, coming from the redactor.³⁷⁶ U. B. Müller sees 1:14, 16 as belonging originally in a miracle Christology and referring only to Jesus' ministry, then taken up and linked by a redactor with the cross as glorification.³⁷⁷

Glorification of Jesus' Human Nature?

Riedl develops a detailed theory taken from Thomas Aquinas according to which the tension between Jesus having glory on earth and his receiving glory at Easter is to be solved by the suggestion that it is the human nature which is glorified at Easter. This suggestion goes back to Cyril of Alexandria. It means taking ἐν αὐτῷ ("in him" or "in himself") in the phrase καὶ ὁ θεὸς δοξάσει αὐτὸν ἐν αὐτῷ ("God will glorify him in himself" in 13:32) to refer not to God but to Christ. Accordingly God glorifies the man Jesus in the Son.³⁷⁸ The glorification includes the filling of Jesus' humanity to the full with divine glory as he reaches the highest level of knowledge of God. Thus the human Jesus asks in 17:1, 5 what he has already as a Son. Riedl de-

---

372. So Schnackenburg, *Johannesevangelium*, 2.503; Whitacre, *Polemic*, 109; Hegermann, "δόξα," 840-41.
   373. Cf. Moloney, *Son of Man*, 227; Pamment, "Doxa," 14.
   374. Wilkens, *Zeichen*, 113.
   375. Richter, *Studien*, 193, 284-85.
   376. Becker, *Johannes*, 518.
   377. Müller, *Christologie*, 32-35.
   378. Riedl, *Heilswerk*, 123-27.

velops this into a three-stage theory: pre-existence, filling the human Jesus, flowing out into the world. There is no addition of glory at any point.[379] But the theory depends heavily upon the assumption that the author operated with a two-nature theory. There is no trace of this in the Gospel. It does not make sense on this theory that the same Jesus in ch. 17 prays as a human being for glory and refers at the same time to glory he received as a gift in pre-existence.

Equally inappropriate is the view according to which glorification attaches primarily to leaving the flesh for the spiritual form of existence[380] or the suggestion that Jesus' reference to former heavenly glory (17:5) and to Isaiah's seeing it (12:41) are merely an apocalyptic way of talking about what is destined for the Son in the task of revelation he is to bear on earth, for both fail to take the context of the glorification sayings seriously.[381]

4.3.1.6 Glorification and Glory: Conclusions

There is therefore a glory which Jesus bears as God's Son and which he manifests in the world to the eyes of faith. This is his revelation of the Father and may be seen in his work and words. It is a glory which enables him to perform miracles. These should not be denied, as did Bultmann,[382] or denied any relevance with Schottroff.[383] Faith in the signs as miracles entails not ignoring the miracles altogether, but seeing in them a pointer to who Jesus is, both as the Son able to perform the miracle itself and as the bearer of life often symbolised in the miracle narrative. Many assume that it was only the glory of miraculous power which had been emphasised in the author's sources. In taking up such sources the author has not denied the miracles as manifestations of power, but has been critical of faith which stopped there.

In the deeds and words which his unique origins enabled him to perform and speak, the Son gives glory, as he gives himself—the revelation—to his disciples. But there is also a heavenly glory which belongs to the presence

---

379. Riedl, *Heilswerk*, 169–71, 178–79. Similarly, Braun, *Jean*, 209–10, 216–17, 220–21; Porsch, *Pneuma*, 76–78; Cadman, *Open Heaven*, 13.

380. Baur, *Kritische Untersuchungen*, 253; Bultmann, *Johannes*, 398.

381. Against Dupont, *Christologie*, 235–36, 267–68, 288–90. See Braun's critique in *Jean*, 201.

382. Bultmann, *Johannes*, 83. So Nicol, *Semeia*, 106; Haenchen, *Johannes*, 106; "Johannesevangelium," 219–21; Schottroff, *Glaubende*, 245–46, 255–56, 259–60; von den Osten Sacken, "Leistung," 161; Bornkamm, "Interpretation," 116; Wilkens, *Zeichen*, 28–29, 44–49; Schulz, *Johannes*, 212; Appold, *Oneness*, 88–91; earlier: Lütgert, *Christologie*, 10.

383. Schottroff, *Glaubende*, 252–59; similarly, Langbrandtner, *Weltferner Gott*, 93–96.

of the Son with the Father in heaven. This lies behind statements which speak of Jesus' glorification through the event of his death and return to the Father. Beside these is the less specific use of glory in the sense of honour, mostly used of the Son's glorifying the Father through the fulfilment of his will, especially through his obedience to the end, to death, but also used of his disciples and of the Paraclete, who through their work glorify both the Father and the Son. Of the two primary uses, both interpret the death of Jesus, one, more by implication, as the completion of the work of revelation,[384] the other quite specifically by portraying the death as the means whereby the Son returns to be glorified in heaven by his Father.

4.3.2 Lifting Up and Exaltation: Text, Language and Tradition

Closely associated with the concept of glorification is the author's use of the exaltation motif. The word ὑψόω ("to lift up, to exalt") occurs in the Gospel in three passages:

> Καὶ καθὼς Μωϋσῆς ὕψωσεν τὸν ὄφιν ἐν τῇ ἐρήμῳ,
> οὕτως ὑψωθῆναι δεῖ τὸν υἱὸν τοῦ ἀνθρώπου,
> ἵνα πᾶς ὁ πιστεύων ἐν αὐτῷ ἔχῃ ζωὴν αἰώνιον.
> And as Moses lifted up the serpent in the wilderness,
> so must the Son of Man be lifted up,
> that all believing may have life in him. (3:14–15)

> ὅταν ὑψώσητε τὸν υἱὸν τοῦ ἀνθρώπου, τότε γνώσεσθε ὅτι ἐγώ εἰμι,
> καὶ ἀπ' ἐμαυτοῦ ποιῶ οὐδέν, ἀλλὰ καθὼς ἐδίδαξέν με ὁ πατὴρ ταῦτα λαλῶ.
> When you have lifted up the Son of Man, then you will know that I am the one, and I do nothing of myself, but as the Father taught me, so I speak. (8:28)

> κἀγὼ ἐὰν ὑψωθῶ ἐκ τῆς γῆς, πάντας ἑλκύσω πρὸς ἐμαυτόν.
> τοῦτο δὲ ἔλεγεν σημαίνων ποίῳ θανάτῳ ἤμελλεν ἀποθνήσκειν.
> Ἀπεκρίθη οὖν αὐτῷ ὁ ὄχλος·
> ἡμεῖς ἠκούσαμεν ἐκ τοῦ νόμου ὅτι ὁ χριστὸς μένει εἰς τὸν αἰῶνα,
> καὶ πῶς λέγεις σὺ ὅτι δεῖ ὑψωθῆναι
> τὸν υἱὸν τοῦ ἀνθρώπου;

---

384. Schwindt, *Herrlichkeit*, 302.

τίς ἐστιν οὗτος ὁ υἱὸς τοῦ ἀνθρώπου;
And I, if I am lifted up from the earth, will draw all to myself.
This he said indicating by what death he was going to die.
The crowd therefore replied to him,
"We have heard from the Law that the Christ remains forever,
and how do you say the Son of Man must be lifted up?
Who is this Son of Man?" (12:32–34)

The word ὑψόω, like its equivalents in Aramaic and Hebrew, can mean a literal lifting up as well as a metaphorical lifting up, an exaltation.[385] It could and did function therefore as a base for puns both in the Semitic languages of Hebrew and Aramaic and also in Greek.[386] It is used to describe exaltation in NT christological tradition of Jesus' exaltation to God's right hand or to heavenly lordship:

τῇ δεξιᾷ οὖν τοῦ θεοῦ ὑψωθείς, τήν τε ἐπαγγελίαν τοῦ πνεύματος τοῦ ἁγίου λαβὼν παρὰ τοῦ πατρός, ἐξέχεεν τοῦτο ὃ ὑμεῖς [καὶ] βλέπετε καὶ ἀκούετε.
Thus being exalted to God's right hand and receiving the promise of the Holy Spirit from the Father, he poured out this which you (both) see and hear. (Acts 2:33)

τοῦτον ὁ θεὸς ἀρχηγὸν καὶ σωτῆρα ὕψωσεν τῇ δεξιᾷ αὐτοῦ [τοῦ] δοῦναι μετάνοιαν τῷ Ἰσραὴλ καὶ ἄφεσιν ἁμαρτιῶν.
God has exalted him as leader and saviour to his right hand to give repentance to Israel and forgiveness of sins. (Acts 5:31)

διὸ καὶ ὁ θεὸς αὐτὸν ὑπερύψωσεν
καὶ ἐχαρίσατο αὐτῷ τὸ ὄνομα τὸ ὑπὲρ πᾶν ὄνομα
Therefore also God highly exalted him
and gave him the name which is above every name. (Phil 2:9)

---

385. See Georg Bertram, "ὑψόω," *TDNT* 7.610 n. 38; Thüsing, *Erhöhung*, 36–37; Moloney, *Son of Man*, 61 n. 102; Gerd Lüdemann, "ὑψόω," *EWNT* 3.982; George R. Beasley-Murray, "John 12,31–32: The Eschatological Significance of the Lifting Up of the Son of Man," in *Studien zum Text und zur Ethik des Neuen Testaments. Festschrift für H. Greeven*, ed. W. Schrage, BZNW 167 (Berlin: de Gruyter, 1986), 71–72.

386. So Wead, *Devices*, 34–35; Meeks, "Man from Heaven," 155 and 171 n. 63.

4.3.2.1 Lifting Up: Crucifixion Only?

In John it certainly refers to Jesus' crucifixion as a lifting up. This is made clear by the author in 12:33, where the author treats the saying as a prediction of the manner of Jesus' death. In 18:32 he refers back to this after noting that Jesus was handed over to Pilate for trial:

ἵνα ὁ λόγος τοῦ Ἰησοῦ πληρωθῇ ὃν εἶπεν σημαίνων
ποίῳ θανάτῳ ἤμελλεν ἀποθνῄσκειν.
so that the word of Jesus might be fulfilled which he spoke indicating by what death he was going to die. (18:32)

This may reflect a concern to deal with the offence created by the crucifixion for belief in his messiahship (cf. 12:34).[387] Crucifixion also matches the image of the lifting up of the serpent in 3:14.[388] In 8:28 Jesus is clearly referring to the crucifixion when he refers to it as an action done by the Jews: "When you have lifted up the Son of Man" (ὅταν ὑψώσητε τὸν υἱὸν τοῦ ἀνθρώπου).[389]

It is possible to let matters rest there. The verb ὑψόω would mean nothing more than the lifting up of Jesus onto the cross and is simply a synonym for "crucify" in each of these verses. In 3:14-15 this would give the meaning either that the actual death itself is the basis for the promise of the healing of eternal life,[390] namely death understood as an expiatory or vicarious sacrifice or as apotropaic, or that crucifixion began an event which through the giving of the Spirit would lead to the gift of life becoming more freely available.[391] As Painter notes, the notion of the Son of Man's being lifted up to draw all people to himself (12:32) "may already be present in the first use of the metaphor in 3:14-15."[392] John 8:28 points to the lifting up as an event as a result of which they would come to know who he is. It is not referring exclusively to the crucifixion at the metaphorical level[393] but includes what

---

387. So Riedl, *Heilswerk*, 100-101; Richter, *Studien*, 61, 74-79, 116; Dauer, *Passionsgeschichte*, 231; Müller, "Bedeutung," 57-58, 67; Müller, *Christologie*, 49-50; Müller, *Menschwerdung*, 71; Wengst, *Gemeinde*, 63-65; Nicholson, *Death*, 143-44.

388. Moloney, "Son of Man Revisited," 187.

389. Moloney, "Son of Man Revisited," 187; Frey, "Theologia crucifixi," 545.

390. Bergmeier, "ΤΕΤΕΛΕΣΤΑΙ," 288; Frey, "Theologia crucifixi," 545.

391. Weidemann, *Tod Jesu*, 376; Schmidl, *Jesus und Nikodemus* 273-76; Carson, *John*, 201-2; Michaels, *John*, 197; Beutler, *Johannesevangelium*, 139.

392. Painter, "Sacrifice and Atonement," 305.

393. Cf. Catherine Cory, "Wisdom's Rescue: A New Reading of the Tabernacles Discourse (John 7:1–8:59)," *JBL* 116 (1997): 106, who writes: "Jesus' vindication and exaltation do not simply follow his death, but rather they *coincide* with the moment of his death, so that his

The Death of Jesus in John

that will inaugurate.³⁹⁴ This would cohere well with the idea of the promised Spirit, bringing knowledge (7:39; 12:16), and especially by interpreting the meaning of Jesus' crucifixion and death as is done in 16:8-11. In this case the knowledge would also bring judgment.³⁹⁵ John 12:32 could contain a reference to Jesus' death understood as an expiatory or vicarious sacrifice or as apotropaic as the basis for the salvation then to be offered to all and so the basis for drawing all. Thüsing argues this unconvincingly on the basis of ποίῳ θανάτῳ (literally: "what kind of death") in 12:33, which he takes to refer to Jesus' death as of a kind that is salvific, whereas 18:32 makes it clear that the mode of execution is intended;³⁹⁶ or it, too, could refer to the crucifixion as the beginning of the event which would lead to the Spirit and to world mission, more likely given the context.

In 3:14 the imagery uses looking at the uplifted one as the source or basis for receiving eternal life, analogous to the Israelites looking to the bronze serpent. Imagery of seeing occurs also in association with reference to Jesus as the Son of Man in 1:51, and 6:62. In 19:37 the author cites Zech 12:10 in relation to the spear thrust: "they shall look on him whom they have pierced,"³⁹⁷ applied to Jesus' parousia in Rev 1:7, but transferred here to his death.³⁹⁸ While a possible allusion to Jesus' death as expiatory or vicarious in 3:14 should not be ruled out—given that one might read 3:16 as alluding to his death—this is by no means clear, especially in the light of the other references to seeing the Son of Man in the future, nor is this the only way of reading the text. Nor should it be, given the other broader occurrences of seeing: seeing (and sharing) Jesus' future glory (17:24), seeing God (1:18; 6:46; and in Jesus 14:7-11; cf. also 5:19), seeing the Son's glory (1:14; 2:11; cf. "come and see!" 1:39).

---

exaltation is his *rescue* from death"; similarly Carson, *John*, 345: "When Jesus is 'lifted up' on the cross, he is being 'lifted up' to his Father's presence, returned to the glory he enjoyed with the Father before the world began (17:5).... The exaltation of Jesus by means of the cross is also the exaltation of Jesus on the cross."

394. Painter, *Quest*, 337; Reynolds, *Apocalyptic Son of Man*, 123-24.
395. Thüsing, *Erhöhung*, 15, 21.
396. Thüsing, *Erhöhung*, 24.
397. On this see Sanghee Michael Ahn, *The Christological Witness Function of Old Testament Characters in the Gospel of John* (Eugene: Wipf and Stock, 2014), 170-73; William Randolph Bynum, *The Fourth Gospel and the Scriptures: Illuminating the Form and Meaning of Scriptural Citation in John 19:37*, NovTSup 144 (Leiden: Brill, 2012), 171-74; Weidemann, *Tod Jesu*, 422.
398. Weidemann, *Tod Jesu*, 129, sees the reference functioning like 3:14 and 1:29, 36 as predicting people's sense of protection when they look on Jesus as the Passover lamb. Frey, "Herrlichkeit," 661-62, links this seeing to 17:24, which he takes not as referring to Jesus' final state, the meaning the context demands, but to his earthly ministry and death.

4.3.2.2 Lifting Up/Exaltation and Isaiah 53?

We have already seen how the idea of Jesus' death as an expiatory or vicarious sacrifice, while present, is not prominent in the author's Christology. This counts against seeing it as the primary reference in 3:14 and 12:32. The same must be said of attempts to make a link between the language of exaltation and glorification and the suffering servant of Isa 53.[399] As already noted, it is very likely that Isa 52:13 has impacted upon the author's usage.[400]

> Ἰδοὺ συνήσει ὁ παῖς μου καὶ ὑψωθήσεται καὶ δοξασθήσεται σφόδρα.
> Behold my servant shall understand and shall be exalted and glorified exceedingly. (Isa 52:13)

In Isaiah this refers to God's response to the servant's suffering and death, not to the suffering and death itself. This corresponds to its use in other Christian tradition cited above (Acts 2:33; 5:31; Phil 2:9) to speak of Jesus' vindication. A similar use of the two verbs ὑψόω and δοξάζω in the context of vindication is also to be found in Isa 5:16; 33:10; 45:25, as Caird and Walter Klaiber point out.[401] The use of ὑψόω and δοξάζω in these contexts supports the idea that in John they are being used similarly but not just to depict what follows Jesus' suffering death, but also to include it as part of the meaning in a manner typical of Johannine irony. The author has exploited the dual reference in ὑψόω.

4.3.2.3 Lifting to the Cross, Exaltation to Glory: Two Ways of Seeing

The world sees a crucifixion; believers see it as exaltation, not in the sense that this is like martyrdom a moment of glory and that is all, a view which, as we saw, did not give a satisfactory account of the author's use of glorification.[402] Rather faith sees in the event of Jesus' crucifixion an exaltation because it knows that in and through this event Jesus will be exalted to God's presence.[403]

---

399. Cf. Pamment, "Doxa," 16, who makes a link with the use of δόξα in Isa 53:2; similarly Reim, "Targum," 2.
400. On the role of Isaiah passages in the development of Christology see Hurtado, *Lord Jesus Christ*, 380–81.
401. Caird, "Glory," 274–75; Klaiber, "Interpretation," 316.
402. Cf. Lincoln, *John*, 153: the Son of Man's humiliation and suffering is his glory.
403. Müller, *Menschwerdung*, 74; Theobald, *Johannes*, 1.264, who notes that crucifixion and exaltation are not identical, the former the beginning of the latter which includes return to the Father.

The word ὑψόω thus enabled the author to describe two realities, the reality of crucifixion and the reality of Jesus' return through this event to exalted glory.[404] Unfaith sees only one reality; faith sees both. We have, therefore, a typical word play of the evangelist which functions powerfully as irony at the heart of the author's Christology. It also accords with the use of ὑψόω in Christian tradition, such as in Acts 2:33; 5:31 and Phil 2:9, to express exaltation, but goes beyond it in that the author creatively uses it already of the death as part of the larger complex event which ends in God's presence.[405] It misreads such creativity to conclude that it can refer only to the death.[406] The author's use of ὑψόω to refer both to crucifixion and to the exaltation of Jesus to God in heaven receives further confirmation when we recall how it belongs within a particular cluster of vocabulary associated with the Son of Man title: glorification, exaltation, ascent, judgment, the "hour," and the greater event motif, as we noted in ch. 3 above.

The context of the exaltation sayings illustrates this connection. John 3:13 has just referred to the ascent of the Son of Man. John 8:28 belongs in the broader context of the Jews' perplexity about where Jesus is going (8:21-24), his return to the Father. John 12:32 follows a statement about the hour of the world's judgment having come when the ruler of the world would be cast out. In the next allusion to the same theme, 16:8-11, the judgment of the world and the vindication of Jesus are related to his death and return to the Father. The wider context of 12:32, stretching back to 12:19, is embraced by the theme of mission and of Jesus' death and return as the event which makes it possible. In this sense the parallels to 12:32 are 12:23 and 24, where, at the coming of the Greeks, Jesus declares,

---

404. So among others Dodd, *Interpretation*, 306; Schulz, *Menschensohn*, 108; *Johannes*, 59-60; Wilkens, *Zeichen*, 103-4, 110; Barrett, *John*, 214, 427; "Paradox," 109; Blank, *Krisis*, 84-85, 261, 287; Schnackenburg, *John*, 1.394-97; *Johannesevangelium*, 2.156, 492-93, 499-502; 4.112; Käsemann, *Letzter Wille*, 46-47; Joseph Coppens, "Le Fils de l'Homme dans l'Évangile johannique," *ETL* 52 (1976): 48; Becker, *Johannes*, 402-4; Müller, "Bedeutung," 56-60; Brown, *John*, 40, 84, 168; Brown, *Introduction*, 256; Smalley, "Son of Man," 291; Maddox, "Function," 191; Appold, *Oneness*, 52-53; Riedl, *Heilswerk*, 364; Bertram, "ὑψόω," 610; Boismard and Lamouille, *Jean*, 51, 124, 319; Nicholson, *Death*, 75, 99-101, 119, 132-36; Lüdemann, "ὑψόω," 982; Gnilka, "Christologie," 104; Bruce, *John*, 88, 182, 267, but cf. 195; O'Day, *Revelation*, 111-12; Beasley-Murray, *John*, lxxxiv-lxxxv, 50-51, 54, 76, 131-32; Beasley-Murray, "John 12,31-32," 71-73; Burge, *Anointed Community*, 132; Burkett, *Son of Man*, 122; Schwindt, *Herrlichkeit*, 316.

405. Ashton, *Fourth Gospel*, 268; Ashton, "Johannine Son of Man," 526, where he writes: "The explanation must lie rather in some sort of mystical experience that allowed the evangelist to see the hoisting-up of Jesus onto the cross as an exaltation."

406. Cf. Schnackenburg, *Person Jesu Christi*, 289; similarly Söding, "Kreuzerhöhung," 13, yet he can also write of the lifting up on the cross as foreshadowing Jesus' return and exaltation to the right hand of the Father.

Ὁ δὲ Ἰησοῦς ἀποκρίνεται αὐτοῖς λέγων·
ἐλήλυθεν ἡ ὥρα ἵνα δοξασθῇ ὁ υἱὸς τοῦ ἀνθρώπου.
ἀμὴν ἀμὴν λέγω ὑμῖν, ἐὰν μὴ ὁ κόκκος τοῦ σίτου πεσὼν εἰς τὴν γῆν ἀποθάνῃ,
αὐτὸς μόνος μένει· ἐὰν δὲ ἀποθάνῃ, πολὺν καρπὸν φέρει.
Jesus responded to them,
"The hour has come for the Son of Man to be glorified.
Truly, truly I tell you unless a grain of wheat falls into the ground and dies,
it remains alone; but if it dies it bears much fruit." (12:23–24)

We have already seen that glorification refers here to Jesus' being brought through death to the glory he once shared in the beginning with the Father. Seen in this light, all three passages cohere impressively and take their place within a cluster of motifs by which the author explicates the significance of Jesus' death and return. Exaltation, with glorification, explicates the significance of Jesus' death and return. Similarly, as our discussion below will show, 13:1 makes it clear that the "hour" includes the time for him to love his own to the death and then to return to the Father. This perspective is present in the references to "the hour" and its equivalents (e.g., "now"; "time") elsewhere.

4.3.2.4 Crucifixion: Paradox of Exaltation and Glorification?

Exaltation in John is, then, another way of the author's saying that, through the event of his death and return, the Son of Man has been glorified with the glory he shared with God before the foundation of the world.[407] This is far more likely than the suggestion that exaltation and glorification have been transferred by the author exclusively to the crucifixion itself, let alone, that, by association with Isa 53, they also include the notion of the expiatory or vicarious sacrifice of Jesus for his own. An explanation of ὑψόω which would see it as having a single meaning, namely only the execution on a cross, and would see crucifixion as the beginning of the total event through which life, the Spirit, mission are made available, would be more coherent with the main structure of the author's theology, but it, too, fails to grasp the full import of the passages by limiting ὑψόω to the crucifixion. For the ascent onto the cross is the beginning of the ascent ultimately to heaven itself. When the

---

407. Ashton, *Fourth Gospel*, 470, who concludes that "'lifting up' and 'glorification' are alternative and complementary ways of speaking of the same event."

world lifts Jesus to the cross and to death, it unwittingly sets in motion an event of far greater significance. For through death he returns exalted and glorified to the Father.

The common misinterpretation which applies exaltation and glorification to the cross arises, in part, from the persistence of the Bultmann model of Johannine Christology which sees exaltation demythologised by the author, so that the crucifixion itself is interpreted as a great Pauline paradox of glorification and exaltation. The result is startling, provocative and immensely challenging: glory in shame, exaltation in humiliation.[408] But, once we concede that glorification cannot be understood like this or be limited to this in John, then the case for taking exaltation as referring exclusively to Jesus' death and not to exaltation to God in heaven, beginning with the crucifixion, is seriously weakened. It does not follow logically that because the literal meaning refers only to the crucifixion, therefore the metaphorical meaning must be similarly restricted, as some have argued.[409] Here we also tread the same ground again in noting that royal messianic imagery in the passion narrative cannot be used to support this kind of interpretation of the cross in John in relation to the exaltation motif, any more than it can in relation to glorification. Nor is there sufficient evidence in it of enthronement Christology, and, even if there were, it is not linked with the exaltation theme.

There is also no evidence in the Gospel for Wolfgang J. Bittner's contention that "lifting up" is primarily a messianic image based on the lifted ensign of Isa 11:11.[410] Similarly Bühner's theory of an action taking place on two levels (simultaneously lifting up on the cross, at one level, heavenly enthronement, on the other) imposes a foreign framework onto the text.[411] This is not to deny we see in John the true king of Israel on the cross nor to ignore the powerful irony expressed in the fact that the mockery of the trial, transposed into the key of faith, plays the melody of faith's affirmation: Jesus is the Christ, the Son of God. But neither the exaltation nor the glorification motifs are made to say this in John, however well they have been so used in theology and edification.

Exaltation entails the entire event from crucifixion to being exalted to God's presence. "The Christian believer is not expected to see the crucifixion as a kind of exaltation or glorification but to see *past* the physical reality of Jesus' death to its true significance: the reascent of the Son of Man to his true

---

408. Bultmann, *Johannes*, 189, 331.
409. Cf. Frey, "Theologia crucifixi," 545; Moloney, "Son of Man Revisited," 187.
410. Bittner, *Zeichen*, 254.
411. Bühner, *Gesandte*, 396–97.

home in heaven."[412] It is not, therefore, exaltation onto the cross without being exaltation through this to heaven.[413] Neither does glorification refer only to Jesus' death on the cross.[414] Margaret Pamment's argument to the contrary, that this language does not occur in 20:17, where Jesus speaks of return or ascent to the Father, and that allusion to Jesus' death in 12:24 means we must take 12:23 as referring to Jesus' death, is not cogent, as passages like 3:13-14 and our review (2.2) of ch. 12 have shown.[415]

There remains, however, a distinctively Johannine paradox in the Fourth Gospel's use of ὑψόω: faith sees the cross, the pathway of suffering, as the pathway to glory. This is part of the author's inspiration,[416] as it was with the extension of glorification to cover Jesus' death, and is not to be seen only as something which followed, which, of course it also included.[417] We shall return to this paradox and its implications for understanding discipleship in John.

---

412. Ashton, *Fourth Gospel*, 471; similarly "Johannine Son of Man," 525; Reynolds, *Apocalyptic Son of Man*, 127, who writes: "The exaltation of the descended one begins at his crucifixion and is completed in his ascent to the right hand of God"; similarly 172, 198; Lee, *Flesh and Glory*, 35, 79; Hahn, *Theologie*, 1.649-50; Weidemann, *Tod Jesu*, 105, 126; Michaels, *John*, 697; Burkett, *Son of Man*, 122; Keener, *John*, 565-66; Chibici-Revneanu, *Herrlichkeit*, 616.

413. Cf. Meeks, *Prophet-King*, 287-92; "Man from Heaven," 156; Thüsing, *Erhöhung*, 1-12; Forestell, *Word*, 63; Riedl, "Menschensohn," 360; Ruckstuhl, "Abstieg," 333; Lindars, *Son of Man*, 146, 156-57; Baum-Bodenbender, *Hoheit*, 265-66, cf. 256; Ellis, *Genius*, 153, 204; Frey, *Eschatologie*, 3.278; Dietzfelbinger, *Johannes*, 2.249; Söding, "Kreuzerhöhung," 13; Thyen, *Johannesevangelium*, 208-9; Francis J. Moloney, in his Editor's notes to R. E. Brown, *An Introduction to the Gospel of John. Edited, Updated, Introduced and Concluded by Francis J. Moloney, S.D.B.*, AncBRL (New York: Doubleday, 2003), dissenting from Brown (256 n. 82; 288 n. 22). Cf. Moloney, *Son of Man*, 60-64, 140-41, 228-29.

414. Cf. Moloney, *Son of Man*, 63, 176-78, 207, 210; Moloney, "Son of Man Revisited," 185; Lindars, "Passion," 79; Lindars, *Son of Man*, 147; Pokorny, "Jesus," 218, 222; Pamment, "Doxa," 13-16; Bittner, *Zeichen*, 248; Bjerkelund, *TAUTA*, 124, 128; Schnelle, *Christologie*, 208, 250; "Tempelreinigung," 366-67.

415. Pamment, "Doxa," 13-14.

416. Ashton, "Johannine Son of Man," 526, speculates that this extension of exaltation to include the event of Jesus' death "can best be accounted for if we suppose that John himself had a vision overwhelming enough to eliminate the painful and humiliating aspects of Jesus' passion and to replace them with signs of exaltation and glory."

417. Cf. de Boer, *Johannine Perspectives*, 170, who writes that at the third stage in his historical reconstruction "language appropriate to resurrection-ascension is being intentionally transferred to the crucifixion." The author hardly then limits such language to the cross. See also Martinus C. de Boer, "Jesus' Departure to the Father in John: Death or Resurrection?" in *Theology and Christology in the Fourth Gospel. Essays by the Members of the SNTS Johannine Writings Seminar*, ed. G. Van Belle, J. G. van der Watt, and P. Maritz, BETL 184 (Leuven: Peeters, 2005), 19; and de Boer, "Johannine History," 313, 318.

4.3.2.5 Exaltation on the Cross: Glorification in Heaven?

A different approach is taken by Thüsing, who distinguishes glorification and exaltation. Jesus is exalted on the cross, so that he continues to rule from the cross. Glorification includes the cross, but refers primarily to his subsequent return to glory.[418] In this way he holds exaltation and glorification apart and yet does so in a way that confuses. He speaks of exaltation, for instance, as a "Bild," a picture or image,[419] and sometimes speaks of it as exaltation to the throne of glory.[420] His diagrammatic representation of exaltation and glorification does in fact equate exaltation and glorification as return to heavenly glory;[421] yet he continues to use the idea of exaltation upon the cross as a "Bild" in such a way that he can say that the Son rules from here and draws people first to the cross and only then into glory.[422]

4.3.3 Ascension, the Son of Man and the "Greater" Event

Both glorification and exaltation interpret Jesus' death in John as his return to the Father, to glory on high. Both are associated with the title Son of Man. They belong together within a cluster of motifs. The review in ch. 3 showed that to this close association of ideas also belongs ascension.[423]

4.3.3.1 John 3:13

The attempts of Moloney and others to deny its presence in 3:13 and 6:62 are unconvincing. Moloney first notes the likelihood that the words "No one has ascended to heaven" (οὐδεὶς ἀναβέβηκεν εἰς τὸν οὐρανόν in 3:13) might reflect a common tradition (reflected in Deut 30:12; Prov 30:4; Bar 3:29; Wis 9:16–18) which the author is using to counter alternate claims to revelation.[424] Such claims were widespread and diverse and might include

---

418. Thüsing, *Erhöhung*, 24–28, 33, 302–303; similarly Jacob Jervell, *Jesus in the Gospel of John* (Minneapolis: Augsburg, 1984), 58, 60, 72; Schillebeeckx, *Christ*, 409–10.
419. Thüsing, *Erhöhung*, 8–9, 24, 26, 33, 293, 302–3, 307.
420. Thüsing, *Erhöhung*, 300.
421. Thüsing, *Erhöhung*, 305–7.
422. Thüsing, *Erhöhung*, 303.
423. Cf. Schnelle. *Johannes*, 303, who seeks to divorce the ideas.
424. Moloney, *Son of Man*, 54–55; John Lierman, "The Mosaic Pattern of John's Christology," in *Challenging Perspectives on the Gospel of John*, ed. J. Lierman, WUNT 2.219

mystical ascents,[425] ascents of Moses or of prophets,[426] apocalyptic visions and visionaries,[427] Philonic ascent,[428] and gnostic revealers.[429] Moloney goes on to argue for a translation which would continue the verse: "but there is one who has descended, the Son of Man" (cf. εἰ μὴ ὁ ἐκ τοῦ οὐρανοῦ καταβάς, ὁ υἱὸς τοῦ ἀνθρώπου). In this way he rules out any allusion in 3:13 to the ascent of the Son of Man.[430]

This runs counter to the natural reading of εἰ μή in 3:13 to mean "except" and is widely rejected.[431] The fact that the usual translation would have Jesus speaking anachronistically here[432] should not, in itself, be a problem, since already 3:11 does so. Furthermore the allusion to Jesus' death and exaltation in 3:14-15 makes the translation most unlikely, even more so, if, unlike Moloney, we understand exaltation to include exaltation to heavenly glory. Attempts to see in 3:13 a pre-existent ascension as part of the process of authorisation, as Bühner and others suggest,[433] or an earthly ecstatic one after the model

---

(Tübingen: Mohr Siebeck, 2006), 212–14; Reynolds, *Apocalyptic Son of Man*, 107–8; Schmidl, *Jesus und Nikodemus*, 250–66.

425. Hugo Odeberg, *The Fourth Gospel* (Uppsala: Almqvist & Wiksells, 1929), 72–78.

426. Meeks, *Prophet-King*, 297, 301; Meeks, "Man from Heaven," 147; Haacker, *Stiftung*, 108–10; Miranda, *Vater*, 80; Peder Borgen, "The Son of Man Saying in John 3:13–14," in *Logos Was the True Light* (Trondheim: Tapir, 1983), 133–38; Whitacre, *Polemic*, 52; Alan F. Segal, *Two Powers in Heaven. Early Rabbinic Reports about Christianity and Gnosticism* (Leiden: Brill, 1977), 213–14; Borgen, "Agent," 131–32; James D. G. Dunn, "Let John Be John—A Gospel for its Time," in *Das Evangelium und die Evangelien*, ed. P. Stuhlmacher, WUNT 28 (Tübingen: Mohr Siebeck, 1983), 326–27.

427. Blank, *Krisis*, 77; Dahl, "Church," 137; Forestell, *Word*, 43; Meeks, "Man from Heaven," 147; Otto Michel, "Der aufsteigende und herabsteigende Gesandte," in *The New Testament Age: Essays in Honor of B. Reicke*, ed. W. C. Weinrich (Macon: Mercer, 1984), 349, 352–53; Dunn, "John," 322–25 (especially Merkabah mysticism); Reim, "Targum," 7 (ascending angels).

428. Peder Borgen, *The Gospel of John: More Light from Philo, Paul and Archaeology: The Scriptures, Tradition, Exposition, Meaning*, NovTSup 154 (Leiden: Brill, 2014), 60, 98–99; Borgen, "Agent," 129–31.

429. Bultmann, *Johannes*, 146–53; Blank, *Krisis*, 77–78.

430. Moloney, *Son of Man*, 54–55, 244; "Son of Man Revisited," where he acknowledges that his translation did not convince but still maintains that no reference to Jesus' ascension is present (190–93). See also E. M. Sidebottom, *The Christ of the Fourth Gospel* (London: SPCK, 1961), 120; Ruckstuhl, "Abstieg," 325; Lindars, *Son of Man*, 150; Moloney, *Love*, 190–93.

431. Specifically in relation to Moloney: Barrett, *John*, 213; "Paradox," 110; Nicholson, *Death*, 93–95; John Painter, "Christology and the Farewell Discourses," *ABR* 31 (1983): 45–62, 59; cf. also Borgen, "Son of Man," 139; Reynolds, *Apocalyptic Son of Man*, 109–10.

432. Against this: Carson, *John*, 200.

433. Bühner, *Gesandte*, 304–7, 380–81, 392–93; Borgen, "Son of Man," 139–41; Jarl E. Fossum, "The Son of Man's Alter Ego: John 1.51, Targumic Tradition and Jewish Mysticism," in *The Image of the Invisible God. Essays on the Influence of Jewish Mysticism on Early Christology*, NTOA 30 (Göttingen: Vandenhoeck und Ruprecht, 1995), 149. For criticism see Dunn, "John,"

of Paul's being caught up into the third heaven,[434] or an allusion to Jesus' ascent from the waters of baptism,[435] or the idea of constant traffic of Jesus between earth and heaven,[436] or to previous descents and ascents recorded in the OT on the basis of Prov 30:1-4,[437] are also unconvincing for this reason. The manuscript tradition which added "who is in heaven" (ὁ ὢν ἐν οὐρανῷ) understood the anachronism perfectly.[438] Jesus is represented here as speaking from a post-Easter perspective[439] or perhaps better we should see these words, indeed the sections, 3:13-21, 31-36, as the words of the narrator.[440]

329-30; Moloney, *Son of Man*, 232-33, 240-41; Schnackenburg, *Johannesevangelium*, 4.105; Schnelle, *Christologie*, 207; Michael Theobald, *Herrenworte im Johannesevangelium*, HBS 34 (Freiburg: Herder, 2002), 205 n. 15; Beasley-Murray, "Mission," 1863.

434. Cadman, *Open Heaven*, 30. Ashton, *John*, writes: "Crucial here is the observation that Jesus bases his claim of being able to transmit his knowledge of celestial realities ('we speak of what we know and bear witness to what we have seen') on *personal experience*, an experience that came not, as is often asserted, from some sort of heavenly pre-existence but from an ascent into heaven that is denied all others" (171). This fails to recognise that the Johannine Jesus does not reveal heavenly secrets and revelations. See also "Johannine Son of Man," where he argues that the author deliberately contrasted Jesus' mystical ascent with Moses' (522; similarly 528), locating it in transfiguration tradition (527); similarly McGrath, *Christology*, 162-65, 226.

435. Frederick H. Borsch, *The Son of Man in Myth and History* (London: SCM, 1967), 273, 275 n. 2.

436. Lütgert, *Christologie*, 42, 46-47; Robert H. Strachan, *The Fourth Gospel*, 3rd ed. (London: SCM, 1941), 137-38; Robinson, *Priority*, 371; cf. also Barrett, *John* 187; "Paradox," 110-11.

437. Burkett, *Son of Man*, 87, proposes that "'the Son of the Man' in Jn 3.13 is the son of 'the Man' in Prov. 30.1-4." Of the "Son of (the) Man" he writes that "the source of the expression itself is a christological interpretation of Prov. 30.1-4, in which Jesus is identified as 'Ithiel,' like the son of 'the Man'" (50). "His reference to Prov. 30.4 permits the recognition that he is speaking of those occasions recorded in the Old Testament when God ascended back to heaven following a visit to earth" (85); in agreement Thyen, *Johannesevangelium*, 202-208; cf. Joong Suk Suh, *The Glory in the Gospel of John: Restoration of Forfeited Prestige* (Oxford, OH: M. P. Publications, 1995), 22-27. This speculative reconstruction fails to take into account the strength of existing Jewish and Christian apocalyptic traditions in part elaborating Daniel 7.

438. So Thüsing, *Erhöhung*, 256; Coppens, "Le Fils de L'Homme," arguing for its originality (35); cf. also Barrett, *John*, 213; Brown, *John*, 16; Schnackenburg, *John*, 1.394; Nicholson, *Death*, 97-98. See also Michael Mees, "Lectio Brevior im Johannesevangelium und ihre Beziehung zum Urtext," *BZ* 12 (1968): 115, and Michael Mees, "Erhöhung und Verherrlichung Jesu im Johannesevangelium nach dem Zeugnis neutestamentlicher Papyri," *BZ* 18 (1974): 34; Painter, *Quest*, 329, who sees it as the *lectio difficilior* and more original (329); similarly Wilckens, *Johannes*, 70.

439. So Barrett, *John*, 213; Brown, *John*, 132; Sanders and Mastin, *John*, 126; Bruce, *John*, 87-88; Haenchen, *Johannes*, 224; Schulz, *Johannes*, 59; Painter, "Christology and the Farewell Discourses," 59.

440. So Painter, *Quest*, 330, who notes that they "are to be understood as the words of the narrator where an ascension perspective is not surprising."

The ascension of the Son of Man is alluded to in 3:13.[441] This is not to deny the difficulty in the flow of thought within the passage. After 3:12, with its contrast between earthly and heavenly revelation, we might expect 3:13 to be countering the claims of rival revealers, and so it does. But if it were as simple as that, then we might well wonder why the author has not formulated 3:13 more clearly and used a simple adversative. The credentials Jesus pits against the rivals are not only his descent. They also include his ascent, but not a preceding ascent. It is the one who descended and also ascended again who is qualified to be the revealer *par excellence*. In his coming he brings revelation to earth ("earthly things" including birth from above, 3:12).

εἰ τὰ ἐπίγεια εἶπον ὑμῖν καὶ οὐ πιστεύετε,
πῶς ἐὰν εἴπω ὑμῖν τὰ ἐπουράνια πιστεύσετε;
If I have told you earthly things and you do not believe,
how will you believe if I tell you heavenly things? (3:12)

In 3:13 Jesus goes on directly to speak of "heavenly things,"[442] namely of the greater event which will occur at the climax of his ministry, his ascent and exaltation.[443] Both events, the revelation through descent and, above all, its abundant availability and greater understanding achieved through ascent, make Jesus the superior revealer. Accordingly the author goes on in 3:14–15 to refer to the latter, and how it will be achieved: through exaltation.[444]

---

441. Dietzfelbinger, *Johannes*, 1.85; Witherington, *John's Wisdom*, 100; Reynolds, *Apocalyptic Son of Man*, 115, prefers a gnomic understanding of the perfect, translating: "No one ascends except the Son of Man, the one who has descended."

442. Thyen, *Johannesevangelium*, 198–202, argues unconvincingly that in 3:12 heavenly and earthly express not serious differentiation but despair at unresponsiveness.

443. Theobald, *Johannes*, 1.257–58; Beutler, *Johannesevangelium*, 136; Moloney, *John* 94–95; Schnelle, *Johannes*, 72; Alexander S. Jensen, *John's Gospel as Witness: The Development of the Early Christian Language of Faith* (Aldersgate: Ashgate, 2004), 109; Cf. Ashton, *Fourth Gospel*, 117: who identifies "the heavenly things" as a reference to the Gospel itself; similarly, Ashton, *John*, 251, although he earlier identifies them as what Jesus had seen (116); and in "Johannine Son of Man" as alluding to the transfiguration (519–20, 528); similarly John Ashton, "Reflections on a Footnote," in *Engaging with C. H. Dodd on the Gospel of John: Sixty Years of Tradition and Interpretation*, ed. T. Thatcher and C. H. Williams (Cambridge: Cambridge University Press, 2014), 213–14; McGrath, *Christology*, 162–65, 194. Reynolds, *Apocalyptic Son of Man*, 106, sees it referring to Jesus' revelation.

444. See also Nicholson, *Death*, 92–93. Moloney, "Son of Man Revisited," 189–90, argues that "1,51; 3,14; 8,28 and 12,32 should be removed from any discussion of the ascent-descent of the Son of Man," and that nine of the thirteen "sayings can be interpreted as associated with the earthly activity of Jesus: the one in whom a lasting revelation takes place (1,51; 6,27), when

4.3.3.2 John 6:62

Moloney offers an unusual interpretation of 6:62 through which he again seeks to deny the presence of the ascension motif.

> ἐὰν οὖν θεωρῆτε τὸν υἱὸν τοῦ ἀνθρώπου ἀναβαίνοντα ὅπου ἦν τὸ πρότερον;
> Then what if you were to see the Son of Man ascending where he was before? (6:62).

Moloney sees here a taunt aimed at popular expectations of ascending revealers. "There will be no ascension to where he was before."[445] But once we allow ascension in 3:13 (it is also present in 20:17), there is no reason to dismiss it here. 6:62 and 3:13 both point to something greater still to come and, like 3:14, which also refers to that coming event, do so using the title Son of Man.[446] An allusion to ascension may well be present ironically in Jesus' exchange with his blood brothers where he speaks of his time to "go up" (ἀναβαίνω) to the feast (7:6–8). The notion of an ascent is also present in 20:17, where the resurrected but not yet ascended Jesus responds to Mary's wanting to cling to him:[447]

> μή μου ἅπτου, οὔπω γὰρ ἀναβέβηκα πρὸς τὸν πατέρα· πορεύου δὲ πρὸς τοὺς ἀδελφούς μου καὶ εἰπὲ αὐτοῖς· ἀναβαίνω πρὸς τὸν πατέρα μου καὶ πατέρα ὑμῶν καὶ θεόν μου καὶ θεὸν ὑμῶν.
> Do not hold onto me, for I have not yet ascended to the Father, but go to my brother and tell them, "I am ascending to my Father and your Father and my God and your God." (20:17)

Within the Johannine narrative this makes best sense if it is understood as a reference to Jesus' ascent to the Father,[448] not, as in Acts, 40 days

---

he is lifted up on a cross (3,14; 6,53; 8,28; 12,34)." Such fragmentation of Johannine Christology does not do justice to the narrative integrity of the writing.

445. Moloney, *Son of Man*, 123, 244–47; Moloney, "Son of Man Revisited," 193–95; in agreement McGrath, *Christology*, 178.

446. Weidemann, *Tod Jesu*, 109; Reynolds, *Apocalyptic Son of Man*, 116, 160; Schnelle, *Johannes*, 303.

447. On clinging see Carson, *John*, 644–45.

448. So de la Potterie, "Genèse," 36–37; D. Bruce Woll, *Johannine Christianity in Conflict*, SBLDS 60 (Chico: Scholars, 1981), 41; Burge, *Anointed Community*, 136–37; Chibici-Revneanu, *Herrlichkeit*, 327; Reynolds, *Apocalyptic Son of Man*, 160–61; Beutler, *Johannesevangelium*, 523;

later,[449] but as occurring on resurrection day, and as belonging to the sequence outlined in the last discourses, that Jesus would return to the Father and then give the Spirit, which he is then shown as doing in 20:22.

4.3.3.3 The Son of Man's Glorification, Exaltation, Ascension, and 1:51

The first occurrence of the title Son of Man in the Gospel, 1:51, must also be considered in this context. Nathanael has confessed Jesus king of Israel and Son of God, a confession substantially the same as that which the Gospel as a whole seeks to elicit (20:31).[450]

> ἀπεκρίθη Ἰησοῦς καὶ εἶπεν αὐτῷ· ὅτι εἶπόν σοι ὅτι εἶδόν σε ὑποκάτω τῆς συκῆς, πιστεύεις; μείζω τούτων ὄψῃ. καὶ λέγει αὐτῷ· ἀμὴν ἀμὴν λέγω ὑμῖν, ὄψεσθε *τὸν οὐρανὸν ἀνεῳγότα καὶ τοὺς ἀγγέλους τοῦ θεοῦ ἀναβαίνοντας καὶ καταβαίνοντας ἐπὶ τὸν υἱὸν τοῦ ἀνθρώπου.*
> Jesus responded and said to him: "Because I said I saw you under the fig tree do you believe? You shall see greater things than these." And he said to him, "Truly, truly, I tell you, you shall see the heaven opened and the angels of God ascending and descending on the Son of Man." (1:50–51)

Some see here a saying which related perhaps at one time to the parousia.[451] Certainly tradition associated the Son of Man with angels (Mark 8:38;

Schnelle, *Johannes*, 303. Cf. De Boer, "Jesus' Departure," 7, who follows Brown in suggesting that "Mary is being asked to give up a prior understanding of Jesus' resurrection and thus to understand Jesus' resurrection as an ascension—*as his departure*—to the Father. For this reason, the resurrected Jesus cannot be 'held on to'"; Brown, *John*, 1014.

449. Cf. Carson, *John*, 655, who harmonistically sees Jesus' action in 20:22 as a kind of active parable pointing to Pentecost; similarly Onuki, *Gemeinde*, 86; Keener, *John*, 1193–94; Michaels, *John*, 1001. Lincoln, *John*, 493, on the other hand writes: "Jesus' words about his ascent are part of the evangelist's attempt to bring this perspective to expression within the constraints of the traditional resurrection accounts."

450. Adela Collins, "Epilogue," in *John's Gospel and Intimations of Apocalyptic*, ed. C. H. Williams and C. Rowland (London: T&T Clark, 2013), 300–307, sees 1:51 as an attempt on the part of the author to divert attention from the politically ambiguous language of messiahship and align the understanding of messiahship with what we find in the Parables of Enoch (1 En. 37–72) and 4 Ezra (301). See also Carson, *John*, 164, for a similar view. The latter connection does make sense of how he combines Messiah and Son of Man, but the evidence for concern with political misunderstanding in John is at most marginal, at least in what is expressed.

451. So Bühner, *Gesandte*, 391–92; Richter, *Studien*, 361–62; Forestell, *Word*, 23–24; Schulz, *Menschensohn*, 102–3; Reynolds, *Apocalyptic Son of Man*, 101–102.

The Death of Jesus in John

13:26-27; Matt 13:41; 25:31). The simplest understanding of the saying is to take it at face value. It refers to angels ascending to and descending to the Son of Man. That does not make sense as a reference to the Son of Man on earth. In any case the angels first ascend not descend, as though he were on earth. What would angels be doing below the Son of Man on earth? Rather the scene is best understood as above the earthly realm as the Son of Man is traditionally depicted. The angels are serving him and, one may assume, adoring him, as they do God. It is most naturally read as a scene of the Son of Man in glory. The motif of ascending and descending angels is drawn from Jacob's vision in Gen 28 and the key link that in the future Nathanael and all who believe (hence the change to plural in 1:51) will see, as Jacob saw, but see something greater. A key link with Jacob's experience at Bethel is the motif of seeing, especially if the author was familiar with etymologies of Israel which emphasised seeing God. In addition, the heavens are not opened for the descent of a dove or for a manifestation to be seen on earth, such as a descent of angels, but to enable the Son of Man to be seen in glory. This is the simplest and most obvious way to read what the author says.

Hearers of the Gospel who would, we must suppose, already know the whole story, would therefore most naturally associate the movement of the angels with adoration and exaltation, and especially those familiar with what follows in the Gospel would surely make connections between the promise of something greater and similar promises throughout the Gospel, often associated with the promise of seeing or knowing and with Jesus as Son of Man. They would know that the promise related not to greater miracles, nor to better faith, as though Nathanael's affirmation were faulty (surely not in the light of 20:31!) and were to be seen as at the level of the believers in 2:23-25 and Nicodemus,[452] nor to Jesus' action on earth such as revelation. Rather as elsewhere it referred to the promise associated with the Son of Man, namely the hour of his exaltation and ascension (3:12-14 and 6:62). For the contrast here in 1:50-51, as in 3:12-15 and 6:62, is between the events of Jesus' earthly ministry and its revelation, on the one hand, and the events of Jesus' death and ascent to the Father, on the other. John 1:51 belongs among those sayings which promise a new seeing and knowing. The simplest explanation of 1:51, then, both of its imagery, and in the light of the motifs associated with Son of Man in the Gospel, is to see it as referring to the exalted and glorified Son of Man.[453] It refers not to the act of

---

452. So rightly Thyen, *Johannesevangelium*, 144.
453. So Maddox, "Function," 190-91; A. B. J. Higgins, *Jesus and the Son of Man* (London: Clarke, 1964), 159-60; Dahl, "Church," 133; John Painter, "The Church and Israel in the Fourth

exaltation and glorification, but to its outcome, namely the status of having been exalted and glorified. The Son of Man is not moving; the angels are, in service and adoration. In this sense, John 1:51 depicts what in 17:24 Jesus prays for: that his own may see him glorified again with the glory he once had from before the foundation of the world and to which he returns (17:1, 5). John 1:14-18 depicts the glory manifest on earth to which the appropriate response is as Nathanael and the Gospel's conclusion express it (20:31), to hail him the Christ, the Son of God. John 1:51 then promises more: seeing the Son of Man in his heavenly glory.

The frequent attempts to see 1:51 as referring to what is to follow in the Gospel, especially Jesus' work of revelation in his ministry,[454] fall foul of the imagery. Most who do so point to a first fulfilment in the miracle at Cana where the evangelist notes that through this sign the disciples saw Jesus' glory.[455] Most struggle to explain the author's particular and selective use of the imagery from the account in Gen 28 of Jacob's vision and often have recourse to later exegetical tradition. Some see Jesus as the ladder (a bridge of revelation between heaven and earth),[456] or as represented in the Jacob figure,[457] or as

---

Gospel: A Response," *NTS* 25 (1978): 109-10; Painter, *Witness*, 55-56; Coppens, "Le Fils de L'Homme," 45; William Loader, "John 1:50-51 and the 'Greater Things' of Johannine Christology," in *Anfänge der Christologie. Für Ferdinand Hahn*, ed. C. Breytenbach and H. Paulsen (Göttingen: Vandenhoeck und Ruprecht, 1991), 255-74; Pryor, *John*, 14; de Boer, *Johannine Perspectives*, 161; Söding, "Kreuzerhöhung," 12.

454. So W. Bauer, *Das Johannesevangelium*, HNT 6 (Tübingen: Mohr Siebeck, 1933), 42; Lütgert, *Christologie*, 47; Cadman, *Open Heaven*, 28; Schulz, *Menschensohn*, 102-3; Bultmann, *Johannes*, 75; Dodd, *Interpretation*, 296; Brown, *John*, 83-84, 97; Haenchen, *Johannes*, 182; Schnackenburg, *John*, 1.321-22, 413; Schnackenburg, "Son of Man," 131; Forestell, *Word*, 67; Reim, *Studien*, 104; Appold, *Oneness*, 53-54; Ferdinand Hahn, "Die Jüngerberufung. Joh 1,35-51," in *Neues Testament und Kirche. Festschrift für R. Schnackenburg*, ed. J. Gnilka (Freiburg: Herder, 1974), 173; Hahn, *Theologie*, 1.632; Lindars, "Passion," 77; Boismard and Lamouille, *Jean*, 99; Bühner, *Gesandte*, 391-92; Olsson, *Structure*, 102-4; Richter, *Studien*, 366; Dunn, "John," 326; Bittner, *Zeichen*, 76; Margaret Pamment, "The Son of Man in the Fourth Gospel," *JTS* 36 (1985): 59; de Jonge, *Stranger*, 13, 59; Schnelle, *Christologie*, 87-88; Burge, *Anointed Community*, 86; Scroggs, *Christology*, 70; Michaels, *John*, 136-37; Beutler, *Johannesevangelium*, 117.

455. Schenke, "Christologie als Theologie," 449; Van Belle, "Death of Jesus," 23-24; similarly Moloney, *Love*, 41.

456. McGrath, *Christology*, 209; Busse, *Johannesevangelium*, 336-37; Robert H. Gundry, *Jesus the Word according to John the Sectarian* (Grand Rapids: Eerdmans, 2002), 12-14; Weidemann, *Tod Jesu*, 426; Lincoln, *John*, 122; Lee, *Flesh and Glory*, 35; Ahn, *Christological Witness*, 66-77. He notes that "the Septuagint clarifies the antecedent of the demonstrative pronoun as it shifts the gender into feminine (ἐπ' αὐτῆς)" (70); cf. the Hebrew of Gen 28:12 which has the ambiguous בֹ that can be understood as a reference to a person, meaning "on him."

457. Ashton, *John*, 142; Ashton, *Fourth Gospel*, 249-51; Müller, *Menschwerdung*, 56-57; Ulrich Busse, *Das Johannesevangelium. Bildlichkeit, Diskurs und Ritual* (Leuven: Peeters, 2002),

Bethel the place of God's presence.[458] The theme of the saying is commonly taken to be Jesus as the revealer.[459] Some have seen in the ladder an allusion to the cross.[460] A number of scholars who espouse the view that 1:51 refers to Jesus' ministry also go on to include the cross as the climax of revelation,[461] confirming that "greater" demands more than the miracles to follow in the ministry. A number note the close link between 1:51 and 3:13.[462] None of these can give a satisfactory account of the imagery which the author has used, instead reading in motifs which he does not mention, such as the ladder, the place of Bethel, or Jacob as somehow prefiguring Jesus. Such interpretation of the imagery is problematic and fails to take into account that the author highlights the movement of the angels towards the Son of Man, and does not highlight the ladder, nor the place, nor speculative associations of the Son of Man, but simply promises that when heaven is opened, believers, the true seeing ones, will see the Son of Man in his heavenly glory. Multivalence in the use of the motif of "the third day" in 2:1, of "the hour" in 2:4, and the eucha-

---

336-37; Dietzfelbinger, *Johannes*, 1.61; Burkett, *Son of Man*, 112-19, 121. On this identification see the critique in Ahn, *Christological Witness*, 66-77, pointing to the contradictory nature of rabbinic traditions usually cited in support and the indications from the context.

458. Beate Kowalski, "Thesen zur johanneischen Christologie," *BN* 146 (2010): 110; Michael Theobald, "Abraham–(Isaak–) Jakob. Israels Väter im Johannesevangelium," in *Israel und seine Heilstraditionen im Johannesevangelium. Festgabe für Johannes Beutler SJ zum 70. Geburtstag*, ed. M. Labahn, K. Scholtissek, A. Strotmann (Paderborn: Ferdinand Schöningh, 2004), 161-62; Knut Backhaus, "'Before Abraham was, I am': the Book of Genesis and the Genesis of Christology," in *Genesis and Christian Theology*, ed. N. MacDonald, M. W. Elliott, and G. Macaskill (Grand Rapids: Eerdmans, 2012), 78; Benny Thettayil, *In Spirit and Truth. An Exegetical Study of John 4:19-26 and a Theological Investigation of the Replacement Theme in the Fourth Gospel*, CBET 46 (Leuven: Peeters, 2007), 376-82; Schnelle, "Tempelreinigung," 369; Schnelle, *Johannes*, 56; Witherington, *John's Wisdom*, 72-73; McHugh, *John*, 169; Coloe, *God Dwells with Us*, 73, 215; see also Busse, *Johannesevangelium*, 336-37.

459. Ashton, *John*, 115; Adele Reinhartz, "Jesus as Prophet: Predictive Prolepses in the Fourth Gospel," *JSNT* 36 (1989): 8; Beasley-Murray, "Mission," 1862; Harris, *Prologue*, 119; Brown, *Introduction*, 255; Moloney, "Son of Man Revisited," 188; Davies, *Rhetoric and Reference*, 179; Wilckens, *Johannes*, 53. Weidemann, *Tod Jesu*, 103-4, 107, but focused especially on the climax of Jesus' ministry (109-10).

460. J. Duncan M. Derrett, *Law in the New Testament* (London: DLT, 1970), 416; Moloney, *Son of Man*, 38-40; Pamment, "Son of Man," 59; L. P. Trudinger, "The Israelite in Whom There Is No Guile," *EvQ* 54 (1982): 119; Bruce, *John*, 88; Collins, "Epilogue," 301.

461. So Brown, *John*, 88; Moloney, *Son of Man*, 38-40; Bruce, *John*, 88; Lindars, *Gospel of John*, 122; *Son of Man*, 148-49; *John*, 84; Ellis, *Genius*, 58; Beasley-Murray, *John*, 35; Carson, *John*, 163-64; Smalley, *John*, 312; Schwindt, *Herrlichkeit*, 331; Theobald, *Johannes*, 1.195; Leung, *Kingship-Cross*, 114.

462. So Moloney, *Son of Man*, 67; Lindars, *Son of Man*, 148-49; Meeks, "Man from Heaven," 146-47.

ristic imagery in what follows, coheres well with this understanding of 1:51 as referring to the outcome of Jesus' death, exaltation and glorification.

4.3.3.4 Glorification, Exaltation, Ascension, and the Son of Man

Closely associated with glorification, exaltation and ascension motifs in John is the Son of Man title. In his 1964 article on the Son of Man Schnackenburg noted this circle of themes.[463] He notes also its traditionally judicial character, reflected in the judgment saying of 5:27,[464] and probably also in the use of the title in 9:35 (cf. 9:39). Schnackenburg argues against seeing the presence of the title behind the use of ὁ ἄνθρωπος, the *ecce homo* saying (19:5), the image of the vine (in the light of Ps 80:8, 14),[465] and the "I am" saying of 8:28.[466] He suggests a possible link with Son of Man tradition in the use of Zech in 19:37,[467] but, beside this—rightly in my assessment—limits the influence of Son of Man tradition to passages where the title occurs. Cullmann suggests that "Son of Man" lies originally behind "flesh" in 1:14 and was avoided by the author because of speculation about the ἄνθρωπος,[468] but of this there is no evidence. Some have suggested that the sealing of the Son of Man in 6:27 refers to his exaltation,[469] but more likely it refers to the Son of Man's authorisation and sending[470] or perhaps his baptism.[471]

According to Schnackenburg the author's contribution lies in having expanded the use of Son of Man in Johannine tradition where it had related primarily to parousia and exaltation. In doing so, he has included the cross as part of the process of exaltation and glorification and has introduced the idea of the descending and ascending Son of Man.[472] Whereas in Paul we see the cross as the paradox of glory in suffering, in John we see the paradox in

---

463. Rudolf Schnackenburg, "Der Menschensohn im Johannesevangelium," *NTS* 11 (1964/65): 126; Schnackenburg, *John*, 1.393; Schnackenburg, *Johannesevangelium*, 2.156, 166–67, 256.

464. Schnackenburg, "Menschensohn," 126; similarly Preiss, *Life in Christ*, 16–17.

465. Against Dodd, *Interpretation*, 245.

466. Schnackenburg, "Menschensohn," 127–28.

467. Schnackenburg, *Johannesevangelium*, 4.173.

468. Oscar Cullmann, *Die Christologie des Neuen Testaments*, 4th ed. (Tübingen: Mohr Siebeck, 1966), 192.

469. So Blank, *Krisis*, 257; Schenke, "Vorgeschichte," 86–87.

470. So Moloney, *Son of Man*, 114.

471. So Schnackenburg, *Johannesevangelium*, 2.50–51; Bruce, *John*, 162.

472. Schnackenburg, "Menschensohn," 129–30, 132; *John*, 1.393; similarly Barrett, "Symbolism," 73–74; Boismard and Lamouille, *Jean*, 51; Nicholson, *Death*, 142.

The Death of Jesus in John

different form. As noted above, the cross is a path of suffering, but to the eyes of faith it is also the ascent to the glory of the Father.[473] Schnackenburg still sees no real distinction in John between the use of "Son" and "Son of Man."[474]

Maddox notes the virtual absence of "Son of Man" in the last discourses (cf. only 13:31-32), but points out a similar infrequency of other titles and notes that its themes continue.[475] He argues, however, rightly, that this also reflects an incomplete assimilation of "Son of Man" and "Son."[476] Moloney emphasises this difference, setting out the differences in parallel columns,[477] but the distinctive character which he attributes to the Son of Man rests heavily on his unconvincing exegesis of ascension in 3:13 and 6:62 and of the concepts of exaltation and glorification. Accordingly, for him Son of Man is primarily the title for Jesus as the revealer on earth, the man announced in 1:51 and fulfilled in the *"ecce homo"* scene of 19:5, which he takes as a Son of Man reference.[478] In this way he virtually eliminates what is the dominant motif associated with Son of Man, namely the event complex which begins on the cross and ends in glory, and reduces all Son of Man sayings to statements about revealing. He also argues that this is the primary focus of the judicial uses in 5:27 and 9:35. Moloney acknowledges glorification (17:1, 5; 11:4) and ascension (20:17), but argues that they mean something different because of the absence of the Son of Man title, though the same concepts also occur with the title earlier in the Gospel.[479] Somewhat in tension with

---

473. Schnackenburg, *Johannesevangelium*, 4.112; similarly, Gnilka, "Christologie," 103.

474. Schnackenburg, "Menschensohn," 136.

475. Maddox, "Function," 201-2; similarly Culpepper, *Anatomy*, 39.

476. Maddox, "Function," 193; similarly James D. G. Dunn, *Christology in the Making* (London: SCM, 1980), 56; Reynolds, *Apocalyptic Son of Man*, who reflects that absences of Son of Man at key points suggest it is not the author's primary Christology (223), though there is some overlap. "This suggests that Loader's 'Son of Man cluster' may be more closely entwined with the 'central structure' of Johannine Christology than primarily in the 'exalt, glorify and ascent' language in the interpretation of the climax of Jesus' ministry" (224 n. 35). Cf. Burkett, *Son of Man*, 95-100, who claims both "designations are used synonymously in all of these respects" (101).

477. Moloney, *Son of Man*, 211-13. See also Lindars, *Son of Man*, 150-51, who largely follows Moloney (so 218 n. 2.). Reynolds, *Apocalyptic Son of Man*, 223, rightly rejects the view that Johannine Son of Man Christology highlights Jesus' humanity and is synonymous with Johannine Son of God Christology and emphasises the apocalyptic background of the Johannine Son of Man sayings, and not merely of 1:51; 3:13; and/or 5:27.

478. Moloney, *Son of Man*, 179, 207.

479. Moloney, *Son of Man*, 226-27. In "Son of Man Revisited" he acknowledges: "If there is no distinction between the Johannine use of 'the Son of Man' and 'the Son (of God)' language, then this is a logical and justifiable conclusion" (196), then they mean what 17:1, 5 mean. "My earlier work created the false impression that the Johannine Son (of God) and Son of Man

this claim is his acknowledgment of this fuller use of glorification in the Son of Man saying in 13:32.[480] Moloney also emphasises humanness as an aspect of the title, a claim for which I see no justification in the Gospel once one abandons Moloney's denial of the role of ascension, glorification and exaltation in the Gospel.[481] Even less can I find an antidocetic orientation in its use as Schnelle suggests.[482]

There can be no denial that revelation in the sense of bringing life is present in John's use of Son of Man, and this is especially evident in the image of the bread which descends from heaven in ch. 6. It must also be present in the notion of descent in 3:13 and belongs to the descent–ascent pattern of καταβαίνω/ἀναβαίνω, which, apart from 20:17, is used consistently in Son of Man contexts. At this point the Son of Man and the Son–Father patterns overlap, though the language of coming and returning is different and much more frequent with the latter. But our analysis in Part One showed that the revealer motif is predominantly associated not with Son of Man but with Son–Father. Leaving aside the overlap which exists, the Son of Man designation and its associated imagery (exaltation, glorification, ascension, the hour, judgment, and the greater things) are used in interpreting the climax of Jesus' ministry, his death and return to the Father, and this is its predominant use in the Gospel.[483]

4.3.3.5 The Son of Man and the "Hour"

As noted above, the motif of the hour and its variants like "the time" or "now" occurs frequently in John and in particular in association with the language characteristic of the Son of Man cluster. This is particularly evident in ch. 12 where Jesus speaks of the hour having come for the Son of Man to be glorified (12:23), for him "now" to face the "hour" of suffering and to

---

Christologies were to be radically separated. This position misunderstands the unity of the Johannine Christology that should not be broken into separate compartments" (201). Moloney, *Love*, 53, 60, 73–89, 93–96, 144–50, 165, repeatedly distinguishes between the exaltation, which he reads as referring only to Jesus' death, and the glorification of the Son of Man, which occurs through the cross as the event which will lead through death, resurrection, and ascent, to his return to the Father with the glory he had with the Father before the world began (17:5).

480. Moloney, *Son of Man*, 195, 229 n. 27.

481. Moloney, *Son of Man*, 202–7; similarly Pamment, "Son of Man," 58, 62, 64; cf. Weidemann, *Tod Jesu*, 104; Reynolds, *Apocalyptic Son of Man*, 107.

482. Schnelle, *Christologie*, 224. Against this: Wilckens, "Lebensbrot," 237; Schnackenburg, *Johannesevangelium*, 2.91.

483. So Weidemann, *Tod Jesu*, 106–7.

glorify God's name (12:27–28), and of "now" being the judgment of the world and his being lifted up as Son of Man (12:31–34). Similarly 13:1 speaks of the "hour" having come for the Son to return to the Father, and 13:31–32 speaks of "now" in relation to the glorification of the Son of Man, echoed in the reference to the coming of the "hour" in 17:1, 5 (similarly 17:13). In each of these the focus is on the event which begins with Jesus' suffering and ends with his return to the Father and its consequences (the sending of the Spirit).[484] None isolate the death as an expiatory or vicarious sacrifice as though the author were to have Jesus say: "Now is the time for me to offer myself as a sacrifice." References to "hour" or "time" which occur earlier in the Gospel have a similar focus, whether in Jesus' words to his mother about his "hour" not yet come (2:40), or to his brothers that his time was not yet (7:6, 8), or in relation to the Jews that his hour had not yet come (7:30; 8:20).

4.3.3.6 Resurrection

The most common way that the author has Jesus speak of the events following his death is in terms of return to the Father, glorification, exaltation, and ascension. These four encompass a single event. By contrast, in the author's narrative, the passion is followed by burial, empty tomb and resurrection appearances. How do the two relate?

Mary and Jesus, Risen, but Not Ascended: 20:17

The point at which the two most clearly come together is in the words of Jesus to Mary Magdalene, discussed above:

> μή μου ἅπτου, οὔπω γὰρ ἀναβέβηκα πρὸς τὸν πατέρα· πορεύου δὲ πρὸς τοὺς ἀδελφούς μου καὶ εἰπὲ αὐτοῖς· ἀναβαίνω πρὸς τὸν πατέρα μου καὶ πατέρα ὑμῶν καὶ θεόν μου καὶ θεὸν ὑμῶν.
> Do not hold onto me, for I have not yet ascended to the Father. But go to my brothers and say to them, "I am ascending to my Father and your Father and my God and your God." (20:17)

Here the promises of the last discourses are echoed, in particular 14:12, 28,

---

484. Chibici-Revneanu, *Herrlichkeit*, 327, 331; Frey, *Eschatologie*, 2.219; Frey, "Theologia crucifixi," 511; Frey, "Edler Tod," 558; Weidemann, *Tod Jesu*, 120; Reynolds, *Apocalyptic Son of Man*, 192.

ὁ πιστεύων εἰς ἐμὲ τὰ ἔργα ἃ ἐγὼ ποιῶ κἀκεῖνος ποιήσει
καὶ μείζονα τούτων ποιήσει, ὅτι ἐγὼ πρὸς τὸν πατέρα πορεύομαι·
He who believes in me, the works which I do he will do
and greater works than these will he do, because I go to my Father.
(14:12)

ἠκούσατε ὅτι ἐγὼ εἶπον ὑμῖν· ὑπάγω καὶ ἔρχομαι πρὸς ὑμᾶς.
εἰ ἠγαπᾶτέ με ἐχάρητε ἂν ὅτι πορεύομαι πρὸς τὸν πατέρα,
ὅτι ὁ πατὴρ μείζων μού ἐστιν.
You heard that I said to you, I go away and return to you.
If you loved me, you would rejoice, that I go to the Father,
because the Father is greater than I. (14:28)

This relates in turn to the gift of the Spirit and the relationship of oneness which it will bring (cf. 14:16-20). The narrative to follow in 20:19-23 will tell of the giving of the Spirit to the disciples.

As we have seen above, the most natural reading of 20:17 is to see expressed in it the assumption that, at the point of her contact with Jesus, he had not yet completed the ascent to the Father and that, by the evening when he appeared to the disciples, he had. There is no need to deny this or to assume ascension must follow later. This reading does not depend on the argument that here touching is not possible whereas in the evening or with Thomas it is,[485] though it makes good sense of it. It depends on what is actually said: "I am ascending," and on what has been said about its implications for the giving of the Spirit. The difficulty of Jesus' enigmatic words, that he has not yet ascended to the Father and that he is about to ascend, should not be harmonised away by a spiritualising or metaphorical interpretation which understands ascent to mean the process of coming and bringing life to the disciples[486] or in some way to mean both return to the Father and return to the disciples simultaneously.[487]

It is much more fruitful to acknowledge the tension which exists and to understand it as arising from the author's use of different traditional ideas.[488] The author does not appear to espouse the view that Jesus ascended directly into heaven from the cross nor that he was exalted or glorified directly at, or

---

485. Against Sanders and Mastin, *John*, 428. So rightly Thüsing, *Erhöhung*, 265; Brown, *John*, 992-94, 1011; Schnackenburg, *Johannesevangelium*, 3.376; Onuki, *Gemeinde*, 86.

486. Kremer, *Osterevangelien*, 173-74, 183; Schillebeeckx, *Christ*, 918; cf. also Brown, *John*, 1011.

487. Schnackenburg, *Johannesevangelium*, 3.376-77; Minear, *John*, 128.

488. See the excellent discussion in Brown, *John*, 1011-16; also *Beloved Disciple*, 54; Schnackenburg, *Johannesevangelium*, 3.378; 4.110; Nicholson, *Death*, 69-73, 199.

from, the point of death, though much of his language could be read in this way.[489] Dodd approaches this view in maintaining that the resurrection is merely an event on the earthly plane corresponding, on his Platonic model of interpretation, to the real heavenly event in the glory of the cross.[490] The language of return, glorification, exaltation and ascent might easily lead to this, but the author remains within the traditional pattern attested by his narrative of death and resurrection on the third day. Wilkens argues that the tradition of the appearances belongs to the narrative source which he posits, and ascension from the cross to the sayings source.[491] Lindars suggests the appearance stories are a concession on the part of the author to faith not fully fledged, pointing to the Thomas episode,[492] but this cannot be said of the other appearances, nor of the Thomas story. The author integrates the two sets of concepts within a narrative which portrays Jesus passing through the following stages. He dies, is buried, is raised, is seen by Mary Magdalene, then ascends to the Father (here we must include glorification and exaltation), and then appears to the disciples. There is no bodiless glorification.[493] The appearances are made after his ascent and return and, consistent with the promises of the last discourses, his return makes possible the giving of the Spirit and the equipping of the disciples for mission.

This is not the pattern of Luke-Acts where an appearance, including assumption into heaven through clouds, commonly referred to as an ascension, completes a series of appearances over a forty-day period, though even Luke's writings may reflect an alternative view according to which Jesus makes his appearances from heaven, as in the case of Paul's encounter with Jesus on the Damascus Road. Luke's typological scheme in Acts, far from being the norm, seems more likely to be the exception, especially when one considers the way in which Ps 110:1 was applied to the Easter event, as God raising Jesus to his right hand, a widespread tradition (Rom 8:34; 1 Pet 3:22; Heb 1:3–4, 13; 8:1; 10:12; Eph 1:20), reflected also in the speeches in Acts (2:34–35; 5:31), and nowhere suggesting a forty-day gap between resurrection and heavenly enthronement. The Johannine pattern of revelation of the risen

---

489. So rightly Lindars, *Gospel of John*, 607–8; Meeks, "Man from Heaven," 159; Zeller, "Ostermorgen," 160; de Boer, "Jesus' Departure," 17. Cf. Dietzfelbinger, *Johannes*, 2.322: who identifies in 20:17 a problem (in fact with his own construction of Johannine Christology rather than the author) when he writes of the crucifixion as entailing already Jesus' resurrection and ascension to the Father. Reynolds, *Apocalyptic Son of Man*, 123–26, misreads my position as embracing this view.

490. Dodd, *Interpretation*, 241–42.

491. Wilkens, *Zeichen*, 113.

492. Lindars, "Passion," 79.

493. So rightly Schillebeeckx, *Christ*, 417; Beasley-Murray, *John*, 73.

one to his own from heaven may well reflect tradition (cf. also Matt 28:18). The peculiarity of John's account becomes then the pre-ascension encounter with Mary.

The somewhat awkward appearance to Mary may reflect a tension between two systems of thought: exaltation, glorification, ascent and return, on the one hand, and resurrection on the third day, on the other. In the author's hand it may also function to make a statement about an appropriate and an inappropriate response of faith, directing attention away from a faith which clings to the earthly form of Jesus and towards life in relation to the exalted and glorified Lord who gives the Spirit,[494] but its focus, as the repetitions show, is clearly on the significance of the ascent. Thereby the author makes the encounter with the disciples the event of paramount importance. The traditional encounter with the woman (or women) becomes its incomplete forerunner. It is at this cost that the author has embellished the tradition, producing the remarkable and powerfully dramatic episode.

Jesus' Resurrection Elsewhere in the Gospel

The Fourth Gospel also refers to Jesus' resurrection within the main body of the Gospel. If there are not hints of it already in the "three days" of 2:1—and there probably are—there is the explicit prediction of 2:19:

> λύσατε τὸν ναὸν τοῦτον καὶ ἐν τρισὶν ἡμέραις ἐγερῶ αὐτόν.
> Destroy this temple and in three days I shall raise it. (2:19)

Typically the author has the Jews take the words literally, adding his own footnote:

> ἐκεῖνος δὲ ἔλεγεν περὶ τοῦ ναοῦ τοῦ σώματος αὐτοῦ.
> He was speaking about the temple of his body. (2:21)

The resurrection becomes, then, the answer to the Jews' quest for a sign of authentication for Jesus' activity (2:18). Consequently the author adds,

> ὅτε οὖν ἠγέρθη ἐκ νεκρῶν, ἐμνήσθησαν οἱ μαθηταὶ αὐτοῦ ὅτι τοῦτο ἔλεγεν,
> καὶ ἐπίστευσαν τῇ γραφῇ καὶ τῷ λόγῳ ὃν εἶπεν ὁ Ἰησοῦς.

---

494. De Boer, *Johannine Perspectives*, 129; De Boer, "Jesus' Departure," 6–10.

The Death of Jesus in John

When therefore he was raised from the dead, his disciples remembered that he had said this and believed the Scripture and the word which Jesus spoke. (2:22)

From this three things are clear. Firstly, Jesus' resurrection is the sign of his vindication and will enable Thomas to proclaim, "My Lord and my God" (20:28). Secondly, Jesus' resurrection functions for the author in the same way as his exaltation, glorification, ascension, and return to the Father. It belongs to this single complex event. This is evident from the way similar understanding on the part of the disciples is said to have come:

ὅτε ἐδοξάσθη Ἰησοῦς τότε ἐμνήσθησαν ὅτι ταῦτα ἦν ἐπ' αὐτῷ γεγραμμένα
καὶ ταῦτα ἐποίησαν αὐτῷ.
When Jesus had been glorified, then they remembered that these things were written about him and that they did these things to him. (12:16)

When Jesus was raised and when he was glorified are functionally equivalent in the two passages (2:22; 12:16). It may be significant that they occur in material which probably belonged closely together in the narrative of the last days of Jesus, as in Mark 14. And thirdly, what comes into being as the result of Jesus' resurrection will replace the temple. In Jesus there is now the possibility of worship in spirit and in truth (4:23) and, more specifically, the promise that because of resurrection, the Son and the Father will come through the Spirit and make their dwelling in the disciples (14:19–23). At the same time this should not be read as implying that Jesus became the dwelling place of God, the temple only after Easter.[495] He was already that during his ministry as 1:14 affirms and indicated in the typologies which depict him in images drawn from the feasts.

Resurrection and the "Greater" Event

The integration of resurrection, along with the exaltation, glorification, ascent and return to the Father, within the total concept of the single event complex is apparent also in 14:19:

ἔτι μικρὸν καὶ ὁ κόσμος με οὐκέτι θεωρεῖ,

---

495. Cf. Thyen, *Johannesevangelium*, 257, 260.

> ὑμεῖς δὲ θεωρεῖτέ με, ὅτι ἐγὼ ζῶ καὶ ὑμεῖς ζήσετε.
> Yet a little while and the world will see me no more,
> but you will see me, because I live, you also will live.

Here the fact of Jesus' being alive is singled out, but done so in a context which assumes his return to the Father and, by the Spirit, his coming with the Father to dwell in the disciples.[496] Similarly 10:17–18 focusses on Jesus' authority to lay down his life and take it up again. This, in turn, is related to the work of mission by which he will gather his sheep into one (10:16).

In both cases taking up life again could be understood without a story of resurrection from an empty tomb on the third day. But the total context of the Gospel demands that this is not the case. Resurrection is how the author portrays Jesus' taking up his life to have occurred. This is the Jesus tradition he has received. Nevertheless, as an event, it is so integrated within the wider event and its significance that characteristically the risen Jesus tells Mary to tell the disciples only that he ascends to his Father and theirs (20:17). For not the resurrection in itself, but the total event, resurrection, exaltation, glorification, ascension, and return to the Father, is the "greater" event to which the ministry looks forward and through which the full impact of the revelation that took place in that ministry will be made known. For through that "greater" event "greater things" become possible through the sending of the Spirit and of the disciples, who are able to confront the world with the truth that Jesus is the Son come from the Father to make him known. At one level therefore the resurrection adds nothing to the revelation, as Bultmann points out;[497] at another, as part of the "greater" event it is resurrection that makes the story of revelation possible.

4.3.3.7 The "Greater" Event and the Spirit

In the discussion of Jesus as "exalted, glorified, ascended" in ch. 3 I drew together texts which showed a pattern within the Gospel according to which, from the standpoint of the earthly ministry of Jesus, something greater would be inaugurated by the event of Jesus' death and return. These were, in particular, 1:50–51, which points to the Son of Man in exaltation; 3:12, promising heavenly things, explicated in the following verses as the ascension and

---

496. Jean Zumstein, "Die Deutung der Ostererfahrung in den Abschiedreden des Johannesevangeliums," *ZTK* 104 (2007): 131–32, 137–38.
497. Bultmann, *Theologie*, 408–11.

exaltation of the Son of Man (3:13–14); 6:61–62, contrasting the descent with the even greater event of the ascent of the Son of Man to where he was before; and 14:12, promising greater works which the disciples would do because Jesus goes to the Father (echoed in 14:28). In 5:20 Jesus promises that God will show him greater works than those which the Father is currently doing through him.[498] He is currently exercising judgment so this cannot be the reference. It could be to greater miracles, such as the raising of Lazarus.[499] It more likely refers to his role in future judgment or perhaps to the climax of his ministry, in which case this reference should also be included among the promises of that greater event.

The "greater" event describes the Son's return and his exaltation, glorification and ascent as Son of Man. Whereas these describe what the event entails, the contrast expressed in each of these texts, which I describe here as the "greater" event motif, gives this total event a special status in relationship to the event of the Son's coming and his work of making known the Father on earth. In this section I want to explore further the nature of this relationship.

Implications of the "Greater" Event

The review of texts relating to Jesus' death and return also showed that references to exaltation, glorification, ascension, and return rarely stand alone without some explanation of their implications. The review set this out simply as the sending of the disciples and the sending of the Spirit to make possible greater understanding, to equip the disciples for mission, and to build up the community of faith. Each of these fruits of the event relates to each other and together they explain why the event is "greater." The Son goes away and sends the Paraclete; the risen Christ also sends the disciples. Both are sent to be bearers of revelation, as the Son was, but it is no independent revelation. It remains the revelation of the Son. Both belong together. The Spirit enables the disciples' recall and leads them to fuller understanding of the Son's words and deeds and of their meaning in the light of Scripture. The Spirit, therefore, makes the mission of the disciples possible. Through them it confronts the world with the meaning of the Son's coming, his death and vindication. The mission of the disciples will bear fruit and lead to the gathering of the Son's community from throughout the world, bringing glory

---

498. See Loader, "John 5,19–47," 158; Keener, *John*, 648.
499. Thyen, *Johannesevangelium*, 311, 313.

to him and to the Father. The Spirit also makes possible the presence of the Father and the risen Son dwelling in the disciples and the communion in unity among them. They enjoy the life which flows from that and feed on it through the sacrament of the Son of Man's flesh and blood.

The "greater" event is "greater," not because it adds to the life and light present in the person of the Son, the revealer. For this revelation is complete in the person of the Son and remains so throughout his ministry up to and including his death on the cross where the crisis it engenders is brought to a head. It is not "greater" because it entails the fruits of one further task, the work of atonement, a benefit not present in the Son's revelation thus far. The author, while using vicarious atonement tradition, does not give it that kind of status and it is absent where the "greater" theme and associated concepts are being used. The "greater" event is "greater" because it makes available for all the true significance of the event of revelation. It represents the Son's vindication and makes possible and accessible in a new way the encounter with the Son who came as the sent one from the Father and made him known in word and deed. The "greater" event has accordingly a hermeneutical function. But it is not just a hermeneutical function for the author. It is an event. The Son has returned to the Father, risen, exalted, glorified, ascended and this is also promise of future heavenly dwelling for the disciples. For the Son it is "greater" because it means his return to glory after the completed task. And it is precisely because of this return that it is "greater" for the disciples, for it enables the story of Jesus to be understood and made known. Thus, return to the Father who is "greater" makes the "greater works" of the disciples possible (14:28, 12; cf. also 20:17).

Life Only after the "Greater" Event through the Spirit's Coming?

Frequently the promise of the greater event is interpreted in an exclusive manner, which suggests that the life which the Son has and is became available only through the Spirit's coming, and was not really available during his ministry.

Haenchen, for instance, argues that there is no true faith, no birth from above, before the giving of the Spirit.[500] Thüsing argues similarly, linking 7:38–39 with 19:34, the flow of water and blood from the side of Jesus.[501] Thompson writes:

500. Haenchen, "Vater," 73, 75; *Johannes*, 109.
501. Thüsing, *Erhöhung*, 161, 164, 324.

The Death of Jesus in John

The actual reception of life seems to be deferred until after Jesus' death. Consequently when Jesus speaks of giving life (e.g., 3:5–8; 6:63), he speaks proleptically of a situation that will obtain only after his death . . . What also needs to be emphasized is that what happens *after* Jesus' death also happens *because of* Jesus' death, whether that be the conferring of life or the giving of the Spirit.[502]

Scholars who, like Thüsing, stress the importance of the death of Jesus as a saving act logically lean towards this position. Dauer even sees an allusion to atonement implicit in 7:37–39,[503] and Schnackenburg says its promise of salvation is accessible only after Easter.[504] Haacker acknowledges the problem in denying that salvation is present in the person of the revealer, but finally argues the necessity of both the Spirit and the work of atonement for salvation.[505] Forestell, who denies atonement plays such a role, nevertheless claims that it is not until the work of revelation is completed by Jesus' death that the benefits of salvation are available.[506] Similarly Becker points to the necessity of victory over the power of death as first needing to be achieved.[507] Dodd argues that the real gift of life is available only after the cross and resurrection.[508] Painter, too, speaks only of a proleptic faith before Easter in John.[509] Nicholson believes that such lack of knowledge continues even in ch. 20 until 20:22 and the giving of the Spirit[510] and for Schillebeeckx any pre-Easter offer of life is but a pledge or preliminary sign of what will become available after Easter.[511] Similarly Johnston argues that the glory of 1:14 and 2:11 can only be understood proleptically of the post-Easter period.[512]

We discussed the specific reference to eternal life as a gift in the future as reflected in 3:14–15 (often linked with 12:32); 6:27, 53 and in some readings of 7:37–39, to which we return below. We also addressed the meaning of "the hour is coming and now is" in relation to the person of Jesus and the possibility of receiving life in him. In each instance there is a future dimension, but they occur within a Gospel which abounds in claims, far more numerous,

502. Thompson, *God*, 178.
503. Dauer, *Passionsgeschichte*, 39.
504. Schnackenburg, *Johannesevangelium*, 2.217; but cf. "Frage," 208.
505. Haacker, *Stiftung*, 164–68, cf. 156, n. 806.
506. Forestell, *Word*, 19.
507. Becker, *Johannes*, 403–405.
508. Dodd, *Interpretation*, 372.
509. Painter, *Witness*, 89–90; Painter, "Eschatology," 50–51; Painter, "Christ and the Church," 361–62.
510. Nicholson, *Death*, 119.
511. Schillebeeckx, *Christ*, 405–6, 410–11.
512. Johnston, "Ecce Homo," 135–36.

which depict Jesus as offering eternal life, as the word, bread, light and life, because of who he is and was already during his ministry in ways that cannot be dismissed within the world of the narrative as proleptic, as though the author did not believe that in himself Jesus was already the bearer of life, as his hearers had once claimed Torah to be. The author preserves narrative integrity by making it very clear that greater understanding both of Jesus' words and of Scripture fulfilment in him came only after Easter when the disciples would receive the indwelling Spirit (2:22; 12:16), but not in a way that implies that Jesus, the bearer of the Spirit, had no eternal life to offer before then.[513]

Hamerton-Kelly says that only after this event can what was eternally present be known.[514] This is closer to what I take to be the Johannine understanding, inasmuch as it does not interpose an additional achievement such as atonement or victory and acknowledges that the revelation was present in the ministry of Jesus, but it is still hard to reconcile such statements with the Gospel narrative which assumes that some did in fact receive the sent one and his revelation. Onuki speaks of a paradox that saving knowledge of Christ's divinity is possible only after his resurrection and yet is mediated by his earthly ministry,[515] but this, like many of the approaches mentioned, confuses the process of growth of awareness in history (our insights into how Christology developed) with the evangelist's understanding that in the person of the earthly Jesus, life was already offered.

"Greater" Event—Deeper Understanding

Here Bultmann is nearer the mark in arguing that nothing is added to the revelation by the coming of the Spirit but deeper understanding.[516]

---

513. So Ashton, *John*, 41, who writes: "In spite of an occasional wobble the evangelist makes an absolute principle of his distinction between all that transpired in Jesus' lifetime—both words and actions—and the quite different situation after his death and resurrection"; Larry W. Hurtado, "Remembering and Revelation: The Historic and Glorified Jesus in the Gospel of John," in *Israel's God and Rebecca's Children: Christology and Community in Early Judaism and Christianity: Essays in Honor of Larry W. Hurtado and Alan F. Segal*, ed. D. B. Capes, A. D. DeConick, H. K. Bond, and T. A. Miller (Waco: Baylor University Press, 2007), 212, who writes: "GJohn distinctively emphasises the contrast between the cognitive possibilities in the pre-resurrection and post-resurrection situations, indicating more explicitly than in the Synoptic Gospels, that in his earthly ministry Jesus did not reveal all that came later to be known of his divine significance."

514. Hamerton-Kelly, *Pre-Existence*, 233-34.

515. Onuki, *Gemeinde*, 206.

516. Bultmann, *Johannes*, 395; similarly Dahl, "Church," 124-25; Brevard Childs, *The New Testament as Canon: An Introduction* (Philadelphia: Fortress, 1984), 135.

More precisely Segovia argues that the disciples do not misunderstand the meaning of Jesus' coming, but only the meaning of his departure.[517] Bultmann promptly demythologises this along the lines of distance producing better perspective,[518] but his basic observation is correct: it is a matter of greater understanding. Already Baur emphasised this.[519] But the issue is less whether there is growth in understanding through the coming of the Spirit, which no one denies, and more whether this implies that no salvation or life, no knowledge that saves, was possible before Easter and therefore that the "greater" event was "greater" because before it no salvation was available.

Porsch vigorously denies such an implication,[520] as does Ibuki, who speaks of development of the truth already there through the activity of the Spirit in the word of Jesus.[521] Hofbeck distinguishes similarly between the promises of life within the Spirit as the gift of the exalted one, and the life and resurrection already present in the work and words of the earthly Jesus.[522] T. E. Müller offers an interesting variant explanation. Acknowledging the problem and emphasising, as he does, the importance of the atoning death, he speaks of a unique and unrepeatable situation existing before Easter where life was given through friendship with the earthly Jesus.[523] Bennema draws attention to the author's use of the Wisdom model to argue that, indeed, the Son offered life already during his ministry.[524] "Jesus, as Wisdom incarnate, is the source of salvation."[525] He writes: "It seems that the disciples had, at times, a sufficient, though not perfect, understanding, and that they had an adequate belief-response and were in a life-giving relationship with Jesus."[526] His answer, consistent with my own, is that Jesus' going to the cross was in

---

517. Fernando. F. Segovia, "The Structure, Tendenz and Sitz im Leben of John 13:31–14:31," *JBL* 104 (1985): 490–91; cf. also Nicholson, *Death*, 68–69.

518. Bultmann, *Johannes*, 430–31; *Theologie*, 395, 437.

519. Ferdinand Christian Baur, *Vorlesungen über neutestamentliche Theologie* (Leipzig: Fues, 1864), 379.

520. Porsch, *Pneuma*, 66–68; similarly de Jonge, *Stranger*, 9; Bennema, *Saving Wisdom*, 34, who writes: "Both Porsch and Loader present a two-stage model of John's pneumatic soteriology—Porsch on pneumatological grounds, Loader on christological. The seminal work of Porsch (but also that of Loader) has been seriously neglected.... Neither has anyone seriously engaged with Loader."

521. Ibuki, *Wahrheit*, 300, 324.

522. Hofbeck, *Semeion*, 147, 177, 219.

523. Müller, *Heilsgeschehen*, 25, 33, 80–82, 132.

524. Bennema, *Saving Wisdom*, 37.

525. Bennema, *Saving Wisdom*, 38, similarly 94–96, 122.

526. Bennema, *Saving Wisdom*, 144.

order to make the life which the historical Jesus had in himself more widely available through the giving of the Spirit.

7:37-39 Life Only after Easter?

The passage 7:37-39 has been one of the main arguments for those denying salvation until after the giving of the Spirit. Jesus calls the thirsty to drink and promises rivers of living water (7:37-38) and the evangelist adds:

> τοῦτο δὲ εἶπεν περὶ τοῦ πνεύματος
> ὃ ἔμελλον λαμβάνειν οἱ πιστεύσαντες εἰς αὐτόν·
> οὔπω γὰρ ἦν πνεῦμα,
> ὅτι Ἰησοῦς οὐδέπω ἐδοξάσθη.
> This he said of the Spirit
> which those who believe in him were about to receive;
> for the Spirit was not yet,
> because Jesus was not yet glorified. (7:39)

On the basis of this statement Thüsing interprets all the images of life and salvation, such as water, bread, light, resurrection, as referring to a reality not available until after the coming of the Spirit.[527] These, he argues, reflect the author's post-Easter perspective, particularly the image "resurrection" which derives from the Easter event.[528] The author had no interest in what might have been available before Easter. He acknowledges that the author would have believed there was life in the earthly ministry, but that how it might have been available to the disciples was as of little interest to him as the issue of how OT saints might have received life.[529] Blank writes in similar terms that the evangelist knew of no proclamation or message of Jesus independent of what the church proclaimed.[530]

But it is precisely this insight which calls Thüsing's interpretation into question. For then the author would have perceived the proclamation of Jesus as being substantially no different from that of the post-Easter community. Our perception that post-Easter perspectives govern the presentation of Jesus in John should not be confused with the issue of how the author

---

527. Thüsing, *Erhöhung*, 161, 164, and esp. 321-24.
528. Thüsing, *Erhöhung*, 283.
529. Thüsing, *Erhöhung*, 164.
530. Blank, *Krisis*, 141.

portrays, and to that degree, believes, the earthly ministry to have been. Besides, it is not so that the author is unaware of difference in understanding between the earthly ministry and the post-Easter church. That is what is at issue. The evidence points in the direction of the author being very interested in what the incarnate Word said and did and being convinced that the word of the Son brought life, while at the same time being aware that fuller understanding was possible only through the gift of the Spirit after Easter. Ultimately the gift of life is centred not in events, but in the person.[531] Soteriology which is essentially Christology renders such distinctions of time irrelevant. As Bennema has shown, John's soteriology is a variant of Wisdom soteriology,[532] based on "pneumatic wisdom Christology,"[533] and when one considers Torah images used of Jesus this makes very good sense.

The Promise of the Indwelling Spirit

Porsch,[534] rightly, draws attention to 14:16–17,

> κἀγὼ ἐρωτήσω τὸν πατέρα καὶ ἄλλον παράκλητον δώσει ὑμῖν,
> ἵνα μεθ' ὑμῶν εἰς τὸν αἰῶνα ᾖ, τὸ πνεῦμα τῆς ἀληθείας,
> ὃ ὁ κόσμος οὐ δύναται λαβεῖν, ὅτι οὐ θεωρεῖ αὐτὸ οὐδὲ γινώσκει·
> ὑμεῖς γινώσκετε αὐτό, ὅτι παρ' ὑμῖν μένει καὶ ἐν ὑμῖν ἔσται.
> And I shall ask the Father and he will give you another Paraclete,
> that he may be with you forever, the Spirit of Truth,
> whom the world cannot receive, because it neither sees nor knows him;
> but you know him, because he remains with you and shall be in you.
> (14:16–17).

Beutler notes here the fulfilment of the promise of the new covenant of Jeremiah 31.[535] The Greek for "remains" can be accented to read either as a present, μένει the most common reading, or as a future, μενεῖ. Some manuscripts have ἐστιν "is" as an alternative to ἔσται "shall be." The text as quoted has strong external support and also makes best sense on internal grounds, since the Spirit is spoken of as a future gift in 14:16 and the text implies a contrast between two

---

531. Bennema, *Saving Wisdom*, 211.
532. Bennema, *Saving Wisdom*, 157.
533. Bennema, *Saving Wisdom*, 100.
534. Porsch, *Pneuma*, 246–47; Boismard and Lamouille, *Jean*, 357, pointing to the parallel in 2 John 2. For a contrary view see Boring, "Christian Prophecy," 114 n. 1.
535. Beutler, *Angst*, 64–65.

modes of the Spirit's presence: the disciples know him (present) and he will be given (future). Accordingly, 14:17 speaks of two modes of the Spirit's presence with the disciples: he remains *with* them and shall be *in* them.[536]

The Spirit in Jesus' Ministry

The Spirit was not absent during the ministry, but present and effective through Jesus, upon whom the Spirit remained (μένον, 1:33, cf. 3:34). The promise of baptism with the Spirit and the indwelling of the Spirit came to fulfilment only after Easter.[537] The presence of the Spirit in Jesus' ministry is attested not only through his baptism, but also in 6:63, where Jesus says of his words:

> τὸ πνεῦμά ἐστιν τὸ ζῳοποιοῦν, ἡ σὰρξ οὐκ ὠφελεῖ οὐδέν·
> τὰ ῥήματα ἃ ἐγὼ λελάληκα ὑμῖν πνεῦμά ἐστιν καὶ ζωή ἐστιν.
> The Spirit makes alive; the flesh is of no use;
> the words which I have spoken to you are spirit and are life. (6:63)

The juxtaposition of this statement with Jesus' prediction of his ascent does, it is true, allow the inference that the author may also have in mind the work of the Spirit after Easter, but primarily he is referring to the words that Jesus has spoken during his ministry, and, shortly after, it is to these words that Peter responds with his confession:

> ῥήματα ζωῆς αἰωνίου ἔχεις,
> καὶ ἡμεῖς πεπιστεύκαμεν καὶ ἐγνώκαμεν
> ὅτι σὺ εἶ ὁ ἅγιος τοῦ θεοῦ.
> You have the words of eternal life
> and we have believed and come to know
> that you are the holy one of God. (6:68–69)

Merging Horizons in John 3

A similar reference to the Spirit in the ministry of Jesus is present in 3:1–11, though here the situation is reversed. The passage speaks of birth of the

---

536. So Porsch, *Pneuma*, 71–72, 208, 246–47.
537. So Porsch, *Pneuma*, 105, 109–10, 144. Zumstein, "Ostererfahrung," 120 and 131, writes of John's Easter cycle as the counterpart of 15:18–26 and its "relecture" in 16:16–22.

Spirit, from above, and continues in a way which clearly reflects the post-Easter situation.

> ἀμὴν ἀμὴν λέγω σοι ὅτι ὃ οἴδαμεν λαλοῦμεν καὶ ὃ ἑωράκαμεν μαρτυροῦμεν,
> καὶ τὴν μαρτυρίαν ἡμῶν οὐ λαμβάνετε.
> Truly, truly I tell you, we speak what we know and we bear witness to what we have seen,
> and you do not receive our testimony. (3:11)

Jesus gathers into the "we" both himself, as the one and only Son who has come from above, from the Father, and those who will be given authority to become children. Here two sets of ideas are merged, the Son and the children; and also the pre-Easter and post-Easter horizons. Statements about birth by water and by Spirit and about witness fit best the post-Easter horizon, but this should not lead us to conclude that therefore the author would have meant that no rebirth and no seeing of the kingdom had been possible during the earthly ministry. The context portrays Jesus in the midst of the disciples as the Spirit-bearing Son of God par excellence.

7:37–39 Life and Its Abundance

7:39 neither means the Spirit was not in existence before Jesus' glorification nor can it mean it was not active in Jesus' ministry in a way that benefitted the disciples. Nor is this the implication of 7:37–39 as a whole. It reads:

> Ἐν δὲ τῇ ἐσχάτῃ ἡμέρᾳ τῇ μεγάλῃ τῆς ἑορτῆς εἱστήκει ὁ Ἰησοῦς
> καὶ ἔκραξεν λέγων· ἐάν τις διψᾷ ἐρχέσθω πρός με καὶ πινέτω.
> ὁ πιστεύων εἰς ἐμέ, καθὼς εἶπεν ἡ γραφή,
> ποταμοὶ ἐκ τῆς κοιλίας αὐτοῦ ῥεύσουσιν ὕδατος ζῶντος.
> τοῦτο δὲ εἶπεν περὶ τοῦ πνεύματος
> ὃ ἔμελλον λαμβάνειν οἱ πιστεύσαντες εἰς αὐτόν·
> οὔπω γὰρ ἦν πνεῦμα, ὅτι Ἰησοῦς οὐδέπω ἐδοξάσθη.
> On the last great day of the feast Jesus stood
> and cried out saying, "If anyone thirsts let him come to me and drink.
> He who believes in me, as the Scripture said,
> out of his belly shall flow rivers of living water."
> This Jesus said about the Spirit

which those who believed on him were going to receive;
for the Spirit was not yet (given), because Jesus was not yet glorified.
(7:37-39)

I have supplied in brackets the words "given" because the sense of the Greek requires it. I have followed the punctuation of Aland's printed text in taking ὁ πιστεύων εἰς ἐμέ ("he who believes in me") with what follows, rather than with what precedes.[538] To do the latter would mean the one who believes in Jesus should come and drink and allows then the interpretation of 7:38 that it is out of Jesus' belly that the rivers of living water will flow, which would refer to the gift of the Spirit by Jesus,[539] and some also take it in addition as an allusion to 19:34, where water and blood flowed from the side of the crucified one.[540] Reading it in this way raises the acute difficulty that Jesus is portrayed as standing before people, inviting them to come to him and drink, but in fact offering them something which the author would be fully aware could not be theirs until after Easter. He would be offering them nothing but promise. Is this tenable?

It is better with Hahn to read 7:38 as promising abundance,[541] related to 4:14

ὃς δ' ἂν πίῃ ἐκ τοῦ ὕδατος οὗ ἐγὼ δώσω αὐτῷ, οὐ μὴ διψήσει εἰς τὸν αἰῶνα,
ἀλλὰ τὸ ὕδωρ ὃ δώσω αὐτῷ γενήσεται ἐν αὐτῷ πηγὴ ὕδατος ἁλλομένου εἰς ζωὴν αἰώνιον.
Whoever drinks the water I shall give him will never thirst,

---

538. So Ferdinand Hahn, "Die Worte vom lebendigen Wasser im Johannesevangelium," in *God's Christ and His People: Studies in Honor of N. A. Dahl*, ed. J. Jervell and W. Meeks (Oslo: Universitetsforlaget, 1977), 53-54; Reim, *Studien*, 85; Coloe, *God Dwells with Us*, 128; Carson, *John*, 324-25; Witherington, *John's Wisdom*, 173-74; Henry M. Knapp, "The Messianic Water Which Gives Life to the World," *HBT* 19 (1997): 114. Cf. Melanie Baffes, "Christology and Discipleship in John 7:37-38," *BTB* 41 (2011): 144-50, who suggests the grammatical ambiguity in verses 37-38 is deliberate to enable it to serve both Christology and ecclesiology (144); similarly Koester, *Symbolism*, 14.

539. So Schnackenburg, *Johannesevangelium*, 2.213-14; Painter, *Witness*, 64-65; Haacker, *Stiftung*, 51; Boismard and Lamouille, *Jean*, 52; Bruce, *John*, 181-82; Beasley-Murray, *John*, 116; Moloney, *John*, 253; Johnson, "Salvation," 96; Thettayil, *In Spirit and Truth*, 403-13; Chanikuzhy, *Jesus, the Eschatological Temple*, 354; Schnelle, "Tempelreinigung," 370; *Johannes*, 148; Wilckens, *Johannes*, 133; Lincoln, *John*, 255; Theobald, *Johannes*, 1.538; Um, *Temple Christology*, 157-59.

540. Thüsing, *Erhöhung*, 161; Brown, *John*, 329; Burge, *Anointed Community*, 91-93.

541. Hahn, "Wasser," 53, 60; Porsch, *Pneuma*, 70; cf. Ibuki, *Wahrheit*, 324.

but the water which I shall give him shall become in him a spring of water
welling up to eternal life. (4:14)

and to 6:35,

ἐγώ εἰμι ὁ ἄρτος τῆς ζωῆς· ὁ ἐρχόμενος πρὸς ἐμὲ οὐ μὴ πεινάσῃ, καὶ ὁ πιστεύων εἰς ἐμὲ οὐ μὴ διψήσει πώποτε.
I am the bread of life. He who comes to me shall never hunger; and he who believes in me shall never thirst. (6:35)

Accordingly 7:37 is not an invitation to drink which cannot be fulfilled until much later. That presses anachronism far beyond what is usual in the Gospel. Rather, in this verse Jesus, speaking like Yahweh and Torah/Wisdom of old, offers drink and nourishment now, just as he had offered bread from heaven in ch. 6 (cf. Isa 55:1; Sir 51:23–25).[542] As water was poured out on the last day of the feast, so Jesus offers the water of life. Yet characteristically 7:38 expands this promise in view of its future abundance made possible through the future coming of the Spirit.[543] It is the equivalent of the shift from παρ' ὑμῖν ("with you") to ἐν ὑμῖν ("in you") in 14:17,[544] and from bread to Eucharist in ch. 6.

The presence of an allusion in 7:38 to the vision of the temple in Ezekiel 47, which many see here, is possible.[545] The parallel with 4:14 may indicate that we may have here an echo of the Jewish tradition which saw Torah like a wellspring in the faithful. The punctuation present in Aland favours the interpretation I offer here. The one who responds and drinks is promised abundance. But even should we read 7:38 christologically, we are not bound necessarily to deny any relevance in 7:37 for the ministry of Jesus. One could see the promise of 7:37 as a real offering during Jesus' ministry and 7:38–39 as the prediction of the "greater event" and its promised abundance. Therefore the use of 7:37–39 to support the argument that faith and life before Easter can only be proleptic stands on weak ground.

---

542. Bennema, *Saving Wisdom*, 186–87, suggests that as with the bread in John 6 "living water" refers to *both* Jesus' revelatory word *and* Spirit at the same time, i.e., *both* before *and* after Jesus' glorification."

543. Coloe, *God Dwells with Us*, 128, who notes that cultic imagery applicable only to Jesus during the narrative time of his ministry will in future apply to believers (133).

544. So Porsch, *Pneuma*, 68–70; Bennema, *Saving Wisdom*, 17.

545. Cf. Hahn, "Wasser," 66–67.

Life before and Abundance Life after the "Greater" Event: Conclusions

The concern of this section so far has been to clarify the extent to which the "greater" event is "greater" and, in particular, to guard against those interpretations which do so at the expense of denying salvific significance to the earthly ministry of the revealer, or, at least, of denying access to its salvific significance at the time of its occurring. We have considered this especially in relationship to the promise of the Spirit. The strongest argument against such an interpretation lies less in passages which promise what the Spirit will do and more in the portrayal of the ministry of the Son in itself as the salvific act. 6.1 will demonstrate the centrality of this as the salvation event. But in the light of it and of the considerations thus far, we can see that the primary significance of the "greater" event for faith is that it gives greater understanding of and access to the revelation event itself, the coming into the world of light, life, and truth in the person of the Son, in his words and his deeds from his baptism to his passion.

The Spirit in Sayings, Discourse and Narrative

Finally I want to comment on the relationship between sayings material and narrative in the way the Spirit is portrayed. The difference is similar to the one we noted between the narrative of resurrection appearances and the statements about Jesus' death and return. In the last discourses the Paraclete is portrayed as personal and personally active in the promises given the disciples. The only exception is 14:16–17 where the neuter pronoun, corresponding to the neuter noun, πνεῦμα, is retained, but in the same discourse the personal "he" appears when the Spirit is referred to a second time in 14:26. Elsewhere in John πνεῦμα is not more closely defined in this regard. The Spirit descends and remains on Jesus (1:32–33); Jesus will baptise with the Spirit (1:33); himself receives the Spirit without measure (3:34); the Spirit is what makes alive (neuter, 6:63) and is related to Jesus' words being "spirit and life" and also to worship of God as "spirit" (4:24) in "spirit and in truth" (4:23–24); disciples are born of the Spirit (3:5–6, 8), and are compared to the wind, the spirit, which blows where it wants to and no one know where it comes from or where it is going (3:8). None of these references makes the Spirit directly personal and this is true also of the author's note in 7:39 about the Spirit being given after Jesus was glorified, though we should assume the personal in the light of the promise expressed in the last discourses. Yet, after the very personal portrait of the Paraclete, Spirit of Truth, in the promises of the last discourses, the event which demands to be seen as its fulfilment in the Gospel, 20:22, again uses very impersonal language:

καὶ τοῦτο εἰπὼν ἐνεφύσησεν καὶ λέγει αὐτοῖς· λάβετε πνεῦμα ἅγιον·
And saying this he breathed on them and said, "Receive the Holy Spirit." (20:22)

Both Thüsing and Porsch note the difficulties in seeing 20:22 as fulfilment of the promises of the Paraclete.[546] On the one hand, they argue, the narrative speaks of the Spirit as breath, has Jesus give the Spirit while on earth during the time of his resurrection appearances, and sets the Spirit in close association with authorisation to bind and loose sins; and on the other hand, in the last discourses the Paraclete is personal, comes in Jesus' absence from the earth, is in fact the mediation of his presence, brings thus the joy which endures in Jesus' absence (16:22), and relates to much more than the authority to bind and loose. While not merely a symbolic event, it functions primarily as a symbol of what now begins and continues in the life of the community.[547] The differences are not to be denied, though some must be qualified. For it is, as we have seen, compatible with the author's Christology that the Spirit be given during the appearances, because Jesus has ascended first to the Father (20:17). We should note also the words of commission which precede, which could not be more characteristic of Johannine sayings material and indicate that the giving of the Spirit equips for mission.

Yet the differences are significant. The uncharacteristic elements continue with 20:23, the promise about binding and loosing sins, a motif not present elsewhere in the Gospel. The differences probably reflect the author's use of traditional sources,[548] so that he takes an account of Jesus' giving the Spirit by breath, and works it into his narrative as a whole in such a way as to enable the reader to find here the fulfilment of the promised Paraclete.[549] It is not "so foreign" as to need to be attributed to a redactor, as Forestell suggests.[550] Nor should the reference to Jesus' giving up his spirit at death be seen as the original gift of the Spirit or its foreshadowing, as we saw in 2.5 and 4.1.2.11 above.

---

546. Thüsing, *Erhöhung*, 263–68; Porsch, *Pneuma*, 249–50, 343, 371–76, 386; see also Dauer, *Johannes und Lukas*, 238–41.

547. So Porsch, *Pneuma*, 374.

548. So Porsch, *Pneuma*, 359–62; Schnackenburg, *Johannesevangelium*, 3.386; Onuki, *Gemeinde*, 89; Dauer, *Johannes und Lukas*, 242–45; Perkins, *Resurrection*, 178.

549. So Thüsing, *Erhöhung*, 274.

550. Forestell, *Word*, 98–101, 157.

The evangelist portrays the gift of the Spirit as something given by Jesus to the disciples on the evening of resurrection day after he had risen and ascended to the Father, as he had promised them. In the sense that the promise of the Spirit is here fulfilled, this is the Johannine "Pentecost."[551] It is not the point of revelation for them, as though they only now understood who he was. It brings, however, the promise of better understanding. They had already welcomed him and seen the resurrection evidence which confirmed the claims they had believed already during his ministry. The Spirit is given in the context of their commission, for their greater works, and with it they carry the authority of their task. If we should also see echoes of the creative breath of life of Genesis here (Gen 2:7), we witness here a new creative beginning. The primary function of the narrative is to announce the promise fulfilled. The "greater" event has taken place and its "greater" blessings are now present for all. The Spirit will bring greater understanding, bring forth the fruit of mission and mediate the presence of the Son and the Father to the believer in the community of faith and sacrament.

4.4 Conclusion

Jesus' death is interpreted, then, consistently within the framework of the central structure of the author's Christology and as such it represents the climax of the Son's fulfilment of his task. As the Son came from the Father, so the Son returns to the Father through death. Our analysis shows that his death is much more than a point of exit. The commission is not completed until death. We explored the suggestion that this means that the author sees the act of vicarious atonement as the final task of the commission, but found this not to be the case, even though the author knows of and makes use of traditions of vicarious atonement. The passion rather brings to a climax the work of revelation inasmuch as the conflict of claim and counter claim reaches the point where through the Jews and Pilate the world rejects the Son, putting him to death. The judgment on the Son becomes at the same time a judgment on the world for its sin and its ruler, for the Son's return to the Father is his vindication.

We also considered the motifs glorification and exaltation and found that they describe the action whereby God raises the Son to his glory in heaven. They are not paradoxical assertions about glory or exaltation in suffering. These terms, together with ascension, the title Son of Man, and

---

551. So Haacker, *Stiftung*, 62, 150; against de la Potterie, "Genèse," 38.

the motif of "something greater," form an association of ideas whereby the author describes the event faith perceives to have occurred at the death of Jesus. The author also integrates this association of ideas with the tradition of resurrection and resurrection appearances. The "greater" event thus described becomes the basis for "greater blessings" which follow. These are made possible through the sending of the Spirit and the sending of the disciples. The Spirit makes greater understanding possible of the fact that the Son came from the Father to make him known. The mission of the disciples, equipped for their witness by the Spirit, bears fruit to the glory of God. Altogether this produces a growing community of believers, who, like the first disciples, enjoy the indwelling of the Father and the Son through the Spirit, are nourished by the sacrament of flesh and blood, and are called to live in communion with one another, with the Son and the Father.

We saw that the "greater" event does not add to the revelation of the Son as if it were incomplete or inaccessible until it had happened. But it takes the knowledge of faith already in existence and deepens it, enabling greater knowledge and scriptural understanding of who Jesus was and is and of what he said and did. The "greater" event serves then also a hermeneutical function and ultimately explains how it is that the author could write the Gospel he did. The centre remains the primary event, the Son's making the Father known, and all else serves this. The Spirit is the primary agent in this hermeneutical function and the author integrates the Paraclete sayings of the last discourses with a traditional account of Jesus' giving the Spirit by breathing on the disciples on the evening of resurrection day.

We also noted how the passion serves as a pattern for the disciples as they follow their Lord. They, too, face suffering and they, too, will find the goal of their journey where he is in the glory of the Father. Despite the heavy emphasis throughout the passion on the Son as the revealer, the true meaning of his messiahship, there is nevertheless sufficient evidence that the author considered the passion a real passion. For the world this is a paradox: the Son of God faces humiliation and death. For faith it is the Son fulfilling the Father's commission in obedience faithfully to the end, and then returning to glory.

We have seen that the centre of Johannine Christology remains the Son's coming to make the Father known. This is the saving event to which all else points. In our next chapter we examine the nature of this saving event.

5 The Salvation Event in John

5.1 The Salvation Event—Revelation?

According to the basic structure of the author's Christology the salvation event consists in the coming of the Son, sent by the Father to make him known in word and deed. The response to this event determines salvation or condemnation. The glorification, exaltation, ascension, and return of the Son to the Father vindicate the Son and judge the world, and confirm that his coming was the salvation event, as the gift of the Spirit makes it possible to understand more fully what this event means. This event is the subject of the disciples' proclamation as they fulfil the commission given them by the Son in all the world. It is the salvation event. But in what does this event consist?

In Part One we noted the wide variety of expressions used to describe the Son's fulfilment of his divine commission. The Son who has come from the Father witnesses to, tells of, what he has seen, heard, been taught, commanded, told. He does the works of the Father, including the signs which both manifest his being as Son and point to his role as the bearer of life and salvation (water, bread, light, resurrection and more). The Son is the Word, as the prologue states in the beginning, and he makes the Father known (1:18). As noted in the previous section, the author can also embrace understandings of Jesus' death as vicarious and victorious, but the primary focus of his saving mission from beginning to end is to make the Father known. Because he speaks the words of God, to see him is to see the Father. In short the Son reveals the Father.

This pattern is one of revelation and it assumes that salvation comes in response to this revelation. On the surface this is straightforward and clear. But when we begin to examine the words and deeds of Jesus, problems emerge. How did the author understand this pattern of revelation? What did the Son reveal?

The Salvation Event in John

5.1.1   Revelation?

5.1.1.1   What Does the Revealer Reveal?

If we look for content in the words and deeds of Jesus, we do not find detailed secrets of the heavenly world. We find some predictions about the future, especially about the future of the Son, the disciples and the Spirit, but these are ancillary to the main work of revelation. For they refer to the "greater" event and its effects through which the revelation in Jesus' ministry is more fully understood and made accessible, not to the revelation itself. We also find claims about the Father, especially about his love, but beyond this there is no passing on of information such as we might expect after a statement like 3:32, "What he has seen and heard, to this he bears witness." Most of the discourses concentrate on Jesus' claims about himself. Jesus proclaims and argues for the truth about himself as the revealer, the Son sent from the Father to make him known. One could speak of a self-revelation, but the content of that self-revelation is that he is the revealer of the Father and only in that sense that he and the Father are one and to have seen him is to have seen the Father.

Already Baur noted that the revelation in the Fourth Gospel is a self-presentation.[1] Wetter and Friedrich Büchsel both stress that the evangelist offers only the fact of the Son's coming from God, not the contents of a revelation.[2] But it was above all Bultmann who repeatedly drew attention to this fact and made it the mainstay of his interpretation of Johannine Christology.[3]

The Revealer Reveals He Is the Revealer

The many statements, formulated in the language of communication of information from the Father, are claims which have no literal fulfilment in the Gospel. Jesus offers no such body of information of what he has seen and heard. There is no detailed programme of ethics, no set of teachings about God, no prophecy of the end time.[4] There is nothing which equates

1. Baur, *Vorlesungen*, 372, 377.
2. Wetter, *Sohn Gottes*, 5–6, 151–52; Friedrich Büchsel, *Das Evangelium nach Johannes*, NTD 4 (Göttingen: Vandenhoeck und Ruprecht, 1934), 16.
3. Bultmann, *Johannes*, 103–104, 111, 188; *Theologie*, 414, 418–20.
4. Cf. Ashton, *John*, 118, who writes: "The basic conviction the evangelist shared with the apocalyptic writers who preceded and followed him was that God had further mysteries to reveal above and beyond the Torah." However, the evangelist sees the substance of these

to the Sermon on the Mount except in the most general terms. There is no preaching of the kingdom of God or teaching in parables, except as part of a wide range of sayings about himself as the revealer Son.

Jesus presents himself with the claim that he is the Son who speaks the Father's words and does his works and that to respond to him is life.[5] If the author uses this revelation pattern without intending that we should understand Jesus as an information bearer, what is really happening? What is salvific here, if it is not revelation or knowledge as we are first led to assume? How should the revelation pattern be understood if not primarily in terms of revelation?

How is the Revealer Model Being Employed? Confronting Paradox?

Bultmann's answer was that the language of revelation is used in the Fourth Gospel as a way of talking about the self-presentation of the Son in encounter. He specifies this even further in the claim that what is presented, using the revelation pattern, is the sheer fact of the human flesh as the place of divine glory, sometimes formulated by him as the mere fact of his coming, the "Dass," not the "Was" (the fact that he came, not what actually happened), though with this formulation we should also note that, according to Bultmann, for the author, statements about coming and going were also only symbols of the paradox, the human and divine glory.[6] It is this offence or paradox which is salvific inasmuch as it calls into question human self-understanding and self-sufficiency.[7]

The Quest for Revelation Content

Dissatisfaction with the description of Jesus' message as merely the fact of his coming had already been expressed long before Bultmann by Wilhelm Lütgert, who argued that, as well as the fact of his coming, also the fact of his sonship was the content of Jesus' revelation and this was manifest par-

---

"mysteries" not in teaching or sets of information but in the event of Christ's coming. Better is his comment in "Intimations," 9, where he writes: "I argued that the Gospel is the reverse of an apocalypse, since its revelations concern events that have already taken place in the world below, not heavenly occurrences foreshadowing what is to come to pass later on earth."

5. So Ashton, "Reflections," 210–11.
6. Bultmann, *Johannes*, 188; *Theologie*, 418.
7. Bultmann, *Theologie*, 420.

The Salvation Event in John

ticularly through his miracles as acts of revelation.[8] But it was above all in reaction to Bultmann that the strongest criticisms have been voiced.

Haenchen argues that the content includes words about God and the fact of God's love.[9] He makes the important observation that the question of who God is becomes central for the Johannine understanding of revelation and rightly calls into question the sheer arbitrariness of the claim as formulated by Bultmann.[10]

Like Lütgert, Käsemann points to sonship and to the nature of the relationship of Father and Son as the content of revelation,[11] and those scholars who attribute a major role to atonement motifs in the Gospel usually claim that revelation must include a reference to it.[12] The first suggestion is surely true, but does not take us far, especially not concerning the revelation itself; for it merely tells of the unique relationship which makes it possible, not about the revelation itself. The connection with atonement is forced and not justified by the actual texts which speak of revelation. This is not to deny that the revealer is also the one who would suffer and that that in itself conveys something of a revelation, much in the sense of Bultmann's paradox, and that in relation to Jesus' death the author includes allusion to its role as vicarious, but this is not addressed in the many statements which depict Jesus as revealer.[13] Brown argues that revelation includes teaching about the creator giving light and life, God's love, the love commandments, the Holy Spirit, baptism and the Eucharist, and even claims that much of the teaching of the Sermon on the Mount is to be found in John.[14] The latter is surely an exaggeration, the sacraments incidental, the Holy Spirit functional, and, beyond that,

---

8. Lütgert, *Christologie*, 17; similarly, Hofbeck, *Semeion*, 190–93.

9. Haenchen, "Vater," 72; *Johannes*, 232; similarly Scroggs, *Christology*, 66–67. To this Moloney devotes his monograph, *Love*.

10. Haenchen, "Johannesevangelium," 222–23, 226.

11. Käsemann, *Letzter Wille*, 47–48, 87–89; Ibuki, *Wahrheit*, 44–46; de la Potterie, *Vérité*, 1011, 240; von den Osten-Sacken, "Leistung," 161; Riedl, *Heilswerk*, 26–27; similarly, Bennema, *Saving Wisdom*, 118; van der Watt, "Salvation," 107, who writes: "If the question were asked, 'From what must a person be saved according to John?,' the answer would be, 'From a lack of spiritual knowledge and blindness in order to be able to see and know the Father and the Son.'" While this is true, it remains too cognitive.

12. So Müller, *Heilsgeschehen*, 112, 135; Blank, *Krisis*, 133–34; Riedl, *Heilswerk*, 314; Wengst, *Gemeinde*, 119–20.

13. As de Boer, "Jesus' Departure," 2, observes, having cited my summary of the Christology's central structure: "the Gospel can summarize Jesus' identity as the life-giving envoy and revealer from above without any reference at all to his death/departure." Similarly van der Watt, "Salvation," 116.

14. Brown, *John*, 32.

we have the light and love which Haenchen affirms. We can scarcely speak of quantitative revelatory data as the model of the revealer-envoy would suggest.

Schnackenburg points to the Son's role in making access possible to the world of God and his uniting two worlds by his incarnation,[15] and in similar vein Becker points to the Son's making known to us our cosmic situation and overcoming the devil.[16] Theobald reads the Gospel as depicting Jesus as pioneering a way out of the realm of death.[17] A dualism is indeed presupposed in the Gospel, but is not itself the revelation, and overcoming the ruler of the world relates primarily to Jesus' death, but not framed as forging an escape route from the world below. Lee suggests that "The notion of the restoration of the divine image (*eikōn*) is central to this understanding of the incarnation,"[18] but such notions are foreign to the text. Weder emphasises that the "how" is as important as the "that," namely that the Son came in flesh and blood;[19] for, he argues, the Gospel is concerned with Jesus' ministry as much as with his death and return, and does not reflect the Pauline focus which is mainly on the single event of the cross and resurrection.[20] This is not to be denied, but none of these suggestions can explain away Bultmann's central observation that in the Gospel the Son speaks like an envoy bearing a communication of what he has seen and heard and been told, but fails to deliver any communication of this kind.

Can the "How" Replace the "What" of Revelation?

Meeks notes Bultmann's puzzle and offers a pertinent sociological observation that this model of Christology arises out of a situation where the community is experiencing alienation and so looks to Jesus as its "stranger,"[21] a term taken up in turn by de Jonge into the title of his collected essays. But beyond its sociological function, how was the myth understood in the Johannine community?

O'Day has recently challenged Bultmann's "Dass" (that) of revelation and the attempts of Käsemann and others to fill out the content of the "Was" (what) of revelation with christological dogma and suggested we look again

---

15. Schnackenburg, *John*, 1.155, 392.
16. Becker, "Auferstehung," 142–44, 149–50.
17. Theobald, *Johannes*, 1.64, 812.
18. Lee, *Flesh and Glory*, 49.
19. Weder, "Menschwerdung," 353.
20. So Schnackenburg, *Johannesevangelium*, 4.114–15; similarly Thüsing, *Erhöhung*, iii.
21. Meeks, "Man from Heaven," 143–46, 154, 161–62; cf. also Charles H. Talbert, "The Myth of the Descending and Ascending Redeemer in Mediterranean Antiquity," *NTS* 22 (1976): 425.

The Salvation Event in John

at the "Wie" (How) of revelation.²² Her study belongs to a rich developing tradition of literary studies of the Gospel concerned to examine how the text works and the importance of narrative in communication of the Gospel. A one-sided emphasis on the literary would easily come to mean: the Word became text and dwells among us! But it is a false and unnecessary antithesis to pit "How" against "What" in this way. The "How" evokes all the more strongly the question: "What?" and shifts the focus in a useful way from "What?" as information data to "What?" in the sense of "What person?" or "Who?" The centre becomes then less the "Dass," the "Was" or the "Wie" and becomes the "Wer?" (Who?).

Revealer-Envoy Language Serving to Express Encounter and Invitation

The word "revelation" does not occur in the Gospel, as Haenchen notes.²³ What we do find is language of communication and language of epiphany (e.g., "I am" sayings) combined in the pattern of the coming and going of an envoy. Schweizer used the Gospel's own forensic term "witness" rather than revealer to characterise the centre of Johannine Christology, thereby highlighting the confrontational component of the Gospel.²⁴ This is hardly the central motif, but its use instead of the language of revelation does enable us to see more clearly in the Gospel the quality of personal encounter and confrontation. This was already implicit in Bultmann's understanding, even the use of witness,²⁵ since he characterised the Son's action as a call or invitation, doubtless with gnostic parallels in mind, but nevertheless accurately representing what the Son in fact does.²⁶

Others, too, have picked up the language of encounter and confrontation.²⁷ Forestell understands the revelation as a communication of that life which the Son receives from the Father²⁸ and speaks of a dynamic intercommunion as

---

22. O'Day, *Revelation*, 35–42, 45–46; similarly Scroggs, *Christology*, 60–61.
23. Haenchen, "Johannesevangelium," 219.
24. Eduard Schweizer, *Jesus Christus im vielfältigen Zeugnis des Neuen Testaments* (Hamburg: Siebenstern, 1968), 160; "Zeuge," 161; cf. also Preiss, *Life in Christ*, 11, 17; Schillebeeckx, *Christ*, 312, 314; Lee, "Witness," 2–9; Söding, "Ich und der Vater," 181. Lincoln, *Truth on Trial*, 210, who writes: "Salvation in the Fourth Gospel's trial comes through the positive verdict of life."
25. So Bultmann, *Johannes*, 116.
26. Bultmann, *Theologie*, 393–94, 415.
27. E.g., Käsemann, "Prologue," 102; Schulz, *Johannes*, 210; Lieu, *Epistles*, 201.
28. Forestell, *Word*, 57.

the character of salvation.²⁹ Similarly Ibuki stresses that the revelation of the relationship of the Father and the Son is not a communication but an event.³⁰ Haacker also tries to get away from the communicative or noetic aspect of revelation. He lays emphasis on the role of the Spirit in association with the word and on personal encounter rather than revelation as information.³¹ His use of the founder motif as an alternative to revealer, partly in order to rehabilitate the place of atonement in John, is not, however, convincing; the motif is foreign to the Gospel and it does not do justice to the presentness which the element of encounter and confrontation demands. T. E. Müller makes a distinction between the time after Easter when salvation comes through encounter with Christ on the basis of his work of atonement and the time before Easter when salvation comes directly through the encounter with his person.³² Anderson notes that "this *theology of encounter* connects the Jesus of Galilee with the risen Christ of the Johannine community."³³ Similarly van der Watt writes: "Looking at these Johannine expressions, namely, birth, life, faith, etc. the common denominator is a *living relationship with God* who is revealed and is made present among his people through Jesus."³⁴

The authors we have considered above rightly emphasise, in one way or other, the importance of confrontation or encounter in John's Christology, an emphasis already highlighted by Bultmann.³⁵ In what follows I want to explore the issue further by examining first how it is that Jesus presents himself, if not as bearer of revelations; and secondly, what happens to people when they respond to the Son, in order to perceive from the perspective of the receivers the nature of the salvation brought by the Son in his making the Father known.

Encounter with What, with Whom?

Jesus presents himself with a claim to the people of his day: he is the one who has come from the Father and calls for faith in himself.³⁶ The claim for

---

29. Forestell, *Word*, 172.
30. Ibuki, *Wahrheit*, 115.
31. Haacker, *Stiftung*, 163–65.
32. Müller, *Heilsgeschehen*, 33, 138–39; Smith, *Theology*, 117; Ashton, "Reflection," 212.
33. Anderson, *Christology*, 164.
34. Jan G. van der Watt, "Eschatology in John: A Continuous Process of Realizing Events," in *Eschatology of the New Testament and Some Related Documents*, ed. J. G. van der Watt, WUNT 2.315 (Tübingen: Mohr Siebeck, 2011), 121.
35. Bultmann, *Johannes*, 190; *Theologie*, 415.
36. Schwankl, "Aspekte," 361, who emphasises that Jesus himself is what is to be communicated.

The Salvation Event in John

allegiance presented in this manner could appear quite arbitrary. Others, too, might present themselves with such absolute claims. This raises the question of their validity. The author does not simply present Jesus with his claims. He begins with the prologue which relates Jesus to God and to creation. The one who is to make such claims is not some arbitrary fanatic, but draws his being from God and has been involved in the creation of all things. He has been the light and life from the beginning of time. The validity is supported also by the witness of John the Baptist, by the witness of Scripture, directly as witness to Israel's Messiah and indirectly through typology and symbol, and by the use of language elsewhere associated with claims of divine representation (life, light, truth, etc.), in particular of Torah, frequently associated or identified with Wisdom.[37]

These are in part the interpretations of the author and in part Jesus' words about himself, as portrayed by the evangelist, so that there is a certain circularity of argument. We are being asked to believe both Jesus' self-claims (mediated by the evangelist) and the claims the evangelist himself makes about him directly. Retrospectively, the evangelist can appeal to the resurrection and return of the Son to the Father as vindication of these claims. Nevertheless the evangelist does present Jesus as making absolute claims about himself, being in that sense his own chief witness, and thematises this in conflict with the Jews.

The apparent arbitrariness of these claims is somewhat modified when we examine their nature. The claims are designed primarily to elevate not Jesus himself but God. Haenchen pointed to the importance of theology in the strictest sense for understanding the nature of the Son's revelation, and the theocentricity of the Gospel is widely recognised.[38] As Moloney puts it, "The Gospel is ultimately about God, not about Jesus."[39] The evangelist builds thus upon the presupposition that God is in some sense known. For all his claims, Jesus does not impart detailed information about God, but speaks on the assumption that God is a word that makes good sense to his hearers. Since this is so, it is equally important to examine the unexpressed

---

37. So rightly Pryor, *John*, 123–24; Bennema, *Saving Wisdom*, 38, 94.

38. So Dodd, *Interpretation*, 194; Haenchen, "Vater," 73; Barrett, *John*, 98; Barrett, "Father," 21–26; Ferdinand Hahn, "Sehen und Glauben im Johannesevangelium," in *Neues Testament und Geschichte. Festschrift für O. Cullmann*, ed. H. Baltensweiler and B. Reicke (Zürich: TVZ; Tübingen: Mohr Siebeck, 1972), 128; *Theologie*, 1.600; Ritt, *Gebet*, 459; Rudolf Schnackenburg, "'Und das Wort ist Fleisch geworden,'" *IKaZ* 8 (1979): 8; Busse, "Theologie oder Christologie," 33; Schwankl, "Aspekte," 352, who rightly notes that with regard to their actual message the Synoptics are theocentric, John, christocentric.

39. Moloney, *Love*, 38.

assumptions about God present in the Gospel, for Jesus' claim and significance are inseparably connected with them.

Direct teaching about God is sparse in the Gospel, largely because Jesus is not presented as offering teaching about God.[40] Some important presuppositions are evident. God is creator.[41] There is no absolute dualism here. "God is Spirit and they who worship him must worship him in spirit and in truth" (4:24)—a rare example of direct teaching about God on the lips of Jesus in the Fourth Gospel. It is important because he uses it to relativise the cultic centres of both Samaritans and Jews. God transcends space in such a way that he is to be worshipped as a spiritual being. Porsch shows that, as Spirit, God himself is the active ground, making a relationship with himself possible.[42] The author assumes God's involvement in history in the past and that he continues to speak to people, teach and draw them to himself in the present. The Father is said to give people the right to become his children. He is also linked with judgment. But by far the most dominant impression is that the Father is concerned and involved in the world of people, giving gifts, and sending people for specific tasks. God's attitude to the world of people is one of love and this motivated the sending of the Son.

The attempts of Käsemann, Schottroff and Lattke to deny that the statement of 3:16, God loved the world, has weight for the evangelist are unconvincing,[43] and rest on the assumption that such a statement stands in tension with the author's dualism. But "world" here is the world of people viewed in their potential for transformation, and in the Gospel as a whole the potential for such transformation is assumed by the act of sending the Son and of his sending the disciples.[44] Ibuki is right in noting that the love between Father and Son is one which reaches dynamically out into the world.[45]

The God we recognise here is largely the God known to us in much of the OT and the writings of the New. God is not uninterested, aloof, divided, distracted, but has involved himself and seeks a relationship between himself and people. God is involved, yet above; engages himself, yet also transcends. It is doubtful whether any of this is distinctively Johannine. What is distinc-

---

40. Thompson, *God*, 225, concludes her discussion of the issue: "John thus presents Jesus as the one through whom worship is directed to God," never as independent of God.

41. Thompson, *God*, 55.

42. Porsch, *Pneuma*, 151.

43. Käsemann, "Prologue," 124; *Letzter Wille*, 107-9; Schottroff, *Glaubende*, 288; Lattke, *Einheit*, 50-51, 70.

44. So Bultmann, *Theologie*, 367; Klaiber, "Interpretation," 319-21; Segovia, *Love Relationships*, 169; Schnelle, *Christologie*, 210-11; Scroggs, *Christology*, 76-77.

45. Ibuki, *Wahrheit*, 174.

The Salvation Event in John

tively Christian is that God is related to Jesus in a special way and what is distinctively Johannine is the particular way this is expressed in the Fourth Gospel.

When, therefore, in the Fourth Gospel Jesus claims to be the Son sent from God the Father, already a lot of information is implied through the use of the word "God." When, therefore, beyond the claim to be the sent one and to enjoy a special relationship with him, Jesus offers not primarily information, but a claim for allegiance, a call to faith, we are not left in a knowledge vacuum. For the Son offers not a new theology, but, as God's representative and envoy, offers God and to offer God is not to offer an abstraction according to the presuppositions of the author, but someone known. The Son's claim for allegiance to himself is a claim for allegiance to God.[46] His mission is not one of revelation, as the revealer-envoy pattern at first suggests, but of encounter and invitation. He offers a relationship with himself and thus with God. The offer is absolute in its claim and at the same time totally without preconditions, in the sense of people needing to establish a level of worthiness or deserving before the offer applies to them.

5.1.1.2 The "What?" and the "Who?" in the Mirror of Response

In the light of these observations the distinctive imagery of the Son's claims makes sense and the nature of salvation may be read from the nature of the response demanded. In ch. 1 the relationship between Jesus and his disciples has two elements. The first is John the Baptist's witness in the presence of the disciples concerning who Jesus is. It is a claim to be believed. The second is the personal following, sometimes at the level of enquiry in response to John, sometimes in response to Jesus' direct command. In the relationship of following there is room for growth and promise of new understanding, as Jesus tells Nathanael. Elsewhere it is clear that following Jesus in the literal sense and acclamation of him as Messiah or prophet on the basis of his miracles may not indicate that a saving relationship has been established. For it must also entail right understanding of who Jesus is, including of his miracles as signs, and response to him on that basis.

The miracles or signs may evoke the response of wonder and at this

---

46. Thompson, *God*, 98, writes: "The Father-Son relationship thus becomes the theological grounding for the predications of the authority and work of the Father given to and embodied in the Son."

level miracle-based faith may go no further than asserting with Nicodemus that Jesus is a teacher from God (2:23–3:2), with the Samaritan woman and the healed people that he is a prophet (4:19; 9:17), or with the 5,000 and the crowd at his entry that he is the prophet or the messianic king (6:14–15; 12:13). That may be a first step,[47] but it remains an inadequate response and the author has Jesus attack it accordingly.[48] It goes little further than the use of miracles in imperial propaganda.[49] Bittner's attempt to turn 4:48 into a positive statement about the need for signs and wonders is unconvincing, especially after 2:23–25 and similar statements in the Gospel.[50] Neither does the evangelist deny the reality of miracles[51] or their relevance.[52] Miracles matter and are not mere symbols.[53] But the boundary to true faith is crossed where faith sees in the performance of the miracle the glory of the revealer, ,and then faith, primarily at the level of the reader, can also see the miracle itself as symbolic of the life and light and truth which he brings and which he is.[54] Kee has noted a similar symbolic use of miracles in the Isis cult,[55] but

---

47. So Bultmann, *Johannes*, 92; Forestell, *Word*, 70; Appold, *Oneness*, 100; Schnackenburg, *John*, 1.506, 519–20; Brown, *John*, 528; Nicol, *Semeia*, 99–103.

48. So Bultmann, *Johannes*, 83 n. 7; 396; Schnider and Stenger, *Johannes*, 82, 84–86; Haenchen, *Johannes*, 107; Richter, *Studien*, 343; Untergassmair, *Im Namen Jesu*, 47; Fortna, "Christology," 493; Barrett, "Symbolism," 76–77; Schnelle, *Christologie*, 202. On miracles and Elijah and prophetic Christology see Ashton, *Fourth Gospel*, 182. More speculatively on their use as representing a stage of the author's faith development, see Anderson, *Christology*, 159. See also Brian C. Dennert, "Hanukkah and the Testimony of Jesus' Works (John 10:22–39)," *JBL* 132 (2013): 431–51, who in relation to John 10 notes the association of Hanukkah with miracles (432, 445, 451).

49. On this see Michael Labahn, "'Heiland der Welt'. Der gesandte Gottessohn und der römische Kaiser—ein Thema johanneischer Christologie?" in *Zwischen den Reichen: Neues Testament und Römische Herrschaft. Vorträge auf der Ersten Konferenz der European Association for Biblical Studies*, ed. M. Labahn and J. Zangenberg, TANZ 36 (Tübingen: Francke, 2002), 163–68.

50. Bittner, *Zeichen*, 128–32.

51. Against Bultmann, *Theologie*, 397. So rightly Wead, *Devices*, 19; Nicol, *Semeia*, 106; Pokorny, "Jesus," 218; Schnelle, *Christologie*, 150.

52. Schottroff, *Glaubende*, 48; Langbrandtner, *Weltferner Gott*, 93–96.

53. So rightly Wead, *Devices*, 24; Gnilka, "Christologie," 99; Schnelle, *Christologie*, 94–98, 148–51, 183, 191.

54. Similarly Hofbeck, *Semeion*, 180, 182; Schnackenburg, "Frage," 205–6; Käsemann, *Letzter Wille*, 17, 53; Segovia, *Love Relationships*, 194; H. E. Lona, "Glaube und Sprache des Glaubens im Johannesevangelium," *BZ* 28 (1984): 179; Fortna, "Christology," 491; van der Watt, "Salvation," 112.

55. Howard C. Kee, "Myth and Miracle: Isis, Wisdom, and the Logos of John," in *Myth, Symbol, and Reality*, ed. B. M. Olson (Chicago: University of Notre Dame Press, 1980), 145–64; Howard C. Kee, "Christology and Ecclesiology: Titles of Christ and Models of Community,"

the parallels which exist fall short of convincing evidence that they have a direct relationship with the Johannine use of miracle stories.

If you believe the works, you must eventually come to believe the words. A progression to full faith is occasionally traceable in narratives. The Samaritan woman (ch. 4) progresses from seeing Jesus as a mere man, to belief he may be a prophet because of the miracle of supernatural knowledge, to belief he is probably the Messiah (on the same basis), to belief with her fellow Samaritans that he is saviour of the world. The blind man (ch. 9) makes a similar journey. One may also note the development of the faith theme in ch. 20, from grief and astonishment to belief in the miracle of resurrection, to letting go of the human appearance of Jesus or forgoing the direct physical contact, to trusting the witness and believing the Son to have returned to the Father and to have given the Spirit.[56]

In itself right understanding is not perceived as an intellectual hurdle, as if it should entail a complete understanding of Christology. For the truth is there for eyes that want to see and ears that want to hear. Essentially right understanding is belief in what constitutes the central structure of the author's Christology, namely that the Son has come as the sent one from the Father to make him known, to do his works and to offer life and light and truth. The disciples grasp this truth and after Easter the Paraclete will lead them to greater understanding.

Beside right understanding the saving relationship also includes faithful allegiance, remaining in the relationship, abiding in the vine, obedience to the Son's commandments, above all, mutual indwelling, loving and being loved by the Son and the Father. These are relationship terms. Coming to faith, being born from above, receiving the right to become a child of God, is the beginning of an ongoing faith relationship in this sense.[57] The author does not address directly the problem of what happens when a believer sins, though indirectly Peter's experience shows that repentance is possible. Ideas of perfectionism, as present in the context of I John, are not evident in the Gospel. The assumption is that the saving relationship is one which continues and grows. But it is also one which may be terminated, as disciples opt to cease the allegiance, perhaps because of the extent of Jesus' claims, perhaps as an act of apostasy and betrayal.

Semeia 30 (1984): 181, 190; Howard C. Kee, *Miracles in the Early Christian World* (New Haven: Yale, 1983), 221.

56. On this see the essay by de la Potterie, "Genèse."

57. Bennema, *Saving Wisdom*, 122, emphasises that Wisdom implies sustained growth.

Predestination and Dualism

Beside these statements about the response of faith must stand others which speak of the Father drawing particular people who are his own to faith and destining others not to believe (3:19-21; 6:44), or, in the case of Judas, to betray. Bultmann argues that the language of predestination never obviates the basic intention of universality of the offer of salvation in John.[58] Response to this offer determines whether people are in darkness or light and are so described as predestined to faith or unfaith, not deterministic dualism. It is not difficult to find statements which speak in determinist categories from which to argue that the evangelist's thought is primarily deterministic. This is argued by Bergmeier, who traces this to Jewish attitudes of the kind found in Qumran and argues that such dualism is found in Gnosticism only through secondary Christian influence, whereas gnostic dualism is not deterministic.[59] Wolfgang Langbrandtner, following earlier observations by Haenchen and Schottroff, succeeds in showing that gnostic soteriology is based upon "Entscheidungsdualismus" ("dualism of decision"),[60] much as that argued for the Fourth Gospel by Bultmann and many others,[61] but denied by him to Gnosticism. While there is evidence for this, Gnosticism is also very diverse and it should not be denied that cosmic anthropological dualism plays a much larger role in gnostic writings generally than in John[62] and should not be overplayed in John to the degree that protology becomes central.[63] Becker traces various stages of development in Johannine dualism from the Qumran type to a gnostic-like dualism of decision supported by an ontological dualism, through to a deterministic dualism evident in relationships with the Jews in John 8 and in relationship with other Christians of different beliefs in the first epistle.[64] In particular, renewed interest in

---

58. Bultmann, *Johannes*, 27-28; Bultmann, *Theologie*, 370, 373-75, 429; similarly Ibuki, *Wahrheit*, 38-54, 114-15; Painter, "John 9," 55; Scroggs, *Christology*, 101-2.

59. Bergmeier, *Glaube*, 213-16; similarly Haenchen, "Johannesevangelium," 224-25.

60. Langbrandtner, *Weltferner Gott*, 91-93; Haenchen, "Johannesevangelium," 223-24; Schottroff, *Glaubende*, 289, 295; Peter Hofrichter, "Gnosis und Johannesevangelium," *BK* 41 (1986): 17-18.

61. Bultmann, *Johannes*, 26-27, 39; Bultmann, *Theologie*, 420, cf. 379; Wilkens, *Zeichen*, 120; Blank, *Krisis*, 96-99, 145-49; Hegermann, "Eigentum," 120; Porsch, *Pneuma*, 128-30; Schottroff, *Glaubende*, 229; Langbrandtner, *Weltferner Gott*, 100 (of the *Grundschrift*).

62. So rightly Onuki, *Gemeinde*, 53. See also H. M. Schenke's review of Schottroff in *ThZ* 97 (1972): 751-55, esp. 755.

63. So rightly Onuki, *Gemeinde*, 54, against Käsemann, *Letzter Wille*, 114.

64. Becker, "Dualismus"; *Johannes*, 147-51; see also Jörg Frey, "Zu Hintergrund und Funktion des johanneischen Dualismus," in *Die Herrlichkeit des Gekreuzigten. Studien zu den*

The Salvation Event in John

reconstructing the history of the Johannine community offers an important resource for understanding Johannine dualism.[65] Fundamentally, despite its cosmic dualistic presuppositions to which we return below, the Gospel has at its centre the importance and possibility of a continuing faith response to the Son.

Salvation Offered and Received

In returning then to the response required and given as an approach to understanding the nature of the salvation which the Son brings, we can note that the benefit of salvation consists primarily in the relationship offered. This includes a cognitive element, namely, belief that the Son is the sent one. In that sense it is right to say that there is revelation content involved, the revelation that the Son has a unique relationship of oneness with the Father and speaks and acts for him. Responding to him means believing this; it also means entering the relationship he offers. The joy of the believers is oneness with the Son. The believers enjoy eternal life now though there is a future element inasmuch as one day they will join the Son in the heavenly presence of the Father and see his glory. The gift of salvation is mostly described using images such as water, bread, light, life, resurrection. The giver is, however, also described as the gift. He is the bread, light, life, resurrection, way, door, truth. The double reference of these images for both the gift and the giver is possible because it is primarily the person and the personal relationship which is at the centre of salvation, not a place, a possession, a body of knowledge, or a set of charismatic powers.

This is widely recognised as a major characteristic of Johannine Christology.[66] Becker, however, disputes it as characteristic of the author of John 17, which speaks of the Son only as giver (of words, name, and glory).[67] But it is doubtful whether absence of a specific identification of gift and giver in John 17 justifies this conclusion, especially because statements about Jesus as bearer of the word are common elsewhere in the Gospel. This is not to deny the elements peculiar to John 17, especially the giving of the name and

---

Johanneischen Schriften I, ed. J. Schlegel, WUNT 307 (Tübingen: Mohr Siebeck, 2013), 409–82; also Ashton, *Fourth Gospel*, 387–417.

65. See, in particular, Nicol, *Semeia*, 146–47; von den Osten-Sacken, "Leistung," 157.

66. So Bultmann, *Theologie*, 394; Preiss, *Life in Christ*, 29; Ibuki, *Wahrheit*, 355; Riedl, *Heilswerk*, 26–27; de la Potterie, *Vérité*, 1011.

67. Becker, "Johannes 17," 76–78; *Johannes*, 519; similarly Langbrandtner, *Weltferner Gott*, 68–69; cf. Untergassmair, *Im Namen Jesu*, 67–68.

of glory. At the same time these motifs, especially, are ways of talking about God himself, and the promise of indwelling also coheres well with the notion of the giver as himself the gift.

Existential Imagery for Salvation

The images used of Jesus as both gift and giver reflect fundamental human need: light, life, water, bread, way. This is emphasised rightly by Bultmann.[68] This was the strength of his existentialist approach to John. They imply that what Jesus brings belongs to the essence of what a human being needs and, conversely, what a human being needs is to be found in Jesus. Bultmann emphasises that the prologue enables us to identify a connection between the Word as agent of creation and the Word as bearer of basic human needs.[69] Human beings do not have revelation through creation; but they do have a certain questioning, a negative knowledge, a sense of dependency which comes to fulfilment in response to the Word and, beyond that, the creation may, as Painter suggests, function as symbol-bearer of the Word.[70] Bultmann writes that creation and redemption stand in continuity because of the prologue.[71] This is a correct observation about consistency within the Gospel, though at no point does the author make it explicit, as he might have. Painter points particularly to the frequency in the Gospel of Torah imagery used christologically as a reflection of conflict with the synagogue. This is probably the most likely medium of many of the existential creation images into Johannine Christology.[72] One of the strengths of the work of Bennema

---

68. Bultmann, *Theologie*, 418; similarly Käsemann, *Letzter Wille*, 109, 116; Haenchen, "Johannesevangelium," 282; Eduard Schweizer, *Ego Eimi*, 2nd ed., FRLANT 56 (Göttingen: Vandenhoeck und Ruprecht, 1965), 132-35; Lieu, *Epistles*, 241-42; Painter, "John 9," 44-46; Gnilka, "Christologie," 101.

69. Bultmann, *Johannes*, 26-27; similarly Käsemann, *Letzter Wille*, 109; von den Osten-Sacken, "Leistung," 159; also Gundry, *Jesus the Word*, 3, who writes: "a Christology of the Word dominates the whole of John's Gospel" (similarly 6-7).

70. Painter, "John 9," 49-55.

71. Bultmann, *Johannes*, 39.

72. On this see also Martin Scott, *Sophia and the Johannine Jesus*, JSNTSup 71 (Sheffield: JSOT, 1992), 159-61; van der Watt, "Salvation," 111; Paul N. Anderson, "The Origin and Development of the Johannine *Egō Eimi* Sayings in Cognitive-Critical Perspective," *JSHJ* 9 (2011): 166; Pryor, *John*, 123; McGrath, *Christology*, 177; Thompson, *God*, 130-36; Colleen M. Conway, "'Behold the Man!' Masculine Christology and the Fourth Gospel," in *New Testament Masculinities*, ed. S. D. Moore and J. C. Anderson, SemeiaSt 45 (Atlanta: SBL, 2003), 178; Andrew T. Glicksman, "Beyond Sophia: The Sapiential Portrayal of Jesus in the Fourth Gospel and Its

The Salvation Event in John

is to have underlined "Saving Wisdom" as the model for understanding Johannine soteriology. He sees the link of Spirit and Wisdom as the key to the major question of *how* this comes about, already during Jesus' ministry.

> First, the Spirit *creates* a saving relationship between the believer and God, i.e., brings a person into such a relationship with the Father and Son, through the mediation of saving wisdom which is itself present in Jesus' revelatory teaching. Second, the Spirit *sustains* this saving relationship between the believer, Father and Son, through further mediation of wisdom that enables the believer to manifest discipleship (as an ongoing belief-response).[73]
>
> The same Spirit and Wisdom that are at work together in creation are also co-operating with one another in salvation.[74]

The gift of salvation in John does not represent an addition to the created human being or a distraction from it, but rather something which belongs to it. This is true, notwithstanding the fact that the existential images are used symbolically of spiritual truth. The relationship offered is with the Son and the Father who is also the Creator. But while the focus is entirely upon the gift of this relationship, it is appropriate to ask to what degree the way in which this gift is expounded in the Gospel implies nevertheless a tension with the notion of creation of all things, presupposed elsewhere in the Gospel. It is legitimate to ask this question because the theme of creation is not developed at any point in the Gospel and because it has a bearing on our understanding of Johannine soteriology.

We have noted that the gift is of a growing and living relationship and that at least two stages may be detected: oneness with the Son and Father on earth and oneness with the Son and Father in heaven. The contrast between heaven and earth is present throughout the Gospel. To be "of the earth" is to be not saved. But this does not imply an ontology according to which sheer physicality is evil. It does however imply a hierarchy of order in God's creation between heaven and earth. To be "of the earth" means limiting oneself to seeing only at an earthly level and failing to see the kingdom of God. Here we meet the complicating factor of election and choice. But both statements are juxtaposed in expressing the belief that some see and some do not and

---

Ethical Implications for the Johannine Community," in *Rethinking the Ethics of John: 'Implicit Ethics' in the Johannine Writings*, ed. J. G. van der Watt and R. Zimmermann, Contexts and Norms of New Testament Ethics 3 (Tübingen: Mohr Siebeck, 2012), 89–95.

73. Bennema, *Saving Wisdom*, 38.
74. Bennema, *Saving Wisdom*, 96.

those who do not carry responsibility for their continuing blindness. The assumption is not, however, that a superhuman capacity is added to people when they are enabled to see, but rather that seeing and hearing is the true state of the human being. In other words, the gift of salvation is primarily to be seen as a relationship within which human beings have life and have it in abundance as they open themselves to the Son and the Father. In this they do not cease to be human beings in order to become superhuman beings, by addition of the divine or subtraction of the human; they become human beings as they were created to be.

The images of salvation express the gift in various ways. Light gives security by showing the way and exposes the wayward; it brings salvation and judgment.[75] Life contrasts with death and almost ceases to be an image since life in its fullness is found only in unity with the Father and the Son. Water quenches thirst and makes life possible; bread nourishes and so also mediates life. Resurrection symbolises transformation from death to life through faith, an image borrowed from literal eschatological hope also present in the Gospel. Door speaks of Jesus as the means of access to relationship with the Father and way is used similarly, though also having in mind the ultimate heavenly destination. Vine brings together emphasis on ongoing relationship with the Son, the notion of bearing fruit in mission, and also unity among the disciples as branches in the vine. Shepherd expresses both leadership and a contrast with false leadership claims; it also entails the themes of mission and unity.

Salvation an Ongoing, Expansive Relationship

The saving relationship is not static and unchanging, as though salvation were thought of as passively receiving a gift. It is dynamic and developing, a relationship which reproduces itself, in much the same way as the relationship between Father and Son led to the offering of a relationship to the world. The saving relationship is therefore one of being commissioned. The mission of the disciples is likewise not primarily one of information-giving, though it includes information about who the Son is, his coming, ministry, death and return, glorified, exalted, and ascended, to the Father. It is a mission which offers relationship. In one sense it is unlike the Son's mission who offered relationship with himself as relationship with the Father. On the other hand, the relationship focus of the salvific gift gives to community in relationship a

---

75. Painter, "Sacrifice and Atonement," 312.

central significance in the Fourth Gospel. This is both what we might deduce, given the author's starting point, and what we find expressed in the Gospel itself. Being Christian means being in relationship with the community and in the community being in relationship with the Father and the Son, being in a communion of love that is forever expansive. Appold rightly shows how the oneness motif expands to include the notion of gathering the children of God (11:52). Less convincing is his attribution of this motif to the pattern of the gnostic redeemer gathering his own.[76]

Accordingly, the gift of salvation in John is primarily a person and a relationship with a person, the Son, and through the Son, a relationship with the Father. In this relationship human beings find their deepest needs to be met. It is a relationship ultimately with God who is creator and with the Son, the Logos active in creation. It is ongoing and finds its ultimate end in the heavenly presence of the Father. Its primary focus is the present, where it is lived out in a community of love and witness, where the spirit gives knowledge and equips for mission.

Salvation, Eschatology and Cosmic Dualism

It is this primary focus on relationship which forms the basis for the author's eschatology. At its centre is the relationship of life, and its ultimate future is the shared presence with the Son and the Father in heaven (17:24). It is therefore not a relationship which reaches its ultimate potential already on earth,[77] though it is a life-giving relationship already on earth. This should not, however, be used as a criterion for denying the presence of elements of traditional collective eschatology in the Gospel. The Gospel still has a place for parousia, resurrection, and judgment day. The individualising application of the parousia tradition of 14:3 in 14:18-22 need not imply denial of the former altogether.[78] But these are no longer central.

76. Appold, *Oneness*, 276-78. And see the criticism by Onuki, *Gemeinde*, 57-62.
77. So rightly Schnackenburg, *Johannesevangelium*, 2.54; Schnackenburg, "Frage," 204; Onuki, *Gemeinde*, 65-70.
78. So Porsch, *Pneuma*, 382; C. F. D. Moule, "A Neglected Factor in the Interpretation of Johannine Eschatology," in *Studies in John. Presented to J. N. Sevenster*, NovTSup 24 (Leiden: Brill, 1970), 159; Forestell, *Word*, 132-34; van Hartingsveld, *Eschatologie*, 153; de Jonge, *Stranger*, 173-74, 188; Schnelle, *Christologie*, 146; Beasley-Murray, *John*, 79; Burge, *Anointed Community*, 143-46; Frey, *Eschatologie*, 2.150-51, 177-78; van der Watt, "Eschatology," 124, 127. Against Günter Fischer, *Die himmlischen Wohnungen*, EHS 23.38 (Frankfurt: Lang, 1975), 330-32, 346-48; Jürgen Heise, *Bleiben. Menein in den Johanneischen Schriften*, HUT 8 (Tübingen: Mohr Sie-

The dualism of heaven and earth, both created spheres, but from one of which it is desirable to escape, lurks beneath the Gospel in a way that could have led potentially to an absolute dualism of a gnostic kind.[79] It has not gone that far in John. There is ontological dualism, but the two parts are not unconnected.[80] They remain God's creation, though the author shows little interest in creation (outside the prologue).[81] There is still some sense of belonging within a history of a God who has acted in relation to figures of the past like Abraham, Moses, Isaiah, even if this past is now seen totally from a christological perspective. It is this God who has sent his Son. Unlike Gnosticism, therefore, the centre of focus is not place and therefore change of place, but a person.[82] Christology or better, theology, not cosmology or anthropology, determines soteriology. There is no room or licence here for multiple redeemers and redeeming acts, because at the centre is not soteriology, but the claim of the person, God, in his Son.

Nor is it correct simply to say that protology has usurped eschatology.[83] Future hope remains important, but the focus of this future is no longer a great cosmic event, but joining the Son where he is with the Father. This is the outworking of the underlying dualism. The dualistic framework determines to that degree the nature of eschatology and soteriology. It may be reflected in the author's use of the tradition about casting out the ruler of the world, as Becker suggests.[84] I doubt that it should be seen as contributing to an understanding of the incarnation as somehow bridging the two realms as Schnackenburg suggests.[85] It remains rather in the background, providing the stage on which the drama is set; at the centre of that stage is the personal claim and declaration of God in his Son. Whereas soteriology, anthropology and cosmology are central for Gnosticism, and saviour figures or saving initiatives may vary and need not even be consistent within a single document, this is not so in John. In John, by contrast, Christology and the soteriology of

---

beck, 1967), 100, 173; Scroggs, *Christology*, 98–99. Coloe, *God Dwells with Us*, interprets many dwelling places as referring to the interpersonal relations made possible by mutual indwelling (163) and so as a replacement of the temple (167), but reference to heavenly hope is more likely.

79. Rightly Scroggs, *Christology*, 58–59; Gnilka, "Christologie," 94–95; Becker, *Johannes*, 147–51; Becker, "Dualismus," 71–87; Becker, "Auferstehung," 147–48; Becker, "Streit der Methoden," 46–47.

80. So Barrett, *John*, 108; cf. Schottroff, *Glaubende*, 272–74.

81. Gnilka, "Christologie," 96–97, 102; Onuki, *Gemeinde*, 41–42; Painter, "John 9," 54; Scroggs, *Christology*, 58–59.

82. So Onuki, *Gemeinde*, 53–54.

83. Against Käsemann, *Letzter Wille*, 114; Evans, "Passion," 65.

84. Becker, "Auferstehung," 149–50.

85. Schnackenburg, *John*, 1.155.

relationship with the person of God through his Son is the constant; beside this it can tolerate side by side both its underlying dualism and traditional elements of eschatology of a very much more diverse nature.

5.1.1.3 Salvation: Conclusion

Salvation is therefore not primarily a place, a reward, a body of knowledge, a gift of powers. Nor is it perceived contractually as a covenant inaugurated or a status restored. Nor is it perceived primarily as the achievement of a sacrifice, or the fruit of the cross and resurrection as in Paul.[86] Nor is it primarily presented on the model of rescue or deliverance. It is presented as the gift of the Son from the Father. By far the most dominant model is that of the Son as envoy of the Father bearing revelatory information. But it is evident that the author is making use of the envoy to make claims not about information, but to present the Son as one who encounters and confronts the world with the offer of a relationship through himself with the Father. He does not make the Father known by imparting information. The author assumes basic knowledge about God. The Son claims an intimacy with the Father, in that sense, knowledge of the Father, and on that basis calls people to believe his claim and so enter a saving relationship with himself and the Father.

Salvation and the "Greater" Event

Accordingly, salvation is present in the person of the Son, the gift of relationship he brings. The Paraclete leads the disciples to greater understanding of the event of the Son's coming. It does not first make the salvation accessible, as though it was present only proleptically in the presence of the Son or as though no one received it during his ministry. Nor is the life first made accessible through Jesus' atoning death.[87] This way of speaking of the work of salvation was known to the author and he uses its imagery from time to time by way of illustration. But it is not dominant and should not be used to deny the saving impact of the Son during his ministry. Nor, as we have seen, should those few passages where Jesus speaks of the gift of life in a future sense (3:14–15; 6:27, 51–58) be made the basis for denying life in the presence

---

86. So rightly Schillebeeckx, *Christ*, 339; Wilckens, "Lebensbrot," 234.
87. Against Müller, *Heilsgeschehen*, 35, 67–70; Thüsing, *Erhöhung*, 132–33; Richter, *Studien*, 43–44, 53, 58–59.

and person of the Son in his ministry. For they predict the availability of life after Easter, particularly in the context of the Eucharist and Son of Man traditions. The manner in which the author perceives the salvation events demands that the life is offered through relationship and this relationship is freely offered in the coming of the Son.

This does not mean that from the standpoint of the post-Easter community the death of Jesus is superfluous. The reality which faced the post-Easter situation was that Jesus' life had come to an end on earth. Had that been anything other than the faithful fulfilment of the divine commission of bearing the revelation of God even to death, then the issue of Jesus' salvific significance would have been called into question. In that sense Jesus' obedience to the end belongs necessarily to the post-Easter proclamation of the message of salvation. In addition the death of Jesus brings this ministry to its climax and becomes the ultimate exposure of the world's sin, Jesus' vindication and the judgment of the world and its ruler. As van der Watt writes: "The essence of their sin is clear: it is not expressed in terms of individual deeds or guilt, but in terms of not accepting (believing in) God as he is revealed in and through Jesus (1:9–11; 5:44–46; 8:24; 10:36–39; 15:23–24)."[88] The centre of salvation remains the person of the Son and life through faith in him.

In the light of this centre we can also see how the author understands the traditional notion of forgiveness of sins. The author does allude to Jesus' death and its role in relation to sins, but for him salvation is much bigger than that and forgiveness is rooted in who Jesus was. Thus forgiveness is primarily the gift of the word and implied in the relationship he offers.[89] Similarly the episode about foot washing symbolises this gift, linking it to the Son's obedience and love from the beginning to the end, not in the sense of foreshadowing a forgiveness not yet available until an act of atonement, but expressing now the gift of cleansing, so that Jesus, then and there, can proclaim them clean.

The central structure of the author's Christology is the pattern of the revealer-envoy. The author employs this to set forth Jesus as the one who calls people to believe his claim and to join in relationship to him and the Father and so find life. This is the event of salvation which reaches its climax in Jesus' death, its vindication in his return to the Father; to this the disciples and the Paraclete bear witness and the Paraclete leads them to greater understanding of its truth. In the following sections we shall explore more

---

88. Van der Watt, "Salvation," 107.
89. So Bultmann, *Theologie*, 408–9; Lattke, *Einheit*, 149; Becker, *Johannes*, 423.

fully the nature of this event, particularly what it implies concerning the nature of the Son.

5.2 The Salvation Event and Pre-existence

A careful examination of the way the author understands the pattern of statements which form the central structure of his Christology has shown that the author has reinterpreted the language of revelation and communication. The salvation event is not literally the Son telling what he has seen and heard, but the presenting of the Father's claim, his personal challenge in the Son, an encounter aimed at the response of faith which enters a relationship with the Father through the Son. Similarly we must ask what role pre-existence plays for the author as he interprets the pattern.

The patterns tells of the Son having seen and heard from the Father in his pre-existence what he has made known on earth. But the fact that in reality the author does not have the Son tell what he has seen and heard, raises the question whether he also means us to take literally the statements about seeing and hearing the Father or in what sense he understood them. And if it is not a passing on of information to which he was privy in pre-existence, how does pre-existence function in relationship to the work of salvation as the author understands it?

5.2.1 Pre-existence–Significant for Johannine Christology?

The question becomes more acute when we note that sometimes the pattern of hearing and seeing the Father is not related to Jesus' pre-existence at all, but is something happening in the present and also in the future. Bultmann made much of this observation in his claim that ultimately the author has demythologised pre-existence, so that in reality it plays no part as such within his Christology at all.[90] Others, like Lütgert, Brun and, more recently, Robinson, make a strong case for taking a large number of those

---

90. Bultmann, *Johannes*, 187–88, 190, 191 n. 5; *Theologie*, 414–15; similarly Cadman, *Open Heaven*, 4–6; cf. also Robinson, *Priority*, 389. Davies, *Rhetoric*, comes unwittingly close to Bultmann (whom she criticises on the basis of misunderstanding), when she writes: "To make sense of the Gospel, it is necessary to understand the language of descent, mission, ascent, arrival and departure not as myth but as metaphors of allegiance" (117); similarly specifically on sending (163–67), giving (167–68), coming and going (170–73), and descending–ascending (174–81).

texts which speak of Jesus' hearing or seeing the Father as references not to pre-existence at all, but to earlier experiences of Jesus on earth.⁹¹ In the following I shall review the relevant texts in the light of our findings thus far, and, in particular, of the insight that not information but encounter forms the central salvation event in John.

5.2.1.1 Pre-existence and 5:19–20

A key text is 5:19–20,

> Ἀπεκρίνατο οὖν ὁ Ἰησοῦς καὶ ἔλεγεν αὐτοῖς· ἀμὴν ἀμὴν λέγω ὑμῖν, οὐ δύναται ὁ υἱὸς ποιεῖν ἀφ᾽ ἑαυτοῦ οὐδὲν ἐὰν μή τι βλέπῃ τὸν πατέρα ποιοῦντα· ἃ γὰρ ἂν ἐκεῖνος ποιῇ, ταῦτα καὶ ὁ υἱὸς ὁμοίως ποιεῖ.
> ὁ γὰρ πατὴρ φιλεῖ τὸν υἱὸν καὶ πάντα δείκνυσιν αὐτῷ ἃ αὐτὸς ποιεῖ, καὶ μείζονα τούτων δείξει αὐτῷ ἔργα, ἵνα ὑμεῖς θαυμάζητε.
> So Jesus replied and told them: "Truly, truly, I tell you, the Son can do nothing of himself, but only what he sees the Father doing; what he does, the Son does these things likewise. For the Father loves the Son and shows him all that he himself is doing, and greater things than these will he show him that you may marvel." (5:19–20)

John 5:30 reads similarly,

> Οὐ δύναμαι ἐγὼ ποιεῖν ἀπ᾽ ἐμαυτοῦ οὐδέν· καθὼς ἀκούω κρίνω, καὶ ἡ κρίσις ἡ ἐμὴ δικαία ἐστίν, ὅτι οὐ ζητῶ τὸ θέλημα τὸ ἐμὸν ἀλλὰ τὸ θέλημα τοῦ πέμψαντός με.
> I can do nothing of myself; as I hear, I judge, and my judgment is just, because I seek not my will, but the will of him who sent me. (5:30)

The Son sees, and the Father shows him in the present, what the Father is doing; and he will do so in the future. The Son hears the Father, and this is the authority for his judgment. Judgment belongs to the "greater things" to be shown the Son according to 5:20.⁹² These texts assume a present seeing

---

91. Lütgert, *Christologie*, 25–30; Brun, "Gottesschau," 1; J. A. T. Robinson, "The Fourth Gospel and the Church's Doctrine of the Trinity," in *Twelve More New Testament Studies* (London: SCM, 1984), 174; Robinson, *Priority*, 368–89; similarly Büchsel, *Johannes*, 15–16; Cadman, *Open Heaven*, 3–4; earlier, D. Willibald Beyschlag, *Neutestamentliche Theologie II* (Halle: Strien, 1896), 417–32.

92. Frey, *Eschatologie*, 2.352, notes that the greater works relate to the work of the post-

The Salvation Event in John

and hearing during the earthly ministry and apparently also a future seeing and hearing on earth.⁹³ Nothing in the context suggests that they refer only to the post-Easter Jesus, as Blank and Thüsing suggest.⁹⁴

5.2.1.2 Past Seeing, Hearing, and Knowing: Pre-existence?

Since this is so, it is possible to argue that passages which refer to such seeing and hearing in the past are also perceived as having taken place on earth, and not during pre-existence at all. These include, it is claimed: "What I have heard from the Father I speak to the world" (8:26); "As my Father taught me, so I speak" (8:28); "I have spoken to you what I have heard from the Father" (8:40); "I have not spoken of myself, but the Father who sent me gave me instruction, what I was to say and speak" (12:49); "All that I have heard from the Father I have made known to you" (15:15); "What we know, we speak, and what we have seen, to that we bear witness" (3:11).⁹⁵

A further argument cited in support of the texts in ch. 8 is the parallel made in 8:38 between Jesus and the Jews: "What I have seen from the Father I speak; and what you have heard from (your) father you do." Clearly the Jews have heard from their father not in any pre-existence, but as human beings on earth and their father is the devil. Accordingly, it is argued, Jesus will have heard from his Father while on earth, if the analogy is to be effective.⁹⁶

Similarly 3:11 includes knowing and seeing of human beings together with the knowing and seeing of the Son himself. It would be strange, it is argued, for the reference in the one case to be to an earthly experience and in the other to a heavenly one.⁹⁷ In 16:13–15 Jesus promises revelation to the disciples through the Spirit while they continue their work. Why, it is argued, should such revelation not have been available to the Son during his earthly ministry?⁹⁸

Easter Jesus, based, as he sees it, on Jesus' saving death (353). Christology rather than eschatology is determinative (398).

93. So Lütgert, *Christologie*, 26–27; Brun, "Gottesschau," 1, 3–4; Büchsel, *Johannes*, 16; Cadman, *Open Heaven*, 4; Robinson, *Priority*, 372; earlier Holtzmann, *Lehrbuch*, 452.

94. Blank, *Krisis*, 117; Thüsing, *Erhöhung*, 213.

95. So Lütgert, *Christologie*, 25–26; Brun, "Gottesschau," 4; Cadman, *Open Heaven*, 4; Holtzmann, *Lehrbuch*, 452.

96. So Lütgert, *Christologie*, 27–28; Brun, "Gottesschau," 4; Cadman, *Open Heaven*, 5; Robinson, *Priority*, 370.

97. So Lütgert, *Christologie*, 30; Brun, "Gottesschau," 1, 17–18; Holtzmann, *Lehrbuch*, 452.

98. So Brun, "Gottesschau," 5.

Some also argue that 3:34-35 should be understood similarly of Jesus' equipping with the Spirit to speak God's word on earth, "Whom God has sent speaks the words of God, for he does not give the Spirit to him by measure. For the Father loves the Son and has given all things into his hands."[99] Accordingly Lyder Brun, reading the longer text, takes 3:32 to refer to an experience on earth: "What he has seen and heard to that he bears witness." Holtzmann had denied this, finding a conflict between the pre-existence tradition found in 3:32 and the tradition of prophetic inspiration in 3:34.[100] But Brun argues, to the contrary, that in the words "of the earth" and "of heaven" (3:31), only a contrast in quality, not one of origin, is expressed, and points to 1:33, where John the Baptist hears words from heaven and speaks them on earth.[101]

Lütgert explains 3:31 on the basis that even on earth the Son can be understood to be in heaven,[102] noting, as does Robinson,[103] that it can also be said of the disciples that they are not "of the earth," but "from above"; though of the Son it refers to eternal generation.[104] He points similarly to 3:13 as indicating Jesus' access to heaven while on earth: "No one has ascended into heaven but the one who descended from heaven,"[105] a text discussed above in 4.3 where we identify the various suggestions about how such an earthly ascent might have been understood, including most recently Ashton's view that the author is adapting transfiguration tradition. Hugo Odeberg explains the passage against the background of Jewish mysticism and proposes that 3:13 refers to a mystical ascent which will, in turn, set a pattern for mystical ascent of the disciples.[106]

Another line of argument runs from 1:18, where the participial phrase, ὁ ὢν εἰς τὸν κόλπον τοῦ πατρός ("the one being in the bosom of the Father"), is read as referring to a permanent state of affairs, including therefore the relationship between Father and Son on earth, so that the participial phrase

---

99. So Lütgert, *Christologie*, 30; Brun, "Gottesschau," 6; Cadman, *Open Heaven*, 6; of receiving revelation on earth, though not denying pre-existence: Strathmann, *Johannes*, 79.

100. Holtzmann, *Lehrbuch*, 452-53.

101. Brun, "Gottesschau," 20-21; similarly Robinson, *Priority*, 371.

102. Barrett, *John*, understands 3:13 similarly (73, 187); Barrett, "Paradox," 110-11; cf. also Dodd, *Interpretation*, 258-59; Kieffer, "L'Espace," 405-406.

103. Robinson, *Priority*, 370-71.

104. Lütgert, *Christologie*, 31, 36-38.

105. Lütgert, *Christologie*, 42, 46-47; similarly Beyschlag, *Neutestamentliche Theologie II*, 100-101; Büchsel, *Johannes*, 16, 53; as possible: Brown, *John*, 17; cf. C. K. Barrett, "Paradox and Dualism," in *Essays on John* (Philadelphia: Westminster, 1982), 98-115, who uses 3:13 with 1:51 to say that the addition to 3:13, "who is in heaven," would be consistent with John's view of the earthly Jesus (110-11).

106. Odeberg, *Fourth Gospel*, 114.

almost takes on a causal quality: "No one has ever seen God; God, the only Son, being in the bosom of the Father, has made him known." Accordingly, it is argued, the basis on which the Son knows the Father is this special relationship and the seeing of the Father in this sense may also have taken place on earth.[107] The view that ὁ ὤν refers to Jesus' earthly life, not just to his present exalted state or present and pre-existent state, is widely held among scholars who do not espouse the approach to pre-existence we are examining.[108]

John 6:46 would, it is argued, also refer to an event on earth: "Not that anyone has seen the Father except he who is from God; he has seen the Father," and similarly 5:37, "You have never heard his voice nor seen his form."[109] Brun also points to the context of 6:46 where Jesus argues that people taught of God come to him (6:45) and also to 8:47, "He who is from God hears the words of God; because of this you do not hear, because you are not from God."[110]

Brun also notes that, while people may hear God and be taught of him on earth, according to the Gospel only the Son sees or has seen God. But, he argues, this cannot mean pre-existent seeing, for it is not unique to the Son to have seen God in heaven. The evangelist, he suggests, was probably fully aware of the wide range of traditions which speak of beings in heaven seeing the face of God. The distinctive seeing denied to all others, he argues, is the seeing of God on earth. Jesus as a man on earth is the sole exception and this is the case because he comes from above. His distinctive origins make it possible for him, as a human being on earth, to see the Father.[111]

This view also claims support from the consistent emphasis during the ministry of the Son's relationship with the Father. On earth he was not left alone, but worked with the Father. On earth he is one with the Father. Surely, it is argued, this must mean more than that he faithfully carried out the Father's commission which he remembered from the days of his pre-existence. Lütgert speaks of a fully conscious communication between Father and Son and Son and Father on earth.[112] Brun prefers to speak of visionary com-

---

107. So Lütgert, *Christologie*, 32; Brun, "Gottesschau," 7–8, 14–16; Beyschlag, *Neutestamentliche Theologie II*, 426; Büchsel, *Johannes*, 16; Cadman, *Open Heaven*, 10; Robinson, *Priority*, 371.

108. Westcott, *John*, 15; Lindars, *Gospel of John*, 99; Käsemann, "Prologue," 163; *Letzter Wille*, 27–28; Schillebeeckx, *Christ*, 361; Beasley-Murray, *John*, 4.

109. So Lütgert, *Christologie*, 34; Brun, "Gottesschau," 7, 10–13, who also takes 8:37-38 in this way (8–9); Holtzmann, *Lehrbuch*, 452; Robinson, *Priority*, 372.

110. Brun, "Gottesschau," 10–11; similarly Robinson, *Priority*, 369–70.

111. Brun, "Gottesschau," 13–14.

112. Lütgert, *Christologie*, 36, 47–48; similarly Büchsel, *Johannes*, 14, 16.

munication similar to what he finds in Philo or is present among inspired prophets who "listen in" on the council of Yahweh.[113] How can the author assume a relationship of oneness exists between Father and Son, such as becomes the model for believers, in which no communication takes place? Had communication between Father and Son ceased at the point of the Son's coming into the world? Is the Son just an envoy a long way from home?

A further argument is found in the common interpretation of 1:51, "You will see heaven opened and the angels of God ascending and descending upon the Son of Man." According to this interpretation Jesus is predicting the revelatory nature of his ministry as a bridge between heaven and earth. It assumes Jesus engages both in receiving and in giving revelation.[114] Bultmann sees in it a symbol of uninterrupted oneness between Father and Son.[115]

5.2.1.3 Significance of Arguments against Pre-existence

The arguments for denying any role of pre-existence in the pattern of revelation deserve fuller attention than they have received in recent research, not least because, as Brun points out, it is in part in response to the issues they raise that Bultmann developed his influential analysis of Johannine Christology.[116] Bultmann responded by declaring statements about pre-existent seeing and hearing and about pre-existence in general as mythological ways of saying that in the Son something beyond this world and beyond human resources is breaking in.[117] The Ἐν ἀρχῇ ("beginning") in 1:1 and ἀπ' ἀρχῆς ("from the beginning") 1 John 1:1 are in effect the same.[118] Before considering such solutions, I first want to re-examine the arguments outlined above for their cogency.

Reviewing the Arguments: Seeing and Hearing

Some of the arguments are particularly unconvincing. To these belong the argument from the analogies between the Jews and the devil, on the one

---

113. Brun, "Gottesschau," 6–8.
114. So Lütgert, *Christologie*, 42; Brun, "Gottesschau," 16 n. 1; Büchsel, *Johannes*, 16; Strathmann, *Johannes*, 53.
115. Bultmann, *Johannes*, 75; similarly Appold, *Oneness*, 53.
116. Brun, "Gottesschau," 1.
117. Bultmann, *Johannes*, 191.
118. Bultmann, *Theologie*, 387.

hand, and the Son and the Father, on the other; and between the disciples and the Son, using 3:11 and parallels. These analogies cannot be pressed beyond the aspects of hearing, allegiance and obedience. There is no indication that the manner and timing of the hearing must be the same, nor that the nature of sonship or of the relationship is identical in each case.

Similarly the argument in relation to 1:18 that God's invisibility relates only to human beings on earth is unconvincing. It is true that the contrast is primarily between Jesus and human beings on earth, but the claim is that the Word made flesh has seen the Father because he was with him in the beginning. The other two passages which speak of the vision of God do so in close relationship to statements about Jesus' pre-existence. "No one has seen the Father except he who is from the Father, he has seen the Father" (6:46).[119] The Son has come from the Father and this must be seen as the ground for the claim that the Son, unlike any other human being, has seen the Father. 5:37–38 is also most naturally understood in this way, "The Father who sent me has borne witness concerning me. His voice you have never heard and his form you have never seen and his word you do not have abiding in you, because in the one he has sent you do not believe."

Seeing and Hearing in the Context of Coming and Being Sent

These claims must be seen and interpreted within the context of the pattern of statements which express the central structure of the author's Christology, as the following sample texts show: "I know him, because I am from him and he sent me" (7:29); "I was born for this and for this I came into the world to bear witness to the truth" (18:37); "I have not spoken of my own accord, but the Father who sent me has given me the command about what I am to say and speak" (12:49); "Now they know that all which you have given me is from you. Because the words which you gave me I have given them, and they have received them and know truly that I came from you and they have believed that you sent me" (17:7–8).[120]

The connection is also very clear in 3:31–32, especially when we follow the shorter reading: "He who comes from above is above all. He who is of the

---

119. Cf. Ashton, *John*, who, based on his interpretation of 3:13 as mystical ascent, denies reference to pre-existence here (175). In "Reflections" he argues that pre-existence came into the Gospel through the late addition of Son of Man sayings (210). It is, however, much more widely attested than that.

120. On the centrality of the notion of sending linked to pre-existence in Johannine Christology see Hahn, *Theologie*, 1.608.

earth is of the earth and of the earth he speaks; he who comes from heaven bears witness to what he has seen and heard." But even the longer text makes the connection evident: "He who comes from heaven is above all. What he has seen and heard to this he bears witness." Similarly in 8:42-44 we see this connection assumed: "If God were your Father, you would love me, for I went out and have come from God; nor have I come of my own accord, but he sent me. Why do you not recognise my message? Because you cannot hear my word. You are of your father, the devil."

5.2.1.4 The Integrity of Time and Space in John's Christology

Such texts as these, which we reviewed extensively in Part One, show that where Jesus speaks of having been taught or having seen or heard the Father in the past, he refers to pre-existence and not to a past event on the earth. This includes the texts like 8:26, 28, 38, 40 cited as arguments above. Nor is there any reason why 3:13 should be an exception and refer to an ascent of the Son of Man while on earth,[121] let alone a constant state of ascending and descending as Lütgert proposes.[122] The reference to ascent is to Jesus' return to the Father as the context shows and the verse is one of a number in the Gospel which contain anachronism (cf. already 3:11). The denial of spatial categories and therefore of categories of movement does not do justice to the Gospel. If the Son remains both in heaven and on earth during his earthly ministry, this would make nonsense of statements of coming and going and rob of any meaning others which imply a movement towards the presence of the Father in heaven as a return to glory. Either the author has completely collapsed the spatial, demythologising it, as Bultmann suggests, or we must take time, place, and movement seriously and consistently.[123]

As far as the phrase ὁ ὢν εἰς τὸν κόλπον τοῦ πατρός ("who is in the bosom of the Father" in 1:18) is concerned, it is best taken as a reference to the present exalted status of Jesus, viewed (like 3:13 and the Baptist's witness in 1:15)[124] from the standpoint of the author,[125] not as a description also of

---

121. Against Odeberg, *Fourth Gospel*, 114.

122. Lütgert, *Christologie*, 42, 46-47.

123. So rightly, Woll, *Johannine Christianity*, 27-28; Reginald H. Fuller, "The Theology of Jesus or Christology? An Evaluation of the Recent Discussion," *Semeia* 30 (1986): 107; against Schillebeeckx, *Christ*, 403; cf. also Robinson, "Christology," 75.

124. So Beutler, *Martyria*, 248; Theobald, *Anfang*, 57; Ignace de la Potterie, "Structure du Prologue de Saint Jean," *NTS* 30 (1984): 363-64, 367.

125. So Thüsing, *Erhöhung*, 209; Schnackenburg, *John 1*, 281; Bühner, *Gesandte*, 376;

The Salvation Event in John

Jesus' earthly relationship with the Father,[126] nor as such, taking εἰς in a dynamic sense to mean turned towards the Father, as de la Potterie and others suggest.[127] It describes the relationship of the Son with the Father in heaven as it now is since Easter and as it was before the Son's coming into the world. In that way it forms an *inclusio* with 1:1-2.

> Ἐν ἀρχῇ ἦν ὁ λόγος, καὶ ὁ λόγος ἦν πρὸς τὸν θεόν, καὶ θεὸς ἦν ὁ λόγος. οὗτος ἦν ἐν ἀρχῇ πρὸς τὸν θεόν.
> In the beginning was the Word and the Word was with God and the Word was God. He was in the beginning with God. (1:1-2)

> Θεὸν οὐδεὶς ἑώρακεν πώποτε· μονογενὴς θεὸς ὁ ὢν εἰς τὸν κόλπον τοῦ πατρὸς ἐκεῖνος ἐξηγήσατο.
> No one has ever seen God. The God, the only Son, who is in the bosom of the Father, he has made him known. (1:18)

At the same time the phrase indicates why the Son can make the Father known: he was with God as the Word and became flesh to make him known. The author assumes a difference between the Son's heavenly being with the Father and his oneness with the Father on earth. This corresponds to our findings on glory and glorification. The Son manifested glory on earth, yet also came from and returned to the glory he had with the Father from the foundation of the world (17:5).

This is not to deny the relationship the Son has with the Father on earth. The Son is not an envoy a long way from home, abandoned by his Father. The Father is present and at work in the works of the Son on earth. They are one. But this no more means that, in the case of Jesus, we should collapse

---

Haenchen, *Johannes*, 132; Theobald, *Anfang*, 119; Painter, "Prologue," 470; earlier Holtzmann, *Lehrbuch*, 450.

126. Against Westcott, *John*, 15; Bultmann, *Johannes*, 56; Käsemann, "Prologue," 163; *Letzter Wille*, 27-28, 124; Lindars, *Gospel of John*, 99; Beasley-Murray, *John*, 4.

127. Ignace de la Potterie, "L'emploi dynamique de εἰς dans S. Jean et ses incidences théologiques," *Bib* 43 (1962): 366-87; de la Potterie, *Vérité*, 73-74; de la Potterie, "Prologue," 369; Moloney, "John 1:18," 65, 67-68. Against this Schnackenburg, *Johannesevangelium*, 2.234; Schnackenburg, "Fleisch," 2 n. 5; Haenchen, *Johannes*, 116; Bruce, *John*, 45; Schnelle, *Christologie*, 233. Caragounis in Jan G. van der Watt and Chrys Caragounis, "A Grammatical Analysis of John 1,1," *Filologia Neotestamentaria* 21 (2008): 137, comments: "Comparisons of this structure with παρά + dative, indicate that πρός + acc. was a late formation which came to be used side by side with the older παρά + dative. The manuscript tradition, too, gives the two expressions πρός + acc. and παρά + dat. as *varia lectiones*. The two structures occur also in lit. after the NT to express normal human relations."

the concept of heaven as the dwelling place of God, than we should in the case of other human beings. There has never been a problem in speaking of a relationship between human beings and God and at the same time believing that this relationship will be richer and fuller in the world to come. The fourth evangelist assumes such a pattern.

Of the remaining arguments, 1:51, which refers to a vision of angels ascending and descending upon the Son of Man, need not refer to the Son as revealer in constantly receiving and giving revelation. It could equally refer to Jesus the revealer being the revelation because of what he has seen and heard already in pre-existence. We prefer, however, to read the verse as a reference to neither, but rather to Jesus' exalted state as Son of Man (see 4.3 above).

John 3:34 need not mean that Jesus gains inspiration for revelation from receiving the Spirit at his baptism, on the analogy with the disciples in 16:13–15. In its present context it cannot be separated from the notion of sending and pre-existence as the basis for revelation: "Whom God sent speaks the words of God, for he does not give the Spirit to him by measure" (3:34 and cf. 3:31–32). Similarly the following verse refers to the Son's pre-existent authorisation in the words "The Father loves the Son and has given all things into his hands."

5.2.1.5 Relating Pre-existence and Continuing Oneness with the Father

The dominant pattern throughout the Gospel is that of the Son's having received revelation in his pre-existence which he brings to the world. Yet this happens only in such a way that the relationship with the Father remains a living one in which communication takes place, at least at the level at which it is possible for human beings to communicate with God, and doubtless more. How do these two aspects relate? The question must be considered in the light of our finding that the language of communication and revelation serves the end of setting forth Jesus as God's Son who presents people not with communication of revealed knowledge, but with himself and through himself with God and his offer of a relationship of allegiance and faith that brings life.

Function of Pre-existent Seeing and Hearing for Christology

Accordingly, statements about pre-existent receiving of revelation serve primarily to underline the fact that the Son has come from the Father, from the

The Salvation Event in John

heavenly unity with the Father. The reference to the pre-existent life with the Father qualifies and validates the Son's claim to speak and act on God's behalf, in his person to offer God himself. Pre-existence remains central for the author's purpose,[128] but he uses the revealer-envoy communication model only as a framework to present the Son's claim. This, then, throws new light on the two exceptions to the normal pattern that statements about seeing and hearing refer to the Son's being with the Father in pre-existence, which have long been noted,[129] namely 5:19–20, 30. These speak in the present tense of Jesus' seeing and hearing, but refer to this not as acquisition of knowledge to be imparted, using the revealer-envoy model, but rather to the Son's ability to judge as the Father judges or to act in accordance with his will. This sounds similar, but it is a different model. Accordingly they should not be made the basis for arguing a different time reference for all other passages and a denial of pre-existence. Nor do they represent a contradiction, as Bultmann supposed.[130]

5.2.2 John 5:19–20, 30 Resolution of a Conflict of Models

When we see that the author is employing the revealer-envoy model in a non-literal sense, the apparent contradiction between statements of this pattern and those like 5:19–20, 30, which focus on the Son's oneness with the Father on earth, is resolved and, with it, one of the major arguments against pre-existence.[131] For in this instance the author is not employing the revealer-envoy pattern, but apprenticeship imagery to describe not primarily revelation, but the giving of life. But ultimately both envoy and apprenticeship family relational imagery serve the same end: to establish the claim that in the Son the Father confronts the world with the opportunity for life.

Real Pre-existence in Space and Time

However, unlike the statements in the revealer-envoy model about information acquisition, those statements which speak of the Son's coming, being

---

128. So Schnackenburg, *Johannesevangelium*, 4.109; Scroggs, *Christology*, 106.
129. So Brown, *John*, 214; Schulz, *Johannes*, 187–88; Beasley-Murray, *John*, 53, 76.
130. Bultmann, *Theologie*, 190–91.
131. For a fuller discussion of the passage with regard to the relationship between the Father and the Son see 5.3 and on the issue of the deviation from envoy Christology here see Loader, "John 5,19–47," 155–64.

sent, and returning show no sign of needing to be taken in a way that robs them of their implied sense of movement in space and time. It would not be consistent to explain the Logos motif, for instance, as expressing only the divine communication in the earthly ministry of Jesus and to deny to it the aspect of pre-existence, as does Dupont,[132] nor to reduce the pre-existent Logos to an anhypostatic Logos which takes hypostatic form in Jesus[133] or enters him at his baptism.[134] Sending statements are not to be reduced to the equivalent of prophetic inspiration,[135] nor, as Mark L. Appold, should we convert statements about Jesus' authorisation into statements about Jesus' continuing relationship with the Father.[136]

The author assumes the pre-existence of the Son[137] and uses it throughout as a basis for asserting the Son's authority to speak and act in a way that confronts the world and offers life in relationship with himself and with the Father. The pre-existence is also assumed in the reference to the descent of Jesus as Son of Man in 3:13,[138] and in 6:62 to his returning to where he was before.[139] Statements like Jesus' existence before Abraham (8:58, hardly to be explained away as a reference to pre-existence of a Jungian "self"),[140] his antedating John the Baptist (1:15, 30), his continuing as Son in the house forever (8:35),[141] his being seen by Isaiah (12:41),[142] his pre-existent glory

---

132. Dupont, *Christologie*, 48–49.

133. Against Robinson, "Trinity," 174; J. A. T. Robinson, "The Use of the Fourth Gospel for Christology Today," in *Christ and Spirit in the New Testament. In Honour of C. F. D. Moule*, ed. B. Lindars and S. S. Smalley (Cambridge: Cambridge University Press, 1973), 75, 77; Robinson, *Priority*, 379–81; cf. also Schillebeeckx, *Christ*, 403, 431; A. E. Harvey, *Jesus and the Constraints of History* (Philadelphia: Westminster, 1982), 178.

134. Against Reginald H. Fuller, "Christmas, Epiphany, and the Johannine Prologue," in *Spirit and Light*, ed. M. L'Engle and W. Green (New York: Seabury, 1976), 70; Piet Schoonenberg, "A Sapiential Reading of John's Prologue," *TheolDig* 33 (1986): 409, 411–12; and most radically, Watson, "Christology," 114–16; cf. Brown, *Beloved Disciple*, 152–53; *Epistles*, 121–22.

135. Against Robinson, "Christology," 75; so rightly de Boer, *Johannine Perspectives*, 114, who observes that the author has transposed prophetic sending and messianic sonship into a higher key through the notion of pre-existence.

136. Appold, *Oneness*, 62.

137. So Haenchen, "Johannesevangelium," 218; Thüsing, *Erhöhung*, 209; Haacker, *Stiftung*, 14; Bühner, *Gesandte*, 378–80; earlier Weiss, *Lehrbuch*, 602, 605–6; Holtzmann, *Lehrbuch*, 451–53.

138. Painter, *Quest*, 332.

139. Reynolds, *Apocalyptic Son of Man*, 160–61.

140. Against Robinson, *Priority*, 389.

141. So Barnabas Lindars, "Slave and Son in John 8:31–36," in *The New Testament Age, Essays in Honor of B. Reicke*, ed. W. C. Weinrich (Macon: Mercer, 1984), 274, 281.

142. Hahn, *Theologie*, 1.621; Burkett, *Son of Man*, 127.

The Salvation Event in John

(17:5, 24) and possibly 8:56[143] and 8:25, if it entails a reference to 1:1,[144] serve only to confirm what is announced in the prologue and presupposed in the central structure of the author's Christology: the Son who was with the Father in the beginning came to make him known.[145]

> John's Christology combines assumptions about the nature of the Son, derived ultimately from wisdom mythology, with the envoy model. The former gives substance to the claim that the Son in his person is God's word and invitation, so that to respond to him is to respond to God. He is thus the light, bread, life, glory, and the revelation of God, that is, to see him is to see the Father. The envoy framework has been adapted to serve that message by drawing attention to the Son's authorisation and commission to come embodying God's word and invitation. It is not dependent for its effectiveness on the assumption of absence, including absence of communication, since what is communicated is not information but the word of invitation to relationship in which is life and the absence is relativised by assumptions about the flexibility of divine spatiality which can assume God's presence through the Spirit while on the journey to the glory of God's heavenly presence.[146]

This throws all the more weight on the nature of this relationship between Father and Son, especially since the revealer-envoy communication model has been shown to be only a motif serving to express this claim. To this we turn in the following section.

5.3 The Nature of the Son in Relation to the Father

The central structure of the author's Christology depends upon the pattern of the revealer-envoy. This serves to underline the Son's claim of a unique relationship with the Father on the basis of which he has come into the world

---

143. So Schnackenburg, *Johannesevangelium*, 2.299; cf. Brown, *John*, 367.
144. Edward L. Miller, "The Christology of John 8,25," *TZ* 36 (1980): 263.
145. McGrath, *Christology*, 223, argues that the idea of pre-existence is associated only with Logos and Son of Man, not with Son or Son of God. He maintains—apart from the questionable demarcation based on titles—"Son" is always implied in statements about sending by the Father. Further, he understands that sending in John in relation to Jesus refers to his having been sent from his pre-existent state. "Son of God," a title still reflecting its origins in royal messianism in John (e.g., 1:49), does not occur in such contexts, but has clearly been integrated by the author into the larger christological structure which accrues the assumption of pre-existence.
146. Loader, "John 5,19–47," 164.

bringing life and light and truth. In this section we shall examine the nature of this unique relationship.

5.3.1 A Relationship Characterised by Love

We begin by noting that throughout the Gospel love is a fundamental characteristic of this relationship. The Father loves the Son. In 3:35 it stands beside statements of equipping and authorisation: "The one whom God sent speaks the words of God, for he does not give the Spirit by measure. The Father loves the Son and has given all things into his hand" (3:34–35). In 5:20 it stands beside the statement that the Father is showing the Son what he is doing. In 10:17 it is said to be in response to the Son's obedient fulfilment of the task given him by the Father to lay down his life that he might take it up again for the sake of the sheep. In 15:9–10 it is the pattern for Jesus, in turn, to give love to his disciples, and for his exhortation that they should remain in that love by keeping his commands, as he remains in that love by keeping the commission given him (cf. also 13:34–35). In 17:23 the goal of the community faith is that its oneness might bring the world to know that the Father sent the Son and that the Father has loved the disciples as he has loved the Son.

The relationship of mutual love between Father and Son is the source and the pattern for the relationships of love which are the goal and content of salvation. The similarity of pattern between the Father's love of the Son and the Son's love of the Father, on the one hand, and the relationships of love between the believers and the Father and the Son, and among believers themselves, on the other, is not a similarity in all respects. For the relationship between Father and Son is primary and pre-existent and the Son, unlike the believers, is pre-existent and unique.

5.3.2 The Prologue—Guide to the Relationship and to the Gospel

How is this unique sonship understood? The author doubtless intends the prologue to offer important information in the light of which the Gospel is to be read, especially information about who the Son is. It was not a puzzle to be understood only at the end of a reading of the Gospel, as it has sometimes become for us. Nor is it the Gospel's first commentary written after it,[147] although many of its major motifs, including its chief motif, Logos,

---

147. Cf. Adolf von Harnack, "Über das Verhältnis des Prologs des vierten Evangeliums

The Salvation Event in John

the theme of Christ and creation, and the incarnation of the Word, to name only a few, do not occur in the rest of the Gospel. Key themes—not least, the motifs associated with Jesus' death—are absent in the prologue.[148] There are, however, significant links with the rest of the Gospel, including the references to Jesus as θεός forming an *inclusio* in 1:1, 18 and 20:28; the motifs of life, light, coming into the world, glory, truth, faith, knowledge, being born, pre-existence, seeing God, and light-darkness dualism,[149] and not least the use of Wisdom mythology which attaches to Jesus motifs originally linked with Torah. It provides the hearer with essential information on the basis of which to understand what follows,[150] including its irony,[151] much as prologues functioned in literature of the time.[152] Without access to the extensive

---

zum ganzen Werk," *ZTK* 2 (1892): 230, who argued the prologue was not to be seen as the key to the Gospel but to prepare the Hellenistic reader. Michael Theobald, *Die Fleischwerdung des Logos: Studien zum Verhältnis des Johannesprologs zum Corpus des Evangeliums und zu 1 Joh*, NTAbh 20 (Münster: Aschendorf, 1988), argued that a redactor added the prologue to counter the Christology behind the conflict in 1 John (295, 491–92), but in his 2009 commentary, *Johannes*, sees it as integral to the evangelist's composition, who uses hymnic tradition to supplement the John the Baptist material of his signs source (101–8). See also Raymond F. Collins, "The Oldest Commentary on the Fourth Gospel," *TBT* 98 (1978): 1771; Peter Hofrichter, *Im Anfang war der "Johannesprolog": Das urchristliche Logosbekenntnis—die Basis neutestamentlicher und gnostischer Theologie*, BU 17 (Regensburg: Pustet, 1986), 13–82. For critical discussion of views seeing the prologue as secondary see Jean Zumstein, "Der Prolog als Schwelle zum vierten Evangelium," in *Der Johannesprolog*, ed. Günter Kruck (Darmstadt: WBG, 2009), 49–75.

148. Noted by Preiss, *Life in Christ*, 10; Beyschlag, *Neutestamentliche Theologie II*, 430–31; Lütgert, *Christologie*, vii; Painter, "Christology and the Farewell Discourses," 48. See also Jensen, *John's Gospel*, 76; Zumstein, "Prolog," 57–58, 61, 62, 69; Ulrich Busse, "Theologie oder Christologie im Johannesprolog?" in *Studies in the Gospel of John and Its Christology: Festschrift Gilbert Van Belle*, ed. J. Verheyden, G. van Oyen, M. Labahn, and R. Bieringer, BETL 265 (Leuven: Peeters, 2014), 35; Beutler, *Johannesevangelium*, 61, 82.

149. Zumstein, "Prolog," 52–55; similarly Christopher Skinner, "Misunderstanding, Christology, and Johannine Characterization: Reading John's Characters through the Lens of the Prologue," in *Characters and Characterization in the Gospel of John*, ed. C. Skinner, LNTS 461 (London: Bloomsbury, 2012), 127.

150. So Holtzmann, *Lehrbuch*, 446; Haacker, *Stiftung*, 17–18; Wengst, *Gemeinde*, 101–3; Hartwig Thyen, "Aus der Literatur zum Johannesevangelium," *ThR* 39 (1974): 1–69, 222–52, 289–330; Schnelle, *Christologie*, 246; Bultmann, *Johannes*, 1; Pollard, *Christology*, 13–14; Dunn, "John," 334; Zumstein, "Prolog," 75; Johannes Beutler, "Der Johannes-Prolog—Ouvertüre des Johannesevangeliums," in *Der Johannesprolog*, ed. G. Kruck (Darmstadt: WBG, 2009), 78–82; Beutler, *Johannesevangelium*, 61, 82; Busse, "Theologie oder Christologie," 35; cf. Beyschlag, *Neutestamentliche Theologie II*, 430–31; Lütgert, *Christologie*, vii.

151. Culpepper, *Anatomy*, 108; Skinner, "Misunderstanding," 112, who notes that "apart from the Beloved Disciple there is no character who fully grasps what the audience has learned from the Prologue."

152. So Zumstein, "Prolog," 59–63; Harris, *Prologue and Gospel*, 189, 195; Jo-Ann A. Brant,

field of meanings shared by the author and his readers or hearers, we must be satisfied with constant cross references within the material of the Gospel and with a consideration of a series of key passages before being able to place the statements of the prologue and others in the Gospel of like kind within what we might claim is near to the Johannine perspective. Accordingly we shall look in particular at the prologue itself; the disputes with the Jews in 5:17–47 and 10:22–39; Jesus' words to his disciples in 14:8–11; and his prayer in ch. 17. In the course of doing so we shall also take into account other references and more general considerations.

5.3.3 The Word Was "God"

The Gospel begins with the words,

> Ἐν ἀρχῇ ἦν ὁ λόγος, καὶ ὁ λόγος ἦν πρὸς τὸν θεόν, καὶ θεὸς ἦν ὁ λόγος. In the beginning was the Word and the Word was with God and the Word was God. (1:1)

"The Word was θεός" must not be isolated and made into a simple equation: the Word was God. Grammatically this is a possible translation, but not the only one. The statement's meaning, and so its translation, must be determined by its context. It could also be translated: "the Word was a god" or "the Word was divine." Grammatical considerations alone fail to decide the question, since all three translations can be defended on grammatical grounds. Chrys Caragounis writes:

> When John wrote καὶ θεὸς ἦν ὁ λόγος, he simply meant "and *God* was the Word." This, expressed according to the English idiom, becomes: "and the Word was God," although the emphasis of the original on θεός is gone. This is the best we can do in English, which, as has already been hinted at, is not an adequate translation of the original. But the reason for this, as we have seen above, is due to the fact that the uses of the Greek article do not coincide with those of the English article.[153]

Dialogue and Drama: Elements of Greek Tragedy in the Fourth Gospel (Peabody: Hendrickson, 2004), 17, who notes significant resemblance to those of Euripides. Morna D. Hooker, "The Johannine Prologue and the Messianic Secret," *NTS* 21 (1974): 45, writes of it as enabling one to resolve the Gospel's "messianic secret"; similarly Busse, "Theologie oder Christologie," 13–15.

153. Van der Watt and Caragounis, "Grammatical Analysis," 123. See also Westcott, *John*, 3; E. C. Colwell, "A Definite Rule for the Use of the Article in the Greek New Testament," *JBL*

5.3.3.1 The Word Was God?

Against the first of these interpretations ("the Word was God") is the fact that the author has just said that the Word was "with" God.[154] If "Word" means little more than "words," then it would be conceivable that the author could say: God's words were with him; they are, as his words, part of God himself, in that sense, they are God. Dupont comes near to this in claiming that the Logos concept refers not to a person but to God's communication of himself.[155] But the author goes on to speak of the Word as a person distinct from God, so that this must be assumed also in the opening verses.

Nor is it likely that the author intends in his opening statement to make a gradual approach to what he wishes to say, so that "the Word was with God" is merely a step along the way to the statement "the Word was God." For it is precisely "the Word was with God" which is repeated in 1:2.

5.3.3.2 The Word Was a God?

The other two translations fit the context more smoothly at one level. Yet their evaluation cannot take place without our making assumptions about the author's wider frame of reference.[156] In particular it is unlikely, given his context within the Christian community and its roots in Judaism, that he would mean that there is more than one God.[157] Langbrandtner reckons with this as the position of the redactor, whereas the *Grundschrift* had thought of

---

52 (1933): 21; C. F. D. Moule, *An Idiom-Book of New Testament Greek* (Cambridge: Cambridge University Press, 1960), 115–16; Philip B. Harner, "Qualitative Anarthrous Predicate Nouns. Mark 15:39 and John 1:1," *JBL* 92 (1973): 75–87; B. A. Mastin, "A Neglected Feature of the Christology of the Fourth Gospel," *NTS* 22 (1975): 35–36; Haenchen, *Johannes*, 118; Bruce, *John*, 31; D. A. Fennema, "John 1.18: 'God the Only Son,'" *NTS* 31 (1985): 128–31; Otfried Hofius, "Struktur und Gedankengang des Logos Hymnus," *ZNW* 78 (1987): 16–17.

154. So Bauer, *Johannes*, 6; Schnackenburg, "Fleisch," 3; Barrett, "Father," 23; Bruce, *John*, 31; Theobald, *Anfang*, 43–44; Hofius, "Struktur," 16; Mastin, "Neglected Factor," 36; Fennema, "God the Only Son," 129–31. Contrast also the translation in Schillebeeckx, *Christ*, 317, "God was the Word."

155. Dupont, *Christologie*, 48–49.

156. See also Caragounis in van der Watt and Caragounis, "Grammatical Analysis," 137, who writes: "The author wanted to emphasize θεός, that is why he put that word first. It is anarthrous because it is predicate. But this for a Greek does not mean 'a God' (which would have been θεός τις or εἷς θεός), nor does it mean 'the God' (ὁ θεός). It means simply 'God.'"

157. So Schnelle, "Trinitarisches Denken," 378.

Jesus more as an extension of God into the world,[158] but such a view on the part of the redactor is unlikely and unsupported elsewhere. It is true, on the most natural reading of the text, that there are two beings here: God and a second who was θεός. This second is related to God in a manner that shows God is the absolute over against which the second is defined. They are not presented as two equal gods.[159]

5.3.3.3 The Word Was Divine?

This leads us to consider the third translation, "divine," the equivalent of θεῖος, suggested already by Origen,[160] and represented often by the phrase "Gott von Art" or "God of a kind."[161] Should the author have been concerned to say the Word was divine, why did he write θεός and not the more usual adjective θεῖος?[162] The order of 1:1c and the lack of the article may be idiomatic in relation to the use of predicate nouns, as E. C. Colwell suggests,[163] or it may, in addition, reflect an emphasis on quality shared without exact reciprocity.[164] This would suggest that the focus here lies not on the person, but on the quality or nature of the Word. Schnackenburg points to 1 John 5:20 ("We know that the Son of God has come and has given us understanding, so that we may know the truth and we are in the truth, in his Son, Jesus Christ. He is the true God and eternal life") and understands the use of θεός for Jesus as expressing that in him God reveals himself and that he has the same nature as the Father.[165]

---

158. Langbrandtner, *Weltferner Gott*, 40–42.

159. So rightly Cullmann, *Christologie*, 317; Schnackenburg, *John*, 1.234-35; Theobald, *Anfang*, 43-45; Fennema, "God the Only Son," 130.

160. Cited in Mastin, "Neglected Factor," 35.

161. So Schulz, *Johannes*, 19; Haenchen, *Johannes*, 117-18. Van der Watt in van der Watt and Caragounis, "Grammatical Analysis," 134, writes: "It seems that the translation 'the Word is divine' is plausible and acceptable, as long as it is interpreted in light of the theology of John and not in light of general thoughts about the divine."

162. So Dodd, *Interpretation*, 280; similarly Schnackenburg, *John*, 1.234-35; Theobald, *Anfang*, 43-44, 47; Hofius, "Struktur," 17.

163. Colwell, "The Use of the Article," 21.

164. So Westcott, *John*, 3; Moule, *Idiom Book*, 115-16; Harner, "Qualitative Anarthrous Predicate Nouns," 75-87; Mastin, "Neglected Factor," 35-36; Fennema, "God the Only Son," 129-30; Beasley-Murray, *John*, 10-11; Hofius, "Struktur," 16-17.

165. Schnackenburg, "Fleisch," 3; Barrett, *John*, 156; Bruce, *John*, 31.

5.3.3.4 What Was "Was"?

But what does "nature" or "quality" mean in this context? The New English Bible translates, "what God was, the Word was." It still leaves open the question: and what and how was that? Brown is right in pointing out that we are dealing with the language of doxology here.[166] Can we go beyond Bultmann's statement that here is paradox?[167] Is, as Haenchen argues, the anarthrous θεός another indication of subordination of the Son to the Father in the Gospel?[168] It would be easy to read 1:1–3 in isolation as a statement that the Logos had once been with, indeed been part of God and had ceased to be so, a kind of emanation, but passages such as 17:5, 24 and those considered at the beginning of this discussion indicate much more of a personal relationship of union and love. The claim of shared originality (in the beginning)[169] and the absence of any notion of the Son Logos as, for instance, "firstborn" or "first created" being, normally associated with Wisdom/Logos tradition, is astounding. It is no surprise that such statements provoke christological reflection in subsequent centuries. But our task must be to interpret as far as possible their meaning within the Gospel without reading back into the text later attempts at a solution.

The nature of the relationship of Son and Father in the Fourth Gospel must rest on more than 1:1 and its grammatical interpretation. The term θεός is applied similarly to Jesus in 1:18, with which it forms an *inclusio*, and comes also in the confession of Thomas in 20:28. But the issue is much wider than the use of θεός even in the prologue, and presents itself as a repeated focus of contention, as the Son makes his claims and the Jews make counter-claims accusing him of ditheism, an accusation constantly repudiated. But we return first to the prologue as presupposition and prelude to the Gospel.

5.3.4 Analogous Relationship in Logos Wisdom Torah Tradition

It is widely recognised that the motif, Word, Logos, belongs within a tradition of thought reaching back to such passages as Prov 8:22–31 and reflecting speculation about wisdom or logos as the highest heavenly power in God's service,[170] and as active in creation. One strand of this tradition identifies

---

166. Brown, *John*, 1047.
167. Bultmann, *Johannes*, 16.
168. Haenchen, *Johannes*, 118.
169. So Theobald, *Anfang*, 49: "Gleichursprünglichkeit."
170. So Craig A. Evans, *Word and Glory: On the Exegetical and Theological Background*

heavenly wisdom with Torah, Law, and so personifies Torah (Sir 24:3-10, 19-23; Bar 3:29-4:2).[171] Wisdom seeks a place to dwell and finds it in Israel and its temple.[172] In this stream Torah is God's and in that sense is God. It is not thought of literally as a person distinct from God, as we have it in the Fourth Gospel, but remains a personification. A related tradition is preserved in the *Parables of Enoch* where Wisdom seeks a place and finds none (1 En 42:1-2), a stance closer to what we find in the prologue (1:10-12).[173] Closer to the notion of Wisdom or the Logos as a person is also the stream which finds expression in Hellenistic Judaism (Wis 7:22-29; Philo).[174] This belongs within a wider tendency in Judaism to speak of the highest beings under God—sometimes to the extent that the kind of interchangeability already present in the OT between the angel of the Lord and the Lord, which Justin later exploited so fully as a christological argument, extended to other high beings—including the Logos.[175] Incipient Gnosticism doubtless heightened this tendency. It, too,

---

of John's Prologue, JSNTSup 89 (Sheffield: Sheffield Academic Press, 1993), 77-114; Zumstein, "Prolog," 64; Beutler, "Johannes-Prolog," 84-85; Glicksman, "Beyond Sophia," 83-101, who notes however that it is never said of Sophia that she becomes incarnate (89), is the truth (90) or life (91) or is universal (91) or is an example (100), so that the author seeks to portray Jesus as "the new *and improved* Sophia" (99). Scott, *Sophia*, 159, sees the author countering identification of Wisdom with Torah. See also Bennema, *Saving Wisdom*, 180, who writes of the Spirit as "life-giving cognitive agent, as the agent of life-bearing wisdom and understanding." Bauckham, "Monotheism," 149-51, argues that the author avoids compromising Jewish monotheism by retelling Gen 1:1-4 in 1:1-5 and referring to God's word impersonally as in Psalm 33:6, a use of "word" which all Jews would recognize. See also Painter, "Prologue," 41-42.

171. See Schnackenburg, *John*, 1.484-85; Brown, *John*, 523-24; Borgen, *Bread from Heaven*, 104; Weder, "Menschwerdung," 340; Dunn, "John," 332-33; Painter, "John 9," 49-50; Ashton, *Fourth Gospel*, 383. On the possible influence of rabbinic traditions concerning the Memra: C. T. R. Hayward, "The Holy Name of the God of Moses and the Prologue of the Fourth Gospel," *NTS* 25 (1978): 16-23; Theobald, *Anfang*, 46; Reim, "Targum," 5-6; Daniel Boyarin, "The Gospel of the Memra: Jewish Binitarianism and the Prologue to John," *HTR* 94 (2001): 243-84; Hurtado, *Lord Jesus Christ*, 366, 381-86; cf. Barrett, *John*, 153, who deems this "a blind alley."

172. Ashton, *Fourth Gospel*, 366-83.

173. Charles H. Talbert, "'And the Word Became Flesh': When?" in *The Future of Christology*, ed. A. J. Malherbe and W. A. Meeks (Minneapolis: Fortress, 1993), 47.

174. See Bultmann, "Prologue," 20-30; Dodd, *Interpretation*, 54-73; Schnackenburg, *John*, 1.485-87; Brown, *John*, 521-23; Theobald, *Anfang*, 98-109; Eugen Ruckstuhl, "Kritische Arbeit am Johannesprolog," in *The New Testament Age: Essays in Honor of B. Reicke*, ed. W. C. Weinrich (Macon: Mercer, 1984), 454; Dunn, *Christology*, 242, 344-45, 349 arguing, I think, unconvincingly that all uses before John are metaphorical; "John," 330-31; cf. Alan F. Segal, "Pre-Existence and Incarnation: A Response to Dunn and Holladay," *Semeia* 30 (1984): 92-94; Fuller, "Theology," 110-11.

175. See further Fuller, "Theology," 110-11; Talbert, "Descending and Ascending Re-

The Salvation Event in John

used the Sophia/Logos speculation.[176] In Philo the Logos is not only portrayed as a person, the highest heavenly being in the service of God, but can also be called θεός, a second god (*Somn.* 1.229–230; *Leg.* 3.207–208; *QG* 2.62).[177] This is all the more interesting since Philo clearly does not understand this as compromising monotheism, which he stoutly defends.[178] Rather the bearing of God's name seems related to the bearing of God's power and functions.[179]

Further Analogies: Angels, Christ, Messiah, Rulers

A similar transfer of God's name to his highest servants is evident in circles of Jewish apocalyptic.[180] It sometimes meant that heavenly beings would be seen as being authorised to exercise divine functions such as the judging Melchisedek in 11QMelch, where "the acceptable day of the Lord" in Isa 61:2 becomes "the acceptable year of Melchisedek" (11QMelch ii 9). The *Apocalypse of Abraham* has the angel Iaoel speak in God's name as one sent by God to Abraham (Apoc.Ab. 8–17).[181] Philo could also use it of Moses (*Mos.* 1.148–58).[182] It also became important within christological traditions of the church already in the period of the New Testament, most notably in the Philippian hymn, where Jesus is given "the name which is above every name, that at the name of Jesus every knee should bow and every tongue confess, that Jesus Christ is KYRIOS, to the glory of God the Father" (Phil 2:11).[183] The practice of giving divine epithets to human rulers was widespread and finds its particular expression in Israel when the king is addressed not only as "Son of God" (Ps 2:7), but also as "God" (Ps 45:6-7). It became attached also to the hope for a future royal figure (Isa 9:6). Within the context of Christian messianic tradition it also came to be applied to Jesus (Heb 1:8–9).[184]

---

deemer," 439; Jarl E. Fossum, "Jewish-Christian Christology and Jewish Mysticism," *VigChr* 37 (1983): 260–87.

176. See esp. R. McL. Wilson, "Nag Hammadi and the New Testament," *NTS* 28 (1982): 298; Craig A. Evans, "On the Prologue and the Trimorphic Protenoia," *NTS* 27 (1981): 399.

177. So Dodd, *Interpretation*, 280; Bauer, *Johannes*, 6; Haenchen, "Johannesevangelium," 218; *Johannes*, 116; Schnelle, *Christologie*, 234; Fuller, "Theology," 110–11; cf. Theobald, *Anfang*, 43–45.

178. So Lindars, *Gospel of John*, 77.

179. So Hurtado, *Lord Jesus Christ*, 388.

180. See Hengel, *Sohn Gottes*, 73–76; Hurtado, *Lord Jesus Christ*, 361.

181. On this see Ashton, *Fourth Gospel*, 87.

182. Theobald, "Gott, Logos und Pneuma," 353.

183. Hurtado, *Lord Jesus Christ*, 388.

184. See Loader, *Sohn und Hohepriester*, 25–26.

Logos, Wisdom, Torah, and the Gospel

The parallels which share most in common with the prologue, however, are those related to Wisdom or Logos. While there is reference to Torah in the final verses of the prologue and many of the images used of Jesus in the Gospel were frequently used of Torah in these contexts,[185] the prologue clearly differentiates Jesus as Logos (Wisdom) from Torah in 1:14-18.[186] The present tense "shines" in 1:5 followed by the reference to John the Baptist in 1:6-8, and the claim that only those responding to the Word could become God's children (1:12-13) make it likely that the author understands the prologue, from at least 1:5 onwards, as referring to the Logos coming in Jesus,[187] not to prior appearances of the Logos in Israel's history.[188] The Logos is here no personification and that is true already in the opening verses of the prologue which have string parallels with passages which use motifs of Wisdom or Logos in relation to creation and the beginning of time. The presence both of the creation and the visitation traditions associated with Wisdom underlines the presence of the Wisdom or Logos tradition in the prologue. The tradi-

---

185. So Brown, *John*, cxxii-cxxv; Weder, "Menschwerdung," 340; Painter "John 9," 49-50; Reim, "Targum," 5-6.

186. Loader, "Law and Ethics," 143-58; Coloe, *God Dwells with Us*, 62; cf. Braine, "Jewishness," 116, who see the author identifying Jesus with Torah; similarly Keener, *John*, who writes: "playing on the link between Torah and Wisdom, the Fourth Gospel presents the logos of its prologue as Torah" (360, similarly 281).

187. See also Beutler, "Johannes-Prolog," 84-89; Theobald, *Johannes*, 1.134-35; *Fleischwerdung*, 371-72; Hahn, *Theologie*, 1.615; Thyen, *Johannesevangelium*, 84; Georg Strecker, *Theologie des Neuen Testaments* (Berlin: de Gruyter, 1995), 501; Gail O'Day, "The Word Become Flesh: Story and Theology in the Gospel of John," in *What Is John?: Volume II; Literary and Social Readings of the Fourth Gospel*, SBLSym 7 (Atlanta: Scholars, 1998), 70; Michaels, *John*, 56, who writes: "What is striking is that he passes over the whole 'biblical' period (what Christians today call the 'Old Testament') in silence" (similarly 63-64).

188. The position represented in the Greek fathers and much of church tradition and in recent times again, for instance, by Walther Eltester, "Der Logos und sein Prophet," in *Apophoreta. Festschrift für E. Haenchen*, BZNW 30 (Berlin: de Gruyter, 1964), 124-34; Haenchen, *Johannes*, 120-33; Hofius, "Struktur," 21; Kysar, *Jesus*, 17; Martin Hengel, "The Prologue of the Gospel of John as the Gateway to Christological Truth," in *The Gospel of John and Christian Theology*, ed. R. Bauckham and C. Mosser (Grand Rapids: Eerdmans, 2008), 272-82; Charles H. Talbert, *Reading John: A Literary and Theological Commentary on the Fourth Gospel and the Johannine Epistles* (New York: Crossroad, 1992), 67, 71-72; Boyarin, "Gospel of the Memra," 262-72, who sees in 1:1-5 a Jewish hymn and in 1:6-18 a Christian expansion; Beasley-Murray, *John*, 1868; Scott, *Sophia*, 104-5; Wilckens, *Johannes*, 29-32. For the likely meaning of the original tradition used by the author see Theobald, *Anfang*, 109-15; Rudolf Schnackenburg, "Logos-Hymnus und johanneischer Prolog," *BZ* 1 (1957): 84-90; Onuki, *Gemeinde*, 105; Ruckstuhl, "Prolog," 452-53; Painter, *Quest*, 137-39.

The Salvation Event in John

tion of Wisdom in creation is attested elsewhere in early Christian hymnic tradition (Col 1:15-16; Heb 1:2-3). Gospel tradition also attests the motif of Wisdom coming with the offer of life like Torah in Sirach 51 (Matt 11:28-30; cf. Sir 51:23-27) or sending prophets (Luke 11:49-51 as Wisdom, but in Matt 23:34 identified with Jesus himself; cf. also Matt 11:19; par. Luke 7:35).

The prologue stands within the stream of Wisdom and Logos. This stream also influences the imagery of the rest of the Gospel elsewhere. Without clarifying further the context in which the stream influences the Fourth Gospel (conflict with the synagogue, influence from speculative Jewish Christianity or contact with early Gnosticism), we can hold to the high probability that this stream lies beneath the prologue.[189] Within this stream, at least in Philo, θεός had been transferred as a title to the Logos without compromise of monotheism. This procedure is also by no means without parallel in Judaism and Christianity. We may with some confidence assert that this also forms the background for the author's statement that "the Word was θεός."

Divine hypostases such as Wisdom, Name, Logos, and Spirit—that derive substantially from divine attributes—are to be distinguished from heavenly divine beings such as angels and the Son of Man of the Parables of Enoch. They should also be distinguished from divinised figures like kings. For hypostases such as Wisdom, Name, Logos, and Spirit reflect a part of the divine being of God, thus both "with God" and "God" in the beginning. Indeed, in that sense, God was never without Wisdom, Name, Logos and Spirit. There is an ontological connection. John's integration of traditions about the Son of Man within a Christology that identifies Jesus as the Logos and employs the family imagery of Father and Son thus goes beyond seeing his exaltation and glorification as reinstatement of his divine being as Son of Man. It describes it as a return to the glory he shared with the Father before the world began, as in 17:5, an echo of 1:1-2.

5.3.5 The λόγος - θεός Son in the Prologue

We are therefore probably correct to assume that the use of the title θεός for the Logos in 1:1 involves at least the understanding that the Logos is in the unique position of exercising functions and powers which belong to God. This would make good sense of the juxtaposition of statements in 1:1-2 and

---

189. It is not clear to me that the use of the Logos/Wisdom tradition was an attempt "to serve as part of a defence of the messiahship of Jesus as understood by many, if not indeed most or all, early Christians," as McGrath, *Christology*, 145, suggests.

in no way jeopardise monotheism.¹⁹⁰ Within the NT the closest parallel outside Johannine literature would be the use of κύριος for Jesus in Phil 2:11. This understanding of 1:1 also coheres well with the way the Gospel presents the Son as primarily making the claim that a response to him is a response to God and as being the bearer of light and life and truth, images of what comes from God, associated in Jewish tradition with Torah understood as Wisdom. In John, Wisdom and Logos are identified not with Torah but with the Son as its embodiment.¹⁹¹ But such an evaluation must wait until other passages have been considered.

If the sense in which the Logos is θεός is to be explained by analogy with the model of Logos and Wisdom, there remains the question: of what nature is then the Logos according to John? On what basis does the Logos bear these powers and functions? Was he thought of as the highest power under God, God's image and reflection, his firstborn, as Philo thought of the Logos, and the Book of Wisdom spoke of Wisdom (7:1–14), terms also used of Jesus in NT hymnic material elsewhere? Was he thought of as the highest angel, or as a being of unique kind, or as a being one with the Father in substance? Is his exercise of divine functions and powers rooted in his nature or in some way the result of authorisation, and, where the latter motif is present, how is it understood? Is it just a symbol? These questions of the Gospel's Christology must not be handled in abstract or answered from the annals of later christological discussion independent of close examination of the Gospel itself.

5.3.5.1 The λόγος - θεός Son in the Prologue: 1:1–13

John 1:2 repeats the statement that the Logos was with God and so confirms that the Logos is thought of primarily as a being distinct from God: "he was in the beginning with God" (οὗτος ἦν ἐν ἀρχῇ πρὸς τὸν θεόν). The repetition suggests that the emphasis is on primordial togetherness, and the closing verse of the prologue, which forms an *inclusio*, matches this emphasis:

Θεὸν οὐδεὶς ἑώρακεν πώποτε·
μονογενὴς θεὸς ὁ ὢν εἰς τὸν κόλπον τοῦ πατρὸς ἐκεῖνος ἐξηγήσατο.

190. Busse, "Theologie oder Christologie," 3–6, suggests that the use of θεός in 1:1 reflects the way he is viewed from the perspective of humanity, namely as the Creator-God, whereas from a divine perspective he is God only in a derivative sense. He summarises 1:1 in that sense as meaning the Logos was God in relation to the world.

191. Pryor, *John*, 123; van der Watt, "Salvation," 110–11; Glicksman, "Beyond Sophia," 91–95.

The Salvation Event in John

No one has ever seen God;
God, the only Son, who is in the bosom of the Father, he has made him known. (1:18)

We shall return to this statement below.

John 1:3-4 tells of the function which the Logos bore as the one through whom all things were made.

πάντα δι' αὐτοῦ ἐγένετο,
καὶ χωρὶς αὐτοῦ ἐγένετο οὐδὲ ἕν.
ὃ γέγονεν ἐν αὐτῷ ζωὴ ἦν,
καὶ ἡ ζωὴ ἦν τὸ φῶς τῶν ἀνθρώπων·
All things were made (came about) through him,
And without him not one thing was made (came about).
What was made (came about) in him was life,
And the life was the light of all people. (1:3-4)

It is possible to take the words at the end of 1:3 not with 1:4 but with what precedes, so that 1:3b would read: "And without him not one thing was made (came about),[192] which has been made (come into being)." The staircase parallelism favours the former division. While one division has life having come about in the Logos and the other simply has it located in the Logos, the import of the statement is that Logos brought life and light to all people. While one might read this at the level of making existence possible, it is better understood as referring already here to the gift of eternal life that the Logos was able to offer. Accordingly, John 1:5 refers not to the continued sustenance of created life, but to what the Logos brought in Christ and so still shines for all as a possibility.[193]

καὶ τὸ φῶς ἐν τῇ σκοτίᾳ φαίνει, καὶ ἡ σκοτία αὐτὸ οὐ κατέλαβεν.
And the light shines in the darkness and the darkness has not accepted it. (1:5)

This best refers to Jesus' rejection.[194] Whether read in this way, or as others

---

192. Ashton, *John*, insists that "the standard rendering of John 1:3, 'all things were made through him' is simply wrong" (149), similarly 146-47; and should read "came to pass," referring to God's plan for humankind (154-55). Wisdom tradition, as in Col 1:16, supports the sense, coming into being, becoming, as in 1:14, rather than coming to pass.

193. So Beutler, *Johannesevangelium*, 88: John 1:5 is about history not just pre-history.

194. So Käsemann, "Prologue," 165-66; Schnackenburg, *John*, 1.227; Schnackenburg, "Pro-

prefer, with reference to the Logos's work in creation before the incarnation,[195] the functions exercised and the qualities borne (life and light) are those belonging to God himself. In 1:6-13 the same assumption is present, again, whether these verses refer already to the Logos in Jesus from his incarnation onwards or, less likely, only to pre-incarnational activity. The Logos stands in the place of God. Yet the distinction is preserved. Faith leads to people becoming not children of the Logos, but children of God.[196]

5.3.5.2 The λόγος - θεός Son in the Prologue: 1:14-18

We shall examine John 1:14-18 in greater detail in discussing the question of Jesus' humanity, but for the present context we note that the Logos tents among his people much as God tents among his people in the wilderness. This motif already belongs to the stream about Wisdom, and elsewhere tradition also speaks of God's Torah or shekinah or glory descending to dwell with his people (Sir 24:3-10, 19-23; Bar 3:29-4:2; cf. 1 En. 42:1-2). There is no confusion of being. The glory of the Son is "glory as of the μονογενοῦς of the Father." This is more than "glory like that of a father's only son," which Robinson and NRSV suggest,[197] for this would be a bland anticlimax. Jesus' glory is related to his being the unique and only Son. It is a derived glory.

The use of μονογενής, "the only one of his kind," for the Logos implies unique sonship (μονογενής of the Father).[198] John 3:16 confirms this

---

log," 40, 42; Ruckstuhl, "Prolog," 452-53; Theobald, *Anfang*, 117-26; Onuki, *Gemeinde*, 42; Ellis, *Genius*, 22; Beutler, *Johannesevangelium*, 86, prefers "comprehend" to "overcome."

195. Schnelle, *Johannes*, 35, of the author's tradition.

196. I am not convinced that 1:13 originally had a singular verb and so referred to Jesus' birth. Cf. Matthew Vellanickel, *The Divine Sonship of Christians in the Johannine Writings*, AnBib 72 (Rome: BibInst, 1977), 112-32; Boismard and Lamouille, *Jean*, 72; de la Potterie, *Vérité*, 206. So M. Mees, "Joh 1,12.13 nach frühchristlicher Überlieferung," *BZ* 29 (1985): 107-15; John W. Pryor, "Of the Virgin Birth or the Birth of Christians? The Text of John 1:13 Once More," *NovT* 27 (1985): 296-318. Hofrichter has since modified his support for the singular reading expressed in Peter Hofrichter, *Nicht aus Blut sondern monogen aus Gott geboren*, FB 31 (Würzburg: Echter, 1978), and argues now for the singular reading having belonged to the original pre-Johannine prologue to which he attributes then unbelievable influence on Christianity and Gnosticism (Peter Hofrichter, *Im Anfang war der Johannesprolog*, BU 17 [Regensburg: Pustet, 1986], 45-54).

197. Robinson, "Christology," 70; Robinson, *Priority*, 321; also citing Dodd in approval: Robinson, "Christology," 78 n. 99. See also the criticism of de la Potterie, *Vérité*, 178.

198. So Ferdinand Hahn, "Beobachtungen zu Joh 1:18, 34," in *Studies in New Testament Language and Text. In Honour of G. D. Kilpatrick*, ed. J. K. Elliott (Leiden: Brill, 1976), 241-44; de la Potterie, *Vérité*, 189-90; John V. Dahms, "John's Use of *monogenēs* Reconsidered," *NTS* 29 (1983): 228, 230; Fennema, "God the Only Son," 126-27.

The Salvation Event in John

where μονογενής is used as an adjective directly qualifying "Son." This verse is related to a tradition evident elsewhere in the NT where the adjective ἀγαπητός ("beloved") expresses the uniqueness of Jesus' sonship (Mark 1:11; 9:7; 12:6; cf. Col 1:13; Eph 1:6; Rom 8:32).[199] It is because of this unique relationship of the Son to the Father that he is the bearer of light and life, and here: glory, glory as of the unique Son of the Father. The closest parallel in the Gospel is 17:22, "The glory you have given to me I have given to them" (κἀγὼ τὴν δόξαν ἣν δέδωκάς μοι δέδωκα αὐτοῖς). John 1:16 belongs with 1:14, δόξαν ὡς μονογενοῦς παρὰ πατρός, πλήρης χάριτος καὶ ἀληθείας ("glory as of the unique Son of the Father, full of grace and truth") . . . ὅτι ἐκ τοῦ πληρώματος αὐτοῦ ἡμεῖς πάντες ἐλάβομεν καὶ χάριν ἀντὶ χάριτος ("Because of his fullness we have all received, even one gift of grace in place of another gift of grace"). This is also close to what we find in 5:26–27:

> ὥσπερ γὰρ ὁ πατὴρ ἔχει ζωὴν ἐν ἑαυτῷ,
> οὕτως καὶ τῷ υἱῷ ἔδωκεν ζωὴν ἔχειν ἐν ἑαυτῷ.
> καὶ ἐξουσίαν ἔδωκεν αὐτῷ κρίσιν ποιεῖν,
> ὅτι υἱὸς ἀνθρώπου ἐστίν.
> As the Father has life in himself,
> so he has also granted the Son to have life in himself
> and he has given him authority to make judgment,
> because he is the Son of Man. (5:26–27)

Light, life, glory, grace, and truth all describe qualities which derive ultimately from God and are mediated through the Son.[200] Accordingly, the author can contrast in 1:17 the two mediators, Moses and Jesus Christ. Sinai imagery is present in 1:14–18, in the tenting, the glory, the reference to Moses and Law, and in the statement about seeing God. The way in which it is used makes it difficult to see Torah wisdom as the primary basis for the prologue, because here Jesus is primarily being set in contrast to Torah. Indeed, as Ruth Edwards has convincingly pointed out,[201] ἀντί in 1:16 means "instead of," so that we see here grace acknowledged as once given in the Law through Moses now replaced and superseded by the grace that has come through Jesus Christ. It is not about grace supplementing grace. One gift has been given. Another now fulfils its promise and takes its place. It is still God's grace.

---

199. See also de Kruijf, "Glory," 114.
200. So also Schnelle, *Christologie*, 342.
201. Ruth Edwards, "χάριν ἀντὶ χάριτος (John 1.16): Grace and the Law in the Johannine Prologue," *JSNT* 32 (1988): 3–15. Further discussion in 6.2.5.4 below.

ISSUES OF JOHANNINE CHRISTOLOGY

Here is new revelation on a new basis. 1:18 makes this clear in bringing the prologue to its climax:

Θεὸν οὐδεὶς ἑώρακεν πώποτε· μονογενὴς θεός [P⁶⁶ ℵ* B; v.l. υἱός A]
ὁ ὢν εἰς τὸν κόλπον τοῦ πατρὸς ἐκεῖνος ἐξηγήσατο.
No one has ever seen God; God the only Son,[202]
who is in the bosom of the Father, he has made him known. (1:18)

θεός is probably the reading to be preferred.[203] It forms an *inclusio* with 1:1 as does ὁ ὢν εἰς τὸν κόλπον τοῦ πατρός ("in the bosom of the Father") with πρὸς τὸν θεόν ("with God" 1:1, 2). μονογενής and "Father" catch up 1:14 μονογενοῦς παρὰ πατρός ("the *monogenēs* of the Father"). The imagery εἰς τὸν κόλπον τοῦ πατρός ("in the bosom of the father") continues the family imagery ("Father," μονογενής, "Son"). While many take the latter to refer to the relationship of the Son and the Father during Jesus' ministry,[204] it more likely refers to his exalted state.[205] Nevertheless the intimacy of Father and Son is in any case strongly evident in the claim made in these concluding verses of the prologue that in the Son we have seen the Father's glory, reiterated in 2:11 (cf. also 17:22–23). Indeed it also constitutes him as God's dwelling place, a temple, and finds echoes in 2:19, 21–22 and 4:23.

The picture is one of closest family intimacy. This image of family intimacy with the designation θεός and the contrast with the "no one" in the beginning of the verse suggest that the author is making the strongest possible distinction between the Son and all others and establishing the strongest possible base for the claim that the Son makes the Father known. But even here the distinctness of Father and Son is maintained. As in 1:1 the same word θεός is used for both. The θεός not only echoes 1:1, but functions within the same framework. There it was best understood along with its context as

---

202. For this translation, see Fennema, "God the Only Son."

203. See the discussion in Cullmann, *Christologie*, 317; Brown, *John*, 17; Lindars, *Gospel of John*, 98–99; Bruce, *John*, 45; Mastin, "Neglected Factor," 37–41; Fennema, "God the Only Son," 126–28, 131; contrast Barrett, *John*, 169; Schnackenburg, *John*, 1.280; Haenchen, *Johannes*, 132; Beasley-Murray, *John*, 2–3; Harris, *Prologue*, 109. Petersen, ". . .wieso sagt ihr: 'Du lästerst,'" 477–83, notes its absence in early translations and that μονογενής usually refers to children. Petersen argues that θεός makes no sense in its context and reflects the emphasis on likeness in second-century philosophical schools. The *inclusio*, however, with 1:1 and the precedent for using "God" of others within a monotheistic context, especially in Wisdom, support θεός. Davies, *Rhetoric*, 123, prefers reading neither θεός nor υἱός.

204. E.g., Thyen, *Johannesevangelium*, 107; Keener, *John*, 648.

205. So also Painter, *Quest*, 156; McGrath, *Christology*, 136–37, 140, who sees here the tradition of exaltation to God's right hand refracted through wisdom (cf. Wis 9:4).

The Salvation Event in John

deriving, at least, from the stream of thought about Wisdom and as referring to the exercise of divine powers and functions by the Logos. Here it belongs in the language of family intimacy, more characteristic of the Gospel as a whole, but similarly relates to the Son as bearer of light, life and revelation, attributes traditionally associated with Torah.

5.3.5.3 The λόγος - θεός Son in the Prologue: Conclusion

The prologue offers us, therefore, an understanding of the Son as one who is life, light, glory, grace, and truth to the world. He is what God is for the world. Thus he bears the designation θεός. Yet in being what God is for the world, he is distinct from God. He was with God in the beginning, as now he shares the same intimacy with him in heaven. He is not another God, but the Son, the only one, deriving what he is for the world from God. By considering other passages in the Gospel we can test what has emerged here and, if possible, supplement it. For anything more that is to be said of the nature of the Son as θεός must be said in the light of the rest of the Gospel. This will include not only the sole further occasion where θεός is used again of Jesus, namely Thomas' confession (20:28), but also passages where Jesus explicates the basis of his claim.

5.3.6 The Son and the Father—John 5:17–30

In ch. 5 Jesus' healing of a lame man on the Sabbath provokes the anger of the Jews (5:16). Jesus responds: "My Father is working up till now and I am working" (5:17). Jesus justifies his work on the Sabbath by appealing to the belief that God also works on the Sabbath. This may well reflect knowledge of discussion about God's activity or otherwise on the Sabbath found already in Aristobulus and also later in Philo and rabbinic tradition.[206] In making this claim Jesus presupposes a special relationship between himself and God which justifies his appeal. Why should a person claim to be able to do something on the basis that God does it? Can God be used as an example to follow in this way? Does this not obliterate the distinction between God and human beings? How can this be justified when it contradicts God's Law for human beings?

Jesus not only appeals to God as an example; he also claims that God

---

206. On this see Borgen, *John*, 47–48, 86; Keener, *John*, 646; Thyen, *Johannesevangelium*, 307.

is his Father and he, God's Son, in a way that goes beyond the usual understanding of these terms in Judaism, where to speak of God as one's father was a commonplace of piety and no offence to faith.[207] For John's Jesus is claiming much more, including more than being like any other obedient agent of God, such as a prophet or John the Baptist. He is claiming to belong to the family of God, a claim articulated most clearly in 8:35:

> ὁ δὲ δοῦλος οὐ μένει ἐν τῇ οἰκίᾳ εἰς τὸν αἰῶνα, ὁ υἱὸς μένει εἰς τὸν αἰῶνα.
> The slave does not remain in the household forever, but the son remains forever. (8:35)

He is the Son sent by the Father to make the Father known. He is the Word who was with God in pre-existence and was God, of a higher order of being. The Jews in John's narrative world understand enough to know that a claim is being made which goes way beyond what they would find acceptable from a human being. It is against this background that we must understand the reaction of the Jews: they seek to kill him,

> ὅτι οὐ μόνον ἔλυεν τὸ σάββατον, ἀλλὰ καὶ πατέρα ἴδιον ἔλεγεν τὸν θεὸν ἴσον ἑαυτὸν ποιῶν τῷ θεῷ.
> because he not only broke the Sabbath, but was also saying that God was his own Father, making himself equal with God. (5:18)

The issue is more than a dispute of interpreting the Law, for Jesus is setting himself apart from all others and in that sense above the Law.[208]

How would the evangelist have understood the Jews' accusation that Jesus was "making himself equal with God" (ἴσον ἑαυτὸν ποιῶν τῷ θεῷ)?[209] This accusation forms the basis for the author's development of Jesus' explanation which follows. Jesus says,

---

207. So McGrath, *Christology*, 89, suggests that the participle ποιῶν be read as concessive: "although [he was] making himself equal with God." This is unnecessary.

208. Lincoln, *John*, 75.

209. Tobias Kriener, *"Glauben an Jesus"—ein Verstoss gegen das zweite Gebot: Die johanneische Christologie und der jüdische Vorwurf des Götzendienstes*, NTDH 29 (Neukirchen-Vluyn: Neukirchener Verlag, 2001) assembles evidence in early rabbinic literature about objections to humans making themselves gods, in particular in relation to the emperor cult (9–24), and sees this kind of response then applied to Jesus in John's account (147). Borgen, *John*, 55, points to Philo's interpretation of Deuteronomy 13 (*Spec.* 1:315–18), noting similarities: the charge of polytheism and execution without a court and as service to God.

The Salvation Event in John

Ἀπεκρίνατο οὖν ὁ Ἰησοῦς καὶ ἔλεγεν αὐτοῖς· ἀμὴν ἀμὴν λέγω ὑμῖν, οὐ δύναται ὁ υἱὸς ποιεῖν ἀφ' ἑαυτοῦ οὐδὲν ἐὰν μή τι βλέπῃ τὸν πατέρα ποιοῦντα·
ἃ γὰρ ἂν ἐκεῖνος ποιῇ, ταῦτα καὶ ὁ υἱὸς ὁμοίως ποιεῖ.
So Jesus replied and told them: "Truly, truly, I tell you, the Son can do nothing of himself, but only what he sees the Father doing;
what he does, the Son does these things likewise. (5:19)

This is not a statement about equality in the sense that it could be reversed to read: The Father can do nothing except what he sees the Son doing.[210] The notion of equality is heavily qualified by the notion of dependence.[211] The equality consists primarily in equal works, which had been the point of Jesus' claim in 5:17. In 5:20 he expands this further:

ὁ γὰρ πατὴρ φιλεῖ τὸν υἱὸν καὶ πάντα δείκνυσιν αὐτῷ ἃ αὐτὸς ποιεῖ, καὶ μείζονα τούτων δείξει αὐτῷ ἔργα, ἵνα ὑμεῖς θαυμάζητε.
For the Father loves the Son and shows him all that he himself is doing, and greater things than these will he show him that you may marvel. (5:20)

Some have read this as a parable, drawing attention to how especially in the world of the time sons learned from fathers.[212] A similar generic analogy informs the translation of 1:14 as "and we beheld his glory as of a father's only son" (καὶ ἐθεασάμεθα τὴν δόξαν αὐτοῦ, δόξαν ὡς μονογενοῦς παρὰ πατρός). Thus 5:19-20 could be read as saying: (In a normal family) "the [a] son cannot do anything on his own accord except what he sees the [his] father doing. What he does, the son also does similarly. The father loves the son and shows him everything he is doing." Accordingly, Jesus would be arguing, what applies in families applies to my relationship with the Father.

---

210. So also Reimund Bieringer, "'. . .because the Father is greater than I' (John 14:28): Johannine Christology in Light of the Relationship between the Father and the Son," in *Gospel Images of Jesus Christ in Church Tradition and in Biblical Scholarship: Fifth International East-West Symposium of New Testament Scholars: Minsk, September 2 to 9, 2010*, ed. C. Karakolis, K.-W. Niebuhr, and S. Rogalsky, WUNT 288 (Tübingen: Mohr Siebeck, 2012), 203.

211. So Bauckham, "Monotheism," 152, who also notes that the Son is exercising divine prerogatives; Thyen, *Johannesevangelium*, 309; Busse, *Johannesevangelium*, 132.

212. So C. H. Dodd, *Historical Tradition in the Fourth Gospel* (Cambridge: Cambridge University Press, 1965), 386; Robinson, "Christology," 71, who see a parable in 5:19-20; Lindars, "Slave," 272, in 5:19 only; Ashton, *Fourth Gospel*, 227; but see Ashton, "Reflections," 207, where he challenges this view.

Such an explanation might help explain the deviation here from the usual reference to the Son's having seen and heard in the past, to the use of the present tense.²¹³ The generic use of the article could be read in this way.

The wider context, however, makes it more likely that we have here primarily a christological claim which employs the imagery of family and apprenticeship.²¹⁴ One could read it along the lines that, as sons learn from fathers, so the Son learned in the past from the Father and has therefore come to do his will and make him known. This, however, would not give appropriate weight to the present tense which implies ongoing instruction and information.²¹⁵ It would also make little sense of 5:20b which speaks of a future showing. In 5:30 the present tense is repeated:

Οὐ δύναμαι ἐγὼ ποιεῖν ἀπ' ἐμαυτοῦ οὐδέν·
καθὼς ἀκούω κρίνω, καὶ ἡ κρίσις ἡ ἐμὴ δικαία ἐστίν,
ὅτι οὐ ζητῶ τὸ θέλημα τὸ ἐμὸν ἀλλὰ τὸ θέλημα τοῦ πέμψαντός με.
I am not able to do anything of myself.
As I hear, I judge, and my judgment is just;
because I do not seek my own will, but the will of him who sent me.
(5:30)

It is clearly christological and confirms the christological reading of 5:19-20.²¹⁶ The following verses continue in similar vein: both Father and Son make alive (5:21); the Father has authorised the Son to judge (5:22), "so that all may honour the Son as they honour the Father. He who does not honour the Son does not honour the Father who sent him" (5:23); the Son has been given the right to have life in himself and so to judge (5:26-27). The references to

---

213. Michaels, *John*, 309, comes close to saying this when he argues that the language of the present tense derives from parable and that the focus is imitation.

214. See Jan G. van der Watt, "Der Meisterschüler Gottes (Von der Lehre des Sohnes)—Joh 5,19-23," in *Kompendium der Gleichnisse Jesu*, ed. R. Zimmermann (Gutersloh: Gütersloher Verlagshaus, 2007), 745, who notes that the literal and metaphorical are intertwined. See also Schnackenburg, *Johannesevangelium*, 2.129; Haenchen, *Johannes*, 276; Frey, *Eschatologie*, 3.324-43; Zimmermann, *Christologie*, 176-83; Ashton, *Fourth Gospel*, 227, who writes: "The Johannine conception of Jesus' sonship comes out of a conceptual world in which the agent appointed by the landowner to look after his estates is thought of as a son (the בן בית) and conversely one in which the firstborn son attains his majority at the very important moment he receives his appointment."

215. Van der Watt, "Meisterschüler," 748-50, notes education's role in Jewish families.

216. Ashton, *Fourth Gospel*, 83, writes: "One might almost say that on Jesus' lips the name 'father' contains *in nuce* the whole of the evangelist's Christology"; van der Watt, "Meisterschüler," 746.

judgment in 5:21–29 apply both to the present and to the future, corresponding to the two tenses in 5:19–20. The formulations ἔρχεται ὥρα καὶ νῦν ἐστιν (5:25) and ἔρχεται ὥρα (5:28) also reflect the dual perspective (cf. 4:21, 23). The reference in 5:20c to the Son's being shown greater things in the future is unclear,[217] but may well refer to the future judgment.[218]

What this means is that the author envisages more than what the envoy model assumes, namely that Jesus communicates what he has seen and heard in the past; he also communicates what he sees and hears in the present.[219] The Son not only does what he was instructed to do at his sending but continues to hear instruction about what God wants. This means a continuing relationship between the Son and the Father which goes beyond what the envoy image can express. The author employs the envoy model to express the Son's coming from the Father, sent by him, but, as already noted, uses the communication, information-giving aspect of the model metaphorically, because basically the Son does not come communicating information but invitation. It is therefore not in tension with the way he appropriates the model to find here references to ongoing communication, communion, between Father and Son, for which he can use the family apprenticeship model. This, in turn, underlines the unique relationship of Father and Son which is far more than a unity of will, as it would have been for a commissioned prophet. Thus the author can continue to employ the envoy model as he does in the rest of the chapter, but always on the assumption of the Son's special status.

Thus the Son has been given power to raise the dead (5:21), and to exercise judgment (5:22), so that all may honour him as the one sent to do so (5:23). This goes beyond authorisation. It is empowerment. The author then has Jesus employ traditional motifs of eschatological judgment, including the role of the Son of Man in judgment (reflected also in 9:35–39), and apply them metaphorically in the present to people's response of faith in him: it effects for them a resurrection from the dead now (5:24–27), which, in turn, does not obviate the literal expectation of a future judgment (5:28–29). In the light of this exposition of 5:19–20 the author then has Jesus return to its claim in 5:30, cited above.

Within the framework of the envoy model, in which Jesus speaks of his authorisation and sending, the author has Jesus speak also of a present com-

---

217. Thyen, *Johannesevangelium*, 311, 313, suggests the reference is to the raising of Lazarus. Keener, *John*, 648, suggests Jesus' resurrection.

218. Schnackenburg, *Johannesevangelium*, 2.125; Brown, *John*, 214, cf. 88; Beasley-Murray, *John*, 76; Thyen, *Johannesevangelium*, 311, 313. Becker, *Johannes*, 236–41, suggests the author applied exaltation tradition to the earthly Jesus (5:19bc, 21–23b).

219. So Ashton, *John*, 175; van der Watt, "Meisterschüler," 747.

munion with God which enables him to know and do God's will. The envoy model continues to inform the verses which follow, which appeal to Jesus' works as testimony for his claim that the Father has sent him (5:31–36), and that he has seen the Father and has God's word and his love abiding in him (5:37–44). The allusions to seeing God and to the Word may have alerted the hearer to the claims of the prologue which declares that Jesus is the Word and that only he has seen the Father (1:18).[220]

Equality Grounded in Complete Obedience Enabled by Unique Being

The Son's equality with the Father is grounded in and defined by his doing the Father's will and fulfilling his commission.[221] This is not just like any other human being doing God's will.[222] For it is also grounded in the claim that he is uniquely qualified to do so, since he is the Son of the Father, different from other people, and his commissioning was not an earthly call but an authorisation and commissioning as the pre-existent Word. His being is distinctive and enables his doing. In his being he is dependent and subordinate; in his doing he is equal. The inequality of dependence of the unique Son is also emphasised as the basis for the equality of deed and word in 5:36–37.

This is substantially also the conclusion of Barrett,[223] and earlier Wetter, who cites this as a major difference between Jesus and other divine figures claiming to be sons of God in the world of the time.[224] Büchsel argues that this subordination applies only to the earthly Jesus and speaks of the unity as the highest achievable by human beings on earth,[225] but this denies both the use of dependency language for the pre-existence (sending, commissioning) and also the difference in the nature of sonship presupposed in this passage. Similarly Wendy Sproston relates subordination only to Jesus' humanity and

---

220. It is therefore more than just empowerment. Cf. Neyrey, *Ideology*, 22, who writes: "5:19–20 argues that Jesus is 'equal to God' for God gave him his creative power."

221. McGrath, *Christology*, who notes that calling God "Father" implies subordination and obedience (85–86); similarly Beth M. Sheppard, "Another Look: Johannine 'Subordinationist Christology' and the Roman Family," in *New Currents through John: A Global Perspective*, ed. F. Lozada and T. Thatcher, SBLRBS 54 (Atlanta: SBL, 2006), 113–17; Frey, *Eschatologie*, 3.351, recognises both elements: equality and subordination; similarly Bauckham, "Monotheism," 152.

222. Cf. Davies, *Rhetoric*, 131, 136–37.

223. Barrett, "Father," 23–24; similarly Brown, *John*, 218–19; Preiss, *Life in Christ*, 25; Moloney, *Son of Man*, 209; Haenchen, *Johannes*, 275–76; John Painter, "Text and Context in John 5," *ABR* 35 (1987): 32; Beasley-Murray, *John*, 74–75; Scroggs, *Christology*, 79.

224. Wetter, *Sohn Gottes*, 174.

225. Büchsel, *Johannes*, 75; cf. also Schillebeeckx, *Christ*, 403, 431.

The Salvation Event in John

not to the Son of the prologue.[226] Lindars comments that the author is not always consistent, sometimes treating the relationship metaphysically, sometimes functionally.[227] By contrast, Riedl suggests that the author operates with a binitarian concept in which the Son as Son is seen as dependent on the Father without suggesting direct subordination.[228] He speaks of a metaphysical unity of being ("Wesenseinheit") and of the eternal generation of the Son.[229] But, as Barrett points out, this kind of interpretation reads later christological formulations into the text.[230] Appold strongly emphasises equality and oneness, but imposes here his own system upon the text when he denies any element of subordination, claiming that 5:18 correctly interprets 5:17.[231] This is the case only if we take 5:19–21 as the key to the understanding of 5:18. There is no reciprocal relationship here. The Father sends and empowers the Son, not vice versa. On the other hand, Reinhold Leistner and Miranda are surely incorrect in arguing that the author denies the substance of the Jews' accusation of equality altogether.[232] With Barrett, we see the author rejecting the Jews' meaning of equality with God, but taking it up, like many statements with double meaning, as true in his own distinctive sense of equality in subordination.[233] These are doubtless also real accusations hurled at the Johannine community by Jewish critics.[234]

5.3.7 The Son and the Father: John 10:22–39

In 10:30–39 the confrontation is similar to that of ch. 5.[235] Jesus claims: "I and the Father are one" (ἐγὼ καὶ ὁ πατὴρ ἕν ἐσμεν in 10:30). This statement has

---

226. Sproston, "Christology," 81–82.
227. Lindars, *Gospel of John*, 56.
228. Riedl, *Heilswerk*, 422.
229. Riedl, *Heilswerk*, 201–2, 213. Cf. also Schnelle, "Trinitarisches Denken," 379–80.
230. Barrett, "Father," 19–22.
231. Appold, *Oneness*, 23.
232. Reinhold Leistner, *Antijudäismus im Johannesevangelium?* (Frankfurt: Lang, 1974), 126; Miranda, *Sendung*, 45.
233. Barrett, "Father," 23–24; *John*, 72; similarly Bultmann, *Johannes*, 184–85; Schnackenburg, *Johannesevangelium*, 2.128; Kysar, *Jesus*, 35.
234. Theobald, "Gott, Logos und Pneuma," 367–68; see also Martijn Steegen, "Raising the Dead in John 5,19–30: Questioning Equality or Subordination in the Relationship between the Father and the Son," in *Resurrection of the Dead: Biblical Traditions in Dialogue*, ed. G. Van Oyen and T. Shepherd, BETL 249 (Leuven: Peeters, 2012), 240. De Jonge, *Stranger*, 148–49, notes the charge was also laid against Caligula.
235. On this see McGrath, *Christology*, 117–19.

often been seen as the hallmark of Johannine Christology and rightly so, but only if it is understood strictly within its context in the Gospel.[236] Appold, for instance, makes it the basis of his claim that oneness and equality are the centre of the Gospel, but does so by denying its context and even asserting that obedience of the Son to the Father is foreign to Johannine Christology.[237] Barrett also warns against reading too much into 10:30[238] and Haenchen cautions similarly, noting that the motif of oneness occurs only here and in ch. 17.[239]

Responding to the Jews' question about his messiahship, Jesus had answered that the works he did in his Father's name bore witness to him, but that the Jews had not believed in him because they were not his sheep (10:24-26). The sheep hear and follow Jesus and he knows them. They are safe in his hands (10:27-28). This statement is then expanded in a way which equates the activity of the Son and Father. In 10:28 Jesus said, "No one shall snatch them from my hand"; in 10:29 he says: "No one can snatch them from the Father's hand." "I and the Father are one" (10:30) is thus primarily related to the work of caring for the disciples.

Unfortunately the statement which lies between the two parallel claims of 10:28 and 10:29 has an uncertain textual tradition. The reading, ὁ πατήρ μου ὃ δέδωκέν μοι πάντων μείζών ἐστιν (Sinaiticus; "My Father who has given (them) to me is greater than all") fits the context well and would make explicit the connection between the two claims. This would also be true of the reading, ὁ πατήρ μου ὃ δέδωκέν μοι πάντων μεῖζόν ἐστιν (A; "My Father, as regards what he has given me, it is greater than all"). The more difficult reading is almost untranslatable because it makes μεῖζόν "greater" refer not to the Father, but to the relative pronoun ὅ, translated above "as regards what." It could read, "As for my Father, what he has given to me is greater than all." It would then imply the Father's love as the motivation for his caring for the Son's disciples, though, nevertheless, also imply indirectly the Son's dependence on the Father. The conjunction of oneness and dependence is very evident in what follows.

---

236. So Schnelle, "Trinitarisches Denken," 376. Bauckham, "Monotheism," 163, suggests that the statement may allude to the Shema (Deut 6:4). The primary focus, however, is functional equivalence which precedes and has its basis in the Son's belonging to the divine family. See also Keener, *John*, 826.

237. Appold, *Oneness*, 23, 24 n. 1, 272.

238. Barrett, "Father," 150.

239. Haenchen, *Johannes*, 107-8.

10:22–39—Oneness in Dependence

In response to Jesus' words the Jews seek his death (10:31). The Son's claim and the Jews' response echo 5:17–18. There Jesus had said, "My Father is working up till now and I am working." The accusations of the Jews arose here, as we have seen, from the Son's claim also to keep his own, as the Father does (10:28–29), and from his assertion that he and the Father are ἕν, one (10:30). The sense of the neuter ἕν is functional unity, compared with the more strongly ontological claim which would be made with the personal masculine εἷς, "one."[240] It assumes that to be in the hands of the Son is to be in the hands of the Father. But it also means more than this. For the disciples are safe only because being in the hands of the Son also means being in the hands of the Father. The identity of caring, or we might say, the equality of caring, is bound to the dependence of Son on Father. The Father guarantees the Son's caring is his caring. In that sense the Father and Son are one.

Jesus' defence of his claim also follows similar lines to his defence in 5:19–20: "I have shown you many works from the Father. For which of them do you want to stone me?" (10:32; cf. 5:20, "The Father loves the Son and shows him all he is doing").[241] Jesus is also referring back to the works mentioned at the beginning of the encounter (10:25). The claim to oneness, like the statement of equality in 5:18, is, therefore, immediately interpreted as a oneness of works and in such a way that they derive from the Father.

The Jews fail to see the connection and retort:

περὶ καλοῦ ἔργου οὐ λιθάζομέν σε ἀλλὰ περὶ βλασφημίας, καὶ ὅτι σὺ ἄνθρωπος ὢν ποιεῖς σεαυτὸν θεόν.
We do not want to stone you because of a good work, but for blasphemy, because you, though you are a human being, make yourself God. (10:33)

The Jews have misunderstood Jesus' words "I and the Father are one" as though Jesus had said: "I am God," in effect, "I am the Father." But the author

---

240. Beasley-Murray, *John*, 174; Brown, *John*, 232–33; Hahn, *Theologie*, 1.609; Frey, *Eschatologie*, 3.350; Bauckham, "Monotheism," 163; Hartwig Thyen, "Erwägungen zu Jesu Prädikationen als ἴσος τῷ θεῷ, θεός und υἱὸς τοῦ θεοῦ," in *Studien zum Corpus Iohanneum*, WUNT 214 (Tübingen: Mohr Siebeck, 2007), 692; Carson, *John*, 394.

241. Neyrey, *Ideology*, 76, notes that the background of 10:37-38 is not envoy Christology but mutual indwelling of Father and Son.

never has Jesus equate himself in this way with the Father.[242] Rather we have before us a typical example of the Johannine use of misunderstanding. Yet the following verses also indicate that their accusation, "you, though you are a human being, make yourself God" (σὺ ἄνθρωπος ὢν ποιεῖς σεαυτὸν θεόν in 10:33), is true at one level, not in the sense that Jesus makes himself God, but that he is θεός. A similar structure of thought is present here as in 5:18 where the accusation proves both false and true.

10:34–39—The Use of Psalm 82

In 10:34–38 Jesus argues the validity of his claim to be θεός. He quotes Ps 82:6,

> ἀπεκρίθη αὐτοῖς [ὁ] Ἰησοῦς· οὐκ ἔστιν γεγραμμένον ἐν τῷ νόμῳ ὑμῶν ὅτι ἐγὼ εἶπα· θεοί ἐστε; εἰ ἐκείνους εἶπεν θεοὺς πρὸς οὓς ὁ λόγος τοῦ θεοῦ ἐγένετο, καὶ οὐ δύναται λυθῆναι ἡ γραφή, ὃν ὁ πατὴρ ἡγίασεν καὶ ἀπέστειλεν εἰς τὸν κόσμον ὑμεῖς λέγετε ὅτι βλασφημεῖς, ὅτι εἶπον· υἱὸς τοῦ θεοῦ εἰμι; εἰ οὐ ποιῶ τὰ ἔργα τοῦ πατρός μου, μὴ πιστεύετέ μοι· εἰ δὲ ποιῶ, κἂν ἐμοὶ μὴ πιστεύητε, τοῖς ἔργοις πιστεύετε, ἵνα γνῶτε καὶ γινώσκητε ὅτι ἐν ἐμοὶ ὁ πατὴρ κἀγὼ ἐν τῷ πατρί.
> Jesus replied to them: "Is it not written in your Law, 'I said, you are gods'? If he called them gods to whom the word of God came, and Scripture cannot be contradicted, you say of the one whom God sanctified and sent into the world, that he blasphemes, because I said, 'I am the son of God.' If I do not do the works of my Father do not believe in me. But if I do, even if you do not believe in me, believe in the works, so that you may come to know and recognise that the Father is in me and I in the Father." (10:34–38)

There are a number of extraordinary features in this reply. Jesus had not made the claim, "I am the Son of God." This must be a rephrasing of "I and the Father are one" (10:30), understood in line with the Jews' accusation of his making himself θεός, but taken in a Johannine way. This is just like 1:18 where being the only Son and being θεός are juxtaposed. Accordingly we are faced with the same question: the nature of the Son as θεός. The use of Psalm 82 is intended to address this, or at least defend Jesus' claim. How does it do so?

---

242. So rightly, Miranda, *Sendung*, 78; Barnabas Lindars, *Behind the Fourth Gospel* (London: SPCK, 1971), 70; Jervell, *Jesus*, 21.

The Salvation Event in John

Psalm 82 in 10:34-39—The People of Israel, the Judges?

Many exegetes point to the use of Psalm 82 in rabbinic tradition, where it is taken as a reference to the people of God at Sinai, to whom indeed the word of God came, who for a short time attained divine status.²⁴³ Accordingly Jesus' argument would be: if it was valid to address the people of God as "gods" at Sinai, then surely it is all the more valid to use this term of the one whom God sanctified and sent into the world.²⁴⁴ In the Psalm those addressed have also been understood as judges and this may be linked with Moses and the judges to whom the people came in the wilderness days, who acted as gods for them (Exod 4:16; 7:1; 21:6; 22:8-9).²⁴⁵ Boismard sees also a link between the coming of the word to the people as judges of Israel, and in that sense, prophets, and the idea of Jesus as the prophet par excellence.²⁴⁶ The contrast with Sinai recalls 1:14-18 of the prologue and would maintain the contrast between the word coming then and the incarnation of the Word in the person of Jesus.

While, on these interpretations, a qualitative distinction between the people of Israel or the judges and Son is presupposed, nevertheless the comparison has the effect of watering down the use of θεός and "Son of God" considerably. It would be a long way below what the author usually means by the term θεός when referring to Jesus.²⁴⁷ The passage can hardly mean that Jesus was as much Son of God as any human being might become, except that Jesus was so from birth onwards, as Lütgert suggests.²⁴⁸ Nor should the lack of article be taken as supporting such an interpretation, as if Jesus were saying, "I am a Son of God," as Robinson proposes.²⁴⁹ Such a use of "Son of

---

243. So Dahl, "Church," 130; Riedl, *Heilswerk*, 260-61; Schnackenburg, *Johannesevangelium*, 2.390; Frédéric Manns, "Exégèse Rabbinique et Exégèse Johannique," *RB* 92 (1985): 532; Beasley-Murray, *John*, 176-77; Anthony T. Hanson, "John's Citation of Ps LXXXII," *NTS* 11 (1965): 160, who also identifies the "Word" as the Logos (161). Against this Schnackenburg, *Johannesevangelium*, 2.391.

244. McGrath, *Christology*, 122-25, sees a link here between Adam, those at Sinai, and Adam typology in the Philippian hymn where Jesus is given the name of God.

245. Brown, *John*, 409-10; Robinson, *Priority*, 373-74.

246. M.-E. Boismard, "Jésus, le Prophète par excellence d'après Jean 10,24-39," in *Neues Testament und Kirche. Festschrift für R. Schnackenburg*, ed. J. Gnilka (Freiburg: Herder, 1974), 170; Boismard and Lamouille, *Jean*, 275.

247. So Barrett, "Father," 25; similarly J. Ernest Davey, *The Jesus of St. John* (London: Lutterworth, 1958), 36-37.

248. Lütgert, *Christologie*, 58-60; Büchsel, *Johannes*, 75; similarly Robinson, *Priority*, 311, 375.

249. Robinson, "Christology," 72.

God" would be something of an anticlimax and stands in tension with the emphasis found in ch. 5 where the quality of Jesus' sonship is contrasted with that of normal human beings.

Psalm 82 in 10:34-39—Angelic Elohim?

Another interpretation avoids the blandness of this approach by referring to the way Psalm 82 is used in Qumran. Emerton drew attention to 11QMelch, where the *elohim* ("gods") among whom God takes his place in council and holds judgment (82:1), whom he rebukes (82:2-5), and whom he addresses with the words, "You are gods, sons of the most high all of you; nevertheless you shall die like men and fall like any human prince" (82:6-7), are heavenly beings, angels.[250] This is also better OT exegesis of the original. For in 11QMelch Melchisedek assumes God's role as judge in the heavenly council. The original psalm itself uses the word *elohim*, which can mean either God, gods or angels, to refer to beings other than God (ii 9). The LXX translates: θεοί. Jesus' argument would then be as follows: if it was valid to address these heavenly beings as "gods" or "sons of God," is it not all the more valid for the one God sanctified and sent into the world, to be so addressed? The use of θεός here would be similar to its use of the Logos in the prologue and would not have the effect of watering down the concept of sonship to the same degree as presupposed in the more common interpretation. It would, however, still conflict with the author's designation of Jesus as μονογενής in 1:18. It is a much more offensive claim than that assumed by the first interpretation, which the Jews should have had no difficulty in accepting. It makes better sense therefore in the context, since the Jews' response was to seek Jesus' arrest (10:39).

Psalm 82 in 10:34-39—Conclusions

On balance, the second interpretation coheres better with the context and the Christology of the Gospel as a whole. It would enable us to view angelology beside Logos wisdom tradition as a possible background against

---

250. So J. A. Emerton, "Some New Testament Notes, I: The Interpretation of Psalm 82 in John 10," *JTS* 11 (1960): 329-32; J. A. Emerton, "Melchizedek and the Gods. Fresh Evidence for the Jewish Background of John X. 34-36," *JTS* 17 (1966): 399-401; similarly Bühner, *Gesandte*, 393-95; Ashton, *Fourth Gospel*, 92.

The Salvation Event in John

which to interpret the nature of the Son as θεός, but does not really lead us beyond that. All of the interpretations of Psalm 82 in 10:34-39 which we have considered imply some qualitative difference between the Son and others, whether they be the people of Israel, judges or other heavenly beings. They imply a claim about the Son's being. This is more than, though it includes, moral unity.[251] There are metaphysical claims implied here,[252] though they stop short of Sproston's assertion that here we have the paradox of full humanity and full divinity.[253] As in 5:19-20, however, the author's argument is primarily about ethical and functional unity.[254]

10:36-39—The Unique Intimacy of Father and Son

In the argument from Psalm 82 the author also uses the shaliach envoy motif in 10:36, where the Son describes himself as the one sanctified and sent into the world.[255] This is the pattern of the familiar revealer-envoy motif. When, therefore, Jesus refers to the claim to be "Son of God" in the same verse, this is also primarily functional, but it also cannot be any less than what was implied in his claim to oneness with the Father and in a Johannine sense to be θεός.[256] The following verses then expound Jesus' claim in characteristically Johannine manner. Jesus says, "If I do not do the works of my Father, do not believe me. If I do, and you do not believe me, believe the works, that you may come to know that the Father is in me and I am in the Father" (10:37-38). The distinction between believing the works and believing in Jesus recalls the distinction Mark has Jesus make between slander against himself, which is forgivable, and slander against the Spirit (evident in the deeds), which is not (3:28-30). Here we see oneness or equality at the level of works and at the same time the explicit claim that there is more here than functional unity; there is something more to believe, namely, the mutual indwelling of Father and Son.[257] While the lan-

---

251. Against Robinson, *Priority*, 375.
252. So Barrett, *John*, 382; Brown, *John*, 408.
253. Sproston, "Christology," 84-85.
254. Barrett, *John*, 382; Brown, *John*, 408; Lindars, *Gospel of John*, 370-71; Busse, "Johannes 10," 524.
255. So Brown, *John*, 411.
256. Petersen, "...wieso sagt ihr: 'Du lästerst,'" 484, speculates that the retreat to "Son of God" from "God" and the use of "My Lord and my God" in 20:28 may reflect sensitivities in debates with Jews and use by the author of claims current in his context, without his necessarily endorsing Thomas' stance.
257. On this see Hurtado, *Lord Jesus Christ*, 374; Bauckham, "Monotheism and Christology," 154. On 10:38 as explaining 10:30 see Klaus Scholtissek, "'Ich und der Vater, wir sind eins'

guage of indwelling is also used of the relationship between believers and the Son, the context here, as in 14:10-11, where mutual indwelling between Father and Son and the distinction between believing in the works and believing in Jesus are repeated, indicates that what is being expressed is above all the unique intimacy of relationship between Father and Son such as we have it in 1:18.[258]

John 5 and 10 and Christology

The controversies of ch. 5 and ch. 10 have their sequel in the trial before Pilate, where the Jews claim Jesus must die because υἱὸν θεοῦ ἑαυτὸν ἐποίησεν ("he has made himself the Son of God" in 19:7). This is more than a false accusation about messianic claims, as Leistner suggests.[259] Pilate is filled with numinous fear, and the evangelist, employing his characteristic narrative skills, has Pilate ask: "Where do you come from?" (19:9), a use of irony which the author has used to great effect also elsewhere (e.g., 2:9; 8:14; 9:29-30). For in truth the readers know that the central focus of his sonship is: he is the Son come from the Father to make him known. It is this developed understanding of sonship which led, according to Martyn, to hefty conflict with the synagogue.[260] For this Christology the community stood trial. The passages considered may also reflect use of material originally at home in the tradition of Jesus' own trial or hearing before the Jews.[261]

As a whole, the christological controversies in ch. 5 and ch. 10 present a remarkably consistent picture. Jewish accusation that Jesus claims equality or identity with God is rejected at one level, but affirmed at another. In the process the author preserves the claim already expressed in the prologue of Jesus' unique sonship and his being θεός, setting him apart from all others. At the same time he possesses this uniqueness of being in dependence upon

---

(Joh 10,30). Zum theologischen Potential und zur hermeneutischen Kompetenz der johanneischen Christologie," in *Theology and Christology in the Fourth Gospel: Essays by the Members of the SNTS Johannine Writings Seminar*, ed. G. Van Belle, J. G. van der Watt, and P. Maritz, BETL 184 (Leuven: Peeters, 2005), 338-39; also Söding, "Ich und der Vater," 199.

258. On "ἕν" language see Borig, *Weinstock*, 210-13, 217; Edward Malatesta, *Interiority and Covenant*, AnBib 69 (Rome: BibInst, 1978).

259. Leistner, *Antijudäismus*, 126-29; cf. also Miranda, *Sendung*, 78.

260. J. Louis Martyn, "Glimpses into the History of the Johannine Community," in *The Gospel of John in Christian History* (New York: Paulist, 1978), 104-5. Cf. also Brown, *Beloved Disciple*, 44-47; de Jonge, *Stranger*, 148-49; Söding, "Ich und der Vater," 183, who notes against Brown that there is no evidence that the debate is with Christians.

261. So Lindars, *Behind the Fourth Gospel*, 70; Lindars, *Gospel of John*, 365; Schnackenburg, *Johannesevangelium*, 2.128, 388; Boismard and Lamouille, *Jean*, 273-74.

The Salvation Event in John

and in subordination to the Father, as on the basis of his distinctive being he does the Father's works and fulfils his commission.

5.3.8 The Son and the Father: John 14:9–11

In 14:9–11 Jesus responds to Philip's request, "Show us the Father" by saying, "Have I been with you so long, Philip, and you do not recognise me?" This is not a claim on the part of Jesus to be the Father. Rather, as the following comments show, he stands for the Father in the world:

> λέγει αὐτῷ ὁ Ἰησοῦς· τοσούτῳ χρόνῳ μεθ᾽ ὑμῶν εἰμι καὶ οὐκ ἔγνωκάς με, Φίλιππε;
> ὁ ἑωρακὼς ἐμὲ ἑώρακεν τὸν πατέρα· πῶς σὺ λέγεις· δεῖξον ἡμῖν τὸν πατέρα;
> οὐ πιστεύεις ὅτι ἐγὼ ἐν τῷ πατρὶ καὶ ὁ πατὴρ ἐν ἐμοί ἐστιν;
> τὰ ῥήματα ἃ ἐγὼ λέγω ὑμῖν ἀπ᾽ ἐμαυτοῦ οὐ λαλῶ,
> ὁ δὲ πατὴρ ἐν ἐμοὶ μένων ποιεῖ τὰ ἔργα αὐτοῦ. πιστεύετέ μοι ὅτι ἐγὼ ἐν τῷ πατρὶ καὶ ὁ πατὴρ ἐν ἐμοί· εἰ δὲ μή, διὰ τὰ ἔργα αὐτὰ πιστεύετε.
> Jesus said to them, "Have I been so long with you and you have not recognised me, Philip? He who has seen me has seen the Father. How can you say, 'Show us the Father'? Do you not believe that I am in the Father and the Father in me? The words which I say to you I do not speak of my own accord, but the Father remaining in me does his works. Believe me that I am in the Father and the Father in me; otherwise believe because of the works themselves. (14:9–11)

Mutual indwelling and doing the works of the Father are motifs we have already encountered in 10:38. Seeing the Father by seeing the Son recalls 1:18, according to which the Son makes the Father known, whom no one except the Son has seen. The new element here, of the Father dwelling in the Son and therefore doing his works in him, is also only a combination of themes already present elsewhere. It also shows how the author goes beyond the envoy model, for it speaks of something ongoing in the present, not just works earlier commissioned. The Son is also not an unconscious mouthpiece of the Father. It is the unique relationship between the two and the Son's willingness that the Father work and speak through him that makes possible the claim: anyone seeing me sees the Father.

The language of indwelling occurs in 14:17 in relation to the Spirit and then in 14:20 about mutual indwelling between the Father, the Son, and the believers (cf. already 6:56 in relation to believers and the Son and similarly in 15:5-7), repeated as the basis of unity in 17:20-23. So the disciples are also sent, as the Son was sent, indeed to do greater deeds (14:12; 20:21), and they share in the unity of indwelling, but this never however leads to a claim that therefore to have seen a disciple is to have seen Jesus, let alone the Father. The distinctive being of the Son in contrast to the disciples is not compromised.

5.3.9 The Son and the Father: John 17

In ch. 17 the Son prays to the Father. In itself this reflects subordination and dependency. Ricca exaggerates in describing Jesus the Son as characteristically the praying Son,[262] but, at least, with Lütgert and Wetter, we can say that it is consistent with the Johannine picture of Jesus the Son as humble and submissive to the Father.[263] The prayer illustrates the distinctiveness of Father and Son and of their relationship and comes closest to 1:1 and 1:18 in describing how the Son had shared the Father's glory before the foundation of the world and would share it again at his glorification. This implies a special claim about the being of the Son, setting him apart from all others. At the same time this distinctive being stands side by side with statements implying subordination. The Son is commissioned, passes on the glory, name, and words of the Father. His bearing the Father's name amounts to saying he bears the function and power of God himself. It comes close to what is expressed by θεός in the prologue.

5.3.10 The Confession of Thomas: John 20:28

In his encounter with the risen Jesus, Thomas hails him with the words, "My Lord and my God" (ὁ κύριός μου καὶ ὁ θεός μου in 20:28), possibly echoing and countering imperial claims.[264] Probably an *inclusio* is intended with

---

262. Ricca, *Eschatologie*, 108.
263. Lütgert, *Christologie*, 92-95, 105; Wetter, *Sohn Gottes*, 176.
264. So Schnelle, "Trinitarisches Denken," 474, who notes that it matches the self-appellation of Domitian as *Dominus et Deus noster* in the latter stages of his reign; similarly Robert J. Cassidy, *John's Gospel in New Perspective. Christology and the Realities of Roman Power* (New York: Orbis, 1992), 36-39, who sees "saviour of the world" similarly (34-35). See also Labahn, "Heiland der Welt," 168, who cautions against placing too much weight on the role of imperial claims in Johannine Christology; Van Belle, "Christology and Soteriology," 456-57;

the use of θεός in 1:1,²⁶⁵ but not in a way that isolates θεός, as, for instance Wengst does, when he sees caught up in it the notion of the suffering God.²⁶⁶ The confession of Thomas should not be seen as different from the confession of Jesus as the Christ, the Son of God in 20:31, in a way that would make the latter an anticlimax.²⁶⁷ For Jesus is θεός because he is the Son of God sent from the Father. Note the similar transition from 10:30, 33 ("one," θεός) to 10:36 ("Son of God"). Jesus is not θεός in a way that obliterates the distinction between Father and Son or denies the subordination of the Son to the Father.

5.3.11 The "I am" Sayings and Christology

Finally we should make mention of the passages where Jesus uses the words ἐγώ εἰμι ("I am") either absolutely, or with a predicate such as light, life, bread. Richard Bauckham identifies two sets of "I am" sayings in John matching the seven occurrences in the OT.²⁶⁸ It has been argued that these, and, in particular, the absolute occurrences, represent an allusion to the divine name,²⁶⁹

---

and Warren Carter, *John and Empire: Initial Explorations* (London: T&T Clark, 2008), 72, who notes that the words used in Greek reports are δεσπότης καὶ θεός.

265. So Zumstein, "Prolog," 52-55.

266. Wengst, *Gemeinde*, 103-4. Neyrey, *Ideology*, 29, speculates that like Philo, John uses "Lord" and "God" to describe God's eschatological and creative power, but I find no evidence for this in John.

267. So rightly, George Mlakuzhyil, *The Christocentric Literary Structure of the Fourth Gospel*, AnBib 117 (Rome: BibInst, 1987), 258.

268. Bauckham, "Monotheism," 157. Cf. Keener, *John*, 318 n. 329, who in response asks: "Would John really have counted the occurrences in the OT (in any case, outside Deutero-Isaiah, who uses it six times)?"

269. So Heinrich Zimmermann, "Das absolute *ego eimi* als neutestamentliche Offenbarungs-formel," BZ 4 (1960): 54-69, 266-76; 60-69; Brown, *John*, 535-38; J. B. Harner, *The "I am" of the Fourth Gospel* (Philadelphia: Fortress, 1970), 6-15; Schnackenburg, *Johannesevangelium*, 2.64-70; Moloney, *Son of Man*, 131-32; Gnilka, "Christologie," 100; H. K. McArthur, "Christological Perspectives in the Predicates of the Johannine ἐγώ εἰμι Sayings," in *Christological Perspectives: In Honor of H. K. McArthur*, ed. R. F. Berkley and S. A. Edwards (New York: Pilgrim, 1982), 80; Beasley-Murray, *John*, 89-90; Harris, *Prologue*, 130-36; Schenke, "Christologie," 456; Hurtado, *Lord Jesus Christ*, 370-73; Dietzfelbinger, *Johannes*, 1.247; Lincoln, *John*, 86, 257; David Mark Ball, *"I am" in John's Gospel: Literary Function, Background and Theological Implications*, JSNTSup 124 (Sheffield: Sheffield Academic Press, 1996), 157-58; Catrin H. Williams, "'I am' or 'I am He'? Self-Declaratory Pronouncements in the Fourth Gospel and Rabbinic Tradition," in *Jesus in Johannine Tradition*, ed. R. T. Fortna and T. Thatcher (Louisville: Westminster John Knox, 2001), 345; Édouard Delebecque, *Évangile de Jean. Texte Traduit et Annoté* (Paris: Gabalda, 1987), who sees allusions to the divine name also in the use of the participle of the verb "to be" in 1:18; 3:13; and also in 8:25. On this see Schnackenburg, *Johannesevangelium*, 2.254.

sometimes portrayed as an aspect of agency that he bears the divine name.²⁷⁰ Usually the suggestion is made that we have here a typical use of double meaning in John, where besides a literal meaning there is a metaphorical one for those with ears to hear.²⁷¹ Indeed they have been seen as the centre of Johannine Christology.²⁷² The problem with this approach is that usually the author leaves hints in the text about double meaning for the hearer/reader, whereas this appears not to be the case with the "I am" sayings. Identifying them as alluding to the divine name depends upon identifying in John some influence from suggested allusions to the divine name in Isaiah and reflected in the LXX ἐγώ εἰμι (Isa 43:11-12),²⁷³ and possibly indirectly from its use in Exodus (Exod 3:14),²⁷⁴ where however the LXX reads: ἐγώ εἰμι ὁ ὤν ("I am the living one"; cf. Hebrew: אהיה אשר אהיה "I am who I am am") thus identifying the divine name not as "I am" (ἐγώ εἰμι) but as "the living one" (ὁ ὤν). Were an allusion to the divine name to be present in John, we should have here the extraordinary situation that Jesus would be pronouncing the divine name and so making the claim, either that he is Yahweh, the "I am," or in this particular way uniquely represents him.

The first occurrence of "I am" occurs on the lips of John the Baptist where he declares that he is not the Christ (1:20). In 4:25-26 in response to the Samaritan woman's reference to the coming of the Messiah, Jesus declares: "I who am speaking to you am he" (ἐγώ εἰμι ὁ λαλῶν σοι in 4:26). The author reports nothing to indicate that this was something other than a claim to be the Messiah such as one might expect had the woman or the hearers of the Gospel been meant to hear Jesus using the divine name of himself.²⁷⁵

The situation could be different in 6:20, where Jesus, walking on the water, reponds to the disciples' fear by declaring: "It is I; don't be afraid" (ἐγώ

---

270. So Bühner, *Gesandte*, 166-80; Becker, *Johannes*, 208; "Auferstehung," 150; McGrath, *Christology*, 106, 114.

271. For instance, Ball, *"I am" in John's Gospel*, on 4:26 (65-66, 177-78), 6:20 (78, 181-85); 18:5 (142); 8:24, 28 (89, 189); 8:58 (196-97); 13:16-19 (199).

272. Schnelle, "Trinitarisches Denken," 378.

273. Bauckham, "Monotheism," 158; Schwankl, "Aspekte," 357.

274. Neyrey, *Ideology*, 214; Bauckham, "Monotheism," 157-59, who points also to Deut 32:39 and notes that use of Exod 3:14 would have to depend on the Hebrew text and therefore prefers the background in Second Isaiah as reflected in Isa 41:4; 43:10, 25; 46:4; and 51:12. "Just as 'I am [he]' in the Hebrew Bible sums up what it is to be truly God, so in John the expression identifies Jesus as truly God in the fullest sense."

275. So Hahn, *Theologie*, 1.646; Silke Petersen, *Brot, Licht und Weinstock. Intertextuelle Analysen johanneischer Ich-bin-Worte*, NovTSup 127 (Leiden: Brill, 2008), 107; Carson, *John*, 227; cf. Burkett, *Son of Man*, 148; Williams, "'I am' or 'I am He,'" 350; Moloney, *John*, 130; Wilckens, *Johannes*, 86; Coloe, *God Dwells with Us*, 102, citing Isa 52:6.

εἰμι· μὴ φοβεῖσθε), similarly attested as Jesus' response in Mark 6:50 ("Be of good courage; it is I; don't be afraid," θαρσεῖτε, ἐγώ εἰμι· μὴ φοβεῖσθε).²⁷⁶ Nothing in what follows indicates astonishment about what he said. This makes it very unlikely that the author implied that the disciples would have heard Jesus' words as claiming the divine name for himself. Nothing in the context suggests that this was by contrast with what the author's hearers were meant to discern,²⁷⁷ even though a divine claim is implied by Jesus' miracle, expressed in the Matthean parallel by acclamation of Jesus as Son of God (Matt 14:33).²⁷⁸

The occurrences in 18:5-7 may provide better evidence. Jesus asks the band from the chief priest and the Pharisees who had come to arrest him, whom they sought and then openly declared: "I am he" (ἐγώ εἰμι). Their response is shock. They fall to the ground. Had they, however, heard use of the divine name, they might also have rent their clothes.²⁷⁹ This makes it likely that we have here a matter of identification in response²⁸⁰ to which—and surely, for the author, to the numinous power of Jesus' presence—those arresting him initially recoil.²⁸¹

276. Barrett, *John*, 281; Barrett, "Theocentric," 12-13; Lindars, *Gospel of John*, 247; Lindars, *John*, 85; Haenchen, *Johannes*, 311-14; Bruce, *John*, 128; Kim, *Truth, Testimony, and Transformation*, 4; Carson, *John*, 275, who writes that John 6:20 "bears no necessary theological baggage."

277. Cf. Schnackenburg, *Johannesevangelium*, 2.36, 68; Brown, *John*, 254-55; Pokorny, "Jesus," 217; Gnilka, "Christologie," 101; Ellis, *Genius*, 110-11 whose structural analysis makes 6:16-21 the centre of the Gospel (108); Hübner, *Biblische Theologie*, 168; Hahn, *Theologie*, 1.646; Burkett, *Son of Man*, 148; O'Day, "John 6:15-21," 8; Schnelle, *Johannes*, 119; Williams, "'I am' or 'I am He,'" 347, who cites the sudden arrival on shore and suggests 6:20 may have been "an important source, if not the basis, for the absolute *egō eimi* declarations that follow." Anderson, "Johannine *Egō Eimi* Sayings," 146-47, seeks to push back the origin of these sayings to the historical Jesus though also acknowledges: "With a strong degree of certainty, the Johannine I-am sayings appear to have been crafted rhetorically in order to convince audiences to believe in Jesus as the Messiah/Christ, targeted at both Jewish and Gentile members of the audience" (165-66).

278. So John Paul Heil, *Jesus Walking on the Sea*, AnBib 87 (Rome: BibInst, 1981), 59, 67, 80.

279. Carson, *John*, 578; Cf. Brown, *John*, 818; Boismard and Lamouille, *Jean*, 406; Schnackenburg, *Johannesevangelium*, 2.253; Bruce, *John*, 341; Ellis, *Genius*, 251; Zimmermann, "*egō eimi*," 54-69, 266-76; Forestell, *Word*, 47; Pancaro, *Law*, 60; Appold, *Oneness*, 82, 126; Reim, *Studien*, 172, 243-44; Dauer, *Passionsgeschichte*, 41-43; Anderson, "Johannine *Egō Eimi* Sayings," 146-47; Burkett, *Son of Man*, 147; Pryor, *John*, 74; Williams, "'I am' or 'I am He,'" 351-52; Moloney, *John*, 485.

280. Lindars, *John*, 86; cf. Brown, *John*, 818; Boismard and Lamouille, *Jean*, 406; Schnackenburg, *Johannesevangelium*, 3.253; Bruce, *John*, 341; Ellis, *Genius*, 251; Zimmermann, "*egō eimi*," 54-69, 266-76; Forestell, *Word*, 47; Pancaro, *Law*, 60; Appold, *Oneness*, 82, 126; Reim, *Studien*, 243-44; Dauer, *Passionsgeschichte*, 41-43.

281. Bultmann, *Johannes*, 494-95; Barrett, *John*, 520; Barrett, "Theocentric," 12; Nicholson,

ISSUES OF JOHANNINE CHRISTOLOGY

The occurrences in 8:24 and 28 come in response to Jesus' conflict with "the Jews" over his identity. In 8:24 he had complained:

ἐὰν γὰρ μὴ πιστεύσητε ὅτι ἐγώ εἰμι, ἀποθανεῖσθε ἐν ταῖς ἁμαρτίαις ὑμῶν.
If you do not believe who I am, you will die in your sins. (8:24b)

The Jews' response gives no indication that they understand this as use of or allusion to the divine name.[282] They fail to understand his claims. In 8:28 he then declares that one day they will, when they have lifted him up, namely brought him to his death by crucifixion.

εἶπεν οὖν [αὐτοῖς] ὁ Ἰησοῦς· ὅταν ὑψώσητε τὸν υἱὸν τοῦ ἀνθρώπου,
τότε γνώσεσθε ὅτι ἐγώ εἰμι,
καὶ ἀπ' ἐμαυτοῦ ποιῶ οὐδέν,
ἀλλὰ καθὼς ἐδίδαξέν με ὁ πατὴρ ταῦτα λαλῶ.
Jesus said to them, "When you have lifted up the Son of Man,
then you shall know that I am (the one I claim to be)
and that I do nothing of my own accord,
but say those things as my Father has taught me." (8:28)

Had this been a use of the divine name, one might have expected charges of blasphemy.[283] Instead the author has Jesus proceed to explain who he is:

καὶ ὁ πέμψας με μετ' ἐμοῦ ἐστιν· οὐκ ἀφῆκέν με μόνον,
ὅτι ἐγὼ τὰ ἀρεστὰ αὐτῷ ποιῶ πάντοτε.
And the one who sent me is with me. He does not abandon me,
because I always do what is pleasing to him. (8:29)

Death, 112; cf. Schnackenburg, *Johannesevangelium*, 3.254; Bauckham, "Monotheism," 161–62, who notes the "ironic level at which the characters act much more significantly than they themselves know or understand." He sees an allusion to Isa 45:18–24, especially 21–24, and the notion that every knee is to bow to Jesus.

282. Cf. Bauer, *Johannes*, 123; Blank, *Krisis*, 230, 246, 227; Forestell, *Word*, 47; Riedl, *Heilswerk*, 234; Dauer, *Passionsgeschichte*, 244; Pancaro, *Law*, 60–61; Harner, "*I am*," 43–45; Lindars, *Gospel of John*, 320–21; Brown, *John*, 350–51; Schnackenburg, *Johannesevangelium*, 2.253–54, 256; Boismard and Lamouille, *Jean*, 230; Moloney, *Son of Man*, 132; Bruce, *John*, 193; Beasley-Murray, *John*, 130; Burkett, *Son of Man*, 159–60; Williams, "'I am' or 'I am He,'" 347; Schnelle, *Johannes*, 263.

283. So Zimmermann, *Christologie*, 132; cf. Burkett, *Son of Man*, 159–60; Van Belle, "Death of Jesus," 22; Bauckham, "Monotheism," 156; Reynolds, *Apocalyptic Son of Man*, 166–68; Carson, *John*, 343–45.

The Salvation Event in John

This is another instance of going beyond a literal understanding of the envoy model. He has come from God and at the same time God is with him. None of this suggests that the ἐγώ εἰμι in 8:28 is a pronouncement of the divine name.[284]

Similarly in 13:19 Jesus promises his disciples that when they see his prediction come true about Judas, they will realise that he is who he claims to be:

ἀπ' ἄρτι λέγω ὑμῖν πρὸ τοῦ γενέσθαι,
ἵνα πιστεύσητε ὅταν γένηται ὅτι ἐγώ εἰμι.
I tell you this now before it happens,
so that when it does happen, you may believe that I am (who I claim to be). (13:19)

It is not impossible that we could have here an allusion to the divine name,[285] but nothing requires it.[286] The response one would have expected, had "I am" been understood as use of the divine name to refer to himself, would be what we do indeed find in 8:58–59, where Jesus' hearers are wanting to stone him.

εἶπεν αὐτοῖς Ἰησοῦς· ἀμὴν ἀμὴν λέγω ὑμῖν, πρὶν Ἀβραὰμ γενέσθαι ἐγώ εἰμί.
Ἦραν οὖν λίθους ἵνα βάλωσιν ἐπ' αὐτόν.
Ἰησοῦς δὲ ἐκρύβη καὶ ἐξῆλθεν ἐκ τοῦ ἱεροῦ.
Jesus said to them, "Truly, truly I tell you: before Abraham came into existence, I have been in existence."
So they took up stones to throw onto him.
Jesus hid himself and left the temple. (8:58–59)

Given that this is not the response to ἐγώ εἰμι elsewhere, it may well not be

---

284. Barrett, *John*, 342; Barrett, "Theocentric," 12; Barrett, "Symbolism," 71–72; Becker, *Johannes*, 208; Nicholson, *Death*, 113, 121.

285. So Brown, *John*, 571; Boismard and Lamouille, *Jean*, 343; Schnackenburg, *Johannesevangelium*, 3.31; Forestell, *Word*, 47; Bruce, *John*, 288; Pokorny, "Jesus," 222; Burkett, *Son of Man*, 146–47; Bauckham, "Monotheism," 156; Moloney, *Love*, 108; Williams, "'I am' or 'I am He,'" 347; Ashton, *Fourth Gospel*, 90, who claims: "The easiest and most straightforward explanation of 8:58, whether the allusion is to Exod 3:14 (Odeberg, Schnackenburg, etc.) or to the divine oracle in Deut 32:39 and Second Isaiah (Barrett, Herner, Williams), is that Jesus is actually claiming the name of Yahweh for himself."

286. So Barrett, "Theocentric," 12–13; Barrett, "Symbolism," 71–72; Becker, *Johannes*, 209; Nicholson, *Death*, 113. Petersen, *Brot, Licht und Weinstock*, 108–9, points out that Origen understands 13:19 similarly and she agrees.

the explanation for their response here either.[287] Offence may well have been taken to the claim that he existed before Abraham, an outrageous claim.[288] Such a claim reflects the author's view of Jesus as Logos incarnate.[289] Thompson concludes:

> There may be a reference to the divine "I am" of the OT in the claim of 8:58, but it is allusive or indirect. Jesus does not say "I am that I am." . . . Thus the link between Jesus' statement and the divine OT 'I am' is through the middle term, life. Jesus claims to share in God's kind of existence, eternal existence, existence that does not "come into being" but that simply 'is.' (8:35; 1:1, 2)[290]

Our review of the texts in which the absolute ἐγώ εἰμι is used has at no point found evidence that required seeing these words as either the divine name or alluding to it.[291] Indeed all the occurrences are capable of alternative explanations which in most cases are more consistent with the context and the hearers' responses and in just one or two provide a more plausible reading. This is not to deny that the author (or his tradition) could not have modelled Jesus' self-declarations on those of Yahweh in Isaiah, but, as there, the primary meaning in John is that Jesus is all he claims to be, as 8:28-29 aptly illustrates.[292] Alleged use of the divine name as a self-appellation by Jesus thus fails to convince. On the other hand, equally unconvincing would be a finding that identified use of the divine for instance in 6:20 or 8:58 and

---

287. Cf. Brown, *John*, 367-68; Schnackenburg, *Johannesevangelium*, 2.300-301; Pokorny, "Jesus," 217; Becker, *Johannes*, 208; Forestell, *Word*, 47; Beasley-Murray, *John*, 139-40; Burkett, *Son of Man*, 146-47; Carson, *John*, 358; Williams, "'I am' or 'I am He,'" 351; Bauckham, "Monotheism," 155, who notes that it is "some kind of claim to divine authority—which is taken by his hearers to be blasphemous." Coloe, *God Dwells with Us*, 142, who suggests "the fivefold repetition of the phrase ἐγώ εἰμί (8:12, 18, 24, 28, 58) in the Temple . . . gives the phrase the character of a theophany."

288. Barrett, *John*, 352; Barrett, "Theocentric," 12; Barrett, "Symbolism," 7-8; Lindars, *Gospel of John*, 336; *John*, 85-86; Petersen, *Brot, Licht und Weinstock*, 107; E. D. Freed, "Who or What Was before Abraham in Jn 8:58?" *JSNT* 17 (1983): 52-53, though his suggestion that we understand here a reference to the pre-existent Messiah Son of Man is not convincing.

289. Moloney, *John*, 284-85.

290. Thompson, *God*, 91-92;

291. Petersen, *Brot, Licht und Weinstock*, notes that Origen did not sense anything special in the absolute "I am" sayings (97) and pointed out that others use the "I am" of themselves (106). Similarly Zimmermann, *Christologie*, notes that the responses in the narrative do not suggest "I am" is understood as a divine claim (132).

292. So Barrett, *John*, 342; Barrett, "Theocentric," 12-13; Barrett, "Symbolism," 69-72; Lindars, *Gospel of John*, 320; Bühner, *Gesandte*, 166-74; Becker, "Auferstehung," 150; *Johannes*, 208.

The Salvation Event in John

then denied its presence elsewhere. Once these instances could be established, then this possibility would have to be considered at least for those open-ended instances like 4:26; 8:24, 28 and 13:19, but this is not our finding.

When, however, Jesus presents himself as bread (6:35, 42, 48, 51), light (8:12; 9:5), life (11:25) and "the way, the truth, and the life" (14:6; cf. also gate: 10:7, 9; good shepherd: 10:11, 14; [true] vine: 15:1, 5),[293] images associated with Torah and Israel, it is clear that a claim is being made that he offered what God alone can offer. These are not divine titles,[294] but the claim entailed in this kind of self-presentation amounts to the assertion, consistently made in the Gospel, that the Son uniquely acts and speaks for the Father.[295] It makes a claim about who the Son is, not just as one sent with a commission, but as in himself bearing what are divine qualities in a way not, for instance, said of disciples (cf. Matt 5:15–16).[296] The closest analogy is in the widespread use of such images to describe what Wisdom offers,[297] in particular Wisdom understood as embodied in Torah. The author has transferred such images to Jesus away from Torah.[298] This makes sense of the depiction of Jesus as the true bread.

οὐ Μωϋσῆς δέδωκεν ὑμῖν τὸν ἄρτον ἐκ τοῦ οὐρανοῦ,
ἀλλ' ὁ πατήρ μου δίδωσιν ὑμῖν τὸν ἄρτον ἐκ τοῦ οὐρανοῦ τὸν ἀληθινόν·
It was not Moses who gave you the bread from heaven,
but my Father gives you the true bread from heaven. (6:32)

---

293. Anderson, "Johannine *Egō Eimi* Sayings," 166, notes that "for Jewish audiences, each of the I-am metaphors echoes a typology of Israel in Hebrew Scripture. As Israel is a light to the nations (Isa. 42.6; 49.6), Israel's leaders are described as shepherds (2 Sam. 5.2; Ps. 78.70–72), Israel is a luxuriant vine (Hos. 10.1), the Torah is associated with bread (Deut. 8.3), etc. Further, each of the nine I-am metaphors and themes in John possesses cross-cultural qualities that address existential needs of humanity, so they would communicate well to Gentile audiences as well." See also Ball, *"I am" in John's Gospel*, who points to the occurrence of many of the images in Second Isaiah (199–236): food in Isaiah 55; 40:6 (214); light in Isa 42:6; 49:6; 51:4–5 (216–19); way in Isa 40:3; 48:17 (233, 236), but also shepherd in Ezekiel and Jeremiah (227), and vine in Ps 80 and Isa 5 (24–44).

294. Against Schweizer, *Ego Eimi*, 125–27, 135; so Zimmermann, "*egō eimi*," 57–58; Wead, *Devices*, 76–77.

295. Zimmermann, *Christologie*, 86, rightly notes that the author's rich imagery is an important medium of expression of his Christology.

296. On the significance of the "I am" sayings in going beyond the envoy model see also Schwankl, "Aspekte," 357–62.

297. Schnelle, *Johannes*, 125; Brown, *Introduction*, 261–62.

298. Thatcher, "Remembering Jesus," 178, describes the "I am" sayings as functioning like negative theology.

Only Jesus is the true bread, the true vine, the good shepherd,[299] and offers the water of life.[300] The claim to embody God's life and offer it is also this claim which lies behind some of the statements without a predicate where Jesus claims he is the one, the one who can do this (8:24, 28; 13:19). The ἐγώ εἰμι "I am" statements reflect therefore the heart of Johannine Christology; but they do not represent a *novum*: Jesus' self-appellation with the name of God.

5.3.12 The Son's Unique Being and Oneness with the Father

The passages considered thus far present a remarkably consistent picture. The first major point to emerge is that the Son has a unique relationship with the Father and has had since the beginning of time. It is a relationship of love. The unique relationship has to do with the unique being of the Son. He is called μονογενής θεός ("God the only Son"), while not identical with God; he is (μονογενής) υἱός, "the only Son," of the Father. As such he is dependent upon and subordinate to the Father; as such he is also uniquely able to fulfil the Father's commission and do his works and thereby present the Father's presence in the world. There is an ontological aspect.[301] Yet the precise nature of his being is left undefined.

5.3.12.1 Monotheism, Christology and Wisdom and Related Traditions

The closest analogy is in the stream of Logos/Sophia, where θεός could also be used of someone other than God without compromising monotheism. This doubtless paved the way for the kind of Christology developed in John, and the second-century apologists pursued the Logos concept further.[302] As Dunn points out, it also helped ensure the preservation of monotheism.[303] Apocalyptic notions of heavenly beings exercising divine functions and so bearing the divine name also offer analogies. Both may have influenced the

---

299. So Schweizer, *Ego Eimi*, 125-35; Ashton, *John*, 190, who speculates that these sayings come from prophets speaking as Jesus, but Ashton, *Fourth Gospel*, 128, notes that the majority "are clearly the product of deliberate composition."

300. Lindars, *John*, 78-79. On the image see Zimmermann, *Christologie*, 144-51.

301. So de Jonge, *Stranger*, 150; Mastin, "Neglected Factor," 49; Fuller, "Theology," 114.

302. So Dunn, "John," 334-35; Grant R. Osborne, "Christology and New Testament Hermeneutics: A Survey of the Discussion," *Semeia* 30 (1984): 58; Fuller, "Theology," 109-10.

303. Dunn, "John," 336-37.

The Salvation Event in John

way in which the Gospel speaks of the Son, but the Gospel falls short of offering more than this.

Judaism had been tolerating a range of ways in which God's action was represented by personifications and presences, including glory, name, Spirit, angel of the Lord, Wisdom, Shekinah, Torah, and these were never used in a way which implied abandonment of monotheism. They were either direct personifications or beings subordinate to God (angels and, mostly, Wisdom and Logos, though this is still in dispute).[304] The Fourth Gospel and its legacy would not have encountered difficulty with monotheism had it remained within such streams of thought. But, as it appropriated and formulated its Christology, it shows a departure from such streams in three respects.

5.3.12.2 Christology and Wisdom: The Differences

First, the Son Logos is co-eternal with the Father, was there "in the beginning," not created like Wisdom Logos, the first of his works of old, as in Prov 8:22. This raises the question of shared being with the Father posed already through the formulation of the Gospel's opening verses, but presumed throughout. This would not in itself be a problem for monotheism of the time, but would force one to the personification option, present in a number of places where wisdom tradition is used in Judaism. In that sense this is not strictly a departure. It becomes such in the light of the Christian use of Wisdom to refer to a separate being. The second, therefore, is this use of Logos/Wisdom to refer to a being whose relationship with the Father can therefore be described in functional terms of obedience, being sent, coming and going. This, too, need not pose a problem if we were to take such statements as personification. God also sends his Spirit who also comes and goes.

The third and crucial departure is the identification of the man Jesus of Nazareth with the personal Logos Son. As Keener notes, "Observers have long noted that virtually everything that John says about the Logos—apart from its incarnation as a particular historical person—Jewish literature said about divine Wisdom."[305] This is not presented in a manner which reduces

---

304. See Dunn, *Christology*, 163–76, who argues for personification in the use of Sophia right up to but not including the fourth evangelist. Countering, rightly, that this sets the limit too late: Segal, "Pre-existence," 93; Fuller, "Theology," 108–11.

305. Keener, *John*, 352; similarly, Glicksman, "Beyond Sophia," 89; McGrath, *Christology*, 76–77, who writes: "The issue does not appear to have been about whether the Johannine Christians were still monotheists, but about whether the one to whom they attributed various

the human Jesus to an appearance, as we shall see in 5.4 below. And as we have seen, the central structure of the author's Christology gives a major place to identity of being between the pre-existent one and the man Jesus. At this point both monotheism and, at the other pole of the paradox, Jesus' human personhood, are threatened. The Gospel does not work out solutions to the paradox and the author was unlikely to have been aware of the complexity of the problem which, above all, his Gospel posed for the Church to follow. But he marked out the ground on which later theological edifices would rise, including the doctrine of the Trinity. He never ultimately surrendered the real human personhood of Jesus and he asserts at the beginning and assumes throughout the kind of intimacy of shared being between Son and Father, otherwise preserved only for Jewish personifications of the divine. But even these poles of the paradox are scarcely defined or precise. For, on the one hand, he sometimes speaks of the Son as if he were a separate pre-existent being. It is hard to understand the envoy descent–ascent model otherwise. And, on the other, he sometimes speaks of the human Jesus as if he were no longer human, as we shall see in 5.4 below. We see Christology in a state of flux or, to change the metaphor, we identify two poles. At times they bend to the point of breaking, but ultimately they remain in place. This was a significant contribution of the Fourth Gospel to the theology and Christology of the Church to follow.

5.3.12.3 The Son and the Father

Not Ditheism

Accordingly the Gospel vigorously defends itself against the charge of ditheism, and, legitimately so.[306] It even turns such accusations around ironically and responds to them always from a point of view which sets Jesus in a functional unity of subordination with the Father, without denying the Son's distinctive being. He does as the Father does, and this also includes exercise of miraculous powers normally reserved for God, such as walking on water, keeping his own, raising the dead, raising himself from the dead and being the bearer of glory.[307] Evans notes that the use of glory is the

---

divine prerogatives and honours was God's appointed agent, or a rebel against God who sought to out himself in God's place" (114); Söding, "Ich und der Vater," 194, 197.

306. So de Jonge, *Stranger*, 148–49; Ellis, *Genius*, 140; Lindars, *Gospel of John*, 77; Schnelle, "Trinitarisches Denken," 379; Schwankl, "Aspekte," 368–69; Söding, "Ich und der Vater," 188–89.

307. So Boismard and Lamouille, *Jean*, 52.

The Salvation Event in John

nearest the Hebrew tradition came to ontology.³⁰⁸ But there is no merging of Jesus into God.³⁰⁹ Nor is Jesus a divine emanation.³¹⁰ Yet neither are there two divine beings.³¹¹

Not Begotten

There is also no word of the Son's eternal generation by the Father,³¹² nor, on the other hand, any mention of a beginning of the Son's existence. Birth from above (3:3) is not such an allusion, but, like 1:12–13, applies only to believers. Neither μονογενής nor 1:13 contains reference to the Son's birth. The former means "only one, the unique one" and in relation to fatherhood and sonship, "the only Son"; the latter would speak of the Son's birth only when the variant singular reading should prove original, and then need mean no more than the human birth of Jesus by a virgin. The allusion to birth from above refers primarily to Christians in ch. 3, and even though there is a close analogy between the Son's being from above and the disciples' being "from above," at no point is the language of birth applied directly to Jesus.³¹³

Not Incarnate Awakened Sonship

There is no indication that sonship belongs to Jesus only since the incarnation, as Lütgert argues, on the grounds that the prologue preserves the word Logos for the pre-existent being.³¹⁴ He treats the birth of Jesus as the point at which he is sent³¹⁵ and speculates that the Logos makes the Son aware of his original divinity.³¹⁶ It is true that the prologue uses the motif Logos of pre-existence, but never elsewhere in the Gospel is there the slightest indication that "Son" (let alone, God as his "Father") is inapplicable to the pre-existence. The sending is regularly associated with commissioning by

---

308. Evans, "Passion," 65.
309. Lieu, *Epistles*, 202.
310. So Haenchen, *Johannes*, 275–76.
311. So Cullmann, *Christologie*, 272–73; Barrett, "Theocentric," 13.
312. Against Riedl, *Heilswerk*, 213; Vellanickel, *Sonship*, 112–13, 130–31.
313. Cf. Nicholson, *Death*, 81.
314. Lütgert, *Christologie*, 60, 64–65, 77.
315. Lütgert, *Christologie*, 24, 41, 60.
316. Lütgert, *Christologie*, 54, 56, 67. Similarly Beyschlag, *Neutestamentliche Theologie II*, 425; Weiss, *Lehrbuch*, 609, 613; Cadman, *Open Heaven*, 11–13, 16; Brun, "Gottesschau," 15.

the Father as an act which must be in pre-existence, for it is on the basis of it that the Son came from above in the first place.

Not Adopted at Birth or Baptism

Lütgert is concerned to ward off views which see the unity of Father and Son as primarily one of will and thought, such as Holtzmann had propounded.[317] But his theory of a unity of being mediated by the Spirit, a position followed by Büchsel and Strathmann, also falls short of the Johannine conception.[318] He ends up with a Spirit-mediated unity on earth, but a substantial unity of the Logos and God in pre-existence.[319] A modern, yet also ancient variant of this view is that propounded by Watson,[320] who identifies, like Fuller earlier,[321] the baptism of Jesus as the point when the anhypostatic Logos enters the human being, Jesus, and takes 1 John 5:6, with its reference to coming by water, to mean coming through baptism, a position therefore akin to Cerinthus.[322] "Son" is also more than a metaphor to describe a functional unity and more than doxological, as if the evangelist is merely describing the human ideal, as Robinson and, earlier, D. Willibald Beyschlag suggest.[323]

Not Later Trinitarian Syntheses

Nor have we indication in the Gospel that Jesus operates with two egos, an "I am" of pre-existence and an obedient human self, as Fuller proposes.[324] The Gospel must be allowed to speak in its own terms without our reading in the Christologies of later centuries.[325] F.-M. Braun and Riedl, for instance, read the Fourth Gospel in line with the developments in later christological

---

317. Holtzmann, *Lehrbuch*, 493-94.

318. Lütgert, *Christologie*, 51-52, 99; cf. Büchsel, *Johannes*, 59; Strathmann, *Johannes*, 79.

319. Lütgert, *Christologie*, 69; similarly Cadman, *Open Heaven*, 16; and earlier, Beyschlag, *Neutestamentliche Theologie II*, 425.

320. Watson, "Christology," 113-14.

321. Fuller, "Christmas," 70; also Schoonenberg, "Prologue," 409-11; Brown, *Beloved Disciple*, 152-53; *Epistles*, 77-78.

322. Watson, "Christology," 118.

323. Robinson, "Christology," 71-72; Robinson, "Trinity," 177; Robinson, *Priority*, 311; Beyschlag, *Neutestamentliche Theologie II*, 425; Harvey, *Constraints*, 178; Schillebeeckx, *Christ*, 431.

324. Fuller, "Theology," 116.

325. So Schnackenburg, *Johannesevangelium*, 2.107; Mastin, "Neglected Factor," 49; Barrett, "Father," 19-21; Dunn, "John," 30-31.

The Salvation Event in John

thought and claim that we have in John a binitarian metaphysical unity, one in which unity of being is combined with awareness of distinct subjects acting in love and oneness.[326] Blank holds the two in tension, speaking of an irreducible separateness in unity to be understood neither in mythological nor pantheistic terms, nor as a statement of simple identity.[327] He speaks of the "christological implication" of the fourth evangelist's portrayal of Jesus.[328] Ibuki similarly stresses unity of being.[329] Schnelle argues that John sees the Son as not only participating in the being of the Father but having the same being as the Father. Accordingly John represents an exclusive monotheism in binitarian form, so that worship of the one God has been extended to include his Son.[330] John is certainly moving in that direction.[331] While the author does not use pneumatology to explicate how the Son tells not only what he has seen (the envoy-communicator model), but also what he sees and hears (the Father-Son apprentice model), namely the oneness during his earthly ministry, there does underlie such thought the assumption that the Spirit abides on and in the Son (1:34; 14:17), thus making the binitarian concept possible and suggesting even a trinitarian direction, as Schnelle has argued.[332]

Not Oneness without Real Subordination

Baur had argued that the Son was not created, but was born of the Father and emphasised that such was the unity that no independent thought was possible,[333] but this denies the assumption of willing obedience we find

326. Braun, *Jean*, 70; Riedl, *Heilswerk*, 421–23, cf. also 201, 205, 277; cf. also Fuller, "Theology," 116.
327. Blank, *Krisis*, 222–24.
328. Blank, *Krisis*, 347.
329. Ibuki, *Wahrheit*, 115, 123, 149, 174, 206.
330. Schnelle, "Trinitarisches Denken," emphasises that the Son is much more than an agent; he shares in the Father's being, which expresses itself in oneness of will and action, a binitarian monotheism (380). The issue is not usurpation (cf. 5:18; 19:7) but proper understanding of God's being (385–86). Ditheism is avoided while differentiation is expressed through the use of θεός and ὁ θεός in 1:1 and the neuter formulation ἕν ἐσμεν in 10:30. Only the Father is εἷς θεός (379).
331. Schnackenburg, *Person Jesu Christi*, 278, notes that the references to mutual indwelling (14:10–11, 20; cf. 17:21, 23) and oneness (10:30) go beyond functional unity and point to an ontological unity.
332. Schnelle, "Trinitarisches Denken," 385–86, who notes the role of pneumatology in bridging the gaps between heaven and earth, time and space, present and future; see also Thyen, "Erwägungen," 693.
333. Baur, *Vorlesungen*, 357–58, 367. Cf. similarly Scroggs, *Christology*, 79, on Jesus' freedom as Son.

throughout the Gospel. It is nevertheless interesting to see the strength of the emphasis on oneness in Käsemann and to find in Appold a survival of the view that obedience and subordination are foreign to Johannine Christology.[334] Yet Appold is hesitant to define the nature of the oneness he stoutly defends. He denies it is metaphysical or trinitarian, claims that more than a moral unity is presupposed for pre-existence, and prefers to speak of a unity in which Father and Son have equivalent status, "equivalent relationality" and mutually conditioned reciprocity.[335] He is right in observing that the Fourth Gospel does not offer a precise definition, though in his analysis he fails to do justice to the element of subordination. Pollard, too, claims the author gives no precise definition.[336] Langbrandtner goes beyond the evidence when he claims that for the *Grundschrift* the Logos is understood as an extension of God, not a separate person, whereas the emphasis on distinct persons comes first through the Redactor's addition of 1:3 and 1:14-18.[337] Scholtissek rightly observes that the author holds together differentiation of the persons of the Father and the Son *ad intra* with identity in their salvific work *ad extra*.[338] Donald A. Carson rightly comments: "The tension between unqualified statements affirming the full deity of the Word or of the Son, and those which distinguish between the Word or the Son from the Father, are typical of the Fourth Gospel and are present from the very first verse."[339]

The Unique Son Subordinate in Oneness with the Father

The second most important point to emerge from our review of the passages is that the Son is consistently presented as subordinate to the Father. This is not to be explained away using two-nature theory or by defining roles within the Trinity on the basis of the implied dependence in the imagery of "Father" and "Son."[340] Nor is subordination something limited to the earthly Jesus, as Lütgert's position assumes.[341] Nor is there a kind of *kenosis* as Ulrich Busse suggests, when he proposes that the Logos surrenders its nature so that only

---

334. Käsemann, *Letzter Wille*, 59, 105; Appold, *Oneness*, 20-22; Osborn, "Theology," 76; Schnelle, "Trinitarisches Denken," 379-80.
335. Appold, *Oneness*, 272, 283, 22.
336. Pollard, *Christology*, 17.
337. Langbrandtner, *Weltferner Gott*, 42, 89-92, 108-109.
338. Scholtissek, "Ich und der Vater," 337.
339. Carson, *John*, 34.
340. Cf. Mastin, "Neglected Factor," 50.
341. Lütgert, *Christologie*, 69; also Cadman, *Open Heaven*, 16; Braun, *Jean*, 141-42.

The Salvation Event in John

through a unity of action may one recognise God.[342] Precisely in his uniqueness of being as the Son of the Father Jesus is also subordinate to the Father.[343]

Subordination and Sending

The Father sent the Son. Above all Miranda and Bühner have emphasised the importance of this motif and by implication the centrality of subordination in the relation of Father and Son.[344] Miranda sees two streams merging in the Gospel, that of messianic and prophetic sending and that of the sonship of Jesus, in such a way that a functional Christology combines with one of distinctive relationship, producing the Christology of obedient sonship of the pre-existent sent one.[345] Bühner identifies in the Fourth Gospel a combination of influences from the judicial shaliach, the common envoy procedures, and the sent prophet and angel, and Becker, importantly, notes that in John this sending stream must be seen as merging with the distinctive wisdom stream.[346] One could say that this merging accounts for much of the tension between the more strongly ontological orientation of the logos traditions and the primarily functional orientation of the sending tradition.[347] Both aspects are present in each, but in different proportion. Subordination is still common to both.

While the author uses the revelation-communication pattern in a non-literal way, he upholds the notion of the Son's obedience to a heavenly commission and his continuing dependence on the Father during his earthly ministry. The author assumes that the Son comes from the Father, from heaven to earth, completes his commission, and then returns. With endless variation the author has Jesus repeat this claim. The sending of the Son is central to Johannine faith.[348]

---

342. Busse, "Johannes 10," 524.

343. So Barrett, "Father," 23–25.

344. So Miranda, *Vater*; Miranda, *Sendung*; Bühner, *Gesandte*; see also Borgen, *Bread from Heaven*, 158–62; Haenchen, *Johannes*, 107–8; Bruce, *John*, 130; Barrett, "Theocentric," 6–7; Robinson, *Priority*, 350; Schnelle, *Christologie*, 209.

345. Miranda, *Sendung*, 34, 38, 41–45, 67; Borgen, *Bread from Heaven*, 158–62; Boismard and Lamouille, *Jean*, 49–50; Bruce, *John*, 167–68; Isaacs, "Prophetic Spirit," 402–403.

346. Bühner, *Gesandte*, 213–15, 233–34, 264–66, 335; Becker, *Johannes*, 55; "Auferstehung," 142; cf. also critically Schnelle, *Christologie*, 209–10, who stresses the wisdom background of sending.

347. So Schnackenburg, *Person Jesu Christi*, 278.

348. Cf. McGrath, *Christology*, 224, who writes: "Both the Word and the Son are sent, but the former designates the divine agent sent from heaven, whereas the latter designates the

Sending and Oneness

Sending should not be seen as rivalling oneness as the centre of Johannine Christology. Both Käsemann, and more particularly, Appold argue that sending is unable to integrate the whole of Johannine Christology as oneness does.[349] At 5:19-20 a different image is employed. But their stress on oneness is given at the expense of motifs of subordination, sending, commissioning and obedience present in the text. Ashton emphasises the oneness between sender and sent one reflecting Jewish laws of agency,[350] but, while this plays a role, oneness in John is much more than this as the bold statements of the prologue demonstrate.[351] The problem with oneness is that it leaves too much undefined.

The oneness between the Son and the Father is beyond dispute in the Gospel. But what kind of oneness is it and in what way is it perceived to function? As a motif it is relatively rare. As a concept applied to the text it does integrate much of what is there in a way that is far more effective than, say, Haacker's notion of Founder. But it is methodologically more satisfactory to identify the underlying structure of the author's thought than to seek one focal motif or to impose one overriding concept. By seeking the underlying structure we have been able to show how both oneness and sending belong, and to show what they mean in the Gospel much more concretely than has been done by Appold. Haenchen's attack on the oneness motif, on the other hand, sees only the occurrence of the motif and fails to perceive the way in which Appold uses the notion.[352] Hahn is right in seeing three key elements in the Gospel: oneness, sending, witnessing,[353] but that, too, does not go far enough, for it fails to show the integrating structure within which they belong. Sending provides the structure of Johannine Christology, but that Christology goes

---

human agent whom the Word becomes." This runs contrary to the many allusions to the Son as the one sent from the Father which assume pre-existence.

349. Käsemann, *Letzter Wille*, 30, 59, 105; Appold, *Oneness*, 20-22, 283; cf. the criticism in Haacker, *Stiftung*, 93 n. 76; Barrett, "Father," 25-26.

350. Ashton, *Fourth Gospel*, 297. Importantly he also observes that agency law is not enough of an explanation "for it leaves unexplained the transition from the idea of a human agent as envisaged by the law (and one must include here the implications of the term 'son of the house') to that of a divine agent to whom God has entrusted his own powers and his own authority" (228). Similarly Theobald, *Johannes*, 1.62.

351. Schnelle, "Trinitarisches Denken," 379-80; Schwankl, "Aspekte," 357.

352. Haenchen, *Johannes*, 107.

353. Hahn, "Prozess," 95; cf. Anderson, *Christology*, 261, who writes: "Subordinationist and egalitarian christological motifs are not central component parts of John's pervasive *agency christology*."

The Salvation Event in John

far beyond a literal application of the envoy model which would simply have the Son as revealer of what he has seen and heard or authorised to act on the Father's behalf,[354] for as especially John 5 and 10 show, the Son is in constant communion with the Father and ultimately he offers not information but a relationship with himself and the Father in which is eternal life.[355]

Christocentric or Theocentric?

It is consistent with the thoroughgoing christocentric interpretation of Käsemann and Appold that they fail to do justice to the notion of subordination and so make Christology not theology the centre of the Gospel. Judith M. Lieu also emphasises the central role of Christ, especially compared with the first epistle where he is cast more in the role of founder and vicarious redeemer, but ultimately this central role of Christ in the Gospel makes sense only because of the Gospel's particularly theocentric approach in regard to its Christology.[356] Haenchen and Becker strongly emphasise the sending motif and therewith theocentricity.[357] Barrett notes that the evangelist has the ministry of Jesus end with an openness for more to be said through the ministry of the Spirit and uses Davey's observations to show that the Son is dependent upon the Father for power and knowledge. Thus Christ remains strongly in the role of the mediator and revealer.[358] Robin Scroggs exaggerates in claiming that we have in John complete subordination and complete equality.[359] Rather, in his unique being, the Son, so superior to all others, acts in a unity of will and obedience with the Father which only his unique being makes possible.

5.3.12.4 The Son and the Father: Conclusions

Accordingly, we find within the Gospel a Christology of Jesus' sonship which does not easily fit the familiar categories. There is a definite ontological claim about the Son's being, which sets him apart from all others. As such, he is

---

354. So rightly Zimmermann, *Christologie*, 192.
355. Bauckham, "Monotheisn and Christology," 153: more than an agent Jesus "exercises the full divine sovereignty as given him by his Father—but as also fully his own."
356. Lieu, *Epistles*, 201–6; similarly Robinson, *Priority*, 350–51.
357. Haenchen, *Johannes*, 107–8; Becker, *Johannes*, 147–48.
358. Barrett, "Theocentric," 6–7; "Father," 22–23; similarly Lieu, *Epistles*, 202.
359. Scroggs, *Christology*, 242.

separate from God, yet as such, also uniquely able to do his works and speak his words. His relationship with the Father is one of love and obedience and, in obedient submission to the Father who sent him, he comes into the world offering to human beings all that the Father offers: light and life and truth. To receive him is to receive him who sent him. To see him is to see the Father. To enter a relationship of love with him is to do so also with the Father. To reject him is to reject the Father. Rejected by the world, he returns, ascending, exalted and glorified to the Father. He is vindicated; the world is judged; the Spirit is given; the disciples sent. He remains the unique Son, at one with the Father, always and obediently concerned to glorify the Father.

The undefined yet impressive emphasis on the unique being of the Son and his relationship with God raises, in turn, the question to what degree the author has defined the nature of this sonship in relationship to Jesus' humanity.

5.4 The Nature of the Son as Jesus of Nazareth

We have considered the statements of the central structure of the author's Christology which deal with the return of the Son to the Father, the nature of his "revelation" as salvation event, the meaning of pre-existence and the nature of the Son in relation to the Father. The latter emphasised the unique being of the Son which also enabled him to fulfil his Father's commission in coming as the sent one into the world. As the sent one, making the Father known through his earthly ministry, he is Jesus of Nazareth. As we examined his nature as unique Son of the Father, so we now examine his nature as Jesus of Nazareth. How is his humanity portrayed in the Gospel? And how is it likely that the author intended it should be understood? I distinguish these two questions, because an examination of what the artist has drawn may well reveal features belonging to the finished product which give an impression different from what the author intended, insofar as intentions are at all evident.

5.4.1   Jesus of Nazareth, the Son Come from the Father

5.4.1.1 Real Pre-existence and Real Coming

I want to begin with findings drawn from our analysis thus far. One is that the Gospel employs revelation-communication language only as a way of

The Salvation Event in John

claiming that the Son represents the Father's offer of life, and not literally as a description of an information-giving process, whereas it uses the language of coming from pre-existent heavenly intimacy with the Father as a description of what actually happened. The Son, pre-existent with the Father, comes into the world, commissioned by him, to bring life to the world. This means, at the same time, that the author works with spatial and temporal categories which enable him to describe movement from heaven to earth and earth to heaven. Believers look forward to the sight of the Son's glory in heaven, a vision not possible as long as they are on earth (17:24–26). Similarly Jesus, while on earth, had looked forward to his return to the Father in glory. Therefore theories of the Son somehow straddling heaven and earth during his earthly ministry or moving constantly between the two, as Lütgert proposed,[360] have no place in the author's Christology. His oneness with the Father on earth never means his presence in heaven on earth. Behind the author's Christology is a cosmological perspective according to which God is active and present on earth, but there exists a heaven in which God's being is more intensively present. This is the view common to all NT writers.

5.4.1.2 Real Continuity of Being

The Son's presence means therefore a departure from this heavenly presence. In this there is loss for the Son. Therefore also he looks forward to his return. In this he shared with human beings life on earth as distinct from life in heaven. Thus Thüsing speaks of the Son's giving up the glory of heaven.[361] The extent to which this represents humiliation will be addressed below when we also take into account the nature of his suffering and death. The Son's coming is a real coming in the sense that he does not cease to be the Son during his earthly ministry, but speaks and acts in full awareness of being the Son sent from the Father. Nowhere does the Gospel indicate that this was an awareness awakened at some specific point in Jesus' ministry, as Lütgert suggested,[362] nor that the Logos or Spirit adopted[363] or became incarnate in him[364] only through the waters of baptism. Nor is there the

---

360. Lütgert, *Christologie*, 49.
361. Thüsing, *Erhöhung*, 222–23, 225; cf. Schnelle, *Christologie*, 93, 182, 254.
362. Lütgert, *Christologie*, 54, 56, 67.
363. Watson, "Christology," 114. So rightly Theobald, *Fleischwerdung*, 295, who sees the prologue as in part countering that view.
364. Fuller, "Christmas," 70; Schoonenberg, "Prologue," 409.

slightest indication of duality in the Son as Jesus of Nazareth.[365] The Son is Jesus of Nazareth and Jesus of Nazareth is the Son, the one subject, the one Son who was with the Father from the beginning. The evangelist reveals no awareness of problems here. He does not ask: would the child Jesus have possessed the same full self-awareness, the same knowledge? His interest is to tell of the Son's confrontation with the world in the event of his ministry and death.

Similarly the interest of the author is not to present Jesus as omniscient, though he tells of occasions of miraculous knowledge, nor as omnipotent, though he tells of miraculous deeds. His interest is to present him as a person demanding faith and allegiance toward himself and so towards God. It is for this that the Son came. And it is for this that he tells of the Son's pre-existence and sending. This consistent perspective throughout the Gospel has important methodological implications. Miracles of knowledge and power have a subordinate role and must be weighted accordingly in examining the author's Christology.

5.4.1.3 The Spirit and Jesus of Nazareth

We begin our analysis by considering the significance of the Spirit for understanding the nature of the Son as Jesus of Nazareth. The fact that the author's account of the earthly life of Jesus concentrates only on the period following his baptism has led to a good deal of speculation about its significance, particularly as a way of explaining continuity of consciousness between the pre-existent Son and the earthly Jesus. This began with early gnostic teachers, like Cerinthus, who proposed that the Son first entered the man, Jesus of Nazareth at this point (Irenaeus *Haer.* I 14:6; Clement of Alexandria *Exc.* 43:5; 61:6). The same suggestion has been put forward again by Watson.[366] Is John the Baptist's cry, "Behold the Lamb of God, who takes away the sin of the world," really saying that here is the body to be sacrificed, which the Son will now take upon himself or into which he will now enter? The narrative of the baptism contains nothing to support this view. For the Baptist goes on to speak of his pre-existence, without any indication of a distinction of persons or of anhypostatic pre-existence only.

---

365. Against Fuller, "Theology," 116.
366. Watson, "Christology," 114. On this see also Talbert, "And the Word Became Flesh," 44, of the Alogi and Theodotus.

The Spirit and Jesus of Nazareth—Establishing Continuity?

More serious attention has been given from time to time to the theory that the coming of the Spirit in baptism established the continuity of consciousness between the Son as the man Jesus of Nazareth and the pre-existent Son as Logos. Cadman argues that the Spirit enabled Jesus to perceive himself as taken up into the Logos of God.[367] Lütgert identifies Spirit and Logos.[368] Weiss distinguishes between Jesus' receiving the Spirit for self-awareness and his having received revelation already before baptism because of the Logos, citing the Baptist's words in 1:30–31.[369] Büchsel sees the receiving of the Spirit as part of the process of incarnation.[370] Such views once had the support of a number of scholars and it is instructive to read the critical discussion in earlier writers like Holtzmann and before him Baur.[371] The baptism narrative also fails to support these views. There is not even the report of a vision, as in Mark. It would be a strange conflict of imagery if Jesus, on the one hand, claims that he tells what he had seen and heard and, on the other, knows that he needed to be reminded by the Spirit.

Jesus' Baptism: Bestowal or Statement of What Is?

Nevertheless the role of the Spirit in relationship to the Son during his earthly ministry is an important issue. The key texts are the Baptist's report of the descent of the Spirit in 1:32–34; the references to birth of the Spirit in 3:1–11; the statement about Jesus' receiving the Spirit in 3:34–35; and the link between Jesus' words and the Spirit in 6:63. According to the Baptist's witness in 1:32–34, the descent of the Spirit enables the Baptist to identify Jesus as the pre-existent one, the Lamb of God, the elect one or Son of God, and the one who baptises with the Holy Spirit. Beside this, the other distinctive feature, in comparison with the Synoptic accounts, is that the narrative explicitly adds that after its descent the Spirit not only descends but also remains on Jesus.

367. Cadman, *Open Heaven*, 6–8.
368. Lütgert, *Christologie*, 25; cf. also Talbert, "And the Word became Flesh," 45, who notes that hearers would link 1:32–34 and 3:34 and might identify this with coming of wisdom as in 1 En. 42:1–2, Wis 10:6, 15–16; 18:15.
369. Weiss, *Lehrbuch*, 613 n. 15, 614.
370. Büchsel, *Johannes*, 40; similarly Fuller, "Christmas," 70; Schoonenberg, "Prologue," 409.
371. Holtzmann, *Lehrbuch*, 451, 464, 508–9; Baur, *Vorlesungen*, 366.

Already Baur argued that for John the descent of the Spirit is nothing more than a sign for the Baptist[372] and Holtzmann notes that already Matthew has turned it into a declaratory act for the sake of others.[373] Does the remaining of the Spirit on Jesus also symbolise his prophetic equipping with the Spirit from that point onwards,[374] or his equipping with the Spirit at his pre-existent commissioning onwards, as Bühner suggests?[375] Or is it a symbolic declaration of the permanent availability to him of the Spirit through his eternal intimacy with the Father or the unique nature of his being? Burge, for instance, while acknowledging the tension which exists between Spirit-possession tradition and the incarnation of the Son, the Logos, suggests that Spirit should be understood here not primarily as a power, but as an attribute of his person.[376] As Thompson puts it, "The Spirit does not make Jesus who or what he is—rather, it is because of *who* Jesus is, the incarnate Word of God, who is with God and is God, that he has the Spirit and gives it to others."[377] The meaning of the dove's descent must be considered in the light of the other important statements about the Son and the Spirit in the Gospel and to these we turn.

The Father Gives the Spirit to the Son without Measure 3:34

In 1.2.1 we discussed the translations of 3:34b and argued for the view that it be understood as a statement about God's giving the Spirit to Jesus, not of Jesus' giving the Spirit to others.

> ὃν γὰρ ἀπέστειλεν ὁ θεὸς τὰ ῥήματα τοῦ θεοῦ λαλεῖ,
> οὐ γὰρ ἐκ μέτρου δίδωσιν τὸ πνεῦμα.
> ὁ πατὴρ ἀγαπᾷ τὸν υἱὸν καὶ πάντα δέδωκεν ἐν τῇ χειρὶ αὐτοῦ.
> He whom God sent speaks the words of God;
> For he does not give (him) the Spirit by measure.
> The Father loves the Son and has given all things into his hands.
> (3:34–35)

---

372. Baur, *Vorlesungen*, 107; similarly Porsch, *Pneuma*, 104; Braun, *Jean*, 68–69; Thompson, God, 161–62.
373. Holtzmann, *Lehrbuch*, 509.
374. Miranda, *Sendung*, 40, 54; similarly Schnackenburg, *John*, 386; Bennema, *Saving Wisdom*, 166, writing of "an empowerment of revelatory wisdom in order to reveal God."
375. Bühner, *Gesandte*, 304.
376. So Burge, *Anointed Community*, 72–73, 87.
377. Thompson, *God*, 160.

The Salvation Event in John

This could refer to a giving of the Spirit at baptism,[378] or in pre-existence at his sending as he is given all things (3:35),[379] but the present tense, δίδωσιν ("he gives"), makes it more likely that it refers to a constant state.[380] It is therefore to be taken closely with the present tense in the statement ὁ πατὴρ ἀγαπᾷ τὸν υἱὸν ("The Father loves the Son") and with the perfect tense of πάντα δέδωκεν ἐν τῇ χειρὶ αὐτοῦ ("and has given all things into his hands" in 3:35). We may detect a tension here between the image of permanent abiding and constant giving, but this should not be pressed and reflects the merging of different traditions. The focus is primarily on the fullness, ἐκ μέτρου ("without measure"; cf. πάντα "all things" 3:35). This would also receive confirmation through 6:63 which shares with 3:34 a reference to Jesus' words and identifies them with spirit and by implication with the work of the Spirit:

τὸ πνεῦμά ἐστιν τὸ ζῳοποιοῦν, ἡ σὰρξ οὐκ ὠφελεῖ οὐδέν·
τὰ ῥήματα ἃ ἐγὼ λελάληκα ὑμῖν πνεῦμά ἐστιν καὶ ζωή ἐστιν.
The Spirit is what makes alive, the flesh is of no profit;
the words which I have spoken to you, they are spirit and they are life.
(6:63)

cf. ὃν γὰρ ἀπέστειλεν ὁ θεὸς τὰ ῥήματα τοῦ θεοῦ λαλεῖ,
οὐ γὰρ ἐκ μέτρου δίδωσιν τὸ πνεῦμα.
He whom God sent speaks the words of God;
for he does not give (him) the Spirit by measure. (3:34)

The presence of the Spirit with the disciples in Jesus (and in them after his return) receives emphasis also in 14:16–17.

κἀγὼ ἐρωτήσω τὸν πατέρα καὶ ἄλλον παράκλητον δώσει ὑμῖν,
ἵνα μεθ' ὑμῶν εἰς τὸν αἰῶνα ᾖ, τὸ πνεῦμα τῆς ἀληθείας,
ὃ ὁ κόσμος οὐ δύναται λαβεῖν, ὅτι οὐ θεωρεῖ αὐτὸ οὐδὲ γινώσκει·
ὑμεῖς γινώσκετε αὐτό, ὅτι παρ' ὑμῖν μένει καὶ ἐν ὑμῖν ἔσται.
And I will ask the Father and he will give you another paraclete,
so that he may be with you forever, the Spirit of Truth,
which the world cannot receive, because it neither sees nor knows it;

---

378. So Büchsel, *Johannes*, 59; Strathmann, *Johannes*, 79; Dodd, *Interpretation*, 311; Schnackenburg, *John*, 1.386; Miranda, *Sendung*, 40.
379. So Lindars, *Gospel of John*, 171; Bruce, *John*, 97; Burge, *Anointed Community*, 83.
380. Thompson, *God*, 170–71.

but you know it, because it remains with you and will be in you. (14:16-17)

John 3:34 favours therefore an interpretation which sees the descent of the dove in John as symbolising a permanent state of affairs.[381] Correspondingly it is the one so identified who can baptise with the Spirit. He was of unique being and John recognises this. As Bennema emphasises, the link between Spirit and Wisdom informs the author's depiction of Jesus' offer of life during his ministry.[382]

The Son, Born of Water and the Spirit? 3:1-11

The earlier sections of ch. 3 should also not be seen as implying that Jesus was equipped or born of the Spirit at his baptism. The issue arises in 3:1-11 because in contrasting Nicodemus, on the one hand, and the disciples, on the other, the author makes statements which identify Jesus so strongly with his disciples that one might easily apply what is said of them also to Jesus himself. This is particularly evident in 3:11, where Jesus says, "What we know we speak and what we have seen to that we bear testimony and you do not receive our testimony." Similarly the use of the wind simile in 3:8 raises questions of origin and destination in a way usually applied to the Son's coming and going. But there is no evidence that we should extend this further and see in 3:3 or 3:5, which describe birth by water and the Spirit, also a christological reference either to the Son's birth or to his receiving the Spirit by baptism.[383]

Permanent Bestowal of the Spirit: Conclusion

The passages considered suggest that we best understand the Spirit as a constant gift of the Father to the Son and Jesus' baptism as a sign of this giving, of its permanence, and as a sign for the Baptist that Jesus is the expected one and the one whose pre-existent glory he affirms. The Gospel does not make explicit whether there was a point when Jesus was first given the Spirit or

---

381. So Thompson, *God*, 175-76.

382. Bennema, *Saving Wisdom*, 100, who speaks of "John's pneumatic wisdom christology"; similarly Rusam, "Lamm Gottes," 77; Theobald, "Gott, Logos und Pneuma," 374.

383. Cf. Nicholson, *Death*, 81; Thyen, *Johannesevangelium*, 188-89, reading 3:3 christologically as a self-reference by Jesus. See the critical discussion in Frances Back, "Die rätselhaften 'Antworten' Jesu. Zum Thema des Nikodemusgesprächs (Joh 3,1-21)," *EvT* 73 (2013): 181-82.

The Salvation Event in John

whether the Spirit, like love, has been the constant gift of the Father to the Son from the beginning. The former might be understood in association with the Son's commissioning and authorisation, offering a close analogy with the disciples' receiving the Spirit and their commissioning. The latter is more probable and would see the Spirit as another way of describing that quality of eternal relationship of Son and Father which enables him to represent the gift of divine life to the world. Nowhere did we find evidence that the Gospel uses Spirit as the mediator of awareness between the human Jesus and the pre-existent Logos or as the means whereby the Logos supposedly enters or takes up the human being Jesus of Nazareth at his baptism or an earlier point in time. The nature of the Son as Jesus of Nazareth is not such that he is a human being possessed of the Spirit, for the Spirit is the Father's gift to the Son. His nature as Jesus of Nazareth comes much more into focus when we turn to the theme of incarnation.

5.4.2 The Word Became Flesh: 1:14a in 1:14–18

The coming of the Son into the world is most frequently defined in association with incarnation, a term based on a single text, 1:14, "And the Word became flesh." It is unique in the Gospel, but its position as part of the climax of the prologue demands that it be considered carefully as a christological statement. The statement in 1:14 may be set out as follows:

Καὶ ὁ λόγος σὰρξ ἐγένετο καὶ ἐσκήνωσεν ἐν ἡμῖν,
καὶ ἐθεασάμεθα τὴν δόξαν αὐτοῦ, δόξαν ὡς μονογενοῦς παρὰ πατρός,
πλήρης χάριτος καὶ ἀληθείας.
And the Word became flesh and tented among us,
and we beheld his glory, glory as of the only (Son) of the Father,
full of grace and truth. (1:14)

It is not itself the climax, but forms the beginning of the prologue's climax which reaches to 1:18. The coming of the Logos into the world in Jesus had already been addressed in the verses which precede,[384] so that the focus here is not the coming but its manner. 1:15 reports the Baptist's witness that the one referred to is the superior pre-existent one. "John bears witness concerning him and has cried out saying, 'This was the one of whom I said, He who

---

384. Michaels, *John*, 76; Beutler, *Johannesevangelium*, 97, who notes that the reference in 1:14 to incarnation makes explicit what had already been indicated.

comes after me is my superior, because he was before me.'" In that sense, 1:15 expands the second half of 1:14 which speaks of the glory and eminence of the Son. 1:16-17, in developing the contrast with the Law, also expands 1:14, taking up πλήρης χάριτος καὶ ἀληθείας ("full of grace and truth"): "Because from his fullness we have all received grace replacing grace; for the Law was given through Moses, grace and truth came through Jesus Christ." We return in 6.2.5.4 to the issue of the Law and the allusion to Sinai (Exod 33-34) within 1:14-18 and its implications for understanding John's approach to the Law.

John 1:18 also focusses on the salvific work of the Son.[385] "No one has ever seen God; God the only Son, who is in the bosom of the Father, he has made him known." At the same time it echoes the language of 1:14 (μονογενοῦς, πατρός) and puts ἐθεασάμεθα τὴν δόξαν αὐτοῦ ("we have seen his glory") in different words, for to see the glory (1:14) is to see the Father made known in the Son. I have translated ἐσκήνωσεν as "tented" (1:14), since it alludes to the divine presence in the wilderness tabernacle. 1:14a (ὁ λόγος σὰρξ ἐγένετο, "the Word became flesh") is the primary link with what precedes, for it is the Logos of 1:1-13 who is being described in 14-18 as the only Son of the Father who makes God known.

The words ὁ λόγος σὰρξ ἐγένετο καὶ ἐσκήνωσεν ἐν ἡμῖν ("the Word became flesh and tented among us") already contain or imply a reference to what is seen on earth (the Word, the tent), but primarily they describe how this comes to be. They are, in that sense, preparatory. The central focus of 1:14-18 is on the presence and presentation of God and God's glory in the Son: καὶ ἐθεασάμεθα τὴν δόξαν αὐτοῦ ("and we beheld his glory"). Already Baur stressed this[386] and the same point has been particularly emphasised by Käsemann.[387]

What significance is to be attached, then, to the particular formulation in 1:14a: Καὶ ὁ λόγος σὰρξ ἐγένετο ("And the Word became flesh")? The author might easily have employed one of the Gospel's more common formulations and said that the Logos came or was sent into the world. The widely held assumption that he uses a traditional source here may well account for the difference of formulation, but this still calls for an explanation how the author might have understand these words and what weight we should give them in explicating his Christology.

385. Dennis, *Death and Gathering*, 141, notes that 1:14-18 express the soteriological benefits resulting from faith "in his name" (1:12).

386. Baur, *Vorlesungen*, 363-64; Baur, *Kritische Untersuchungen*, 94-96.

387. Käsemann, *Letzter Wille*, 23-24; similarly Schnackenburg, *Johannesevangelium*, 2.511-12; Hamerton-Kelly, *Pre-Existence*, 206; Bergmeier, *Glaube*, 210-11; Haacker, *Stiftung*, 26-27.

5.4.2.1 The Word Became Flesh: 1:14a and What Precedes

When we read 1:14a also in relation to what precedes, we find that the prologue has already spoken of the coming of the Logos into the world: Ἦν τὸ φῶς τὸ ἀληθινόν, ὃ φωτίζει πάντα ἄνθρωπον, ἐρχόμενον εἰς τὸν κόσμον ("The true light, which gives light to every person, was coming into the world"; 1:9); εἰς τὰ ἴδια ἦλθεν, καὶ οἱ ἴδιοι αὐτὸν οὐ παρέλαβον ("He came to his own and his own did not receive him" (1:11). Some interpret these as references not to his coming in Jesus, but to his work in the world of creation and with Israel.[388] Then 1:14a would be a climax and emphasise that the Word came in a new way, "in the flesh," in Jesus. I think it very likely that the author's tradition might have meant this once, when it existed as a variant of the Wisdom story applied to Jesus.[389] But in its present form the prologue refers already in 6–8 to John the Baptist and uses the present tense of φαίνει ("shines") in 1:5, so that the verses 9–11 most naturally read as already descriptions of the coming of the Son in Jesus of Nazareth.[390] Accordingly 1:14a represents another way of referring to the same event and not a contrast with previous ways in which the Logos might have come.

5.4.2.2 The Word Became "Flesh"—Meaning?

If 1:14a represents a climax, on the former view, or, on the latter, a contrast with the previous descriptions of the same event of the Logos's coming into the world, there is still the question what the author means or intends by the word σάρξ ("flesh)." Bultmann identifies here a deliberate paradox, the central theme of the Gospel, the presence in human flesh of the divine Logos.[391] He also identifies it as deliberately antidocetic.[392] Richter identifies 1:14a

---

388. So Eltester, "Logos," 124–34; Hofius, "Struktur," 21; Kysar, *Jesus*, 17.

389. So also Schnackenburg, "Logos-Hymnus," 84–89; Theobald, *Anfang*, 109–15; Ruckstuhl, "Prolog," 452–53.

390. So Bultmann, *Johannes*, 26–38; Schnackenburg, *John*, 1.227; Käsemann, "Prologue," 165–66; Theobald, *Anfang*, 117, 126; Ruckstuhl, "Prolog," 452–53.

391. So Bultmann, *Johannes*, 40–41; Bultmann, *Theologie*, 403; similarly Bousset, *Kyrios Christos*, 220; Bauer, *Johannes*, 22; Braun, *Jean*, 65; Hamerton-Kelly, *Pre-Existence*, 199, 207; Christoph Demke, "Der sogenannte Logos-Hymnus im johanneischen Prolog," *ZNW* 58 (1967): 63; Schnackenburg, "Fleisch," 5; Schnackenburg, *John*, 1.266; Heinrich Zimmermann, "Christushymnus und johanneischer Prolog," in *Neues Testament und Kirche. Festschrift für R. Schnackenburg*, ed. J. Gnilka (Freiburg: Herder, 1974), 262–63; Weder, "Menschwerdung," 352, 256; Barrett, "Paradox," 105; Painter, "Prologue," 470; Hofius, "Struktur," 24.

392. Bultmann, *Johannes*, 41–42; Bultmann, *Theologie*, 392; similarly Bauer, *Johannes*,

as belonging to an antidocetic redaction of the Gospel, of which he finds evidence also in 19:34-35, 39-40; 20:24-29; 20:2-10; 6:51-58, and Hartwig Thyen and Langbrandtner argue similarly.[393] If an emphasis on paradox, with or without the antidocetic motive, is present, then it is strange that the author passes away from it so quickly to place all the attention on glory and that in referring back to 1:14 in 1:15-18 he never returns to this theme.[394] This also counts against seeing 1:14a as a major focus either as a climax or a contrast with the previous description of the coming of the Logos (Son) into the world. 1:14a serves rather to underline the coming of the Logos in humanity, in the human person Jesus,[395] where it could be seen and experienced.[396] According to Ruckstuhl the incarnation is implied, but carries no emphasis since it is already assumed in what has been said.[397] One could see flesh as merely the basic wherewithal for communication among people, the manner of appearance, as Käsemann argued[398] and the statement does not seem primarily to be highlighting a paradox,[399] as Bultmann suggests, nor countering antidocetic views.[400] What follows in 1:14-18 suggests, rather, that the focus lies in enabling the glory to be seen and experienced.

23; Schnackenburg, *John*, 1.170, 269; Lindars, *Gospel of John*, 79, 94; Fritz Neugebauer, *Die Entstehung des Johannesevangeliums*, AzTh I 36 (Stuttgart: Calwer, 1968), 29; Bruce, *John*, 39; Gnilka, "Christologie," 103-4; Hofrichter, *Im Anfang*, 52; Schnelle, *Christologie*, 242-43, arguing that "tented" is also antidocetic.

393. Richter, *Studien*, 157-58, also 110-11, 134, 179-82; Thyen, "Brüder," 532, and 534; "Entwicklungen," 260-61; Langbrandtner, *Weltferner Gott*, 44, 108, and 9-10, 17, 32, 36; similarly Anderson, "Interfluential," 13; Beutler, "Johannes-Prolog," 96; see also John Painter, "The 'Opponents' in 1 John," *NTS* 32 (1986): 31-47, 65, 68.

394. So Theobald, *Fleischwerdung*, 385; Zumstein, "Prolog," 51, 75; Müller, *Menschwerdung*, 64-65, 70, who argues that the author has integrated the idea of incarnation within his envoy Christology (71). See also Ashton, *Fourth Gospel*, 165, who notes the issue of how to relate the two, given its absence in the rest of the Gospel.

395. Theobald, *Anfang*, 55.

396. So de Jonge, *Stranger*, 207-8; Marianne Thompson, *The Humanity of Jesus in the Fourth Gospel* (Philadelphia: Fortress, 1988), 51-52.

397. Ruckstuhl, "Prolog," 451.

398. Käsemann, "Prologue," 159-60; Käsemann, *Letzter Wille*, 24; similarly Müller, *Menschwerdung*, 44-45.

399. So also Hamerton-Kelly, *Pre-Existence*, 207; Nicol, *Semeia*, 131-33; Dupont, *Christologie*, 51-52.

400. So also Käsemann, *Letzter Wille*, 27; Schottroff, *Glaubende*, 276-77; Müller, *Christologie*, 25; Bergmeier, *Glaube*, 210; Theobald, *Anfang*, 35; Becker, *Johannes*, 77; "Auferstehung," 140-41; Painter, "Christology and the Farewell Discourses," 50; Klaus Berger, "Zu 'Das Wort ward Fleisch' Joh I 14a," *NovT* 16 (1974): 166; Schnackenburg, *Johannesevangelium*, 4.113; Thyen, *Johannesevangelium*, 91.

The Salvation Event in John

5.4.2.3 The Word "Became" Flesh—Meaning?

There is a variety of possible interpretations of the word ἐγένετο in 1:14. The most common meaning of γίνομαι is "become," so that 1:14a is regularly translated: "The Word became flesh." But what does it mean to "become"? It cannot mean a transformation of being in which the Logos became only what flesh is and ceased to be what flesh is not, for the author assumes a continuity of consciousness. This is widely recognised.[401] Büchsel therefore says it must mean that the Logos took upon himself human flesh.[402] But what does that mean? Weiss argued that "flesh" is always personal, equipped with a soul ("beseelt").[403] This was in part a reaction against Baur, who had pointed out that the author might have written ἄνθρωπος (a human being) instead of "flesh" and, accordingly, claims that "flesh" here should be understood as a covering ("Hülle").[404] This would allow a close parallel with 1:14b where tent imagery is present, tent being a common image for the human body. To see here, on the other hand, a kenotic Christology of the kind found in Phil 2:6–11 scarcely fits the following context according to which what happened in 1:14 made divine glory visible.[405] The author offers us not a Son emptied of divine powers, but on the contrary one who is full of all authority and in himself brings divine life and light. The only loss the author speaks of is the loss of having to depart from the intimacy of the heavenly divine presence.[406] The Son remains the Son on earth and never distinguishes between his nature and obedience as Son on earth and his nature and obedience as Son in heaven.

Käsemann returned to the position substantially represented already by Baur (see above), in arguing that 1:14a is primarily speaking of manner of appearance, human guise.[407] He reinforced his claim by correctly highlighting the centrality of 1:14c and thus challenged the role Bultmann and others had given to 1:14a. He went on to argue that the picture of Jesus in John's Gospel

---

401. So Hamerton-Kelly, *Pre-Existence*, 206; Büchsel, *Johannes*, 32; Schnackenburg, "Fleisch," 4; Barrett, *John*, 169.

402. Büchsel, *Johannes*, 32.

403. Weiss, *Lehrbuch*, 612–13; similarly Holtzmann, *Lehrbuch*, 464.

404. Baur, *Kritische Untersuchungen*, 233. Cf. Cullmann, *Christologie*, 192, who argues that ἄνθρωπος was not used because of possible associations with Anthropos figures.

405. So Ibuki, *Wahrheit*, 190–91; Wilkens, *Zeuge*, 110; Riedl, *Heilswerk*, 155; earlier Beyschlag, *Neutestamentliche Theologie II*, 432.

406. So Haenchen, *Johannes*, 144–45; Wilkens, *Zeichen*, 110; Painter, "Prologue," 57–58; Hera, *Christology*, 131, but limiting glorification to the cross, on which see 4.3 above.

407. Käsemann, *Letzter Wille*, 24; similarly Schulz, *Johannes*, 31–32, 212; Müller, *Menschwerdung*, 46, 50, 62.

is naively docetic.[408] But his espousal of the Baur interpretation of 1:14a is hardly convincing. The word ἐγένετο usually carries with it more than this. It can mean little more than appearance (cf. 1 John 1:2)[409] and this is how later gnostic Christians interpreted this verse (cf. NH XIII 50.12–15; I 113.37; I.44.13–14);[410] and, as Klaus Berger shows,[411] the verb can mean "come" of the Lord's coming into people (Barn. 6:14–16) or "come to appear" as in Justin's description of Logos appearing as the fire of the burning bush (*Dial.* 127–128). Many argue that here it must mean something like "came on the scene of history"[412] or be similar to Gal 4:4.[413] The verb ἐγένετο with σάρξ suggests a change in mode of being[414] and some see this as emphatically stressing a full entry into the human condition,[415] including its vulnerability and death.[416]

5.4.3 The Word Became Flesh—
To Be Read in the Context of the Gospel

On the other hand, the problem posed by 1:14a can never be solved in isolation from the rest of the Gospel.[417] Its interpretation has suffered far too much by people treating it as a key to the Gospel, but not reading it first within the wider context to which it belongs. Accordingly, I shall consider the wider issue of Jesus' humanity in the Gospel as a whole, bearing in mind the questions raised by 1:14a. In doing so, I want to keep in mind both aspects of the question with which we began: how does the portrait look to us and what, if anything, can we know of how the author would have interpreted it, assuming that the answer may not necessarily be identical in each case?

408. Käsemann, *Letzter Wille*, 61–62.
409. So Schulz, *Johannes*, 32; similarly Schillebeeckx, *Christ*, 365.
410. So Elaine H. Pagels, *The Johannine Gospel in Gnostic Exegesis: Heracleon's Commentary on John*, SBLMS 17 (Nashville: Abingdon, 1973), 37; Brown, *Beloved Disciple*, 111–12, 152–53; Majella Franzmann and Michael Lattke, "Gnostic Jesuses and the Gnostic Jesus of John," in *Gnosisforschung und Religionsgeschichte. Festschrift für Kurt Rudolph zum 65. Geburtstag*, ed. H. Preissler and H. Seiwert (Marburg: Diagonal-Verlag, 1994), 147.
411. Berger, "Word," 162.
412. Barrett, *John*, 169.
413. Painter, "Prologue," 37; Painter, "Christology and the Farewell Discourses," 49; Müller, *Christologie*, 25.
414. Schnackenburg, *John*, 1.267; Hofius, "Struktur," 24.
415. Cranfield, "John 1:14," 215; Dunn, "John," 347; Beasley-Murray, *John*, 13–14; Schnelle, *Christologie*, 241–42; Lee, *Flesh and Glory*, 34.
416. Painter, "Sacrifice and Atonement," 295.
417. So Schillebeeckx, *Christ*, 365.

5.4.3.1 Jesus, a God at Play in Galilee?

The problems of the Johannine picture of the humanity of Jesus have long concerned exegetes and came to the fore once again through the explosive essay of Käsemann.[418] Already earlier, scholars like Baur, Wrede, Holtzmann, Wetter, and Wilhelm Bousset had described the Son as being like a God striding across the world, rather than a human being.[419] The following features have led many to deny that we can speak of a real humanity of Jesus in the Fourth Gospel.

Supernatural Knowledge and Power: Tradition and Heightening

Jesus appears to have extraordinary capacity to know what is usually beyond the humanly possible.[420] He sees Nathanael under the fig tree when it was impossible for him normally to have seen him. He knows of the husbands of the Samaritan woman. He also has extraordinary miraculous power beyond what is evident in the Synoptic Gospels. He not only feeds the 5,000 and walks on the water; he also changes water into wine, raises Lazarus from the dead after four days, and performs a healing miracle at very great distance from the scene.

Some of these miracles show signs of having already been heightened before the author came to retell them, as in the Johannine version of the centurion's servant/official's son's healing at Capernaum. But, while the author constantly warns against faith centred solely on Jesus as miracle worker, he never suggests that the miracles did not happen, nor diminishes their fantastic character. At times it seems he has himself heightened them.[421] He has also heightened the degree of Jesus' supernatural knowledge (e.g., 5:6; 6:6, 15a; 11:11; 16:19; 18:4).[422] The author is doubtless responsible for a number of

---

418. Käsemann, *Letzter Wille*.

419. Baur, *Kritische Untersuchungen*, 87, 313; Wrede, *Charakter*, 39; Holtzmann, *Lehrbuch*, 458; Wetter, *Sohn Gottes*, 149; Bousset, *Kyrios Christos*, 217–18; cf. also Käsemann, *Letzter Wille*, 22; Schulz, *Johannes*, 211; Miranda, *Vater*, 54; Martyn, "Glimpses," 102; Langbrandtner, *Weltferner Gott*, 38, 95–96 (of the *Grundschrift*); and with extensive character illustration: Culpepper, *Anatomy*, 108–12.

420. So already Baur, *Kritische Untersuchungen*, 233; Baur, *Vorlesungen*, 358; Holtzmann, *Lehrbuch*, 453–58; similarly Nicol, *Semeia*, 132.

421. So Wrede, *Charakter*, 7–8; Wetter, *Sohn Gottes*, 71; Käsemann, *Letzter Wille*, 17; Schulz, *Johannes*, 212; Klaiber, "Interpretation," 317; Schnelle, *Christologie*, 105, 116, 183; see also Hegermann, "Eigentum," 113.

422. So Fortna, "Christology," 394; Schnelle, *Christologie*, 184.

passages of typical Johannine irony, which often entail a heightening of the miraculous for their effect.

5.4.3.2 Miracles and the Evangelist

Wilkens notes that the raising of Lazarus as a miracle is made to perform an important role in his description of what led to the passion.[423] Wengst notes the role of Jesus' miraculous foreknowledge in assuring the reader that Jesus' passion was not an accident.[424] Langbrandtner argues that the author (of the *Grundschrift*) both heightens and criticises miracles (e.g., 9:6-7), while at the same time maintaining that the miracles in themselves are irrelevant for faith.[425] Becker sees the author using a miracle source, but correcting its *theios aner* Christology.[426] Fortna sees the author doing little to combat *theios aner* Christology and, unlike Becker, sees the Signs Gospel (which includes Becker's signs source material and more) as already docetic, with the evangelist heightening both the divinity and the humanity of Jesus and portraying the ministry more as an epiphany than had his source.[427] Schottroff speaks of the author retaining miracles in full force, but seeing in them the innerworldly irrelevant aspect of reality which calls forth a false innerworldly miracle-based faith.[428] But they are hardly irrelevant for the author, for he himself heightens them. Nor, therefore, are they to be seen with Bultmann as merely a concession to human weakness.[429]

At the other extreme, Käsemann argues that the author would even find the miracles inadequate since they reflect so little of the divine glory.[430] Schnelle argues that the miracles serve the Gospel's antidocetic purpose, but does so mostly in the form of assertions in summaries, with very little grounding in the text.[431] I fail to see how in John the miracles serve to emphasise the reality of the incarnation in a sense which could be seen as antidocetic by heightening their massive character, as he suggests.[432] At most,

---

423. Wilkens, *Zeichen*, 51-52.
424. Wengst, *Gemeinde*, 104-105.
425. Langbrandtner, *Weltferner Gott*, 94-95.
426. Becker, *Johannes*, 119-20.
427. Fortna, "Christology," 493, 495-96.
428. Schottroff, *Glaubende*, 251, 254, 269.
429. Bultmann, *Johannes*, 173.
430. Käsemann, *Letzter Wille*, 53 n 59; cf. also Appold, *Oneness*, 95.
431. Schnelle, *Christologie*, 94, 140, 148, 184-85, 188, 194.
432. Against Schnelle, *Christologie*, 94-95, 148.

The Salvation Event in John

in this regard, they identify Jesus as the Christ who did these things and manifested divine glory, but that begs the question about the nature of this Jesus in regard to docetism. More relevant to an antidocetic stance would be Gnilka's comment that Jesus as miracle-worker shows traits of humanity such as weeping and that miracles such as those of the Fourth Gospel are not found in Gnosticism.[433]

Miracles Remain Miracles: Manifestations of Glory and Symbols

There is little doubt that the miracles remain miracles in John and so present us with a Jesus of extraordinary knowledge and power. We are to read them as evidence that he is indeed the Son who has come from the Father. This is so even though their primary function for the reader is to be signs of the one who brings the bread of life, light, life, and resurrection, which they symbolise. At times, Baur claimed, real humanity almost disappears from view, as in 7:10, 15; 8:59; 10:39, and ceases to be human flesh.[434] Consistent with this power Jesus has authority to lay down his life and take it up again in resurrection and return to the Father (10:18; 2:19–22).

Miracles and the Issue of Real Humanity

In itself the performance of miracles, including miracles of foresight, did not, according to the popular anthropology of the day, carry with it the implication that a wonder-worker was not a human being. Sometimes miracles were claimed as evidence that someone possessed divine nature and so ceased to that extent to be a mortal human being.[435] But often such miracles were seen as possibilities for human beings who, as prophets or wonder-workers, were gifted with divine powers or with the Spirit of God. In that sense the presence of such phenomena within the life of human beings in no way compromised their humanity. The difference between such figures and the Jesus of the Fourth Gospel is that Jesus is not pictured as one gifted with divine powers received on earth, but as a divine being acting in this way amongst men and women in the world with his own divine power. As Barrett puts

---

433. Gnilka, "Christologie," 99.
434. Baur, *Vorlesungen*, 304–5, 365; similarly H. J. Holtzmann, *Lehrbuch*, 458–61.
435. See the extensive material gathered by Wetter, *Sohn Gottes*, 6–8; see also Bauer, *Johannes*, 23–24; Käsemann, *Letzter Wille*, 17; and Kee, *Miracles*.

it, he is both too human and too divine to be a *theios aner*.⁴³⁶ At the same time, the observation that miracles need not necessarily have been seen as compromising humanity leaves open the possibility that the author could in some way still hold that the Son who so worked was also human flesh and blood and did not compromise what he perceived as humanity.

5.4.3.3 The Discourses and Dialogues and the Issue of Real Humanity

More than the miracles exhibit superhuman ability: the discourses and dialogues pose real problems for a human picture of Jesus. For in these we see Jesus constantly taunting his opponents with double meaning as he asserts an authority based on a premise they do not share, and behaving toward his conversation partners in a way that takes full advantage of his superior knowledge and their ignorance of his meaning to a degree that Robinson, for instance, speaks of an impression of arrogance and megalomania.⁴³⁷ The woman of Samaria is hopelessly at sea with Jesus' cryptic remarks which she cannot have been expected to understand. The Jesus of the dialogues and discourses is distanced and many see him lacking any warmth of character.⁴³⁸ Above all, Culpepper has documented this emotional distance in John's characterisation: Jesus lacks compassion and humanising traits, never really hungers, is little influenced by those around him, seems incapable of giving a straight answer, knows shrewdly when to withdraw, and has no real need of prayer except for confirmation and always remains in control.⁴³⁹ The humanity of the Lazarus episode is an exception.⁴⁴⁰

5.4.3.4 The Son's Divine Self-awareness in Life and Death

Leaving aside the value judgments which often fall against the Johannine Christ because of such behaviour, we note that the stance of superior knowl-

---

436. Barrett, "Theocentric," 13; similarly Fortna, "*Christology*," 495. See also Ashton, *Fourth Gospel*, 161–62, who notes that the sources for the *theios aner* motif are too late.

437. Robinson, "Christology," 68; similarly Strathmann, *Johannes*, 3; Käsemann, *Letzter Wille*, 22–23, 48.

438. Lindars, *Gospel of John*, 53–54, 62; cf. also Käsemann, *Letzter Wille*, 22–23, 48.

439. Culpepper, *Anatomy*, 108–12; similarly Käsemann, *Letzter Wille*, 22–23; Brown, *Beloved Disciple*, 114–16; Jan A. du Rand, "The Characterization of Jesus as Depicted in the Narrative of the Fourth Gospel," *Neot* 19 (1985): 29.

440. Culpepper, *Anatomy*, 111.

edge derives from Jesus' awareness of who he is. He is God's only Son who was pre-existent with the Father and has come bearing his gift of life to the world. This is superhuman knowledge. The author never attempts to show Jesus as having only the knowledge available to a mere mortal. That would make the mission of the Son impossible. It is true, the Son is not imparting heavenly revelations, as the story pattern at first suggests; but he nevertheless offers himself as standing for God because he knows himself as God's only Son come as the sent one from above.

This supreme confidence and awareness explains how sometimes his prayers take the form of demonstrations for the sake of others, of who he is (so 11:41–42; cf. 12:30).[441] It also explains his attitude toward his death. For Jesus approaches death aware of his authority to lay down his life and take it again. He knows his hour is coming. He knows he will return to the Father. Confidence of return to the Father and so confidence in the face of death can also characterise human beings, particularly those with a firm assurance of life beyond. At that level Jesus sets a pattern of confident faith for his disciples to follow. In itself, therefore, such confidence does not conflict with the claim to be human. Yet the confidence of the Son is not the same as that of believers. His is based in his own nature and awareness as Son. It is assurance divinely given and knowledge supernaturally available. Accordingly Jesus approaches his passion, conducts himself before the Jews and before Pilate, and spends the last moments on the cross in the supreme confidence derived from his self-knowledge. In that sense it is, indeed, a triumphant exit from life, with no cry of forsakenness, only a declaration that the task had been completed.[442] The more important issue is whether his suffering was real or just apparent and to this we shall return.

5.4.3.5 Jesus of Nazareth a Real Human Being

On the other side of the ledger there are indications in the Gospel that the author understands Jesus' humanity to be real. Jesus' conversation partners and his opponents always treat him as a human being[443] and Jesus never takes exception to this assumption. Even though he may at times have Jesus

---

441. So Appold, *Oneness*, 123, 205–6.
442. So Nicol, *Semeia*, 132; Appold, *Oneness*, 136, 120, 125–26; Müller, "Bedeutung," 54, 56; Strathmann, *Johannes*, 3; Lattke, *Einheit*, 142; Haenchen, "Vater," 77; Langbrandtner, *Weltferner Gott*, 96 (of the *Grundschrift*); Wengst, *Gemeinde*, 104–5.
443. So Bousset, *Kyrios Christos*, 219–20; Barrett, "Theocentric," 3; Wengst, *Gemeinde*, 100–101; Scroggs, *Christology*, 80–81.

scold them for seeing him only in terms of human parentage, the author never has Jesus deny his human origins.[444] It is possible, as David W. Wead suggests,[445] that the author knew of controversies surrounding Jesus' birth and therefore knew the tradition of the virginal conception; but it is equally possible he did not. The Gospel gives no clear indication. What is apparent is that the offence Jesus caused was because of two facts which the author will not see compromised: the Son came from above and he is also Jesus, the man from Nazareth.[446]

Traits of Humanity

Similarly Jesus does exhibit characteristic human needs. He is hungry, tired, thirsty; he loves, cries, is angry, needs and receives information, and possibly even changes his plans (11:6, 11?). It is not convincing to argue that when in 4:34 Jesus speaks of having food to eat of which the disciples do not know, the will of God, he is thereby denying his need to eat.[447] Nor is it likely that his request of the Samaritan woman for a drink was a mere ploy for setting up his claims to be the water of life.[448] Sometimes statements about the Son's subordination to the Father are cited as evidence of Jesus' humanity, but as we have seen this belongs rather already to his relation as Son with the Father in pre-existence and has no implication for humanity in this sense.[449]

A Suffering Humanity

He approaches the passion with confidence, but also, in words which reflect Ps 6:3-4 and probably draw on Gethsemane tradition, speaks of being deeply troubled (12:27). Was this τετάρακται ("he was troubled") an uncertainty about what he should pray? That in itself would be a human trait. Was it

---

444. So Holtzmann, *Lehrbuch*, 467–68; Baur, *Vorlesungen*, 365; Nicol, *Semeia*, 132; de Jonge, *Stranger*, 92–94; Schweizer, *Jesus*, 156; John F. O'Grady, "The Human Jesus in the Fourth Gospel," *BTB* 14 (1984): 63; Robinson, *Priority*, 367; Johnston, "Ecce Homo," 130.

445. Wead, *Devices*, 62–63.

446. So Dewailly, "D'où es-tu?," 493–94; Weder, "Menschwerdung," 356.

447. Against Käsemann, *Letzter Wille*, 22–23; Culpepper, *Anatomy*, 109–10; Cf. Nicol, *Semeia*, 132.

448. Against, for instance, Dauer, *Passionsgeschichte*, 287.

449. So rightly Baur, *Vorlesungen*, 367–68; Wetter, *Sohn Gottes*, 119; de la Potterie, *Vérité*, 990 n. 254. See 5.3 above.

of the nature of despairing anxiety, as Lütgert suggests ("ratlose Angst")?[450] But this would deny Jesus' foreknowledge of events to come. Nor should the passage be seen as an embarrassment for the evangelist's Christology.[451] Maybe it was Jesus' anxiety concerning his disciples whose suffering he had predicted.[452] But it is more likely that we have to do here directly with the prospect of the suffering which awaits him in his nonetheless confident journey through the cross to the Father. Confidence and real suffering are not incompatible. That real suffering is in view receives support from the fact that the author has added OT passages which reflect suffering into the passion narrative.[453] Thüsing goes further and writes that the troubledness of 12:27 remains with Jesus throughout the passion, but there is little trace of this.[454] Fortna suggests that whereas the Signs Gospel (which he postulates as the evangelist's source) had an unmediated relationship between the miracles and the passion narrative, the author uses passages such as 12:27 and the last discourses to mediate between them in a way that directly emphasises Jesus' humanity.[455]

The author never mentions details of how Jesus' suffering pained him. The crucifixion is only briefly described. The mockery is portrayed in all its cruelty, but nothing is said of what Jesus felt. We can only speculate: would the author have believed that Jesus felt nothing of the horror and pain of all of this?[456] Or would he have believed that Jesus did experience it all, but saw it through in triumphant confidence? We cannot be absolutely sure, but the latter is more likely,[457] especially when taken together with Jesus' troubledness in prayer (12:27) and his view of what lay before him as a cup to be drunk (18:11).[458] Accordingly the wretchedness of the mocked one to

---

450. Lütgert, *Christologie*, 101.
451. Against Schnackenburg, *Johannesevangelium*, 2.485.
452. So Nicholson, *Death*, 128.
453. So Beutler, *Angst*, 25–36; Whitacre, *Polemic*, 63.
454. Thüsing, *Erhöhung*, 81; cf. Lütgert, *Christologie*, 101.
455. Fortna, "Christology," 501–2.
456. Cf. Evans, "Passion," 62.
457. So Lütgert, *Christologie*, 110; Schnackenburg, *Johannesevangelium*, 2.512; Bornkamm, "Interpretation," 114; Wilkens, *Zeichen*, 62, 67; Barrett, "Theocentric," 11; Schweizer, *Jesus*, 156; Onuki, *Gemeinde*, 203; Baum-Bodenbender, *Hoheit*, 268–70; Johnston, "Ecce Homo," 134; Xavier Léon-Dufour, "'Père, fais-moi passer sain et sauf à travers cette heure' (Jean 12,27)," in *Neues Testament und Geschichte. Festschrift für O. Cullmann*, ed. H. Baltensweiler and B. Reicke (Tübingen: Mohr Siebeck, 1972), 162–65, who suggests Jesus prays to be brought through the hour.
458. So Jörg Frey, "Leiblichkeit und Auferstehung im Johannesevangelium," in *Die Herrlichkeit des Gekreuzigten. Studien zu den Johanneischen Schriften I*, ed. J. Schlegel, WUNT 307 (Tübingen: Mohr Siebeck, 2013), 711; Frey, "Theologia Crucifixi," 538.

whom Pilate points with the words "Behold the man" (19:5) is real,[459] even if at the same time the reader knows the irony of the situation and knows Jesus' confidence. I am not, however, convinced by Moloney who sees here an allusion to the Son of Man title and evidence that Son of Man emphasises Jesus' humanity.[460] Nor conversely do I see any need to read 5:27 as a reference not to the Son of Man in his role as judge but to Jesus simply as a human being,[461] nor to see that title as emphasising Jesus' humanity.[462]

If there is some real humanity present on the part of Jesus in the mockery, the same then must also be said of the crucifixion. The reference to blood and water flowing from the side of Jesus, secured by an eyewitness, also belongs here. Its meaning is debated (see 4.1.2.9), but it most likely refers primarily either to the fact that Jesus really did die,[463] or to the fact that he really was flesh and blood,[464] and did not in some docetic way escape death.[465]

5.4.3.6 Antidocetic Interests in the Gospel?

The context of either claim concerning 19:35 demands some opposing notion, such as that Jesus had not really died or that he was not fully human or both. This is an unusual emphasis in the Gospel, rarely found elsewhere, or found in material seemingly the most recent in the Gospel and similar to the apparent concerns of 1 John.[466] Because we are concerned to find the strength of the Gospel's portrait of Jesus' humanity, we shall consider here those theories which find an antidocetic thrust in the Gospel.

459. Litwa, "Behold Adam," 136, suggests that the statement "recalls Adam's alienation and death—keynotes of his very *human* existence," but goes beyond this at the level of irony to claim "Pilate's 'Behold the man!' is not really a statement meant to excite pity or ridicule, but a statement expressing Jesus' divine sovereignty over his whole trial" (141).

460. Moloney, *Son of Man*, 254-55; Moloney, "Son of Man Revisited," 181; Davies, *Rhetoric*, 188, 190-92; Thyen, *Johannesevangelium*, 149.

461. So rightly Reynolds, *Apocalyptic Son of Man*, 135-36; cf. Burkett, *Son of Man*, 44-45; Davies, *Rhetoric*, 190-92.

462. So rightly Weidemann, *Tod Jesu*, 104; Reynolds, *Apocalyptic Son of Man*, 107, 220-23.

463. So Brown, *John*, 948-49; Boismard and Lamouille, *Jean*, 451.

464. So Richter, *Studien*, 134.

465. So Barrett, "Theocentric," 13-14; de Jonge, *Stranger*, 210-11; Klos, *Sakramente*, 80; Schweizer, "Herrenmahl," 350-51; Bruce, *John*, 376; Beasley-Murray, *John*, 356-57; Gnilka, "Christologie," 105; Schnelle, *Christologie*, 229.

466. Anderson, *Christology*, 241-43, suggests that the grounds for some believers departing in 1 John 2:19 was reaction to ditheism, but much more likely is their docetism, which he notes in 1 John 4:1-3 and which would potentially sit well with ditheism. See also Thatcher, "Remembering Jesus," 185.

The Salvation Event in John

Many see it as the work of redaction. Thorwald Lorenzen argues for an antidocetic interest in the beloved disciple material, securing the reality of Jesus' suffering, death and resurrection.[467] Neugebauer, followed by Thyen and, more recently, Schnelle, argues for an antidocetic reading of 20:31 so that in essence it would be claiming (I think, quite unexpectedly, compared with similar confessional statements in 1:35-49; 11:27) that the Christ is Jesus, the man.[468] Richter and Thyen argue also for an antidocetic purpose in the Thomas episode which precedes[469] and a similar concern is suggested behind 6:51-58.[470] But in none of these is this, to my mind, finally convincing. Schnelle's major attempt to prove that the Gospel is written after the epistle and in the light of the docetic problems it encountered has assembled a comprehensive range of arguments to support the hypothesis. But his attempt by its comprehensiveness succeeds on my assessment in being counterproductive of the hypothesis he seeks to prove. The argument from the use of the miracles, already alluded to above, and forming the major part of the book,[471] convincingly shows that miracles matter as an expression of the author's Christology, but not that they are antidocetic. We are left then with the sacramental passages and with 1:14 discussed earlier. Where we might most expect the emphasis to show, namely in the major discourses, it is absent. As Menken observes, "anti-docetic elements in John which Schnelle indicates, are hardly explicitly anti-docetic; it rather appears that Jesus' humanity has not yet constituted a problem in the Gospel."[472]

As it stands in the Gospel, the commentary on the water and blood seems to me, nevertheless, to be strong evidence for an emphasis on Jesus' humanity as real humanity and his death as a real death. Whoever wanted to emphasise this would certainly have understood 1:14 as indicating this real humanity, whether or not it, too, carries antidocetic character.

---

467. Thorwald Lorenzen, *Der Lieblingsjünger im Johannesevangelium*, SBS 55 (Stuttgart: KBW, 1971), 106-8; similarly Onuki, *Gemeinde*, 203.

468. Neugebauer, *Entstehung*, 28-29; Thyen, "Entwicklungen," 260-61; Schnelle, *Christologie*, 155. Against this reading: de Jonge, *Stranger*, 207.

469. Thyen, "Brüder," 534; Richter, *Studien*, 180; Schnelle, *Christologie*, 160. Against this: de Jonge, *Stranger*, 207; Pokorny, "Jesus," 219; Dauer, *Johannes und Lukas*, 293.

470. So Schenke, "Vorgeschichte," 86-87; Beutler, "Heilsbedeutung," 192; Weder, "Menschwerdung," 348-49; Schnelle, *Christologie*, 223; Schnelle, *Johannes*, 138; Anderson, *Christology*, 242-43; Borgen, *Bread from Heaven*, 183-92, but see his change of mind in *John*, 21. Against this view see also: Schnackenburg, *Johannesevangelium*, 2.91-92; Wilckens, "Lebensbrot," 238-39; Moloney, "Sacraments," 23; Painter, "Death of Jesus," 340-41; cf. also de Jonge, *Stranger*, 208-9.

471. Schnelle, *Christologie*, 87-194.

472. Menken, "Christology," 308.

5.4.3.7 The Passion Narrative: Triumphant Exit as Käsemann?

The role of the passion narrative and its significance for the reality of incarnation in Johannine Christology have been discussed already in relation to 12:27 and its implications. I want here to review briefly the debate which Käsemann's evaluation of the Johannine passion narrative has occasioned, before offering a summary evaluation and returning to the question raised by 1:14.

Käsemann sees the passion in John as an account of the Son's triumphant exit.[473] As such the passion, he says, fits awkwardly into Johannine Christology and would have become an irrelevant appendix for the author, had he not sprinkled it liberally with traits of victory. U. B. Müller suggests that the author employs the passion narrative not to depict real suffering, but to show up Jesus' opponents and that in doing so he has made use of a tradition Müller identifies in 1:14, 16, which had seen the miracles as manifestations of divine glory.[474]

The Passion Narrative: Responses to Käsemann

By contrast, Bultmann had spoken of the *theologia crucis* as not only including the passion narrative, but also as extending over the entire ministry and as stated in its sharpest form in 1:14.[475] Thüsing had borrowed Kähler's phrase and described the Gospel as "a passion narrative with an extended introduction."[476] He also affirms that both *theologia crucis* and *theologia gloriae* are to be found in the Gospel. In this way he distinguishes Johannine theology, therefore, from that of the Philippian hymn.[477] De la Potterie does similarly and attacks Käsemann's posing of the options as either glorious exit, or humiliation and exaltation on the model of Philippians 2,[478] preferring to speak of a humiliation of obedience. The Fourth Gospel presents us with the unique Son who has come and returns, but in obedient fulfilment

---

473. Käsemann, *Letzter Wille*, 23, 49 n. 53; similarly Schulz, *Johannes*, 237; Müller, "Bedeutung," 65; Appold, *Oneness*, 52, 103, 123; and against this Schweizer, *Jesus*, 156.

474. Müller, "Bedeutung," 65–67.

475. Bultmann, *Theologie*, 403, 405, 411.

476. Kähler, "Historical Jesus," 80; Thüsing, *Erhöhung*, 222; similarly Schnelle, *Christologie*, 256; cf. de Boer, *Johannine Perspectives*, 20, noting that the Gospel's "focus is not on Jesus' (passive) suffering but on his (active) control of the situation (cf. 19:11)."

477. Thüsing, *Erhöhung*, 3.

478. De la Potterie, *Vérité*, 990 n. 254.

The Salvation Event in John

of his commission also endures suffering. Thus Schnackenburg points out that the focus of the passion narrative is neither on proofs of divinity, on the one hand, nor on humiliation of the kind found in Philippians, on the other, but on fulfilment of the revelatory task.[479] Wilkens and Barrett speak of the movement from heavenly glory as indicating loss and real exposure to abuse.[480]

Ibuki also denies the presence of humiliation Christology, emphasising the centrality of the glory of a constantly shared relationship, thereby also countering the triumphant portrait Käsemann gives, but as we have seen, this fails to take into account the nuances of "glory."[481] Similarly Riedl imports foreign concepts into the Gospel when he describes incarnation as the taking up of humanity into the divine or as the extension of divine glory into human flesh, even in its suffering, without compromising either.[482] From a different angle Wengst, too, imposes a foreign construction on the Gospel in his thesis that the passion depicts the story of a suffering God.[483] Sproston is closer to the mark in emphasising Christ's suffering as a model for the disciples' suffering.[484] Hegermann, in response to Käsemann, relates elements of victory in the passion to the fact that Jesus goes on to take away sin by exposing its full extent, though this motif is more implicit than explicit in the narrative.[485] Leistner comes nearer to the reality of the Fourth Gospel when he admits the elements of victory and power noted above, but claims that at the same time the author believed in a real suffering and a real death.[486]

Our analysis above would confirm those who see in the Johannine passion narrative neither triumphant exit nor abject humiliation, but a path of real suffering, endured, however, with all the self-confidence of the returning Son. The author neither depicts subjective suffering as such (apart from 12:27) nor indicates that the occurrences of affliction were any different in their effect on Jesus as a human being than they would have been on any other person. The lack of interest of the evangelist at this point counts rather for a normal human experience than against it. There are no hints of the later triumphant "playing" of the Christ with his tormentors, such as we find

---

479. Schnackenburg, *Johannesevangelium*, 2.512; Forestell, *Word*, 225.
480. Wilkens, *Zeichen*, 110; Barrett, "Father," 32; also Haenchen, *Johannes*, 144–45.
481. Ibuki, *Wahrheit*, 191–96; and see 4.3 above.
482. Riedl, *Heilswerk*, 155.
483. Wengst, *Gemeinde*, 102–3.
484. Sproston, "Christology," 79–80. Anderson, "Interfluential," 13, notes, "if a non-human Jesus neither suffered nor died, his followers *need not be expected* to do the same."
485. Hegermann, "Eigentum," 116–17, 119.
486. Leistner, *Antijudäismus*, 145–50.

when Christ and Jesus are no longer seen as one, as they are still in John. It is probably right to assume that the author was naively unaware of anything in his Christology which would count against these being real experiences. But characteristically his interest centres on portraying Jesus as knowing himself to be God's only Son in every situation which confronts him and remaining faithful to his mission to the end.

5.4.4 Returning to 1:14a in the Light of the Gospel as a Whole

What then does 1:14a mean in the light of the Gospel? It cannot mean that human flesh is like a garment, a mere disguise to make communication possible. On the other hand, we can speak of a real humanity only in a qualified sense. For the Son who is Jesus of Nazareth remains the Son in full awareness of his being and of his commission to leave the intimacy of his heavenly glory with the Father and enter the world, and in full awareness that his deeds are wrought with the power that derives from his being as Son of the Father from the beginning of time.

5.4.4.1 Naive Docetism?

Barrett speaks rightly of a struggle between the Logos idea and the author's belief in the real humanness of Jesus which threatens to undermine the humanness.[487] He suggests the author is, therefore, at the same time, both naively docetic and even more naively antidocetic.[488] Davey, too, had spoken of a tension without synthesis.[489] Others have responded to Käsemann's charge of naive docetism by noting its applicability to only certain parts or to sources. Baum-Bodenbender denies it is applicable to the passion narrative. She argues that what Käsemann proposes is appropriate as a description of the source of the body of the Gospel, whereas Bultmann's notion of paradox in incarnation fits the Gospel itself.[490] Similarly Thyen and Langbrandtner describe the *Grundschrift* of the Gospel in docetic terms.[491] Fortna, on the other hand, argues that the description, naive docetism, fits both the "signs

---

487. Barrett, "Theocentric," 11–12.
488. Barrett, "History," 129–30; similarly Lieu, *Epistles*, 204–5.
489. Davey, *Jesus*, 14.
490. Baum-Bodenbender, *Hoheit*, 284–86.
491. Thyen, "Brüder," 536; Langbrandtner, *Weltferner Gott*, 38, 95–96; similarly Martyn, "Glimpses," 110.

The Salvation Event in John

Gospel" and the Fourth Gospel as we have it.[492] Scroggs sees the Gospel standing in a tradition in which the memory of the human Jesus acts as a restraint on what otherwise would quickly become a docetic Christology.[493]

While the presence of miraculous powers need not be (or be seen by the author to be) in conflict with the claim that Jesus was a human being in the full sense, greater difficulties are created by the presence of the kind of self-knowledge which the Son possesses. This might be somewhat alleviated with an anthropology which includes pre-existence for all humans, but that does not seem to apply here.

The author portrays Jesus as a man with human passions and emotions.[494] He affirms both: the real man who dies a real death with a real human body; and the Son with divine powers and knowledge, the unique pre-existent being who comes in obedient fulfilment of his Father's commission and through death returns to his former glory. The author never suggests that the Son's divine powers and awareness are compromised or lessened by his humanity, nor that we should think of Jesus of Nazareth as not a human being. We, from our standpoint, are aware of implications of one for the other. He, in his context, appears never to address this as an issue and may have been quite unaware of it. Against the Jews he constantly has Jesus assert his unique sonship, but never by denying his humanity. Assertion of Jesus' humanity against those who would deny it appears only rarely as an issue in the Gospel, probably only in the reference to blood and water flowing from the side of Jesus and possibly indirectly in 1:14a. The author gives no indication of how precisely he would see Jesus' humanity and his unique sonship in relation to one another.[495] I think, had we asked him, he would have answered uncompromisingly that Jesus was truly human. But he would not have surrendered his faith that here is also the Son come from the Father.[496]

We can only wonder, then, how he might have solved the conflict which his portrait raises. He has similarly left open the relation of the Son to the Father. His portrait raised problems for generations to come. It is not that it is

---

492. Fortna, "Christology," 494.

493. Scroggs, *Christology*, 61.

494. On this see Voorwinde, *Jesus' Emotions*, on Jesus' love (150–62), joy (162–68), anger (168–77), being troubled (177–82), tears (182–84). Schnelle, "Tempelreinigung," 171, notes that John has more about Jesus' feelings than the other three Gospels.

495. Conway, "Behold the Man!" 163, writes that "the desire to show the true divinity of Jesus . . . results in a particularly masculine Christology."

496. Ashton, *Fourth Gospel*, 161, observes, "John would have been surprised to be asked whether Jesus was human." He "was not greatly concerned with Jesus' human traits: what preoccupied him above all (Käsemann was right about this) was his glory."

consistently docetic, even naively so. Nor is it consistently setting forth Jesus as fully human. It has elements of both. Viewed within the perspective of the anthropology of the day, the docetic tendencies lie really in the claims of Jesus to self-awareness as the pre-existent Son come from the Father and not primarily in the miracles. Viewed within our contemporary understanding of humanity, it is above all the massively miraculous elements combined with the way they are related to Jesus' self-awareness which seem to compromise the claim to normal humanity.[497] We may dub their anthropology naive; but we must acknowledge, it seems to me, that the portrait still contains many clear indications that he was a human being and that the author saw him thus.[498]

5.4.4.2 Portrait and Intention

It is instructive to distinguish between the portrait itself and the more elusive intention of the author. In response to Käsemann, Bornkamm had emphasised, amongst other things, that the Johannine Christology is a projection of post-Easter faith upon the ministry of the earthly Jesus.[499] Accordingly, he argued that the Gospel must be seen from the perspective of Easter and the Paraclete, a perspective which understands the cross as paradox. It is this post-Easter perspective, he argues, which leads to tension in the Gospel's christological statements.[500] The bearing of this observation will vary, depending upon whether we are evaluating the portrait for its possible docetism or for the author's own intention or Christology. All it does for the former is explain how the portrait came to be. It in no way invalidates an examination of the portrait with a view to evaluating its docetic character as Käsemann has done. As Schweizer pointed out, a post-Easter perspective may produce a Gospel where Jesus still cries the cry of dereliction on the cross, as in Mark, or produce one in which post-Easter glory casts its

---

497. Schwankl, "Aspekte," notes that the strong emphasis on Jesus' divinity overshadows the human characteristics of Jesus in John's account (373, 352); similarly Müller, *Menschwerdung*, 77; Ashton, "Johannine Son of Man," 528. McGrath, *Christology*, 222, notes that "no explicit answer is given to the question of how the Son of Man and Wisdom related to one another prior to their union as the human being Jesus."

498. Söding, "Ich und der Vater," 193; Hurtado, *Lord Jesus Christ*, 394–96.

499. Bornkamm, "Paraklet," 89; "Interpretation," 114; similarly Robinson, "Christology," 67.

500. Bornkamm, "Interpretation," 117; similarly Haenchen, "Vater," 75–76; Hegermann, "Eigentum," 113; Onuki, *Gemeinde*, 200.

The Salvation Event in John

splendour on the earthly life in a way which endangers the historical Jesus, as in John.[501]

5.4.4.3 The Son as Jesus of Nazareth in the Author's Christology

Acknowledgment of the post-Easter perspective is, however, relevant for the way we evaluate the author's intention, in that sense, his Christology. This is particularly the case in John, because there are indications that he was aware in part of this process of projection, both in direct footnotes, such as 2:22 and 12:16, and in the creative shaping of his source material, to which we return below.

In that sense we can agree with Nicol that the author has some awareness of the tension which results.[502] This is also the weakness of Käsemann's work, where he claims naive docetism without acknowledging the tension within the Gospel.[503] The same must be said of Schottroff who denies the presence of docetism in the Gospel because full real humanity is never denied by the author; it is only irrelevant;[504] though later she describes the Johannine Jesus as an inhuman figure, "unmenschliche Gestalt."[505] Von den Osten Sacken is nearer the mark in claiming that the author's intention was not docetic, but that the product of his work shows docetic features.[506] Nicol also rightly notes how the author's christological concern threatens to absorb history and so produce docetism, while, at the same time, the same concern gives the earthly Jesus of history a great importance, for it was in history that the glory was manifest.[507]

My assessment of the elusive intention of the author suggested that it would not have compromised either the unique sonship or the real humanity and was probably unaware of the problem in making both statements at once. Within the parameters which both offer he portrays the pre-Easter Jesus from a post-Easter perspective, without, it seems, intending to compromise either. For him, it seems, neither is dispensable, neither irrelevant. Yet the resultant portrait raises problems of its own. Here traits of real humanity and unique sonship appear before us largely unmediated. If we fix our gaze

---

501. Schweizer, "*Zeuge*," 167–68.
502. Nicol, *Semeia*, 135–36.
503. Käsemann, *Letzter Wille*, 61–62.
504. Schottroff, *Glaubende*, 274.
505. Schottroff, *Glaubende*, 290–91.
506. Von den Osten Sacken, "Leistung," 157.
507. Nicol, *Semeia*, 136; similarly Schweizer, "*Zeuge*," 145.

at one point, we see Jesus the human figure; if we look at another, we see a divine being. This is the strength of Käsemann's use of the word "naive" to describe the docetism that appears, though my analysis suggests that even this is too simple and one-sided in the way Käsemann presents it and fails to acknowledge the full extent of the tension in the portrait. In John's Gospel we see Christology in the making, with many tensions unresolved. In the next section I suggest that the resultant portrait is all the more complicated because of the author's creative and celebratory literary style, which has produced in many ways a timeless icon of faith. This will, in turn, have bearing on our evaluation of the author's sense of history and understanding of the historical Jesus.

The Fourth Gospel leaves unresolved the relationship of the unique Son and the humanity of Jesus.[508] It simply asserts both. Subsequent history demanded closer definition and the Johannine Jesus became, not surprisingly, the central figure both of docetist Christianity and eventually of those who opposed it. More recently many have constructed a history of the Johannine community which sees the division in the Johannine community resulting in part from these two potential readings of the Gospel and addressed by the members of one side in 1 John and perhaps already through redactional additions to the Gospel itself.[509] In the following section I suggest that it is crucial to define carefully the nature of this document, for failure to do so leads, and has led, to major distortion of its message.

508. So also Theobald, *Johannes*, 1.64.
509. So Richter, *Studien*, 112, 141, 357; David Mealand, "The Christology of the Fourth Gospel," *SJT* 31 (1978): 453; Nicol, *Semeia*, 149; Thyen, "Brüder," 536; Langbrandtner, *Weltferner Gott*, 38, 95-96; Brown, *Beloved Disciple*.

6 The Fourth Gospel in the Light of Its Christology

6.1 The Gospel and the Jesus of History

How did the author mean his portrait of Jesus to be understood? We do not, of course, have access to the thoughts and intentions of ancient authors except in so far as they have left direct or indirect indications of them in their writings. In this chapter I shall be examining these indications with the questions: Did the author write his Gospel believing he was writing an accurate report of the events of the ministry of Jesus, including Jesus' words? Was he deliberately and consciously using the setting of the earthly historical Jesus in order to portray the Christ of the community's faith as experienced and understood in the period after Easter? Was he at all concerned about the Jesus of history or only about the Christ of faith? Would he have been aware of such a distinction?

6.1.1 John and History

It seems to me that the possible answers may be set out as follows:

6.1.1.1 Objectively Reliable Historical Reporting

The author believed he was writing an accurate report of the events of the ministry of Jesus, including Jesus' words, and occasionally makes his own commentary, which is clearly identified as such. The author was right in what he believed he was doing. This is substantially the position of Morris, Cadman and Riesenfeld.[1]

---

1. Morris, *John*, 41–46; Cadman, *Open Heaven*, 203–4; Riesenfeld, "Gospel Tradition," 151; Temple, *Core*, 286; Delebecque, *Jean*, 18–19; cf. Schnackenburg, *John*, 1.19–22.

6.1.1.2 Intentionally Reliable Historical Reporting

This option is similar to the above except for the concluding sentence. Scholars holding this position admit that the author would have been unaware that, in the process of writing, he was portraying Jesus in the light of his own and his tradition's post-Easter faith. Thus Grundmann writes of the author taking over inspired words of the exalted Jesus from early Christian prophets as words of the earthly Jesus.[2]

6.1.1.3 Intentionally Creative Portrait Using Historical Tradition

The third position holds that the author was aware of using traditions which he believed faithfully depicted the words and deeds of Jesus or had their basis in authentic memory, but not only added commentary; he also expanded, re-created or created from afresh dialogues and discourses in order to give new expression to who he believed Jesus to have been and to be; he worked over narrative material similarly; and he believed his work to be inspired by the activity of the Spirit in the community.

Thus E. M. Sidebottom quotes with approval Burkitt's claim that the author seems to have been aware where the historical Jesus tradition stopped and his own thoughts of what he "must have said" began.[3] A number of scholars see the author operating thus at two levels, one, that of the story in history, the other, that of deeper christological insight. Thus, Smalley, for instance, speaks of the author adding to his historical tradition of Jesus' words and deeds a layer of theological interpretation. In this he refers to Martyn's work, who emphasised above all, that the interpretative level reflected the situation facing the Johannine church and not only its Christology.[4] Smalley also draws attention, like Dodd before him,[5] to the author's concern to present the eternal in the temporal, so that the historical details are reworked in the light of the deeper meaning of the whole. Already Baur had noted that the author lives more with the idea than with history.[6]

---

2. Grundmann, *Zeugnis*, 14; cf. Schnackenburg, *John*, 1.23–24.
3. F. C. Burkitt in *History of Christianity in the Light of Modern Knowledge*, 3 vols., ed. Cyril Bailey et al. (London: Blackie & Son, 1929), 209, cited in Sidebottom, *Christ*, 11; similarly Ricca, *Eschatologie*, 28; Müller, *Heilsgeschehen*, 79.
4. Smalley, *John*, 192–95; similarly Müller, *Heilsgeschehen*, 79. Cf. also Martyn, *History and Theology*; Martyn, "Source Criticism," 103–14; Nicholson, *Death*, 157–59; Onuki, *Gemeinde*, 99, 165.
5. Dodd, *Interpretation*, 142–43, 444–45.
6. Baur, *Kritische Untersuchungen*, 314.

The Fourth Gospel in the Light of Its Christology

Two recent variants of this approach assume single authorship and employ notions of memory. They have been developed in part over against the plethora of hypotheses about sources which the Gospel writer employed, proposed to explain tensions among the author's statements about Christology. Thatcher exaggerates playfully when he writes: "Many modern scholars, overwhelmed by the conflicting christological claims of the Fourth Gospel, have simply torn the text in despair."[7] But equally many have simply sought to explain how the situation came about. The question of sources is legitimate in and of itself. Thatcher assumes a single author for the Gospel and the Epistles. He writes:

> John did not, in other words, reflect on things that Jesus did and then try to decide whether his words and deeds meant that he was equal to God or subordinate to God, etc. Instead, John refers to the process by which he painted his portrait as a "memory" of Jesus, a "witness" to Jesus' true identity. A coherent theory about the way this witness and memory worked is critical to any study that seriously seeks to understand John's Christology on its own terms.[8]

Importantly he adds:

> For John, Christian "memory" is not a simple act of recalling information about things that Jesus said or did. Rather, Christian memory is a complex combination of the recall of the historical Jesus, post-resurrection faith, and a Christian interpretation of the Hebrew Bible—all melted together by the heat of the Holy Spirit. This charismatic memory is the generative matrix that produced all of John's statements about Jesus, and what we today call John's "Christology" is the image of Jesus that this memory matrix produced under the specific circumstances in which the Johannine books were written.[9]

It is, of course, possible that we are dealing with a single author, but this cannot be assumed, nor can the data which have led so many to sources theories be dismissed lightly, especially where a case can be made not just for rethinking but significant correction.

Anderson goes even further claiming a single author, who he would

---

7. Thatcher, "Remembering Jesus," 167.
8. Thatcher, "Remembering Jesus," 171.
9. Thatcher, "Remembering Jesus," 172.

like to believe was an eyewitness, one of the disciples, sometimes arguing as much,[10] sometimes acknowledging that this may not have been so.[11] He, too, takes a modern individualist approach, like Thatcher, a position which the latter otherwise critiques,[12] and employs modern theories of western individual stages of faith growth as developed by Fowler,[13] and responses to trauma developed by Loder,[14] to speculate about the author's personal and theological development, which he argues leaves its trace in the document, as he "matured over the years."[15] He suggests, for instance, that the author was present at the event of Jesus' walking on water, which he treats as historical, but read it differently from Peter (and so, he alleges, the Synoptics, led by Mark): "at least two of Jesus' followers understood his mission and ministry in significantly different ways, and some of these differences extended well into the sub-apostolic era."[16] On this basis he argues that "what we appear to have in Mark and John is two 'bi-optic' perspectives on the events and implications of Jesus' Gospel ministry."[17] He rightly notes that some of the imagery linked with the "I am" sayings is also to be found in the Synoptic tradition,[18] but his historical reconstruction strains credibility when it asks us to believe that Jesus did openly make the christological claims during his ministry found in John, but that some disciples heard them and some did not.[19] It is much more

---

10. Anderson, "Johannine *Egō Eimi* Sayings," 202–3.

11. Thus Anderson, *Christology*, 192, writes: "The evangelist's dialogue with his tradition may best be understood as his reflection upon either his own experiences or traditional stories about Jesus' ministry"; similarly Anderson, "Johannine *Egō Eimi* Sayings," 173.

12. Cf. Thatcher, "Remembering Jesus," 170, who writes: 'Essentially, source-critical and developmental approaches begin with a taxonomy of categories that reflect the Western philosophical and theological tradition. The text of the Fourth Gospel is dissected, and each distinct unit or theme is sorted into one of the familiar christological categories."

13. Anderson, *Christology*, 142–48.

14. Anderson, *Christology*, 148–51. James E. Loder, *The Transforming Moment: Understanding Convictional Experiences* (Colorado Springs: Helmers and Howard, 1989).

15. Anderson, *Christology*, 261.

16. Anderson, *Christology*, 255; similarly 260.

17. Anderson, "Interfluential," 25; similarly, Anderson, "Johannine *Egō Eimi* Sayings," 170.

18. In Anderson, *Christology*, 256, he writes: "The kind of material most characteristic of John (a large quantity of non-symbolic, illustrative detail) is *precisely* the kind of material omitted by Matthew and Luke." This assumes known material deliberately omitted. Use of Mark as a test case does not support this. There is however validity in the observation that "John's omission of exorcisms and his existentializing view of Jesus' signs suggest that implicit in Jesus' correcting Peter in John 6:70 is an ideological disagreement between the Johannine and Petrine traditions regarding the character of God's reign on earth" (259), but that reflects views at the time of the author.

19. See also the criticism in Marinus de Jonge, "Christology, Controversy and Community

The Fourth Gospel in the Light of Its Christology

plausible to argue that John incorporates traditions which reflect independent evidence of historical data, such as in *realia*, dating, and length of ministry.[20]

6.1.1.4 Furthering a Tradition of Intentionally Creative Portrayal of the Earthly Jesus of History

The fourth position is very close to the third, except that it is more willing to concede that already the author's traditions included elements which had been transferred back onto the earthly Jesus.

For instance, Mussner emphasises the historical witness which was borne by the apostolic office and which already combined memory plus interpretative anamnesis.[21] "Apostolic office" narrows the role of the disciples inappropriately,[22] but others, too, identify a tradition of interpretation borne by disciples. Bornkamm emphasised the importance of the Paraclete sayings as illustrating the way the author would have seen his relationship, but also the relationship of those before him, to historical tradition.[23] Indeed the Paraclete sayings serve as a justification or rationale for the creative shaping which has produced the Gospel.[24] Similarly Hahn speaks of a merging of

---

in the Gospel of John," in *Christology, Controversy and Community: New Testament Essays in Honour of David R. Catchpole*, ed. D. G. Horrell and C. M. Tuckett, NovTSup 99 (Leiden: Brill, 2000), 212–13, who writes: "I do not think that one can really speak of an individual person responsible for the Gospel or that it is possible to delineate an independent 'Johannine way back to Jesus'—let alone that we may assume that the evangelist was an eye-witness. Also Anderson's picture of the process that finally resulted in John 6 in its present form, is at least as complicated and, therefore disputable, as those of his predecessors."

20. Paul N. Anderson, "Why This Study Is Needed, and Why it is Needed now," in *John, Jesus, and History, Volume 1: Critical Appraisals of Critical Views*, ed. P. N. Anderson, F. Just, and T. Thatcher, SBLSym 44 (Atlanta: SBL, 2007), 70, mentions data concerning John the Baptist's ministry; Jesus' visits to Jerusalem; his three-year ministry; early events in his ministry; positive reception in Galilee, among Samaritans, women, and Gentiles; the Judean ministry, archaeologically confirmed data; the dating of Jesus' last meal and his death; the cleansing of the temple as at the beginning; not all of which are beyond dispute. I see the location of the expulsion as theologically motivated despite the protestations in Anderson, "Interfluential," 24. See also James Charlesworth, "The Historical Jesus in the Fourth Gospel: A Paradigm Shift?" *JSHJ* 8 (2010): 3–46.

21. Mussner, *Sehweise*, 23, 42–43; Mussner, "Parakletsspruche," 154–55.

22. So Käsemann, *Letzter Wille*, 70–71; Haacker, *Stiftung*, 157–61, in criticism of Mussner and Käsemann.

23. Bornkamm, "Paraklet," 87–88; Bornkamm, "Interpretation," 114, 117; similarly Nicol, *Semeia*, 27; de Jonge, *Stranger*, 11–12; Klauck, "Gemeinde," 213–14.

24. Jakob Kremer, "Jesu Verheissung des Geistes. Zur Verankerung von Joh 16,13 im Leben Jesu," in *Die Kirche des Anfangs. Für H. Schürmann*, ed. R. Schnackenburg, J. Ernst, and

horizons ("Horizontverschmelzung") and of the importance of the figure of the beloved disciple as a link with historical tradition,[25] the "implied author," as Culpepper brings out.[26] Becker vividly illustrates the former by speaking of two slides projected onto a single screen.[27] Blank, too, notes, that the author would not naively believe that the words of Jesus in ch. 5 were spoken by the earthly Jesus.[28] In discussing the narrative of the wedding feast at Cana, Olsson speaks of a screening of the text, through which both salvation-historical perspectives and post-Easter perspectives leave their mark on the narrative, and describes this as a deliberate process on the part of the author, inspired by the Paraclete.[29] The Paraclete and the beloved disciple are not merged into one; rather the beloved disciple stands out in the Johannine tradition in which the Paraclete is given to all.[30]

In both the third and fourth position scholars acknowledge a sensitivity to history on the part of the author despite the subsequent layers of tradition and interpretation. Mussner, in appealing to "apostolic office," and Hahn, for instance, in pointing to the function of the beloved disciple, are emphasising this. Similarly Haacker argues against Käsemann's diminishing of the link with history[31] and Hegermann points out that the author has not chosen to speak of the exalted one as presented, for instance, in the early chapters of Revelation, but has written a Gospel centred on the earthly historical Jesus.[32] Schnelle argues that the Gospel form, which roots faith in history and links it with the earthly Jesus, also reflects an antidocetic concern of the evangelist.[33] Onuki points out that the merging of horizons is the author's way of maintaining historical continuity and holding together the pre- and post-Easter image of Jesus.[34] Cullmann sees here an alternative method to

---

J. Wanke (Freiburg: Herder, 1978), 259–60; Painter, "Farewell Discourses," 531; Dietzfelbinger, "Paraklet," 405, 407.

25. Hahn, "Sehen," 140; similarly Onuki, *Gemeinde*, 12–14, 203; Frey, *Eschatologie*, 2.256, of the farewell discourses, John 3 and all the speeches.

26. Culpepper, *Anatomy*, 47; cf. also his work R. Alan Culpepper, *The Johannine School: An Evaluation of the Johannine-school Hypothesis Based on an Investigation of the Nature of Ancient Schools*, SBLDS 26 (Missoula: Scholars, 1975).

27. Becker, *Johannes*, 57.

28. Blank, *Krisis*, 117.

29. Olsson, *Structure*, 271, 279, 281.

30. So Klauck, "Gemeinde," 213–14.

31. Haacker, *Stiftung*, 159–60.

32. Hegermann, "Eigentum," 129; similarly Barrett, "Theocentric," 7; Onuki, *Gemeinde*, 50–51, 205; Klaiber, "Interpretation," 306.

33. Schnelle, *Christologie*, 250.

34. Onuki, *Gemeinde*, 202, 205.

that of Luke, who writes two successive volumes, noting how in John 3 the author moves almost imperceptibly from the pre- to the post-Easter words of Jesus.[35] While Schnackenburg rightly observes that this particular kind of merging is confined to this chapter,[36] Cullmann's overall assessment of continuity combined in one volume without abandonment of the earthly historical Jesus has strong support. Brown notes how the signs have a similar duality of reference and points out that this includes also an awareness of time before and after Easter.[37] Similarly Onuki argues for the author's consciousness of historical distance,[38] and, like many others, points to passages like 2:21–22 and 12:16–17 where we have a more explicit expression of the issue of distance and difference in time between pre- and post-Easter than in any of the other Gospels.[39] Others point also to the description of the Paraclete which implies historical awareness, especially in its function of bringing to remembrance what Jesus said,[40] although the overlap is present in the Paraclete's mediating also the words of the exalted Lord. Wead also points out that beside the beloved disciple there is also the community itself represented by the author's "we" in 1:14, which illustrates historical awareness.[41] Culpepper, in particular, has analysed the importance of the author's statements on time in an excellent discussion which includes comments on the "historical prolepses," such as 2:22 and 12:16, mentioned above.[42]

The presence of historical tradition in John has been especially emphasised by Robinson, following the lead of Dodd, though this also derives, in part, from Robinson's hypothesis of a very early date for the Gospel.[43] The issue of the presence of historically accurate material in the Gospel need not logically hang together with the issue of date, and the historical material is much better explained, to my mind, as coming to the author through the nature of his traditions than through direct authorship memory. Robinson, too, however, notes deliberate anachronism in the Gospel with the resultant impression of

---

35. Oscar Cullmann, *Salvation as History* (London: SCM, 1967) 271; similarly Childs, *Canon*, 135.

36. Schnackenburg, "Frage," 205.

37. Brown, *John*, 530; similarly Cullmann, *Salvation*, 272–73; Schnackenburg, "Frage," 205–6.

38. Onuki, *Gemeinde*, 12–14, 165.

39. Onuki, *Gemeinde*, 58–59; similarly Robinson, *Priority*, 35; Franck, *Revelation*, 48; Cullmann, *Salvation*, 274; Woll, *Johannine Christianity*, 28–29; Nicholson, *Death*, 157–58.

40. So Lieu, *Epistles*, 177–78; Burge, *Anointed Community*, 216.

41. Wead, *Devices*, 10–11.

42. Culpepper, *Anatomy*, 54–70, esp. 67.

43. J. A. T. Robinson, *The Redating of the New Testament* (London: SCM, 1976), 254–311, and, most extensively: Robinson, *Priority*.

docetism.⁴⁴ The author's awareness of temporal distance between his own day and the earthly Jesus is upheld by many. It is a different question to what degree this difference is discernible in specific passages, and a different question again to what degree what the author might have considered historical is in fact so.

Ashton's most recent work emphasises the role of the Spirit in the way the author underlines "the essential difference between the reception of Jesus' words and actions during his lifetime and the enhanced understanding of these words and actions that was available to him and his community."⁴⁵ Accordingly he sees the author in response to apocalyptic hope making the claim that "the new revelation is the Gospel itself, a story set on earth—which is why it may be called an apocalypse in reverse."⁴⁶ With regard to this he writes that "just as the Old Testament tells of men and women too, who spoke with the voice of God, there were some in the Johannine community who spoke with the voice of Jesus."⁴⁷ Accordingly he explains:

> Here we have the most likely explanation of the extraordinary difference between his portrait of Jesus and that of the Synoptics. It had nothing to do with a decision to present a docetic Christ, but arose from his constant awareness, which he shared with the members of his community, that they were living in the presence of the Glorified One. So dazzling was his glory that any memory of a less-than-glorified Christ was altogether eclipsed.⁴⁸

The resort to charismatic prophecy to explain John does not do justice to the careful literary work.

6.1.1.5 Furthering a Tradition of Creative Portrayal of the Living Christ Without Particular Interest in the Earthly Jesus of History

The fifth option is to deny that the author had any concern with the question of history at all and to maintain that the author used the traditions at his

---

44. J. A. T. Robinson, *The Human Face of Jesus* (London: SCM, 1973), 67–68; Robinson, *Priority*, 35.
45. Ashton, *John* 43.
46. Ashton, *John*, 118.
47. Ashton, *John*, 189. "All these sayings come from members of the community with the gift of prophecy speaking with his voice" (190).
48. Ashton, *John*, 198; similarly Ashton, *John*, 201–2; Hurtado, "Remembering and Revelation," 206, who writes of charismatic utterances in Jesus' name being understood by the author as a "fuller disclosure of what he was all along" (similarly 207–10).

disposal and his own creative genius to portray the living Christ as experienced in the community of faith, and that he did so believing his work was the fruit of the Spirit which had been working in this way in the community.

Bultmann's assertion that only the "Dass," the sheer fact of Jesus' coming, not the "Was," the details, matters for the author,[49] comes close to this position. Similarly Heinrich Schlier notes there is no historical development in the Johannine picture of Jesus and suggests that the author has no interest in history, but seeks only to focus on the person of the Son.[50] Käsemann's position is similar, who speaks of the author clothing the dogmatic Christ in the earthly Jesus with no interest in the historical Jesus,[51] though he can argue against Bultmann that the miracles were not merely symbols.[52]

Against this option Barrett points out that the author was not satisfied with a timeless mediator in the manner of Philo, but remains committed to the human person Jesus as mediator.[53] Here, too, belong those who believe that the merging has gone to such a degree that the author virtually knew of no other Jesus than the exalted one and so can sometimes have Jesus use tenses, as in 3:13 about ascension, inappropriate for the earthly Jesus.[54] Others, like Nicholson, acknowledge the fictional quality of much of the author's presentation of the earthly Jesus, but argue that the author has not created the fiction without also being concerned about the historical link.[55] The expansion of the Jesus tradition, not only through the revelations of the post-Easter exalted Lord mediated by the Paraclete, but in particular through devices literary and otherwise to enhance communication and celebration, should also be noted here (on this see below).

6.1.2 What Degree of Historical Interest?

I have identified five positions for the sake of overview. There is considerable variety within each and points where they merge, one into the other. There is a continuum of positions. Along that continuum the degree of interest in the earthly Jesus of history attributed to the author varies from the minimal

---

49. Bultmann, *Theologie*, 419.
50. Schlier, "Christologie," 86–87.
51. Käsemann, *Letzter Wille*, 96 n. 37; Lattke, *Einheit*, 143; cf. Wead, *Devices*, 24; Nicholson, *Death*, 157–59.
52. Käsemann, *Letzter Wille*, 54.
53. Barrett, "Theocentric," 9–10.
54. So Thüsing, *Erhöhung*, 256; Riedl, *Heilswerk*, 154.
55. Nicholson, *Death*, 157–59.

position of Bultmann to those in the first position in whose mind it is one of the author's vital concerns. Was the author's interest only in the "Dass," as Bultmann would have us believe? Does it include every detail recorded in the Gospel? The answer lies, it seems to me, at neither extreme. We must also allow that the author may have weighted various historical elements differently.

Historical Intention and Historical Achievement

Again, as in our discussion of the issues of the humanity of Jesus, we need to distinguish between the presence of what we, for our part, adjudge historically valuable material in the Gospel and what the author, for his part, might have sensed as being historical, as distinct, for instance, from what he knew to be his own or the community's interpretative additions and embellishments. The focus of the present discussion is not on the historicity of John or Johannine tradition from our standpoint, but from the author's. What value did he place on the earthly Jesus as a historical figure? To what degree is his Gospel history and to what degree conscious elaboration and embellishment of the tradition which lay before him?

Asking the Questions

In what follows I shall defend a version of the fourth option and, in the course of doing so, present arguments which tell against the other four. I shall be pursuing the questions: what evidence is there that the author was aware of development in the Jesus tradition and, if so, how did he understand such development? What indications are there of the way he might have evaluated the products of this development, including his own Gospel, in relation to historicity? And are there indications of criteria or of methods which the author employed when engaging in the interpretative process?

6.1.3 The Paraclete: Evidence for Awareness of Historical and Interpretative Issues

In the last discourses Jesus promises the gift of the Paraclete to his disciples:

ὁ δὲ παράκλητος, τὸ πνεῦμα τὸ ἅγιον, ὃ πέμψει ὁ πατὴρ ἐν τῷ ὀνόματί

The Fourth Gospel in the Light of Its Christology

μου, ἐκεῖνος ὑμᾶς διδάξει πάντα καὶ ὑπομνήσει ὑμᾶς πάντα ἃ εἶπον ὑμῖν [ἐγώ].
The Paraclete, the Holy Spirit, which the Father will send in my name, he will teach you all things and bring all things to your memory which I have said to you. (14:26)

Ὅταν ἔλθῃ ὁ παράκλητος ὃν ἐγὼ πέμψω ὑμῖν παρὰ τοῦ πατρός,
τὸ πνεῦμα τῆς ἀληθείας ὃ παρὰ τοῦ πατρὸς ἐκπορεύεται,
ἐκεῖνος μαρτυρήσει περὶ ἐμοῦ·
When the Paraclete comes whom I will send you from the Father, the Spirit of Truth, which comes out of the Father, he will bear witness concerning me. (15:26)

Καὶ ἐλθὼν ἐκεῖνος ἐλέγξει τὸν κόσμον περὶ ἁμαρτίας καὶ περὶ δικαιοσύνης καὶ περὶ κρίσεως·
And when he comes he will convince the world with regard to sin, righteousness, and judgment. (16:8)

ὅταν δὲ ἔλθῃ ἐκεῖνος, τὸ πνεῦμα τῆς ἀληθείας,
ὁδηγήσει ὑμᾶς ἐν τῇ ἀληθείᾳ πάσῃ·
οὐ γὰρ λαλήσει ἀφ᾽ ἑαυτοῦ, ἀλλ᾽ ὅσα ἀκούσει λαλήσει
καὶ τὰ ἐρχόμενα ἀναγγελεῖ ὑμῖν.
ἐκεῖνος ἐμὲ δοξάσει, ὅτι ἐκ τοῦ ἐμοῦ λήμψεται καὶ ἀναγγελεῖ ὑμῖν.
πάντα ὅσα ἔχει ὁ πατὴρ ἐμά ἐστιν·
διὰ τοῦτο εἶπον ὅτι ἐκ τοῦ ἐμοῦ λαμβάνει καὶ ἀναγγελεῖ ὑμῖν.
When he comes, the Spirit of Truth,
he will lead you into all truth.
For he will not speak of his own accord, but what he hears he will speak and he will declare to you the things which are coming.
He will glorify me because he will take what is mine and declare it to you.
All the Father has is mine;
therefore I said, he will take what is mine and declare it to you. (16:13–15)

These logia reveal an awareness on the part of the evangelist that memory of the historical earthly Jesus and his words is an issue of relevance for the disciples.[56] As Porsch points out, this includes awareness that the disciples

---

56. So Bornkamm, "Paraklet," 87–89.

had not fully understood Jesus during his earthly ministry.[57] 16:13–15 also leaves open the possibility that not only the words of the earthly Jesus but also those of the risen Jesus will be mediated by the Spirit.[58]

6.1.3.1 Bearers of the Paraclete—Not a Select Few

There is no indication here of a select group, the apostolate, being made bearers of such revelation, as Mussner proposes,[59] as though the Paraclete were to be given to a chosen few. The verses may indicate the presence of inspired prophets in the Johannine community and in its tradition.[60] Schulz, for instance, suggests this in explaining the background of the "I am" and the Son of Man sayings;[61] and Karl Kundsin pointed to the parallels between the "I am" sayings and the words of the exalted Jesus in Rev 1–3.[62] But there is no indication that we should see the Paraclete promise as relating only to Christian prophets,[63] nor, with Minear, see the last discourses as applying only to the wandering charismatic disciple group.[64] Modelled perhaps on the succession from Moses to Joshua,[65] the promise of the Paraclete is to all the disciples without specifying a particular ministry. All are to abide in the vine and bear fruit; all need the comfort and encouragement of the second Paraclete, because all have been left by the earthly Jesus. Recall of what Jesus said and did is, of course, relevant only for those who were

---

57. Porsch, *Pneuma*, 262, 264–65.

58. Frey, "Johannes und die Synoptiker," notes that the author would have been aware of the processes of reinterpretation which underlay his work (286).

59. Mussner, "Parakletssprüche," 154–55.

60. So Karl Kundsin, "Charakter und Ursprung der johanneischen Reden," *Acta Universitatis Latviensis Teologijas Fakultatis Serija* 1.4 (1939): 268–84; Käsemann, *Letzter Wille*, 70–71; Leroy, *Rätsel*, 180; David E. Aune, *The Cultic Setting of Realized Eschatology in Early Christianity*, NovTSup 18 (Leiden: Brill, 1972), 101; D. Moody Smith, "Johannine Christianity: Some Reflections on Its Character and Delineation," *NTS* 21 (1975): 244; Onuki, *Gemeinde*, 80–81; Boring, "Christian Prophecy," 113–14; Franck, *Revelation*, 120–22; Minear, *John*, 20–23; cf. Schnackenburg, *Johannesevangelium*, 4.56–58.

61. Schulz, *Johannes*, 86, 91–94; see also his earlier work, Schulz, *Menschensohn*.

62. Kundsin, "Reden," 268–84; similarly Boring, "Christian Prophecy," 115; cf. Burge, *Anointed Community*, 218.

63. So rightly Klauck, "Gemeinde," 213–14; Franck, *Revelation*, 127–29; Isaacs, "Prophetic Spirit," 406–7; Schnackenburg, *Johannesevangelium*, 4.57–58; against Boring, "Christian Prophecy," 113.

64. Against Minear, *John*, 20–23.

65. Ashton, *John*, 42.

The Fourth Gospel in the Light of Its Christology

with Jesus, but the promise of 16:13-15 goes beyond memory of what was said and done.[66]

6.1.3.2 Paraclete and *Methurgeman*?

Franck seeks further elucidation of the function of the Paraclete in the community and its tradition with a novel theory which combines the idea of prophet and teacher or interpreter of Scripture. He suggests, somewhat speculatively, that the Paraclete was modelled in a special way in the Johannine community on the person of the *methurgeman*, who traditionally translated the Scripture into targum in the synagogue and so indirectly also preached.[67] The analogy is interesting and is consistent with the suggestions of Reim[68] and others concerning targumic traditions in the Fourth Gospel. It would also explain, by analogy, the relationship of the work of the Paraclete and its bearers to the Jesus tradition and its interpretation. I am not convinced, however, that there is more than an analogy or parallel present.

6.1.3.3 Paraclete—An Open Door for New Claims of Revelation?

Being led into all truth and being told of things to come (16:13) might, if isolated from the context, seem to open the door for all manner of new revelation and, accordingly, Käsemann sees here a claim of charismatic enthusiasts.[69] But, as Haacker and Nicol point out, the context ties this revelation very closely to Jesus and may mean no more than the promise of greater understanding of who Jesus was and is.[70] Nicol includes in this both what Jesus once said and what he might well have said in the light of the full truth of who he is.[71] Schnackenburg speaks of a continuing revelation

---

66. Thatcher, "Remembering Jesus," 174-75, writes: "'Christology' is the image that emerges when a Christian interprets events from Jesus' life through the lens of the resurrection against the backdrop of the Hebrew Bible under the guidance of the Holy Spirit."
67. Franck, *Revelation*, 132-40.
68. See Reim, "Targum."
69. Käsemann, *Letzter Wille*, 70-71.
70. Haacker, *Stiftung*, 154-55, 158-60; Nicol, *Semeia*, 126, 130; similarly Mussner, "Parakletssprüche," 150-52; de la Potterie, *Vérité*, 424, 438; Porsch, *Pneuma*, 295; Ibuki, *Wahrheit*, 300-301; Müller, *Heilsgeschehen*, 83; Franck, *Revelation*, 74.
71. Nicol, *Semeia*, 126, 130; similarly Scroggs, *Christology*, 88, 91.

in the person of the exalted Jesus, but bound to him.⁷² This leaves open the extent to which such revelation not only interprets the earthly historical Jesus, but also adds new christological insight. Boring argues similarly that Johannine prophetic activity retained the link with the historical Jesus and was never free-floating.⁷³ Kremer sees the passage not as opening, but rather closing doors, especially against all other truth claims.⁷⁴ This may be so. On the other hand, I find Woll's thesis, in this regard, that much of the last discourses is aimed at countering the growing authority of charismatic prophets by subordinating the disciples, by highlighting the prior ascent and higher exaltation of Jesus and by tying the Paraclete promise to him, to be a construction going far beyond what the text justifies.⁷⁵

6.1.3.4 The Paraclete and "the things that are coming"—Meaning?

The promise that the Paraclete would also declare τὰ ἐρχόμενα ("the things that are coming") might also indicate teaching in addition to what was given by the earthly Jesus. The expression may reflect Isa 41:22–23, as de la Potterie and Porsch suggest, where it is used of future prediction.⁷⁶ It might refer to prophecy of the last days, such as we find in Revelation, but the relatively minor place of themes of future eschatology in John make this unlikely,⁷⁷ unlikely, at least, for the evangelist. It may have conveyed this meaning once in an earlier form, if one existed. Thüsing takes the expression to refer to the time of the Spirit,⁷⁸ which might include the ordeals to face the disciples.⁷⁹ It is also possible to see in it a reference to the events immediately to come in Jesus' ministry, namely Jesus' death and return to the Father, which the Spirit would interpret for the disciples,⁸⁰ perhaps seen also as eschatological judgment.⁸¹

---

72. Schnackenburg, *Johannesevangelium*, 3.154.
73. Boring, "Christian Prophecy," 117–18.
74. Kremer, "Verheissung," 256.
75. D. Bruce Woll, "The Preparation of 'the Way': The First Farewell Discourses in the Gospel of John," *JBL* 99 (1980): 237–38; Woll, *Johannine Christianity*, 105, 124.
76. de la Potterie, *Vérité*, 450; Porsch, *Pneuma*, 298.
77. So rightly Schnackenburg, *Johannesevangelium*, 3.154.
78. Thüsing, *Erhöhung*, 151–52.
79. So de Jonge, *Stranger*, 25; similarly in part Kremer, "Verheissung," 258.
80. So Kremer, "Verheissung," 258; Onuki, *Gemeinde*, 150–51; Burge, *Anointed Community*, 215.
81. So Isaacs, "Prophetic Spirit," 398.

6.1.4 Historical Awareness Evident in "Footnotes"

However we measure the extent of any additional revelation to be given according to 16:13–15, all of the Paraclete sayings demonstrate a degree of historical awareness. This same awareness is also apparent in what Olsson and others have called Johannine "footnotes."[82] De Jonge points, in particular, to the following as illustrating awareness of two periods of history: 2:21–22; 12:16; 13:7; 14:7b; and 20:9.[83] This tells against the view that the author had no interest in the historical Jesus. The author also reveals in passages like 20:29; 17:20; 10:16; 11:51–52 an awareness of the "generation gap," as Nicholson puts it, between his own and earlier times, including the time of the historical Jesus and the disciples.[84]

6.1.4.1 John 2:22

ὅτε οὖν ἠγέρθη ἐκ νεκρῶν, ἐμνήσθησαν οἱ μαθηταὶ αὐτοῦ ὅτι τοῦτο ἔλεγεν,
καὶ ἐπίστευσαν τῇ γραφῇ καὶ τῷ λόγῳ ὃν εἶπεν ὁ Ἰησοῦς.
When Jesus was raised from the dead, the disciples remembered that he was saying this, and believed the Scripture and the word which Jesus spoke. (2:22)

They remembered Jesus' temple saying and believed it, because it had come true, but the author also implies, by his explanation of its meaning in 2:21, that they did not understand it until after Jesus' resurrection. The Scripture they believed was doubtless Ps 69:9, which the disciples remembered, possibly during the incident of the temple expulsion, but more probably after Easter, "Zeal for your house will consume me" (2:17). They saw its application to Jesus after Easter. The coming of the Paraclete made this possible.

---

82. Olsson, *Structure*, 262; similarly Wead, *Devices*, 6–9; Nicholson, *Death*, 32–33; Bjerkelund, *Tauta*, 97; Minear, *John*, 9–10.

83. So de Jonge, *Stranger*, 8, 17.

84. Nicholson, *Death*, 36–37; similarly O'Day, "The Word Become Flesh," 73; Hurtado, "Remembering the Revelation," 212.

6.1.4.2 John 12:16

Similarly 12:16 displays historical sensitivity:

> ταῦτα οὐκ ἔγνωσαν αὐτοῦ οἱ μαθηταὶ τὸ πρῶτον,
> ἀλλ' ὅτε ἐδοξάσθη Ἰησοῦς τότε ἐμνήσθησαν
> ὅτι ταῦτα ἦν ἐπ' αὐτῷ γεγραμμένα καὶ ταῦτα ἐποίησαν αὐτῷ.
> The disciples did not know these things at first;
> but when Jesus was glorified, then they remembered
> that these things were written concerning him and that they did these things to him. (12:16)

It refers to Jesus' entry into Jerusalem, acclaimed by the crowds as royal messiah, and to the Zechariah prophecy, "Fear not, daughter of Zion; behold your king comes, sitting upon the foal of an ass" (12:14–15). This is all the more extraordinary since the Synoptic accounts present the narrative as messianic as though the disciples were fully part of the acclamation. The fourth evangelist distinguishes here between history and reflection. Again the coming of the Paraclete made this reflection possible.

6.1.4.3 John 8:28; 13:7; 20:9; 14:20; 16:25

John 8:28 has Jesus address the Jews:

> ὅταν ὑψώσητε τὸν υἱὸν τοῦ ἀνθρώπου, τότε γνώσεσθε ὅτι ἐγώ εἰμι, καὶ ἀπ' ἐμαυτοῦ ποιῶ οὐδέν, ἀλλὰ καθὼς ἐδίδαξέν με ὁ πατὴρ ταῦτα λαλῶ.
> When you have lifted up the Son of Man, then you shall know that I am the one and I do nothing of my own accord, but as the Father taught me so I speak. (8:28)

This, too, promises (as a possibility) that knowledge of who Jesus is as the Son sent from the Father will come to some as a fruit of the exaltation. Similarly Jesus tells Peter in 13:7, "What I am doing you do not know now, but afterwards you will" (ὃ ἐγὼ ποιῶ σὺ οὐκ οἶδας ἄρτι, γνώσῃ δὲ μετὰ ταῦτα). He will perceive the meaning of the foot washing. According to 20:9 the disciples did not understand the empty tomb because they had not yet understood the Scripture about Jesus. Similarly in 14:20 Jesus promises the disciples that one day they shall know that he is in the Father, and 16:25 promises deeper understanding.

The Fourth Gospel in the Light of Its Christology

The promise to Nathanael of the vision of the Son of Man (1:50–51) probably also belongs here, as does 6:62 with its promise of greater seeing, the ascension of the Son of Man. This would all be made possible through the Paraclete.

6.1.4.4 "The hour is coming and now is"

Some would include here the sayings introduced with the formula, "The hour is coming and now is" (4:23; 5:25; cf. 16:32). Thus Forestell and Thüsing take "now is" as the author's own comment about the period following Easter.[85] But Blank is more convincing when he explains the "now" as a claim being made by the earthly Jesus based on his personal presence, and Porsch points out that the narrative of Jesus' meeting with the Samaritan woman assumes that then and there the hour of fulfilment and hope was present.[86] Frey's major investigation reaches similar conclusions where he emphasises that "now is" relates to what is present in the person of Jesus, which while perceived from a post-Easter perspective, for the author is also true of the earthly Jesus, because its truth is based on who Jesus is and was.[87] Accordingly these sayings do not reflect a distinction between pre- and post-Easter in the author's Christology.

6.1.4.5 The Significance of Texts Reflecting Awareness of Two Periods in History

Whether indirectly in the words of Jesus or directly in his own words, the author often makes a clear distinction between two periods of time, between which is a watershed in understanding marked by Jesus' death, return to the Father, and the giving of the Spirit. None of the texts needs mean anything more than that the author sees himself preserving authentic Paraclete-aided memory of what the historical Jesus actually said, plus enlightened comment and reflection, including OT reflection, on what is reported. But there are indications within the Gospel that this picture is inadequate. For, on the one hand, some changes have taken place within the tradition of which the author may have been aware, and on the other hand, he himself has effected significant changes which altered the tradition.

---

85. Forestell, *Word*, 34; Thüsing, *Erhöhung*, 98, 163; Dahl, "Church," 125–26.

86. Blank, *Krisis*, 136; Porsch, *Pneuma*, 139, 143, 147–48; similarly Riedl, *Heilswerk*, 20–22; Bornkamm, "Paraklet," 88; Bornkamm, "Theocentric," 15.

87. Frey, *Eschatologie*, 2.152, notes that the author assumes the Son's person transcends time (similarly 3.487).

6.1.5 Identifying Distinctively Johannine Tradition and Interpretation

The distinction between what is the author's and what is tradition is difficult. Comparison with the Synoptics enables us at least to identify elements peculiar to, or receiving a distinctive shape in, the Fourth Gospel. There is no need here to rehearse the evidence in full. Of primary importance is the pattern of christological statements we identified in Part One as the central structure of the author's Christology. While the designations "Father" and "Son" are not absent in the Synoptic Gospels, there is no comparison with the extensiveness of their use in the Fourth Gospel. This is even more the case with statements about pre-existence, sending, coming and returning, which are either totally absent or used quite differently in the other three Gospels. It is not just the presence of statements reflecting the revealer-envoy pattern of the author's Christology in the Gospel itself, which sets John and the Synoptics apart, but also their presence as explicit claims on the lips of Jesus. Whatever links may exist with the traditions present in these Gospels, the Johannine Gospel reflects a distinctive development. The Johannine Christ speaks Johannine language[88] and makes the christological claims of the Johannine community.[89] Neither the language nor the claims, in the way they are set forth here, can claim to represent accurately the Jesus of history. The language and Christology of the Synoptics would be scarcely explicable, should we have to assume their tradition reached back to the Johannine Christ.

6.1.5.1 The Gospel in Community

Community is an important perspective from which to understand the Gospel. Meeks has shown this in pointing to the way the Johannine pattern of the descending–ascending revealer serves more than christological affirmation. It also helps to reinforce the identity of the community estranged from the synagogue and from the world.[90] It represents a substantial modification of the Jesus tradition. Onuki has observed that the two parts of the Gospel, Jesus' coming in chs. 1–12 and Jesus' going 13–21, also reflect the two-fold movement of the community of faith: its reaching out into the world, where

---

88. So Schnackenburg, *John*, 1.21–22; similarly Leroy, *Rätsel*, 46–47, 71–73, 79; Olsson, *Structure*, 282; Culpepper, *Anatomy*, 86; Onuki, *Gemeinde*, 26.

89. Mussner, *Sehweise*, 84.

90. Meeks, "Man from Heaven," 162–63; cf. the critical appropriation of the thesis in de Jonge, *Stranger*, 99. See also Thatcher, "Remembering Jesus," 176–77, on conflict with the synagogue as influencing the development of the author's Christology.

The Fourth Gospel in the Light of Its Christology

it also faces strangeness and alienation, and its withdrawing from the world for consolation and strength.[91] These help explain the shape of the Gospel and the relevance of its Christology to the community. But beside these dynamics which operate at a less conscious level in the community's development, there is also abundant evidence that the Jesus tradition has been quite consciously shaped and transformed to address its needs.

6.1.5.2 The Author's Creative Development and Embellishment of the Tradition

While we cannot be sure of the extent to which the author would have been aware of the distinctive language of the Johannine tradition about Jesus, we are on surer ground when speaking of his own contribution.

Culpepper notes, for instance, how the language the author uses in the so-called Johannine footnotes (e.g., 7:39; 12:16; 21:19; 7:30; 8:20) also corresponds largely to that of the last discourses,[92] and Fortna postulates that these are the particular contribution of the author to bring together the disjointed parts of the "signs Gospel," the ministry and the passion narrative, in a way which spoke to the immediate needs of the Johannine community.[93] Onuki, too, stresses that the last discourses are primarily about the Johannine community and its situation.[94]

It is particularly through literary analysis that the creative skill of the evangelist is being given the attention it deserves. Olsson, for instance, has shown through an analysis of the account of the wedding feast at Cana that this is a carefully composed piece of work written in the language of insiders.[95] Similarly Leroy has expounded the author's use of the techniques of misunderstanding and double meaning, their dependence for effect on a common in-group language and their function in reinforcing a sense of community.[96] He also shows how the author applies his technique sometimes in a way that the partners of Jesus are deliberately portrayed in a way that cannot have corresponded to reality.[97] Wead also highlighted the use of mis-

---

91. Onuki, *Gemeinde*, 110–14.
92. Culpepper, *Anatomy*, 36.
93. Fortna, "Christology," 503.
94. Onuki, *Gemeinde*, 165.
95. Olsson, *Structure*, 282.
96. Leroy, *Rätsel*, 46–47, 71–73, 79, 158–60; similarly Culpepper, *Anatomy*, 152–97, esp. 164, 179–80; Duke, *Irony*, 142–47; Richard, "Double Meaning."
97. Leroy, *Rätsel*, 62.

understanding, and emphasised the use of irony and metaphor in the Gospel.[98] Similarly Lindars listed many of the deliberate techniques used by the author.[99] The recognition of literary technique in the Fourth Gospel is not new.[100] But in recent years it has come very strongly to the fore, represented especially through the work of Culpepper, Duke and O'Day, and scholars like de la Potterie.[101] They also emphasise the degree to which the effectiveness of such techniques depends heavily on a knowing community. This is especially so with the author's use of dramatic irony which both assumes a conversant group of hearers and reinforces their identity as community.[102] This Gospel speaks the language of insiders for insiders.[103]

This is not the place to discuss the range of contributions being made in recent studies towards understanding the literary techniques of the Gospel.[104] But for the immediate purpose they offer abundant evidence of conscious literary skill on the part of the author with which he has shaped, composed, and created the material of the Gospel,[105] including creative use of symbolism.[106] Instances of this skill are endless. The following are some examples: the author's use of symbolic allusion, for instance, in the Cana wedding pericope; the use of double meaning in the dialogue with Nicodemus, where ἄνωθεν ("from above" or "again") works only in Greek; the drama of the Samaritan woman's meeting with Jesus, which depends so much for its effectiveness on double meaning and irony; the symbolic use of the feeding of the 5,000; the brilliant multilevel drama of the healing of the blind man, a story of the light of the world and the blindness of those who oppose it; and not least the powerful irony woven into the passion narrative.[107]

From beginning to end the author's hand is to be seen in the reshaping of narrative and discourse. This is not to deny that literary techniques such

98. Wead, *Devices*, 30–70, 71–93.
99. Lindars, "Traditions," 111–12.
100. E.g., Strathmann, *Johannes*, 59.
101. Culpepper, *Anatomy*; Duke, *Irony*; O'Day, *Revelation*; de la Potterie, "Genèse"; de la Potterie, "Prologue."
102. So Culpepper, *Anatomy*, 179–80; Duke, *Irony*, 27; O'Day, *Revelation*, 30.
103. So Meeks, "Man from Heaven," 162; Culpepper, *Anatomy*, 28; Minear, *John*, 19.
104. E.g., Brant, *Dialogue and Drama*, 17; and Zumstein, "Prolog," 63, on the role of the prologue in creating the basis for irony.
105. So also Frey, "Johannes und die Synoptiker," 284.
106. See, for instance, the contributions in Frey, van der Watt, and Zimmermann, eds., *Imagery in the Gospel of John*. See also Zimmermann, *Christologie*; Lee, *Flesh and Glory*.
107. See also Xavier Léon-Dufour, "Towards a Symbolic Reading of the Fourth Gospel," *NTS* 27 (1981): 443–45.

The Fourth Gospel in the Light of Its Christology

as irony may not have been already present in the sources he used, such as, to some degree, surely in the passion narrative, as the Synoptic parallels show, and we must reckon with the possibility that such techniques had become the stock in trade of teachers and preachers of the Johannine community. But, for all of this, there can scarcely be any doubt that the author plays a major part in their being in the Gospel.

6.1.5.3 Implications of Evidence of Creative Literary Techniques for Understanding the Nature of the Gospel and Its Relation to History

The recognition of conscious literary shaping of the kind spoken of above, with its necessary impact on narrative and discourse content, has implications for the questions we face. It means that the author would have been to that degree aware that what he was producing was not primarily a historical report of what Jesus once said and did. At the same time we have to place beside this the author's concern for the Jesus of history. The Gospel's central theme is that the Son of God has come from the Father to bring life. The fact of the historical Jesus, the event of the Son's coming in history, is of fundamental importance. This also means that the author would have believed that this Jesus would have made such claims. He probably saw himself as expanding upon a central christological claim already going back to Jesus himself. But beyond this, he also felt inspired and free to expand upon and elaborate the traditions he had received and saw this as part of the continuing work of the Paraclete. Accordingly it is doubtful that he would have understood the Paraclete promises to relate only to memory of the earthly Jesus.

6.1.5.4 Implications for Understanding the "Unreal" Elements in the Portrait of Jesus' Humanity

The author's use of literary and dramatic technique, such as irony, misunderstanding, and double meaning, also has a profound influence on the portrait of Jesus as a human being, as we have briefly noted in the previous section. On the one hand, much of the superiority, indeed arrogance, seen in Jesus' behaviour in encounter with his contemporaries, is the product of the author's style of presentation. Such passages should not, therefore, be read as literal descriptions of the historical Jesus, nor should they be taken as indicators for the author's view of Jesus' actual humanity. Wead points out that it would be irrelevant to ponder what Nicodemus might have understood, as though ch. 3 were historical dialogue, or what the disciples might have understood of 6:51–58.[108] As Brandt observes:

> The tragic genre from which the Gospel seems to have emerged as a new literary form but to which it still bears affinity exaggerates conflict and demands characterization of some of its citizens as hostile or ignorant, but it should not necessitate the vilification of one side of the context. That step is taken when a reader fails to recognize the dramatic conventions at work.[109]

On the other hand, it is likely that the author develops such scenes in the belief that what they convey has a basis in the historical reality of Jesus as he perceived it. Above all, the author would have believed that the underlying Christology reflected in these scenes was a valid one and truly corresponded to what was claimed by the historical Jesus himself. He was the Son from the Father. At most we may suggest that the manner of word play and other dramatic techniques of presentation, developed in order to assert this basic truth of the earthly historical Jesus, in end-effect creates a story of Jesus in which unwittingly, that is, naively, the author makes it seem that Jesus is far less human than his own Christology presupposes. This means saying that the medium affects the message, which then comes through in a way that the author did not realise.

Alternatively one would have to argue that the medium was christologically consistent with the message and that the author actually believed Jesus would have responded to people in exactly the way he presents. None of the indications of his awareness of the change in development between the time of the earthly Jesus and the post-Easter period need imply otherwise. On such an alternative view, we have before us much more than unwittingly docetic tendencies. On balance, I think the awareness we must presuppose in the author's conscious employment of literary techniques counts against this. The question remains to what extent, then, he would have understood his creations as consistent with the way he would have thought Jesus to have been in reality during his earthly ministry.

---

108. Wead, *Devices*, 8–9.
109. Brant, *Dialogue and Drama*, 187.

The Fourth Gospel in the Light of Its Christology

6.1.6 The Centrality of the Historical Event of the Ministry of Jesus

To return to the issue of the author and the Jesus of history, the chief concern of the author is the one reflected in what we have traced as the central structure of his Christology. It is not only the truth about the post-Easter Christ of faith, nor is it simply that truth projected back into the scenery of the historical Jesus. Otherwise, as Haacker notes, we should expect a Gospel focussing primarily on words to the disciples.[110] It is the story of the coming into the world of the Son of the Father, sent to bear the Father's challenge to the world. The Son's death and return to the Father represents not only the climax of this work, but also underlines its authenticity and significance, a perception given by the Spirit to the post-Easter community.

The author is thus aware of history and of a development in understanding marked by Easter. But the event of fundamental importance is the Son's coming. Therefore the facts of Jesus' coming as the Son of the Father, his ministry in encounter with men and women, especially the Jews, his suffering and death on the cross at the hands of Pilate through the Jews, and his resurrection and return to the Father, these facts and a good many others are important for the author as historical events and necessary to his understanding of the Gospel.

6.1.6.1 A Hierarchy of Significant Historical Data

The fact that Jesus encountered men and women is absolutely essential, though the details of each episode are not. The fact of Jesus' encounter with the Jews, in particular, is important because of its significance for his own community's relation with Judaism, though the details are not. This is why he can handle details of narrative and discourse so freely. Similarly the passion is essential for the author's historical claims; but details often reflect not history, but devotional edification.

There is for the author a complex hierarchy of historical data. He can take the trouble to inform readers of the detail of Jewish customs. He can also freely reconstruct narrative sources so that a bare torso of the original remains. The encounters of the historical Jesus with men and women, with Jews, with the world are central, even if the details are not. The basic fact of the coming of the Son, the sent one, is so much the centre, that the Gospel is an endless variation on this theme, a persistence which already Baur noted,

---

110. Haacker, *Stiftung*, 59–60.

many in his day described as monotonous.[111] Jesus stories, like OT stories, now serve this higher end.

6.1.6.2 Radical Simplification and Centring of the Tradition

However we evaluate it, the effect of the author's undertaking is to simplify. This is true of the constant recurrence of the same pattern, as we noted in Part One. The encounters always centre around Jesus' claim to be the sent one and his call to receive what he offers in relationship with himself. The simplicity is also present in the symbols reflecting central human need like life, light, water, and bread. None of these is without an extensive traditio-historical background. But at the level of the evangelist's composition, they are consistently used to focus the message of the Gospel on the gift of life in the Son.

The simplicity is more than a technique of communication; it reflects a centring or focussing upon what the author holds to be essential in such a way that other elements of the tradition are put in perspective in relation to that centre, even to the extent of being omitted altogether. This represents a theological method which has wide implications, not least for understanding what the Gospel is and is not.

Accordingly the Gospel is a presentation of a simple truth: the coming of the Son and so the coming of life through faith in him. It is interested in history in that it places this event firmly in history in the ministry of Jesus of Nazareth and assumes encounters like those present in the Johannine community. But beyond this, history is not the author's concern and stories and discourses serve not primarily, or even at all, to report what actually happened on this or that occasion, but to convey what happens and happened through the coming of the Son into the world. Each episode portrays the total event or an aspect of it as such.

6.1.6.3 The Gospel as Celebration of Faith

The dramatic irony, the word plays, the misunderstandings, so characteristic of the author's method, demand an audience which both knows the story

---

111. Baur, *Kritische Untersuchungen*, 295; cf. also Wrede, "Charakter," 13; Wrede, *Sohn Gottes*, 135; Strathmann, *Johannes*, 2; W. Sanday, *The Criticism of the Fourth Gospel* (Oxford: Clarendon, 1914), 206; Preiss, *Life in Christ*, 10; Hengel, "Cana," 87.

The Fourth Gospel in the Light of Its Christology

and understands the Johannine language. In the scenes of ch. 4 where Jesus encounters the Samaritan woman, one can almost hear the laughter of the audience as the woman consistently fails to see what they had known all along and had been summarised for them also in the prologue. Many of the Gospel episodes seem to be written like dramas to be acted out before a live audience.[112] Yet the Gospel is not primarily dramatic entertainment. Nor is it primarily evangelistic, for it depends so much for its effects on having readers or hearers who understand. It is primarily the telling of a story to those who already know it. In that sense it does, indeed, resemble the great Greek dramas.[113] But its purpose seems much more to be the vehicle for edification and celebration. Duke speaks of devotional pleasure created through the fellowship of irony, considering as only a secondary possibility the persuasion of crypto-Christians.[114] Culpepper speaks of the readers' enjoyment.[115] O'Day notes that the effect of the author's literary technique is to facilitate vision and emphasises the narrative mode as the vehicle of revelation.[116]

Faith's Icon

The Gospel is thus primarily faith celebrating faith and so making faith stronger. It is like an icon. Its context is the community of faith. It is doing, and doubtless sets out to do, precisely what was promised of the Paraclete: it calls to remembrance, leads into all truth about Christ, and takes what is his and declares it. But like the pattern of the revealer-envoy, the focus is not primarily knowledge or information; it is encounter and relationship. The Gospel is itself a work of Christology, a portrait presented to the believer as a vehicle for evoking deeper faith commitment.

A Mirror of Unfaith

On the negative side it is a mirror of unfaith in which believers can see the conflicts of their own day. This accounts for the negative simplification and stereotyping of unbelievers. Such portrayals are to serve as comfort and encouragement for believers in their conflict with the world. Accordingly the

112. Similarly Nicholson, *Death*, 38.
113. Cf. Strachan, *Fourth Gospel*, 32–34.
114. Duke, *Irony*, 152, 154.
115. Culpepper, *Anatomy*, 175–76.
116. O'Day, *Revelation*, 31.

issue of the Jews in history must be seen in much the same light as the issue of the Jesus of history within the Gospel. The same unhistorical, simplifying elaboration overlays the stories based on actual conflicts, which the author believed Jesus faced during his ministry and in his passion. Here, too, it is the total response of rejection which shapes each episode and in such a generalising way that the hearers can make the connections with their own day. To read these narratives as history would be a gross distortion.

The Last Discourses and the Gospel

The Fourth Gospel is thus a stylised presentation of the central significance of Jesus as the author sees it to have been, both in the earthly ministry and in the author's own day. It is stylised for the celebration and comfort of the faithful. For this reason the last discourses perform a distinctive role within this function. Bornkamm wrote that they help the community come to terms with the distance of history.[117] They also aid reflection on Jesus' ministry in terms of the central structure of the author's Christology, offer comfort and hope, and set the terms of reference for the community of faith as called to be a community of love and commissioned to continue the Son's work in the world in the power of the Spirit. The final two chapters expand particular aspects of these themes, particularly those concerned with mission, order and historical distance.

6.1.7   John and the Synoptics

6.1.7.1 John and the Synoptics—Similarities

The distinctiveness of the Fourth Gospel as a christological statement is evident when we compare it with the first three Gospels. They, too, are written from a post-Easter perspective. They, too, seek to come to terms with the tension between faith's growth in perception before and after Easter, Mark doing so, in particular, through the use of the motif of the messianic secret. Barrett notes therefore a common artificiality.[118] Leroy points to the presence of epiphany and misunderstandings in Mark.[119] Many of the questions we

---

117. Bornkamm, "Interpretation," 112.
118. Barrett, *John*, 32; on the use of the messianic secret motif in John see also Barrett, "Paradox," 108; Schnackenburg, "Menschensohn," 126; Hooker, "Prologue," 46–51; Schillebeeckx, *Christ*, 368; Fortna, "Christology," 503.
119. Leroy, *Rätsel*, 163 n. 14.

The Fourth Gospel in the Light of Its Christology

asked of the Fourth Gospel can be asked equally of the Synoptics. The Synoptic evangelists without doubt believed that when they wrote they included information about what actually happened during the ministry of Jesus. They, too, would have taken some traditions as historically accurate which had already been shaped and substantially modified by processes in the post-Easter period of which they were unaware. They were also aware that after Easter there had been growth in understanding of who Jesus was. They, too, engaged in shaping, reordering, and supplementing the Jesus material that had come to them. And they, too, must have at least accepted the possibility that they were not the first to have done so.[120] This is particularly evident in the way authors created and developed the depiction of Jesus' last words in the testamentary genre, from Mark 13, which echoes in John 14, to Matthew's 24–25, Luke's assembling tradition to create Jesus' parting words (22:21–38), and the apparent sequence of elaborations behind John 13:31–17:26.

6.1.7.2 John and the Synoptics—Differences

What then is the difference between their work and that of the fourth evangelist? Schnackenburg argues that there is no essential difference, except that in John statements are taken to their extreme ("Spitze").[121] Strathmann describes the three evangelists as painters, the fourth, as one who has produced a drawing or sketch.[122] Haacker points to the greater number of confessional statements in John.[123] Käsemann stresses the greater emphasis on divine glory.[124]

We have already noted the distinctive Johannine language. To this may be added major differences in the content and form of the material, in chronology, the absence in John of parables of the usual Synoptic kind, of the kingdom of God as a central theme, and, conversely, in the Synoptics, the absence of the kind of christological statements and symbols typical of John. Some of these differences will be explained by the distinctive history

---

120. On the complex issue of (i) the author's knowledge of the Synoptics or (ii) at least as having once performed Mark or (iii) as independent, see on (i) Van Belle, "Return of John"; similarly Beutler, *Johannesevangelium*, 60–61; on (ii) Ian D. Mackay, *John's Relationship with Mark*, WUNT 2.182 (Tübingen: Mohr Siebeck, 2004); Mark Jennings, "The Fourth Gospel's Reversal of Mark in John 13,31–14,3," *Biblica* 94 (2013): 210–36; on (iii) Anderson, "Interfluential."
121. Schnackenburg, *Johannesevangelium*, 1.14; *John* I, 24; similarly Smalley, *John*, 213.
122. Strathmann, *Johannes*, 4.
123. Haacker, *Stiftung*, 58 n. 258.
124. Käsemann, *Letzter Wille*, 22–23, 28.

of the Johannine tradition and the Johannine community. But some major differences are doubtless attributable to the evangelist. These include the author's method of radically simplifying and centring and the extensiveness and nature of his reshaping of narrative and discourse material to serve as vehicles of a single christological statement. None of the other evangelists do this on anything like the same scale. There is in the Synoptics some use of irony, above all in the passion narratives (e.g., the title, "King of the Jews"), and some use of symbolism (e.g., in the feeding miracles, the stilling of the storm, and healings), but nothing on the scale of the Fourth Gospel. In the others we can identify christological concerns and trace redaction through preferred expressions and particular themes, but compared with John these are mere traces in what is basically a very conservative handling of the tradition.

Different Soteriology and Christology

It accords with these observations that another major distinction lies in the kind of soteriology which becomes central in the Johannine christological programme. While the author knows the wider tradition, his centre is the offer of life in relationship with the Father through the Son. Johannine salvation is thus relationship-centred. Not definitive interpretation of Torah by God's Messiah, nor the promise of God's reign, nor the achievement of atonement, nor the gift of knowledge, nor defeat of the powers stands at the centre, but the coming of a person and the gift in that person to all who believe, of life in relationship. Thus Blank emphasises the resolution of the traditional tensions between the now and not yet through a change of focus from eschatological hope to the person of Jesus.[125] This centrality of the person, in turn, makes central what in the other Gospels is absent, namely the origin of the Son in pre-existent splendour with the Father and his heavenly commissioning.

The Fourth Gospel is unique among the Gospels in its Christology and soteriology. It shares with them the concern to tell the story of Jesus of Nazareth. It is even more explicitly aware of the issues of growth in understanding than they are, through the Paraclete sayings and through frequent references to historical distance throughout the Gospel. It reflects a distinctive methodology, both in its simplification and centring and in its extensive freedom in reshaping traditional material using literary techniques such as irony and

125. Blank, *Krisis*, 165–67; similarly Käsemann, *Letzter Wille*, 42.

The Fourth Gospel in the Light of Its Christology

double meaning, all to state over and over again the central christological statement of the Son's coming with the gift of life. The result is a portrait of Jesus which has the character of an icon, a celebration and focus of faith. There is strong evidence that this is also how the author viewed his work. The Jesus of history remains central, not simply the fact of his coming, but also key encounters in which he engaged. Yet there the concern with history stops and faith's drama begins, in which scene by scene the central issues are rehearsed. This unique Gospel demands to be understood in this light. Whenever people have approached its pages as if it were primarily history or doctrine or have failed to appreciate it as a celebration of faith, it has become a seedbed of controversy and conflict.

6.2 The Gospel, Its Christology and Its Community

The Fourth Gospel belongs to a community of faith. It spoke the language of that community. It encouraged, consolidated and celebrated the faith of the community through its unique portrayal of Jesus. It reinforced the community's identity as in, but not of, the world. It also challenged and confronted faith and understanding. Within all of this its Christology played an important part.

The major part of this book has been considering the broad structure of Johannine Christology and the issues of interpretation which arise within it. In it we have focussed on the text of the Gospel as transmitted, which was once also the text of a community in the late first century. I want in this section to ask about the relationship between the author's Christology and the community to which it once belonged. In doing so, I want also to take into account the important issues of the history of that community, the history of its Christology and the history of the composition of the Gospel itself. One short chapter cannot adequately treat the complex issues of any one of these three aspects. There exist excellent reviews of current research in these areas.[126] Rather it is my intention to begin with the structure of the

---

126. See Kysar, "Fourth Gospel," 2389–480; Becker, "Streit der Methoden." See also Anderson, *Christology*, who argues that the author underwent stages of faith reflected in different christological emphases within the Gospel and that "the author of the Johannine Epistles was the editor of the finalized Gospel (impressive stylistic convergences exist between the material in the Gospel's supplementary material and the style of the Epistles). Then 1, 2 and 3 John were probably written between the gathering of the first edition (ca. 80 CE) and the finalization of the Gospel around 100 CE after the death of the Beloved Disciple" (20). Among significant attempts to posit stages of development in the community after the initial work of Martyn and

author's Christology and note questions and implications which I perceive arising in relationship to it.

The author's Christology represents a synthesis. It combines various streams of thought. Sometimes these are identifiable and we can observe the degree to which they have merged. Occasionally we have detected tensions within the text between different traditions. By identifying these tensions and streams of thought, we can go on to ask how they arose and what they indicate about the development and background of Christology, about the history and issues of the community, and perhaps, also about the history of composition of the Gospel itself. In effect this means beginning with questions which emerge ultimately from the text itself and from the christological structure we have identified within it.

6.2.1 The Revealer-Envoy Model

6.2.1.1 The Dominance of the Revealer-Envoy Model

The most important and outstanding feature of the author's Christology is the dominance of the pattern of the revealer-envoy—the coming and going of the Son from and to the Father—a structure enunciated within the framework of a cosmic dualism of heaven, above, and earth, below. On the basis of this model the author reinterprets eschatology, integrates diverse christological traditions, focusses soteriology, and develops his pneumatology.

Thus eternal life, resurrection, and judgment are now in relationship with the Son. Arguments with Jews about different kinds of messiahship are ultimately irrelevant and serve only to highlight their alleged blindness to the one messiahship, which consists in Jesus' being the Son sent from the Father. Hopes for a prophet cease to be meaningful except in so far as they point to the one sent from above to tell what he has seen and heard. Here

---

Brown are Neyrey, *Ideology*, 122–55; de Boer, *Johannine Perspectives*, 77–90; Painter, "Death of Jesus," 337; Ashton, *John*, who assumes a missionary signs source (11) and affirms Martyn's analysis of John 5 and 9 (93) and suggests that a second edition of the Gospel added the prologue and chapters 6, and 15 –17 (127, 164). See also his critical response to Bauckham's questioning of the validity of speaking of Gospel communities in Bauckham, "For Whom Were the Gospels Written?" 75–83; similarly Bauckham, *Fourth Gospel*, 28–30; and pursuing Bauckham's line: David Lamb, *Text, Context and the Johannine Community: A Sociolinguistic Analysis of the Johannine Writings*, LNTS 477 (London: Bloomsbury, 2014). See also the radical attempts of Urban van Wahlde to identify stages now elaborated in von Wahlde, *Gospel and Letters*.

is much more than a Mosaic prophet teacher. Similarly the descent of the Spirit at Jesus' baptism is now only a sign of what is already his and a means of identification for the Baptist.

The distinctive imagery of Wisdom and Logos in the prologue also serves now to portray him from the beginning as the one who came to make God known. The traditions of family intimacy of the *monogenēs* Son of God and his sending serve the same end. Imagery of the Torah as water, bread, light, and life, with which Jesus presents himself, now serves to express the gift of salvation which is relationship with the person of the Son. He is ("I am") the one who comes thus. Even the passion narrative with its strongly messianic colouring has been overlaid with the simplicity of the claim of the Son sent from the Father to bear witness to the truth. Likewise the miracles in their splendour manifest his glory and in their symbolism illustrate the life he brings.

Similarly he uses its pattern of sending also to describe the sending of the Spirit and the disciples. The Spirit Paraclete will be sent to make known what is the Son's word, to bring all that he has said to their memory and to lead the disciples into all truth. The disciples have been sent, as the Son was sent. They are to bear faithful witness with the aid of the Spirit of truth. The Spirit is not a second revealer; even less so are the disciples. The Paraclete and the disciples are witnesses to the one original and one only Son who has come as revealer-envoy and returned. The Gospel itself is the product of the Paraclete and the disciple fulfilling this work. Thus the pattern of the revealer-envoy pattern lends itself, in part, to the description of their sending, but retains its own absolute priority and dominance.

By using this model the author has radically simplified and centralised eschatology, Christology, and pneumatology. The dominance of the model calls for an explanation. In seeking that explanation we should note also its role in simplifying and centralising soteriology.

6.2.1.2 The Modified Revealer-Envoy Model

In appropriating the model of the revealer-envoy, the evangelist (or maybe already the tradition before him) has modified it in a significant way. The model logically demands the language of communication and revelation; the revealer reveals; the envoy tells what he has seen and heard. Whereas the author consistently employs the model using such language, he uses it now not primarily about revelation as information giving but as a means of portraying epiphany and encounter. What the Son comes to offer is primarily the gift of life in relationship with himself and with the Father. Only occasionally does he break from his dominant model, such as when he uses the apprenticeship pattern of the Father and Son in 5:19-20. When he does, it is possible because of the distinctive modification of the model's basic statement. The primary focus in the modified revealer-envoy model is life-giving encounter. The coming and going remains intact, as does the cosmic dualism;[127] but the salvific event is not information-giving; it is the offer of a life-giving faith relationship.

This modification also brings with it, therefore, a modification of soteriology. The author's soteriology still includes the promise of following on the path that the redeemer has gone. In other words, going on after death to where he is and to belong to him is not to belong to this world; it is to be born from above. Yet, the primary focus in the soteriology is not belonging to, and finally going to, the heavenly world, but life now in relationship with the Son and through the Son with the Father. The centre of focus moves from ascent to the heavenly world, transmortal salvation that one might expect to be the focus of the message of a heavenly revealer-envoy, to relationship with the person of the Son through faith. This relativises the significance of the cosmic dualism.

There is a strangeness here. Why is it that the pattern of the revealer-envoy is both dominant and yet also appears as something which has had to be especially adapted? What has happened or what is the background for this? The question becomes more acute and more complex when we consider the understanding of the death of Jesus in relationship to the author's modified revealer-envoy Christology.

6.2.1.3 The Modified Revealer-Envoy Model and the Death of Jesus

The revealer-envoy model, both when it is taken literally as a communication revelation model and when it is understood in a modified way as in the Gospel, assumes by its structure that coming and going correspond and reflect little more than change of place, entry to and exit from earthly life. Our analysis has shown that the language of coming and going is frequently used throughout the Gospel of the Son and his mission from the Father. Only exceptionally does the author go beyond the language of departure or going away when speaking of the end of the mission of Jesus as the Son.

---

127. On cosmic dualism and Johannine Christology see Becker, "Dualismus"; Becker, *Johannes*, 147-51; Becker, "Auferstehung," 142-43; Becker, "Streit der Methoden," 46-47.

We might think of the use of language of glorification in relation to Jesus as the Son in 11:4 and, by implication, in 17:1, 5; but this kind of language to describe the end of Jesus' earthly life belongs within a distinctive cluster of terms associated with the title Son of Man. To these we shall return below. However, the fact remains that the model of the revealer-envoy—which the author uses primarily in association with the language of Son and Father and which speaks of the Son's coming from and returning to the Father—has by its very structure little to say about Jesus' death and return to the Father beyond that it represents this return. It has little place for a soteriological significance to be attributed to Jesus' death. Structurally, persistence through suffering, even to death, need mean no more than faithful fulfilment of the revelatory task, without reneging under pressure. At most, the cross might reveal the extent to which the Son was willing to go and so might function symbolically as representative of the whole ministry. Structurally, it need mean no more than this.

Even with the author's own adaptation of the pattern, so that it represents the Son in encounter offering life in relationship to himself and not primarily information, this remains the case. For if the gift is already given by his presence, what more can his death and return add, especially when his presence is replaced or re-presented by the Spirit? In itself, the envoy Christology presents the Son as the all-sufficient life and nourishment and nothing more is to be done, except to ensure continuity and greater accessibility of the offer.

6.2.1.4 The Modified Revealer-Envoy Model and Vicarious Atonement

Yet there are other statements in the Gospel which attribute a more significant role to Jesus' death than this assumes. These stand in a certain tension with the model of the revealer-envoy, even in its modified form. For instance, the model of the revealer-envoy has no need, structurally, of vicarious atonement through an act of sacrifice or representative self-giving on the part of the Son. For life is in the person of the Son and in relationship with him; the Logos is received or not received. Accordingly, we might expect that when they are used, they are largely incidental to the argument and this we found to be so. Then why are they even present? As we have argued above, they are part of what the author would have affirmed as one way of expressing how sin has been dealt with, an aspect but not the whole of his concerns which are focused on the offer of life in relationship, offered in the person of Christ. The author could embrace this tradition without making it central.

6.2.1.5 The Modified Revealer-Envoy Model and the Casting Out of the World's Ruler

Another tradition in the Gospel which interprets the climax of Jesus' earthly life sees his death as the casting out of the ruler of the world. It is located more centrally than the vicarious atonement traditions, since it is one of a number of statements which stand at the climax of a series of predictions about the "hour" or "time" to come and are introduced by the words, "The hour has come" or "Now is." It appears in one of these, 12:31; it reappears in the summary of the Paraclete's proclamation to the world (16:11) and apart from that it is hinted at in 14:31 and, anachronistically, in 16:32.

But why is this tradition there at all? Does the author indicate by it a particular achievement which actually changed cosmic power structures?[128] Is it such that, without it, the earthly gift of the Son could not have benefitted the recipients? Does it represent in some way the overcoming of the barrier between earth and heaven, for instance, the disempowerment of the one who bars the way, and thus the breaking open of the way? This would, indeed, fit the basic model of the revealer-envoy in its unmodified form, whose focus is access to the heavenly and transmortal salvation. Such a soteriology might well entail the necessity that revelation of the heavenly home be supplemented by an act which pioneered its access.[129] But, were we to posit it as significant for the evangelist's soteriology, it would be extraordinary that an event of such crucial salvific significance is thematised only here in the Gospel. It is much more likely, as we have argued above, that the author has now fully appropriated it to his modified model of the revealer-envoy in a way that understands the disempowerment as exposure of the evil power in the event of Jesus' death for the evil that it is, as 16:8–11 suggests. With regard to the path to the Father, in John it is Jesus himself who is the way in his person, as he is also the door, the truth, and the life.

Nevertheless the tradition of 12:31 still sits unevenly in its wider context and alerts us to its different character and origin. If traditions of atonement and of casting out the world's ruler are very much subordinated to the dominant model of the revealer-envoy, this cannot be said in the same way of the cluster of ideas around the Son of Man.

---

128. So Forestell, *Word*, 165 and see the discussion in 4.2 above.
129. E.g., Theobald, *Johannes*, 1.64, 814.

6.2.2 The Modified Revealer-Envoy Model and "the Son of Man Cluster"

We noted in ch. 3 and 4.3 the concentration of Son of Man sayings and associated motifs on and around the climax of Jesus' ministry, his death and return, in what I have described earlier as "the Son of Man cluster."[130] Included in this cluster are the title "Son of Man," itself; lifting up/exaltation (ὑψόω), glorification, ascending and descending (ἀναβαίνω/καταβαίνω) as distinctive vocabulary (whereas Son/Father sayings use other verbs); the judgment motif; the "hour" (sometimes "the time" or "now"); and the promise of "greater things." These motifs occur often in association with "Son of Man," individually, and sometimes in combination. Already this raises the questions: why this particular association of ideas? Where does it come from? Why concentrate on Jesus' "hour"?

6.2.2.1 Different Foci

It is more than the presence of such a cluster of ideas and their concentration on the climax of Jesus' ministry which are noteworthy here. These also reflect a different focus in the application of key salvific motifs. On the one hand, the envoy model points to the saving presence of Jesus in his ministry, proclaims the glory of the Son manifest on earth, announces the offer of life as present in his person, and declares judgment to have come at the point of response to the encounter he brings. On the other hand, the language of the Son of Man cluster points forward to the "hour" to come, looks upward to the glory of heaven with which the Son of Man will be glorified, promises the gift of life as something the Son of Man will give after his exaltation through his flesh and blood, and declares judgment to have taken place at the climax of Jesus' ministry.

6.2.2.2 Merging Traditions

I analysed in 4.3.1 the way in which the author integrates, for instance, the two notions of glory, and in 4.3.3 have shown how the "greater" component of the "hour" is set forth by the author largely in terms of the greater

---

130. William Loader, "The Central Structure of Johannine Christology," NTS 30 (1984): 196-99.

understanding brought by the Spirit and the mission this makes possible. Nevertheless there is evidence here of the envoy model and the cluster around the Son of Man being two different associations of ideas, represented by distinct language. In the Gospel we see the two streams coming together. Why is this so and what does it mean? How does the model of the revealer-envoy, which assumes such a dominant role in the author's Christology, relate to the Son of Man cluster of ideas? The closest the two sets of ideas come to merging is in John 17 where cluster terminology (e.g., glorification) and Father-Son terminology are no longer distinguishable (as it still is, for instance, earlier in the last discourse material in 13:31–14:31). We must also ask why this is so at this point in the Gospel. But we return first to the relation between the revealer-envoy model and the cluster in the Gospel as a whole.

6.2.2.3 Not Merely Vestiges of Tradition

The Son of Man cluster is particularly interesting because its language is present in clearly identifiable authorial footnotes, such as 7:39 and 12:16, referring to the coming of the Spirit who would mediate life and bring understanding. It cannot therefore be dismissed as a mere vestige of tradition and it is too well integrated to be seen as secondary redaction, especially when we see both envoy and Son of Man cluster merged in John 17. What is its present relationship to the model of the revealer-envoy which the author adapts?

While I detect tension between these models, I do not find evidence of the author using one against the other. I see no evidence that he is using the title "Son of Man" to highlight the humanity of Jesus, perhaps even correctively over against the envoy model.[131] This ignores that we are dealing with a cluster of ideas, not a title alone, and these do not point in such a direction; nor has the title this connotation in the Gospel. It suggests the opposite. The evidence would be consistent, rather, with his approaching an already established revealer-envoy model for portraying Jesus' ministry and supplementing it with the Son of Man material. Why has he done so? What did this cluster of ideas offer? Why was there need to offer any more than the revealer-envoy Christology anyway, given its presentation of an all-sufficient salvation in the person of Jesus himself?

---

131. Cf. Moloney, *Son of Man*, 247–56.

6.2.2.4 Meeting Points

We come a step further when we look at passages where revealer-envoy Christology and Son of Man Christology stand side by side. There is something slightly odd where this happens, as can be seen, for instance, in the contrasts between 1:49 and 1:50–51; 3:1–11 and 3:12; 6:60–61 and 6:62; 7:37 and 7:38–39. The relationship is not polemical, nor corrective. But is the author really interested only in informing the reader of the historical differentiation between what the disciples understood before and after Easter? Or does the author point the reader to an even deeper understanding than that represented by Nathanael's traditional confession, Jesus' offer of new birth, and his gift of the bread and the water of life? What is the "greater" represented by the vision of the Son of Man in heaven (1:51), the "heavenly things" (which must include the Son of Man's ascension and exaltation of 3:13–15), the ascent of the Son of Man to where he was before (6:62), or the giving of the Spirit (7:38–39)?

As we saw in 4.3.3, the author expounds the promise of the "greater" event primarily in terms of what the Spirit makes possible and brings to the community of faith. The greater event of the Son of Man's heavenly exaltation, glorification, and ascent will result in the drawing of everything to himself as well as the possibility of a deeper understanding of himself—his coming and return, the events of his ministry, and of Scripture's witness to him. It will do so above all through making possible the Spirit. This is what Jesus means by his promise that the disciples will do "greater" works than he (14:12). What then is the author doing, when he juxtaposes the model of the revealer-envoy and the cluster around the Son of Man in such a way that the former is central and foundational and the latter is somehow "greater"?

6.2.2.5 The Gift Then and Its Promised Availability and Abundance in the Community of Faith

The most probable explanation is that the author wants to stress the importance of the presence of the gift of life now being available and abundant in the post-Easter community. He is not setting the event which the Son of Man cluster describes over against the earthly Jesus, but, on the contrary, using it as the means whereby to underline that what the Son brought then is now accessible for all in the community of faith. Occasionally this post-Easter availability is mentioned directly such as in the promise in ch. 6 that the Son of Man will give life in his eucharistic flesh and blood (6:53; cf. 6:27; 3:14–15);

mostly it is simply presupposed. The gift of life then is the gift of life now. The Paraclete will mediate the gift of the presence of Christ, himself the gift, to the disciples and bring them deeper understanding (14:16–17). Nowhere does the author suggest that the salvation set forth in the christological model of the revealer-envoy is inadequate or inferior. Confessing Jesus as the king of Israel and Son of God (1:49), being born from above (3:1–11), and receiving the bread and the water of life (6:50–51; 7:37) are not now supplanted. But they now abound to all and they abound in and through the community of faith. And they are only possible now through the work of the Paraclete in this community. Or to use language which the author uses to link both together, the glorification of the Son of Man will make possible God's glorification in and through the disciples in mission, even as Jesus glorified God by his faithful fulfilment of his mission.

The author would, then, on my understanding, have employed the Son of Man cluster of ideas to point readers to the appropriation of all that Jesus already was in his earthly ministry now through the Spirit in the Church's mission and in its community. He sees the community of faith as the present place of the life and light Christ brought and therefore highlights this as the focus of the "greater works," the fruit of "the greater event" to which the Son himself looked forward and which he promised. The concern was not primarily with a competing view or a competing Christology. Rather, it was with the life and light which the Son brought by his incarnation and through the greater event has enabled to be present and available in the faith community.

6.2.2.6 The Ecclesial Dimension of Johannine Christology

This coheres well with the ecclesiological implications of the author's Christology as a whole. For where the author employs the modle of the revealer-envoy, adapting it to focus primarily on relationship, this focus on relationship necessarily brings with it an increased focus on relationship, and thus on community as the vehicle of mission and the place of the life and presence of Christ. Meeks has shown also how the pattern of the descending–ascending revealer might also reinforce community among those who, facing adversity and rejection of their mission, also identified themselves as strangers in the world.[132] The role of the Son of Man cluster would partly confirm this and

---

132. Meeks, "Man from Heaven," 163; similar Neyrey, *Ideology*, 115–16; de Boer, *Johannine Perspectives*, 39.

speak to the community's vulnerability, but we should also note mission and fruit-bearing as an important component in the Son of Man cluster or association of ideas (e.g., 12:23-24, 32). This points to an understanding of the community of faith as being much more actively the bearer of light and life to the world than Meeks's hypothesis of a withdrawn sectarian community envisages.[133]

This emphasis on the post-Easter community's mission is also found above all in the first of the final discourses, where Jesus promises "greater works" and speaks of the Spirit (14:12-17). In the remaining final discourse material in chs. 15-17 it continues, though with a much stronger emphasis on the maintenance of the community itself. The Gospel is surprisingly ecclesiological in both the final discourses and in the final two chapters. This emphasis is also reflected in the author's concern to validate the community's integrity and witness through the Paraclete, the beloved disciple, the "treasured legacy" of the mother of Jesus, the dependence on eyewitnesses and the reliability and adequacy of resourcing of the Gospel itself.

6.2.2.7 The Son of Man Cluster—Its Background

If this adequately accounts for the author's juxtaposition of the revealer-envoy model and the Son of Man cluster, it raises at the same time important historical questions about the nature of these traditions. The relatively distinct association of motifs clustered around the Son of Man title indicates in all probability a pre-existing tradition. There is a strong concentration of exaltation Christology within it and such Christology elsewhere uses ὑψόω and glorification terminology, usually however in association with a form of messianic Christology (Acts 2:33; 5:31; Heb 5:5; Phil 2:11). There appears here to have been an association rather with Son of Man, perhaps also because of authorisation motifs (e.g., 3:35) which originally belonged to an understanding of Jesus' exaltation[134] and are reflected in Matt 28:18 (cf. Dan 7:13-14; perhaps originally the sense also of Matt 11:27a; Luke 10:22a). Traditional forensic associations of Son of Man are also evident in the Gospel (5:27; 9:35, 39) and perhaps the parousia associations of the term have bequeathed the motifs of angelic service and heavenly glory (cf. 1:51; Mark 8:38; 13:26; 14:62). Beside this, there is the major expansion of Son of Man Christology into pre-existence, evident in 3:13 and 6:62, which in the light of its distinctive

---

133. So de Jonge, *Stranger*, 99-100; see also Onuki, *Gemeinde*, 110-14.
134. So Becker, *Johannes*, 158.

vocabulary (present also in the manna discourse), must have already been established in the author's tradition. This expansion also results in some overlap with the revealer-envoy model inasmuch as the "descent" of the Son of Man is also related to revelation and the offer of life in both 3:13 and ch. 6. The Johannine Son of Man tradition demands closer research along these lines than space here permits.

The author has, therefore, employed the Son of Man cluster of ideas in order to point readers to the reality that the life then is even more fully present now in the post-Easter mission and community of faith which lives from the benefits which flow from the Son's return to the Father, as the exalted, glorified, ascended Son of Man.

6.2.3 The Modified Revealer-Envoy Model, the Spirit and the Miracles

We have noted above how the revealer-envoy model integrates both the miracle tradition and the tradition of the giving of the Spirit. The miracles reveal the glory of the Son and symbolise who he is; the Spirit Paraclete bears witness to him. But in the process of integration, the understanding of Spirit and miracle tradition is seriously modified in a way which raises important questions about the nature of the Johannine Christology and its community. It is striking that the work of the Spirit in John remains almost entirely at the level of information giving, acquaintance and confrontation with the truth, and mediation of presence in a personal way.[135] Where are the signs and wonders? Where are the charismatic gifts? There seems to be a concentration on teaching. Where are the public charismatic manifestations, traditionally the markers for mission?

This is all the more striking because, by contrast, the Gospel tells us that Jesus' ministry was one of signs enough to fill a universe of books, and the selection we have contains the most massively miraculous of all the canonical Gospels. What has happened? Does this way of understanding the Spirit imply a similar balance should apply to our understanding the christological material, the miracles of the Gospel? What does this tell us, in turn, about the Johannine community? What has happened, that the community with the "best" miracles of Jesus least sees the Spirit, and we may assume its community in the Spirit, in charismatic miraculous terms? Why have they lost their relevance?

---

135. See also Dietzfelbinger, "Paraklet," 402.

The Fourth Gospel in the Light of Its Christology

6.2.3.1 Miracles and the "Agenda" of Salvation

The question of miracles includes more than the contrast between pneumatology and the account of Jesus' ministry in the body of the Gospel. For the presentation of Jesus at many points exhibits a tension between what is happening in the miracles and what the revealer-envoy model understands to be the mission of Jesus. Some of the miracles alleviate human sickness; one brings resuscitation of a dead person; others make provision for human need by way of food and drink; some more directly relate to Jesus' actions in regard to himself. At no point is there a suggestion that they should be doubted. On the contrary, they must be believed. Yet, aside from the miracles, there is nothing which indicates that the kind of agenda Jesus announces in the Lukan story to his home synagogue (Luke 4:16-20) and which is consistent with the portrait of Jesus in the other two Synoptic Gospels, is an agenda here in John. The miracles, as signs or works, manifest the Son's power and symbolise who and what he is, but, beyond that, they have ceased to be of paradigmatic value for the disciples, either in relation to a mission of healing and liberation or in relation to the manner in which such a mission should be exercised. The "greater works" promised in 14:12 seem to bear no relation to signs and wonders of the apostolic church of Paul or of Luke;[136] they indicate rather the fullness of life available through the Paraclete in the church and its fruit-bearing mission.

6.2.3.2 The Place of the Miracles in Johannine Christology and Community

The miracles are not out of place in John, but they take their place in a manner which calls into question both their caritative role and their apologetic significance. The latter is present, but amid controversy, and frequently the wrong christological conclusions are drawn. The author implies that people should have read the miracles as proving that Jesus is what he claimed to be, as set out in the sayings material. Anything less than that is inadequate (2:23-3:3; 4:48; 6:14-15).[137] But, beyond that, he overlays them or through sayings material supplements them with symbolic interpretation, bringing them into line with, and making them serve, the central christological claim,

---

136. Cf. Keener, *John*, 947.
137. Michael Theobald, "Das Johannesevangelium—Zeugnis eines synagogalen 'Judenchristentums'?" in *Paulus und Johannes. Exegetische Studien zur paulinischen und johanneischen Theologie und Literatur*, ed. D. Sänger and U. Mell, WUNT 198 (Tübingen: Mohr Siebeck, 2006), 109-18.

that Jesus is the Son sent from the Father, even to the extent that the original story is left behind in the process (e.g., 11:27). What lies behind this? Is this more than the will to integrate such stories within the dominant christological pattern? Does it reflect community conflict? How does the Johannine community relate to the kind of Christianity, so much evident elsewhere in the NT writings and their situations, for which signs and wonders and works of healing are manifestations of the Spirit and of the work of the apostles and have their natural precedent in the story of Jesus?

6.2.4 The Modified Revealer-Envoy Model and Other Traditions

One of the remarkable features of Johannine Christology is the dominance of the modified revealer model, on the one hand, as the centrepiece of its salvific message, and the presence, on the other hand, of traditions which might easily have been deemed on the basis of it to be superfluous. We have noted this already in relation to traditions about Jesus' death as vicarious or victorious and in relation to Spirit and miracle tradition. It is also the case in relation to other traditions. Probably some, at least, of the references to traditionally future eschatology belong here.[138] They are now almost superfluous; for, since soteriology and eschatology necessarily follow Christology, future hope for believers will be fulfilled when they join their Lord where he is (17:24); yet traditional motifs of eschatology persist.

6.2.4.1 The Persistence of the Tradition of Jesus as a Real Human Being

More importantly, the revealer-envoy model does not require more than an appearance of the envoy among people in a form which makes communication or encounter possible. There is strictly no need for a fully human Jesus. Yet the Gospel holds to both. The author adapts this model into the Jesus tradition which speaks of a real human being. The "play" of the Son with his contemporaries always threatens to evaporate the humanity, and the concentration of the full meaning of his coming into each single encounter makes human characterisation of Jesus almost impossible. But the author seems in no doubt that the full meaning of the incarnation includes the real human being, Jesus of Nazareth.

---

138. Schnackenburg, *Johannesevangelium*, 4.94, sees some future eschatology statements as redactional.

6.2.4.2 The Persistence of the Tradition of Passion, Resurrection and Bestowal of the Spirit by the Risen One

Similarly, the conclusion of the mission of the envoy need be no more than an exit, but the author tells of suffering and real death. The model also had no particular need for a human birth, nor for a descent of the Spirit. Yet these are present, the latter sitting now somewhat awkwardly in the author's scheme. It is no surprise that one solution of this tension, which the author does not adopt, was to see this as the moment of the descent of the revealer-envoy, leaving open the possibility that ascent also occurred before the crucifixion. Such positions were consistent (though not necessary) extrapolations of the revealer-envoy model. This model would most naturally see death as the point of return to the Father and find no place for a passion narrative nor for an account of resurrection on the third day. It would be consistent with the tradition of appearances of Jesus from heaven to his disciples, but would need no separate act of bestowing the Spirit on earth by breath. Yet the author persists in reaffirming these traditions, even though the "rough edges" of merged traditions sometimes show, as in the account of Jesus' words to Mary Magdalene in 20:17. The model might also leave room for subsequent revealers, but the second Paraclete never becomes this in John. It has no need for salvation-historical perspectives,[139] nor for a doctrine of creation, but these, too, seem, nevertheless, part of the author's theology.[140]

6.2.4.3 Conclusion

Our discussion in the larger part of this book has explored the way the author combines these traditions or streams of thought. Occasionally we have seen how the perception of what the revealer-envoy model requires has determined what scholars have argued must be so in John. I have sought to weigh the significance of the diverse ideas within John's Christology and examine the degree of integration. At the same time this has exposed tensions. The author holds together diverse traditions. He makes central the revealer-envoy model in a modified form, but uses it within a distinctively

---

139. As the Johannine position: Becker, *Johannes*, 58; Walter Schmithals, "Der Prolog des Johannesevangeliums," *ZNW* 70 (1979): 39–40; Haenchen, *Johannes*, 35; Schnelle, *Christologie*, 43.

140. Cf. Becker, *Johannes*, 148, who cautions against interpreting Johannine dualism on the basis of creation statements of the prologue.

Christian setting. This surely explains the persistence of elements like the real humanity, suffering and death of Jesus, his baptism and the descent of the Spirit, his resurrection on the third day and his breathing of the Spirit, and the presence, incidentally, of traditions like that of vicarious atonement. These stand together with the basic Christology: the revealer-envoy model which proclaims the salvation event and the Son of Man cluster which secures and assures its ongoing availability and abundance in the community of faith. The "rough edges" are apparent from time to time in the text and the integration is incomplete. The Christology of the Gospel is Christology in development. The potential for greater dominance of the revealer-envoy model at the expense of other traditions is already apparent and will be realised in Gnosticism. The existence of this state of affairs calls for reflection on the story of this complex Christology and its community.

6.2.5 Johannine Christology and the Johannine Community

The Christology of the Fourth Gospel has developed in a community of faith and reflects its story. In it there are traces of early conflicts with the synagogue over the claims for Jesus' messiahship and this has doubtless left its mark on the retelling of stories from the Jesus tradition.

6.2.5.1 Jesus as Messiah

While the author has integrated the motif of messiahship within the broader central structure of his Christology,[141] the motif remains of significance and will have played a significant role both in past conflicts within the synagogue community and in continuing conflicts outside it, and also in the task of reinforcing the identity of the community of believers of whom many will

---

141. Bultmann, *Theologie*, 389; Dahl, "Church," 127–28; de Jonge, *Stranger*, 52, 57–60, 63–66, 84–85, 96–97; Appold, *Oneness*, 68–69; Schnackenburg, *John*, 1.155; Brown, *Beloved Disciple*, 29; Painter, "Christology and the Farewell Discourses," 45; Painter, "John 9," 37; Dunn, "John," 321, 328–29; Schnelle, *Christologie*, 117, 123; Mlakyzhyil, *Structure*, 256–58; Van Belle, "Signs of the Messiah," 165, 169–70, 174; similarly Van Belle, "Death of Jesus," 36; de Boer, *Johannine Perspectives*, 114; Bauckham, "Jewish Messianism," 238; Johannes Beutler, *Neue Studien zu den johanneischen Schriften / New Studies on the Johannine Writings*, BBB 167 (Göttingen: Vandenhoeck und Ruprecht, 2012), 135. Ashton, *John*, 138, writes: "The concept of Jesus' messiahship was not one that fully engaged the evangelist's own interests"; similarly Bauckham, *Fourth Gospel*, 148.

have strong Jewish roots.¹⁴² It is therefore not by chance that in the first chapter the issue arises¹⁴³ and that it comes to expression in the climax¹⁴⁴ where the author declares:

ταῦτα δὲ γέγραπται ἵνα πιστεύ[σ]ητε
ὅτι Ἰησοῦς ἐστιν ὁ χριστὸς ὁ υἱὸς τοῦ θεοῦ,
καὶ ἵνα πιστεύοντες ζωὴν ἔχητε ἐν τῷ ὀνόματι αὐτοῦ.
These things are written so that you may believe
that Jesus is the Christ the Son of God
and that believing you may life in his name. (20:31)

One can still see in John the traditional association of messiahship with notions of the messiah as king and as adopted Son of God.¹⁴⁵ Within the framework of his Christology the author's use of "Son of God" means so much more and, as both 10:30, 36 and the link between Thomas' affirmation (20:28) and 20:31 show, the author can treat θεός and "Son of God" as equivalent.¹⁴⁶ The author is also sensitive to the political dimensions of Jewish messiahship, as is evident in 6:14-15 and in the passion narrative, where bearers of the tradition¹⁴⁷ of the passion narrative had to continue to differentiate Jesus as messiah, Son of God, and King of the Jews from the likely understanding which had him crucified in the first place. John stands in the succession

---

142. Ashton, *Fourth Gospel*, 150-54.

143. So Ashton, *John*, 11; Van Belle, "Signs of the Messiah," 165.

144. McGrath, *Christology*, 145, writes: "We have found no reason to deny or qualify the Evangelist's statement of his purpose in 20.31."

145. Hahn, *Theologie*, 1.624-28; Ashton, *Fourth Gospel*, 166, 220; Hurtado, *Lord Jesus Christ*, 359, who writes of Lamb of God and Son of God: "These latter two designations are to be taken as complementary ways of referring to Jesus as Messiah." See also the review of royal messianism in Leung, *Kingship-Cross*, 22-44; Ahn, *Christological Witness*, 22-33 and his discussion of the thesis of Margaret Daly-Denton, *David in the Fourth Gospel: The Johannine Reception of the Psalms* (Leiden: Brill, 2000), who points to alleged Davidic allusions in Jesus' crossing the Kidron (2 Sam 15:23); in the Greeks' coming (12:20-26), echoing Ittai the Gittite's pledge to follow David (2 Sam 15:19-22); in Caiaphas' proposal that Jesus die for the people echoing Ahithophel's advice to Absalom (2 Sam 17:3), and in John the Baptist's not knowing the Messiah, echoing Samuel's not knowing whom to anoint (1 Sam 16:1-13). Ahn concludes: "As convincing as the suggested analogies might sound, however, these allusions still appear to be too subtle, so that it is altogether questionable whether the originally intended audience would have immediately detected those connections without difficulty" (143).

146. On 20:31 Van Belle, "Christology and Soteriology," 457, argues that it gives expression to what he agrees is the central structure of the author's Christology as outlined above; similarly Beutler, *Neue Studien*, 135.

147. See Collins, "Epilogue," 301, on 1:51; Ahn, *Christological Witness*, 155.

of tradition-bearers who continue to exploit its irony, extrapolating upon the tradition to have Jesus declare that his kingdom comes from elsewhere and that his claims to messiahship have to do with his having come to bear witness to the truth. The author incorporates verbal conflicts about Jesus' messiahship into the frame of reference of the central structure of Christology, so that in essence to acclaim him as Messiah is to acknowledge that he is the one sent from the Father to make him known.[148]

When, therefore, in 20:31 the author declares the Gospel's purpose, this broader understanding of his Christology is assumed.[149] Claims that Jesus was the Messiah would not have been sufficient ground to explain the split from the synagogue.[150] Claims that he was the Son of God in the broader sense, the Son of the Father, even θεός, however understood and misunderstood, would have been; and we see this reflected in the conflicts especially in ch. 5 and 10. As Ashton notes, "The uncompromising opposition to traditional Judaism expressed in the Prologue would have been inconceivable before the separation of the two parties in the synagogue, and consequently the Prologue must have been composed quite late in the long history of their many disagreements."[151] The charges brought against Jesus in the Synoptic trial tradition and in John throughout Jesus' ministry[152] are more reflective of the charges laid against believers in latter decades of the first century,[153]

---

148. Schnackenburg, *Johannesevangelium*, 2.152; Scroggs, *Christology*, 68. Ulrich Busse, "Metaphorik und Rhetorik im Johannesevangelium: Das Bildfeld vom König," in *Imagery in the Gospel of John: Terms, Forms, Themes, and Theology of Johannine Figurative Language*, ed. J. Frey, J. G. van der Watt, and R. Zimmermann, WUNT 200 (Tübingen: Mohr Siebeck, 2006), 317, argues that hellenistic models of kingship have also contributed to the Johannine notion of kingship. See also Joachim Kügler, *Der andere König. Religionsgeschichtliche Perspektiven auf die Christologie des Johannesevangeliums*, SBS 178 (Stuttgart: KBW, 1999), on kingship motifs in relation to Johannine motifs of logos, bread, and shepherd.

149. Van Belle, "Death of Jesus," writes that it entails: "the Messiah or the Christ, the true king and true prophet, but also as the Son of God and the Son of Man" (35), which, he argues, are ultimately interchangeable (36). Cf. Adelbert Denaux, "The Twofold Purpose of the Fourth Gospel: A Reading of the Conclusion to John's Gospel (20,30-31)," in *Studies in the Gospel of John and Its Christology: Festschrift Gilbert Van Belle*, ed. J. Verheyden, G. van Oyen, M. Labahn, and R. Bieringer, BETL 265 (Leuven: Peeters, 2014), 534, who argues that the author chose the two titles to express the horizontal and vertical.

150. So Painter, "Point of John's Christology," 233; Adele Reinhartz, "Judaism in the Gospel of John," *Interp* 63 (2009): 389; Theobald, "Johannesevangelium," 152-53; Theobald, *Johannes*, 61; cf. de Boer, *Johannine Perspectives*, 77, 137.

151. So Ashton, *John*, 167; similarly Neyrey, *Ideology*, xi, 35; Frey, "Juden," 374-75; McGrath, *Christology*, 50-53; Söding, "Ich und der Vater," 183; Kriener, *Glauben an Jesus*, 151-52.

152. Lincoln, *Truth on Trial*, 23; Söding "Ich und der Vater," 181.

153. Lincoln, *Truth on Trial*, 302.

than any laid against Jesus himself. These claims, enunciated in the prologue and assumed throughout, rest heavily on christological developments informed by the Sophia myth, much more than those associated with belief in Jesus as Son of Man.[154]

6.2.5.2 Jesus as Son of Man

Son of Man does not occur directly in the context of conflict and appears to have more to do with the community developing its own faith and identity, perhaps also to avoid the political associations of messiahship.[155] Nothing suggests an attempt to counter alternative understandings of the Son of Man idea,[156] even though that figure is heavenly and is set in contrast in 3:13 to claims of mystical ascent by Moses and others.[157] Association of Son of Man and royal messianic images in the latter decades of the first century[158] will have helped inform its usage in John, but the figure itself is limited primarily in relation to Jesus' heavenly origin,[159] his role as judge, and the meaning of the sequence of events surrounding his death,[160] and is therefore hardly to

---

154. McGrath, *Christology*, 220, notes the association of wisdom and Son of Man in 1 En. 49:3. See also Theobald, *Herrenworte*, 589; Harris, *Prologue*, 127, 129.

155. As Painter, "Death of Jesus," 338, suggests, does Mark; similarly Carson, *John*, 164; Collins, "Epilogue," 301.

156. McGrath, *Christology*, 193, comments: "We have not seen any firm evidence that John's legitimation Christology against charges of 'blasphemy' is presupposed in his legitimation of his Christology in relation to the Moses issue, nor any real indication that the reverse is true." This is so in relation to the Son of Man, but surely not in relation to the prologue's Christology which informs the high claims which evoke charges of blasphemy.

157. Theobald, *John*, 1.259; Ensor, "Glorification," 238; Ashton, *John*, 171-72; Borgen, *John*, 256, who notes mystical ascent claims occurred also beyond the Jewish world (98).

158. Ashton, *Fourth Gospel*, 264; Bauckham, "Jewish Messianism," 233; Reynolds, *Apocalyptic Son of Man*, 60, 85.

159. Weidemann, *Tod*, 104; Ensor, "Glorification," 238.

160. Cf. McGrath, *Christology*, argues that John uses the traditional depiction of Jesus as Son of Man "to reinterpret others, such as messiah/Christ, king of Israel, and prophet" (193), seeing a parallel use in Mark 8:27-31; 14:61-62 (194). This is true but only to a limited degree, since Son of Man is limited in its focus. Cf. Burkett, *Son of Man*, argues that Son of Man and Son of God are equivalent in John (85-89); similarly Moloney, "Johannine Son of Man," 201. Rhea, *Son of Man*, 69, sees the author using Son of Man differently from the transcendent Son of Man image of Jewish apocalyptic literature." Better, Reynolds, *Apocalyptic Son of Man*, 223: "The Johannine Son of Man Christology does not highlight Jesus' humanity, whether purely human or divinely human, nor is it synonymous with Johannine Son of God Christology. The Johannine Son of Man is a heavenly being, and his apocalyptic

be seen as the climax of the author's Christology.¹⁶¹ It is above all the elaboration of Christology under the influence of the Sophia myth which provides the integrating structure of the author's Christology of the Son having been sent by the Father to make him known.¹⁶²

6.2.5.3 Jesus as Prophet

More pertinent to the claims and counterclaims that appear to have marked the relationship with the synagogue are those related to Jesus as prophet (1:21, 25; 4:19, 44; 6:14; 7:40, 52; 9:17),¹⁶³ validated by miracles,¹⁶⁴ and also important in Samaritan tradition.¹⁶⁵ That, too, is a claim which need not have been seen as too outlandish. It also merged well with claims about messiahship, especially in the light of the fact that signs had also become a feature of messianic claims and hope,¹⁶⁶ as one might expect given the role of

---

nature is evident in the context of each of the Son of Man sayings in the Gospel of John and not merely 1.51; 3.13; and/or 5.27."

161. Cf. Moloney, *Son of Man*, 40, 183–84, 210. So rightly Pryor, *John*, 136; Reynolds, *Apocalyptic Son of Man*, 233. De Boer, *Johannine Perspectives*, 102–5, suggests that Son of Man sayings are additions and do not fit well in their contexts. He further maintains they were added in response to persecution (230); similarly De Boer, "Johannine History," 299, 313; Ashton, "Reflections on a Footnote," 210.

162. Cf. McGrath, *Christology*, who makes the extraordinary claim that when the author depicts Jesus as claiming to have been sent from the Father and designating himself Son he does not refer to a pre-existent sending (223). He adds to the confusion in writing: "but did not find such ideas associated with the designation 'Son of God'" (223), ignoring the different traditional origins of Son and Son of God.

163. Ashton, *John*, sees an emphasis in what he understands as the Signs Source on Jesus as a prophet like Elijah and Moses, citing 1:19–2:11 (11); similarly *Fourth Gospel*, 182, 185–94. McGrath, *Christology*, points to an emphasis on Jesus as the prophet like Moses promised in Deut 18:15–18 (188); see also Anderson, *Christology*, 185; Reinhartz, "Jesus as Prophet," 10–11; Pryor, *John*, 119; Schnackenburg, *Person Jesu Christi*, 303; Sukmin Cho, *Jesus as Prophet in the Fourth Gospel* (NTM 15; Sheffield: Phoenix, 2006) 231, who writes: "The apologetic christological role of the Johannine Jesus as prophet contributes to providing a proper balance between the high-Christology and the low-Christology in Johannine Christology" (283).

164. McGrath, *Christology*, 188–89; Pryor, *John*, 120; Lierman, "Mosaic Pattern," 213–13; Ashton, *John*, 140.

165. Ashton, *John*, 12; and *Fourth Gospel*, where he notes the lateness of sources often used to reconstruct Samaritan expectations (201).

166. On this see Van Belle, "Signs of the Messiah," who notes the association of signs and messiahship in early Christian tradition (Matt 11:2–6 and Mark 13:22), in contrast to other Jewish tradition, especially in relation to the Son of David motif in Matthew (167), pointing

miracles in political propaganda. Its notion of commissioning could then be transformed in the author's Christology into a pre-existent commissioning, the Father's sending the Son into the world.[167] Moses typology is significant for the author. Lierman observes: "When John's christological portrait is analysed as a whole, no one besides Moses even comes close as a precedent for what John has to say about Jesus and it turns out that Moses comes a lot closer than many would imagine."[168] He points to Moses the disciple-maker (John 9:28), the heavenly advocate (5:45).[169] Ashton notes the succession of Jesus and the Paraclete as matching that of Moses and Joshua.[170] Coloe suggests that "just as Moses took specially prepared oil and anointed the tabernacle, Mary anoints Jesus, whose flesh is the tabernacle of God's presence."[171] Anderson attributes a major role to Moses Christology developed, as he believes, by a follower of Jesus in contributing to unity and disunity in John's Christology.[172]

The matter becomes contentious, however, where affirmations about Jesus are informed by Moses typology in order to show Jesus as greater than Moses. As Harris notes, in pressing Moses into service as one who represented the wide diversity of Judaism, the author thereby placed Moses "in an uneasy relationship with the new figure Jesus."[173] According to Ashton "the Gospel represents a deliberate decision to supplant Moses and to replace him with Jesus, thereby substituting one revelation, and indeed one religion, with

---

to the equivalence of prophet and Messiah in 1:19, 20, 25 (171), and arguing that they are integrated within what I had identified as the central structure of the author's Christology (174). He also notes that some see the presence of miracles in association with the anointed figure in 11QMelch and 4Q521, with allusions to Ps 146:7–8 and Isa 61:1 (170–71); similarly Bauckham, "Monotheism and Christology," 234–35. See also Cho, *Jesus as Prophet*, on the relationship between the motifs of prophet and kingship/messiahship (265–66) and Son of Man (267–71); Rhea, *Son of Man*, who believes the author derived his messianic use of Son of Man from prophetic background and tradition (70).

167. De Boer, *Johannine Perspectives*, 114; Theobald, *Herrenworte*, 592; Beasley-Murray, "Mission," 1865.

168. Lierman, "Mosaic Pattern," 233–34.

169. Lierman, "Mosaic Pattern," 224–25.

170. Ashton, *John*, 42.

171. Coloe, "Anointing the Temple of God," 114

172. Anderson, *Christology*, 192, 260. Lierman, "Mosaic Pattern," emphasises Mosaic rather than Davidic Christology (223). See also Cho, *Jesus as Prophet*, 260–63. While noting the positive role of Moses, Ahn, *Christological Witness*, writes: "One can make a tenable case for the presence of recurrent exodus themes in John 6, but those imageries scarcely constitute a Mosaic Christological typology" (272). Paradoxically, while depicted as losing his authority, Moses assumes the role of accuser of his own (273–74).

173. Harris, *Prologue*, 89.

another."[174] He speculates that the author may stand in Enochic tradition which challenged Moses' authority.[175] The prologue shows Jesus as a gift of God's grace which both fulfils and so replaces God's former gift of Torah, something which the author has developed in association with the Sophia myth, transferring its attributes from Torah to Christ.

The author also appears to counter claims of Moses' mystical ascent (1:18; 3:13) and clearly reflects the great gulf which exists between his community and the synagogue over the claims now made for Jesus, reflected in the charges over ditheism.[176] Conflict has moved progressively from persecution, to synagogue expulsion and finally to formal denunciation[177] and is still current,[178] but from a distance. In that respect John's Gospel exhibits a similarly bitter, yet already distanced, confrontation with Judaism as Matthew's Gospel, yet gives less attention to justification of the Christian claim from the OT. This is because the issue has ceased to be fought and rationalised on grounds of messianism and now focusses on transcendental claims about Jesus. The Fourth Gospel has not abandoned the OT, but it is seen through the eyes of an author who stands within a stream which has linked Torah, wisdom and logos, and has begun to do what Justin did much more fully. It has begun to find the OT heroes witnessing to and acquainted with the divine logos. They bore witness to the new which would replace the old. Failure to perceive this was to reject that same Logos.

---

174. Ashton, *John*, 3, similarly 7, and he sees the same expressed in John 9 (141). He also argues for "6:32 strongly contrasting Moses and God" (19) and sees 6:14 as indicating that the "people see him as replacing Moses" (20). See also Ashton, "Johannine Son of Man," 519-20; Dennis, *Death and Gathering*, 143; Thatcher, "Remembering Jesus," 179-80; Ahn, *Christological Witness*, 253, 261; Kriener, *Glauben an Jesus*, 149; Thatcher, "Remembering Jesus," 181-83.

175. Ashton, *John*, 111, a position which could be supported by the fact that both 1 En. 42 and the prologue share a pessimistic view of the response of God's people to wisdom, compared with Sirach 24. He suggests that belief in Jesus as prophet led to belief that he superseded Moses (143), but much more was in play, including the status of Torah.

176. So Martyn, "Source Criticism," 105-6; Onuki, *Gemeinde*, 33; L. Th. Witkamp, "The Use of Traditions in John 5:1-18," *JSNT* 25 (1985): 33.

177. On the historical issues of synagogue expulsion and the cursing of the *minim* and Nazoreans in the 18 Benedictions see William Horbury, "The Benediction of the Minim and Early Jewish-Christian Controversy," *JTS* 33 (1982): 19-61; Lincoln, *Truth on Trial*, 266-78. Ashton, *John*, 93, sees the separation reflected in "disciples of Moses" (9:28), a term which he argues would have been unthinkable during Jesus' lifetime and much time after that.

178. Against Käsemann, *Letzter Wille*, 102 n. 41; Schnelle, *Christologie*, 42.

6.2.5.4 Jesus and Torah[179]

One of the most notable features of the prologue is the way in which it uses imagery associated with wisdom, which in Jewish tradition had been linked with Torah, and differentiates between Jesus as Logos and Torah, but without disparaging the latter.

The word ὁ νόμος occurs fifteen times in John, linked with Moses (1:17; 1:45; 7:19, 23; cf. Moses alone: 7:22; 5:45–46; 9:28; cf. 5:39), referring to a provision within the law (7:51; 8:17) or legal system (18:31; 19:7; cf. also 7:49). "Your law" appears in 8:17; 10:34; similarly 15:25. The author also uses ὁ νόμος to refer also to the Psalms (10:34; 12:34). Scripture (γραφή) is used seven times in relation to specific predictions (2:22; 7:38; 7:42; 13:18; 17:12; 19:24, 34) and more generally in that sense in 5:39 and 10:35. Fulfilment is usually expressed through use of the verb πληρόω (12:38; 13:18; 15:25; 17:12; 19:24, 36); cf. τελειόω 19:28. "It is written" functions similarly (2:17; 6:45; 12:14; 12:16; 15:25), but sometimes also in argument about what Scripture reports (6:31) or, as Law, requires (8:17).

"In the Fourth Gospel the Logos (= Wisdom), just as in Baruch, 'appeared on earth and lived among men,' but took the place of the Law as the source of life to all who accept the message of Jesus."[180] The differentiation is carried through consistently within the Gospel as the author uses images traditionally associated with Torah to portray the gift of life which Jesus brings, not least in the "I am" statements which portray Jesus as bread, light, life and way. For instance, the author uses the imagery of the feast of Tabernacles, poured water, and light, to portray a new pouring of water (7:37–38; cf. Ezek 47:1–12; Zech 14:8), and Jesus as the light (8:12; cf. Zech 14:7). Thus Coloe writes: "The glory of the God of Israel, revealed in Jesus, permanently leaves the temple. The cultic institutions of Israel are left emptied of the reality they once symbolized and celebrated."[181] Similarly, as Torah could be seen as like a well of water (cf. Ps 36:9a; Prov 18:4; Isa 12:3; CD 6.7), Jesus now offers the

---

179. See my earlier discussions in Loader, *Jesus' Attitude towards the Law*, 432–91; Loader, "'Your Law'—the Johannine Perspective"; Loader, "Jesus and the Law in John"; Loader, "Law and Ethics"; Loader, "Significance of the Prologue for Understanding John's Soteriology," 46–54.

180. Ashton, *Fourth Gospel*, 383; similarly McGrath, *Christology*, 153; Pryor, *John*, 123–24; Scott, *Sophia*, 159–61; cf. Hooker, "Creative Conflict," 136: "There is no contradiction between old and new, since the same divine λόγος, which spoke in creation and through Moses, was 'made flesh' in Christ (1:14)"; Braine, "Jewishness," 116, 119; Keener, *John*, 334, 350–51, 354–55, 360; Moloney, *Love*, 152.

181. Coloe, *God Dwells with Us*, 155; see also 65, 119–22; Lincoln, *John*, 77.

water of life, and, as Torah could be seen as heavenly manna, so Jesus is the manna from above. He, not Torah, is the way to life. As Lincoln puts it, "For Jewish believers who have been cut off from the celebration of the law's festivals, what Jesus signifies now fulfils the meaning of these festivals and takes their place."[182] The differentiation is not one which disparages or denounces Torah (as, arguably, in Mark 7:1-5; Heb 7:18; 10:4; cf. also Rom 2:25-29), but rather sees it as God's gift through Moses, now replaced by God's greater gift through Jesus. This comes to expression clearly in the prologue, where the author writes:

> ὅτι ἐκ τοῦ πληρώματος αὐτοῦ ἡμεῖς πάντες ἐλάβομεν
> καὶ χάριν ἀντὶ χάριτος·
> ὅτι ὁ νόμος διὰ Μωϋσέως ἐδόθη,
> ἡ χάρις καὶ ἡ ἀλήθεια διὰ Ἰησοῦ Χριστοῦ ἐγένετο.
> Because of his fullness we have all received,
> even one gift in place of another gift
> Because the Law was given through Moses,
> grace and truth came through Jesus Christ. (1:16-17)

The word ἀντί in the expression χάριν ἀντὶ χάριτος is to be read in the usual sense of "instead of" or "in place of."[183] There is no need to construe it as indicating supplementation, as though the meaning were "in addition to,"[184] and certainly no need to do so for dogmatic or apologetic reasons. *We* may deem supersessionism inappropriate, but that is no reason for denying it in John.

---

182. Lincoln, *John*, 77. Cf. Thompson, *God*, 219: "Thus, rather than saying that 'Jesus supersedes the great pilgrim festivals,' it would be more precise to argue that even as the great pilgrim festivals celebrate God's work, so too Christians commemorated God's acts of salvation—here, the act of eschatological salvation in Christ."

183. So Edwards, "χάριν ἀντὶ χάριτος," 3-15; Coloe, *God Dwells with Us*, 28; Ahn, *Christological Witness*, 241-44; Francis J. Moloney, *Belief in the Word: Reading the Fourth Gospel: John 1-4* (Minneapolis: Fortress, 1993), 47-48, 96, 102, but cf. 152; Moloney, *John*, 46; McHugh, *John*, 64-67; Theobald, *Anfang*, 60-61.

184. So again most recently Beutler, "Johannes-Prolog," 97; Beutler, *Johannesevangelium*, 95; Busse, "Theologie oder Christologie," 24; Harris, *Prologue*, 52, "unfolded in ever-changing variety"; Theobald, *Johannes*, 1.133-35; Michaels, *Johannes*, 90; Martin Vahrenhorst, "Johannes und die Tora: Überlegungen zur Bedeutung der Tora im Johannesevangelium," *KD* 54 (2008): 28-29; Keener, *John*, 1.421. Carson, *John*, 134, confuses Word and Torah when he writes: "But the law that was *given* through Moses, and the grace and truth that *came* through Jesus Christ (v. 17), alike sprang from the fullness of the Word (v. 16), whether in his pre-existent oneness with the Father, or in his status as the Word-made-flesh. It is from that 'fulness' that we have received 'one grace replacing another'"; similarly Thyen, *Johannesevangelium*, 105, who has John believing the Logos Son appeared also in OT times, citing 8:56; 12:41; 5:46 (310).

The Fourth Gospel in the Light of Its Christology

As de la Potterie showed, the sole instance one can cite to support a meaning other than replace (Philo, *Post.* 145) does not in fact support it, but refers to one gift of God replacing another in succession:

> Wherefore God ever causes his earliest gifts to cease before their recipients are glutted and wax insolent; and storing them up for the future gives others in their stead (ἑτέρας ἀντ' ἐκείνων), and a third supply to replace (ἀντί) the second, and ever new in place of (ἀντί) earlier boons, sometimes different in kind, sometimes the same.[185]

The juxtaposition (not technically a contrast since there is no δέ in the Greek, unless we follow P66)[186] is not of something bad and something good, but between something good, given by God,[187] and something better,[188] and reflects an understanding of divine intent to give now in the new what the old had foreshadowed, an understanding related to but expressed differently in Hebrews. On 1:17 Ashton writes: "In attributing grace and truth to Christ rather than to Moses, the author of this sentence knew—cannot but have known—that he was dissociating himself from Judaism in any of its forms."[189] Underlying 1:14-18 is the depiction of the revelation to Moses in Exodus (cf. Exod 33:7-23; 34:6),[190] and its reflection in Sir 24:8; 43:31,[191] but the author

---

185. De la Potterie, *Vérité*, 143. See also the linguistic discussion in Konrad Pfuff, *Die Einheit des Johannesprologs* (Frankfurt: Peter Lang, 2013), 99–103.

186. Keener, *John*, 422, notes however that "the lack of adversative conjunction here does not eliminate the contrast." "Context must dictate the *force* of contrast."

187. Contrast Schnackenburg, *John*, 1.277, who understands Moses as the giver; see also Andreas Lindemann, "Mose und Christus: Zum Verständnis des Gesetzes im Johannesevangelium," in *Das Urchristentum, in seiner literarischen Geschichte: FS J. Becker*, ed. U. Mell and U. B. Müller, BZNW 100 (Berlin: de Gruyter, 1999), 332.

188. So Lincoln, *John*, 75–76; Wolfgang Kraus, "Johannes und das alte Testament. Überlegungen zum Umgang mit der Schrift im Johannesevangelium im Horizont Biblischer Theologie," ZNW 88 (1997): 18.

189. Ashton, *John*, 22.

190. On this see Schnackenburg, "Fleisch," 7–8; Hooker, "Prologue," 53–58; Theobald, *Anfang*, 38–39; H. Mowvley, "John 1:14-18 in the Light of Exodus 33:7–34:35," *ExpT* 95 (1984): 135–37; Thyen, "Brüder," 533; Bühner, *Gesandte*, 375; Vahrenhorst, "Johannes und die Tora," 30; Stefan Schapdick, "Autorität ohne Inhalt: Zum Mosebild des Johannesevangeliums," ZNW 97 (2006): 182; Beutler, "Johannes-Prolog," 95–96; Dennis, *Death and Gathering*, 142–44, who sees the author using Exodus to claim that in Jesus God's glory has been restored to his people in a new Exodus.

191. Thyen, *Johannesevangelium*, 104; Jörg Frey, "God's Dwelling on Earth: Shekinah-Theology in Revelation 21 and in the Gospel of John," in *John's Gospel and Intimations of Apocalyptic*, ed. C. H. Williams and C. Rowland (London: T&T Clark, 2013), 94–96. Cf. also 1 En. 42:1–2.

deliberately transfers "grace and truth" to Jesus, while acknowledging the former revelation of the Law as God's gift, for only in Christ do we have one who has seen God and can make him known (cf. also 3:13; 5:37; 6:46).[192] Thus even if on doubtful grounds one opts to read "grace upon grace," the ultimate meaning has to be the same, for the new does what the old could not do.[193]

The author never disparages the Law, its rituals and festivals. The six stone jars for purification are not an item for ridicule, even though they are now transformed into bearers of wine. There is nothing wrong with six;[194] but it falls short of seven, the perfect number,[195] significant given the ancient world's interest in numerology. Jesus is portrayed as being concerned with the temple, calling it in his own words, "My Father's house,"[196] and as attending the festivals (2:13-14; 5:1; 6:4; 7:8-9; 12:12).[197] Jews are not disparaged over their relationship with the Samaritans (4:9). The author mentions purification in relation to the Passover (11:55; 18:28), a motif informing the discussion of the foot washing (13:8). While there is an implied criticism that the leaders are concerned with such observance (18:28) when they should have been concerned with the impending killing of Jesus, the Passover with its purity

---

192. So Theobald, *Fleischwerdung*, 259; Schapdick, "Autorität ohne Inhalt," 183. Ashton, *John*, 141; similarly Ashton, "Reflections," 211; Witherington, *John's Wisdom*, 49; Lincoln, *John*, 75; Matthias Gawlick, "Mose im Johannesevangelium," *BN* 84 (1996) 29-35, 32; Moloney, *Love*, 94, 96, 102.

193. Beutler, *Johannesevangelium*, notes the irony that "grace and truth" is derived from the account of the giving of the Law (96).

194. Vahrenhorst, "Johannes und die Tora," 16. On their likely use for purification of the hands before eating see R. Deines, *Jüdische Steingefässe und pharisäische Frömmigkeit: Eine archäologisch-historischer Beitrag zum Verständnis von Joh 2,6 und der jüdischen Reinheitshalacha zur Zeit Jesu*, WUNT 2.52 (Tübingen: Mohr Siebeck, 1993), 247-51, 263-75; Eyal Regev, "Non-Priestly Purity and Its Religious Aspects according to Historical Sources and Archaeological Findings," in *Purity and Holiness: The Heritage of Leviticus*, ed. M. J. H. M. Poorthuis and J. Schwartz; (Leiden: Brill, 2000), 232.

195. Cullmann, *Salvation*, 279; Cullmann, *Worship*, 69-70; Brown, *John*, 104; Lindars, *Gospel of John*, 128, 134; Ellis, *Genius*, 42-43; Mussner, "Kultische Aspekte," 137; Brown, *John*, 110; Kee, *Miracles*, 234; Hengel, "Cana," 102; as the work of the redactor: Langbrandtner, *Weltferner Gott*, 72; Heekerens, *Zeichen-Quelle*, 71-76; Loader, "Law and Ethics," 144-45; Moloney, *John*, 68; Coloe, *God Dwells with Us*, 69, 99.

196. The attack echoes Zech 14:21 (cf. also Ezek 8:1-18; 9:1-2, 6), and is on merchandising not the temple. So Bruce G. Schuchard, *Scripture within Scripture: The Interrelationship of Form and Function in the Explicit Old Testament Citations in the Gospel of John*, SBLDDS 133 (Atlanta: SBL, 1992), 25; Cf. Gale A. Yee, *Jewish Feasts and the Gospel of John*, Zacchaeus Studies (New Testament; Wilmington: Liturgical, 1989), 62, who suggests "fundamental opposition to the temple itself."

197. Vahrenhorst, "Johannes und die Tora," 17.

provisions is not being demeaned.[198] Nicodemus also charged that the Jews acted unlawfully in relation to Jesus (7:50–51). Similarly concern with not leaving a corpse hanging overnight and on the Sabbath (19:31) and concern with burial after the Sabbath (19:40, 42)[199] imply no disparagement. The author even believes the high priest could have prophetic inspiration (11:51).

On the other hand, he makes clear that Jesus in his person is the true temple which will be torn down and then raised up (2:19–22).[200] Salvation is, indeed, "from the Jews" (4:22), but the person of Jesus is now the sacred temple, no longer the temple on Zion or Mt Gerizim. The issue is not reform but replacement.[201] This in part addresses the crisis created by its destruction in 70 CE.[202] It also fulfils widespread Jewish eschatological expectation, often associated, as in Mark 11–13, with royal messiahship.[203] Thus Dennis notes the promise of

> a renewed or new Temple where God's glory will once again dwell, the gathering and unification of Israel and Israel's deliverance from oppressors (cf. Isa 44–49; 31; 66; Ezek 34–37; 40–48; Zech 2; Hag 2). Later expectations of an eschatological (heavenly) temple held together, more or less the same basic constellation of these elements of eschatological restoration (cf. Tob 13–14; Sir 36; Jub. 1; 1 En. 89–90; 1QS, 4QFlor., *Temple Scroll* and *Descriptions of the New Jerusalem*).[204]

Temple and temple cult are central to Torah, not something separate. Replacing temple reflects and implies replacing Torah, now that what it promised has come true. Accordingly, Coloe writes,

> A possible reason why the temple cleansing is so early in the Fourth Gospel is because this pericope provides the reader with both an explicit hermeneutical key for interpreting the Johannine Jesus as the new 'temple,' and a paradigm for further scenes in the use of Johannine symbolism and misunderstandings.[205]

---

198. Vahrenhorst, "Johannes und die Tora," 18–19; Söding, "Macht der Wahrheit," 39.
199. Vahrenhorst, "Johannes und die Tora," 18–19.
200. Ashton, *John*, 142.
201. Söding, "Ich und der Vater," 179.
202. Dennis, *Death and Gathering*, 183; Thettayil, *In Spirit and Truth*, 347.
203. Dennis, *Death and Gathering*, 163; Coloe, *God Dwells with Us*, 186–87, 201, pointing to Zech 6:10–13; Leung, *Kingship-Cross*, 2, 72–75, 81–92; Chanikuzhy, *Jesus, the Eschatological Temple*, 331.
204. Dennis, *Death and Gathering*, 163.
205. Coloe, *God Dwells with Us*, 84.

Thus Jesus replaces the festivals. "For Jewish believers who have been cut off from the celebration of the law's festivals, what Jesus signifies now fulfils the meaning of these festivals and takes their place."[206] On the libation ceremony at the Feast of the Tabernacles, Coloe writes: "The God of Israel's festivals has become incarnate in their midst, no longer in symbols or rituals but in the *sarx* of Jesus."[207] Similarly Chanikuzhy observes: "Now, it is on the background of such a significant water ceremony that Jesus makes his claim. Understood in the light of this background Jesus' claim to be the source of living waters amounts to a claim to be the new rock, the eschatological Jerusalem and the eschatological temple."[208] The Temple motif plays a major role in the Gospel,[209] and is implicit in the allusion in the prologue to the Logos becoming human flesh and so revealing God's glory.[210] The author's attitude towards Torah and more broadly to Scripture mirrors his attitude towards John the Baptist. Both are seen and valued as witnesses to the one who has now come.[211] He is the one to whom Moses and prophets testified (1:45).[212] The Scriptures and Torah are not in themselves the bearers of life but point to the one who now brings life to the world.[213] John has Jesus make this clear:

> ἐραυνᾶτε τὰς γραφάς, ὅτι ὑμεῖς δοκεῖτε ἐν αὐταῖς ζωὴν αἰώνιον ἔχειν·
> καὶ ἐκεῖναί εἰσιν αἱ μαρτυροῦσαι περὶ ἐμοῦ·
> καὶ οὐ θέλετε ἐλθεῖν πρός με ἵνα ζωὴν ἔχητε.
> You search the Scriptures because you think you have eternal life in them
> and they are the ones which bear witness about me.
> And you are not willing to come to me so that you may have life.
> (5:39-40)

---

206. So Lincoln, *John*, 77.
207. Coloe, *God Dwells with Us*, 155.
208. Chanikuzhy, *Jesus, the Eschatological Temple*, 370, who sees temple allusions also in Jesus' reference to his consecration and sending in 10:36, given the context of the Hanukkah festival (383-95). Cory, "Wisdom's Rescue," 96, emphasises the allusions to the Wisdom/Sophia tradition in the Tabernacles discourse. On Hanukkah see also Dennert, "Hanukkah," who suggests that Jesus' claims to divinity there may echo those of Antiochus Epiphanes, also a shepherd/ruler (433-34), also relevant because it matches the emphasis on shepherds as rulers (434), though does not see replacement intended (451).
209. So Busse, *Johannesevangelium*, 332-34; Coloe, *God Dwells with Us*, 23-27, who emphasises replacement (62); earlier: Brown, *John*, 32-34.
210. Um, *Temple Christology*, 155.
211. Schapdick, "Autorität ohne Inhalt," 191.
212. Vahrenhorst, "Johannes und die Tora," 26; Schapdick, "Autorität ohne Inhalt," 186.
213. So Schapdick, "Autorität ohne Inhalt," 189, on 3:14 on Moses as prefiguration.

Had they believed the Scriptures, Jesus charges, they would have believed him (5:46). As such they, or their spokesperson, Moses, will charge the unbelieving Jews with not having believed on the Son to whom they pointed (5:45-47). Similarly John has Jesus contrast Moses and himself as the true bread.

> εἶπεν οὖν αὐτοῖς ὁ Ἰησοῦς· ἀμὴν ἀμὴν λέγω ὑμῖν, οὐ Μωϋσῆς δέδωκεν ὑμῖν τὸν ἄρτον ἐκ τοῦ οὐρανοῦ, ἀλλ᾽ ὁ πατήρ μου δίδωσιν ὑμῖν τὸν ἄρτον ἐκ τοῦ οὐρανοῦ τὸν ἀληθινόν·
> Jesus said to them, "Truly, truly, I tell you, it was not Moses who gave you the bread from heaven, but my Father who gives you the true bread from heaven." (6:32)

Both through fulfilment of Scripture and through typological correspondence, as here with the manna, the author depicts the Scriptures as foreshadowing Jesus' coming and the gift of life he brings.[214]

There are occasions which can be read as debate about halakhah, as though the author sees Jesus and his community as still Torah-observant and so concerned with its application.[215] One such is the controversy about the healing of the lame man on the Sabbath (5:8-10, 16). Part of the defence employs Jewish speculation about what God did or did not do on the seventh day (Gen 2:3; Exod 20:11; Philo *Cher.* 86-89; *Leg.* 1.5-6; Ps. Aristeas 210; Mek. Šabb. 2:25; Gen. Rab. 11:5,11,12),[216] but in effect Jesus makes the claim to override the Sabbath law because of his status as God's Son.[217] Similarly in John 9, Jesus' status overrides Sabbath law (9:14).[218] In both instances there is an element of arguing the unreasonableness of the critics' concerns, but beyond that the assumption is of a new order, at least in the person of Jesus who is above the Law.[219]

In 7:19-24 the dispute about Sabbath law finds a sequel where indeed Jesus employs halakic argument, pointing to circumcision on the Sabbath,[220]

---

214. Schapdick, "Autorität ohne Inhalt," 194; Lindemann, "Mose," 318; Thatcher, "Remembering Jesus," 180. Cf. Markku Kotila, *Umstrittener Zeuge: Studien zur Stellung des Gesetzes in der johanneischen Theologiegeschichte* (Helsinki: Suomalainen Tiedeakatemia, 1988), 170-71.

215. Pancaro, *Law*, 15-19, 29, 45-47; Thyen, *Johannesevangelium*, 394.

216. Vahrenhorst, "Johannes und die Tora," 21-22.

217. Lincoln, *John*, 75.

218. Pancaro, *Law*, 18-19.

219. Cf. Vahrenhorst, "Johannes und die Tora," 22-23, who notes that in both instances we have to weigh whether this should still be seen as a new very liberal Sabbath halakhah.

220. On rabbinic tradition which saw circumcision as healing see t. Šabb. 15,16; b. Yoma 85b; m. Šabb. 18:3; 19:2-3; m. Ned. 3:11.

but this should not be read as evidence for Torah observance.[221] Rather it is an exposure of inconsistency on the part of his critics.[222] When Jesus uses the term "your Law" to refer to Torah, this is not disparagement.[223] It is, however, a distancing because for John, Jesus and now the followers of Jesus, are no longer bound by that Law, but have redefined its role in God's purposes.[224] That same spirit is evident in its use in the dispute in 10:22-39. When he asserts that Scripture cannot be abrogated, he does so to appeal to its evidence which helps justify his claim, not in order to rehabilitate or assert Torah observance.[225] The same may be said of his appeal in 8:17 to the rule about evidence from two witnesses, where he confronts his opponents on the basis of their law.[226]

The cumulative evidence, not least the replacement of the temple and its associated rituals, but also the transfer of Torah imagery to Jesus, indicates that the author has been part of a reassessment of the status of Law and more broadly Scripture. The Son and his commands are now the basis for ethics (13:34-35; 15:9-17),[227] not Torah,[228] though core values enunciated in Torah

---

221. Cf. Vahrenhorst, "Johannes und die Tora," 22; Schapdick, "Autorität ohne Inhalt," 198-99.

222. So Jürgen Becker, *Johanneisches Christentum* (Tübingen: Mohr Siebeck, 2004), 185; Lincoln, *John*, 75; Ashton, *John*, 287-99.

223. So Jörg Augenstein, "'Euer Gesetz'—Ein Pronomen und die johanneische Haltung zum Gesetz," *ZNW* 88 (1997): 311-13, who points to how Moses and Joshua spoke to the people: "Your God, your fathers, your land" (Deut 2:30; 4:23; Josh 1:11, 13-14) similarly Thyen, *Johannesevangelium*, 424; Vahrenhorst, "Johannes und die Tora," 25-26; Schapdick, "Autorität ohne Inhalt," 204.

224. So Lincoln, *John*, 76; Kraus, "Johannes und das alte Testament," 18; Pryor, *John*, 118.

225. Cf. Hengel, "Old Testament in the Fourth Gospel," 386.

226. As already Bultmann, *Johannes*, 212. Cf. Thyen, *Johannesevangelium*, 502; Vahrenhorst, "Johannes und die Tora," 25.

227. On the "new" commandment (13:34-35; cf. 1 John 2:7-8), see Johannes Beutler, "Das Hauptgebot im Johannesevangelium," in *Das Gesetz im Neuen Testament*, ed. K. Kertelge, QD 108 (Freiburg: Herder, 1986), 222-236, who notes use of covenant language ("keeping the commandments" or "keeping the word"; cf. Deut 7:9), but not to refer to Torah, despite likely influence of Lev 19:18 (224-25); similarly Michèle Morgen, "'Votre Loi, mon commandement': Etude de la place accordée à la Loi et au commandement dans l'évangile de Jean," in *Raconter, Interpréter, Annoncer. Parcours de Nouveau Testament: Mélanges offerts à Daniel Marguerat pour son 60ème anniversaire*, ed. E. Steffek and Y. Bourquin, MdB 47 (Geneva: Labor et Fides, 2003), 199, 205-206; Johannes Nissen, "Community and Ethics in the Gospel of John," in *New Readings in John: Literary and Theological Perspectives: Essays from the Scandinavian Conference on the Fourth Gospel Aarhus 1997*, ed. J. Nissen and S. Pedersen, JSNTSup 182 (Sheffield: Sheffield Academic Press, 1999), 202-3; R. Alan Culpepper, "Anti-Judaism in the Fourth Gospel as a Theological Problem for Christian Interpreters," in *Anti-Judaism and the Fourth Gospel*, ed. R. Bieringer, D. Pollefeyt, and F. Vandecasteele-Vanneuville (Louisville: Westminster John Knox, 2001), 80; Lincoln, *John*, 77.

228. Cf. Vahrenhorst, "Johannes und die Tora," 33-34; Pancaro, *Law*; Johnson, "Salvation" 88, 90, who argues that "while John rejects the particular Jewish understanding of the Jewish institutions, he accepts the institutions themselves. In particular, he understands these Jewish

inform those commands.[229] This is clearly evidenced in the last discourses where the author does not have Jesus appeal to Torah (except in 15:25),[230] an approach mirrored in the ethical exhortations in 1 John (except for the sole reference about Cain). The Law belongs to the past and like John's witness, is to be honoured, pointing to what is to come.[231] In a sense its temple and associated rituals both foreshadow what was to come and do so at the level of the flesh or material, something not despised in John,[232] now fulfilled at the level of the spirit in John. While 6:62 may seem to come close to disparaging the flesh, this relates only to its inability to bring new life. The same contrast is present in Jesus' conversation with Nicodemus whose thinking remains at the level of the flesh (3:3, 5–8). The flesh itself is not evil, but to remain with its worship structures and law, when what they foreshadowed has come, is evil. In that sense the Law on the Johannine reading predicts its own eclipse by Jesus. Paradoxically the claim to continuity with Torah and to its faithful interpretation matters greatly to the author as doubtless to his community, but that now means redefining its role as a witness from the past, not as a rule for the present. To ignore its status and treat it as remaining in force would be to reject the new gift according to John.[233]

Unlike Matthew, for whom not a stroke of the Law is to fall, but every part to be kept and done in accordance with its interpretation by Jesus (5:17–19), and

---

institutions as the appropriate way to describe the identity of Jesus" (98), whom he sees as "fulfilling both the place and function of the temple and the feasts and who is significantly superior to the prophets, Moses, Jacob, and the other heroes of Israel's history" (99, similarly 96); Lee, *Flesh and Glory*, 68, who writes that in John, Judaism is "not discarded but rather elevated to a new level of meaning" (similarly 84).

229. Thus Jey J. Kanagaraj, "The Implied Ethics of the Fourth Gospel: A Reinterpretation of the Decalogue," *TynB* 52 (2001): 36–37.

230. U. Luz in R. Smend and U. Luz, *Gesetz*, Biblische Konfrontationen 1015 (Stuttgart: Kohlhammer, 1981), 119–28, raises the important question whether in the way John treats the Law and Scripture as a whole they become mere repositories for testimony and symbolism and effectively lose reference to their own story (125).

231. Marion Moser, "Genügt ein christologische Verständnis der Schrift im Johannesevangelium? Überlegungen zum Kontext der expliziten Schriftbelege," in *Narrativität und Theologie im Johannesevangelium*, ed. J. Frey and U. Poplutz, BS[N] 130 (Neukirchen-Vluyn: Neukirchener Verlag, 2012), 59, notes that while the Scripture retains its authority, it is being interpreted in a way which clearly distances it from Judaism.

232. Hahn, *Theologie*, 1.623.

233. Jan G. van der Watt, "Ethics of/and the Opponents of Jesus in John's Gospel," in *Rethinking the Ethics of John: "Implicit Ethics" in the Johannine Writings*, ed. J. G. van der Watt and R. Zimmermann, Contexts and Norms of New Testament Ethics 3 (Tübingen: Mohr Siebeck, 2012), 175–91, suggests that the issue is not with the Law in itself but with how it is interpreted (185; similarly 189), but the Johannine interpretation completely reframes its role.

unlike Mark, for whom keeping at least the ten commandments as interpreted by Jesus is the way to inherit eternal life (10:17–21), for John only faith in Jesus matters and that is seen not as disowning one's Jewish past, as would have been an issue for many in his community, but reappropriating it as fulfilling the role of witness and prefiguration in God's plan. This still does not alter the fact that, as with Paul, who declares believers no longer under the Law, values informed by Torah (and also generally shared by surrounding cultures of the time) shape John's ethical assumptions. Paul can accordingly claim in that sense to uphold Torah and via the route of the Spirit more than fulfil what it intended (Gal 5:16–23; Rom 8:1–4), but in John that concern with continuity is not expressed.

The evidence for Jewish heritage in the Johannine community is strong. The bitterness is hardly just paradigmatic and must spring from memory of hurt, rejection and also persecution. The Jewish heritage is also present in the earlier messianic concerns, the use of traditions later present in Targums, the apparent reaction to Jewish mystical claims about Moses, and the use of the Logos hymn and of images traditionally associated with personified wisdom as Torah in the discourses.

Samaritan Influence?

How far Samaritan traditions, let alone Samaritan Christianity, played a role in the formation of the community is uncertain, though the author assumes a link with Samaritan Christians in ch. 4.[234] I am not convinced that the early chapters of the Gospel reflect its history[235] nor that there is sufficient evidence to show that the higher Christology is due to Samaritan influence.[236] Links with early forms of Hellenistic Jewish Christianity of the type represented by Stephen are possible, but must remain hypothetical. Nor has it been convincingly shown that John the Baptist sectarians, against whom the Gospel occasionally directs its attention, gave the Gospel a significant legacy.

6.2.6 Johannine Christology and the Emerging Church

The representation of a range of christological traditions within the Gospel, including those used incidentally, and the inheritance of material like that

---

234. Cf. Meeks, *Prophet King*, 216–20; Schillebeeckx, *Christ*, 312–17.
235. Against Brown, *Beloved Disciple*, 26–50.
236. Cf. Cullmann, *Johannine Circle*, 43–56; Brown, *Beloved Disciple*, 36–40.

of the Synoptic tradition, not least the passion narrative, indicate that the Johannine church has had relationships with the wider Christian community, despite being sufficiently isolated for its distinctive forms to develop. The role given to Peter in relation to the beloved disciple suggests a continuing relationship, even if it assumes the Johannine group outruns the rest in wisdom and understanding,[237] and John 21 may reflect a stage of cautious realignment and affirmation of belonging with the wider Church.[238]

Distinctive developments of earlier tradition are apparent in: the Son of Man Christology, both its focus on exaltation and its inclusion of pre-existence; the expansion of Spirit witness tradition through the Paraclete cycle; the use of wisdom Torah motifs to portray the significance of Jesus' ministry; and, above all, the expansion of Father-Son revelation imagery into a full-blown revealer-envoy model with pre-existence playing a major role, and ontology assuming a heightened significance. But the Johannine community seems still in loose association with the wider church as well as having received its early traditions, and this traditional commitment continues to operate within the Gospel with an established authority.

6.2.6.1 Johannine Christology and Miracle-Oriented Christianity

There are also indications within the Gospel of criticism over against responses to Jesus which express themselves using largely messianic affirmations,[239] but which fail to go on to the insight that Jesus is the sent one from above. These are typically represented in Nicodemus (3:2; cf. also 2:23-25; 4:48).[240] The criticism is not an attack on miracles or on miracle-based faith in itself, but it does attack a form of such faith which fails to draw the right conclusions and, given the observations already made about Johannine attitudes to the charismatic in Christianity, we may justifiably, I think, assume that these Christians belonged to such a miracle-oriented group, whose Christology kept it miracle-focussed.[241] I do not consider the author to be concerned here with political zealot hopes linked with popular prophetic ex-

---

237. See Brown, *Beloved Disciple*, 81-88.
238. So Klauck, "Gemeinde," 216.
239. So Fortna, *Gospel of Signs*, 228; similarly Nicol, *Semeia*, 88-90; and contrast Becker, *Johannes*, 117-20, emphasising *theios aner* Christology.
240. So de Jonge, *Stranger*, 39-40; cf. also Painter, "John 9," 37.
241. See also Martyn, "Source Criticism," 106-7, who sees the author both correcting signs-based faith of the "signs Gospel" and securing christological affirmation against its vulnerability to Jewish argument.

pectation, as Bittner suggests,²⁴² nor to be pitting a Moses against a Davidic messiahship, as Schillebeeckx argues.²⁴³ His revealer-envoy Christology transcends such concerns. This miracle-oriented messianic Christianity is inadequate because it fails to confess the one come from above. The evangelist had no qualms in using traditions they doubtless treasured, whether they existed as a collection or as individual units, and even heightened the impressiveness of their miracles, but for him the miracles were now past evidences of the heavenly envoy, manifestations then of the person who now meets them in community, not models of a continuing phenomenon for the faithful. The tensions with Christians of this kind are, I believe, reflected in the split portrayed in 6:60–71.

6.2.6.2 Johannine Christology and Revealer-Envoy Christology

It is another question whether there had also existed a form of Johannine Christianity which had used the revealer-envoy model in a more thoroughgoing and literal sense than the evangelist, as, for instance, Langbrandtner suggests in arguing for a gnostic *Grundschrift*.²⁴⁴ This is not the place to pursue in detail possible gnostic influence in John or its extent. I have made some brief comments above in 5.1. But two further observations are relevant. The model of the revealer-envoy with its cosmic dualism, which the author has adapted, has a major place in the Gospel and the author's merging of it with a developed Son of Man tradition in no way indicates that he has abandoned it. If gnostic influence lies behind the pattern of the revealer-envoy that the author has adapted, he seems unaware or unconcerned about it, even though its application to Jesus is bound to lead to some degree of docetism. Religio-historical research continues to explore the sources the author or his tradition employed in adopting this as the primary model, and early Gnosticism must be counted as a serious option.

The Envoy-Messenger Motif

At the same time I do not want to deny the possibility that the pattern of the revealer-envoy—which in its existing form is based on cosmic dualism—has

---

242. Bittner, *Zeichen*, 285–89.
243. Schillebeeckx, *Christ*, 312–21.
244. Langbrandtner, *Weltferner Gott*.

a complex history. The role of the "shaliach" and messenger in the contemporary world, their stereotype protocol, and the application of these models to heavenly figures have been explored fully by Bühner;[245] they have probably contributed to the Johannine pattern of the sent one. Directly within the Christian community were also sent ones, namely, apostles and missionaries. The language of sending and authorisation was applied early both to Jesus and his disciples (e.g., Matt 10:40; Luke 10:16; John 13:20). One might also compare the revealer function associated with Father-Son language in Matt 11:27; Luke 10:22. Perhaps the charismatic prophet-teacher model has, in its turn, at some stage influenced the portrait of Jesus in the tradition of the Gospel. According to Boismard, the model of the Mosaic prophet shaped the Christology of the earliest form of the Gospel and continued its influence in the successive stages of its development.[246] Perhaps also the sending of prophets associated with the Wisdom tradition lies in the background (Luke 11:49–51). The tradition of the sending of the chosen or beloved Son appears in Johannine form in 3:16–17 and this is close to Gal 4:4 and Rom 8:3. But the form of sending Christology which we have in John goes considerably beyond these and is different in the dualism it presupposes, in its soteriology, and above all, in its understanding of the role of pre-existence.[247]

While Paul presupposes pre-existence and later Pauline literature uses wisdom models of Christology which presuppose it, in John pre-existence is made to be personally significant for the Son and soteriologically significant. In the revealer-envoy model it is the basis on which the revealer has something to tell and in the modified form of the author it remains of major significance in expounding his origin and authority. This is something much closer to forms of early Gnosticism as we know them. We noted above that the Gospel leaves us with the distinct impression that the author modifies an existing model. While descent–ascent patterns were common[248] and had already influenced his tradition, as illustrated by the Son of Man cluster, the foreignness of the model, which the modification presupposes, raises of necessity the question of influence, at least, from a community of ideas not fully compatible with the author's own and where cosmic dualism played a more significant role. This would be compatible with early gnostic influence.[249]

245. Bühner, *Gesandte*; see also Miranda, *Sendung*.
246. Boismard and Lamouille, *Jean*.
247. Against deriving the revealer-envoy model from Wisdom: Becker, *Johannes*, 55.
248. So Talbert, "Descending and Ascending Redeemer."
249. So Martyn, "Source Criticism," 114–15; Becker, *Johannes*, 53–54; cf. also K. M. Fischer, "Der johanneische Christus und der gnostische Erlöser," in *Gnosis und Neues Testament*, ed. K. W. Tröger (Berlin: EvVerlagsanstalt, 1973), 245–66; C. K. Barrett, "The Theological Vocab-

6.2.6.3 Johannine Christology and Docetism

At one or possibly two points there seems to be a concern on the part of the author to emphasise Jesus' humanness as though it were being called into question. These are 19:34-35 and, just possibly, 1:14.[250] The former, particularly 19:35, is strikingly odd and this gives it all the more weight. It has all the marks of a footnote added to the Gospel to counter doubts or doctrines which called into question Jesus' real humanity and death. If this had been a major issue for the evangelist we should have more indication of it in the dialogues and discourses, but in these we find none, unless 6:51c-58 be read in this way. Even then its absence elsewhere in thematic material counts strongly against the hypothesis of Schnelle, for instance, who argues that the Gospel has this as a major focus and follows the time of the epistle.[251] It seems to me more likely that the Gospel writer is still innocently unaware of how a radical use of his envoy model could imperil the tradition and that this awareness arose at a later date, causing some supplementation, though I am not convinced that the supplements are as extensive as Langbrandtner has proposed.[252]

The Gospel without antidocetic supplements could lead some directly to a one-sided emphasis of the model and so to gnostic Christology. Traditionally, 1 John has been adduced as evidence of this development having occurred and of a split in the community having taken place over this issue. Horst Balz and Lieu may be right in arguing that we misread the epistle when we find in its confessions allusions to docetic doctrine.[253] Denying that Jesus came in the flesh may mean little more than denying Christ. On the other hand, the behavioural characteristics which the author addresses are consonant with a group whose Christology had radicalised the dualistic envoy model, developed a triumphalist Christology and consequently, like the Corinthians, have come to place a low value on human belonging and community.[254]

Given the importance of the post-Easter community noted above and

---

ulary of the Fourth Gospel and the Gospel of Truth," in *Essays on John* (Philadelphia: Westminster, 1982), 50-64; Beasley-Murray, *John*, lv-lvi.

250. See the evaluation of possible antidocetic passages by de Jonge, *Stranger*, 207-10.
251. Schnelle, *Christologie*; similarly Strecker, "Anfänge," 31-47.
252. Langbrandtner, *Weltferner Gott*, 108-13; cf. also Thyen, "Entwicklungen"; Richter, *Studien*, 357-58, 409-10.
253. Lieu, *Epistles*, 81-82, 211; Horst Balz, "Johanneische Theologie und Ethik im Lichte der 'letzten Stunde,'" in *Studien zum Text und zur Ethik des Neuen Testaments. Festschrift für H. Greeven*, ed. W. Schrage, BZNW 167 (Berlin: de Gruyter, 1986), 53-55. See also the brief discussion in Loader, *Johannine Epistles*, 62-69.
254. Similarly Balz, "Theologie," 55-56.

the movement in focus in the last discourses from mission in the first, to community maintenance in chs. 15–17, we might well see the development of these chapters as a response to this emerging situation reflected in 1 John.[255] Lieu points out, for instance, that both in 1 John and in John 17 there is a tendency to focus on the message as once given and the community as its preserver, though differences between the two, such as the use of "truth" and the understanding of revelation, make common authorship unlikely.[256] The increased focus on ecclesiology, especially in ch. 21, and in the person of the beloved disciple, may similarly reflect a later phase when the implications of an exalted and dualistic Christology and soteriology threatened unity. Significantly, the epistle seems to have left behind the revealer-envoy Christology.[257] Correspondingly, its salvific focus moves to Jesus' death as vicarious and to traditional futuristic eschatology. It also shows no indication of tensions with Judaism. Its primary interest is with community identity and its maintenance by mutual love.

6.2.7 Johannine Christology and the Composition of the Gospel

Johannine Christology also raises questions about the history of the Gospel itself.[258] In his review of theories of composition Ashton advocates at least two editions of the Gospel, rejects theories of displacement of an ecclesiastical redactor, and sees the author as responsible for the entire composition (except the final chapter and "a few relatively insignificant glosses"), while using a signs source and a hymn to wisdom in the prologue.[259] He also writes of "the unorthodox or dissenting Jewish tradition within which the seeds of the Gospel were first found"[260] and of being "at the cusp between the twin

---

255. For discussion of stages of composition in the last discourses relating to the situation of 1 John see Segovia, *Love Relationships*, 191–95; Fernando F. Segovia, "The Theology and Provenance of John 15:1–18," *JBL* 101 (1982): 125–26; Fernando F. Segovia, "John 15:18–16:4a: A First Addition to the Original Farewell Discourse?" *CBQ* 45 (1983): 210–30; Painter, "Farewell Discourses"; J. Ph. Kaefer, "Les discours d'adieu en Jean 13:31–17:26," *NovT* 26 (1984): 253–82; cf. also Becker, "Streit der Methoden," 29–31.

256. Lieu, *Epistles*, 179, 211–15.

257. Lieu, *Epistles*, 199–200.

258. See the discussion of method and theories in Becker, "Streit der Methoden," 28–39; and Schnackenburg, *Johannesevangelium*, 4.90–102; and the defence of the traditional position on John in Martin Hengel, *The Johannine Question* (London: SCM; Philadelphia: Trinity, 1989), and my review in *Kings Theological Review* 13 (1990): 50–52.

259. Ashton, *Fourth Gospel*, 53.

260. Ashton, *Fourth Gospel*, 61.

currents of Jewish tradition, one destined to emerge in rabbinic Judaism, the other branching off in a different direction."[261]

Van Belle's review of proposals for a signs source and of source theories concludes that neither the numbering of signs, nor 20:30–31, nor style, nor form, nor ideological argument (e.g., assuming critique of miracles) serves as sufficient evidence singly or cumulatively.[262] He writes:

> The language and style of the Gospel *is* so homogenous and the craftsmanship of the evangelist is *so* creative that it is impossible to distinguish alternative sources or traditions apart from the Synoptics. The homogenous Christological and theological language of the evangelist, his symbolism, and the structure of the text, lead us to see, within the framework of Christology and Soteriology, the word made flesh, that is, not the historical *Jesus*, but the faith of the Johannine community: Jesus is the Messiah, the "Son of God," who was sent to the world for our salvation.[263]

Here I can do little more than indicate what my analysis of the Gospel Christology might indicate. I have noted already the likelihood that 19:35 is a later addition and that christological considerations suggest the same for the final discourses beyond 13:31–14:31. There are other well-known literary grounds to corroborate this, such as the ending of the latter and its easy connection with 18:1. 15:1–18 is also clearly composed differently from the rest of the Gospel and speaks in the present tense about post-Easter phenomena. Such straight anachronisms are surprisingly uncommon in John, even if, as a whole, the Gospel portrait is materially anachronistic in the sense of having the earthly Jesus presented as we believe only the post-Easter community came to know him. Similar straight anachronisms occur mainly in ch. 3, ch. 4 and ch. 6 and these may reflect supplementation. Odd loosely attached pieces, such as those with which I began my study in Part One (3:31–36 and 12:44–50), reflect a process of composition. They reflect the revealer-envoy model in summary form, perhaps from the hand of the evangelist, perhaps from earlier material, but now assume positions of major importance in the transmitted text.

The process of composition also reaches backward to earlier forms and I can only refer to discussion of the various theories. It is beyond the scope

---

261. Ashton, *Fourth Gospel*, 90–91.
262. Van Belle, *Signs Source*, 370–77.
263. Gilbert Van Belle, "The Return of John to Jesus Research," *Louvain Studies* 32 (2007): 47. See also Thatcher, "Remembering Jesus," 167–70.

The Fourth Gospel in the Light of Its Christology

of this chapter to examine the various accounts of the origin of the miracle stories. From the perspective of Christology they all seem to have been through a process of heightening, which would be consistent with their having been treasured and transmitted in the hands of those whose Christology the author wants to supplement as inadequate,[264] but the author owns their massiveness and continues to heighten them through overlaying them with his own Christology. This makes discussion of their possibly existing together as a separate body of material difficult; they could equally have been taken up singly[265] or in smaller groupings, such as the Cana miracles,[266] and at different times.[267] If so, we should then have to explain their common christological orientation as one existing within or in relationship to the author's community, and not as something separate. The former seems also likely because of the degree to which there is indication that their use in relationship to discourses has itself a history and is not first the creation of the evangelist.

Source theories should also take into account the evident modification on the author's part of an existing scheme and the degree to which this was reflected already in his sources, the degree to which Son of Man tradition reflects his redaction of earlier material, and the form in which the older Jesus tradition had reached him, which still keeps the new revealer-envoy model from cutting adrift.

6.2.8 Conclusion

The issues of the history and tradition of the Johannine community, its background and setting, and the history of the formation of the Gospel, continue to be a field of intensive research and have been alluded to here only in summary form. The study of the Christology of the Gospel in the transmitted text underlines the importance of such research and raises central questions relevant for such study. At the same time it shows that the Fourth Gospel represents a stage in a history of developing Johannine Christology in which dominant patterns are emerging and tensions are apparent. The Jesus tradition of John, heavily influenced by its Jewish heritage,

---

264. So Becker, *Johannes*, 119–20.
265. So Barrett, "Symbolism," 76.
266. Cf. Schnelle, *Christologie*, 107, 170–82; and Bjerkelund, *TAUTA*, 65, who argue that the traditional markers of a signs source, 2:11 and 4:54, derive from the author.
267. Cf. Heekerens, *Zeichen-Quelle*, 43, who argues that the Cana signs have been introduced into the Gospel at the stage of the final redaction.

is merging with a stream of cosmic dualistic thought which sees salvation made possible by the coming of a revealer-envoy who tells of a heavenly place of rest. The distinctive adaptation of this revealer-envoy model and the cosmic dualism it presupposes into the pattern of the envoy Son who offers life in relationship with himself and with the Father, dominates the Gospel's Christology.

It is hardly a thorough synthesis, but it illustrates a compromise between this dualism and the Jesus tradition to the extent that the focus is moved from revelation to personal encounter, from place and heavenly station to person and personal relationship with him in the community of faith. This modified revealer-envoy model linked with the Son of Man cluster forms the framework within which the author can reshape narrative and sayings tradition using creative literary skill and so making of the Gospel both a proclamation and a celebration of faith. The focus itself on relationship and the use of Son of Man tradition in particular emphasises the Gospel community of faith and its mission as the place of the mediated presence of the Son. Community and its maintenance emerge even more strongly in the later farewell discourses, where the distinctive traditions of Son of Man and Son have now merged. Perhaps these already reflect concern with the outworkings of an interpretation of the Gospel which diminished the earthly and human community. Beyond the Gospel we see a broken community regrouping in 1 John with a Christology, by contrast, largely modified, focused now not on the model of the revealer-envoy, but more directly on God and the community itself and on Christ as its founder and saviour.

The Gospel and its Christology have continued their formative influence to our own day. In the section which follows I offer reflections on its use and abuse and the opportunities it affords for faith's celebration and communication today.

6.3 Johannine Christology and the Gospel Today

In this final section I wish to offer some reflections on the significance of the Christology of the Gospel for the life of faith in today's world. These include positive as well as negative comments about its influence and use, and hopefully some helpful suggestions about appropriate use of the Gospel in the community of faith in the modern world.

6.3.1 The Gospel and Faith

6.3.1.1 Faith and History

The fourth evangelist demonstrates a way of handling issues of faith and history which, I believe, deserves more serious attention. He remains committed to the fact of the earthly Jesus in history and the event of his ministry as the centre of faith. Yet he does not make faith dependent upon more than some basic details of history. The basic fact is that Jesus confronted his contemporaries with a claim that in him God offers to all people the gift of life in relationship to himself.

The Gospel has Jesus express this claim in a distinctively Johannine way and has him make extensive personal claims to justify his authority. These include claims about his own being and origin in particular, such as we do not find in the other Gospels and which have little claim to historical authenticity. Yet it seems to me that in having Jesus ultimately make the claim of God upon people in the form of offering them a life-giving relationship, the evangelist accurately reproduces the central significance of Jesus for faith. He presented and embodied God's total claim. In him the claim and promise of God's reign presented itself.

By reducing or centering the message of Jesus upon this single claim, the author chooses a point of orientation for Christian proclamation which faithfully represents the essence of the message of Jesus.[268] The centre of Christian faith is thus, for John, a relationship with God the Father through Jesus Christ. The formal character of the Johannine claim about Jesus as the one sent from God, which comes to expression in so many variants in the Gospel, has the effect of throwing all the weight upon theology in the strict sense. And the Johannine theology is of a God who loves and involves himself on behalf of the world which he has created. This, too, is simple.[269] It has a present and a future; but in both the focus is on the relationship and the reward is the person of God himself and his glory.

Paradoxically, by putting so much focus on the person of the Son, the author has simultaneously produced a theology in which Jesus is eclipsed, or, to put it another way, has been absorbed into the being of God, to the extent that relating to the Son and relating to God are equivalent, indeed, effectively the same. Later the church would seek to give expression for this in the doctrine of the Trinity and at the same time to protect its faith from

---

268. So Blank, *Krisis*, 349.
269. So similarly Gnilka, "Christologie," 101.

ISSUES OF JOHANNINE CHRISTOLOGY

the dangers that Jesus is lost sight of as truly a human being and his sonship is not understood as ditheistic. Thus while John's high Christology is at one level a cause of division, as already with its community of origin, its effect is to produce a spirituality which returns God rather than single achievements or transactions to the centre and so has more in common with the spirituality and theology of its community of origin within Judaism, than much else in the emerging Christian movement. To this and implications for Jewish-Christian dialogue we return below.

By centering the Gospel in this way the author makes faith less dependent upon history. The claim and the relationship are timeless in their relevance and so transcend the limits of history. Yet they are not timeless in the sense of not being involved in time and space. For it is in real history and a real person that this claim was brought to expression and the claim meets people today in real time and space. Hegermann is right in arguing that the Fourth Gospel does not present us with a timeless Jesus.[270] Bultmann, too, affirms that the revelation remains historical event, encounter with the preached word, not a matter of content, and argues that to make this possible the historical Jesus had to depart.[271] This must not, however, be played off against a significant informational content, which is basic for the author. Nevertheless, as Blank points out, it is the author's tendency to formulate words of Jesus in the light of the whole event which has the effect of liberating the word of Jesus from the confines of history.[272] And similarly, as Riedl notes, the death and resurrection free the event of revelation from its historical immanence in the event of the earthly Jesus.[273]

6.3.1.2 Theology and Community

The understanding of salvation as primarily life in relationship, rather than a status or achieved security, makes the character of God central. God is loving. God is creator. Accordingly, when the Gospel spells out the meaning of salvation it uses relationship language, such as love and mutual indwelling. Thus Forestell draws attention to salvation in John as a state of dynamic intercommunion, something much richer than forgiveness of sins.[274] And Bultmann and others have drawn attention to the explication of salvation in

270. Hegermann, "Eigentum," 129.
271. Bultmann, *Johannes*, 238–39, 261, 430–32.
272. Blank, *Krisis*, 139–40.
273. Riedl, *Heilswerk*, 21.
274. Forestell, *Word*, 122, 155.

terms which embody basic human need: life, light, water, bread, truth, and way.²⁷⁵ While these function metaphorically, they convey the insight that what is offered by God in Christ is what the human being and the human community need for the sake of their humanity before God, not a promise of distraction or escape from being human.

The centering upon relationship with God extends, consistently, to include relationships among believers and so lays the foundation for a profoundly community-oriented understanding of the life of faith. This aspect comes too short in Bultmann's individualising existentialist interpretation. The evangelist also treats the community dimension of faith very simply, offering virtually no indication of how it should be worked out in reality. Concrete instructions are missing. In their place is the commandment of love. There are hints of sacramental life and real indications of a concern with order which authenticates the Gospel, especially in the figures of Peter and the beloved disciple and in the writing of the Gospel itself with its appeal to be trusted; but as a whole, the community receives only one simple rule of ethics, to love as they have been loved.

6.3.1.3 Faith and Relationship

The Johannine understanding of faith is not one of obedience to laws; nor of adherence to a range of beliefs, except to the central one about who Jesus is and whom he represents. The focus of Johannine salvation is not a place of escape. In this it differs in emphasis from Gnosticism with whose formulations it has otherwise much in common. Its salvation is not an experience, visionary or ecstatic. Nor does it centre upon forgiveness of sins, though it includes this; for this would be to remain at the level of dealing with the effects of unfaith, not its root and, on the Fourth Gospel's understanding, sin is primarily rejection of the gift of the person of Jesus. Nor is Jesus' death as atonement central, though this tradition is present in the Gospel. The same must be said of the motif of casting out the ruler of this world. And even though the Gospel employs stories of astounding miracles, in contrast to most other NT accounts, there is remarkably no hint whatever that the promised Spirit, the Paraclete, would guarantee such miraculous phenomena in the time of the Church.²⁷⁶ The primary focus throughout is upon salvation as relationship in life with a person who loves and goes on loving even in the

---

275. Bultmann, *Theologie*, 418; Käsemann, *Letzter Wille*, 106, 112.
276. So Dietzfelbinger, "Paraklet," 402.

face of rejection and death and the living out of that relationship in Christian community.[277] This informs an understanding of ethics modelled on such love and expressed in mutual love, which must also have had concrete implications such as material support, as the protest of the writer of 1 John indicates (3:16–17).[278]

6.3.1.4 Faith and Symbol

The Johannine Gospel, more than any other, transposes faith into the language of existential symbolism, the language of metaphor, and so recognises that symbol and metaphor are the most effective language of faith's expression and communication. The use of this kind of language belongs together with the other tendencies we have been noting and would not really be possible without them. This is particularly so of the Gospel's treatment of history, its method of simplification and centering, and its focus on relationship. The rich use of symbol and metaphor has won the Gospel a major place in Christian history. It is precisely because it is less historical that it is historically more effective and, arguably, more faithful in portraying the meaning of the event of Jesus. It is a naive misuse of the Gospel to preach it as history,[279] liable to lead to naively docetic Christianity. In its real character the Gospel offers its own distinctive model for communication of faith today and challenges us to move away from strongly cognitive and intellectual formulations of faith to creative forms of self-expression and communication that live in the language of art and symbol, the language of dream and metaphor where the deeper levels of our being find expression. The Gospel invites emulation in the way it celebrates faith in the dramatic retelling of the stories of Jesus and the subtle irony with which it engages its audience in the tensions and the wonder of the Word in the world, including their contemporary one. Yet the balance of the Gospel is to be preserved. It employs metaphor and myth in full awareness that here is also something to be believed; for something took place within real history and takes place within real history.

---

277. So also van der Watt, "Eschatology," 75, 133.
278. On ethics and good news for the poor in John see William Loader, "What Happened to 'Good News for the Poor' in the Johannine Tradition?" in *Glimpses of Jesus through the Johannine Lens*, vol. 3 of *John, Jesus, and History*, ed. P. N. Anderson, F. Just, and T. Thatcher, ECL 18 (Atlanta: SBL, 2016), 469–80.
279. So rightly Dunn, "John," 314.

6.3.2 Faith and Danger

6.3.2.1 "In my Father's house"

The Fourth Gospel also has its dangers. While at its base is a theology of God as involved and loving, the future dimension of faith's hope, God's presence in its most intimate sense, is in heaven above and not in this world. Traditional eschatology is no longer the centre of faith, because faith's ultimate goal is the divine presence in heaven. This easily becomes: faith's ultimate goal is heaven, a place of escape from this world. The words "In my Father's house are many dwelling places" (14:2) are among the best known of the Gospel and have frequently projected themselves to the centre of popular Christianity. The Gospel does not put the focus here. Its dualism of "above" and "below" is subordinate to faith in the person, rather than the place, of God. One can cease to be "from below" through responding to the challenge of God's offer in the Son. To be "from above" is then primarily a way of describing a relationship with God, not a relationship with a place, even though the author still retains the spatial and temporal distinction between life now on earth and then in heaven. But when the emphasis is reversed, so that instead of God, the issues of space and time become central, something happens to people's attitude to the world. The world becomes merely a staging post and at worst a creation of evil powers.

6.3.2.2 Unearthed Eschatology?

This danger is also an indirect result of the replacement of traditional apocalyptic eschatology. Where salvation includes submission in faith to the God who promises to establish his reign of justice and peace, raise people from the dead, and transform heaven and earth, and where this is seen as an event already breaking into the present, there remains a lively concern with what is to be, and is being, transformed: heaven and earth, body and spirit, justice and peace now. The danger of reducing all of this to the simplicity of a relationship with its ultimate goal as God's heavenly presence is loss of these traditional perspectives. This lays open the possibility that the world will be devalued in itself. There is also the danger that Jesus himself is seen as not really a human being and the further consequence that concern with what belongs to human flesh, from human sexuality to human welfare and social justice in the widest sense, comes to be seen as irrelevant (cf. 1 John 3:17). The author's dramatic technique contributes further to this danger, since it often lifts Jesus above normal humanity and human interaction. The image of an unreal humanity in the dramatic portrayal of Jesus easily spawns unreal expectations of humanity, such that Christians who follow their master should always be at peace, never troubled, never depressed.

6.3.2.3 Political Awareness?

David Rensberger's observations about underlying political attitudes in the passion narrative which show Christ's kingship pitted against Jewish authority and against Roman authority are pertinent,[280] but nowhere are these political attitudes in direct focus and they remain incidental and at the level of general stance.[281] Meeks's observations about the self-consciously withdrawn character of the community and its Christology more accurately portray the tone of the Gospel,[282] though, it seems to me, mission to the world is still part of the community's self-understanding more than Meeks allows. Carter offers the most comprehensive discussion of ways in which John reflects the tensions and pressures of the imperial context.[283] Here it is important to distinguish between recognising phenomena as typical of responses to such situations and awareness on the part of authors that these responses are indeed directly addressing the political. Frequently this is not the case, but clearly both in relation to Jewish leaders and in relation to Pilate the issue is far from peripheral. The Gospel proffers an alternative and the implications are far reaching with regard also to the political. Its focus is however not one particular form of darkness, but the light that shines and challenges all.

My concern is not to say that the Fourth Gospel must lead to such conclusions, but that it can. For it is a Gospel with loose ends. It does not present us with a rounded, systematically consistent, picture of Jesus. It reflects Christology in a state of flux. The particular methods employed in its production, especially centering, simplifying, and literary techniques such as dramatic irony, mean that it can easily be misread and has been.

---

280. David Rensberger, "The Politics of John: The Trial of Jesus in the Fourth Gospel," *JBL* 103 (1984): 411.

281. See the critical assessment in Labahn, "Heiland der Welt," 163–68.

282. Meeks, "Man from Heaven."

283. Carter, *John and Empire*.

6.3.2.4 Dualism or Theology?

The dualism which seeks escape from this world can interpret the relationship-centred salvation entirely in its own terms as "making right connections" for eternal security. But relationship-oriented faith includes relationship with God, with Christ, and with fellow believers. The key to the quality of that life in relationship is the understanding of God. Where God is thought of as promising an alternative to life in the world, then the community of faith will understand itself as community constituted by its not belonging to the world. Brotherly love becomes mutual support for survival and defence. The formal character of relationship-oriented faith is thus vulnerable at the point of its theological premise, in the strict sense. This is why Lattke, following Käsemann, must explain away the usual sense of John 3:16, for their theories of the Johannine community see it as just such a community as we have described,[284] hardly one whose God loves the world as 3:16 might suggest. Where a community of faith is a self-reproducing, self-supporting, community, bent on escape from the world, its contacts with non-believers will be limited to the invitation to them to join them in the flight. The Fourth Gospel has been, and is frequently, made to serve such a pattern of religion. Meeks notes that the combination of antiworldly sectarian self-understanding with the Logos Sophia myth sets the stage for a Valentinian kind of Gnosticism.[285] This is all the more possible because the Gospel has no direct teaching about ethics outside of the community of faith. Traditional values preserved in apocalyptic eschatology, such as peace among the nations, justice for the poor and oppressed, redemption and transformation of the creation, are largely absent.

6.3.2.5 John 3:16—Rescuing the World's Inhabitants?

Does, therefore, John 3:16 mean anything more than an indication of God's initiative to help people escape the world? Is mission, as Appold suggests, not unlike the gnostic preoccupation with gathering people out of the world?[286] Or do mission and fruit-bearing mean being sent to share the gift of life now

---

284. Lattke, *Einheit*, 2, 50–51, 162–169, 188; Käsemann, *Letzter Wille*, 124–25, 139. See the criticism in Miranda, *Sendung*, 22–23; Thyen, "Brüder," 537; Thyen, "Liebe," 467–68; Segovia, *Love Relationships*, 169; Klaiber, "Interpretation," 319–20; Schnelle, *Christologie*, 210–11.

285. Meeks, "Man from Heaven," 165.

286. Appold, *Oneness*, 266, 278, 288.

in the world, as Thüsing argues?[287] Much depends on the weight given to elements which do not share centre stage whether we see in the Gospel an early form of gnostic faith or one more rooted in traditional Christianity. These elements include the statement about the creation of all things in the prologue, the extent of Jesus' real humanity, and the degree to which the gift of salvific life is related not only to the heavenly world, but, through the Logos and through God as creator, to creation itself. In my view these are sufficiently present as to indicate that the dualism has not gone so far as to deny inherent value to human life on earth and to Jesus' humanity.

As far as creation is concerned, I would agree with Schottroff that it is not denied by the author, though it does not come into his concerns.[288] But for the reasons set out above, I dispute her conclusion that the Gospel is already gnostic in its dualism.[289] The matter is, however, by no means straightforward and the story which is at the centre of the author's Christology, without its props, would grace a gnostic stage without too much modification, as history has shown. Already the first epistle of John is understood by many as attacking a form of Johannine Christianity which displays in reality many of the dangers we have noted. The author attacks a lack of concern for temporal needs, an apparent denial of the human Jesus, and a spiritual perfectionism which results from an unrealistic view of ethics and spirituality.

6.3.2.6 The Centrality of Love

The focus in the last discourses, in particular, is not on recruiting disciples who shall go on a numbers drive to fill heavenly places, but on a quality of life lived already on earth in community. This is where the author's focus on person and personal relationship rather than place transcends dualistic concerns. While the notion of enabling grace, such as we find in Paul, is not so elaborated in John, there can be little doubt that the central story of Johannine Christology is about an initiative of love in which through the Son, God also offers life and love, calls people into relationship with himself, and sends them to be bearers of this life and love in the world.[290] Despite its formal structure it is not a story about revelation of special gnosis, nor primarily a story about a promised future time or place. The dynamic quality

---

287. Thüsing, *Erhöhung*, 138-40.
288. Schottroff, *Glaubende*, 233.
289. Against Schottroff, *Glaubende*, 236-41.
290. See above all the monograph of Moloney, *Love*.

of this life and love is so central that it strongly relativises any underlying dualism of time and place.

6.3.2.7 Antisemitism?

A further matter of concern has been the Gospel's portrait of the Jews, which has left it open to be used as a vehicle of antisemitism. Ashton[291] argues convincingly against the view that "Jews" symbolise the world, or that Judeans are meant (because Josephus reflects its use also for Judeans dispersed throughout his world [*A.J.* 12.48]), or only Jewish leaders are meant, making the case that the term refers primarily to those leading Judaism after 70 CE.[292] It is one thing to grapple with the wonder of divine grace and seek an explanation in the direction of predestination of the astonishing blindness of people to its light. It is another when this is turned as a weapon to defame opponents and bolster one's self-identity. Many find this happening in the author's presentation of Jesus' confrontation of the Jews in John 8,[293] and the same kind of confrontation is undertaken in 1 John against fellow believers, those who, the author tells us, "have gone out from among us" (2:19).

It is, of course, an error to take "Jews" as a reference to all Jews by race or religion and find John to be antisemitic in that sense. The Johannine com-

---

291. Ashton, *Fourth Gospel*, 60–78.

292. See also Reimund Bieringer, "'Ihr habt weder seine Stimme gehort noch seine Gestalt je gesehen' (Joh 5,37): Antijudaismus und johanneische Christologie," in *Studies in the Gospel of John and Its Christology: Festschrift Gilbert Van Belle*, ed. J. Verheyden, G. van Oyen, M. Labahn, and R. Bieringer, BETL 265 (Leuven: Peeters, 2014), 165–88; D. François Tolmie, "The Ἰουδαῖοι in the Fourth Gospel: A Narratological Perspective," in *Theology and Christology in the Fourth Gospel: Essays by the Members of the SNTS Johannine Writings Seminar*, ed. G. Van Belle, J. G. van der Watt, and P. Maritz, BETL 184 (Leuven: Peeters, 2005) 377–97; Cornelis Bennema, "The Identity and Composition of οἱ Ἰουδαῖοι in the Gospel of John," *TynBull* 60 (2009): 239–63; and the following contributions in the volume *Antijudaism and the Fourth Gospel*, ed. R. Bieringer, D. Pollefet, and F. Vandecasteele-Vanneuville (Louisville: Westminster John Knox, 2001): Culpepper, "Anti-Judaism," 61–82; Henk Jan de Jonge, "'The Jews' in the Gospel of John," 121–40; Raymond F. Collins, "Speaking of the Jews: 'Jews' in the Discourse Material of the Fourth Gospel," 158–75; Martinus C. de Boer, "The Depiction of 'the Jews' in John's Gospel: Matters of Behavior and Identity," 141–57; Adele Reinhartz, "'Jews' and Jews in the Fourth Gospel," 213–30; Urban C. von Wahlde, "'You Are of Your Father the Devil' in Its Context: Stereotyped Polemic in Jn 8:38–47," 418–44.

293. Ashton, *John*, 142, writes that "nowhere else in the Gospels is the right to be children of Abraham denied as in 8:37–44," though one should not overlook the Q tradition of John the Baptist's challenge to those claiming to be Abraham's children (Matt 3:9; Luke 3:8). See also Theobald, "Abraham," 179, 182.

munity itself probably included a large number of Jews and the Johannine Christ declares that salvation is of the Jews (4:22).[294] Much of the time the author attacks the leaders of the Jewish people.[295] As Thatcher observes, the term "the Jews"

> is inherently ambiguous, since almost every character in the Fourth Gospel, including Jesus, is Jewish by race and religion. In some instances it seems that John is thinking of "the Jews" as the Jewish religious leaders who oppose Jesus (John 5:10; 9:22); yet on other occasions it appears that a "Jew" is any Jewish person who does not accept Jesus' claims about himself (6:41–42; 8:48–59; 10:24–39). Whatever their specific identity, "the Jews," like "the world," are generally hostile to Jesus and the disciples, a fact that comes with little surprise since they are "children of the devil" (8:44–45).[296]

The author's overall methodology of simplification and dramatic enrichment has also produced a radically simplified and stereotyped image of the Jews whom Jesus confronted, and failure to perceive the author's method and therefore the nature of the Gospel leads, here, too, to dangerous distortion. As Culpepper observes:

> The Christology of the Fourth Gospel is thoroughly Jewish. It is also disconcertingly anti-Jewish . . . the more Jewish the Christology, the more it is apt to be anti-Jewish. Claims of fulfilment easily mutate into claims of replacement, that is, apart from its fulfilment in Jesus, Judaism is no longer valid.[297]

6.3.3 Faith's Witness in Faith's Community

The NT witness reaches the heights in the Johannine portrait of Jesus the Son, who has come as the sent one from the Father to bear his word of life to all. The simplicity and power of the Johannine portrait, its daring strokes and colours, make it a centrepiece and icon of faith. But the artist's achievement is at the expense of imprecision and ambiguity. The Fourth Gospel needs the

---

294. Johnson, "Salvation," 83–99.
295. Ashton, *Fourth Gospel*, 78.
296. Thatcher, "Remembering Jesus," 176.
297. Culpepper, "Anti-Judaism," 72.

Epistles. It also needs the rest of the NT. It is primarily a document of faith's celebration, a drama enriching the community's self-understanding, and must be handled as such. Because it is so powerfully faith's self-expression, it is also powerfully faith's witness. It is a dangerous Gospel when read without this understanding. But properly understood, it succeeds more than any other NT writing in identifying the heart of Christian faith, as life in relationship with the Son and the Father in the communion of love, love sent out into the world.

Conclusion

The concern of this study has been to approach the issues of Johannine Christology by first analysing its central structure. This first step included noting christological structures in select passages, tracing the elements of these structures and collating their occurrence in the Gospel, identifying christological summaries in the Gospel, and reviewing the Gospel as a whole in the search for significant structures. The central structure of Johannine Christology, which emerged from these findings, may be expressed as follows:

> The Father
> sends and authorises the Son,
> who knows the Father,
> comes from the Father, makes the Father known,
> brings light and life and truth,
> completes his Father's work,
> returns to the Father,
> exalted, glorified, ascended,
> sends the disciples
> and sends the Spirit
> to enable greater understanding,
> to equip for mission,
> and to build up the community of faith.

On the basis of this analysis we turned to an examination of the major issues which have emerged in Johannine research and which were identified in the Introduction. We also took into account questions which had been raised during the investigation of the structure of the Christology in Part One.

Conclusion

We began with a consideration of statements related to the death of Jesus and his return to the Father. We noted that the pattern of the Son's coming and return need, in itself, give no more significance to the death of Jesus than to see it as the point of exit. We saw, however, that it assumes a greater significance for the author. It represents the fulfilment of the Son's mission. We then considered whether this means that the author saw that fulfilment in terms of an act of vicarious or sacrificial atonement. We found this not to be so. The author uses traditions of vicarious atonement in the Gospel, but mostly in an incidental manner and never as a major theme. Finishing the Father's work means faithfully fulfilling to the end the task of making the Father known and of presenting the world with his offer of light and life. Accordingly, the cross is the point at which the issues of this claim come to a head: the world passes judgment on the Son. It is also the moment of supreme revelation. For in it the world and its ruler judged, sin is revealed and the Son vindicated.

In the context of discussing Jesus' death we considered also the motifs of exaltation and glorification. We saw that they are best understood in the traditional sense of exaltation of the Son to the presence of God and to divine glory. The Pauline paradox of the cross as both suffering and glory is not found in John. Nor is the dual meaning of ὑψόω, to lift up and to exalt, an indication that the cross itself is being interpreted in this way, namely, as the Son's exaltation. The Johannine paradox does employ the dual meaning of ὑψόω, but it does so by portraying the path to exaltation as the way of the cross. The world sees only the lifting up on the cross; faith sees exaltation through the event of the cross to the divine presence.

We found this understanding of Jesus' return to the Father as exaltation to glory to be also the most probable meaning of the heavenly vision promised believers in Jesus' words to Nathanael in 1:51. We noted also the association of exaltation with the motif of Jesus' ascent (and descent) and the regular association of these motifs with the title Son of Man. We identified, thus, a "Son of Man cluster" of motifs which include: the title Son of Man; exaltation; glorification; ascension (and descent); "the hour," "the time," "now"; judgment; and the promise of a "greater" event to come. Son of Man, while used sometimes of Jesus' earthly ministry, seems primarily associated in John with motifs which describe the climax of Jesus' ministry, in particular his exaltation and its implications.

We then considered the resurrection tradition in the Gospel and saw how the motif of the Son's coming and return had not produced, as it might have, a Christology according to which Jesus ascended directly from the cross; rather, traditions of return and resurrection merge, if sometimes awk-

CONCLUSION

wardly. As evidenced in Jesus' words to Mary, a pattern is preserved of death, resurrection on the third day, ascent to the glory of the Father, appearances of the exalted glorified risen one, and the giving of the Spirit—the Johannine Pentecost.

The event, so described, is the "greater" event to which the Son points forward during his ministry, often using the motifs of the Son of Man cluster. It is the "greater" heavenly vision of the Son of Man served by angels in 1:51, which is greater than the confession of Jesus as Son of God. It is the "heavenly things" of 3:12, explicated in 3:13-15 as the Son of Man's ascent and exaltation, greater than the "earthly things" Jesus has been speaking of in 3:1-11, the announcement of new birth. It is the Son of Man ascending where he was before (6:62), greater than his descending as bread from heaven. It is the basis for "greater works" by the disciples (14:12), greater than the works of the Son, because he goes to the Father.

We saw that the promise of the "greater" event focusses not on the addition of a greater gift of life than was present in Jesus' ministry, nor on the realisation of what some see as only a proleptic offer of life during Jesus' ministry, nor on the fruits of an atonement not yet complete. Rather it interprets Jesus' return to the Father and the sending of the Spirit as the basis for greater availability, abundance and understanding of that gift of life, present in the person of the Son. The notion of greater availability and abundance includes reference to mission and to the presence of the Son and the Father in the believers through the Spirit. Greater understanding includes the work of the Paraclete which calls to remembrance the words and work of Jesus, interprets them in the light of Scripture, mediates the words of the exalted Lord to the community, and leads the disciples into all truth concerning who Jesus is and the meaning of his death and return to the Father. Ultimately the "greater" event is what constitutes the community of faith as the place of the presence of the light and life made manifest in the incarnation of the Son. We also saw that the path of Jesus through suffering set a pattern for the community's own self-understanding. Theirs, too, is the promise to follow that path and find themselves also where he is and share in his heavenly glory.

We turned then to the salvation event itself, the Son's making the Father known, and saw that the author uses, but significantly modifies, the revealer-envoy model. The Son offers not information or revelation, but relationship. He presents himself as the light and life and invites the response of faith. This is the primary meaning of the "I am" sayings, with and without predicate. The "I am" of Isa 43 may stand as analogy, but "I am" is not, itself, a pronunciation of the divine name, as often supposed. In the dialogues, the Son repeatedly asserts that "he is the one" who has come from the Father to make him known. His miracles, the signs, are to be understood as achievements indicative of his divine glory as Son of God sent from above, and true faith sees them as such. They also function as symbols of the life he brings.

The modification of the revealer-envoy model to one of encounter and of the offer of life in relationship also focusses attention away from salvation as place and so also modifies the significance of the dualistic framework in which it is expressed. Faith still looks to a future presence with the Son in heaven, but the relationship and the person are the centre, not time and place. Similarly salvation is not primarily contractual achievement through atonement, victory over powers, or imparting ecstatic experience, but the offer of life in a person. Christology is the centre of soteriology and also of eschatology.

The salvation event, considered as the presence of the Son, raises questions about who the Son is. In particular, we explored whether the author also modified the revealer-envoy model in relationship to statements about the Son's pre-existence in a way that dissolved them. We found the evidence for this was not strong. The noted discrepancy between the common statements about the Son's hearing and seeing in pre-existence what he says and does on earth and 5:19–20, which speaks of a present seeing and hearing on earth, dissolves when it is realised that the language of seeing and hearing belongs to the envoy-messenger motif which the author has modified. John 5:19–20 use apprenticeship imagery; the other statements use messenger imagery. Both are employed for the single purpose of saying that the Son represents the Father and does his work.

We found pre-existence to be important in the author's Christology, not to explain how the Son received information and revelation, as a literal understanding of the revealer-envoy would suggest, but for the Son's authorisation, origin, and ultimately, his being. We considered the question of the Son's being, both in relationship to the extraordinary statements of the prologue that he is θεός and in relation to the way in which his being is asserted and defended in the dialogues. We saw a consistent defense against the charge of ditheism by appeal to the way the Son acted in complete obedience and subordination to the Father's will. Claims to be one or equal with the Father were always explained in these terms. On the other hand, we also saw that this went far beyond a functional Christology which might see in Jesus a human being like any other, but perfectly in harmony with God. For the author presupposes an ontology which sets the Son apart from all mortals. It is his distinctive being, his distinctive origin, which enables him to come as the sent one and to be the light and life of God on earth.

The author never surrenders monotheism, and accusations in this direction are treated almost playfully as a bad joke and exploited dramatically by the author. Yet the precise character of the Son's being θεός is not defined. Its context in Wisdom Logos tradition suggests the analogy with these and other Jewish figures who may bear the title without surrender of monotheism, but such figures range from personifications to representative angels and kings. None brings together the two poles of reality present in Johannine Christology: a real human being and an eternally existent heavenly Son. We rejected attempts to force a compromise in the Johannine material by, for instance, interpreting the pre-existent logos as anhypostatic. Johannine Christology marks out the ground for later controversy and construction, but also in some sense sets the rules by affirming together: monotheism, the Son as distinct, yet θεός, and the Son as Jesus of Nazareth.

Our discussion of the Son as Jesus of Nazareth took into consideration the battles fought over "The Word became flesh" and its meaning and over the alleged naive docetism of the Gospel. We found strong indications that the author would have affirmed Jesus' real humanity, including his real suffering and death. On the other hand, we also had to acknowledge that the Jesus of John's Gospel is portrayed in ways which would normally call any claim to real humanity into question. This need not have been the case with the massive miracles, given the analogies of possessed human beings working wonders, but, because this is not the Johannine model and because the author constantly presents Jesus with both superhuman power and superhuman knowledge of his past and future, even in first-century terms, John's Jesus would have been easily read as a mere appearance of a man. Both streams of thought are present: Jesus, remembered as a real human being, and Jesus, the eternally existent Son.

The Johannine Gospel also, therefore, sets the rules, as it were, here for subsequent discussion: it affirms Jesus as Son and affirms his real humanity. We found it also useful to make a clear distinction between what the author probably intended in his portrayal and what was the result. Explanations that the post-Easter perspective of faith influenced the portrayal help us with the former, not with the latter. We cannot help but see a much-modified humanity in the portrait. But our discussion argued that in intention the author would not have denied Jesus' real humanity. The situation is further complicated by clear evidence of deliberate literary technique on the part of the author, with which he must have been aware he was modifying the portrait in ways that were unhistorical, even if not "un-human."

This latter observation also became important for understanding the author's approach to history in the Gospel and for understanding the nature of the Gospel itself. We noted the author's regular indications that Easter made a difference to the disciples' understanding of Jesus. The "greater" event motif highlights this. The author seems aware of standing within a living tradition inspired by the work of the Paraclete who is leading him and his community into all truth concerning Jesus, past and present. But especially the self-conscious literary techniques demanded that we saw the Gospel not as history, but as a communication within a knowing community which has enough inside information to appreciate the irony and other devices being used.

The centrality of the Son's coming, his making the Father known, offering light and life and truth, makes the earthly Jesus of history of paramount importance: hence the writing of a Gospel. The freedom to reshape the tradition for the community's celebration and to edify its faith by creating a dramatic, almost stereotypical presentation of Jesus and his conversation partners, scene after scene, means that the author's commitment to history was limited. We noted that the same simplifying and centering tendency evident in the author's understanding of the salvation event correspondingly affects his interest in history. Not the sheer fact of Jesus in history is enough. It is important that the story of his encounters be told and that of his death and resurrection; but the contours suffice. Details can vary with the artist's brush. The Johannine Gospel is an icon of faith's celebration. Everywhere one looks, one sees a reflection of the whole. And what one sees is nothing less, the author would contend, than the light and life of the Son which shone among the disciples.

The analysis of the structure of the Christology and its major issues also raises questions about the background of that Christology and its community. This study focussed deliberately on the transmitted text of the Gospel as it has been received. This was in part my not wanting to have the reader wade through a jungle of "ifs" and "buts." It was also on methodological grounds: start first with the received text; then go beyond it. I am aware that this is not the only option. We undertake research in constant interplay between text and tradition. Nevertheless my aim in beginning this way was also to allow questions to arise from the analysis of the Christology which might be pertinent to the issues of Johannine history, tradition, and community.

We observed there that significant streams of christological thought merge in the Gospel, but that at many points we can still see indications of where they have come from and sometimes see signs of turbulence where they mix. We noted first the dominance of the revealer-envoy model and the way the author uses it to integrate a wide range of traditions. It is the overlay which covers the author's tradition, from the announcements of John the Baptist to the passion narrative. Prophetic, messianic, miracle-focused

Christology all served its primary message to declare Jesus the Son sent from the Father. Miracles in particular are not denied, but seem so totally transcended, both in the portrait of Jesus and in the description of the work of the Paraclete, that all the indications point to a complete absence of the charismatic miraculous in the Johannine church. It is also the context into which the author adapts wisdom Christology. Even the sending of the Spirit and of the disciples is portrayed after the envoy pattern. We also saw the effect of this dominance on the author's understanding of salvation, eschatology and pneumatology, particularly in the modified form of the model which the author makes the centrepiece of his Christology.

We noticed, too, the role of the Son of Man cluster in bridging the hermeneutical distance between the ministry of Jesus and the time of the evangelist, and above all, in underlining the importance of the community as the place of the presence of Jesus after Easter. We saw that the Son of Man traditions had already been expanded to include first exaltation and then also pre-existence. It was noteworthy that the Son of Man version of pre-existence and post-existence employed the distinctive descent–ascent language. This probably indicated a development having taken place before the Gospel, since in the Gospel coming and returning is usually associated with the title Son, and with a different set of verbs of movement.

The merging of the Son of Man cluster and the central story of the coming of Jesus as the revealer-envoy still shows that both have an independent origin. This is particularly indicated by the fact that the author, while using the revealer-envoy model with its dualistic cosmology, must significantly adapt it. Its independent existence seems also to be indicated by the way in which the author uses the distinctive Son of Man cluster to expand it and by the tensions which that produces in the understanding of such motifs as glory, judgment, and life. Altogether it is an extraordinary feature of John's Gospel that it has at its centre a model which requires the death of Jesus to mean nothing more than his exit and his life on earth to be nothing other than an appearance; yet we find in the same Gospel the persistence of a wide range of traditions including many vital to the author, like those attesting Jesus' humanity, death, and resurrection—beside others, somewhat incidental, like vicarious atonement. The author obviously stands well rooted in the Jesus tradition and daringly adapts new material in the light of it.

We considered briefly indications of Jewish influence, reflections of a history of bitter conflict with the synagogue, and suggestions of Samaritan or Baptist traditions. We noted the significance of miracle-based messianic Christianity, the relations with the wider church, the possibility of gnostic dualism as a background for the revealer-envoy model and the suggestions of antidocetic emphasis in the Gospel. In particular we noted the author's adaptation of wisdom mythology to identify Jesus as Logos and Wisdom and to dissociate this claim from Torah. Affirming Torah as God's gift through Moses, the author transfers images traditionally associated with Torah to Jesus, whom he depicts as alone the bread, water, life, and light. He alone is the Logos. He alone is the source of salvation but also of ethics, no longer Torah. This reflects both the strongly Jewish background of the author and his community and what must have been severe turbulence as claims about Jesus escalated beyond simple messiahship and interpretation of the Law to become irreconcilable conflict and separation. Part of coming to terms with the pain and dissonance that would have been engendered is reflected now paradoxically in the employment of the OT and the Law as a repository for justifying the split as fulfilling divine intent and portraying the continuing synagogue in harshly negative terms, which lent themselves beyond this context to anti-semitism.

In the course of time the diverse and structurally divergent tendencies latent in the Gospel would inevitably lead to new resolutions among its users, and some would be effected where the Jesus tradition was not so strong as it appears to be for the author. The Christology of the Gospel could be resolved in the direction of a strongly exalted Christology like that at Corinth, if not like that of later docetism, and we recognised the probability, both that something like this will have occurred by the time of 1 John, and that response to it may already have led to expansion of the Gospel through the later discourses and the antidocetic footnote of 19:35. In 1 John itself we see a reassertion of themes like vicarious atonement and future eschatology as reflecting an attempt to steer a community back into the mainstream and a resultant marginalising of the revealer-envoy model.

Finally we turned to the understanding and use of the Gospel today, noting the strength of its simplifying, centring approach to Christology for understanding history and faith. We also noted the dangers of reading (let alone preaching) it without some awareness of its special character, and discussed the negative implications of its cosmic dualism and person-centred salvation which left out of account the vision of a transformed world of justice and peace, present in Jesus' message of the kingdom. Nevertheless we saw in the Gospel a challenge and a pattern for faith's celebration, a vehicle to enrich and stimulate faith, a unique witness which is to be treasured and read within the context of the canonical tradition and in the continuing community of faith. For this is the place of the presence of Jesus, according to its thought, and here its perspectives can be appreciated, its dangers counterbalanced, and its rootedness in Jesus tradition upheld.

CONCLUSION

It is particularly instructive to compare John's soteriology with that of others. For Mark, John the Baptist offers universal forgiveness of sins through repentance (1:4). Thus Jesus offers something more than that. He will baptise with the Holy Spirit (1:8), expounded as a task of liberating people from the powers which oppress them through exorcisms, healings and teaching, as well as through declaring God's forgiveness (2:9-10). This is signalled already by the immediate confrontation with Satan (1:12-13). One inherits eternal life by keeping the commandments as expounded and interpreted by Jesus, which in Mark assumes primarily the Decalogue (10:17-22), whereas other commandments are either relegated to secondary importance (2:1-3:6) or dispensed with, indeed, as not having made sense (7:1-23). For, it argues, what enters from outside cannot make one unclean (7:15-19). At the same time Mark has Jesus identify his servant role as giving his life as a ransom for many (10:45) and this finds its echo in the vicarious understanding of his death in the last supper tradition (14:24).

Luke retains the latter tradition (22:15-20), but puts the focus on Jesus as bringing good news for the poor, especially Israel in its need (4:16-20; 6:20-21; 7:22-23), on Jesus as in future fulfilling the cry of the faithful for Israel's liberation and restoration (1:30-33, 47-55, 68-79; 2:25, 38; Acts 1:6-7; 3:19-21) and on his being judge of all (Acts 17:30-31). Acts tells how this hope now includes Gentiles who can be incorporated into Israel, and proclaims that future judgment will be based on response to Israel's Messiah who was rejected but then vindicated, as the summary speeches in Acts emphasise. Like Mark, Luke understands that one inherits eternal life by keeping the commandments (10:25-37; 18:18-23) and so, following Jesus, but for him that means, as in Q, every stroke (16:17), with just a few divinely mandated exceptions. Omitting Mark 7's dismissal of purity and clean-unclean laws altogether, in Acts he narrates how circumcision of Gentiles was waived (Acts 10-15).

Matthew similarly preserves the Q emphasis on keeping every stroke of the Law (5:17-18), while clearly distinguishing greater and lesser commandments (5:19), and hails complete obedience as the way of salvation/eternal life (19:16-22; 7:24-27; 5:20). Matthew accordingly depicts Jesus as expounding Torah, indeed as exercising the role of Wisdom itself (23:34, 37-39; cf. Luke 11:49). He depicts him also as the judge to come, the one announced by John the Baptist. In his role as judge to come his good news is in part to expound the basis of judgment in advance (3:11-12; 12:15-21; 25:31-46). On the other hand, Matt 1:21 announces that Jesus will save his people from their sins. Read atomistically without the broader understanding noted above, this verse has led many to suppose that for Matthew the good news is that Jesus

Conclusion

came to die for people's sins, indeed, in much the same way as John 1:29 has functioned for many in interpreting John. They have argued therefore that salvation is achieved not through keeping Torah, but through Jesus' death on the cross. Supporting this view is the claim that Matthew adds "for the forgiveness of sins" to Jesus' words over the cup in the last supper narrative (26:28) and removes it from the description of John the Baptist's baptism (cf. Mark 1:4). There can be no doubt that this reflects an understanding of Jesus' death as vicarious.

Matthean scholarship therefore faces a dilemma: is salvation achieved only through Jesus' death on the cross or is it based on keeping Torah as expounded by Jesus? Too often resolutions to the dilemma seek to deny either one aspect or the other. Clearly elements of both are present. Jesus' death is vicarious and in his ministry he does offer the way to life as through keeping Torah. In addition, despite what many redactional critics often assumed, while not taking up Mark's formulation of John's baptism as one of repentance "for the forgiveness of sins" (Mark 1:4), Matthew must still have understood John's baptism as effective in relation to forgiving sins. First-century hearers would not have assumed that people confessed their sins (Matt 3:6) on the assumption that some months or years later they would be able to be forgiven through Jesus' death. Furthermore, already in Jesus' ministry we hear of him declaring forgiveness of sins (Matt 9:2–8) and teaching a prayer for forgiveness (Matt 6:12) with a corollary about forgiving others (Matt 6:14–15). The division among scholars over Matthean soteriology is similar to the divide among Johannine scholars over Johannine soteriology.

How was it possible for Matthew to speak of Jesus' death as for sins and yet already speak of God's forgiving sins before that? The answer may well lie in a better understanding of the Jewish context to which both these writings belonged. For Jews of the time similarly held together diverse notions in relation to forgiveness of sins. God forgives sins in answer to prayer and in response to cultic acts, but also as the result of the suffering of the righteous (Isa 53) and martyrs, and even through John's baptism which, though controversial, was never depicted or assailed as contrary to Torah. Thus Jews of the time could hold together what our intellectual concerns with tidiness might want to depict as contradictions or mutually exclusive. The reason why they could do so was probably in part because forgiveness of sins, while important, was not centre stage in their spirituality. What was central was relationship with the God of grace expressed through keeping the commandments. Matthew was, therefore, in that sense very Jewish, as one should expect, given its strongly Jewish context. For Matthew, too, therefore, the means of God's forgiveness could be variously expressed, including both as a fruit of

CONCLUSION

Jesus' death and as offered to the penitent by John the Baptist and by Jesus during his ministry. These all cohered within a broader context or a more fundamental concern, namely the ongoing relationship with God expressed through keeping God's commandments, now interpreted appropriately by Jesus. Indeed many Jews would have affirmed Jesus' particular emphasis on how that relationship of obedience should be expressed and still do. The point of division between Matthew and his Jewish contemporaries lay beyond this in the absolute claims made about Jesus as a person.

In these respects Matthew and John, also very Jewish, are similar, while standing at opposite ends of the spectrum in relation to how they view Torah. For John's Jesus does not come as spokesperson for Torah, like Matthew's, but as the one to whom Torah pointed when, as John understands it, it foreshadowed its own demise through a greater gift (1:16–18). Thus while the core ethical values of the Decalogue are assumed in John, eternal life is depicted as coming not through keeping the commandments, but through responding to the offer of a relationship with God through Jesus and later mediated through the Paraclete, keeping his new commandment of love, and becoming an active part of his community of mission and love. The good news in John is primarily not a proclamation, but the person of the Son and the relationship he offers. That is the logic of the prologue, but also of the Gospel as a whole and so much of its imagery. He is light and life and truth. That relationship assumed also forgiveness of sins, but that is a theme rarely addressed in the Gospel. It matters, but is not as central as the relationship itself, and in that sense mirrors perspectives typical of Judaism of the time and paralleled in Matthew.

Within this understanding it was not seen as a problem to attribute vicarious benefit to Jesus' death in relation to sins and at the same time to speak of life offered already in encounter with the Son in his ministry, which also included forgiveness of sins. The author, informed by what was typical of Jewish spirituality could embrace both: life through response to God's grace, in John expressed in Jesus rather than Torah, and belief in the benefits of forgiveness through Jesus' death. For the evangelist, eternal life in relationship with God was not the fruit of transaction, but the gift of a person. In a very real sense John's soteriology is grounded in its Christology. It is based on the coming and departure of the Son, the presence of life, and then its mediation through the Paraclete. This can be recognised and affirmed, however, without our needing to dismiss or explain away the significance of Jesus' death, just as, conversely, reference to Jesus' vicarious death can be recognised and affirmed without our needing to dismiss any possibility of eternal life before it. Both belong, but the major focus, as in

Jewish spirituality, is on the relationship, not on the aspect of forgiveness of sins.

Person, the person of Jesus, is important, especially because John's Jesus has usurped the role of Torah. But beside person, process is also important. Jesus was not just an epiphany of God in the flesh. In addition, there is, in the depiction of Jesus' earthly ministry, a constant focus on its climax. In part, that is the climax of his life lived for his own, all the way to his death. He sustained this commitment to the end when he declared, "It is finished" (19:30). In that sense he lived and died for his own. But there is clearly more to it than that, mostly expressed in terms of the complex total event, which included not only his death, but also his exaltation, glorification, return to the Father, and giving of the Spirit. That event would achieve something greater, as John has Jesus emphasise. For now, equipped with the Spirit, the disciples will take the offer of life to the world (14:12). Thus the shepherd lays down his life in order to take it up again (10:17), making all this possible through returning to the Father and giving the Spirit.

Within the narrative context of Jesus' death, John, with typical creativity, also depicts that event as judgment, drawing on the traditional eschatological motif of victory over Satan (12:31; 14:30; 16:11, 33). For the event lays bare what sin is and what goodness is, for all to see (16:9–10). The return to the Father through suffering and death also serves to provide comfort to the hearers, who must have faced similar prospects (12:24–25; 13:36) and can embrace similar hope.

The author also knows the tradition about the Last Supper (6:51–58) and while not recounting the story, includes some references which indicate awareness that this death was also understood as vicarious and possibly as a sacrifice to deal with sin (6:51c; 11:52; 10:11, 15; cf. 10:17; possibly 1:29). The extent to which this is so is debated, as we have seen. It is not made the focus of attention when the author comes to narrate the events surrounding Jesus' death, but it is there in John and not to be denied. Thus for John both person and process are important but with the primary focus throughout on the person, for Jesus himself is the light and life and hope.

As with Matt 1:21, therefore, it is important not to use the presence of references to the achievement of Jesus' death in order to "tidy up" John, and so to make his account fit our dogmatic or intellectual concerns for order by turning vicarious atonement, for instance, into the heart of the Gospel's message, and reducing all references to Jesus as offering life before then as proleptic. Equally, however, it is important not to use the clear references to Jesus as offering light and life during his ministry to explain away the significance of statements about his death. John holds both together, as in a different way does Matthew, as aspects of their Christology, just as their fellow Jews did in the way they saw various aspects of forgiveness belonging within the broader understanding of what it meant to be in relationship to God. An overemphasis on forgiveness of sins has too often led to distorted understandings which pose exclusive alternatives unnecessarily, and fail to do justice to the emphases in the texts themselves and to Judaism of the time.

Thus as other Jews saw relationship with God as the centre, expressed through obedience to Torah, for John relationship is central, expressed through obedience to the Son who now takes the role of Torah. As other Jews could hold together belief that God forgives sin, in response to prayer, sacrifice, or special vicarious acts, without need to synthesise them into watertight consistency, so John could embrace the message of God's forgiving grace, including through Jesus' death, but without needing to argue its absence up to that point or make his death the heart of his message. For ultimately John's soteriology is rooted in his Christology and his Christology is ultimately and profoundly, in the strictest sense, theological. For as the Son sent from the Father, what he offers is life in relationship with God.

The overall effect of John's Christology, therefore, is to create a soteriology with a typically Jewish structure of spirituality, such as we find in Matthew, but now with a different medium, not Torah, but Jesus and his command, primarily the command to love. Its use of Torah-Wisdom images now to portray the offer as one addressing human existential needs, water, bread, life, light, endears this Gospel to all who seek a deep connection with God. Despite what many experience as the stumbling block of its big claims, it can serve as a major source for ecumenical exchange among diverse peoples and cultures, especially because its heart is to express an understanding of God as love and love in community as the way of true spirituality.

Bibliography

Ahn, Sanghee Michael. *The Christological Witness Function of Old Testament Characters in the Gospel of John*. Eugene: Wipf and Stock, 2014.

Anderson, Paul N. "Aspects of Historicity in the Fourth Gospel: Consensus and Convergences." Pages 379–86 in *John, Jesus, and History, Volume 2: Aspects of Historicity in the Fourth Gospel*. Edited by P. N. Anderson, F. Just, and T. Thatcher. ECL 2. Atlanta: SBL, 2009.

———. *The Christology of the Fourth Gospel: Its Unity and Disunity in the Light of John 6*. 3rd ed. Eugene: Wipf and Stock, 2010.

———. "The Cognitive Origins of John's Unitive and Disunitive Christology." *HBT* 17 (1995): 1–24.

———. "Interfluential, Formative, and Dialectical—A Theory of John's Relation to the Synoptics." Pages 19–58 in *Für und wider die Priorität des Johannesevangeliums*. Edited P. Hofrichter. Hildesheim: Olms, 2002.

———. "The Origin and Development of the Johannine *Egō Eimi* Sayings in Cognitive-Critical Perspective." *JSHJ* 9 (2011): 139–206.

Appold, Mark L. *The Oneness Motif in the Fourth Gospel*. WUNT 2.1. Tübingen: Mohr Siebeck, 1976.

Ashton, John. *The Gospel of John and Christian Origins*. Minneapolis: Fortress Press, 2014.

———. "Intimations of Apocalyptic: Looking Back and Looking Forward." Pages 3–35 in *John's Gospel and Intimations of Apocalyptic*. Edited by H. Williams and C. Rowland. London: T&T Clark, 2013.

———. "The Johannine Son of Man: A New Proposal." *NTS* 57 (2011): 508–29.

———. "Reflections on a Footnote." Pages 203–15 in *Engaging with C. H. Dodd on the Gospel of John: Sixty Years of Tradition and Interpretation*. Edited by T. Thatcher and C. H. Williams. Cambridge: Cambridge University Press, 2014.

———. *Understanding the Fourth Gospel*. 2nd ed. Oxford: Oxford University Press, 2007.

Augenstein, Jörg. "'Euer Gesetz'—Ein Pronomen und die johanneische Haltung zum Gesetz." *ZNW* 88 (1997): 311–13.

Aune, David E. *The Cultic Setting of Realized Eschatology in Early Christianity*. NovTSup 18. Leiden: Brill, 1972.

Back, Frances. "Die rätselhaften 'Antworten' Jesu. Zum Thema des Nikodemus-gesprächs (Joh 3,1–21)." *EvT* 73 (2013): 178–89.

Backhaus, Knut. "'Before Abraham was, I am': The Book of Genesis and the Genesis of Christology." Pages 74–84 in *Genesis and Christian Theology*. Edited by N. MacDonald, M. W. Elliott, and G. Macaskill. Grand Rapids: Eerdmans, 2012.

Baffes, Melanie. "Christology and Discipleship in John 7:37–38." *BTB* 41 (2011): 144–50.

Bailey, Cyril, et al, ed. *History of Christianity in the Light of Modern Knowledge*. London: Blackie & Son, 1929.

Ball, David Mark. *"I am" in John's Gospel: Literary Function, Background and Theological Implications*. JSNTSup 124. Sheffield: Sheffield Academic Press, 1996.

Balz, Horst. "Johanneische Theologie und Ethik im Lichte der 'letzten Stunde'." Pages 35–56 in *Studien zum Text und zur Ethik des Neuen Testaments. Festschrift für H. Greeven*. Edited by W. Schrage. BZNW 167. Berlin: de Gruyter, 1986.

Barrett, C. K. "Christocentric or Theocentric? Observations on the Theological Method of the Fourth Gospel." Pages 1–18 in *Essays on John*. Philadelphia: Westminster, 1982.

———. "'The Father is greater than I': John 14.28: Subordinationist Christology in the New Testament." Pages 19–36 in *Essays on John*. Philadelphia: Westminster, 1982.

———. *The Gospel according to St. John*. 2nd ed. London: SPCK, 1978.

———. "Paradox and Dualism." Pages 98–115 in *Essays on John*. Philadelphia: Westminster, 1982.

———. "Symbolism." Pages 65–79 in *Essays on John*. Philadelphia: Westminster, 1982.

———. "The Theological Vocabulary of the Fourth Gospel and the Gospel of Truth." Pages 50–64 in *Essays on John*. Philadelphia: Westminster, 1982.

Bauckham, Richard. "For Whom Were the Gospels Written?" Pages 9–48 in *The Gospels for All Christians*. Grand Rapids: Eerdmans, 1998.

———. "Jewish Messianism according to the Gospel of John." Pages 207–38 in *The Testimony of the Beloved Disciple: Narrative, History, and Theology in the Gospel of John*. Grand Rapids: Baker, 2007.

———. "Monotheism and Christology in the Gospel of John." Pages 148–66 in *Contours of Christology in the New Testament*. Edited by R. Longenecker. MNTS 7. Grand Rapids: Eerdmans, 2005.

Bauer, Walter. *Das Johannesevangelium*. HNT 6. Tübingen: Mohr Siebeck, 1933.

Baum-Bodenbender, Rosel. *Hoheit in Niedrigkeit. Johanneische Christologie im Prozess Jesu vor Pilatus (Joh 18,28–19,16a)*. FB 49. Würzburg: Echter, 1984.

Baur, F. C. *Kritische Untersuchungen über die kanonischen Evangelien*. Tübingen: Fues, 1847.

———. *Vorlesungen über neutestamentliche Theologie*. Darmstadt: WBG, 1973.

Beasley-Murray, George R. *Gospel of Life: Theology in the Fourth Gospel*. Peabody: Hendrickson, 1991.

———. *John*. 2nd ed. WBC 36. Nashville: Thomas Nelson, 1999.

———. "John 12,31–32: The Eschatological Significance of the Lifting Up of the Son of Man." Pages 70–81 in *Studien zum Text und zur Ethik des Neuen Testaments. Festschrift für H. Greeven*. Edited by W. Schrage. BZNW 167. Berlin: de Gruyter, 1986.

———. "The Mission of the Logos-Son." Pages 1855–68 in *The Four Gospels 1992. Festschrift for Frans Neirynck*. Edited by F. van Segbroeck, C. M. Tuckett, G. Van Belle, and J. Verheyden. BETL 100. Leuven: Peeters, 1992.

Becker, Jürgen. "Beobachtungen zum Dualismus im Johannesevangelium." *ZNW* 65 (1974): 71–87.

———. *Das Evangelium des Johannes*. ÖTK 4.1–2. Gütersloh: Mohn, 1979–1981.

———. "Ich bin die Auferstehung und das Leben. Eine Skizze der johanneischen Christologie." *TZ* 39 (1983): 138–51.

———. *Johanneisches Christentum. Eine Geschichte und Theologie im Überblick.* Tübingen: Mohr Siebeck, 2004.

———. "Das Johannesevangelium im Streit der Methoden (1980–1984)." *TRu* 51 (1986): 1–78.

———. "Wunder und Christologie." *NTS* 16 (1969/1970): 130–48.

Bennema, Cornelis. *Encountering Jesus: Character Studies in the Gospel of John.* Milton Keynes: Paternoster, 2009.

———. "The Identity and Composition of οἱ Ἰουδαῖοι in the Gospel of John." *TynBull* 60 (2009): 239–63.

———. *The Power of Saving Wisdom: An Investigation of Spirit and Wisdom in Relation to the Soteriology of the Fourth Gospel.* WUNT 2.148. Tübingen: Mohr Siebeck, 2002.

Berger, Klaus. "Zu 'Das Wort ward Fleisch' Joh I 14a." *NovT* 16 (1974): 161–66.

Bergmeier, Roland. *Glaube als Gabe nach Johannes.* BWANT 12. Stuttgart: Kohlhammer, 1980.

———. "ΤΕΤΕΛΕΣΤΑΙ Joh 19,30." *ZNW* 79 (1988): 281–90.

Bernhard, J. H. *A Critical and Exegetical Commentary on the Gospel of St. John.* 2 vols. ICC. Edinburgh: T&T Clark, 1929.

Berrouard, M. F. "Le Paraclete, Défenseur du Christ devant la conscience du croyant (Jo. XVI.8–11)." *RSPT* 33 (1949): 301–49.

Bertram, Georg. "ὑψόω." *TDNT* 7:606–13.

Beutler, Johannes. *Habt keine Angst. Die erste johanneische Abschiedsrede (Joh 14).* SBS 116. Stuttgart: KBW, 1984.

———. "Das Hauptgebot im Johannesevangelium." Pages 222–36 in *Das Gesetz im Neuen Testament.* Edited by K. Kertelge. QD 108. Freiburg: Herder, 1986.

———. "Die Heilsbedeutung des Todes Jesu im Johannesevangelium nach Joh 13, 1–20." Pages 188–204 in *Der Tod Jesu. Deutungen im Neuen Testament.* QD 74. Edited by K. Kertelge. Freiburg: Herder, 1976.

———. *Das Johannesevangelium.* Freiburg: Herder, 2013.

———. "Der Johannes-Prolog—Ouvertüre des Johannesevangeliums," Pages 77–106 in *Der Johannesprolog.* Edited G. Kruck. Darmstadt: WBG, 2009.

———. *Martyria. Traditionsgeschichtliche Untersuchungen zum Zeugnisthema bei Johannes.* FraTS 10. Frankfurt: Knecht, 1972.

———. *Neue Studien zu den johanneischen Schriften / New Studies on the Johannine Writings.* BBB 167. Göttingen: Vandenhoeck und Ruprecht, 2012.

———. "Psalm 42/43 im Johannesevangelium." *NTS* 25 (1979): 33–57.

Beyschlag, D. Willibald. *Neutestamentliche Theologie II.* Halle: Strien, 1896.

Bieringer, Reimund. "'. . .because the Father is greater than I' (John 14:28): Johannine Christology in Light of the Relationship between the Father and the Son." Pages 181–204 in *Gospel Images of Jesus Christ in Church Tradition and in Biblical Scholarship: Fifth International East-West Symposium of New Testament Scholars: Minsk, September 2 to 9, 2010.* Edited by C. Karakolis, K.-W. Niebuhr, and S. Rogalsky. WUNT 288. Tübingen: Mohr Siebeck, 2012.

———. "'Ihr habt weder seine Stimme gehört noch seine Gestalt je gesehen' (Joh 5,37): Antijudaismus und johanneische Christologie." Pages 165–88 in *Studies in the Gospel of John and Its Christology: Festschrift Gilbert Van Belle.* Edited by J. Verheyden, G. van Oyen, M. Labahn, and R. Bieringer. BETL 265. Leuven: Peeters, 2014.

---. "Das Lamm Gottes, das die Sünde der Welt hinwegnimmt (Joh 1,29): Eine kontextorientierte und redaktionsgeschichtliche Untersuchung auf dem Hintergrund der Passatradition als Deutung des Todes Jesu im Johannesevangelium." Pages 199–232 in *The Death of Jesus in the Fourth Gospel*. Edited G. Van Belle. BETL 200. Leuven: Peeters, 2007.

Bittner, Wolfgang J. *Jesu Zeichen im Johannesevangelium*. WUNT 2.26. Tübingen: Mohr Siebeck, 1987.

Bjerkelund, C. J. *TAUTA EGENETO. Die Präzisierungssätze im Johannes-evangelium*. WUNT 2.40. Tübingen: Mohr Siebeck, 1987.

Blank, Josef. *Krisis. Untersuchungen zur johanneischen Christologie und Eschatologie*. Freiburg: Lambertus, 1962.

---. "Die Verhandlung vor Pilatus. Joh 18,28–19,16 im Lichte johanneischer Theologie." *BZ* 3 (1959): 60–81.

Blinzler, Josef. *Der Prozess Jesu*. 4th ed. Stuttgart: KBW, 1969.

Boismard, M.-E. "Le caractère adventice de Jo., XII, 45–50." Pages 189–92 in *Sacra Pagina II*. Paris: Gemloux, 1959.

---. "Jésus, le Prophète par excellence d'après Jean 10,24–39." Pages 160–72 in *Neues Testament und Kirche. Festschrift für R. Schnackenburg*. Edited by J. Gnilka. Freiburg: Herder, 1974.

Boismard, M.-E., and A. Lamouille. *L'Évangile de Jean. Synopse des Quatres Évangiles en Français, Tome III*. Paris: Cerf, 1977.

Bond, Helen. "Discarding the Seamless Robe: The High Priesthood of Jesus in John's Gospel." Pages 183–94 in *Israel's God and Rebecca's Children: Christology and Community in Early Judaism and Christianity. Essays in Honor of Larry W. Hurtado and Alan F. Segal*. Edited by D. B. Capes, A. D. DeConick, H. K. Bond, and T. A. Miller. Waco: Baylor University Press, 2007.

Borgen, Peder. *Bread from Heaven. An Exegetical Study of the Concept of Man in the Gospel of John and the Writings of Philo*. NovTSup 10. Leiden: Brill, 1965.

---. "God's Agent in the Fourth Gospel." Pages 121–32 in *Logos Was the True Light*. Trondheim: Tapir, 1983.

---. *The Gospel of John: More Light from Philo, Paul and Archaeology: The Scriptures, Tradition, Exposition, Meaning*. NovTSup 154. Leiden: Brill, 2014.

---. "The Son of Man Saying in John 3:13–14." Pages 133–48 in *Logos Was the True Light*. Trondheim: Tapir, 1983.

---. "The Use of Tradition in John 12:44–50." Pages 54–66 in *Logos Was the True Light*. Trondheim: Tapir, 1983.

Borig, Rainer. *Der wahre Weinstock*. SANT 16. München: Kösel, 1967.

Boring, M. E. "The Influence of Christian Prophecy in the Johannine Portrayal of the Paraclete and Jesus." *NTS* 25 (1978): 113–23

Bornkamm, Günther. "Die eucharistische Rede im Johannes-Evangelium." Pages 60–67 in *Geschichte und Glaube. Erster Teil. Gesammelte Aufsätze*. vol. 3. Munich: Kaiser, 1968.

---. "Der Paraklet im Johannes-Evangelium." Pages 68–89 in *Geschichte und Glaube. Erster Teil. Gesammelte Aufsätze*. vol. 3. Munich: Kaiser, 1968.

---. "Vorjohanneische Tradition oder nachjohanneische Bearbeitung in der eucharistischen Rede Johannes 6." Pages 51–64 in *Geschichte und Glaube. Zweiter Teil. Gesammelte Aufsätze*. vol. 4. Munich: Kaiser, 1971.

---. "Zur Interpretation des Johannesevangeliums." Pages 104–21 in *Geschichte und Glaube. Erster Teil. Gesammelte Aufsätze*.vol. 3. Munich: Kaiser, 1968.

Borsch, Frederick H. *The Son of Man in Myth and History*. London: SCM, 1967.
Bousset, Wilhelm. *Kyrios Christos*. Nashville: Abingdon, 1970.
Boyarin, Daniel. "The Gospel of the Memra: Jewish Binitarianism and the Prologue to John." *HTR* 94 (2001): 243–84.
Braine, David D. C. "The Inner Jewishness of St. John's Gospel as the Clue to the Inner Jewishness of Jesus." *SNTU* 13 (1988): 101–55.
Brant, Jo-Ann A. *Dialogue and Drama: Elements of Greek Tragedy in the Fourth Gospel*. Peabody: Hendrickson, 2004.
Braun, F.-M. *Jean le Théologien*. Vol. 3 Paris: Gabalda, 1966.
Breuss, Josef. *Das Kana-Wunder. Hermeneutische und pastorale Überlegungen aufgrund einer phänomenologischen Analyse von Johannes 2,1–12*. BibB 12. Fribourg, SwitzerlandKBW, 1976.
Brown, Raymond E. *The Community of the Beloved Disciple*. New York: Paulist, 1979.
———. *The Epistles of John*. AB 30. New York: Doubleday, 1983.
———. *The Gospel according to John*. 2 vols. AB 29/29A. New York: Doubleday, 1966/1970.
———. *An Introduction to the Gospel of John*. Edited, Updated, Introduced and Concluded by Francis J. Moloney, S.D.B. ABRL. New York: Doubleday, 2003.
Bruce, F. F. *The Gospel of John*. Grand Rapids: Eerdmans, 1983.
Brun, Lyder. "Die Gottesschau des johanneischen Christus." *SO* 5 (1927): 1–22.
Büchsel, Friedrich. *Das Evangelium nach Johannes*. NTD 4. Göttingen: Vandenhoeck und Ruprecht, 1934.
Bühner, Jan. *Der Gesandte und sein Weg im 4. Evangelium*. WUNT 2.2. Tübingen: Mohr Siebeck, 1977.
Bultmann, Rudolf. "Die Bedeutung der neuerschlossenen mandäischen und manichäischen Quellen für das Verständnis des Johannesevangeliums." Pages 402–65 in *Johannes und sein Evangelium*. Wege der Forschung 82. Edited by K. H. Rengstorf. Darmstadt: WBG, 1973.
———. "Die Eschatologie des Johannes-Evangeliums." *Zwischen den Zeiten* 6 (1928): 4–22.
———. *Das Evangelium des Johannes*. KEKNT. Göttingen: Vandenhoeck und Ruprecht, 1968.
———. "Johannesevangelium." *RGG* 3 (1959): 840–50.
———. "Der religionsgeschichtliche Hintergrund des Prologs zum Johannesevangelium." Pages 3–26 in *EUCHARISTERION. Festschrift für H. Gunkel. 2. Teil*. Göttingen: Vandenhoeck und Ruprecht, 1923.
———. *Theologie des Neuen Testaments*. Tübingen: Mohr Siebeck, 1953.
———. "Untersuchungen zum Johannesevangelium." *ZNW* 27 (1928): 113–63.
———. "Untersuchungen zum Johannesevangelium." *ZNW* 29 (1930): 169–92.
———. "Zur Interpretation des Johannesevangeliums." *TLZ* 87 (1962): 1–8.
Burge, Gary M. *The Anointed Community: The Holy Spirit in the Johannine Tradition*. Grand Rapids: Eerdmans, 1987.
———. *Interpreting the Gospel of John*. Grand Rapids: Baker, 1992.
Burkett, Delbert. *The Son of Man in the Gospel of John*. JSNTSup 56. Sheffield: Sheffield Academic Press, 1991.
Burney, Charles F. *The Aramaic Origin of the Fourth Gospel*. Oxford: Clarendon, 1922.
Burrows, F. W. "Did John the Baptist Call Jesus 'Lamb of God'?" *ExpT* 85 (1974): 245–49.
Busse, Ulrich. *Das Johannesevangelium. Bildlichkeit, Diskurs und Ritual*. BETL 162. Leuven: Peeters, 2002.

———. "Metaphorik und Rhetorik im Johannesevangelium: Das Bildfeld vom König." Pages 279–317 in *Imagery in the Gospel of John: Terms, Forms, Themes, and Theology of Johannine Figurative Language*. Edited by J. Frey, J. G. van der Watt, and R. Zimmermann. WUNT 200. Tübingen: Mohr Siebeck, 2006.

———. "Offene Fragen zu Johannes 10." *NTS* 33 (1987): 516–31.

———. "Theologie oder Christologie im Johannesprolog?" Pages 1–36 in *Studies in the Gospel of John and Its Christology: Festschrift Gilbert Van Belle*. Edited by J. Verheyden, G. van Oyen, M. Labahn, and R. Bieringer. BETL 265. Leuven: Peeters, 2014.

Bynum, William Randolph. *The Fourth Gospel and the Scriptures: Illuminating the Form and Meaning of Scriptural Citation in John 19:37*. NovTSup 144. Leiden: Brill, 2012.

Byrne, Brendan. "The Faith of the Beloved Disciple and the Community in John 20." *JSNT* 23 (1985): 83–97.

Cadman, W. H. *The Open Heaven*. Oxford: Blackwell, 1969.

Caird, George B. "The Glory of God in the Fourth Gospel." *NTS* 15 (1968/1969): 265–77.

Caragounis, Chrys, and Jan G. van der Watt. "A Grammatical Analysis of John 1,1." *Filologia Neotestamentaria* 21 (2008): 91–138.

Carson, Donald A. *The Gospel according to John*. Grand Rapids: Eerdmans, 1991.

Carter, Warren. *John and Empire: Initial Explorations*. London: T&T Clark, 2008.

Cassidy, Robert J. *John's Gospel in New Perspective: Christology and the Realities of Roman Power*. New York: Orbis, 1992.

Chanikuzhy, Jacob. *Jesus, the Eschatological Temple: An Exegetical Study of Jn 2,13–22 in the Light of the Pre-70 C.E. Eschatological Temple Hopes and the Synoptic Temple Action*. CBET 58. Leuven: Peeters, 2012.

Charlesworth, James. "The Historical Jesus in the Fourth Gospel: A Paradigm Shift?" *JSHJ* 8 (2010): 3–46.

Chibici-Revneanu, Nicole. *Die Herrlichkeit des Verherrlichten. Das Verständnis der δόξα im Johannesevangelium*. WUNT 2.231. Tübingen: Mohr Siebeck, 2007.

Childs, Brevard. *The New Testament as Canon: An Introduction*. Philadelphia: Fortress, 1984.

Cho, Sukmin. *Jesus as Prophet in the Fourth Gospel*. NTM 15. Sheffield: Phoenix, 2006.

Collins, Adela. "Epilogue." Pages 300–307 in *John's Gospel and Intimations of Apocalyptic*. Edited by C. H. Williams and C. Rowland. London: T&T Clark, 2013.

Collins, Raymond F. "The Oldest Commentary on the Fourth Gospel." *TBT* 98 (1978): 1769–75.

———. "Speaking of the Jews: 'Jews' in the Discourse Material of the Fourth Gospel." Pages 158–75 in *Antijudaism and the Fourth Gospel*. Edited by R. Bieringer, D. Pollefet, and F. Vandecasteele-Vanneuville. Louisville: Westminster John Knox, 2001.

Coloe, Mary L. "Anointing the Temple of God: John 12:1–8." Pages 105–18 in *Transcending Boundaries: Contemporary Readings of the New Testament: In Honour of Professor Francis Moloney, S.D.B.* Edited by R. M. Chennattu and M. L. Coloe. Rome: LAS Publications, 2005.

———. *God Dwells with Us: Temple Symbolism in the Fourth Gospel*. Collegeville: Liturgical, 2001.

Colwell, E. C. "A Definite Rule for the Use of the Article in the Greek New Testament." *JBL* 52 (1933): 12–21.

Conway, Colleen M. "'Behold the Man!' Masculine Christology and the Fourth Gospel." Pages 163–80 in *New Testament Masculinities*. SemeiaSt 45. Edited by S. D. Moore and J. C. Anderson. Atlanta: SBL, 2003.

Coppens, Joseph. "Le Fils de l'Homme dans l'Évangile johannique." *ETL* 52 (1976): 28–81.

Corell, Alf. *Consummatum Est: Eschatology and Church in the Gospel of John.* London: SPCK, 1970.
Cory, Catherine. "Wisdom's Rescue: A New Reading of the Tabernacles Discourse (John 7:1–8:59)." *JBL* 116 (1997): 95–116.
Cullmann, Oscar. *Die Christologie des Neuen Testaments.* 4th ed. Tübingen: Mohr Siebeck, 1966.
———. *Early Christian Worship.* SBT 1.10. London: SCM, 1953.
———. *Salvation as History.* London: SCM, 1967.
Culpepper, R. Alan. *The Anatomy of the Fourth Gospel.* Philadelphia: Fortress, 1983.
———. "Anti-Judaism in the Fourth Gospel as a Theological Problem for Christian Interpreters." Pages 61–82 in *Anti-Judaism and the Fourth Gospel.* Edited by R. Bieringer, D. Pollefeyt, and F. Vandecasteele-Vanneuville. Louisville: Westminster John Knox, 2001.
———. "The Johannine *Hypodeigma*: A Reading of John 13." *Semeia* 53 (1991): 133–52.
———. *The Johannine School: An Evaluation of the Johannine-School Hypothesis Based on an Investigation of the Nature of Ancient Schools.* SBLDS 26. Missoula: Scholars, 1975.
———. "Reading Johannine Irony." Pages 193–207 in *Exploring the Gospel of John: In Honor of D. Moody Smith.* Edited by R. A. Culpepper and C. C. Black. Louisville: Westminster John Knox, 1996.
Dahl, Nils A. "The Johannine Church and History." Pages 122–40 in *The Interpretation of John.* Edited by J. Ashton. Philadelphia: Fortress, 1986.
Dahms, J. V. "John's Use of *monogenēs* Reconsidered." *NTS* 29 (1983): 222–32.
Daly-Denton, Margaret. *David in the Fourth Gospel: The Johannine Reception of the Psalms.* AGJU 47. Leiden: Brill, 1999.
D'Angelo, Mary Rose. "A Critical Note: John 20.17 and Apocalypse of Moses 31." *JTS* 41 (1990): 529–36.
Danker, Frederick W., Walter Bauer, and William F. Arndt. *A Greek-English Lexicon of the New Testament and Other Early Christian Literature.* 3rd ed. Chicago: University of Chicago Press, 2000.
Dauer, Alfons. *Johannes und Lukas.* FB 50. Würzburg: Echter, 1984.
———. *Die Passionsgeschichte im Johannesevangelium.* SANT 30. Munich: Kösel, 1972.
Davey, J. E. *The Jesus of St John.* London: Lutterworth, 1958.
Davies, Margaret. *Rhetoric and Reference in the Fourth Gospel.* JSNTSup 69. Sheffield: Sheffield Academic Press, 1992.
de Boer, Martinus C. "The Depiction of 'the Jews' in John's Gospel: Matters of Behavior and Identity." Pages 141–57 in *Antijudaism and the Fourth Gospel.* Edited by R. Bieringer, D. Pollefet, and F. Vandecasteele-Vanneuville. Louisville: Westminster John Knox, 2001.
———. "Jesus' Departure to the Father in John: Death or Resurrection?" Pages 1–19 in *Theology and Christology in the Fourth Gospel: Essays by the Members of the SNTS Johannine Writings Seminar.* Edited by G. Van Belle, J. G. van der Watt, and P. Maritz. BETL 184. Leuven: Peeters, 2005.
———. "Johannine History and Johannine Theology: The Death of Jesus as the Exaltation and the Glorification of the Son of Man." Pages 293–326 in *The Death of Jesus in the Fourth Gospel.* Edited by G. Van Belle. BETL 200. Leuven: Peeters, 2007.
———. *Johannine Perspectives on the Death of Jesus.* CBET 17. Kampen: Pharos, 1996.

Deines, R. *Jüdische Steingefässe und pharisäische Frömmigkeit: Eine archäologisch-historischer Beitrag zum Verständnis von Joh 2, 6 und der jüdischen Reinheitshalacha zur Zeit Jesu.* WUNT 2.53 Tübingen: Mohr Siebeck, 1993.

de Jonge, Henk Jan. "'The Jews' in the Gospel of John." Pages 121–40 in *Antijudaism and the Fourth Gospel.* Edited by R. Bieringer, D. Pollefet, and F. Vandecasteele-Vanneuville. Louisville: Westminster John Knox, 2001.

de Jonge, Marinus. "Christology and Theology in the Context of Early Christian Eschatology Particularly in the Fourth Gospel." Pages 1835–53 in *The Four Gospels 1992: Festschrift Frans Neirynck: Volume III.* Edited by F. van Segbroeck, C. M. Tuckett, G. Van Belle, and J. Verheyden. BETL 100. Leuven: Peeters, 1992.

———. "Christology, Controversy and Community in the Gospel of John." Pages 209–29 in *Christology, Controversy and Community: New Testament Essays in Honour of David R. Catchpole.* Edited by D. G. Horrell and C. M. Tuckett. NovTSup 99. Leiden: Brill, 2000.

———. *Jesus: Stranger from Heaven and Son of God.* SBLMS 10. Missoula: Scholars, 1977.

de Kruijf, T. C. "'The Glory of the Only Son' (John I 14)." Pages 111–23 in *Studies in John. Presented to J. N. Sevenster.* NovTSup 21. Leiden: Brill, 1970.

de la Potterie, I. "L'emploi dynamique de εἰς dans S. Jean et ses incidences théologiques." *Bib* 43 (1962): 366–87.

———. "Genèse de la Foi Pascal d'après Jn 20." *NTS* 30 (1984): 26–49.

———. "Jésus roi et juge d'après Jn 19,13." *Bib* 41 (1960): 217–47.

———. "Structure du Prologue de Saint Jean." *NTS* 30 (1984): 354–81.

———. *La Vérité dans Saint Jean.* AnBib 73/74. 2 vols. Rome: BibInst, 1977.

Delebecque, Édouard. *Évangile de Jean. Texte Traduit et Annoté.* Paris: Gabalda, 1987.

Demke, Christoph. "Der so genannte Logos-Hymnus im johanneischen Prolog." *ZNW* 58 (1967): 45–68.

Denaux, Adelbert. "The Twofold Purpose of the Fourth Gospel: A Reading of the Conclusion to John's Gospel (20,30–31)." Pages 519–36 in *Studies in the Gospel of John and its Christology: Festschrift Gilbert Van Belle.* Edited by J. Verheyden, G. van Oyen, M. Labahn, and R. Bieringer. BETL 265. Leuven: Peeters, 2014.

Dennert, Brian C. "Hanukkah and the Testimony of Jesus' Works (John 10:22–39)." *JBL* 132 (2013): 431–51.

Dennis, John A. *Jesus' Death and the Gathering of True Israel: The Johannine Appropriation of Restoration Theology in the Light of John 11.47–52.* WUNT 2.217. Tübingen: Mohr Siebeck, 2006.

———. "Jesus' Death in John's Gospel: A Survey of Research from Bultmann to the Present with Special Reference to the Johannine Hypertexts." *CurBR* 4 (2006): 331–63.

———. "The 'Lifting Up of the Son of Man' and the Dethroning of the 'Ruler of This World': Jesus' Death as the Defeat of the Devil in John 12,31–32." Pages 677–92 in *The Death of Jesus in the Fourth Gospel.* Edited by G. Van Belle. BETL 200. Leuven: Peeters, 2007.

Derrett, J. D. M. *Law in the New Testament.* London: DLT, 1970.

Dewailly, L. M. "'D'où est tu?' (Jean 19,9)." *RB* 92 (1985): 481–96.

———. *Das Evangelium nach Johannes.* 2nd ed. Zurich: TVZ, 2004.

Dietzfelbinger, Christian. "Paraklet und theologischer Anspruch im Johannesevangelium." *ZTK* 82 (1985): 389–408.

Dodd, C. H. *Historical Tradition in the Fourth Gospel.* Cambridge: Cambridge University Press, 1965.

———. *The Interpretation of the Fourth Gospel.* Cambridge: Cambridge University Press, 1953.

Duke, Paul D. *Irony in the Fourth Gospel*. Atlanta: Knox, 1985.
Dunn, James D. G. *Christology in the Making*. London: SCM, 1980.
———. "Let John Be John—A Gospel for Its Time." Pages 309–39 in *Das Evangelium und die Evangelien*. WUNT 28. Edited by P. Stuhlmacher. Tübingen: Mohr Siebeck, 1983.
———. "The Washing of the Disciples' Feet." *ZNW* 61 (1970): 246–52.
Dupont, Jacques. *Essais sur la Christologie de Saint Jean*. Bruges: Saint-André, 1951.
du Rand, Jan A. "The Characterization of Jesus as Depicted in the Narrative of the Fourth Gospel." *Neot* 19 (1985): 18–36.
Edwards, Ruth. "The Christological Basis of the Johannine Footwashing." Pages 367–83 in *Jesus of Nazareth: Lord and Christ. Essays on the Historical Jesus and New Testament Christology*. Edited by J. B. Green and M. Turner. Grand Rapids: Eerdmans, 1994.
———. "χάριν ἀντὶ χάριτος (John 1.16): Grace and the Law in the Johannine Prologue." *JSNT* 32 (1988): 3–15.
Ellis, Peter F. *The Genius of John: A Compositional Critical Commentary on the Fourth Gospel*. Collegeville: Liturgical, 1984.
Eltester, Walther. "Der Logos und sein Prophet." Pages 109–34 in *Apophoreta. Festschrift für E. Haenchen*. BZNW 30. Berlin: de Gruyter, 1964.
Emerton, J. A. "Melchizedek and the Gods: Fresh Evidence for the Jewish Background of John X. 34–36." *JTS* 17 (1966): 399–401
———. "Some New Testament Notes, I: The Interpretation of Psalm 82 in John 10." *JTS* 11 (1960): 329–32.
Ensor, Peter. "The Glorification of the Son of Man: An Analysis of John 13:31–32." *TynBul* 58 (2007): 229–52.
Evans, C. F. "The Passion of John." Pages 50–68 in *Explorations in Theology 2*. London: SCM 1977.
Evans, Craig A. "On the Prologue and the Trimorphic Protenoia." *NTS* 27 (1981): 395–401.
———. "On the Quotations Formula in the Fourth Gospel." *BZ* 26 (1982): 79–83.
———. *Word and Glory: On the Exegetical and Theological Background of John's Prologue*. JSNTSup 89. Sheffield: Sheffield Academic Press, 1993.
Fennema, D. A. "John 1.18: 'God the Only Son.'" *NTS* 31 (1985): 124–35.
Fischer, Günter. *Die himmlischen Wohnungen*. EHS 23.38. Frankfurt: Lang, 1975.
Fischer, K. M. "Der johanneische Christus und der gnostische Erlöser." Pages 245–66 in *Gnosis und Neues Testament*. Edited by K. W. Tröger. Berlin: Ev. Verlagsanstalt, 1973.
Forestell, J. Terence. *The Word of the Cross*. AnBib 57. Rome: BibInst, 1974.
Fortna, Robert T. "Christology in the Fourth Gospel: Redaction-Critical Perspectives." *NTS* 21 (1975): 489–504.
———. *The Gospel of Signs: A Reconstruction of the Narrative Underlying the Fourth Gospel*. SNTSMS 11. Cambridge: Cambridge University Press, 1970.
Fossum, Jarl E. "Jewish-Christian Christology and Jewish Mysticism." *VigChr* 37 (1983): 260–87.
———. "The Son of Man's Alter Ego: John 1.51, Targumic Tradition and Jewish Mysticism." Pages 135–51 in *The Image of the Invisible God: Essays on the Influence of Jewish Mysticism on Early Christology*. NTOA 30. Göttingen: Vandenhoeck und Ruprecht, 1995.
Fowler, James. *Stages of Faith: The Psychology of Human Development and the Quest for Meaning*. San Francisco: HarperCollins, 1981.

Franck, Eskil. *Revelation Taught: The Paraclete in the Gospel of John*. ConBNT 14. Lund: Gleerup, 1985.

Franzmann, Majella, and Michael Lattke, "Gnostic Jesuses and the Gnostic Jesus of John." Pages 143-54 in *Gnosisforschung und Religionsgeschichte. Festschrift für Kurt Rudolph zum 65. Geburtstag*. Edited by H. Preissler and H. Seiwert. Marburg: Diagonal-Verlag, 1994.

Freed, E. D. "The Son of Man in the Fourth Gospel." *JBL* 86 (1967): 402-9.

———. "Who or What Was before Abraham in Jn 8:58?" *JSNT* 17 (1983): 52-59.

Frey, Jörg. "Das Bild als Wirkungspotential. Ein rezeptionsgeschichtlicher Versuch zur Funktion der Brot-Metapher in Johannes 6." Pages 381-406 in *Die Herrlichkeit des Gekreuzigten. Studien zu den Johanneischen Schriften I*. Edited by J. Schlegel. WUNT 307. Tübingen: Mohr Siebeck, 2013.

———. "'dass sie meine Herrlichkeit schauen' (Joh 17,24). Zu Hintergrund, Sinn und Funktion der johanneischen Rede von der δόξα Jesu." Pages 639-62 in *Die Herrlichkeit des Gekreuzigten. Studien zu den Johanneischen Schriften I*. Edited by J. Schlegel. WUNT 307. Tübingen: Mohr Siebeck, 2013.

———. "Edler Tod–wirksamer Tod–stellvertretender Tod–heilschaffender Tod. Zur narrativen und theologischen Deutung des Todes Jesu im Johannesevangelium." Pages 555-84 in *Die Herrlichkeit des Gekreuzigten. Studien zu den Johanneischen Schriften I*. Edited by J. Schlegel. WUNT 307. Tübingen: Mohr Siebeck, 2013.

———. "'Ethical' Traditions, Family Ethos, and Love in the Johannine Literature." Pages 767-802 in *Die Herrlichkeit des Gekreuzigten. Studien zu den Johanneischen Schriften I*. Edited by J. Schlegel. WUNT 307. Tübingen: Mohr Siebeck, 2013.

———. "God's Dwelling on Earth: *Shekinah*-Theology in Revelation 21 and in the Gospel of John." Pages 79-103 in *John's Gospel and Intimations of Apocalyptic*. Edited by C. H. Williams and C. Rowland. London: T&T Clark, 2013.

———. *Die johanneische Eschatologie I-III*. WUNT 96, 110, 117. Tübingen: Mohr Siebeck, 1997-2000.

———. "'Die Juden' im Johannesevangelium und die Frage nach der 'Trennung der Wege' zwischen der johanneischen Gemeinde und der Synagoge." Pages 339-77 in *Die Herrlichkeit des Gekreuzigten. Studien zu den Johanneischen Schriften I*. Edited by J. Schlegel. WUNT 307. Tübingen: Mohr Siebeck, 2013.

———. "Leiblichkeit und Auferstehung im Johannesevangelium." Pages 699-738 in *Die Herrlichkeit des Gekreuzigten. Studien zu den Johanneischen Schriften I*. Edited by J. Schlegel. WUNT 307. Tübingen: Mohr Siebeck, 2013.

———. "Die 'theologia crucifixi' des Johannevangeliums." Pages 485-554 in *Die Herrlichkeit des Gekreuzigten. Studien zu den Johanneischen Schriften I*. Edited by J. Schlegel. WUNT 307. Tübingen: Mohr Siebeck, 2013.

———. "Das vierte Evangelium auf dem Hintergrund der älteren Evangelientradition. Zum Problem Johannes und die Synoptiker." Pages 239-94 in *Die Herrlichkeit des Gekreuzigten. Studien zu den Johanneischen Schriften I*. Edited by J. Schlegel. WUNT 307. Tübingen: Mohr Siebeck, 2013.

———. "Zu Hintergrund und Funktion des johanneischen Dualismus." Pages 409-82 in *Die Herrlichkeit des Gekreuzigten. Studien zu den Johanneischen Schriften I*. Edited by J. Schlegel. WUNT 307. Tübingen: Mohr Siebeck, 2013.

Frey, Jörg, Jan G. van der Watt, and Ruben Zimmermann, eds. *Imagery in the Gospel of John. Terms, Forms, Themes, and Theology of Johannine Figurative Language*. WUNT 200. Tübingen: Mohr Siebeck, 2006.

Füglister, Notker. *Die Heilsbedeutung des Pascha*. SANT 8. Munich: Kösel, 1963.
Fuller, Reginald H. "Christmas, Epiphany, and the Johannine Prologue." Pages 63–73 in *Spirit and Light*. Edited by M. L'Engle and W. Green. New York: Seabury, 1976.
———. "The Theology of Jesus or Christology? An Evaluation of the Recent Discussion." *Semeia* 30 (1986): 105–16.
Gawlick, Matthias. "Mose im Johannesevangelium." *BN* 84 (1996): 29–35.
Giblin, C. H. "John's Narration of the Hearing Before Pilate." *Bib* 67 (1986): 221–39.
Glicksman, Andrew T. "Beyond Sophia: The Sapiential Portrayal of Jesus in the Fourth Gospel and Its Ethical Implications for the Johannine Community." Pages 83–101 in *Rethinking the Ethics of John: 'Implicit Ethics' in the Johannine Writings*. Edited by J. G. van der Watt and R. Zimmermann. Contexts and Norms of New Testament Ethics 3. Tübingen; Mohr Siebeck, 2012.
Gnilka, Joachim. "Zur Christologie des Johannesevangeliums." Pages 92–107 in *Christologische Schwerpunkte*. Edited by W. Kasper. Düsseldorf: Patmos, 1980.
Gourgues, Michel. "'Mort pour nos péchés selon les écritures': Que reste-t-il chez Jean du credo des origins? Jn 1,29, Chaînon unique de continuité." Pages 181–97 in *The Death of Jesus in the Fourth Gospel*. Edited by G. Van Belle. BETL 200. Leuven: Peeters, 2007.
Grigsby, Bruce H. "The Cross as an Expiatory Sacrifice in the Fourth Gospel." *JSNT* 15 (1982): 51–80.
Grundmann, Walter. *Zeugnis und Gestalt des Johannes-Evangeliums*. Stuttgart: Calwer, 1960.
Gundry, Robert H. *Jesus the Word according to John the Sectarian: A Paleo-fundamentalist Manifesto for Contemporary Evangelicalism, Especially Its Elites, in North America*. Grand Rapids: Eerdmans, 2002.
Haacker, Klaus. *Die Stiftung des Heils. Untersuchungen zur Struktur der johanneischen Theologie*. AzTh 47. Stuttgart: Calwer, 1972.
Haenchen, Ernst. "Das Johannesevangelium und Sein Kommentar." Pages 208–34 in *Die Bibel und Wir*. Tübingen: Mohr Siebeck, 1968.
———. *Johannesevangelium. Ein Kommentar*. Edited by U. Busse. Tübingen: Mohr Siebeck, 1980.
———. "'Der Vater, der mich gesandt hat.'" Pages 68–78 in *Gott und Mensch*. Tübingen: Mohr Siebeck, 1965.
Hahn, Ferdinand. "Beobachtungen zu Joh 1:18,34." Pages 239–45 in *Studies in New Testament Language and Text. In Honour of G. D. Kilpatrick*. Edited by J. K. Elliott. Leiden: Brill, 1976.
———. "'Das Heil kommt von den Juden.' Erwägungen zu Joh 4,22b." Pages 67–84 in *Wort und Wirklichkeit. Festschrift für E. L. Rapp,*. Weisenheim: Anton Hain, 1976.
———. "Die Juden im Johannesevangelium." Pages 430–38 in *Kontinuität und Einheit. Für Franz Mussner*. Freiburg: Herder, 1981.
———. "Die Jüngerberufung. Joh 1,35–51." Pages 172–90 in *Neues Testament und Kirche. Festschrift für R. Schnackenburg*. Edited by J. Gnilka. Freiburg: Herder, 1974.
———. "Der Prozess Jesu im Johannesevangelium." Pages 23–96 in *EKK Vorarbeitsheft 2*. Neukirchen: Neukirchener Verlag; Zürich: Benziger, 1970.
———. "Sehen und Glauben im Johannesevangelium." Pages 125–41 in *Neues Testament und Geschichte. Festschrift für O. Cullmann*. Edited by H. Baltensweiler and B. Reicke. Zürich: TVZ; Tübingen: Mohr Siebeck, 1972.
———. *Theologie des Neuen Testaments*. 2 vols. Tübingen: Mohr Siebeck, 2002.
———. "Das Verständnis des Opfers im Neuen Testament." Pages 51–91 in *Das Opfer Jesu*

Christi und seine Gegenwart in der Kirche. Edited by K. Lehmann and E. Schlink. Freiburg: Herder; Göttingen: Vandenhoeck und Ruprecht, 1983.

———. "Die Worte vom lebendigen Wasser im Johannesevangelium." Pages 51–70 in *God's Christ and His People: Studies in Honor of N. A. Dahl*. Edited by J. Jervell and W. Meeks. Oslo: Universitetsforlaget, 1977.

Hamerton-Kelly, R. G. *Pre-Existence, Wisdom and the Son of Man*. SNTSMS 21. Cambridge: Cambridge University Press, 1973.

Hanson, Anthony T. "John's Citation of Ps LXXXII." *NTS* 11 (1965): 158–62.

Harner, J. B. *The "I am" of the Fourth Gospel*. Philadelphia: Fortress, 1970.

Harner, Philip B. "Qualitative Anarthrous Predicate Nouns: Mark 15:39 and John 1:1." *JBL* 92 (1973): 75–87.

Harris, Elizabeth. *Prologue and Gospel: The Theology of the Fourth Evangelist*. JSNTSup 107. Sheffield: Sheffield Academic Press, 1994.

Harvey, A. E. *Jesus and the Constraints of History*. Philadelphia: Westminster, 1982.

———. *Jesus on Trial: A Study in the Fourth Gospel*. Atlanta: Knox, 1976.

Hayward, C. T. R. "The Holy Name of the God of Moses and the Prologue of the Fourth Gospel." *NTS* 25 (1978): 16–23.

Heekerens, Hans-Peter. *Die Zeichen-Quelle der johanneischen Redaktion. Ein Beitrag zur Entstehungsgeschichte des vierten Evangeliums*. SBS 113. Stuttgart: KBW, 1984.

Hegermann, Harald. "δόξα, δοξάζω." *EWNT* 1:832–43.

———. "'Er kam in sein Eigentum.'" Pages 112–31 in *Der Ruf Jesu und die Antwort der Gemeinde. Festschrift für J. Jeremias*. Göttingen: Vandenhoeck und Ruprecht, 1970.

Heil, John Paul. *Jesus Walking on the Sea*. AnBib 87. Rome: BibInst, 1981.

Heise, Jürgen. *Bleiben. Menein in den Johanneischen Schriften*. HUT 8. Tübingen: Mohr Siebeck, 1967.

Hengel, Martin. "The Interpretation of the Wine Miracle at Cana: John 2:1–11." Pages 83–112 in *The Glory of Christ in the New Testament: Studies in Christology: In Memory of G. B. Caird*. Edited by L. D. Hurst and N. T. Wright. Oxford: Clarendon, 1987.

———. *The Johannine Question*. London: SCM; Philadelphia: Trinity, 1989.

———. "The Old Testament in the Fourth Gospel." Pages 380–95 in *The Gospels and the Scriptures of Israel*. JSNTSup 104. Edited by C. A. Evans and R. W. Stegner. Sheffield: Sheffield Academic Press, 1994.

———. "The Prologue of the Gospel of John as the Gateway to Christological Truth." Pages 265–94 in *The Gospel of John and Christian Theology*. Edited by R. Bauckham and C. Mosser. Grand Rapids: Eerdmans, 2008.

———. *Der Sohn Gottes. Die Entstehung der Christologie und die jüdisch-hellenistische Religionsgeschichte*. Tübingen: Mohr Siebeck, 1977.

Hera, Marianus Pale. *Christology and Discipleship in John 17*. WUNT 2.342. Tübingen: Mohr Siebeck, 2013.

Higgins, A. B. J. *Jesus and the Son of Man*. London: Clarke, 1964.

Hofbeck, Sebald. *Semeion. Der Begriff des "Zeichens" im Johannesevangelium unter Berücksichtigung seiner Vorgeschichte*. 2nd ed. Münsterschwarzach: Turme, 1970.

Hofius, Otfried. "Die Erzählung von der Fusswaschung Jesu: Joh 13,1–11 als narratives Christuszeugnis." *ZTK* 106 (2009): 156–76.

———. "Struktur und Gedankengang des Logos Hymnus." *ZNW* 78 (1987): 1–25.

Hofrichter, Peter "Gnosis und Johannesevangelium." *BK* 41 (1986): 15–21.

———. *Im Anfang war der Johannesprolog*. BU 17. Regensburg: Pustet, 1986.

———. *Nicht aus Blut sondern monogen aus Gott geboren*. FB 31. Würzburg: Echter, 1978.
Holtzmann, Heinrich J. *Lehrbuch der neutestamentlichen Theologie II*. 2nd ed. Tübingen: Mohr Siebeck, 1911.
Hooker, Morna D. "Creative Conflict: The Torah and Christology." Pages 116–36 in *Christology, Controversy and Community: New Testament Essays in Honour of David R. Catchpole*. Edited by D. G. Horrell and C. M. Tuckett. NovTSup 99. Leiden: Brill, 2000.
———. "The Johannine Prologue and the Messianic Secret." *NTS* 21 (1974): 40–58.
Horbury, William. "The Benediction of the Minim and Early Jewish-Christian Controversy." *JTS* 33 (1982): 19–61.
Hoskyns, Edwyn C., and Francis N. Davey, eds. *The Fourth Gospel*. London: Faber and Faber, 1967.
Hübner, Hans. *Biblische Theologie des Neuen Testaments*. 3 vols. Göttingen: Vandenhoeck und Ruprecht, 1990–1995.
Hunt, Steven A. "And the Word became Flesh—Again? Jesus and Abraham in John 8:31–59." Pages 81–109 in *Perspectives on Our Father Abraham: Essays in Honor of Marvin R. Wilson*. Edited by S. A. Hunt. Grand Rapids: Eerdmans, 2010.
Hurtado, Larry W. *Lord Jesus Christ: Devotion to Jesus in Earliest Christianity*. Grand Rapids, Eerdmans, 2003.
———. "Remembering and Revelation: The Historic and Glorified Jesus in the Gospel of John." Pages 195–214 in *Israel's God and Rebecca's Children: Christology and Community in Early Judaism and Christianity. Essays in Honor of Larry W. Hurtado and Alan F. Segal*. Edited by D. B. Capes, A. D. DeConick, H. K. Bond, and T. A. Miller. Waco: Baylor University Press, 2007.
Ibuki, Yu. *Die Wahrheit im Johannesevangelium*. BBB 39. Bonn: Hanstein, 1972.
Isaacs, Marie E. "The Prophetic Spirit in the Fourth Gospel." *HeyJ* 24 (1983): 391–407.
Jennings, Mark. "The Fourth Gospel's Reversal of Mark in John 13,31–14,3." *Bib* 94 (2013): 210–36.
Jensen, Alexander S. *John's Gospel as Witness: The Development of the Early Christian Language of Faith*. Aldersgate: Ashgate, 2004.
Jeremias, Joachim. "ἀμνός." *TDNT* 1:338–41.
———. "παῖς θεοῦ." *TDNT* 5:654–717.
Jervell, Jacob. *Jesus in the Gospel of John*. Minneapolis: Augsburg, 1984.
Johnson, Brian D. "*Ecce Homo*: Irony in the Christology of the Fourth Evangelist." Pages 125–38 in *The Glory of Christ in the New Testament: Studies in Christology: In Memory of G. B. Caird*. Edited by L. D. Hurst and N. T. Wright. Oxford: Clarendon, 1987.
———. "'Salvation is from the Jews': Judaism in the Gospel of John." Pages 83–99 in *New Currents through John. A Global Perspective*. Edited by F. Lozada and T. Thatcher. SBLRBS 54. Atlanta: SBL, 2006.
———. *The Spirit Paraclete in the Gospel of John*. SNTSMS 12. Cambridge: Cambridge University Press, 1970.
Johnston, George. "Ecce Homo. Irony in the Christology of the Fourth Evangelist." Pages 131–35 in *The Glory of Christ in the New Testament: Studies in Christology. In Memory of G. B. Caird*. Edited by L. D. Hurst and N. T. Wright. Oxford: Clarendon, 1987.
———. *The Spirit Paraclete in the Gospel of John*. SNTSM 12. Cambridge: Cambridge University Press, 1970.
Kaefer, J. Ph. "Les discours d'adieu en Jean 13:31–17:26." *NovT* 26 (1984): 253–82.

Kähler, Martin. *The So-Called Historical Jesus and the Historic, Biblical Christ.* Philadelphia: Fortress, 1966.

Kanagaraj, Jey J. "The Implied Ethics of the Fourth Gospel: A Reinterpretation of the Decalogue." *TynBul* 52 (2001): 33–60.

Käsemann, Ernst. *Jesu Letzter Wille nach Johannes 17.* 3rd ed. Tübingen: Mohr Siebeck, 1971.

———. "The Structure and Purpose of the Prologue to John's Gospel." Pages 138–67 in *New Testament Questions of Today.* London: SCM, 1969.

Kee, Howard C. "Christology and Ecclesiology: Titles of Christ and Models of Community." *Semeia* 30 (1984): 171–92.

———. *Miracles in the Early Christian World.* New Haven: Yale, 1983.

———. "Myth and Miracle: Isis, Wisdom, and the Logos of John." Pages 145–64 in *Myth, Symbol, and Reality.* Edited by B. M. Olson. Chicago: University of Notre Dame Press, 1980.

Keener, Craig S. *The Gospel of John. A Commentary.* 2 vols. Peabody: Hendrickson, 2005.

Kieffer, René. "L'Espace et le Temps dans l'Évangile de Jean." *NTS* 31 (1985): 393–409.

Kim, Yung Suk. *Truth, Testimony, and Transformation: A New Reading of the I Am Sayings of Jesus in the Fourth Gospel.* Eugene: Cascade, 2014.

Klaiber, Walter. "Die Aufgabe einer theologischen Interpretation des vierten Evangeliums." *ZTK* 82 (1985): 300–24.

Klauck, Hans-Josef. "Gemeinde ohne Amt? Erfahrungen mit der Kirche in den johanneischen Schriften." *BZ* 29 (1985): 193–220.

Klos, Herbert. *Die Sakramente im Johannesevangelium.* SBS 46. Stuttgart: KBW, 1970.

Knapp, Henry M. "The Messianic Water Which Gives Life to the World." *HBT* 19 (1997): 109–21.

Knöppler, Thomas. *Die theologia crucis des Johannesevangeliums. Das Verständnis des Todes Jesu im Rahmen der johanneischen Inkarnations- und Erhöhungschristologie.* WMANT 69. Neukirchen-Vluyn: Neukirchener Verlag, 1994.

Koester, Craig. *Symbolism in the Fourth Gospel: Meaning, Mystery, Community.* Minneapolis: Fortress, 1995.

Kohler, Herbert. *Kreuz und Menschwerdung im Johannesevangelium. Ein exegetisch-hermeneutischer Versuch zur johanneischen Kreuzestheologie.* ATANT 72. Zürich: TVZ, 1987.

Kossen, H. B. "Who Were the Greeks of John 12,20?" Pages 97–110 in *Studies in John: Presented to J. N. Sevenster.* NovTSup 21. Leiden: Brill, 1970.

Köstenberger, Andreas J. *A Theology of John's Gospel and Letters.* Grand Rapids: Zondervan, 2009.

Kotila, Markku. *Umstrittener Zeuge. Studien zur Stellung des Gesetzes in der johanneishcen Theologiegeschichte.* Helsinki: Suomalainen Tiedeakatemia, 1988.

Kovacs, Judith. "'Now Shall the Ruler of this World Be Driven Out': Jesus' Death as Cosmic Battle in John 12:20–26." *JBL* 114 (1995): 227–47.

Kowalski, Beate. "Thesen zur johanneischen Christologie." *BN* 146 (2010): 107–23.

Kraus, Wolfgang. "Johannes und das alte Testament. Überlegungen zum Umgang mit der Schrift im Johannesevangelium im Horizont Biblischer Theologie." *ZNW* 88 (1997): 1–23.

Kremer, Jacob. "Jesu Verheissung des Geistes. Zur Verankerung von Joh 16,13 im Leben Jesu." Pages 247–76 in *Die Kirche des Anfangs. Für H. Schürmann.* Edited by R. Schnackenburg, J. Ernst, and J. Wanke. Freiburg: Herder, 1978.

———. *Lazarus. Die Geschichte einer Auferstehung.* Stuttgart: KBW, 1985.

———. *Die Osterevangelien. Geschichten um Geschichte.* Stuttgart: KBW, 1981.

Kriener, Tobias. *"Glauben an Jesus"—ein Verstoss gegen das zweite Gebot: Die johanneische*

Bibliography

Christologie und der jüdische Vorwurf des Götzendienstes. Neukirchener Theologische Dissertationen und Habilitationen 29. Neukirchen-Vluyn: Neukirchener Verlag, 2001.
Kügler, Joachim. *Der andere König. Religionsgeschichtliche Perspektiven auf die Christologie des Johannesevangeliums*. SBS 178. Stuttgart: KBW, 1999.
———. "Das Johannesevangelium und seine Gemeinde. Kein Thema für Science Fiction." *BN* 23 (1984): 48-62.
Kühl, J. *Die Sendung Jesu und der Kirche nach dem Johannesevangelium*. St Augustin: Steyler, 1967.
Kuhn, Hans-Jürgen. *Christologie und Wunder. Untersuchungen zu Joh 1,35-51*. BU 18. Regensburg: Pustet, 1988.
Kundsin, Karl. "Charakter und Ursprung der johanneischen Reden." *Acta Universitatis Latviensis Teologijas Fakultatis Serija* 1.4 (1939): 185-301.
Kysar, Robert. "The Fourth Gospel: A Report on Recent Research." *ANRW* 2.25.3: 2389-480. Part 2, *Principat* 25.3. Edited by H. Temporini and W. Haase. Berlin: de Gruyter, 1985.
———. *John's Story of Jesus*. Philadelphia: Fortress, 1984.
Labahn, Michael. "Bedeutung und Frucht des Todes Jesu im Spiegel des johanneischen Erzählaufbaus." Pages 431-56 in *The Death of Jesus in the Fourth Gospel*. Edited by G. Van Belle. BETL 200. Leuven: Peeters, 2007.
———. "'Heiland der Welt.' Der gesandte Gottessohn und der römische Kaiser—ein Thema johanneischer Christologie?" Pages 147-73 in *Zwischen den Reichen: Neues Testament und Römische Herrschaft. Vorträge auf der Ersten Konferenz der European Association for Biblical Studies*. Edited by M. Labahn and J. Zangenberg. TANZ 36. Tübingen: Francke, 2002.
———. *Offenbarung in Zeichen und Wort*. WUNT 2.117. Tübingen: Mohr Siebeck, 2006.
Lamb, David. *Text, Context and the Johannine Community: A Sociolinguistic Analysis of the Johannine Writings*. LNTS 477. London: Bloomsbury, 2014.
Langbrandtner, Wolfgang. *Weltferner Gott oder Gott der Liebe*. BET 6. Frankfurt: Lang, 1977.
Lattke, Michael. *Einheit im Wort*. SANT 41. Munich: Kösel, 1975.
Le Déaut, Roger. *La nuit pascale*. AnBib 22. Rome: BibInst, 1963.
Lee, Dorothy A. *Flesh and Glory: Symbolism, Gender and Theology in the Gospel of John*. New York: Crossroad, 2002.
———. "Paschal Imagery in the Gospel of John: A Narrative and Symbolic Reading." *Pacifica* 24 (2011): 13-28.
———. *The Symbolic Narratives of the Fourth Gospel*. JSNTSup 95. Sheffield: JSOT, 1994.
———. "Witness in the Fourth Gospel: John the Baptist and the Beloved Disciple as Counterparts." *ABR* 61 (2013): 1-17.
Leistner, Reinhold. *Antijudäismus im Johannesevangelium?* Frankfurt: Lang, 1974.
Léon-Dufour, Xavier. "'Père, fais-moi passer sain et sauf à travers cette heure' (Jean 12,27)." Pages 157-66 in *Neues Testament und Geschichte. Festschrift für O. Cullmann*. Edited by H. Baltensweiler and B. Reicke. Tübingen: Mohr Siebeck, 1972.
———. "Towards a Symbolic Reading of the Fourth Gospel." *NTS* 27 (1981): 439-56.
Leroy, Herbert. *Rätsel und Missverständnis*. BBB 32. Bonn: Hanstein, 1968.
Leung, Mavis M. *The Kingship-Cross Interplay in the Gospel of John: Jesus' Death as Corroboration of His Royal Messiahship*. Eugene: Wipf and Stock, 2011.
Lierman, John, "The Mosaic Pattern of John's Christology." Pages 210-34 in *Challenging Perspectives on the Gospel of John*. Edited by J. Lierman. WUNT 2.219. Tübingen: Mohr Siebeck, 2006.
Lieu, Judith M. *The Second and Third Epistles of John*. Edinburgh: T&T Clark, 1986.

Lincoln, Andrew T. *The Gospel According to Saint John*. BNTC 4. London: Continuum, 2005.
———. *Truth on Trial: The Lawsuit Motif in the Fourth Gospel*. Peabody: Hendrickson, 2000.
Lindars, Barnabas. *Behind the Fourth Gospel*. London: SPCK, 1971.
———. *The Gospel of John*. London: Oliphants, 1972.
———. *Jesus Son of Man*. London: SPCK, 1983.
———. *John*. NTG. Sheffield: JSOT, 1990.
———. *New Testament Apologetic*. London: SCM, 1961.
———. "The Passion in the Fourth Gospel." Pages 71–86 in *God's Christ and His People: Studies in Honor of N. A. Dahl*. Edited by J. Jervell and W. Meeks. Oslo: Universitetsforlaget, 1977.
———. "Slave and Son in Joh 8:31–36." Pages 271–86 in *The New Testament Age: Essays in Honor of B. Reicke*. Edited by W. C. Weinrich. Macon: Mercer, 1984.
———. "Word and Sacrament in the Fourth Gospel." *SJT* 29 (1976): 49–63.
Lindemann, Andreas. "Mose und Christus: Zum Verständnis des Gesetzes im Johannesevangelium." Pages 309–34 in *Das Urchristentum, in seiner literarischen Geschichte: FS J. Becker*. Edited by U. Mell and U. B. Müller. BZNW 100. Berlin: de Gruyter, 1999.
Litwa, M. David. "Behold Adam: A Reading of John 19:5." *HBT* 32 (2010): 129–43.
Loader, William. "The Central Structure of Johannine Christology." *NTS* 30 (1984): 188–216.
———. *The Christology of the Fourth Gospel: Structure and Issues*. 2nd ed. BET 23. Frankfurt: Peter Lang, 1992.
———. "Jesus and the Law in John." Pages 135–54 in *Theology and Christology in the Fourth Gospel: Essays by the Members of the SNTS Johannine Writings Seminar*. Edited by G. Van Belle, J. G. van der Watt, and P. Maritz. BETL 184. Leuven: Peeters, 2005.
———. *Jesus' Attitude towards the Law: A Study of the Gospels*. WUNT 2.97. Tübingen: Mohr Siebeck, 1997.
———. *The Johannine Epistles*. London: Epworth, 1992.
———. "John 1:50–51 and the 'Greater Things' of Johannine Christology." Pages 255–74 in *Anfänge der Christologie. Für Ferdinand Hahn*. Edited by C. Breytenbach and H. Paulsen. Göttingen: Vandenhoeck und Ruprecht, 1991.
———. "John 5,19–47: A Deviation from Envoy Christology." Pages 149–64 in *Studies in the Gospel of John and Its Christology: Festschrift Gilbert Van Belle*. Edited by J. Verheyden, G. van Oyen, M. Labahn, and R. Bieringer. BETL 265. Leuven: Peeters, 2014.
———. "The Law and Ethics in John's Gospel." Pages 143–58 in *Rethinking the Ethics of John: 'Implicit Ethics' in the Johannine Writings*. Edited by J. G. van der Watt and R. Zimmermann. Contexts and Norms of New Testament Ethics 3. Tübingen; Mohr Siebeck, 2012.
———. Review of *The Johannine Question* by Martin Hengel. *Kings College Review* 13 (1990): 50–52.
———. "The Significance of 1:14–18 for Understanding John's Approach to Law and Ethics." *Review of Rabbinic Judaism* 19 (2016): 194–201.
———. "The Significance of the Prologue for Understanding John's Soteriology." Pages 46–56 in *The Prologue of the Gospel of John: Its Literary and Philosophical Context: Papers Read at the Colloquium Ioanneum 2013*. Edited by J. G. van der Watt, R. A. Culpepper, and U. Schnelle. WUNT 359. Tübingen: Mohr Siebeck, 2016.
———. *Sohn und Hohepriester. Eine traditionsgeschichtliche Untersuchung zur Christologie des Hebräerbriefes*. WMANT 53. Neukirchen: Neukirchener Verlag, 1981.
———. "What Happened to 'Good News for the Poor' in the Johannine Tradition?" Pages 469–80 in *John, Jesus, and History; Volume 3, Glimpses of Jesus through the Johannine Lens*. Edited by P. N. Anderson, F. Just, and T. Thatcher. ECL 18. Atlanta: SBL, 2016.

———. "What Is 'Finished'? Revisiting Tensions in the Structure of Johannine Christology." Page 457–68 in *The Death of Jesus in the Fourth Gospel*. Edited by G. Van Belle. BETL 200. Leuven: Peeters, 2007.
———. "Wisdom and Logos Traditions in Judaism and John's Christology." Forthcoming.
———. "'Your Law'—the Johannine Perspective." Pages 63–74 in *"was ihr auf dem Weg verhandelt habt": Beiträge zur Exegese und Theologie des Neuen Testaments. Festschrift für Ferdinand Hahn zum 75. Geburtstag.* Edited by P. Müller, C. Gerber, and T. Knöppler. Neukirchen-Vluyn: Neukirchener Verlag, 2001.
Loder, James E. *The Transforming Moment: Understanding Convictional Experiences*. Colorado Springs: Helmers and Howard, 1989.
Lona, Horacio E. "Glaube und Sprache des Glaubens im Johannesevangelium." *BZ* 28 (1984): 168–85.
Lorenzen, Thorwald. *Der Lieblingsjünger im Johannesevangelium*. SBS 55. Stuttgart: KBW, 1971.
Lüdemann, Gerd. "ὑψόω." *EWNT* 3:981–82.
Lütgert, Wilhelm. *Die Johanneische Christologie*. 2nd ed. Gütersloh: Bertelsmann, 1916.
Luz, Ulrich. "Das Neue Testament." Pages 58–156 in *Gesetz*. Edited by R. Smend and U. Luz. Stuttgart: Kohlhammer, 1981.
Mackay, Ian D. *John's Relationship with Mark*. WUNT 2.182. Tübingen: Mohr Siebeck, 2004.
MacRae, George W. "The Ego Proclamations in Gnostic Sources." Pages 122–34 in *The Trial of Jesus: In Honour of C. F. D. Moule*. Edited by E. Bammel. SBT 2.13. London: SCM, 1970.
Maddox, Robert L. "The Function of the Son of Man in the Gospel of John." Pages 184–204 in *Reconciliation and Hope: Festschrift for L. Morris*. Edited by R. Banks. Exeter: Paternoster, 1974.
Malatesta, Edward. *Interiority and Covenant*. AnBib 69. Rome: BibInst, 1978.
Manns, Frédéric. "Exégèse Rabbinique et Exégèse Johannique." *RB* 92 (1985): 525–38.
Martyn, J. Louis. "Glimpses into the History of the Johannine Community." Pages 90–121 in *The Gospel of John in Christian History*. New York: Paulist, 1978.
———. *History and Theology in the Fourth Gospel*. 3rd ed. Louisville: Westminster John Knox, 2003.
———. "Source Criticism and Religionsgeschichte in the Fourth Gospel." Pages 99–121 in *The Interpretation of John*. Edited by J. Ashton. Philadelphia: Fortress, 1986.
Mastin, B. A. "A Neglected Feature of the Christology of the Fourth Gospel." *NTS* 22 (1975): 32–51.
Matera, Frank J. "Christ in the Theologies of Paul and John: A Study in the Diverse Unity of New Testament Theology." *TS* 67 (2006): 237–56.
McArthur, H. K. "Christological Perspectives in the Predicates of the Johannine ἐγώ εἰμί Sayings." Pages 74–94 in *Christological Perspectives: In Honor of H. K. McArthur*. Edited by R. F. Berkley and S. A. Edwards. New York: Pilgrim, 1982.
McGrath, James F. *John's Apologetic Christology: Legitimation and Development in Johannine Christology*. SNTSMS 11. Cambridge: Cambridge University Press, 2001.
McHugh, John F. *John 1–4*. ICC. London: T&T Clark, 2009.
McNamara, Martin J. *The New Testament and the Palestinian Targum to the Pentateuch*. AnBib 27. Rome: BibInst, 1966.
Mealand, David. "The Christology of the Fourth Gospel." *SJT* 31 (1978): 449–67.
Meeks, Wayne. "The Man from Heaven in Johannine Sectarianism." Pages 141–73 in *The Interpretation of John*. Edited by John Ashton. Philadelphia: Fortress, 1986.
———. *The Prophet-King*. NovTSup 14. Leiden: Brill, 1967.

Mees, Michael. "Erhöhung und Verherrlichung Jesu im Johannesevangelium nach dem Zeugnis neutestamentlicher Papyri." *BZ* 18 (1974): 32–44.

———.

Menken, Martinus J. J. "The Christology of the Fourth Gospel: A Survey of Recent Research." Pages 292–320 in *From Jesus to John: Essays on Jesus and New Testament Christology in Honour of Marinus de Jonge*. Edited by Martinus C. de Boer. JSNTSup 84. Sheffield: JSOT, 1993.

———. "John 6.51c–58. Eucharist or Christology?" Pages 183–204 in *Critical Readings of John 6*. Edited by R. Alan Culpepper. Leiden: Brill, 1997.

Metzner, Rainer. *Das Verständnis der Sünde im Johannesevangelium*. WUNT 122. Tübingen: Mohr Siebeck, 2000.

Michaels, J. Ramsey. *The Gospel of John*. NICNT. Grand Rapids: Eerdmans, 2010.

Miller, Edward. L. "The Christology of John 8,25." *TZ* 36 (1980): 257–65.

Minear, Paul S. "Diversity and Unity: A Johannine Case Study." Pages 162–75 in *Die Mitte des Neuen Testaments. Festschrift für E. Schweizer*. Edited by U. Luz and H. Weder. Göttingen: Vandenhoeck und Ruprecht, 1983.

Minear, Paul S. *John: The Martyr's Gospel*. New York: Pilgrim, 1985.

———. "'We Don't Know Where...' John 20:2." *Int* 30 (1976): 125–29.

Miranda, Juan P. *Die Sendung Jesu im vierten Evangelium*. SBS 87. Stuttgart: KBW, 1977.

———. *"Der Vater, der mich gesandt hat."* 2nd ed. EHS 23.7. Frankfurt: Peter Lang, 1976.

Mlakuzhyil, George. *The Christocentric Literary Structure of the Fourth Gospel*. AnBib 117. Rome: BibInst, 1987.

Moloney, Francis J. *Belief in the Word: Reading the Fourth Gospel: John 1–4*. Minneapolis: Fortress, 1993.

———. *Glory not Dishonor: Reading John 13–21*. Minneapolis: Fortress, 1998.

———. *The Gospel of John*. SP 4. Collegeville: Liturgical, 1998.

———. "The Johannine Son of God." *BTB* 6 (1976): 175–89.

———. *The Johannine Son of Man*. 2nd ed. BSR 14. Rome: Las, 1978.

———. "The Johannine Son of Man Revisited." Pages 177–202 in *Theology and Christology in the Fourth Gospel: Essays by the Members of the SNTS Johannine Writings Seminar*. Edited by G. Van Belle, J. G. van der Watt, and P. Maritz. BETL 184. Leuven: Peeters, 2005.

———. *Love in the Gospel of John: An Exegetical, Theological, and Literary Study*. Grand Rapids: Baker, 2013.

———. *Signs and Shadows: Reading John 5–12*. Minneapolis: Fortress, 1996.

———. "When Is John Talking about the Sacraments?" Pages 109–30 in *"A Hard Saying": The Gospel and Culture*. Collegeville: Liturgical, 2001.

Morgan-Wynn, J. E. "The Cross and the Revelation of Jesus as ἐγώ εἰμί in the Fourth Gospel." Pages 219–26 in *Studia Biblica 1978: II. Papers on the Gospels: Sixth International Congress on Biblical Studies*. Edited by E. A. Livingstone. JSNTSup 2. Sheffield: JSOT, 1978.

Morgen, Michèle. "'Votre Loi, mon commandement': Etude de la place accordée à la Loi et au commandement dans l'évangile de Jean." Pages 195–206 in *Raconter, Interpréter, Annoncer. Parcours de Nouveau Testament: Mélanges offerts à Daniel Marguerat pour son 60ème anniversaire*. MdB 47. Edited by E. Steffek and Y. Bourquin. Geneva: Labor et Fides, 2003.

Morris, Leon. *The Gospel according to John*. Grand Rapids: Eerdmans, 1971.

Moser, Marion. "Genügt ein christologisches Verständnis der Schrift im Johannesevangelium? Überlegungen zum Kontext der expliziten Schriftbelege." Pages 41–66 in *Narrativität und Theologie im Johannesevangelium*. Edited by J. Frey and U. Poplutz. BibS[N] 130. Neukirchen-Vluyn: Neukirchener Verlag, 2012.

Moule, C. F. D. *An Idiom-Book of New Testament Greek*. Cambridge: Cambridge University Press, 1960.

———. "A Neglected Factor in the Interpretation of Johannine Eschatology." Pages 155–60 in *Studies in John. Presented to J. N. Sevenster*. NovTSup 24. Leiden: Brill, 1970.

Mowvley, H. "John 1:14–18 in the Light of Exodus 33:7–34:35." *ExpTim* 95 (1984): 135–37.

Müller, T. E. *Das Heilsgeschehen im Johannesevangelium*. Zürich: Gotthelf, n.d.; Diss. Bern, 1961.

Müller, Ulrich B. "Die Bedeutung des Kreuzestodes im Johannesevangelium." *KD* 21 (1975): 49–71.

———. *Christologie in der Johanneischen Gemeinde*. SBS 77. Stuttgart: KBW, 1975.

———. *Die Menschwerdung des Gottessohnes. Frühchristliche Inkarnationsvorstellungen und die Anfänge des Doketismus*. SBS 140. Stuttgart: KBW, 1990.

———. "Die Parakletenvorstellung im Johannesevangelium." *ZTK* 71 (1974): 31–77.

Mussner, Franz. *Die johanneische Sehweise*. QD 28. Freiburg: Herder, 1965.

———. "Die johanneischen Parakletssspruche und die apostolische Tradition." Pages 146–58 in *Praesentia Salutis*. Düsseldorf: Patmos, 1967.

———. "'Kultische' Aspekte im Johanneischen Christusbild." Pages 133–45 in *Praesentia Salutis*. Düsseldorf: Patmos, 1967.

Neugebauer, Franz. *Die Entstehung des Johannesevangeliums*. AzTh 36. Stuttgart: Calwer, 1968.

Neyrey, Jerome H. *The Gospel of John in Cultural and Rhetorical Perspective*. Grand Rapids: Eerdmans, 2009.

———. *An Ideology of Revolt: John's Christology in Social-Science Perspective*. Philadelphia: Fortress, 1988.

Nicholson, Godfrey. *Death as Departure: The Johannine Descent-Ascent Schema*. SBLDS 63. Chico: Scholars, 1982.

Nicol, Willem. *The Semeia in the Fourth Gospel*. NovTSup 32. Leiden: Brill, 1972.

Nissen, Johannes. "Community and Ethics in the Gospel of John." Pages 194–212 in *New Readings in John: Literary and Theological Perspectives: Essays from the Scandinavian Conference on the Fourth Gospel Aarhus 1997*. Edited by J. Nissen and S. Pedersen. JSNTSup 182. Sheffield: Sheffield Academic Press, 1999.

O'Day, Gail R. "'I Have Overcome the World' (John 16:33): Narrative Time in John 13–17." *Semeia* 53 (1991): 153–66.

———. *Revelation in the Fourth Gospel*. Philadelphia: Fortress, 1986.

———. "The Word Become Flesh: Story and Theology in the Gospel of John." Pages 67–78 in *What is John: Volume II; Literary and Social Readings of the Fourth Gospel*. Edited by F. Segovia. SBLSymS. Atlanta: Scholars, 1998.

Odeberg, Hugo. *The Fourth Gospel*. Uppsala: Almqvist & Wiksells, 1929.

O'Grady, John F. "The Human Jesus in the Fourth Gospel." *BTB* 14 (1984): 63–66.

Olsson, Birger. "The Meanings of John 13,10: A Question of Genre?" Pages 317–26 in *Studies in the Gospel of John and Its Christology: Festschrift Gilbert Van Belle*. Edited by J. Verheyden, G. van Oyen, M. Labahn, and R. Bieringer. BETL 265. Leuven: Peeters, 2014.

———. *Structure and Meaning in the Fourth Gospel*. ConBNT 6. Lund: Gleerup, 1974.

Onuki, Takashi. *Gemeinde und Welt im Johannesevangelium*. WMANT 56. Neukirchen: Neukirchener Verlag, 1984.
Osborn, Eric. "Negative and Positive Theology in John." *ABR* 31 (1983): 72–80.
Osborne, Grant R. "Christology and New Testament Hermeneutics: A Survey of the Discussion." *Semeia* 30 (1984): 49–62.
Pagels, Elaine H. *The Johannine Gospel in Gnostic Exegesis: Heracleon's Commentary on John*. SBLMS 17. Nashville: Abingdon, 1973.
Painter, John. "Christ and the Church in John 1,45–51." Pages 359–62 in *L'Évangile de Jean. Sources, Rédaction, Théologie*. Edited by M. de Jonge. BETL 44. Leuven: Gombleux, 1977.
———. "Christology and the Farewell Discourses." *ABR* 31 (1983): 45–62.
———. "Christology and the History of the Johannine Community in the Prologue of the Fourth Gospel." *NTS* 30 (1984): 460–73.
———. "The Church and Israel in the Fourth Gospel: A Response." *NTS* 25 (1978): 103–22.
———. "The Death of Jesus in John: A Discussion of the Tradition, History, and Theology of John." Pages 327–62 in *The Death of Jesus in the Fourth Gospel*. Edited by G. Van Belle. BETL 200. Leuven: Peeters, 2007.
———. "Eschatological Faith in the Gospel of John." Pages 36–52 in *Reconciliation and Hope: Festschrift for L. Morris*. Edited by R. Banks. Exeter: Paternoster, 1974.
———. "The Farewell Discourses and the History of Johannine Christianity." *NTS* 27 (1981): 525–43.
———. "John 9 and the Interpretation of the Fourth Gospel." *JSNT* 28 (1986): 31–61.
———. *John: Witness and Theologian*. 3rd ed. Melbourne: Beacon Hill, 1986.
———. "The 'Opponents' in 1 John." *NTS* 32 (1986): 31–47.
———. "The Point of John's Christology: Christology, Conflict and Community in John." Pages 231–52 in *Christology, Controversy and Community: New Testament Essays in Honour of David R. Catchpole*. NTS 99. Edited by D. G. Horrell and C. M. Tuckett. Leiden, Brill, 2000.
———. "The Prologue as an Hermeneutical Key to Reading the Fourth Gospel." Pages 37–60 in *Studies in the Gospel of John and Its Christology: Festschrift Gilbert Van Belle*. Edited by J. Verheyden, G. van Oyen, M. Labahn, and R. Bieringer. BETL 265. Leuven: Peeters, 2014.
———. *The Quest for the Messiah: The History, Literature and Theology of the Johannine Community*. 2nd ed. Edinburgh: T&T Clark, 1993.
———. "Sacrifice and Atonement in the Gospel of John." Pages 287–313 in *Israel und seine Heilstraditionen im Johannesevangelium*. Edited by M. Labahn, K. Scholtissek, and A. Strotmann. Paderborn: Ferdinand Schöningh, 2004.
———. "Text and Context in John 5." *ABR* 35 (1987): 28–34.
Pamment, Margaret. "The Meaning of Doxa in the Fourth Gospel." *ZNW* 74 (1983): 12–16.
———. "The Son of Man in the Fourth Gospel." *JTS* 36 (1985): 58–66.
Pancaro, Stephen. *The Law in the Fourth Gospel: The Torah and the Gospel, Moses and Jesus, Judaism and Christianity according to John*. NovTSup 42. Leiden: Brill, 1975.
Perkins, Pheme. *Resurrection: New Testament Witness and Contemporary Reflection*. New York: Doubleday, 1984.
Petersen, Silke. *Brot, Licht und Weinstock. Intertextuelle Analysen johanneischer Ich-bin-Worte*. NovTSup 127. Leiden: Brill, 2008.
———. "'...wieso sagt ihr: "Du lästerst", weil ich gesagt habe: "Sohn des Gottes bin ich"?' (Joh 10,36)—oder: Wie 'göttlich' ist der johanneische Jesus?" Pages 470–85 in *Fragen wider die*

Antworten. Edited by K. Schiffner, S. Leibold, M. L. Frettlöh, J.-D. Döhling, and U. Bail. Gütersloh: Gütersloher Verlagshaus, 2010.

Pfuff, Konrad. *Die Einheit des Johannesprologs*. Frankfurt: Peter Lang, 2013.

Pokorny, Petr. "Der irdische Jesus im Johannesevangelium." *NTS* 30 (1984): 217–28.

Pollard, T. E. *Johannine Christology and the Early Church*. SNTSMS 13. Cambridge: Cambridge University Press, 1970.

Porsch, Felix. *Pneuma und Wort*. FrankTS 16. Frankfurt: Knecht, 1974.

Preiss, Theo. *Life in Christ*. SBT 1.13. London: SCM, 1954.

Pryor, John W. *John: Evangelist of the Covenant Community: The Narrative and Themes of the Fourth Gospel*. Downers Grove, IL: InterVarsity Press, 1992.

———. "Of the Virgin Birth or the Birth of Christians? The Text of John 1:13 Once More." *NovT* 27 (1985): 296–318.

Quek, Tze-Ming. "A Text-Critical Study of John 1.34," *NTS* 55 (2009): 22–34.

Radermakers, Jean. "Mission et Apostolat en Jean." Pages 100–21 in *Studia Evangelica II*. Berlin: de Gruyter, 1964.

Rahner, Johanna. *"Er aber sprach vom Tempel seines Leibes." Jesus von Nazaret als Ort der Offenbarung Gottes im vierten Evangelium*. BBB 117. Bodenheim: Philo, 1998.

Regev, Eyal. "Non-Priestly Purity and Its Religious Aspects according to Historical Sources and Archaeological Findings." Pages 223–44 in *Purity and Holiness: The Heritage of Leviticus*. Edited by M. J. H. M. Poorthuis and J. Schwartz. Leiden: Brill, 2000.

Reim, Günter. *Studien zum alttestamentlichen Hintergrund des Johannesevangeliums*. SNTSMS 22. Cambridge: Cambridge University Press, 1974.

———. "Targum und Johannesevangelium." *BZ* 27 (1983): 1–13.

———. "Zur Lokalisierung der johanneischen Gemeinde." *BZ* 32 (1988): 72–86.

Reinhartz, Adele. "Jesus as Prophet: Predictive Prolepses in the Fourth Gospel." *JSNT* 36 (1989): 3–16.

———. "'Jews' and Jews in the Fourth Gospel." Pages 213–30 in *Antijudaism and the Fourth Gospel*. Edited by R. Bieringer, D. Pollefet, and F. Vandecasteele-Vanneuville. Louisville: Westminster John Knox, 2001.

———. "Judaism in the Gospel of John." *Int* 63 (2009): 382–93.

Rengstorf, Karl Heinrich. "ἀποστέλλω." *TDNT* 1:398–447.

Rensberger, David. "The Messiah Who Has Come into the World: The Message of the Gospel of John." Pages 15–24 in *Jesus in Johannine Tradition*. Edited by R. Fortna and T. Thatcher. Louisville: Westminster John Knox, 2001.

———. "The Politics of John: The Trial of Jesus in the Fourth Gospel." *JBL* 103 (1984): 395–411.

Rese, Martin. "Johannes 3,22–36: Der taufende Jesus und das letzte Zeugnis Johannes des Taufers." Pages 89–98 in *Studies in the Gospel of John and Its Christology: Festschrift Gilbert Van Belle*. Edited by J. Verheyden, G. van Oyen, M. Labahn, and R. Bieringer. BETL 265. Leuven: Peeters, 2014.

Reynolds, Benjamin E. *The Apocalyptic Son of Man in the Gospel of John*. WUNT 2.249. Tübingen: Mohr Siebeck, 2008.

Rhea, Robert. *The Johannine Son of Man*. ATANT 76. Zürich: TVZ, 1990.

Ricca, Paolo. *Die Eschatologie des Vierten Evangeliums*. Zürich: Gotthelf, 1966.

Richard, E. "Expressions of Double Meaning and Their Function in the Gospel of John," *NTS* 31 (1985): 96–112.

Richter, Georg. *Die Fusswaschung im Johannesevangelium*. BU 1. Regensburg: Pustet, 1967.

———. *Studien zum Johannesevangelium*. BU 13. Regensburg: Pustet, 1977.

Riedl, Johannes. *Das Heilswerk nach Johannes*. FTS 93. Freiburg: Herder, 1973.
Riesenfeld, Harald. "The Gospel Tradition and Its Beginnings." Pages 131–53 in *The Gospels Reconsidered: A Selection of Papers Read to the International Congress on the Four Gospels, 1957*. Oxford: Blackwell, 1969.
Ritt, Hubert. *Das Gebet zum Vater*. FB 36. Würzburg: Echter, 1979.
Robinson, John A. T. "The Fourth Gospel and the Church's Doctrine of the Trinity." Pages 171–80 in *Twelve More New Testament Studies*. London: SCM, 1984.
———. *The Human Face of Jesus*. London: SCM, 1973.
———. *The Priority of John*. London: SCM, 1985.
———. *The Redating of the New Testament*. London: SCM, 1976.
———. "The Use of the Fourth Gospel for Christology Today." Pages 61–78 in *Christ and Spirit in the New Testament: In Honour of C. F. D. Moule*. Edited by B. Lindars and S. S. Smalley. Cambridge: Cambridge University Press, 1973.
Ruckstuhl, Eugen. "Abstieg und Erhöhung des johanneischen Menschensohnes." Pages 314–41 in *Jesus und der Menschensohn. Für Anton Vögtle*. Edited by R. Pesch and R. Schnackenburg. Freiburg: Herder, 1975.
———. "Kritische Arbeit am Johannesprolog." Pages 443–54 in *The New Testament Age: Essays in Honor of B. Reicke*. Edited by W. C. Weinrich. Macon: Mercer, 1984.
———. *Die literarische Einheit des Johannesevangeliums*. Studia fribourgensia NF 3. Freiburg, Switzerland: Paulus, 1951.
Rusam, Dietrich. "Das 'Lamm Gottes' (Joh 1,29.36) und die Deutung des Todes Jesu im Johannesevangelium." *BZ* 49 (2005): 60–80.
Sanday, W. *The Criticism of the Fourth Gospel*. Oxford: Clarendon, 1914.
Sanders, J. N., and B. A. Mastin, *A Commentary on the Gospel according to St. John*. BNTC. London: Black, 1968.
Schapdick, Stefan. "Autorität ohne Inhalt: Zum Mosebild des Johannesevangeliums." *ZNW* 97 (2006): 177–206.
Schenke, H. M. "Review of L. Schottroff, *Der Glaubende und die feindliche Welt*." *TLZ* 97 (1972): 751–55.
Schenke, Ludger. "Christologie als Theologie. Versuch über das Johannesevangelium." Pages 445–65 in *Von Jesus zum Christus. Christologische Studien. Festgabe für Paul Hoffmann zum 65. Geburtstag*. BZNW 93. Edited by R. Hoppe and U. Busse. Berlin: de Gruyter, 1998.
———. "Die literarische Vorgeschichte von Joh 6,26–58." *BZ* 29 (1985): 68–89.
Schillebeeckx, Edward. *Christ: The Christian Experience in the Modern World*. London: SCM, 1980.
Schlier, Heinrich. "In Anfang war das Wort: Zum Prolog des Johannesevangeliums." Pages 274–87 in *Die Zeit der Kirche. Exegetische Aufsätze und Vorträge*. Freiburg: Herder, 1968.
———. "Zur Christologie des Johannesevangeliums." Pages 85–101 in *Das Ende der Zeit. Exegetische Aufsätze und Vorträge III*. Freiburg: Herder, 1971.
Schlund, Christine. *"Kein Knochen soll gebrochen werden": Studien zu Bedeutung und Funktion des Pesachfests in Texten des frühen Judentums und im Johannesevangelium*. WMANT 107. Neukirchen-Vluyn: Neukirchener Verlag, 2005.
———. "Schutz und Bewahrung als ein soteriologisches Motiv des Johannesevangeliums." Pages 529–36 in *The Death of Jesus in the Fourth Gospel*. BETL 200. Edited by G. Van Belle. Leuven: Peeters, 2007.
Schmidl, Martin. *Jesus und Nikodemus. Gespräch zur johanneischen Christologie. Joh 3 in schichtenspezifischer Sicht*. BU 28. Regensburg: Pustet, 1998.

Bibliography

Schmithals, Walter. *Johannesevangelium und Johannesbriefe. Forschungsgeschichte und Analyse.* BZNW 64. Berlin: De Gruyter, 1992.

———. "Der Prolog des Johannesevangeliums." *ZNW* 70 (1979): 16–43.

Schnackenburg, Rudolf. "Die ecce-homo-Szene und der Menschensohn." Pages 371–86 in *Jesus und der Menschensohn. Für Anton Vögtle.* Edited by R. Pesch and R. Schnackenburg. Freiburg: Herder, 1975.

———. "Ist der Gedanke des Sühnetodes Jesu der einzige Zugang zum Verständnis unserer Erlösung durch Jesus Christus?" Pages 205–30 in *Der Tod Jesu. Deutungen im Neuen Testament.* QD 74. Edited by K. Kertlege. Herder: Freiburg, 1978.

———. "Johannesevangelium als hermeneutische Frage." *NTS* 13 (1967): 197–210.

———. *Das Johannesevangelium. I. Teil. Einleitung und Kommentar zu Kap. 1–4.* 5th ed. HThKNT 4.1. Freiburg: Herder, 1981.

———. *Das Johannesevangelium. II. Teil. Kommentar zu Kap. 5–12.* 2nd ed. HThKNT 4.2. Freiburg: Herder, 1977.

———. *Das Johannesevangelium. III. Teil. Kommentar zu Kap. 13–21.* 4th ed. HThKNT 4.3. Freiburg: Herder, 1982.

———. *Das Johannesevangelium. IV. Teil. Ergänzende Auslegungen und Exkurse.* HThKNT 4.4. Freiburg: Herder, 1984.

———. "Logos-Hymnus und johanneischer Prolog." *BZ* 1 (1957): 69–109.

———. "Der Menschensohn im Johannesevangelium." *NTS* 11 (1964/65): 123–37.

———. *Die Person Jesu Christi im Spiegel der vier Evangelien.* HThKS 4. Freiburg: Herder, 1993.

———. "'Und das Wort ist Fleisch geworden.'" *IKaZ* 8 (1979): 1–9.

Schneiders, Sandra. *The Johannine Resurrection Narrative: An Exegetical and Theological Study of John 20 as a Synthesis of Johannine Spirituality.* Rome: Gregorian University Press, 1975.

Schnelle, Udo. *Antidoketische Christologie im Johannesevangelium. Eine Untersuchung zur Stellung des vierten Evangeliums in der johanneischen Schule.* Göttingen: Vandenhoeck und Ruprecht, 1987.

———. "Cross and Resurrection in the Gospel of John." Pages 127–51 in *The Resurrection of Jesus in the Gospel of John.* Edited by C. Koester and R. Bieringer. Tübingen: Mohr Siebeck, 2008.

———. *Das Evangelium nach Johannes.* THNT 4. Berlin: Evangelische Verlagsanstalt, 1998.

———. "Markinische und johanneische Kreuzestheologie." Pages 233–58 in *The Death of Jesus in the Fourth Gospel.* Edited by G. Van Belle. BETL 200. Leuven: Peeters, 2007.

———. "Die Tempelreinigung und die Christologie des Johannesevangeliums." *NTS* 42 (1996): 359–73.

———. "Trinitarisches Denken im Johannesevangelium." Pages 367–86 in *Israel und seine Heilstraditionen im Johannesevangelium. Festgabe für Johannes Beutler SJ zum 70. Geburtstag.* Edited by M. Labahn, K. Scholtissek, and A. Strothmann. Paderborn: Ferdinand Schöningh, 2004.

Schnider, Franz, and Werner Stenger. *Johannes und die Synoptiker.* Munich: Kösel, 1971.

Scholtissek, Klaus. "'Eine grössere Liebe als diese hat niemand, als wenn einer sein Leben hingibt für seine Freunde' (Joh 15,13): Die hellenistische Freundschaftsethik und das Johannesevangelium." Pages 413–39 in *Kontexte des Johannesevangeliums. Das vierte Evangelium in religions- und traditionsgeschichtlicher Perspektive.* Edited by J. Frey and U. Schnelle. WUNT 175. Tübingen: Mohr Siebeck, 2004.

BIBLIOGRAPHY

———. "'Ich und der Vater, wir sind eins' (Joh 10,30). Zum theologischen Potential und zur hermeneutischen Kompetenz der johanneischen Christologie." Pages 315–45 in *Theology and Christology in the Fourth Gospel: Essays by the Members of the SNTS Johannine Writings Seminar*. Edited by G. Van Belle, J. G. van der Watt, and P. Maritz. BETL 184. Leuven: Peeters, 2005.

Schoonenberg, Piet. "A Sapiential Reading of John's Prologue." *TD* 33 (1986): 403–21.

Schottroff, Luise. *Der Glaubende und die feindliche Welt*. WMANT 37. Neukirchen: Neukirchener Verlag, 1970.

Schröter, Jens. "Sterben für die Freunde: Überlegungen zur Deutung des Todes Jesu im Johannesvangelium." Pages 263–87 in *Religionsgeschichte des Neuen Testaments. Festschrift für Klaus Berger zum 60. Geburtstag*. Edited by A. von Bobbeler, et al. Tübingen: Francke, 2000.

Schuchard, Bruce G. *Scripture within Scripture: The Interrelationship of Form and Function in the Explicit Old Testament Citations in the Gospel of John*. SBLDS 133. Atlanta: Scholars, 1992.

Schulz, Siegfried. *Das Evangelium nach Johannes*. NTD 4. Göttingen: Vandenhoeck und Ruprecht, 1972.

———. *Untersuchungen zur Menschensohn-Christologie im Johannesevangelium*. Göttingen: Vandenhoeck und Ruprecht, 1957.

Schürmann, Heinz. "Joh 6,51c—ein Schlüssel zur grossen johanneischen Brotrede." *BZ* 2 (1959): 244–62.

Schwankl, Otto. "Aspekte der johanneischen Christologie." Pages 347–75 in *Theology and Christology in the Fourth Gospel: Essays by the Members of the SNTS Johannine Writings Seminar*. Edited by G. Van Belle, J. G. van der Watt, and P. Maritz. BETL 184. Leuven: Peeters, 2005.

Schweizer, Eduard. *Ego Eimi*. 2nd ed. FRLANT 56. Göttingen: Vandenhoeck und Ruprecht, 1965.

———. *Jesus Christus im vielfältigen Zeugnis des Neuen Testaments*. Hamburg: Siebenstern, 1968.

———. "Jesus der Zeuge Gottes." Pages 161–66 in *Studies in John: Presented to J. N. Sevenster*. NovTSup 24. Leiden: Brill, 1970.

———. "Das johanneische Zeugnis vom Herrenmahl." *EvT* 12 (1952/1953): 341–63.

———. "Der Kirchenbegriff im Evangelium und in den Briefen des Johannes." Pages 363–68 in *Studia Evangelica I*. TU 73. Berlin: de Gruyter, 1959.

Schwindt, Rainer. *Gesichte der Herrlichkeit. Eine exegetisch-traditionsgeschichtliche Studie zur paulinischen und johanneischen Christologie*. HBS 50. Freiburg: Herder, 2007.

Scott, E. F. *The Fourth Gospel: Its Purpose and Theology*. Edinburgh: T&T Clark, 1908.

Scott, Martin. *Sophia and the Johannine Jesus*. JSNTSup 71. Sheffield: JSOT, 1992.

Scroggs, Robin. *Christology in Paul and John*. Philadelphia: Fortress, 1988.

Segal, Alan F. "Pre-Existence and Incarnation: A Response to Dunn and Holladay." *Semeia* 30 (1984): 83–95.

———. *Two Powers in Heaven: Early Rabbinic Reports about Christianity and Gnosticism*. Leiden: Brill, 1977.

Segovia, Fernando. F. *The Farewell of the Word: The Johannine Call to Abide*. Minneapolis: Fortress, 1991.

———. "John 13:1–30. The Footwashing in the Johannine Tradition." *ZNW* 73 (1982): 31–51.

———. *Love Relationships in the Johannine Tradition*. SBLDS 58. Chico: Scholars, 1982.

―――. "The Structure, Tendenz and Sitz im Leben of John 13:31–14:31." *JBL* 104 (1985): 471–93.
―――. "The Theology and Provenance of John 15:1–18." *JBL* 101 (1982): 115–28.
Seynaeve, Jean. "Les verbes ἀποστέλλω et πέμπω dans le vocabulaire théologique de Saint Jean." Pages 385–89 in *L'Évangile de Jean. Sources, Rédaction, Théologie*. Edited by M. de Jonge. BETL 44. Leuven: Peeters, 1977.
Sheppard, Beth M. "Another Look: Johannine 'Subordinationist Christology' and the Roman Family." Pages 101–19 in *New Currents through John: A Global Perspective*. SBLRBS 54. Edited by F. Lozada and T. Thatcher. Atlanta: SBL, 2006.
Sidebottom, E. M. *The Christ of the Fourth Gospel*. London: SPCK, 1961.
Skinner, Christopher W., ed. *Characters and Characterization in the Gospel of John*. LNTS. London: T&T Clark, 2013.
Smalley, Stephen S. "Johannes 1,51 und die Einleitung zum vierten Evangelium." Pages 300–13 in *Jesus und der Menschensohn. Für Anton Vögtle*. Edited by R. Pesch and R. Schnackenburg. Freiburg: Herder, 1975.
―――. *John: Evangelist and Interpreter*. Exeter: Paternoster, 1978.
Smith, D. Moody. "Johannine Christianity: Some Reflections on Its Character and Delineation." *NTS* 21 (1975): 225–48.
―――. *The Theology of the Gospel of John*. Cambridge: Cambridge University Press, 1997.
Söding, Thomas. "Einsatz des Lebens: Ein Motiv johanneischen Soteriologie." Pages 363–84 in *The Death of Jesus in the Fourth Gospel*. Edited by G. Van Belle. BETL 200. Leuven: Peeters, 2007.
―――. "'Ich und der Vater sind eins' (Joh 10,30). Die johanneische Christologie vor dem Anspruch des Hauptgebotes (Dtn 6,4f)." *ZNW* 93 (2002): 177–99.
―――. "Kreuzerhöhung. Zur Deutung des Todes Jesu nach Johannes." *ZTK* 103 (2006): 2–25.
―――. "Die Macht der Wahrheit und das Reich der Freiheit: Zur johanneischen Deutung des Pilatus-Prozess (Joh 18,28–19,16)." *ZTK* 93 (1996): 35–58.
Sproston, Wendy E. "'Is not this Jesus, the son of Joseph?' (John 6:42): Johannine Christology as a Challenge to Faith." *JSNT* 24 (1985): 77–97.
Steegen, Martijn. "Raising the Dead in John 5,19–30: Questioning Equality or Subordination in the Relationship between the Father and the Son." Pages 229–48 in *Resurrection of the Dead: Biblical Traditions in Dialogue*. Edited by G. van Oyen and T. Shepherd. BETL 249. Leuven: Peeters, 2012.
Stevens, G. B. *The Theology of the New Testament*. Edinburgh: T&T Clark, 1889.
Strachan, Robert. H. *The Fourth Gospel*. 3rd ed. London: SCM, 1941.
Strathmann, Hermann. *Das Evangelium nach Johannes*. 10th ed. NTD 4. Göttingen: Vandenhoeck und Ruprecht, 1963.
Strecker, Georg. "Die Anfänge der johanneischen Schule." *NTS* 32 (1986): 31–47.
―――. *Theologie des Neuen Testaments*. Berlin: de Gruyter, 1995.
Stuhlmacher, Peter. *Biblische Theologie des Neuen Testaments*. 2 vols. Göttingen: Vandenhoeck und Ruprecht, 1992–1999.
Sturdevant, Jason S. *The Adaptable Jesus of the Fourth Gospel: The Pedagogy of the Logos*. NovTSup 162. Leiden: Brill, 2015.
Suggit, John. "John 19:5. 'Behold the Man.'" *ExpTim* 94 (1983): 333–34.
Suh, Joong Suk. *The Glory in the Gospel of John: Restoration of Forfeited Prestige*. Oxford, OH: M. P. Publications, 1995.
Talbert, Charles H. "'And the Word Became Flesh': When?" Pages 43–52 in *The Future of Christology*. Edited by A. J. Malherbe and W. A. Meeks. Minneapolis: Fortress, 1993.

———. "The Myth of the Descending and Ascending Redeemer in Mediterranean Antiquity." *NTS* 22 (1976): 418–39.

———. *Reading John: A Literary and Theological Commentary on the Fourth Gospel and the Johannine Epistles*. New York: Crossroad, 1992.

Temple, Sydney. *The Core of the Fourth Gospel*. London: Oxford University Press, 1975.

Thatcher, Tom. "Remembering Jesus: John's Negative Christology." Pages 165–89 in *The Messiah in the Old and New Testaments*. Edited by S. E. Porter. Grand Rapids: Eerdmans, 2007.

Theobald, Michael. "Abraham—(Isaak—) Jakob. Israels Väter im Johannesevangelium." Pages 158–83 in *Israel und seine Heilstraditionen im Johannesevangelium. Festgabe für Johannes Beutler SJ zum 70. Geburtstag*. Edited by M. Labahn, K. Scholtissek, and A. Strotmann. Paderborn: Ferdinand Schöningh, 2004.

———. *Das Evangelium nach Johannes Kapitel 1–12*. Regensburg: Pustet, 2009.

———. *Die Fleischwerdung des Logos: Studien zum Verhältnis des Johannesprologs zum Corpus des Evangeliums und zu 1 Joh*. NTAbh 20. Münster: Aschendorf, 1988.

———. "Gott, Logos und Pneuma. 'Trinitarische' Rede von Gott im Johannesevangelium." Pages 349–88 in *Studien zum Corpus Iohanneum*. WUNT 267. Tübingen: Mohr Siebeck, 2010.

———. *Herrenworte im Johannesevangelium*. HBS 34. Freiburg: Herder, 2002.

———. *Im Anfang war das Wort. Textlinguistische Studie zum Johannesprolog*. SBS 106. Stuttgart: KBW, 1983.

———. "Das Johannesevangelium—Zeugnis eines synagogalen 'Judenchristentums'?" Pages 107–58 in *Paulus und Johannes. Exegetische Studien zur paulinischen und johanneischen Theologie und Literatur*. WUNT 198. Edited by D. Sänger and U. Mell. Tübingen: Mohr Siebeck, 2006.

Thettayil, Benny. *In Spirit and Truth: An Exegetical Study of John 4:19-26 and a Theological Investigation of the Replacement Theme in the Fourth Gospel*. CBET 46. Leuven: Peeters, 2007.

Thompson, Marianne. *The God of the Gospel of John*. Grand Rapids: Eerdmans, 2001.

———. *The Humanity of Jesus in the Fourth Gospel*. Philadelphia: Fortress, 1988.

———. *The Incarnate Word: Perspectives on the Fourth Gospel*. Peabody: Hendrickson, 1988.

Thüsing, Wilhelm. *Die Erhöhung und Verherrlichung Jesu im Johannesevangelium*. 3rd ed. NTAbh 21. Münster: Aschendorff, 1979.

Thyen, Hartwig. "Aus der Literatur zum Johannesevangelium." *TRu* 39 (1974): 1–69, 222–52, 289–330; 42 (1977): 211–70; 43 (1978): 328–59; 44 (1979): 97–134.

———. "'... denn wir lieben die Brüder' (1 Joh 3,14)." Pages 527–42 in *Rechtfertigung. Festschrift für E. Käsemann*. Edited by G. Friedrich et al. Tübingen: Mohr Siebeck, 1976.

———. "Entwicklungen innerhalb der johanneischen Theologie und Kirche im Spiegel von Joh 21 und der Lieblingsjüngertexte des Evangeliums." Pages 259–99 in *L'Évangile de Jean. Sources, Rédaction, Théologie*. Edited by M. de Jonge. BETL 44. Leuven: Peeters, 1977.

———. "Erwägungen zu Jesu Prädikationen als ἴσος τῷ θεῷ, θεός und υἱὸς τοῦ θεοῦ." Pages 692–96 in *Studien zum Corpus Iohanneum*. WUNT 214. Tübingen: Mohr Siebeck, 2007.

———. *Das Johannesevangelium*. HNT 6. Tübingen: Mohr Siebeck, 2005.

———. "μονογενής und die frühe Rezeptionsgeschichte des Lexems." Pages 429–33 in *Studien zum Corpus Iohanneum*. WUNT 214. Tübingen: Mohr Siebeck, 2007.

———. "'Niemand hat grössere Liebe als die, dass er sein Leben für seine Freunde hingibt' (Joh 15,13)." Pages 467–81 in *Theologia Crucis—Signum Crucis. Festschrift für E. Dinkler*. Edited by C. Andresen and G. Klein. Tübingen: Mohr Siebeck, 1979.

Bibliography

Tolmie, D. François. "The Ἰουδαῖοι in the Fourth Gospel: A Narratological Perspective." Pages 377-97 in *Theology and Christology in the Fourth Gospel: Essays by the Members of the SNTS Johannine Writings Seminar*. Edited by G. Van Belle, J. G. van der Watt, and P. Maritz. BETL 184. Leuven: Peeters, 2005.

Tovey, Derek. *Narrative Art and Act in the Fourth Gospel*. JSNTSup 151. Sheffield: Sheffield Academic Press, 1997.

Trites, Alison A. *The New Testament Concept of Witness*. SNTSMS 31. Cambridge: Cambridge University Press, 1977.

Trudinger, L. Paul. "The Israelite in Whom There Is No Guile." *EvQ* 54 (1982): 117-20.

Turner, Max. "Atonement and the Death of Jesus in John—Some Questions to Bultmann and Forestell." *EvQ* 62 (1990): 99-122.

Um, Stephen T. *The Theme of Temple Christology in John's Gospel*. LNTS 312. London: T&T Clark, 2006.

Untergassmair, Franz. *Im Namen Jesu*. FB 13. Stuttgart: KBW, 1973.

Vahrenhorst, Martin. "Johannes und die Tora: Überlegungen zur Bedeutung der Tora im Johannesevangelium," *KD* 54 (2008): 14-36.

Van Belle, Gilbert. "Christology and Soteriology in the Fourth Gospel: The Conclusion to the Gospel of John Revisited." Pages 435-61 in *Theology and Christology in the Fourth Gospel: Essays by the Members of the SNTS Johannine Writings Seminar*. Edited by G. Van Belle, J. G. van der Watt, and P. Maritz. BETL 184. Leuven: Peeters, 2005.

———. "The Death of Jesus and the Literary Unity of the Fourth Gospel." Pages 3-64 in *The Death of Jesus in the Fourth Gospel*. BETL 200. Edited by G. Van Belle. Leuven: Peeters, 2007.

———. "The Return of John to Jesus Research." *LS* 32 (2007): 23-48.

———. "The Signs of the Messiah in the Fourth Gospel: The Problem of a 'Wonder-Working Messiah.'" Pages 159-78 in *The Scriptures of Israel in Jewish and Christian Tradition: Essays in Honour of Maarten J. J. Menken*. Edited by B. J. Koet, S. Moyise, and J. Verheyden. NovTSup 148. Leiden: Brill, 2013.

———. *The Signs Source in the Fourth Gospel*. BETL 96. Leuven: Peeters, 1994.

van der Watt, Jan G. "Eschatology in John: A Continuous Process of Realizing Events." Pages 109-40 in *Eschatology of the New Testament and Some Related Documents*. Edited by J. G. van der Watt. Tübingen: Mohr Siebeck, 2011.

———. "Ethics of/and the Opponents of Jesus in John's Gospel." Pages 175-91 in *Rethinking the Ethics of John: "Implicit Ethics" in the Johannine Writings*. Edited by J. G. van der Watt and R. Zimmermann. Contexts and Norms of New Testament Ethics 3. Tübingen: Mohr Siebeck, 2012.

———. *Family of the King: Dynamics of Metaphor in the Gospel according to John*. BI 47. Leiden: Brill, 2000.

———. *An Introduction to the Johannine Gospel and Letters*. London: T&T Clark, 2007.

———. "Der meisterschüler Gottes (Von der Lehre des Sohnes)—Joh 5,19-23." Pages 745-54 in *Kompendium der Gleichnisse Jesu*. Edited by R. Zimmermann. Gütersloh: Gütersloher Verlagshaus, 2007.

———. "Salvation in the Gospel According to John." Pages 101-31 in *Salvation in the New Testament: Perspectives on Soteriology*. NovTSup 121. Edited by J. G. van der Watt. Leiden: Brill, 2005.

———. "Symbolism in John's Gospel: An Evaluation of Dodd's Contribution." Pages 66-85 in *Engaging with C. H. Dodd on the Gospel of John: Sixty Years of Tradition and Interpretation*. Edited by T. Thatcher and C. H. Williams. Cambridge: Cambridge University Press, 2014.

van der Watt, Jan G., and Chrys Caragounis, "A Grammatical Analysis of John 1,1." *Filologia Neotestamentaria* 21 (2008): 91–138.

van Hartingsveld, Lodewijk. *Die Eschatologie des Johannesevangeliums*. Assen: Van Gorcum, 1962.

Vellanickel, Matthew. *The Divine Sonship of Christians in the Johannine Writings*. AnBib 72. Rome: BibInst, 1977.

Vermes, Geza. *Scripture and Tradition in Judaism*. Leiden: Brill, 1961.

Von den Osten-Sacken, Peter. "Leistung und Grenze der johanneischen Kreuzestheologie." *EvT* 36 (1976): 154–76.

von Wahlde, Urban C. *The Gospel and Letters of John*. 3 vols. Grand Rapids: Eerdmans, 2010.

———. "'You Are of Your Father the Devil' in Its Context: Stereotyped Polemic in Jn 8:38–47." Pages 418–44 in *Anti-Judaism and the Fourth Gospel*. Edited by R. Bieringer, D. Pollefet, and F. Vandecasteele-Vanneuville. Louisville: Westminster John Knox, 2001.

Voorwinde, Stephen. *Jesus' Emotions in the Fourth Gospel: Human or Divine?* SNTSup 284. London: T&T Clark, 2005.

Watson, Francis. "Is John's Christology Adoptionist?" Pages 113–24 in *The Glory of Christ in the New Testament: Studies in Christology. In Honour of G. B. Caird*. Edited by L. D. Hurst and N. T. Wright. Oxford: Clarendon, 1987.

Wead, David W. *The Literary Devices in John's Gospel*. Basel: Reinhardt, 1970.

Weder, Hans. "Die Menschwerdung Gottes." *ZThK* 82 (1985): 325–60.

Weidemann, Hans-Ulrich. *Der Tod Jesu im Johannesevangelium. Die erste Abschiedsrede als Schlüsseltext für den Passions- und Osterbericht*. BZNW 122. Berlin: de Gruyter, 2004.

Weiss, Bernhard. *Lehrbuch der Biblischen Theologie des Neuen Testaments*. 5th ed. Berlin: Wilhelm Kerk, 1888.

Wengst, Klaus. *Bedrängte Gemeinde und verherrlichter Christus*. BibS[N] 5. Neukirchen-Vluyn: Neukirchener, 1981.

———. *Christologische Formeln und Lieder des Urchristentums*. Gütersloh: Mohn, 1972.

Westcott, B. F. *The Gospel according to John*. London: Clarke, 1958.

Wetter, G. P. *Der Sohn Gottes*. FRLANT 26. Göttingen: Vandenhoeck und Ruprecht, 1916.

Whitacre, Rodney A. *Johannine Polemic*. SBLDS 67. Chico: Scholars, 1982.

Wilckens, Ulrich. "Der eucharistische Abschnitt der johanneischen Rede vom Lebensbrot (Joh 6,51c–58)." Pages 220–48 in *Neues Testament und Kirche. Festschrift für R. Schnackenburg*. Edited by J. Gnilka. Freiburg: Herder, 1974.

———. *Das Evangelium nach Johannes*. NTD 4. Göttingen: Vandenhoeck und Ruprecht, 1998.

Wilkens, Wilhelm. *Zeichen und Werke*. ATANT 55. Zürich: Zwingli, 1969.

Williams, Catrin H. "'He Saw His Glory and Spoke about Him': The Testimony of Isaiah and Johannine Christology." Pages 53–80 in *Honouring the Past and Shaping the Future: Religious and Biblical Studies in Wales. Essays in Honour of Gareth Lloyd Jones*. Leominster: Gracewing, 2003.

———. "'I am' or 'I am He'? Self-Declaratory Pronouncements in the Fourth Gospel and Rabbinic Tradition." Pages 343–52 in *Jesus in Johannine Tradition*. Edited by R. T. Fortna and T. Thatcher. Louisville: Westminster John Knox, 2001.

Williams, J. T. "Cultic Elements in the Fourth Gospel." Pages 339–50 in *Studia Biblica 1978. II.*

Bibliography

Papers on the Gospels: Sixth International Congress on Biblical Studies. Edited by E. A. Livingstone. Sheffield: JSOT, 1980.
Wilson, R. M. "Nag Hammadi and the New Testament." *NTS* 28 (1982): 289–302.
Witherington, Ben, III. *John's Wisdom: A Commentary on the Fourth Gospel*. Louisville: Westminster John Knox, 1995.
Witkamp, L. Th. "The Use of Traditions in John 5:1–18." *JSNT* 25 (1985): 19–47.
Woll, D. Bruce. *Johannine Christianity in Conflict*. SBLDS 60. Chico: Scholars, 1981.
———. "The Preparation of 'the Way': The First Farewell Discourses in the Gospel of John." *JBL* 99 (1980): 225–39.
Wrede, William. *Charakter und Tendenz des Johannesevangeliums*. 2nd ed. Tübingen: Mohr Siebeck, 1933.
Yee, Gail A. *Jewish Feasts and the Gospel of John*. Zacchaeus Studies: New Testament. Wilmington: Glazier, 1989.
Zeller, Dieter. "Der Ostermorgen im vierten Evangelium." Pages 145–61 in *Auferstehung Jesu und Auferstehung der Christen*. Edited by H. Oberlinner. QD 105. Freiburg: Herder, 1986.
Zimmermann, Heinrich. "Das absolute *egō eimi* als neutestamentliche Offenbarungsformel." *BZ* 4 (1960): 54–69, 266–76.
———. "Christushymnus und johanneischer Prolog." Pages 249–65 in *Neues Testament und Kirche. Festschrift für R. Schnackenburg*. Edited by J. Gnilka. Freiburg: Herder, 1974.
Zimmermann, Ruben. *Christologie der Bilder im Johannesevangelium. Die Christopoetik des vierten Evangeliums unter besonderer Berücksichtigung von Joh 10*. WUNT 171. Tübingen, Mohr Siebeck, 2004.
Zumstein, Jean. "Die Deutung der Ostererfahrung in den Abschiedreden des Johannesevangeliums." *ZTK* 104 (2007): 117–41.
———. "L'interprétation johannique de la mort du Christ." Pages 2119–28 in *The Four Gospels 1992. Festschrift for Frans Neirynck*. Edited by F. van Segbroeck, C. M. Tuckett, G. Van Belle, and J. Verheyden. BETL 100. Leuven: Peeters, 1992.
———. "Der Prolog als Schwelle zum vierten Evangelium." Pages 49–75 in *Der Johannesprolog*. Edited by G. Kruck. Darmstadt: WBG, 2009.

Index of Modern Authors

Ahn, Michael, 243, 256, 437, 441–44
Anderson, Paul N., 10, 11, 13, 17, 25, 32, 35, 43, 169, 288, 292, 296, 349, 353, 362, 374, 384–85, 387, 395–97, 419, 421, 440–41
Appold, Mark L., 11–13, 21, 43, 112, 147, 149, 157, 173, 175–76, 181, 208, 229–30, 235–36, 239, 245, 256, 292, 299, 308, 314, 337–38, 349, 360, 362–63, 378, 381, 386, 436, 467
Ashton, John, 10, 11, 14, 18, 19, 23, 27, 34, 47, 149, 154, 157, 162–63, 168–69, 200, 211, 219, 224–25, 245–46, 248, 251, 252, 256–57, 270, 283–84, 288, 292, 294, 306, 309, 322–23, 327, 333–35, 342, 351, 354, 362, 374, 380, 389–90, 400, 404, 421, 436–43, 445–47, 450, 457–58, 469–70
Augenstein, Jörg, 450
Aune, David E., 404

Back, Frances, 370
Backhaus, Knut, 257
Baffes, Melanie, 276
Bailey, Cyril, 394
Ball, David Mark, 347–48, 353
Balz, Horst, 456
Barrett, C. K., 398, 401, 418, 455, 459,
Bauckham, Richard, 36, 321, 324, 333, 336, 338–39, 343, 347–48, 350–52, 363, 422, 436, 439, 441
Bauer, Walter, 159, 256, 319, 323, 350
Baum-Bodenbender, 112, 161, 205–6, 248, 383, 388

Baur, Rosel, 12, 236, 239, 271, 283, 359, 367–68, 372, 375–77, 379, 382, 394, 415–16
Beasley-Murray, George R., 25, 47–49, 74, 82, 91, 103, 112, 152, 157, 165, 170, 179–82, 186, 188, 205, 210, 214, 218, 221, 223, 229, 241, 245, 250, 257, 263, 276, 299, 307, 311, 313, 320, 324, 330, 335–36, 339, 341, 347, 350, 352, 376, 384, 441, 456
Becker, Jürgen, 12, 15, 24, 29, 33, 35, 42, 44, 47, 52, 60, 68, 74, 82, 91, 104–5, 147, 149, 157, 172, 176, 189, 196, 210–11, 229, 236, 238, 245, 269, 286, 294–95, 300, 302, 335, 348, 351–52, 361, 363, 374, 378, 398, 421, 424, 431, 435, 450, 453, 455, 457, 259
Bennema, Cornelis, 33, 36, 271, 273, 277, 285, 289, 293, 296–97, 322, 368, 370, 469
Berger, Klaus, 374, 376
Bergmeier, Roland, 21, 24, 179–80, 188, 190, 242, 294, 372, 374
Bernhard, J. H., 234–35
Berrouard, M. F., 104
Bertram, Georg, 241, 245
Beutler, Johannes, 46–48, 95, 97, 110–12, 157, 163, 169, 172, 174, 176, 179, 184–86, 188, 200, 217, 219, 229, 233, 242, 252–53, 256, 273, 310, 317, 322, 324, 327–28, 371, 374, 383, 385, 419, 436–37, 444–46, 450
Beyschlag, D. Willibald, 304, 306–7, 317, 357–58
Bieringer, Reimund, 150–54, 333, 469

Index of Modern Authors

Bittner, Wolfgang J., 217, 228, 247–48, 256, 292, 454
Bjerkelund, C. J., 218, 248, 459
Blank, Josef, 22, 27–28, 30, 46, 48, 59, 95, 103, 112, 156, 205–6, 210–11, 214, 230, 237, 245, 250, 258, 272, 285, 294, 305, 350, 359, 398, 409, 420, 461–62
Blinzler, Josef, 112
Boismard, M.-E., 34, 48, 52, 74, 111, 113, 115, 152, 157, 162, 165, 169, 172, 186, 203, 206, 217, 245, 256, 258, 273, 276, 341, 344, 349–51, 356, 361, 384, 455
Bond, Helen, 113, 162, 182, 270
Borgen, Peder, 23, 32, 52, 169, 250, 322, 331–32, 361, 385, 439
Borig, Rainer, 100–101, 344
Boring, M. E., 97, 101, 135, 273, 404, 406
Bornkamm, Günther, 11, 13, 14, 18, 21, 27, 44, 46–47, 82, 136, 196, 204, 224, 236, 239, 383, 390, 397, 403, 409, 418
Borsch, Frederick H., 251
Bousset, Wilhelm, 12, 373, 377, 381
Boyarin, Daniel, 322, 324
Braine, David D. C., 165, 324, 443
Brant, Jo-Ann A., 317, 412, 414
Braun, F.-M., 156–57, 176, 179, 188, 205, 237, 239, 358–60, 368, 373
Breuss, Josef, 43, 74, 188
Brown, Raymond E., 25, 33–35, 48, 50–52, 60, 68, 74–75, 77, 81–82, 86, 91, 95, 104, 106, 112–13, 115–16, 152, 157, 162, 169, 182, 184–86, 188–89, 196, 206, 214, 219, 222–23, 229, 245, 248, 251, 254, 256–57, 262, 276, 285, 292, 306, 313–15, 321–22, 324, 330, 335–36, 339, 341, 343, 347, 349–53, 358, 376, 380, 384, 392, 399, 422, 436, 446, 448, 452–53
Bruce, F. F., 49, 82, 153, 157, 161, 170, 174, 184, 186, 214, 218, 223, 236, 245, 251, 253, 257, 258, 276, 311, 319–20, 330, 349–51, 361, 369, 374, 384, 406, 446
Brun, Lyder, 17, 303–8, 357
Büchsel, Friedrich, 283, 304–8, 336, 341, 358, 367, 369, 375
Bühner, Jan, 23, 32, 44, 59, 135, 205, 235, 247, 250, 254, 256, 310, 314, 342, 348, 352, 361, 368, 445, 455

Bultmann, Rudolf, ix, 1-10, 12–15, 18-22, 24, 25, 27–33, 37, 41–42, 44, 49, 75, 82, 84, 95, 101, 103–4, 145, 147–149, 157, 162, 165, 172, 179, 182, 184–85, 190, 197, 205, 207, 211, 214, 218, 220, 224, 228, 235, 236, 239, 247, 250, 256, 266, 270–71, 283–88, 290, 294–96, 302–3, 310–11, 313, 317, 321–22, 337, 349, 373–75, 378, 386, 388, 401–2, 436, 450, 462–63
Burge, Gary M., 48–49, 82, 97, 103, 136, 157, 186, 188, 245, 253, 256, 276, 299, 368–69, 399, 404, 406
Burkett, Delbert, 217, 229, 245, 248, 251, 257, 259, 314, 348–52, 384, 439
Burkitt, F. C., 394
Burney, Charles F., 153
Burrows, F. W., 155
Busse, Ulrich, 11, 15, 157, 172, 186, 256–57, 289, 317–18, 326, 333, 343, 360–61, 438, 444, 448
Bynum, William Randolph, 243
Byrne, Brendan, 115–16

Cadman, W. H., 17, 67, 236, 239, 251, 256, 303–7, 357–58, 360, 367, 393
Caird, George B., 219, 236, 244
Caragounis, Chrys, 311, 318–20
Carson, Donald A., 48, 103–4, 153, 180, 184, 186, 188, 211, 219, 234, 242, 250, 254, 257, 276, 339, 348–49, 352, 360, 439, 444
Carter, Warren, 347, 466
Cassidy, Robert J., 346
Chanikuzhy, Jacob, 182, 185–86, 447–48
Charlesworth, James, 397
Chibici-Revneanu, Nicole, 203, 233, 235, 248, 253, 261
Childs, Brevard, 270, 399
Cho, Sukmin, 440
Collins, Adela, 254, 257, 437, 439,
Collins, Raymond F., 317, 469
Coloe, Mary L., 157, 159, 162–63, 181–82, 185, 188, 257, 276–77, 300, 324, 348, 352, 441, 443–44, 446–48
Conway, Colleen M., 296, 389
Coppens, Joseph, 84, 245, 251, 256
Corell, Alf, 43
Cory, Catherine, 242, 448

INDEX OF MODERN AUTHORS

Cullmann, Oscar, 74, 153, 258, 320, 330, 375, 398–99, 446
Culpepper, R. Alan, 36, 58, 65, 184, 188, 200, 259, 317, 377, 380, 382, 399, 410–12, 417, 450, 469–70

Dahl, Nils A., 27, 218, 235, 250, 270, 341, 409, 436
Dahms, J. V., 328
Daly-Denton, Margaret, 437
D'Angelo, Mary Rose, 116
Danker, Frederick W., 159
Dauer, Alfons, 26, 27, 110, 112, 116, 148, 156, 161, 165, 173, 179, 205–6, 208, 210, 228, 230, 242, 269, 279, 349, 350, 382, 385
Davey, J. E., 218, 341, 363, 388
Davies, Margaret, 10, 15, 157, 257, 303, 330, 336, 384
de Boer, Martinus C., 14, 34, 36, 168–70, 174, 177, 184–86, 190–91, 197, 208, 225, 248, 254, 256, 263–64, 314, 386, 422, 430, 436, 438, 440–41, 469
de Jonge, Henk Jan, 469
de Jonge, Marinus, 14, 18, 22, 25, 35, 44, 58–59, 74–75, 116, 135, 186, 205, 217, 256, 271, 286, 299, 337, 344, 354, 356, 374, 382, 384–85, 396–97, 406–7, 410, 431, 436, 453, 456
de Kruijf, T. C., 157, 329
de la Potterie, I., 104, 112, 115–16, 181–82, 187, 230, 236–37, 253, 280, 285, 293, 295, 310–11, 328, 382, 386, 405–6, 412, 445
Deines, R., 446
Delebecque, Édouard, 347, 393
Demke, Christoph, 373
Denaux, Adelbert, 438
Dennert, Brian C., 292, 448
Dennis, John A., 14, 25, 156, 163–64, 172, 174–75, 195, 198, 200, 205, 208, 210, 223, 372, 442, 445, 447
Derrett, J. D. M., 257
Dewailly, L. M., 58, 382
Dietzfelbinger, Christian, 27, 95, 103–4, 157, 185, 190, 210, 230, 236, 248, 252, 257, 263, 347, 398, 432, 463
Dodd, C. H., 20, 30, 46, 52, 74, 81, 152–53, 155, 161, 165, 175, 205–6, 224, 229, 235, 245, 252, 256, 258, 263, 269, 289, 306, 320, 322–23, 328, 333, 369, 394, 399
Duke, Paul D., 36, 76, 86, 166, 205, 411–12, 417
Dunn, James D. G., 184, 188, 250, 256, 259, 317, 322, 354–55, 358, 376, 436, 464
Dupont, Jacques, 217, 230, 239, 314, 319, 374
du Rand, Jan A., 380

Edwards, Ruth, 184, 329, 347, 444
Ellis, Peter F., 74, 81, 157, 174, 179, 181–82, 185, 218, 222, 248, 257, 264, 328, 349, 356, 402, 411, 446
Eltester, Walther, 324, 373
Emerton, J. A., 342
Ensor, Peter, 225, 439
Evans, Craig A., 227, 321, 323, 356
Evans, C. F., 206, 300, 383

Fennema, D. A., 319–20, 328, 330
Fischer, Günter, 299
Fischer, K. M., 455
Forestell, J. Terence, 12, 26, 27, 30, 44, 112, 147–49, 152–54, 156–57, 161, 165, 170, 172, 175–76, 181, 186, 188, 194, 204–5, 210, 229–30, 237, 248, 250, 254, 256, 269, 279, 287–88, 292, 299, 349–52, 387, 409, 426, 462
Fortna, Robert T., 33, 165, 198, 292, 347, 377–78, 380, 383, 388–89, 411, 418, 453
Fossum, Jarl E., 323
Fowler, James, 17, 396
Franck, Eskil, 136, 155, 292, 399, 404–5
Franzmann, Majella, 376
Freed, E. D., 85, 197, 352, 420, 477
Frey, Jörg, 13, 25, 26, 47, 147–50, 152–53, 155–58, 163–64, 168–70, 173, 175–81, 183–85, 187, 193–99, 205, 211, 217–19, 225, 228–29, 234, 242–43, 247–48, 261, 294, 299, 304, 334, 336, 339, 383, 398, 404, 409, 412, 438, 445
Füglister, Notker, 159
Fuller, Reginald H., 310, 314, 322–23, 354–55, 358–59, 365–67

Gawlick, Matthias, 446
Giblin, C. H., 112, 206

Index of Modern Authors

Glicksman, Andrew T., 296, 322, 326, 355
Gnilka, Joachim, 157, 169, 186, 206, 245, 256, 259, 292, 296, 300, 341, 347, 349, 373–74, 379, 384
Gourgues, Michel, 162
Grigsby, Bruce H., 157, 161, 179
Grundmann, Walter, 18, 394
Gundry, Robert H., 256, 296

Haacker, Klaus, 13, 18, 24, 42–44, 156–57, 170, 172, 176, 204, 250, 269, 276, 280, 288, 314, 317, 362, 372, 397–98, 405, 415, 419
Haenchen, Ernst, 11, 18, 20–23, 30, 33, 34, 48, 59, 83, 111, 149, 157, 169, 179, 239, 251, 256, 268, 285, 286–87, 289, 292, 294, 296, 311, 314, 319–21, 323, 330, 334, 336, 349, 357, 361–63, 375, 381, 387, 390, 435
Hahn, Ferdinand, 23, 27, 32, 109, 112, 157, 180, 200, 205, 208, 217, 248, 256, 276–77, 289, 309, 314, 324, 328, 339, 348, 349, 362, 367, 397, 398, 437, 451
Hamerton-Kelly, R. G., 218, 223, 224, 270, 372–75
Hanson, Anthony T., 341
Harner, J. B., 347, 350
Harner, Philip B., 319, 320
Harris, Elizabeth, 47, 152, 257, 317, 330, 347, 439, 441, 444
Harvey, A. E., 208, 314, 358
Hayward, C. T. R., 322
Heekerens, Hans-Peter, 74, 446, 459
Hegermann, Harald, 11, 26, 27, 152, 208, 227, 230, 236, 238, 294, 377, 387, 390, 398, 462
Heil, John Paul, 349
Heise, Jürgen, 299
Hengel, Martin, 23, 74, 187, 323–24, 416, 450, 457
Hera, Marianus Pale, 230
Higgins, A. B. J., 255
Hofbeck, Sebald, 43
Hofius, Otfried, 183, 319
Hofrichter, Peter, 294, 317, 328, 374
Holtzmann, Heinrich J., 12, 42, 197, 234, 305–7, 311, 314, 317, 358, 367–68, 375, 377, 379, 382
Hooker, Morna D., 318, 418, 443, 445
Horbury, William, 442

Hoskyns, Edwyn C., 218, 234
Hübner, Hans, 165, 349
Hunt, Steven A., 157
Hurtado, Larry, 151, 175, 225, 233, 244, 322–23, 343, 347, 390, 400, 407, 437

Ibuki, Yu, 15, 21, 27, 44, 49, 95, 102, 110, 181, 230, 237, 271, 276, 285, 288, 290, 294–95, 359, 375, 387, 405
Isaacs, Marie E., 135–36, 261, 404, 406

Jennings, Mark, 419
Jensen, Alexander S., 252
Jeremias, Joachim, 11, 153, 157
Jervell, Jacob, 249, 340
Johnson, Brian D., 162, 188, 276, 450, 470
Johnston, George, 49, 235, 269, 382–83

Kaefer, J. Ph., 457
Kähler, Martin, 13, 204, 386
Kanagaraj, Jey J., 451
Käsemann, Ernst, 11–15, 18, 21, 24, 26, 29, 42, 67, 147, 149, 190, 207, 229, 237, 245, 285–87, 290, 292, 294, 296, 300, 307, 311, 327, 360, 362, 372–77, 379, 380, 382, 386–92, 397–98, 401, 404–5, 419, 420, 442, 463, 467
Kee, Howard C., 292–93, 379, 446
Keener, Craig S., 25, 47–48, 77, 112, 158, 164–65, 180, 184, 186, 225, 229, 248, 254, 267, 324, 330–31, 335, 338, 347, 355, 433, 443–45
Kieffer, René, 58
Kim, Yung Suk, 190, 349
Klaiber, Walter, 200, 204, 244, 290, 377, 398, 467
Klauck, Hans-Josef, 35, 397–98, 404, 453
Klos, Hebert, 161, 186, 384
Knapp, Henry M., 276
Knöppler, Thomas, 24, 157, 170, 172, 175
Koester, Craig, 36, 186, 205, 276
Kohler, Herbert, 10, 13, 20–21, 179, 187
Kossen, H. B., 220
Kotila, Markku, 449
Kovacs, Judith, 200
Kowalski, Beate, 257
Kraus, Wolfgang, 445, 450

517

INDEX OF MODERN AUTHORS

Kremer, Jacob, 115–16 185, 222, 262, 397, 406
Kriener, Tobias, 332, 438, 442
Kügler, Joachim, 35, 438
Kühl, J., 23, 44, 59, 156, 205
Kundsin, Karl, 404
Kysar, Robert, 1, 205, 219, 324, 337, 373, 421

Labahn, Michael, 198, 223, 292, 346, 466
Lamb, David, 422
Lamouille, A., 34, 48, 74, 111, 113, 115, 152, 157, 162, 165, 169, 172, 186, 203, 206, 217, 245, 256, 258, 273, 276, 341, 344, 349–51, 356, 361, 384, 455
Langbrandtner, Wolfgang, 12, 14, 21, 24, 33–34, 147, 239, 292, 294–95, 319–20, 360, 374, 377–78, 381, 388, 392, 446, 454, 456
Lattke, Michael, 12, 147, 172, 179, 290, 302, 376, 381, 401, 467
Le Déaut, Roger, 157
Lee, Dorothy, 36, 158, 161–63, 168, 170, 184–85, 205, 208, 232, 248, 256, 286–87, 376, 412, 451
Leistner, Reinhold, 337, 344, 387
Léon-Dufour, Xavier, 383, 412
Leroy, Herbert, 16, 404, 410–11, 418
Leung, Mavis M., 14, 151, 174, 257, 437, 447
Lierman, John, 249, 440–41
Lieu, Judith M., 34, 287, 296, 357, 363, 388, 399, 456–57
Lincoln, Andrew T., 25, 27, 47, 49, 157, 172, 174, 186, 208, 217, 219, 228, 244, 254, 256, 276, 287, 332, 347, 438, 442–46, 448–50
Lindars, Barnabas, 27, 48–49, 77, 82–83, 106, 115, 125, 149, 153, 157, 162, 170, 172–76, 179, 181–83, 194, 195, 198, 204–5, 218, 221–22, 224, 228, 230, 248, 250, 256–57, 259, 263, 307, 311, 314, 323, 330, 333, 337, 340, 343–44, 349–50, 352, 354, 356, 369, 374, 380, 412, 446
Lindemann, Andreas, 445, 449
Litwa, M. David, 206, 384
Loader, William, 19, 22, 25, 181, 184, 186–87, 225, 256, 259, 267, 271, 313, 315, 323–24, 427, 443, 446, 456, 464
Loder, James E., 396
Lona, Horacio E., 292
Lorenzen, Thorwald, 385

Lüdemann, Gerd, 241, 245
Lütgert, Wilhelm, 43–44, 157, 176, 179, 210, 236–37, 239, 251, 256, 284–85, 303–8, 310, 317, 341, 346, 357–58, 360, 365, 367, 383
Luz, Ulrich, 451

Mackay, Ian D., 419
MacRae, George W., 125
Maddox, Robert L., 86, 176, 179, 245, 255, 259
Malatesta, Edward, 344
Manns, Frédéric, 341
Martyn, J. Louis, 16, 33–35, 126, 227, 344, 377, 388, 394, 421–22, 442, 453, 455
Mastin, B. A., 47, 116, 219, 251, 262, 319–20, 330, 354, 358, 360
Matera, Frank J., 59
McArthur, H. K., 347
McGrath, James F., 11, 25, 43, 205, 251, 253, 256, 296, 315, 325, 330, 332, 336–37, 341, 348, 355, 361, 390, 437–40, 443
McHugh, John F., 168, 257, 444
McNamara, Martin J., 157
Mealand, David, 392
Meeks, Wayne, 27, 32, 35, 46, 75, 82, 111, 179, 205, 206, 208, 229, 241, 248, 250, 257, 263, 286, 322, 410, 412, 430–31, 452, 466–67
Mees, Michael, 251, 328
Menken, Maarten M. J., 25, 169, 170, 385
Metzner, Rainer, 24, 156–57, 196, 201
Michaels, J. Ramsey, 47–49, 152, 180, 203, 219, 225, 242, 248, 254, 256, 324, 334, 371, 444
Miller, Edward L., 113, 270, 315
Minear, Paul S., 101, 115, 135, 186, 227, 229, 262, 404, 407, 412
Miranda, Juan P., 23, 24, 44, 59, 148, 156, 172, 174, 176, 179, 181, 250, 337, 340, 361, 368–69, 377, 455
Mlakuzhyil, George, 347
Moloney, Francis J., 27, 43–44, 46–47, 49, 67, 185, 188–90, 197, 203, 205–6, 217, 219, 221–22, 224, 228, 230, 233, 238, 241–42, 247–53, 256–60, 276, 285, 289, 311, 347–52, 384–85, 428, 439–40, 443–44, 446, 468
Morgan-Wynn, J. E., 204

Index of Modern Authors

Morgen, Michèle, 450
Morris, Leon, 16, 393
Moser, Marion, 451
Moule, C. F. D., 299, 319–20
Mowvley, H., 445
Müller, T. E., 24, 30, 104, 148, 156, 170, 172, 174, 176, 179, 181, 271, 285, 288, 301, 394, 405
Müller, U. B., 13, 15, 26–27, 29, 33–34, 104, 147, 149, 179–80, 374–76, 381, 386, 390, 445
Mussner, Franz, 16, 32, 101, 113, 135, 161, 397–98, 404–5, 410, 446

Neugebauer, Franz, 274, 385
Neyrey, Jerome H., 34, 336, 339, 347–48, 422, 430, 438
Nicholson, Godfrey, 28, 44, 58, 74–75, 88, 106, 112, 115, 179–80, 204, 208, 210, 214, 218, 221, 223, 242, 245, 250, 252, 258, 262, 269, 271, 351, 357, 370, 383, 394, 399, 401, 407, 417
Nicol, Willem, 11, 12, 74, 203, 222, 235, 237, 239, 292, 295, 374, 377, 381–82, 391–92, 397, 405, 453
Nissen, Johannes, 450

O'Day, Gail R., 36, 182, 209, 324
O'Grady, John F., 382
Odeberg, Hugo, 250, 306, 310, 351
Olsson, Birger, 16, 43, 46, 52, 74, 183–84, 256, 398, 407, 410–11
Onuki, Takashi, 18, 21, 35, 97, 101, 103–4, 116, 204, 236, 254, 262, 270, 279, 294, 299–300, 324, 328, 383, 385, 390, 394, 398–99, 404, 410–11, 431, 442
Osborn, Eric, 235, 360
Osborne, Grant R., 354

Pagels, Elaine H., 376
Painter, John, 26, 47, 103–4, 151–55, 158, 159, 163, 165, 166, 189, 170–75, 180, 185, 198, 203, 210, 218–19, 234, 242–43, 250–51, 255–56, 269, 276, 294, 296, 298, 300, 311, 314, 317, 322, 324, 330, 336, 373–76, 385, 398, 419, 422, 436, 438–39, 453, 457

Pamment, Margaret, 179, 214, 218, 238, 244, 248, 256–57, 260
Pancaro, Stephen, 156, 165, 349, 350, 449, 450
Perkins, Pheme, 116, 279
Petersen, Silke, 43, 330, 343, 348, 351–52
Pfuff, Konrad, 445
Pokorny, Petr, 228, 248, 292, 349, 351–52, 385
Pollard, T. E., 42, 317, 360
Porsch, Felix, 29, 50, 74, 82–83, 97, 102, 104, 112, 136, 152, 154, 156–57, 181, 186, 188, 205, 228, 239, 271, 273–74, 276–77, 279, 290, 294, 299, 368, 403–6, 409
Preiss, Theo, 27, 103, 208, 210, 258, 287, 295, 317, 336, 376, 416
Pryor, John W., 113, 174, 182, 256, 289, 296, 326, 328, 349, 440, 443, 450

Quek, Tze-Ming, 154

Radermakers, Jean, 59
Rahner, Johanna, 10, 14, 20
Regev, Eyal, 446
Reim, Günter, 35, 156, 165, 217, 229, 244, 250, 256, 276, 322, 324, 349, 405
Reinhartz, Adele, 257, 438, 440, 469
Rengstorf, Karl Heinrich, 2, 23, 59
Rensberger, David, 198, 466
Rese, Martin, 47
Reynolds, Benjamin E., 170, 201, 205, 211, 218, 220–21, 225, 243, 248, 250, 252–54, 259–61, 263, 314, 350, 384, 439–40
Rhea, Robert, 229, 439, 441
Ricca, Paolo, 43, 230, 346, 394
Richard, E., 36, 229, 347, 411
Richter, Georg, 14, 24, 33, 34, 43, 46, 148, 156, 184, 186, 238, 242, 254, 256, 292, 301, 373, 384–85, 392, 456
Riedl, Johannes, 22–24, 28, 29, 44, 59, 84, 95, 148, 156–57, 170, 172, 179, 181, 188, 214, 230, 237–39, 242, 245, 248, 285, 295, 337, 341, 350, 357–59, 375, 387, 401, 409, 462
Riesenfeld, Harald, 16, 393
Ritt, Hubert, 67, 181, 289
Robinson, John A. T., 15, 17, 44, 161, 165, 251,

INDEX OF MODERN AUTHORS

303–7, 310, 314, 328, 333, 341, 343, 358, 361, 363, 380, 382, 390, 399–400
Ruckstuhl, Eugen, 34, 43, 170, 205, 237, 248, 250, 322, 328, 373–74
Rusam, Dietrich, 150–52, 159, 162, 168, 200, 370

Sanday, W., 416
Sanders, J. N., 47, 116, 219, 251, 262
Schapdick, Stefan, 445–46, 448–50
Schenke, Hans-Martin, 21, 294
Schenke, Ludger, 15, 191, 256, 258, 294, 347, 385
Schillebeeckx, Edwards, 26, 52, 179, 205, 214, 230, 234, 236, 249, 262–63, 269, 287, 301, 307, 310, 314, 319, 336, 358, 376, 452, 454
Schlier, Heinrich, 12, 15, 237, 401
Schlund, Christine, 154, 158–63, 165, 173, 175, 183
Schmidl, Martin, 47, 242, 250
Schmithals, Walter, 435
Schnackenburg, Rudolf, 11, 12, 18, 25, 28–29, 35, 43–44, 46, 48–49, 51–52, 60, 68, 74, 82, 85, 91, 93, 95, 101, 103, 105, 112–113, 115–16, 135, 156–57, 162, 165, 168, 170, 172, 174–76, 179–80, 184, 186, 188–91, 198, 200, 204–6, 210–11, 214, 217–19, 221–23, 229, 234, 236–38, 245, 251, 256, 258–60, 262, 269, 276, 279, 286, 289, 292, 299–300, 310–11, 313, 315, 319, 320, 322, 324, 327, 330, 334–35, 341, 347, 349, 350–52, 358–59, 361, 368–69, 372–76, 383, 385, 387, 393–94, 397, 399, 404–6, 410, 418, 419, 424, 436, 440, 445, 457, 486
Schneiders, Sandra, 116
Schnelle, Udo, 22, 24, 27, 34, 35, 42, 47, 49, 74, 82, 86, 148, 156–57, 163, 168, 170, 184–86, 188, 190, 196, 198, 205, 228, 234, 248–49, 251–54, 256–57, 260, 276, 290, 292, 299, 311, 317, 319, 323, 328–29, 337–38, 346, 348–50, 353, 356, 359–62, 365, 374, 376–78, 384–86, 389, 398, 435–36, 442, 456, 459, 467
Schnider, Franz, 156, 170, 172, 179, 292
Scholtissek, Klaus, 156, 198–99, 201, 343, 360

Schoonenberg, Piet, 358, 365, 367
Schottroff, Luise, 12, 21
Schröter, Jens, 155
Schuchard, Bruce G., 446
Schulz, Siegfried, 14, 15, 18, 29, 47, 82, 147, 172, 179, 218, 223, 229, 239, 245, 251, 254, 256, 287, 313, 320, 375–77, 386
Schürmann, Heinz, 82, 170
Schwankl, Otto, 25, 288–89, 348, 356, 362, 390
Schweizer, Eduard, 13, 14, 186, 229, 287, 296, 353–54, 382–84, 386, 390–91
Schwindt, Rainer, 11, 205, 217, 219, 233, 240, 245, 257
Scott, E. F., 194
Scott, Martin, 296, 322, 324, 443
Scroggs, Robin, 102, 180, 221, 256, 285, 287, 290, 294, 300, 313, 336, 359, 363, 381, 389, 405, 438
Segal, Alan F., 250, 322, 355
Segovia, Fernando, 179, 184, 196, 218, 271, 290, 292, 457, 467
Seynaeve, Jean, 69
Sheppard, Beth M., 336
Sidebottom, E. M., 250, 394
Skinner, Christopher W., 36, 317
Smalley, Stephen S., 16, 26, 43, 74, 229, 236, 245, 257, 314, 394, 419
Smith, D. Moody, 27, 172, 180, 184, 198, 230, 288, 404
Söding, Thomas, 27, 172, 174, 176, 208, 233, 245, 248, 256, 287, 344, 356, 390, 438, 447
Sproston, Wendy E., 224, 336–37, 343, 387
Steegen, Martijn, 337
Stenger, Werner, 156, 170, 172, 179, 292
Stevens, G. B., 194
Strachan, Robert H., 251, 417
Strathmann, Hermann, 210, 306, 358, 369, 380–81, 412, 416, 419
Strecker, Georg, 34, 35, 324, 456
Stuhlmacher, Peter, 157, 250
Sturdevant, Jason S., 36
Suggit, John, 206
Suh, Joong Suk, 251

Talbert, Charles H., 286, 322, 324, 366–67, 455

Index of Modern Authors

Temple, Sydney, 16, 17
Thatcher, Tom, 185, 353
Theobald, Michael, 22, 47, 251, 257, 317, 433
Thettayil, Benny, 257, 276, 447,
Thompson, Marianne, 26, 201, 268–69, 290–91, 296, 352, 368–69, 370, 374, 444
Thüsing, Wilhelm, 13, 251
Thyen, Hartwig, 14, 47, 139, 317, 339, 374
Tolmie, D. François, 469
Tovey, Derek, 36
Trites, A. A., 103, 208
Trudinger, L. P., 257
Turner, Max, 147–48, 156, 184

Um, Stephen T., 185, 448
Untergassmair, F., 95, 214, 292, 295

Vahrenhorst, Martin, 444–50
Van Belle, Gilbert, 11, 33, 440, 458
van der Watt, J. G., 20, 23, 197–98, 234, 285, 288, 292, 296, 299, 302, 318, 320, 326, 334–35, 451, 464
van Hartingsveld, Lodewijk, 97, 205, 210, 299
Vellanickel, Matthew, 328, 357
Vermes, Geza, 157
von den Osten-Sacken, Peter, 11, 13–14, 204, 224, 285, 295–96, 391
von Harnack, Adolf, 316
von Wahlde, Urban C., 34, 422, 469
Voorwinde, Stephen, 10, 389

Watson, Franics, 15, 314, 358, 365–66
Wead, David W., 125, 241, 292, 353, 382, 399, 401, 407, 411–12, 414

Weder, Hans, 42–43, 81–82, 170, 229, 286, 322, 324, 373, 382, 385, 469
Weidemann, Hans-Ulrich, 157, 159, 161–65, 185–88, 219, 221, 225, 242–43, 248, 253, 257, 260–61, 384, 439
Weiss, Bernhard, 235, 314, 357, 367, 375
Wengst, Klaus, 35, 42, 166, 180, 227, 242, 285, 317, 347, 378, 381, 387
Westcott, B. F., 206, 234, 307, 311, 318, 320
Wetter, G. P., 44, 283, 336, 346, 377, 379, 382
Whitacre, Rodney A., 48, 162, 196, 218, 238, 250, 383
Wilckens, Ulrich, 47, 81–82, 157–58, 168–69, 179, 191, 251, 257, 260, 276, 301, 324, 385
Wilkens, Wilhelm, 11, 13–14, 24, 74, 148, 156–57, 165, 172, 186, 205, 214, 237–39, 245, 263, 294, 375, 378, 383, 387
Williams, C. H., 154, 168, 218, 229, 347–52
Williams, J. T., 113, 156, 163, 166, 170, 172, 174
Wilson, R. McL., 323
Witherington, Ben, 47, 252, 257, 276, 446
Witkamp, L. Th., 442
Woll, D. Bruce, 253, 310, 399, 406
Wrede, William, 197, 377, 416

Yee, Gail A., 446

Zeller, Dieter, 115, 263
Zimmermann, H., 347, 349, 353–54, 373,
Zimmermann, Ruben, 36, 152, 168, 172, 334, 350, 352, 354, 412, 438, 451
Zumstein, Jean, 150, 163, 266, 274, 317, 322, 347, 374, 412

Index of Subjects

Above–Below, 80, 135, 254–57, 456
Abraham, 33, 85, 90, 122, 125, 157–58, 300, 314, 352
Adam, 111, 116, 206, 341, 384
Adoptionism, 15, 358, 365, 437
Agent. *See* Revealer envoy
Andrew, 88, 139
Angels, 255–57, 308, 312, 323–25, 355, 476
Angels and Son of Man, 130, 132, 254–57, 325
Annas, 109
Anti-semitism. *See* Judaism/anti-Judaism
Apprentice, 76–77, 123, 313, 334–35, 359, 424
Arrest, 108–111, 349
Ascension, 6–7, 23, 83, 213, 225, 228, 249–55, 258–67, 280, 429
Atonement. *See* Death of Jesus

Baptism, 143, 151, 153–54, 183, 185, 481
Baptism of Jesus, 15, 117, 143, 153, 183, 251, 258, 274, 278, 285, 312, 314, 358, 366–71, 423, 436
Baptist, John the, 47–50, 59–60, 72–73, 78, 114, 117, 122, 125, 149–56, 201, 289, 291, 310, 314, 366–73, 448, 452, 477–78, 480–82
Barabbas, 110, 118
Beloved disciple, 113, 115, 118, 120, 139, 143, 385, 398–99, 431, 453, 457, 463
Below. *See* Above–Below.
Betrayal, 92, 98, 108, 137, 293

Blasphemy, 85–87, 339–352
Brothers of Jesus, 83, 115, 128, 261

Caiaphas, 87, 109, 139, 173, 175
Church, 113–18, 143, 149, 197, 227, 273, 356, 394, 430, 433, 452–53, 461, 463, 478
Circumcision, 449, 480
Commandment, 54, 60, 96–97, 140–41, 285, 293, 452, 463, 480–82
Community, 2, 16–19, 32–26, 95, 107, 113, 118–20, 141–44, 174, 267, 286–88, 299, 337, 392, 401–5, 410–84
Creation, 31, 72, 78, 117, 122, 289, 296–97, 300, 317, 321, 324–25, 328, 373, 435, 486

Darkness, 19, 20, 54–56, 85, 153, 160, 166, 180, 194, 210, 228, 294, 317, 327
David, 454
Death of Jesus: apotropaic, 148, 162, 173–76, 183, 194, 221, 242, 243; revelation, 6, 24, 73, 87–91, 173, 175, 189, 190, 202–13, 302, 473; sacrificial, 24–26, 148–159, 162–210, 242–246, 261, 298, 301, 484, 495; vicarious, 24, 26–27, 30, 37, 42, 71, 81, 86–87, 91, 107, 109, 126, 146, 148, 155, 158, 164, 168–80, 183, 189, 190, 194–203, 209–10, 242–246, 268, 280, 282, 425–26, 434–36, 473, 480–84
Determinism, 21, 32
Devil/Satan, 31, 91–92, 200, 202, 209–10, 286, 305, 308, 310, 470, 480, 483

Index of Subjects

Docetism, 12, 14, 34, 35, 186, 196, 260, 373–79, 384–85, 388–92, 398, 400, 414, 454, 456, 464, 476, 479
Double meaning, 16, 36, 337, 348, 380, 411–13, 431
Drama, 204, 264, 300, 412–17, 421, 464–71, 476–77
Dualism, 3, 5, 20–21, 286, 290, 294–95, 299–301, 317, 422, 424, 454–55, 460, 467–69, 478–79

Election. *See* Determinism
Elijah, 73, 79, 150
Emotions, 380, 389
Eschatology, 8, 97, 143, 200, 213, 234, 299–301, 406, 422–23, 434, 457, 465, 467, 475, 479
Eternal life, 18, 35, 64, 70, 76–79, 91, 93, 117, 134, 189–90, 196, 199–207, 210, 212, 220, 223, 252–53, 279–80, 305, 337, 373, 432, 462, 490, 492
Ethics, 283, 450, 463–64, 467–68, 479
Eucharist, 74, 80–81, 91, 118, 120, 134, 142–43, 165, 169–71, 185–86, 191–92, 199, 201, 277, 285, 302, 429
Exaltation, 3–6, 9, 27–32, 37, 60, 73, 79, 83, 85, 88, 91, 109–10, 118, 134, 140, 145, 175–76, 179, 192, 205, 211–13, 220, 228–29, 240–82, 325, 386, 406, 408, 427–31, 453, 473–74, 478, 483

Faith, 5–21, 75–76, 86, 89, 91, 105–7, 115–20, 177, 191–92, 204–6, 239, 245–48, 264–69, 281, 292–95, 328, 332, 335, 378, 393–96, 416–18, 421–25, 429–32, 460–68, 470–80
Family, 76–77, 161, 313, 325, 330–38, 423
Feast, 74, 79, 126, 142, 160, 162, 253, 265, 277, 398, 411, 443, 448
Flesh: incarnation, 72, 150, 309, 311, 371–76, 448, 483; spirit, 138, 239, 274, 367–70, 451
Foot washing, 93, 129, 142, 183–84, 219, 227, 302, 408, 446
Friends, 101, 107, 176, 194, 199, 207, 271

Galilee, 232, 288, 377
Gentiles, 139, 174–75, 480
Gethsemane, 109, 214, 382

Glory/Glorification, 28, 67–68, 88, 92–94, 104, 129, 133, 182, 213–20, 223, 225, 238, 240, 261, 364
Gnosticism, 3, 4, 13, 20, 21, 294, 300, 322, 379, 436, 454, 455, 463, 467
God Monotheism Ditheism, 323, 325–26, 354–56, 359, 475–76
"Greater" Event, 75, 77, 79, 83, 91, 128, 252, 255, 302, 405, 429
Greeks, 84, 88–89, 128, 139, 220, 245

Healing, 16, 76, 78–79 85, 90, 140, 197, 242, 331, 337, 412, 420, 433–34, 449, 480
Heavenly Council, 342
Heaven, 3–4, 6, 28, 48, 60, 73, 75, 81–83, 123, 205, 224, 238–41, 246–57, 262–64, 297–300, 305–12, 361, 365, 375, 424, 426–27, 465, 474–76
High priest, 87, 113, 138, 174, 181–82, 199, 447
History in John, 16–19, 391–420, 461–64, 476–79
Historical Jesus, 5, 7, 19, 272, 391–420, 462, 464
Hour, 8, 60, 67, 74, 79, 83, 88, 91, 103, 128–30, 193, 203, 208, 214, 218, 220, 246, 260–61, 409, 426–27
Humanity of Jesus, 4–5, 15–16, 18–19, 24, 29, 187, 238, 328, 336, 364, 376, 378, 387, 389–90

I am, 80, 217, 347–354
Incarnation. *See* Flesh
Irony, 36, 73–76, 81, 83–84, 87–88, 90, 94, 111–12, 118, 123, 125, 127, 139, 169, 205, 224–25, 244–47, 317, 344, 378, 384, 412–13, 416–17, 420, 438, 464, 466, 477
Israel, 31–32, 73, 164, 174–75, 199, 341, 353, 443, 447, 480

Jacob, 255–57
Jesus as "God", 318–21, 327–40, 346–54, 356–64
Jews, 29, 43, 44, 76, 81–86, 93, 109–13, 119, 127, 137, 160, 169, 216, 226, 305, 332, 337–44, 415, 447, 469–70, 481–84
Judaism/anti-Judaism, 23, 32, 34, 202, 319,

523

INDEX OF SUBJECTS

322, 325, 332, 355, 415, 438, 441–45, 457, 458, 462, 469–71
Judea, 83, 469
Judas, 91–92, 97, 98, 100, 108–9, 137, 138, 219, 294, 351
Judgment, 27, 31, 51–55, 75, 77–79, 85–86, 103, 112, 124, 134, 200, 202, 207–11, 245, 267, 280, 304, 335, 427, 473, 480–81

King of Israel, 73, 88, 110, 150–51, 205, 247, 254, 323, 430
King of the Jews, 109–13, 119, 204, 420, 437, 470

Lamb, 73, 80, 114, 149–68, 173, 185, 188, 199, 366–67
Law, 19, 42, 201, 241, 322, 329, 331–32, 340, 362, 372, 443–52, 479–80
Lazarus, 8, 65, 87, 126, 133, 222, 231, 267, 377–78, 380
Light, 19, 26, 45–46, 54–57, 62, 66, 79, 85, 89–90, 121, 123–24, 143–44, 147, 152, 194, 196, 201, 278, 289, 292–93, 295, 302, 316–17, 320, 326, 329, 331, 353, 364, 416, 423, 463, 472, 474, 477, 482
Literary, 36, 150, 153, 156, 160, 287, 392, 400–401, 411–17, 420, 458, 460, 466, 48–78
Logos, 15, 31, 66, 72, 78, 314–31, 342, 354–55, 357–58, 360, 367, 371–76, 388, 442–43, 476, 479
Love, 8, 60, 64, 70, 96–101, 105, 115, 118, 120, 141, 148, 153, 171, 179, 190, 203–4, 235, 237, 285, 290, 316, 333, 364, 398, 457, 463–64, 467–69, 484
Luke, 116, 139, 196, 263, 399, 419, 433, 480

Mark, 7, 13, 80, 151, 160, 166, 188, 196, 367, 390, 396, 418, 452, 480–81
Martha, 87, 231
Mary, 113, 116, 119, 138, 253, 264, 266, 441, 474
Mary Magdalene, 98, 114–15, 134, 261, 263, 435
Matthew, 139, 196, 201, 442, 451, 480–84
Melchisedek, 323, 342
Messiah/the Christ, 73, 76, 78, 109–12, 125, 137, 145, 150–53, 155, 165, 206, 281, 291, 293, 323, 325, 338, 348, 420, 422, 436–41, 454, 458, 479
Messianic Secret, 42, 418
Miracle, 5, 9, 11, 12, 75, 78–81, 87, 126, 223, 237, 239, 291–93, 349, 377–80, 432–34, 453–54, 478
Mission, 78, 91–92, 95, 96, 100, 101, 107, 119, 139–41, 144, 172–76, 220, 267, 299, 424, 430–33, 467
Moses, 15, 32–33, 42, 78, 85, 142, 146, 157–58, 250, 300, 323, 329, 372, 404, 439, 441–49
Mother, 83, 113, 120, 138, 261, 431

Name, 69, 88, 95, 98, 102, 122, 125, 203, 241, 295, 323, 325, 346–52, 354
Nicodemus, 48, 65, 78, 80, 82, 105, 110, 126, 131, 142, 179, 255, 292, 370, 412, 414, 447, 451, 453

Paraclete. *See* Spirit
Paradox, 5, 6, 205, 224, 227, 228, 248, 258, 284, 356, 374, 473
Parousia, 7, 9, 30, 77, 97, 118, 143, 243, 258, 299, 431
Passover, 109, 114, 157–68, 188, 446
Peter, 83, 94, 115, 118, 177, 226
Pharisees, 55, 88, 139, 349
Philip, 88, 95, 139, 345
Pilate, 6, 58, 60, 64, 109–14, 118–19, 160, 204, 207, 228, 242, 280, 344, 381, 384, 415, 466
Political, 437, 439, 441, 453, 466
Poor, 467, 480
Prayer, 65, 70, 87, 93, 105, 140, 181–82, 217, 346, 481
Pre-existence, 9, 15, 17, 20–24, 37, 239, 303–15, 317, 357–58, 364, 366, 455, 475, 478
Prologue, 31, 66, 72, 123, 150, 152, 155, 296, 314–18, 321–22, 324–26, 330–31, 357, 371, 438, 442–44
Prophet, 15, 32, 79, 292, 341, 361, 404–6, 440–42, 455
Purity, 446, 480

Redaction, 8, 43, 45–46, 91, 194, 196, 238, 374, 385, 392, 420, 428, 459, 481

Index of Subjects

Resurrection, 8, 31, 74, 87, 97, 116, 193, 254, 261, 263–66, 269–72, 278–82, 295, 379, 435, 473
Return. *See* Parousia
Revealer envoy, 78, 122–23, 136, 145, 286, 313, 315, 363, 422–36, 453–55, 458–60, 474–75, 477–79
Revelation, 3–6, 9, 22–24, 27, 30, 36, 37, 78, 102, 110, 144, 197, 202–7, 210–13, 224, 239, 252, 255–57, 266–70, 280–91, 295, 305, 312, 364, 404–7, 423, 462
Ruler/Prince of this world, 8, 89, 98, 103, 124, 129, 152, 163, 176, 178, 189–90, 199–200, 202, 208–12, 245, 280, 286, 300, 302, 342, 426, 448, 463, 473

Sabbath, 76, 114, 160–61, 331–32, 447, 449
Salvation, 30–32, 54, 194–95, 202, 204, 210, 269, 271–72, 282–314, 462–63, 465, 475, 479, 481
Salvation and Easter, 30, 170, 202, 210, 269, 271–72, 276, 288, 293, 302, 305, 311, 391, 398–99, 458, 478
Samaritan, 32, 76, 290, 397, 440, 446, 452, 478
Samaritan Woman, 79–80, 139, 142, 292, 293, 348, 377, 382, 409, 412, 417
Sanhedrin, 87, 208
Secret believers, 216, 233
Shepherd, 62, 86, 91, 171–73, 176, 298, 353, 354, 483
Signs, 11, 33, 75, 89–90, 126, 237, 239, 282, 291–92, 377–79, 383, 388, 399, 411, 432–34, 440, 457–58, 475
Sin, 148–205, 211, 480–84
Sinai, 154, 232, 329, 341, 372
Son of God, 43, 52, 58–60, 62, 66–67, 73, 75, 76, 86–87, 110, 114, 117, 119, 122, 124, 126, 133, 150–51, 154–55, 186, 222, 239, 247, 300, 323, 325, 328, 332, 341, 343, 347, 372, 381, 430, 438, 475
Son of Man, 79–81, 85, 91–93, 111, 126, 130, 134, 136, 138, 191, 206, 213–20, 241, 243, 245–47, 250, 253–57, 259, 261, 267, 280, 302, 307, 310, 312, 320, 325, 430, 439, 460, 473–74
Space and time, 310–14, 462, 465
Spirit, 18, 50, 59, 96–99, 102, 104, 106, 117, 135–36, 138, 140–42, 188, 211–13, 221, 262–81, 293, 355, 358, 366–71, 403–6, 423, 430–32, 435–36, 463, 474, 483
Synagogue, 16, 208, 296, 325, 344, 405, 410, 433, 436, 438, 440, 442, 478–79
Synoptic Gospels, 17, 160, 165, 377, 410, 418, 420, 433

Temple, 33, 74–75, 79, 88–89, 142, 164, 183, 193, 201, 227, 265, 277, 322, 330, 407, 443, 446–48, 450–51
Thomas, 66, 103, 116–17, 119, 138, 262–63, 265, 321, 331, 346–47, 385, 437
Tradition, 7, 8, 30–34, 149–60, 166, 171, 178, 195, 199–202, 258, 262–64, 299, 306, 321–26, 377, 382, 394–402, 405, 410–23, 426, 428, 431–32, 434–38, 452–60, 473–83
Trial, 33, 109, 110–11, 118, 160, 207–8, 242, 247, 344, 438, 442

Wedding, 43, 74, 79, 126, 142, 171, 235, 398, 411–12
Wisdom, 19, 23, 146, 201, 271, 273, 277, 289, 297, 317, 321–22, 324–31, 342, 353–55, 361, 370, 373, 423, 442–43, 452–53, 455, 457, 476, 478–80, 484
Witness, 48–49, 55–56, 61, 75, 78, 80, 102, 106, 118, 136, 138, 150, 186, 287, 289, 309–10, 371, 395, 423, 431, 442, 451, 470
Women, 264, 379, 400, 415
Works, 61, 62, 77, 78, 85–87, 90, 94–95, 99–100, 126, 131, 136, 140, 210, 221, 267–68, 279–80, 282, 293, 311, 333, 336, 338–40, 343, 345, 354–55, 364, 429–31, 433–34, 474

525

Index of Ancient Sources

OLD TESTAMENT

Genesis
1:1–4	322
2:1	187
2:3	449
2:7	117, 280
3:22	206
28:12	256

Exodus
3:14	348, 351
4:16	341
7:1	341
12:5 LXX	158
12:10	114
12:22	161
12:46	114
12:46 LXX	161
20:11	449
21:6	341
22:8–9	341
29:9	51
29:29	51
29:35	51
29:38–41	159
33–34	372
33:7–23	445
34:6	445

Leviticus
8:33	51
9:3	159
12:6	159
14:4–6	161
14:10–13	159
14:21–24	159
14:49–52	161
16:10	124
23:18–20	159

Numbers
9:2–3	160
19:18	161

Deuteronomy
2:30	450
4:23	450
6:4	338
7:9	450
18:15–18	32, 440
30:12	249
32:39	348, 351

Joshua
1:11	450
1:13–14	450

1 Samuel
16:1–13	437

2 Samuel
12:3	154
15:23	437
17:3	437

2 Chronicles
35:3	163

Psalms
2:7	153, 323
6:3–4	382
33:20–21 LXX	161
34:19–20	161–62
34:21	114
36:9a	443
45:6–7	323
69:9	79, 137, 188
69:22	188
80:8	258
80:14–17	174
80:17	258
82	340–43
82:6	86, 340
110:1	263
146:7–8	441

Proverbs
8:22	355
8:22–31	321
18:4	443
30:1–4	251

Index of Ancient Sources

30:4	249	Daniel		2 Maccabees	
		7:13–14	431	7:14	201
Song of Solomon					
3:1–4	116	Zechariah		Testaments of the Twelve Patriarchs	
		9:9	137		
Isaiah		12:10	161, 243	*Testament of Joseph*	
5:16	244	12:14–15	408	19:8–9	151
6:10	89, 91	14:7	443		
9:6	323	14:21	446	Wisdom of Solomon	
11:11	247, 377			7:1–14	326
12:3	443	Malachi		7:22–29	322
33:10	244	3:1	75	9:4	330
40:3	353			9:16–18	249
41:4	348			10:6	367
41:22–23	406	**OLD TESTAMENT APOCRYPHA AND PSEUDEPIGRAPHA**		10:15–16	367
42	154, 157, 166			18:15	367
42:1	153–54, 166–67				
42:6	353	Apocalypse of Abraham		**DEAD SEA SCROLLS**	
43:10	125, 348	8–17	323		
43:11–12	348			CD (Damascus Document)	
43:25	348	Apocalypse of Moses			
45:18–24	350	31:3–4	116	6.7	443
45:25	244				
46:4	348	Pseudo-Aristeas		4Q521 (Halakhah A)	441
48:17	353	210	449		
49:6	174, 353			11QMelchizedek	
51:4–5	353	Baruch		ii 9	323
51:12	348	3:29–4:2	322, 328		
52:6	348				
52:13	167, 175–76, 229, 244	Ben Sira / Sirach		**NEW TESTAMENT**	
53	157, 166, 244	24	442		
53:1	90	24:3–10	322, 328	Matthew	
53:4–6	167–68	24:8	445	1:21	152, 480, 483
53:12	168	43:31	445	3:2	201
55:1	277	51:23–27	325	3:6	201
61:1	441			3:12	152
		1 Enoch		3:17	153
Jeremiah		42:1–2	322, 328, 367, 445	5:15–16	353
31	273	49:3	220, 439	5:17–19	451
		90:38	151	6:12	481
Ezekiel				6:14–15	481
8:1–18	446	1 Esdras		7:24–27	480
9:1–2	446	1:3	163	9:2–8	481
9:6	446			10:40	455
47:1–12	443	Life of Adam and Eve		11:19	325
		13:3	206	11:27	51, 431, 455

527

INDEX OF ANCIENT SOURCES

11:28–30	325
12:15–21	480
13:41	255
14:33	80, 349
19:16–22	480
23:34	325, 480
23:37–39	480
24–25	419
25:31–46	480
26:28	201, 481
27:50	188
28:18	68, 264, 431

Mark

1:4	481
1:11	153, 166, 329
2:1–3:6	480
2:9–10	480
3:23–30	151
3:28–30	343
6:50	80, 349
7:1–23	480
7:1–5	444
8:38	254, 431
9:7	329
10:17–21	452
10:45	480
11–13	447
12:6	329
13	419
13:11	102
13:26–27	255
14	265
14:1	160
14:12–25	160
14:24	480
14:36	109
14:62	431
15:25	160
15:33	160
15:37	188

Luke

1:30–33	480
1:47–55	480
1:68–79	480
2:25	480
2:38	480
3:8	469
3:17	152
3:22	153
4:16–20	433, 480
6:20–21	480
7:22–23	480
7:35	325
10:16	455
10:22	51, 431, 455
10:25–37	480
11:49–51	325, 455
16:17	480
18:18–23	480
22:15–20	480
22:15	160
22:21–38	419
23:46	188

John (a selection)

1–5	72, 78
1:1–2	122, 217, 311, 325
1:1–13	326, 372
1:1	319
1:3	327
1:3–4	327
1:5	327
1:10–12	322
1:11–12	49
1:12–13	135, 324, 357, 480
1:14	5, 14, 15, 29, 42–43, 57, 62, 66, 75–76, 79, 89, 122–24, 133, 150, 154, 158, 180, 190, 205–6, 216, 224, 230, 232–33, 235–38, 243, 258, 265, 269, 327, 329, 330, 333, 371–76, 456
1:14–18	256, 324, 328, 329, 341, 360, 371–72, 374, 445
1:15	48, 58, 73, 78, 122, 150, 310, 314, 371–72
1:16–17	372, 444
1:17	42, 329, 443, 445
1:18	44, 61, 62, 67, 78, 122–23, 138, 180, 202, 217, 232, 243, 282, 306, 309–11, 321, 327, 329, 330, 336, 340, 342, 344–47, 372, 442
1:19–27	150
1:20	79, 348
1:29	163, 165, 166, 211, 243
1:30–31	367
1:32–33	50, 117, 192, 278
1:34	79, 154, 167, 359
1:36	163, 165, 166, 211, 243
1:41	125, 150
1:45	125, 150
1:48	58
1:49	73, 110, 126, 150, 315, 429, 430
1:50–51	73, 77–78, 83, 95, 98, 130, 132, 254–56, 266, 409, 429
1:51	5, 43, 79, 132, 150, 243, 254–59, 306, 308, 312, 429, 431, 437, 473–74
2:1–11	74
2:9	58, 74, 78, 123, 344, 480
2:11	29, 74, 79, 133, 231, 232
2:13	159
2:19	74, 79, 193, 264, 330, 469
2:19–22	379, 447
2:22	88, 91, 115, 137, 193, 197, 222, 265, 270, 391, 399, 407, 443
2:23	159
2:23–3:2	292
2:23–3:3	433
3:1–11	75, 274, 367, 370, 429–30, 474
3:2	57, 61, 65, 75, 78, 123, 453
3:3	48, 110, 135, 138, 370, 451
3:3–8	50, 135
3:3–11	134
3:11	61,

528

Index of Ancient Sources

	75–76, 80, 197, 250, 275, 305, 309–10, 370, 480	
3:12–13	83	
3:13	58, 76–77, 115, 123, 133, 245, 249, 250, 252–53, 259, 260, 306, 309–10, 314, 347, 401, 431–32, 439, 442, 446	
3:13–14	248, 267	
3:13–15	75, 429, 474	
3:13–21	46, 47, 57, 251	
3:14–15	4, 142, 179, 180, 190–91, 240, 242, 250, 252, 269, 301, 429	
3:14–16	178	
3:16	59, 76, 80, 122, 135, 154, 158, 176, 178–80, 191, 207, 213, 243, 290, 328, 467	
3:16–17	180, 455, 464	
3:16–21	76	
3:17–21	124, 179, 180, 207	
3:18	76	
3:18–21	79, 124	
3:27–30	48	
3:27	60	
3:31–32	4, 309, 312	
3:31–36	51–53, 55, 63	
3:32	44, 48–49, 55, 61, 75, 122, 283, 306	
3:32–33	51, 102	
3:34	49–50, 59–60, 117, 151, 192, 274, 278, 306, 312, 316, 367–70	
3:34–35	59, 68, 70, 306, 316, 367–68	
3:35	44, 49–51, 59–60, 92, 107, 111, 122, 310, 316, 369, 431	
3:36	51, 53–54	
4:14	276–77	
4:19	76, 79	
4:19–26	142, 257	
4:21	335	
4:22	31, 447, 470	
4:23	335	
4:23–24	278	
4:25–26	348
4:33	58
4:34	58, 61, 65, 76, 78, 114, 122, 126, 148, 189, 204, 382
4:48	79, 292, 433, 453
5:7	29
5:8–10	449
5:16	449
5:17–19	451
5:17–23	119
5:17–30	78, 331
5:19–21	337
5:25	193, 335, 409
5:26–27	60, 124, 329, 334
5:28–29	77, 124, 143, 213, 335
5:30	122, 304, 334–35
5:36	59, 61, 78, 122, 126, 148
5:36–37	336
5:37–38	309
5:39	443
5:39–40	124, 448
5:44	78, 216, 223
5:45	78–79, 124, 143, 441
5:44–46	302, 443
5:45–47	449
6–12	80–91
6:4	159, 165
6:5	58, 123
6:14–15	32, 80, 82, 90, 292, 433, 437, 481
6:20	80, 90, 125, 348, 349, 352, 480
6:27	4, 81, 91, 124, 134, 142, 170, 190–91, 258, 269, 301, 429
6:32	353, 442, 449
6:35	4, 125, 169, 277, 353
6:39–40	143, 213
6:44	58, 143, 213, 294
6:46	61, 81, 122, 243, 307, 309, 446
6:51	81, 126, 165, 169, 170–71, 178, 199
6:54	143
6:51–56	191
6:51–58	8, 26, 43, 81, 91, 165, 170, 187, 191, 374, 385, 414, 456, 483
6:61–62	267
6:62	6, 85, 90, 91, 95, 99, 115, 132–33, 142, 170, 191, 243, 249, 253, 255, 259, 314, 409, 429, 431, 451, 474
6:62–63	82, 138
6:63	50, 91, 124, 269, 274, 278, 367, 369
6:65	60
6:66	44
6:68–69	66, 83, 90, 274
7:16	29, 61, 83, 90
7:17	61–62, 122, 181
7:27–29	58, 61
7:27–28	58
7:33–34	84, 90, 93, 140,
7:37–39	26, 84, 186, 192, 269, 272, 275–78
7:42	58
8:12–19	55–57, 78, 84,
8:14	55, 58, 93, 109, 123, 126, 173–75, 344
8:17	443, 450
8:21–22	90, 104, 127
8:21–24	245
8:21–29	44
8:24	125, 348, 353–54
8:25	84, 90, 315, 347
8:26	44, 58, 61, 84, 122, 135, 310
8:28	84, 122, 125, 136, 310, 348, 353–54
8:28–29	63, 84, 91, 137, 352
8:32	62
8:32–36	153
8:35	314, 332, 352
8:40	44, 85, 305
8:42–43	57–58, 61
8:47	307
8:49–50	215
8:54	215–16, 223

529

INDEX OF ANCIENT SOURCES

8:54–55	85, 133	12:27	58, 88, 91, 109, 127, 129, 148, 205, 227–28, 382–83, 386–87	13:36	93, 94, 99, 135, 226, 483
8:56	315, 444			14:3	94, 97, 98–100, 106, 143, 148, 233, 299, 349
8:58	352				
8:58–59	351	12:27–28	261		
9:4	58, 197	12:28	88, 91, 133, 214, 230	14:7–11	61, 62, 122–23, 125, 135, 243
9:17	86, 90, 292, 440	12:30	88, 90, 381		
9:24	216	12:31	89, 91, 98, 103, 107, 123, 134, 152, 163, 176, 190, 199–200, 208–11	14:9–11	345
9:29–30	58, 344			14:10	44, 61, 95, 122–23, 125
9:35–39	77, 89, 335				
10:11	86, 91, 126, 171–73, 176, 353, 483	12:31–32	129	14:10–11	62, 87, 344, 359
		12:32	89, 91, 133, 140, 175–76, 179, 191, 220–23, 231, 242–45, 269	14:10–13	159
10:15	171–73			14:12–17	221, 431
10:17–18	86, 171–73			14:12	127, 261
10:22–39	292, 318, 337–39			14:13	215
		12:32–34	261, 426, 483	14:13–14	95, 99, 105, 107, 140
10:29	60, 86, 209, 338	12:33	109, 118, 129, 242–43		
10:29–39	90	12:41	89–90, 122, 133, 216–18, 239, 314, 444	14:16	50, 59, 136, 140, 226, 273
10:31–39	119				
10:32–38	62, 122	12:43	89, 133, 216, 233	14:16–17	96, 103, 136, 140, 142, 273, 278, 369–70, 430
10:36	70, 181–82	12:44–50	46, 52, 54, 63, 89, 458		
10:36–38	87				
10:36–39	90, 302, 343–44	12:49–50	44, 53–54, 122	14:16–20	262
11:4	91, 133, 222–23, 231	13–17	182	14:17	84, 136, 141, 151, 192, 193, 274, 277, 345, 359
11:27	51, 58, 66, 87, 90, 125, 385, 431, 434, 455	13–14	91–100		
		13:1	91, 99, 109, 114, 126, 129, 159, 160, 190, 203, 207	14:19–23	265
11:40	91, 133, 222–23, 231			14:20	62, 100, 107, 345, 408
11:41–42	87, 90, 231, 381				
11:50	109	13:1–3	184	14:20–21	127
11:50–52	139, 173–75	13:3	99	14:26	59, 98–99, 102, 104, 136, 140, 278, 403
11:55–57	160	13:7	18, 92, 407, 408		
12:1	160	13:10	163, 165, 171, 173, 178, 180, 183	14:28	127, 261
12:13	58, 88, 292			14:30	98, 163, 190, 199, 208, 483
12:13–15	90, 125	13:12–17	92, 227, 246, 261		
12:16	88, 91, 115, 133, 137–38, 193, 197, 211, 221–22, 243, 265, 270, 391	13:12–20	101	14:30–31	61, 64, 212
		13:16	58–59, 92, 99	14:31	98–100, 106, 138, 148, 207, 426
		13:16–19	348		
12:16–17	18, 88, 91, 115, 132, 137–38, 193, 197, 211, 221, 399, 407–8, 411, 428, 443	13:18	443	14:36	138
		13:18–19	109	15–16	100–107
		13:19	92, 98, 100, 102, 108, 124, 137, 351, 353–54	15:1–18	457
				15:3	184
		13:31–32	92, 100, 129, 189, 218, 219, 223, 225, 259, 261	15:8	100, 133, 215
12:23	83, 88, 91–92, 128, 139, 176, 220, 223, 225, 245, 248, 260			15:9–10	96, 316
				15:9–17	450
		13:33	93, 94, 96–99, 103–6, 127, 226	15:10	60–61, 101, 106, 122, 135, 140
12:23–24	246, 431				
12:24	88, 91, 100, 139–40, 175–76, 220, 226, 248	13:34–35	94, 96, 101, 107, 135, 140–41, 316, 450	15:13	101, 107, 109, 126, 176, 199, 207, 227
12:24–25	483				

Index of Ancient Sources

15:15	44, 61, 101, 122, 305	17:24	60, 68, 93–94, 107, 127, 135		117, 119, 124–25, 254–56, 347, 385, 437–38
15:25	160, 443, 451	17:24–26	365	21:18–19	94, 135, 214
15:26	50, 59, 103, 106, 136, 138, 221, 403	17:25	123		
15:26–27	102, 136, 140	18–21	108–20	**Acts**	
16:8–11	103, 135–36, 243, 245, 426	18:1–11	108, 205, 228, 458	1:6–7	480
		18:5–7	349	1:11	116
16:11	106–7, 124, 152, 163, 190, 199, 208–10, 426, 483	18:8	108, 171–73	2:33	241, 244–45, 431
		18:11	60, 108, 114, 119, 122, 127, 148, 383	2:34–35	263
				3:19–21	480
16:13–15	136, 305, 312, 403–5, 407	18:14	109, 126, 173, 175	5:31	241, 263, 336, 431
		18:15	367	5:31–36	336
16:25	105, 408	18:19–24	109	8:32–33	167
16:27–28	57–58, 64, 105–6	18:28	109, 112, 160, 183, 187, 446	17:30–31	480
16:32	409, 426	18:28–19:16	109, 160	**Romans**	
16:33	103, 107, 124, 182, 208–9	18:32	89, 118, 242–43	2:25–29	444
		18:37–38	62	8:1–4	452
17	67–71, 107, 142, 181–83, 203, 226, 295, 346, 428, 457	19:5	111–12, 119, 164, 205, 228, 258–59, 384	8:3	455
				8:32	154, 329
		19:7	111, 119, 344, 359, 443	8:34	263
17:1	60, 93, 182, 216, 221, 230, 238, 256, 259, 261, 425	19:11	60, 111, 386		
		19:19	204	**1 Corinthians**	
		19:19–22	113	5:7	159, 165
17:1–5	189, 203	19:30	43, 61, 65, 109, 113–14, 119, 122, 126–27, 148, 187–88, 190, 203, 221, 483		
17:2	51, 59–61, 107, 122			**Galatians**	
17:2–3	107			4:4	178, 376, 455
17:3	59, 60, 69, 107, 134, 189,			5:16–23	452
17:4	60, 182, 189, 203	19:34–35	185, 374, 456	**Ephesians**	
17:5	15, 68, 108, 122, 130, 132, 216–19, 221, 225, 236, 239, 243, 260, 311, 315, 321, 325	19:37	114, 119, 243, 258	1:6	329
		20:9	115, 119, 138, 185, 407, 408	1:20	263
				5:2	178
		20:17	98, 115–16, 119, 134, 203, 221, 248, 253, 259–64, 266, 268, 279, 435	**Philippians**	
17:6	60–61, 69, 107, 134, 233			2:6–11	375
17:7	60	20:21	58–59, 117		
17:7–8	65, 69, 309	20:21–22	119, 134–36, 227, 346	**Colossians**	
17:11–12	43, 69, 122, 135			1:13	329
17:14	57, 70, 135, 140, 151	20:22	114, 135, 142, 187–88, 221, 254, 269, 279	1:15–16	325
17:20–23	70, 135, 346				
17:21	87, 359	20:22–23	135, 151	**Hebrews**	
17:21–23	141	20:23	117, 187, 201, 279	1:2–3	325
17:22	60–61, 107, 135, 233, 237, 329	20:28	66, 72, 117, 265, 317, 321, 331, 343, 346–47, 437	1:3–4	263
				1:8–9	323
17:22–23	330			1:13	263
17:23	70, 107–8, 135, 316	20:31	43, 66, 73,	5:5	431

531

INDEX OF ANCIENT SOURCES

7:18	444
8:1	263
10:4	444
10:12	172, 263

1 Peter
1:19	165
3:22	263

1 John
1:1	308
1:2	376
1:9	184
2:1	198
2:19	384
3:16	176–79, 199
5:6	186, 358
5:7–12	186
5:20	320

2 John
2	273

Revelation
1:7	243
5:6	155
5:12	155
7:17	151
14:1	155
17:14	151

OTHER WRITINGS

Barnabas
6:14–16	376

Clement of Alexandria
Excerpta ex Theodoto
43:5	366
61:6	366

Irenaeus
Adversus Haereses
I 14:6	366

Josephus
Antiquitates judaicae
2.312	159
3.161	113
12.48	469

Justin
Apology
1.35:6	111

Dialogue
127–28	376

Gospel of Peter
3:17	111

Nag Hammadi
I 44.13–14	376

I 113.37	376
XIII 50.12–15	376

Philo
De cherubim
86–89	449

Legum allegoriae
1.5–6	449
3.207–8	323

De vita Mosis I, II
1.148–58	323

De posteritate Caini
145	445

Quaestiones et solutiones in Genesim
2.62	323

De somniis I, II
1.229–30	323, 445

RABBINIC LITERATURE

Mekilta
Šabb. 2:25	449

Midrash Rabbah
Genesis Rabbah
11:5	449
11:11	449
11:12	449

www.ingramcontent.com/pod-product-compliance
Lightning Source LLC
Chambersburg PA
CBHW030102010526
44116CB00005B/65